EVOLUTION IN INVESTMENT TREATY LAW AND ARBITRATION

International investment law is in a state of evolution. With the advent of investor–State arbitration in the latter part of the twentieth century – and its exponential growth over the last decade – new levels of complexity, uncertainty and substantive expansion are emerging. States continue to enter into investment treaties, and the number of investor–State arbitration claims continues to rise. At the same time, the various participants in investment treaty arbitration are faced with increasingly difficult issues concerning the fundamental character of the investment treaty regime, the role of the actors in international investment law, the new significance of procedure in the settlement of disputes, and the emergence of cross-cutting issues. Bringing together established scholars and practitioners, as well as members of a new generation of international investment lawyers, this volume examines these developments and provides a balanced assessment of the challenges being faced in the field.

CHESTER BROWN is Associate Professor at the Faculty of Law, University of Sydney and a barrister. He is also a door tenant at Essex Court Chambers, London, and Maxwell Chambers, Singapore. He has previously worked as Assistant Legal Adviser at the Foreign and Commonwealth Office, London, and as Senior Associate in the International Law and International Arbitration Group of Clifford Chance LLP, London.

KATE MILES is a senior lecturer at the Faculty of Law, University of Sydney. She currently serves on the International Law Association's New Study Group on the Role of Soft Law Instruments in International Investment Law. She is also a Research Fellow of the Centre for International Sustainable Development Law, Montreal, and co-ordinates the International Investment Law Network for the Society of International Economic Law.

EVOLUTION IN INVESTMENT TREATY LAW AND ARBITRATION

CHESTER BROWN and KATE MILES

CAMBRIDGE
UNIVERSITY PRESS

CAMBRIDGE UNIVERSITY PRESS
Cambridge, New York, Melbourne, Madrid, Cape Town,
Singapore, São Paulo, Delhi, Tokyo, Mexico City

Cambridge University Press
The Edinburgh Building, Cambridge CB2 8RU, UK

Published in the United States of America by Cambridge University Press, New York

www.cambridge.org
Information on this title: www.cambridge.org/9781107014688

First published 2011

Printed in the United Kingdom at the University Press, Cambridge

A catalogue record for this publication is available from the British Library

Library of Congress Cataloging-in-Publication Data
Evolution in investment treaty law and arbitration / [edited by] Chester Brown
and Kate Miles.
p.   cm.
ISBN 978-1-107-01468-8 (Hardback)
1. Investments, Foreign–Law and legislation.   2. Arbitration and award, International.
3. Commercial treaties.   I. Brown, Chester, 1972–   II. Miles, Kate, 1971–
K3830.E96 2011
346.′092–dc23
2011018536

ISBN 978-1-107-01468-8 Hardback

CONTENTS

CONTRIBUTORS

SIR FRANKLIN BERMAN KCMG QC is a barrister and arbitrator, Essex Court Chambers, London; a member of the Permanent Court of Arbitration; a member of the ICSID Panel of Arbitrators; and a Visiting Professor of International Law at the University of Oxford and the University of Cape Town. He was the legal adviser to the Foreign and Commonwealth Office, London, from 1991–9, and has been a judge ad hoc on the International Court of Justice.

PROFESSOR ANDREA BJORKLUND is Professor of Law at the School of Law, University of California, Davis. She is co-rapporteur of the International Law Association's Study Group on the Role of Soft Law Instruments in International Investment Law. Professor Bjorklund has written extensively on investor–State arbitration issues. Prior to entering the academy, Professor Bjorklund worked on the NAFTA arbitration team in the US Department of State's Office of the Legal Adviser, and also worked for Commissioner Thelma J. Askey on the US International Trade Commission and in private practice at Miller & Chevalier in Washington DC.

JONATHAN BONNITCHA is a D.Phil. candidate at the University of Oxford and, during 2010, was a Visiting Fellow at the Crawford School of Economics and Government of the Australian National University. He holds the degrees M.Phil. (Oxon), BCL (Oxon), LLB (Hons) (Syd), and BEc (Hons) (Syd).

DR CHESTER BROWN is Associate Professor at the Faculty of Law, University of Sydney, a barrister and a door tenant at Essex Court Chambers, London, and Maxwell Chambers, Singapore. He previously served as Assistant Legal Adviser at the Foreign and Commonwealth Office, London, and prior to that he was Senior Associate in the International Law and International Arbitration Group of Clifford Chance LLP, London. He is the author of *A Common Law of International Adjudication* (2007), which was awarded the ASIL Certificate of Merit. He was educated at the Universities of Melbourne, Oxford and Cambridge.

DR MARKUS BURGSTALLER is a Senior Associate at Hogan Lovells in London. He represents both investors and States in international disputes. Previously, he served as international legal adviser to the Austrian Chancellor. He was educated at the Universities of Vienna, Stockholm and New York. He is qualified as an attorney and counsellor at law in New York and as a solicitor in England and Wales. He is a member of the ICSID Panel of Conciliators.

DR PAUL JAMES CARDWELL is a Senior Lecturer at the School of Law, University of Sheffield. He holds degrees in law and political science from the Universities of Edinburgh and Warwick, UK, and Sciences Po Bordeaux, France. He has also studied in Japan and previously worked at the Delegation of the European Commission, Tokyo. His principal research area is the external relations of the European Union and he has published widely on the subject, including *EU External Relations and Systems of Governance* (2009) and a forthcoming edited collection, *EU External Relations Law and Policy in the Post-Lisbon Era* (2012).

LEE CARROLL is a Senior Associate at Clayton Utz, Melbourne, and holds the degrees BA (UWA), LLB (Hons) (UWA), BCL (Oxon), and the Diploma in International Commercial Arbitration (Chartered Institute of Arbitrators). Prior to joining Clayton Utz, she was an associate at Allen & Overy LLP, London and was associate to the Hon. Justice Hayne AC of the High Court of Australia from 2005 to 2006.

ANTONY CROCKETT is a lawyer at Clifford Chance LLP in the International Arbitration and International Law Group. He holds the degrees LLB (Hons) (Melb), BSc (Melb), and LLM (LSE). Prior to joining Clifford Chance, he completed an internship at the United Nations Office of Legal Affairs (Vienna), within the UNCITRAL Secretariat. He has represented the Arbitration Committee of the IBA as an observer delegate to Working Group II of UNCITRAL.

JONATHON DEBOOS is a lawyer at Clayton Utz, Melbourne, and holds the degrees BSc (Melb), Grad. Dip. Biotech (Melb), and LLB (Hons) (Deakin). During his time at Clayton Utz, he has worked on arbitrations under the ICC, ICSID, DIAC and SIAC Rules of Arbitration on disputes relating to major infrastructure projects, commercial property, power plants and foreign investment. Since 2006, he has served as the Deputy Secretary-General of ACICA and on the Executive Committee of AFIA.

SIMON FOOTE is a barrister at Bankside Chambers, Auckland, New Zealand, focusing on commercial and construction litigation and international commercial arbitration. He holds the degree of LLB (Hons) (University of Canterbury) and the Diploma in International Commercial Arbitration (Chartered Institute of Arbitrators). He is a Fellow of the Chartered Institute of Arbitrators and the Arbitrators' and Mediators' Institute of New Zealand.

PROFESSOR DUNCAN FRENCH is Professor of International Law at the School of Law, University of Sheffield. He holds degrees from the University of East Anglia, the University of Nottingham and the University of Wales, Cardiff. Professor French is director of the Sheffield Centre for International and European Law and deputy head of the School of Law. He is the co-rapporteur of the International Law Association Committee on International Law on Sustainable Development.

NICK GALLUS is a counsel in the Trade Law Bureau of the Department of Foreign Affairs and International Trade, Government of Canada, and Assistant Professor at Queen's University in Canada. He has published widely on investment treaties, including a book entitled *The Temporal Scope of Investment Protection Treaties* (2009). He has degrees in law (with first-class honours) and economics from Flinders University, Australia. He also has a Bachelor of Civil Law (with distinction) and Masters of Philosophy in Economics from Oxford University.

DR OMAR E. GARCÍA-BOLÍVAR is an international lawyer, public policy consultant and arbitrator. He is president of BG Consulting in Washington DC, specialising in law and development consultancy. Dr García-Bolívar is an arbitrator before ICSID, WIPO, and a member of the panel of arbitrators of the AAA, the ICC and CIETAC. He is admitted to legal practice in Venezuela, New York, Washington DC and the US Court of International Trade. He holds law degrees from Universidad Católica Andrés Bello in Venezuela; Southern Methodist University, Dallas, Texas; and the University of Edinburgh, United Kingdom.

ALEXANDRA HARRINGTON is a Doctor of Civil Law candidate at McGill University.

DANIEL KALDERIMIS leads the international arbitration and trade law practice of New Zealand law firm Chapman Tripp. He is listed, the only lawyer from a New Zealand firm, in *The International Who's Who of Commercial Arbitration* for 2010 and 2011. He is also an adjunct lecturer at Victoria University of Wellington Law School, where he teaches international economic law; a field in which he is widely published. He was previously a Fulbright Scholar and Associate-in-Law at Columbia Law School in New York, and a senior associate in the International Arbitration Group of Freshfields Bruckhaus Deringer LLP in London.

AVIDAN KENT (LLB (Haifa University), LLM (McGill University)) is a Ph.D. candidate in the Department of Politics and International Studies at the University of Cambridge, and an Associate Fellow with the Centre of International Sustainable Development Law in the Trade, Investment and Competition Law Research Programme. His research interests include the field of international trade and investment law and its intersection with other legal disciplines such as competition law and climate-change law. He is a member of the Israeli Bar.

DR CHRISTINA KNAHR has recently joined the Austrian Federal Ministry of Economy. Prior to that she has been a post-doctoral researcher at the Department for European, International and Comparative Law at the University of Vienna. She holds Master's degrees in law from the University of Vienna and in public administration from Harvard University, as well as a Doctorate in law from the University of Vienna. She has published several articles and co-edited three books on international investment arbitration, and has given a number of presentations in this field. She is a member of the ILA Committee on Non-State Actors and a member of the Organizing Panel of the SIEL Investment Network.

JUDITH LEVINE is legal counsel at the Permanent Court of Arbitration. From 2003 to 2008, she was an attorney in the Arbitration Group at White & Case LLP in New York where she represented corporations and sovereign States in ICSID, ICC, AAA and UNCITRAL arbitrations. Her prior roles include serving as law clerk at the International Court of Justice, adviser to the Australian Attorney-General, associate at the High Court of Australia, lecturer at UNSW and for the Chartered Institute of Arbitrators and she also served on the Australian delegation to UNCITRAL Working Group II. She holds a BA (UNSW), LLB (University Medal) (UNSW), and LLM (NYU).

DR SAM LUTTRELL is an Associate in the International Arbitration Group at Freshfields Bruckhaus Deringer, Paris, and holds the degrees LLB/BA (Hons) (UWA), and Ph.D. (Murdoch).

DR KATE MILES is a Senior Lecturer at the Faculty of Law, University of Sydney. She currently serves on the International Law Association's New Study Group on the Role of Soft Law Instruments in International Investment Law. She is also a Research Fellow of the Centre for International Sustainable Development Law, Montreal, and co-ordinates the International Investment Law Network for the Society of International Economic Law. She has also practiced in leading commercial law firms in Auckland and Sydney, including at Allens Arthur Robinson.

DR ALEX MILLS is Slaughter and May Lecturer in Law, Selwyn College, University of Cambridge, where he teaches public international law and conflict of laws. He has a BA (Hons) and LLB (Hons) from the University of Sydney, and an LLM and Ph.D. from the University of Cambridge, and has practised as a solicitor in Australia. He is the author of *The Confluence of Public and Private International Law: Justice, pluralism and subsidiarity in the international constitutional ordering of private law* (Cambridge University Press, 2009).

ANDREW NEWCOMBE is Associate Professor, Faculty of Law, University of Victoria, British Columbia, Canada. Prior to joining the Faculty in 2002, he worked in the International Arbitration and Public International Law Groups of Freshfields Bruckhaus Deringer in Paris. Professor Newcombe's research focuses on investment treaty law and arbitration. He is the co-author of *Law and Practice of Investment Treaties: Standards of treatment* (2009) and co-editor of *Sustainable Development in World Investment Law* (2010). He created and maintains ita (http://ita.law.uvic.ca), a research website focused on international investment treaty law, practice and dispute resolution.

DR MARTINS PAPARINSKIS is a Junior Research Fellow at Merton College, University of Oxford. He has been a Hauser Research Scholar at New York University. Dr Paparinskis has varied research interests in the field of general international law. He has published on different aspects of investment law, including in the *British Year Book of International Law.* His forthcoming publications include *International Minimum Standard and Fair and Equitable Treatment* and *Basic Documents on International Investment Protection.*

DR SERGIO PUIG is a Teaching Fellow at Duke University Law School. From 2007 to 2010 he was a counsel at the World Bank and ICSID. He holds a law degree from ITAM (Mexico), as well as a JSM and JSD from Stanford (USA). Prior to joining the World Bank Group, he worked as a legal consultant in Mexico and the United States.

DR HENNING GROSSE RUSE-KHAN is a Senior Research Fellow at the Max Planck Institute for Intellectual Property and Competition Law in Munich, Germany. He previously worked as a lecturer in international trade law at the University of Leicester. His research and teaching focuses on international intellectual property protection and development issues, law and organisation of the WTO and other issues of international economic law. He teaches at the Ludwig Maximilian University of Munich, the International Max Planck Research School for Competition and Innovation, at the Centre for International Intellectual Property Studies, Strasbourg and the Munich Intellectual Property Law Centre.

PROFESSOR PHILIPPE SANDS QC is Professor of Law and director of the Centre on International Courts and Tribunals at the Faculty of Laws, University College London, and a barrister at Matrix Chambers, London. He has extensive experience litigating cases before the International Court of Justice, the International Tribunal for the Law of the Sea, the International Centre for Settlement of Investment Disputes, and the European Court of Justice. He also appears regularly before the English courts. More recently, Philippe has accepted appointments as an arbitrator is several cases under the ICSID and UNCITRAL rules.

PROFESSOR M. SORNARAJAH is CJ Koh Professor of Law, National University of Singapore, and Tunku Abdul Rahman Professor of Public International Law, University of Malaya, Kuala Lumpur.

SUZANNE SPEARS is a counsel in the International Arbitration Group at Wilmer Cutler Pickering Hale and Dorr LLP, London. Earlier in her career, Ms Spears worked with the Council on Foreign Relations, the Inter-American Institute of Human Rights, Amnesty International and the United Nations. She received a JD from Columbia Law School, an MIA from Columbia's School of International and Public Affairs and a BA in International Relations from Tufts University. She was a Fulbright Scholar in Spain.

ANDREW STEPHENSON heads the International Arbitration Group and Construction Group in Melbourne of Clayton Utz. He is also a member of the Clayton Utz National Board. He has over thirty years of experience in contentious matters relating to all types of major projects. He is a Senior Fellow of the University of Melbourne Law School, and the Australian correspondent to the International Construction Law Review. He has been lead partner or counsel in arbitrations with various seats including Geneva, Singapore, Vancouver, Dubai, London, Sydney and Melbourne.

ANASTASIA TELESETSKY is Associate Professor, College of Law, University of Idaho. As an attorney, she has worked on cases involving international arbitration. She is a former Bosch Fellow, and worked in Germany for the Ministry of Foreign Affairs on drafting guidelines for the implementation of the right to food. Her current research interests include food security, climate-change adaptation and international environmental governance.

DR KYLA TIENHAARA is a Research Fellow at the Regulatory Institutions Network (RegNet), Australian National University. Her research is focused on the public-policy implications of investment agreements and investment arbitration. In particular, she has examined disputes between investors and States that have concerned environmental regulation. She is the author of *The Expropriation of Environmental Governance: Protecting foreign investors at the expense of public policy* (Cambridge University Press, 2009).

EMMA TRUSWELL holds degrees in economics and law from the University of Sydney, and completed her studies on exchange at Cornell Law School in 2009. She is currently working for the Australian Government, having previously worked at Herbert Smith LLP in London and Freehills in Sydney. She has undertaken research in international law, including international investment law and refugee law, at Sydney Law School and the University of New South Wales.

DR J. ROMESH WEERAMANTRY is an Associate Professor at the City University of Hong Kong. His professional experience includes work in international arbitration, dispute resolution and public international law at the Iran–United States Claims Tribunal, the United Nations Compensation Commission and at a leading Swiss law firm. He has also been an international law consultant to several international organisations. His first book, *International Commercial Arbitration: An Asia-Pacific perspective* (co-authored with Simon Greenberg and Chris Kee) was published by Cambridge University Press in 2010. His Ph.D. thesis on the interpretation of investment treaties will be published in 2011 by Oxford University Press.

DAVID A. R. WILLIAMS QC is a barrister and arbitrator at Bankside Chambers, Auckland and Essex Court Chambers, London. He is an Honorary Professor of Law at the University of Auckland and holds an LLB (Auckland), and LLM (Harvard). He has been involved in over one hundred international arbitrations and has extensive experience as an arbitrator in investment treaty cases. From 1992 to 1994, he was a judge of the High Court of New Zealand. He serves part-time as a Justice of the Cook Islands Court of Appeal and as a Justice of the DIFC Court in Dubai, UAE. He is presently a member of the International Council for Commercial Arbitration (ICCA).

CLAIRE WILSON is a legal consultant in the insurance sector advising on corporate restructuring within major Hong Kong and United Kingdom corporations. She has an LLB (Hons) degree from Nottingham Trent University Law School, United Kingdom, and a Masters of International Economic Law with distinction from the City University of Hong Kong. She is currently writing her doctorate in the field of international investment arbitration at the City University of Hong Kong.

EDITORS' PREFACE AND ACKNOWLEDGEMENTS

The publication of this volume has been a collaborative effort made possible as a result of various types of support and financial assistance that we have received from a number of sources, and we are pleased to record, in this formal way, our thanks to those people and institutions.

Many of the chapters in this volume were first presented at a conference, entitled 'Investment Treaty Law and Arbitration: Evolution and Revolution in Substance and Procedure', which was hosted by Sydney Law School, the University of Sydney, Australia, on 19–20 February 2010. That conference was made possible by a Research Development Grant under the New Capacity Programme from the Institute of Social Sciences at the University of Sydney, a Conference Seeding Grant from Sydney Law School and further financial assistance from the Sydney Centre for International Law; the Centre for Asian and Pacific Law at the University of Sydney; and the Parsons Centre of Commercial, Corporate and Taxation Law, each of which are housed within Sydney Law School. Additional sponsorship for the conference was generously provided by Allens Arthur Robinson, Blake Dawson, Clayton Utz and Mallesons Stephen Jaques.

We also wish to record our appreciation to all of the participants who came to Sydney and contributed to the success of the conference. Special thanks go to our keynote speaker and distinguished speakers, namely Professor Philippe Sands QC, Professor Sir Franklin Berman KMCG QC and Professor M. Sornarajah. We are also particularly grateful to the Dean of Sydney Law School, Professor Gillian Triggs, for her support of the conference and this project.

The editing of this book took place at Sydney Law School, the Lauterpacht Centre for International Law at the University of Cambridge, where Dr Miles spent the latter half of 2010 as a Visiting Fellow, and Harvard Law School, which Dr Brown visited during January–February 2011. Dr Miles is grateful to the director of the Lauterpacht Centre, Professor James Crawford, and subsequently Professor Marc Weller, as well as the

Fellows of the Lauterpacht Centre for having hosted her stay. Dr Brown wishes to express his thanks to Professor Bill Alford and those involved in Harvard Law School's International Legal Studies Programme who facilitated his visit. The editorial work was supported by a Legal Scholarship Support Fund Grant from Sydney Law School, and a Donation from the Edward and Emily McWhinney Foundation. We are greatly indebted to our two research assistants, Emanuel Blum and Marty Bernhaut, who worked with us, tirelessly and cheerfully, throughout the editing process.

We also wish to express our sincere thanks to Finola O'Sullivan and Nienke van Schaverbeke at Cambridge University Press for their support of this project, their assistance as this book came together, and also for having seen this volume so efficiently through the production process.

Last, but definitely not least, Chester is immensely grateful to his wife Catherine and his daughter Caroline for their love, support and encouragement, and Kate wishes to thank her husband, Matthew, and son, Samuel, for their love, patience and support throughout this project.

* * *

For the sake of economy in referencing, the editors note that the various bilateral investment treaties, multilateral investment treaties and investment treaty awards which are referred to throughout this edited collection are largely retrievable from publicly available websites such as Investment Treaty Arbitration (http://ita.law.uvic.ca), the website of the International Centre for Settlement of Investment Disputes (www.worldbank.org/icsid), the UNCTAD compendium of investment instruments online (www.unctadxi.org/templates/DocSearch.aspx?id=780) and NAFTA claims (www.naftalaw.org).

The views expressed in this volume are those of the various contributors, and are not necessarily those of any institutions or organisations with which the editors have been or are presently affiliated.

Chester Brown and Kate Miles

TABLE OF CASES

Decisions of ICSID and investment treaty tribunals

xix

Decisions of other international courts and tribunals

Decisions of national courts

TABLE OF TREATIES

Bilateral investment treaties

Multilateral Investment Treaties and Free Trade Agreements

Other international conventions

PART I

Introduction

1

Introduction: Evolution in investment treaty law and arbitration

CHESTER BROWN AND KATE MILES

International investment law is a well-established discipline grounded in principles of customary international law that stretch back into the nineteenth century. In recent times, however, it has become quite evident that the law is in a state of flux. In particular, with the advent of investor–State arbitration in the latter part of the twentieth century, new levels of complexity, uncertainty and substantive expansion have been emerging. Indeed, in many ways, a discrete field of investment treaty law has developed, largely driven by the exponential growth in investment treaty arbitration over the last decade. Together with the continued proliferation of bilateral investment treaties (BITs) as well as the more recent trend of States concluding free trade agreements (FTAs) containing investment chapters, the now often very detailed reasoning set out in an increasingly large number of arbitral awards has contributed to rapid developments in the field. Such change has reached into almost all areas of investment treaty law and practice, encompassing the interpretation of substantive obligations, an intensified focus on procedural matters, the participation of new actors and the more nuanced content of recent BITs. In many investment treaty awards, the tribunals undertake a close examination of previous investment treaty decisions, leading to the creation of what is now being regularly described as an investment treaty jurisprudence.[1]

This acceleration of activity does not, however, indicate consensus. On the contrary, investment treaty law and arbitration has very much become a high-profile area of contestation. In this regard, the controversy is not only reflected in the continuing debates on the implications

---

[1] See e.g. the terminology used throughout Campbell McLachlan, Laurence Shore and Matthew Weiniger, *International Investment Arbitration: Substantive principles* (Oxford University Press, 2007).

of substantive rules, but there has also been a discernible shift towards the consideration of systemic issues, such as the 'legitimacy' of the investment treaty system, its interaction with other areas of international law, the role of economic development in the regime, the problem of inconsistencies in awards and related procedural issues such as challenges to arbitrators and the need for greater transparency. It is, therefore, an opportune moment to take stock of the point at which investment treaty law and arbitration has arrived and to reflect on the processes currently unfolding within the field.

The multiplicity of this evolutionary process is the core theme for this volume. Having been struck by the breadth, complexity and pace of the changes occurring within the field, we convened a conference in February 2010 at the University of Sydney, Australia, to explore the implications of these issues and of the sense that individual developments were linked as manifestations of a more fundamental evolutionary shift in the law: 'Investment Treaty Law and Arbitration: Evolution and Revolution in Substance and Procedure'. Reflecting the many different voices within the field, the presenters were drawn from Europe, the United Kingdom, Asia, North America, South America, Australia and New Zealand; from academia, practice, arbitral institutions, civil society and arbitrators themselves. Significantly, there was also a blend of emerging scholars and practitioners together with the more established figures within the discipline. Indeed, it became quite apparent at this gathering that a new generation of experts in international investment law is emerging with new perspectives and new ideas. Many contributions in this volume are based upon presentations at that conference. They have been carefully selected to reflect both the substantive theme of the book (i.e. the 'evolution' in the field of investment treaty law and arbitration) and, symbolically, the simultaneous evolution of the identity of the authors writing on investment treaty law and arbitration.

Within the framework theme of evolution, the chapters examine ways in which investment treaty law is developing, analyse the most significant contemporary issues in the field, and consider the future direction of investment treaty law and arbitration. What has emerged in the course of these analyses, in particular, is the interaction between public and private law, interests and governance. This interface appears throughout the chapters in this volume in any number of manifestations, ranging from the more conceptual discussions on systemic issues through to the practice-oriented points on procedure. Excavating the many forms of this public–private relationship is a common thread linking the specific topics addressed in this volume. It is clear that these are issues without straightforward solutions. As they concern questions of fundamental importance on how to reconcile 'the public' and 'the private' within the law's own substance, structures and institutions, these issues will, undoubtedly, continue to occupy scholars and practitioners for many years still to come.

Structurally, the book has been organised to address four key subject areas within investment treaty law: shifts in fundamental character, actors in international investment law, the new significance of procedure and engagement with cross-cutting issues. Following on from this intro- ductory section, Part II of the book explores shifts of a systemic nature and considers issues arising out of the conceptualisation, and, indeed, re-conceptualisation, of international investment law. It opens with a chapter from Professor Philippe Sands QC addressing the notion of ethics and conflicts of interest within the investment treaty regime. Such matters can not only impact upon procedural and substantive issues, but also on conceptual questions related to the 'public' and the 'private' character of investment treaty law, and, perhaps, ultimately most signifi- cantly for the future legitimacy of the regime, on the practice of the law. His central theme also reflects the changing nature of our assumptions and understandings of the law as he extends the concept of conflict (until recently, largely concerned with conflict over substantive legal issues) to the 'internal' areas of contestation within the system, in particular, to the formal conflicts of interest that arise for counsel and arbitrators in investment disputes. In the course of his enquiry, Professor Sands focuses on questions about the less formal, but equally 'conflicted', nature of the arbitral system and the position of its participants, such as the ease with which counsel, arbitrators and expert witnesses switch from one role to another in successive disputes. Professor Sands argues strongly for the introduction of rules precluding the continuation of these practices, counteracting the standard objections, such as the pro- position that not everyone is in a financial position to elect to accept appointments as solely an arbitrator or counsel, with a condemnation of self-serving economic justifications when it is a fundamental matter of principle that is at stake – and one that is, indeed, increasingly seen as a source of disquiet more broadly at the operation of the investment arbitration.

The critique of the investment treaty regime as a whole is continued throughout the remainder of the chapters in Part II of this volume. Professor David A. R. Williams QC and Simon Foote consider recent developments in the very concept of 'investment' within the treaty system. The authors examine the divergent methodologies used to determine whether there is an 'investment' within the scope of the Convention for the Settlement of Investment Disputes between States and Nationals of other States (ICSID Convention),[2] and explore the current tensions created by the co-existing, yet conflicting, prescriptive and broader approaches to interpretation. From a systemic perspective, it is indicative of the depth of the ruptures currently within the field that discord of this nature has developed around such a foundational concept within investment treaty law. The accommodation of conflicting approaches is also explored by Dr Martins Paparinskis, albeit with a different emphasis. In his chapter, Dr Paparinskis analyses attempts to interpret investment treaties by reference to customary international law, identifying disagreement as to the relevance of such rules as a key source of inconsistency in the case law. Interestingly, although Dr Paparinskis confines his detailed analysis to the interaction between investment treaty law and 'general customary investment protection law', he also alludes to its wider application, almost as a case study for the future development of more generalised rules on interpretation by reference to custom.

The theme of 'the public' and 'the private' within international investment law is, perhaps, most overtly articulated in the chapter by Dr Alex Mills. Appraising the investment treaty system from a conceptual perspective, Dr Mills explores its inherent public–private dualities and argues that this innately contradictory character is located in its foundations and is at the heart of current controversies. It is this duality that allows either characterisation to be adopted as an essentially 'public' or 'private' system, leading to the development of the law in ostensibly conflicting directions. Dr Mills contends that as the system is neither wholly that of a public or private orientation, but simultaneously a complex coming together of both, a focus on one to the exclusion of the other has resulted in the emergence of explicable, but ultimately incomplete and inaccurate, representations. A systemic analysis of investment treaty arbitration is also undertaken by Jonathan Bonnitcha, although in his chapter, he brings a philosophical perspective to issues of interpretative methodology. He develops a normative framework for the

---

[2] Convention for the Settlement of Investment Disputes between States and Nationals of other States, opened for signature 18 March 1965, 575 UNTS 159 (entered into force 14 October 1966).

evaluation of the different approaches adopted by arbitral tribunals, exploring the theories of, amongst others, Bentham, Epstein and Rawls, and grounding his proposal in the work of Amartya Sen. In essence, Bonnitcha presents an assessment of the consequences of applying different interpretations to the protections guaranteed under investment treaties and an evaluation of the desirability of the various approaches. Again, in the chapter by Daniel Kalderimis, questions of a systemic nature are addressed. The focus for his investigation is the recently emerged conceptual framing of investment treaty arbitration as 'global administrative law'. In particular, Kalderimis presents the viewpoint of a practitioner, considering what the implications of this characterisation might be in practice. Ultimately, he argues, it is most likely that arbitrators of investment disputes will be called upon to contribute to the development of this new field of global administrative law and the formation of further regulatory principles.

The authors in Part II address a variety of topics. However, there is a shared approach that links their chapters. Each author takes a holistic view of the investment treaty regime and is concerned with matters of a systemic or fundamental nature. In particular, the issues identified and questions asked reflect recent trends away from a sole focus on individual points of substantive law towards enquiries into questions of legal theory, conceptual framings, and systemic legitimacy. Indeed, in many respects, this shift in mode of analysis is, in itself, a further manifestation of the current evolutionary state of affairs within international investment law. As the field of investment treaty law expands and develops, it is quite apparent that attention is turning from the immediately controversial issues to reflect also on questions of a more fundamental character. The chapters in Part II represent just such a transition.

Part III of this book focuses on another key area of transformation – actors in international investment law. In recent times, not only have new actors emerged within investment treaty arbitration, significantly changing the face of investment disputes, but important new issues for host States and investors have also materialised. Each of the chapters in Part III addresses an aspect of this dramatically shifting landscape. Opening the discourse, Dr Markus Burgstaller examines one of the most striking recent developments in the character of investors, being the escalation of transnational commercial activity by sovereign wealth funds. He argues that recent shifts in the investment strategies of many sovereign wealth funds, particularly the intensified focus on foreign rather than domestic investment, have fuelled host State anxieties regarding national security issues and economic influence over key sectors. In considering the implications of these trends, Dr Burgstaller discusses 'best practice' soft law initiatives developed by the Organisation for Economic Cooperation and Development and the International Monetary Fund so as to stave off a backlash against the activities of sovereign wealth funds. He also draws attention to restrictive regulation increasingly introduced by host States to limit the reach of sovereign wealth funds and explores whether such domestic measures contravene international investment law.

Pursuing the enquiry into new circumstances for existing actors in the field, Associate Professor Andrew Newcombe examines the changing environment for investors, in which the spotlight has recently turned from a sole focus on the conduct of host States to include also that of investors. Associate Professor Newcombe paints a picture of a 'quantum of solace' that must exist between the host State and the investor for the investment relationship to thrive, but explains that it is a mode of interaction that also impacts on the resolution of disputes. Exploring the ambiguities of reciprocal levels of trust between these participants, he argues for the adoption of differentiated responses to investor misconduct rather than treating the issue as a matter of jurisdictional exclusion.

A significant new actor in the investment treaty regime is the European Union (EU) – and, interestingly, in a number of capacities. As discussed by Dr Christina Knahr in Part IV of this volume in the section on procedural developments, the EU has recently appeared as *amicus curiae* in several investment treaty disputes filed against its Member States. In Part III, Dr Paul James Cardwell and Professor Duncan French analyse the EU's role as an actual party to investment treaties. In this capacity, the EU has recently concluded Economic Partnership Agreements that contain investment provisions with African, Caribbean and Pacific States. The authors examine the implications of the EU as a 'global investment actor', exploring both the ostensible synergies, and innately problematic relationship, between foreign investment as a development assistance tool and as a means to promote market liberalisation. Their analysis of the EU's approach to foreign investment is also considered against the backdrop of the unique set of pressures under which the EU must operate more generally.

Examining what has recently become a particularly controversial protection guarantee, Nick Gallus explores the fair and equitable treatment standard from the perspective of the host State, and, in particular, the relevance of the host State's level of economic development. He argues that the inconsistency in recent awards of the interpretation of States' obligations under the standard has led to uncertainty for host States. Based on arbitral awards, he identifies factors which are relevant in assessing whether the fair and equitable treatment standard may be applied in a differentiated way, in light of the circumstances faced by the host State. Similarly approaching current questions in the law from the viewpoint of the host State, Avidan Kent and Alexandra Harrington examine the recent engagement of investment arbitral tribunals with the customary international law defence of necessity. Kent and Harrington discuss recent awards addressing the doctrine and then consider the application of the defence to investment issues arising out of the most recent Global Financial Crisis, focusing in particular on the circumstances faced by Iceland. In the course of their enquiry, Kent and Harrington assert that the necessity doctrine is not only an important tool for States in times of crisis, but is also an essential instrument in their recovery trajectories. In arguing that the current application of the doctrine does not meet the contemporary needs of States, the authors suggest that, through an 'evolutive' approach to treaty interpretation,[3] several of the doctrine's conditions should be modified so as to produce more just outcomes for host States. Again linked in with the circumstances of the host State, one of the most contentious issues within investment treaty law and arbitration to date has been how to take better account of the public interest within investment treaties, host State–investor contracts, and the resolution of disputes. Suzanne Spears addresses this topic, highlighting the controversy surrounding the potential impact of investment treaty protections on host State regulation. She examines key substantive treaty protections and the implications of recent awards involving non-investment issues. In particular, she focuses on the shift in emphasis seen in the so-called 'new generation BITs'. She speculates that these investment treaties, which display a more balanced consideration of issues from the host State perspective, could, perhaps, prove to be the salvation of the regime, providing a much-needed boost to its internal legitimacy and, in the process, rescuing it from both its most blinkered 'cheerleaders' and most ardent critics.

---

[3] i.e. recognising that the meanings of certain terms may change with time: see e.g. C. Brown, 'Bringing sustainable development issues before Investment Treaty Tribunals' in M.-C. Cordonnier-Segger, M. Gehring and A. Newcombe, *Sustainable Development in World Investment Law* (The Hague: Kluwer, 2011), pp. 171, 185–7; and C. Brown, *A Common Law of International Adjudication* (Oxford University Press, 2007), pp. 46–9.

Exploring the theme of actors within international investment law from a unique angle, Professor Andrea Bjorklund poses the question whether the investment treaty regime would be strengthened by enhancing the role of sub-national government entities, such as State rather than federal governments, within investment arbitration. In particular, she considers the possibility of provincial governments appearing as disputing parties or *amicus curiae* in investment disputes, together with both the public-interest implications and the problematic aspects of doing so. Professor Bjorklund discusses recent examples of an expansionary approach to participation in investment arbitration, focusing on the Quechan tribe submission in *Glamis Gold* v. *United States of America*[4] and the argument that the federal government could not fully represent the tribe's perspective. She also points to the recent intervention of the EU as *amicus curiae* in investor claims made against its Member States. From this, Professor Bjorklund argues that, in the future, it is also likely that local and provincial governments will seek to appear in investor–State disputes on the basis that their interests are separate from, and not adequately represented by, the national government.

The chapters in Part III of this volume reveal a dynamic and changing environment in which new actors are emerging, previously inconceivable possibilities are taking shape and new issues are confronting those more established participants within the investment treaty field. What continues to manifest, even if indirectly, throughout the enquiries in this section, is the sense that so many aspects of the investment treaty regime are really only just beginning to grapple with the exact nature of the public–private relationship within the law and its processes. This underlying preoccupation is also quite clear in the remainder of the book with its addressing of the acceleration of procedural developments in investor–State arbitration and the multitude of cross-cutting issues with which investment treaty law comes into contact.

Part IV considers an intriguing development that has crept up almost unnoticed and taken the field somewhat by surprise – the new significance of procedure, which now rivals the participants' focus on the content of substantive obligations arising under BITs. It is, perhaps, the intensity of the recent focus on procedure and its application to investment arbitration, rather than the notion itself, that is surprising. Litigators have always been aware of the importance of procedural

---

[4] *Glamis Gold Ltd* v. *United States* (Application for Leave to File a Non-Party Submission of 19 August 2005).

matters. Indeed, it is well-understood that substantive disputes are often won or lost at interlocutory hearings. However, investment arbitration has, until recently, been characterised by an approach traditionally seen in international commercial arbitration, being that of a simple desire for a quick and inexpensive decision to resolve the dispute. The attention of practitioners and commentators was more likely to be focused on the resolution of the substantive issues in dispute, rather than any procedural complexities that arose along the way. As the chapters in Part IV demonstrate, however, that approach has quite clearly changed. In fact, the new appreciation of the importance of procedure has been one of the most significant shifts in the recent practice of investment treaty arbitration. And, from the complex nature of the procedural disputes now regularly heard in investor–State arbitration, it is evident that a willingness to explore the implications of procedural rules, as well as the potential tactical advantages presented by preliminary procedural points, has been embraced wholeheartedly.

Again, however, it can be seen from the chapters in Part IV that the conflicted public–private character of international investment law is also playing out in current schisms within the field over recent procedural developments. Dr Christina Knahr explores this ambivalence in her investigation into the application of the 2006 amendments to the ICSID rules on the participation of non-disputing parties and transparency. She argues that the new rules achieve a balance between public-interest requirements and the needs of the disputing parties in maintaining an efficient hearing of the dispute. Dr Knahr draws attention, however, to some, perhaps unexpected, consequences of the opening up of participation restrictions, namely the appearance of the EU as *amicus curiae* in several recent disputes. Dr Sergio Puig's chapter illustrates the new significance being placed on procedural issues, explaining the current impact of procedure on substantive treaty law. Specifically, he argues that the procedural mechanisms in Chapter 11 of the *North American Free Trade Agreement*[5] have encouraged systemic coherence within the field, counteracting the fragmentation that has been fostered by decentralised dispute-resolution systems. Judith Levine also explores the procedural rules used in investment arbitration. In particular, she examines the less well-known realm of investor–State arbitration under the United Nations Commission on International

---

[5] North American Free Trade Agreement, signed 17 December 1992), United States–Canada–Mexico (1993) 32 ILM 289, 605 (entered into force 1 January 1994) (NAFTA).

Trade Law (UNCITRAL) Arbitration Rules,[6] highlighting both the differences and similarities in approach as compared with the ICSID rules,
discussing the recent revision of the UNCITRAL rules, and analysing
controversial procedural issues such as transparency, non-disputing
party participation and challenges to arbitrators.

Continuing the in-depth examination of contemporary issues of
procedure, Dr J. Romesh Weeramantry and Claire Wilson call attention
to a significant issue that is increasingly appearing in investment treaty
disputes, but about which there has been little commentary to date. The
authors explore the implications of 'amount of compensation' clauses
and the divergent lines of authority on whether these clauses allow
the consideration of substantive questions or render the tribunal confined solely to assessing quantum. Presenting a viewpoint from practice,
Andrew Stephenson, Lee Carroll and Jonathon DeBoos analyse an issue
in which, again, contemporary trends in the melding of procedure and
substance can be seen. The authors discuss the enforcement of awards
made pursuant to investment treaties, the interference of local courts in
international arbitration and whether a refusal to enforce an award or
the conducting of a merits review, in themselves, constitute a substantive
breach of investment treaty obligations. Together with several others in
this volume, the chapter by Dr Sam Luttrell bridges the perspectives of a
practitioner and scholar. It also serves to connect Parts IV and V of the
book, reflecting both the new prominence of procedural matters within
investment treaty arbitration and recent controversies surrounding
investment law and its interaction with cross-cutting issues. In this
regard, Dr Luttrell addresses the recent prevalence of bias challenges
against arbitrators in investor–State arbitration, enquiring as to what
can be learnt from such challenges in international commercial arbitration. Drawing from experiences in the commercial arbitration field, he
argues that there are several factors at play in the increase of such
challenges. While these reasons certainly include a new appreciation of
the strategic advantages offered by procedural rules, Dr Luttrell also
identifies decidedly less benign elements. In particular, he points to the
competiveness amongst law firms, generational conflict and the desire to
remove an arbitrator, or most recently even now counsel, from the case
for less than legitimate reasons.

---

[6] UNCITRAL Arbitration Rules (1976), available at www.uncitral.org/pdf/english/texts/
arbitration/arb-rules/arb-rules.pdf (last accessed 15 February 2011). The UNCITRAL Arbitration Rules were revised in 2010: see www.uncitral.org/uncitral/en/uncitral_texts/
arbitration.html (last accessed 15 February 2011).

Over the last decade, there has been an intensification of concern at the way in which investment treaty law and arbitration interacts with non-investment law, policy and issues. This not only remains one of the most contested areas of international investment law, but new manifestations of such conflict continue to emerge. Part V of this volume explores these cross-cutting issues, which span across a diverse range of subjects from the more commercially oriented disciplines, such as intellectual property, to those more traditionally grounded in the public interest such as human rights, environmental protection and development. From the analyses in Part V, it is evident that, within the investment field, responses to the challenges posed by cross-cutting interaction are still very much in the process of unfolding. Dr Henning Grosse Ruse-Khan opens this section with an examination of investment treaty protections and their relationship with intellectual property rights. In particular, focusing on public-health issues and the pharmaceutical industry, he delves into the question of whether, when applied to intellectual property rights, the protections regularly contained in investment treaties go beyond those set out in multilateral intellectual property agreements. This analysis is set against a background of the wider discourse on regime fragmentation and coherence in public international law.

Whether investment treaty protections have the potential to impact negatively on the sustainable development trajectories of host States has also proven to be a particularly controversial issue. Stabilisation clauses contained in host State–investor contracts have often been at the centre of those concerns. In his chapter examining drafting models for stabilisation clauses, Antony Crockett moves the debate forward by considering practical avenues to minimise the potential for conflict within the contract itself and, in so doing, also contributes to the wider discourse on how to reconcile the foreign investor's requirement for a stable and predictable legal framework with the host State's right to regulate. The remaining chapters in Part V also address the interaction of investment treaty protections with development issues and the obligations of States to meet the public welfare needs of their citizens in the future, albeit in very different forms from that discussed by Crockett. Anastasia Telesetsky examines the recent escalation of large-scale foreign land leases in Africa and Asia. She discusses the dynamics of agribusiness in developing States, the impacts of such land leases on local environments and communities and the more long-term concerns over food security issues. Telesetsky also considers whether there are likely to be any repercussions under international investment law in the future if host States seek to terminate these leases for reasons related to environmental concerns or public welfare needs, such as local food shortages, and makes a series of drafting suggestions to take better account of such needs within investment treaties.

The interaction between human rights issues and international investment law is multi-layered, complex and controversial. In her contribution to this volume, Emma Truswell addresses a particularly contentious aspect of this interface, and one that is likely to remain of significant concern well into the future – water. Truswell examines the co-existing qualities of freshwater as a biological necessity and a tradeable commodity, discussing the movement towards recognition of water as a human right, the economics of water pricing and the innate difficulties in the provision of water services by the private sector. She analyses the treatment of water-related investment disputes by arbitral tribunals, highlighting the fact that consistent approaches have not, as yet, emerged to govern water service contracts. Given the unique character of water, Truswell argues for the development of mechanisms to enable more effective management of foreign-owned water services and principles of differentiated treatment for water contracts under international investment law. Consideration of the development needs of the host State is also very much the focus of the chapter by Dr Omar E. García-Bolívar in which the role of economic development in the definition of 'investment' is examined. Indeed, Dr García-Bolívar argues that not only is the 'contribution to economic development a measurable concept, but that it is, in fact, the most important element in ascertaining what constitutes an investment under the ICSID Convention'.

In a literal adoption of the term 'cross-cutting', Dr Kyla Tienhaara blends disciplines and applies the perspective of a scholar in international relations to analysing the impact of investor–State arbitration on host State policy space and the capacity to regulate in the public interest. She provides a detailed investigation into the issue of regulatory chill, addressing the key arguments often used to discount claims of regulatory chill resulting from the threat of investment arbitration. Setting out specific case studies in her chapter, Dr Tienhaara draws attention to the fact that many investor–State conflicts do not proceed to an actual arbitral hearing and calls for the conducting in the future of more interdisciplinary research into the affects of non-progressing investor claims on host States.

Part VI concludes this volume with chapters by Professor M Sornarajah and Sir Franklin Berman KCMG QC that provide a broader evaluation of the state of play within investment treaty law and arbitration together with projections for the future. In essence, these chapters encapsulate the sense of changing understandings, evolving principles, and emerging uncertainties that characterise the field at the present time. Professor Sornarajah frames the current position as one of 'normlessness', in which persistent conflict manifests in expansive arbitral awards giving effect to neoliberal ideology on the one hand, and differing arbitral interpretations and restrictive State responses on the other, leading to conceptual chaos. He provides an extensive assessment of the 'malaise' that exists within investor–State arbitration, arguing that the excess and greed of multiple actors have, over time, subverted the system. Sir Franklin Berman depicts a system very much in the process of developing, as one in the midst of responding to both internal and external pressures. In particular, it is a system grappling with challenges to its own legitimacy, uncertainties around its fundamental tenets, contradictory conceptualisations of its public–private nature and a need to reconcile the conflict that is present in countless forms. At the same time, Sir Franklin observes that many of the criticisms levelled at investor–State arbitration are not unique, and that similar difficulties are experienced in the development of many dispute-settlement regimes. Sir Franklin discusses a number of current issues, including ways in which the further development of the system might be safeguarded, including an awareness of professional responsibilities, of proper application of the rules of treaty interpretation, of the importance of the quality of awards, of correctly identifying the applicable law and of the responsibilities incumbent upon all those operating within the system. He poses many questions for which there are no straightforward answers. It is, however, an opportunity to reflect on those questions, and on the numerous issues raised throughout this volume.

This volume seeks to survey the terrain of investment treaty arbitration and take stock at a time of great activity and rapid development. Some in the field have the tendency to descend into hyperbole. It is the purpose of this volume, however, to provide a balanced assessment of the challenges being faced in the development of international investment law. As is clear from the foregoing review of the various chapters in this volume, those challenges are many, and include conflicting conceptual understandings of the very nature of the investment treaty regime, the emergence of new actors affected by investment treaty law, the development of complex procedural issues in investment arbitration and the interaction between international investment law with multi-layered issues of sustainable development and obligations arising under other international regimes. These challenges are difficult, and it is

apparent that accommodating the various interests in the further development of international investment law will require a great deal of effort
from all stakeholders in the system. Ultimately, it is our hope that this
volume will contribute to this process, and to the better understanding
of what is a fascinating and important period in the evolution of
international investment law.

PART II

Shifts in fundamental character

2

Conflict and conflicts in investment treaty arbitration: Ethical standards for counsel

PHILIPPE SANDS QC[*]

I would like to begin by thanking the editors for inviting me to contribute this chapter to this volume, and in particular for their efforts in contributing to the creation of the new generation that will take forward this area of the law.

I Personal considerations

The international law of foreign investment law is a subject of considerable personal interest. It is the matter addressed by my first academic position, back in 1984, working with Elihu Lauterpacht at the newly established Research Centre for International Law at Cambridge University. For four years we worked together on a project on investment treaty arbitration; much time, I recall, was spent trying to reconstitute what had happened in the old Delagoa Bay Railway arbitration,[1] one of the very first cases to address now familiar issues. A foreign investment dispute was also the subject of the first set of instructions I ever received as a barrister, back in 1986: it was a 'hand-me-down' from Sir Ian Sinclair, the early ICSID case of *Southern Pacific Properties* v. *Egypt*;[2] I recall spending about three days on some remote part of the case that most likely had no role in the outcome. Since then, investment disputes have been a regular feature of my workload, some more memorable than others. Few cases can beat *Tradex Hellas* v. *Albania*,[3] not least for the way in which that case arrived. I recall sitting in my office at the School of

---

[*] I would like to thank Ioana Hyde for her assistance in preparing the published version of the lecture.
[1] *United States and Great Britain* v. *Portugal (Delagoa Bay Railway)*, Moore, International Arbitrations, vol. II, 1865; Henri La Fontaine, *Pasicrisie Internationale* (1900), p. 397.
[2] *Southern Pacific Properties* v. *Egypt* (ICSID Case No. ARB/84/3, Award of 20 May 1992).
[3] *Tradex Hellas* v. *Albania* (ICSID Case No. ARB/94/2, Award of 29 April 1999).

Oriental and African Studies (SOAS) in Russell Square in London, in 1994, receiving a phone call from a former student, Stephen Hodgson, to let me know that he was in the Legal Adviser's Office in the Ministry of Agriculture in Tirana, Albania. He had come across a locked cupboard in the legal adviser's office that he had gained access to, and found a number of unopened Federal Express packages sent by Ibrahim Shihata, the general counsel of the World Bank also responsible for ICSID. The letters notified Albania about pending proceedings. The Fedex packages seem to have been ignored. A first procedural hearing had been set. Albania appeared to have taken no action. Was I in a position to help? James Crawford, Ruth Mackenzie and I took on the case, one in which Albania eventually prevailed on the merits. I believe that the total costs of counsel for the entire case – comprising a jurisdiction phase and a merits phase, several rounds of written pleadings and two hearings – came to less than £100,000. No case has been more memorable!

Since those days the world of investment disputes seems to have changed rather dramatically, not least in relation to costs. ICSID was little known, the Permanent Court of Arbitration was inactive; twenty-five years later the situation is transformed, with investment treaty arbitration being amongst the most vibrant and exciting areas of international law. You only need to look at the large number of awards to be able to appreciate the richness of the legal issues, and also to recognise the range of strongly held views about many of the key issues of the day: the meaning of expropriation and of fair and equitable treatment, the effect of a most-favoured nation (MFN) clause and the implications of an umbrella clause. These are issues that will be familiar to anyone involved in investment treaty arbitrations. Alongside these issues of substance are also some growing issues of legitimacy, as some States withdraw from the ICSID system against a background of concerns as to the adequacy of the system's ability to balance the legitimate interests of investors, on the one hand, and of States, on the other. Over the long term, such balance will be indispensable to the well-being of the system. I have been privileged to observe these changes over the past two decades, having been involved as counsel in a number of cases, and – since 2008 – sitting as arbitrator in several more.

II   The growing importance of imposing limits on arbitration roles

In this chapter I will address one aspect that touches on the legitimacy and effectiveness of the ICSID system, one that goes to heart of the subject of this volume: it concerns the question of the propriety of lawyers acting simultaneously as counsel and arbitrator – in different cases of course – in cases that largely raise the same or similar legal issues. In October 2009, I participated in a lively and well-reported session on this issue at the meeting of the International Bar Association in Madrid. The room was full, and deeply split on this subject, with a range of strongly held views being aired and reported.[4]

Until 2007, having acted in a number of investment treaty arbitrations, acting on both sides, for claimant and respondent, I declined approaches to act as arbitrator. In the summer of 2007, I decided to make a switch and accepted, for the first time, appointment as arbitrator in an ICSID case. In so doing it seemed appropriate to cease to act as counsel in cases that raised similar issues to those that might come before me. I would see through the existing case load, which would be resolved before any decision would have to be made on the merits of a case in which I was sitting as an arbitrator. On the website of my chambers a notice was posted indicating that henceforth I would not accept new instructions 'to act as counsel in proceedings brought pursuant to Article 36 of the ICSID Convention'. This followed a practice adopted by a number of other colleagues.

What caused such a decision to be taken? One influence may have been the experience of the *Pinochet* proceedings before the House of Lords in 1998, when that highest court's landmark judgment – on the ability of a former head of State to claim immunity from the jurisdiction of the English courts in circumstances alleging involvement in an international crime – was set aside following information that one of the law lords had a connection with one of the intervenors that had not been disclosed.[5] The need to maintain a perception of absolute independence of the adjudicating panel on that most vital of cases had a big impact. It caused many involved in those proceedings to step outside the narrow community of lawyers of which we are a part and ask ourselves how others in the broader community might see us: how does the man or woman on the Clapham omnibus perceive a judge's independence? The case provided a salutary reminder that lawyers have a broader set of responsibilities, beyond the narrow legal community of which we are a

---

[4] See e.g. the 'Double Hat' debate in International Arbitration, *The New York Law Journal* (14 June 2010), available at www.dechert.com/library/070101031Dechert.pdf (last accessed 13 February 2011).

[5] *R v. Bow Street Metropolitan Stipendiary Magistrate, ex p. Pinochet Ugarte (No. 2)*, 2 WLR 272 (HL 1999).

part. As lawyers we are also bound to inform ourselves about broader public perceptions as to the legitimacy of the international arbitration system as a whole.

It must be said that as counsel, I, and others, had also on occasion experienced issues that raised concerns. In one hearing, for example, a distinguished and thoroughly decent opponent prepared to address before an arbitral tribunal a case in which he had sat as arbitrator. Is it appropriate for counsel to do that? It was suggested to him that he may want to proceed with caution before referring to a case in which he had been privy to the internal deliberations of the arbitral tribunal, a situation which might disadvantage the other party. An informal objection was made. The opponent acted impeccably, indicating that he had not thought of the point and, having now had a chance to reflect on it, he recognised its merit and would not proceed further in addressing that case. In another case, my equally distinguished opponents invoked an award in which one of their counsel had sat as arbitrator and handed down an award directly touching upon a legal issue that arose in our case. The earlier award had been handed down in the period between the start of our case, and the conduct of the hearings. This raised the possibility that a reasonable observer might conclude that the award might have been influenced by the issues arising in the forthcoming case. The point was raised as follows:

> A reasonable observer might conclude that counsel is relying on his own award, and this gives rise to conflict between activities as an arbitrator on the one hand, and counsel on the other hand. The standard to be applied is one that's been identified by the Appellate Chamber of the International Criminal Tribunal for the Former Yugoslavia in the case of *Prosecutor* v. *Furundzija* (2000): 'there is a general rule that a Judge should not only be subjectively free from bias, but also that there should be nothing in the surrounding circumstances which objectively gives rise to an appearance of bias.'[6] The Respondent submits that this principle is equally applicable to an arbitrator. Where an arbitrator has given an award in respect of legal issues arising in one case and where he or she is at the same time acting as counsel in another case in circumstances in which his client may obtain benefit from the award that he has given as arbitrator, then facts may objectively give rise to an appearance of bias. An objective person might reasonably conclude that there was a risk that the arbitrator might be influenced by his other professional commitments.

[6] *Prosecutor* v. *Furundzija* (ICTY Appeals Chamber, Case No. IT-95–17/1-A, Judgment of 21 July 2000), para. 189.

The arbitral tribunal was invited to make no reference to that part of the previous arbitral award that addressed the legal point in dispute. Although the tribunal did make a mention of the award in question, no reference was made to that part of the award that had given rise to the expression of concern.

The issue that arises seems reasonably clear: it is possible to recognise the difficulty that may arise if a lawyer spends a morning drafting an arbitral award that addresses a contentious legal issue, and then in the afternoon as counsel in a different case drafts a pleading making arguments on the same legal issue. Can that lawyer, while acting as arbitrator, cut herself off entirely from her simultaneous role as counsel? The issue is not whether she thinks it can be done, but whether a reasonable observer would so conclude. Speaking for myself, I find it difficult to imagine that I could do so without, in some way, potentially being seen to run the risk of allowing myself to be influenced, however subconsciously. That said, a number of my closest colleagues and friends take a different view.

This has come to be known as an 'issue conflict', on which significant literature has been developing over the past few years. A recent article by Professor Rusty Park addresses new categories of possible conflict that may suggest themselves, concluding that increasing concern has been expressed about 'issue conflict' and its sibling of 'role confusion'. Professor Park's experience is mainly in commercial arbitration, although he has considerable experience in investment treaty arbitration. He describes 'issue conflict' and 'role confusion' as representing a special form of pre-judgment:

> On occasion, an arbitrator must address, in the context of an arbitration, the very same issue presented to him or his law firm as advocate in another case, or to himself as scholar in academic writings. It is not difficult to see why such situations might compromise the integrity of the arbitral process. The arbitrator might be tempted, even subconsciously, to add a sentence to an award that could later be cited in another case. Such an *arrière pensée* might lead to disparaging or approving some legal authority or argument regularly presented in similar disputes, and thus intended to persuade in a different matter where the arbitrator's firm acts as counsel. The flip side of the coin might also present itself, with an arbitrator influenced by his or her position while acting as counsel in another case.[7]

---

[7] W. R. Park, 'Arbitrator integrity: The transient and the permanent', *San Diego Law Review*, 46 (2009), 692–704.

We are bound to recognise that at the heart of many investment treaty cases, the outcome will turn on the same issues: expropriation, fair and equitable treatment, full protection and security, the effect of MFN clauses, of 'umbrella clauses' and so on. This feature distinguishes the field of investment treaty arbitration from commercial arbitration: in the latter, the same legal issues do not come out with such regularity or frequency, in part because the applicable law will often differ. Special attention is required in investment treaty arbitration because of particular features of this area, including the fact that the applicable law is invariably the same set of rules of public international law, coupled with the point that investment arbitration cases often raise issues that are of particular political sensitivity to the States involved whilst directly affecting the economic interests of the investor. Both constitute legitimate concerns that require protection and special prudence in the field of investment treaty arbitration, an area that cannot be characterised as being exclusively commercial in character: investment treaty arbitration also has a core public law function.

III Domestic case law

These issues have been broadly rehearsed in the domestic context and States have, largely speaking, raised different standards: either the 'justifiable doubts' standard or the 'real danger' test when assessing whether an arbitrator is disqualified on the basis of 'issue conflict'. Most jurisdictions apply the 'justifiable doubts' test, which requires a showing of objective facts that a reasonable, well-informed person would regard as constituting bias on the arbitrator's part. A minority of jurisdictions – including England, Wales, Northern Ireland and the United States – utilise a 'real danger' test which requires a showing that there is a real manifestation of subjective bias before an arbitrator is removed.[8] This is a higher threshold.

In England, Wales and Northern Ireland, an arbitrator will not generally be deemed to have 'issue bias' if the arbitrator expresses an opinion on the law implicated in a case in extra-curricular academic writings.

---

[8] Although the England and Wales Arbitration Act 1996 specifically refers to 'justifiable grounds' being needed for removal of an arbitrator, courts have interpreted this requirement to require a higher threshold before an arbitrator is removed due to lack of impartiality (see *AT&T Corp.* v. *Saudi Cable* [2000] 2 All ER (Comm) 625, holding that there must be a 'real danger' that an arbitrator will not be impartial before the arbitrator will be removed by the court).

Removal of an arbitrator due to 'issue bias' requires that she has expressed her views in 'intemperate terms', such that one party to the proceedings would clearly be seen as being favoured by the adjudicator. In *Locabail* v. *Bayfield Properties*,[9] for example, a barrister specialising in pro-claimant personal injury litigation presided as the judge over a personal injury case. He disclosed his membership in an association which ordinarily represented claimants rather than defendants, and the parties waived the conflict. Subsequently, the defendant discovered an article written by the presiding judge that expressed views in trenchant terms in favour of claimants and critical of defendants and their insurers. On appeal, the English court held that, although extra-curricular comment in textbooks and articles was not incompatible with the discharge of judicial functions and would not ordinarily of itself give rise to a real danger of bias, the intemperate terms in which the recorder had expressed views critical of defendants and their insurers could have given rise to the possibility that, in resolving the case, the judge had favoured the claimant against the defendant. The presiding judge was deemed to have demonstrated impermissible bias.

More recently, the House of Lords has addressed 'role confusion' in the case of *Lawal* v. *Northern Spirit Limited*.[10] The issue examined by the court was whether the appeal hearing before the Employment Appeal Tribunal (EAT) was impermissibly biased due to the fact that counsel for one party had previously sat in his capacity as a part-time EAT judge with one or both of the lay EAT members currently hearing the appeal. The House of Lords made clear that it was the appearance of bias, rather than actual bias, that was implicated in the case. The pertinent test was whether 'a fair-minded and informed observer' would believe that the circumstances were such that there was a 'real possibility of subconscious bias'. The House of Lords concluded that there was a real possibility that such an observer would conclude that the tribunal was biased. Much like the prohibition against judges serving as counsel before the same jury members due to the danger of undue weight being given to the arguments of the judge acting as counsel, an impartial observer would believe that the lay members of the tribunal would likewise look for legal guidance to the EAT judge serving as counsel in a case before them, and be unduly swayed by the QC's arguments. If this arrangement is allowed to continue, public confidence in the administration of justice in

[9] *Locabail* v. *Bayfield Properties* [2000] 1 All ER 65.
[10] *Lawal* v. *Northern Spirit Limited* [2003] UKHL 35.

EAT cases would be eroded. The court further noted that what was once acceptable to the public may no longer be so today. The House of Lords agreed with the dissenting judge in the Court of Appeals,[11] ruling that the current 'revolving door' system should be discontinued by imposing a requirement that part-time EAT judges not be allowed to also serve as counsel before an EAT panel comprising one or two lay members with whom (s)he had previously sat.

In the United States, a party who alleges arbitrator bias must show 'evident partiality' as stipulated in the Federal Arbitration Act[12] and must meet a fairly high threshold before the award will be set aside. In a case dealing with a challenge to arbitrator impartiality, the US Supreme Court held that arbitrators must disclose not only circumstances that amount to arbitrator bias, but also circumstances that may create the appearance of bias. In *Commonwealth Coatings Corp.* v. *Continental Casualty Co.,*[13] for example, the dispute involved a subcontractor who sued the sureties on the prime contractor's bond to recover money allegedly due for a painting job. Pursuant to the arbitration agreement, each party appointed an arbitrator, who then appointed a third arbitrator. The petitioner challenged the arbitral award due to the third arbitrator being an engineering consultant whose services had been utilised by the respondent over a period of four to five years in exchange for approximately $12,000. This information had not been disclosed by the third arbitrator to the parties. The lower courts refused to vacate the arbitral award, but the US Supreme Court disagreed and reversed. In a split decision, a four-judge plurality endorsed the broad 'appearance of bias' test, stating

---

[11] *Ibid.*, paras. 19–23. Dissenting Judge Pill LJ states,

> The fair-minded and informed lay observer will readily perceive, I have no doubt, the collegiate spirit in which the Appeal Tribunal operates and the degree of trust which lay members repose in the presiding judge. It is in my judgment likely to diminish public confidence in the administration of justice if a judge who enjoys that relationship with lay members, with the degree of reliance placed on his view of the law, subsequently appears before them as an advocate. The fair-minded observer might well reasonably perceive that the litigant opposed by an advocate who is a member of the Tribunal and has sat with its lay members is at a disadvantage as a result of that association. A litigant's doubt about impartiality . . . would, for the reasons given, be a legitimate doubt. In my view, the procedure does not inspire public confidence.

[12] Federal Arbitration Act, 9 USC sec. 10(2) (Amended 2010).
[13] See *Commonwealth Coatings Corp.* v. *Continental Casualty Co.*, 393 US 145 (1968).

that 'arbitrators [must] disclose to the parties any dealings that might create an impression of possible bias'.[14] Justice Black noted, in dictum, that courts should be even more careful of ensuring the impartiality of arbitrators than of judges since, unlike judicial officers, arbitrators 'have completely free rein to decide the law as well as the facts and are not subject to appellate review'.[15] Whilst not expected to sever all ties with the business community since arbitrators are not likely to be able to earn a livelihood from arbitration alone, arbitrators must disclose to the parties 'any dealings that might create an impression of possible bias'.[16] The concurring judges, however, indicate in dictum that the court did not decide in this case that arbitrators are held to the same standard as judges. Unlike judges, arbitrators may continue to have business relationships that may touch on issues or parties involved in an arbitration, but have a duty to disclose such dealings. Three judges dissented on the grounds that there was no actual bias alleged on the arbitrator's part, and that the parties had agreed to a methodology for selecting arbitrators that had been followed in this case and should therefore be given effect.

In the broader European context, Article 6(1) of the European Convention on Human Rights (ECHR) is relevant.[17] It has been interpreted to require arbitrator disqualification if his public statements are such as to justify the applicant's reasonable fear that the decision-maker would not be impartial.[18] In *Buscemi* v. *Italy*, for example, the presiding judge in a child protection and custody case and the father of the child in the case pending before the judge had a series of exchanges in the local newspaper regarding the proceedings.[19] The judge expressed the view

---

[14] *Ibid.*, p. 149.   [15] *Ibid.*   [16] *Ibid.*

[17] European Convention for the Protection of Human Rights and Fundamental Freedoms, opened for signature 4 November 1950, 213 UNTS 221 (entered into force 3 September 1953), Art. 6(1) (ECHR).

[18] *Buscemi* v. *Italy* (European Court of Human Rights, Case No. 29569/95, Court Decision of 16 December 1999).

[19] On 24 June 1994, the presiding judge made general comments about the work of the court, including that they were not child snatchers and sought to protect children from suffering. The child's father submitted a response, published on 11 July 1994, stating, inter alia, that: 'In such a case I doubt whether the President, Judge L., . . . can say "we have released a child from its suffering" or "we are not child-snatchers".' The Judge replied on 8 August 1994:

> [The applicant's] account of events is inaccurate as regards the fundamental circumstances of the case . . . Custody of the child was awarded not to the father but to the mother. At home, both on account of the disputes between the parents and other circumstances of which I cannot give details, she was living in very difficult conditions, which led to episodes

that there had been good reasons to remove the child from the father, and the father sought to remove the judge from the pending case due to his statements in the press. The European Court of Human Rights found that there was a violation of ECHR Article 6(1) since the judge's statement was such as to justify the applicant's reasonable fear that the judge would not be impartial.

IV Cases before international investment tribunals

The standard for 'issue conflict' has not been addressed, as such, in the ICSID or UNCITRAL rules. The ICSID Convention has a standard of 'manifest lack of quality' in Articles 14, 57 and 58.[20] Article 14(1) provides that arbitrators 'shall be persons of high moral character and recognized competence . . . who may be relied upon to exercise independent judgment'.[21] Article 57 provides a mechanism by which a party may seek disqualification of an arbitrator by showing 'a *manifest* lack of the qualities required by paragraph (1) of Article 14'.[22] This is a higher standard than the UNCITRAL rules, Article 10(1) of which provides: 'Any arbitrator may be challenged if circumstances exist that give rise to justifiable doubts as to the arbitrator's impartiality or independence.'[23]

There is also guidance, frequently referred to but in no way dispositive, from the International Bar Association Guidelines on Conflicts of Interest.[24] The standard to be applied is whether the existing factors, 'from a reasonable third person's point of view having knowledge of the relevant facts, give rise to justifiable doubts as to the arbitrator's

---

of violence, even physical violence, and which, over time, genuinely undermined the child's physical and psychological stability. It was absolutely necessary to remove her precisely in order to release her from an oppressive situation . . . She was very happy to be somewhere quiet and peaceful at last. Clearly, if and when the parents overcome the difficulties in their relationship, the child will be able to go home. I guarantee that everyone who has worked on and is working on this case is highly qualified: specialist juvenile judges, social workers, psychologists . . .

[20] Convention for the Settlement of Investment Disputes between States and Nationals of other States, opened for signature 18 March 1965, 575 UNTS 159 (entered into force 14 October 1966), Arts. 14, 57–8 (ICSID Convention).

[21] *Ibid.*, Art. 14(1).

[22] *Ibid.*, Art. 57 (emphasis added).

[23] UNCITRAL Rules of Arbitration, Art. 10(1), available at www.uncitral.org (last accessed 12 February 2011).

[24] International Bar Association, 'IBA Guidelines on Conflicts of Interest in International Arbitration' (22 May 2004).

impartiality or independence'.[25] The IBA Guidelines explain that: 'Doubts are justifiable if a reasonable and informed third party would reach the conclusion that there was a likelihood that the arbitrator may be influenced by factors other than the merits of the case as presented by the parties in reaching his or her decision.'[26] A number of non-exhaustive examples are given to illustrate situations where doubts are justifiable, but the Guidelines do not deal with 'issue conflict' as such.

With these considerations in mind, let me now turn to some recent cases that may be pertinent to 'issue conflict'. It is notable that recently there has been an increase in challenges to arbitrators in investment treaty disputes. In addressing these cases, and the topic of 'issue conflict' generally, it must be emphasised that I do not want to be taken as suggesting that any of these arbitrators have acted otherwise than in good faith and with complete integrity. The absence of guidance, and the apparent novelty of the issues, gives rise to cases of the kind that we now face with growing frequency.

A Telekom Malaysia Berhad v. Republic of Ghana

The first case is *Telekom Malaysia Berhad* v. *Republic of Ghana*.[27] This was an UNCITRAL arbitration case before the Permanent Court of Arbitration. The petitioner challenged the propriety of one of the arbitrators, Professor Gaillard, to serve in that capacity while also serving as counsel in the *RFCC/Morocco* dispute that involved a similar claim of expropriation where Professor Gaillard was alleged to be likely to take on a position that was adverse to the petitioner and which was alleged would create arbitrator bias. The tribunal held that one cannot concomitantly serve as an arbitrator and as a lawyer in different arbitrations raising similar issues in dispute due to the existence of the appearance of bias. However, one can serve as arbitrator if willing to resign as counsel in the parallel case; in other words, if the arbitrator resigns as counsel, there will be no automatic disqualification from the role as arbitrator. Professor Gaillard was given ten days from the date of judgment to elect whether he wished to stop serving as arbitrator or preferred to stop serving as

---

[25] *Ibid.*, Art. 2(b).   [26] *Ibid.*, Art. 2(c).

[27] *Telekom Malaysia Berhad* v. *Republic of Ghana* (UNCITRAL Case No. HA/RK 2004, 667, Decision of the District Court of the Hague of 18 October 2004); and *Telekom Malaysia Berhad* v. *Republic of Ghana* (UNCITRAL Case No. HA/RK 2004, 788, Decision of the District Court of the Hague of 5 November 2004).

counsel, and he elected the latter. The test applied was whether, from an objective point of view, 'justified doubts exist with respect to his impartiality and independence',[28] a standard that includes an examination of the appearance of bias. The tribunal concluded that there were justified doubts in this situation.

B   Eureko v. Republic of Poland

The second case is *Eureko* v. *Republic of Poland*,[29] an ad hoc arbitration with arbitrator appointments governed by Belgian law. Following the rendering of an arbitral award in favour of Eureko, the Republic of Poland challenged the impartiality of one of the arbitrators, Mr Schwebel, due to the publication of what was subsequently determined to be erroneous information linking Mr Schwebel to the Washington DC office of Sidley Austin, a law firm that had participated in litigation against the Republic of Poland. The arbitrator had not, in fact, been involved in the prior case against Poland and his only connection to Sidley Austin was that their offices were in the same building. Applying Belgian law, the Brussels Court of First Instance held that the request for recusal of the arbitrator was without merit, finding that the factors alleged in this case were insufficient to maintain a suspicion with regards to the arbitrator's independence and impartiality. On appeal before the Belgian Court of Appeal,[30] Poland made an additional objection to Mr Schwebel's impartiality, alleging that he was acting as co-counsel with Sidley Austin in an unrelated concurrent ICSID arbitration, *Vivendi* v. *Argentina*, where, representing the investor, Mr Schwebel's legal team had cited the *Eureko* award as authority for certain propositions made before the tribunal. Poland argued that Mr Schwebel's impartiality was affected by his participation as arbitrator in rendering an award in the *Eureko* case which subsequently aided his arguments in his capacity as counsel in the other case. The Brussels Court of Appeal avoided the issue. It refused to consider the additional objection because Poland had failed to raise it before the Court of First

[28] *Ibid.*, Pt. 4, para. 6.
[29] *Eureko* v. *Republic of Poland* (R.G. 2006/1542/A, Decision of the Brussels Court of First Instance of 22 December 2006).
[30] *Eureko* v. *Republic of Poland* (R.G. 2007/AR/70, Decision of the Belgian Court of Appeal of 29 October 2007), as discussed in S. Luttrell, *Bias Challenges in International Commercial Arbitration: The need for a 'real danger' test* (The Hague: Kluwer, 2009), pp. 63–127, especially p. 92.

Instance and therefore the Court of Appeal indicated it was barred from considering it.[31]

C   Hrvatska Elektroprivreda *v.* Republic of Slovenia

The third case is *Hrvatska Elektroprivreda* v. *Republic of Slovenia,* an ICSID arbitration.[32] The respondent disclosed, shortly before the commencement of the oral hearing, its intention to add David Mildon QC to its legal team. Mr Mildon was based at the same barrister's chambers as the President of the Tribunal. The ICSID tribunal discussed both the IBA rules regarding prompt disclosure, which did not occur in the present case, and ICSID Article 56 regarding the immutability of properly constituted tribunals, which does not allow a party to modify its legal team if doing so would imperil the tribunal's status or legitimacy. The tribunal held that a party may not change the composition of its legal team at the last moment when the proposed new counsel is from the same chambers as an arbitrator, particularly when no prompt disclosure of such representation had been made and the addition would cause the President of the Tribunal to recuse himself (there had been another case, less well publicised, in which a member of that chambers serving as arbitrator had recused himself when it emerged that one of the counsel appearing before the tribunal was a lawyer with whom the arbitrator had ongoing professional ties).[33] The test applied by the ICSID tribunal in *Hrvatska* was whether the situation would lead a reasonable observer to form justifiable doubts regarding the tribunal's impartiality and independence, concluding, in this case, that it would. Here, of course, the decision was not directed against an arbitrator, but rather against a counsel appearing before the arbitral tribunal, but the concern was motivated by the fact that absent such a decision determining that counsel could not act, the arbitrator may be in the position of having to recuse himself.

---

[31] The Belgian Court of Appeal also noted that Poland failed to notify the arbitrators in accordance with the Belgian procedural rules, and this too affected the court's ability to examine the new objection.

[32] *Hrvatska Elektroprivreda* v. *Republic of Slovenia* (ICSID Case No. ARB/05/24, Tribunal's Ruling of 6 May 2008 regarding the Participation of David Mildon QC in Further Stages of the Proceedings).

[33] *Vannessa Ventures Ltd* v. *Bolivarian Republic of Venezuela* (ICSID Case No. ARB(AF)/04/6 (ongoing case). Arbitrator Veeder resigned in 2007: see *Investment Treaty News* (15 November 2007), www.iisd.org/pdf/2007/itn_nov15_2007.pdf (last accessed 13 February 2011).

D   CEMEX Caracas Investments BV & CEMEX Caracas II Investments BV v. Bolivarian Republic of Venezuela

A fourth case is *CEMEX Caracas Investments BV & CEMEX Caracas II Investments BV* v. *Bolivarian Republic of Venezuela*, another ICSID arbitration involving a foreign investor's claims of expropriation.[34] Venezuela sought disqualification of Mr von Mehren on the basis that he was a retired partner of a law firm representing another company that had brought arbitration proceedings against Venezuela for alleged expropriation in a different case. Although retired, Mr von Mehren maintained an office with the law firm, was listed on their website, and maintained an e-mail account in the firm. Venezuela brought this challenge three weeks before the tribunal's scheduled first session and almost three months after the tribunal was constituted. As provided under ICSID rules, the remainder of arbitrators ruled on the application for disqualification of Mr von Mehren. The tribunal found that where the arbitrator challenge is not promptly brought, the requesting party is deemed to have waived its right to request disqualification. Here, the ICSID tribunal held that the request to disqualify Mr von Mehren was not prompt because all the material information was known to Venezuela at least six months prior to its proposal for arbitrator disqualification. Unlike UNCITRAL, there is no set deadline for filing arbitrator disqualification petitions, and instead whether such petition is timely will be determined on a case-by-case basis.

E   Perenco Ecuador v. Republic of Ecuador & Empresa Estatal Pertoleos Del Ecuador

The next case, *Perenco Ecuador* v. *Republic of Ecuador & Empresa Estatal Pertoleos Del Ecuador*, was another ICSID arbitration.[35] Similar to the cases already mentioned, *Perenco Ecuador* is another variation on the theme concerning the arbitrator's relationship with one of the parties' counsel. Here, the challenged arbitrator was Charles Brower. This case presented the peculiarity that the parties desired the resolution of any disputes pertaining to arbitrators to be resolved not by the remainder of

---

[34] *CEMEX Caracas Investments BV and CEMEX Caracas II Investments BV* v. *Bolivarian Republic of Venezuela* (ICSID Case No. ARB/08/1, Decision of 6 November 2009 on the Respondent's Proposal to Disqualify a Member of the Tribunal).
[35] *Perenco Ecuador* v. *Republic of Ecuador & Empresa Estatal Pertoleos Del Ecuador* (PCA Case No. IR-2009/1, Decision on Challenge to Arbitrator of 8 December 2009).

arbitrators, but by the Permanent Court of Arbitration Secretary-General, by reference to the IBA Guidelines. After the arbitral tribunal was constituted and Mr Brower was appointed as an arbitrator, he was interviewed by a publication about, inter alia, the most pressing issues in international arbitration. Mr Brower indicated that it was the issue of State acceptance and willingness to continue participation in arbitration, and he referred to Ecuador as an example of a failure by a State to comply with orders issued by ICSID tribunals and the fact that investors would become reluctant to invest in such States. Ecuador challenged Mr Brower, and the PCA Secretary-General applied the 'appearance of bias' test contained in the IBA Guidelines. The Secretary-General found that there was an appearance of bias on the part of the arbitrator when he used words such as 'recalcitrant host countries', that were deemed to have been in reference to Ecuador, when he compared Ecuador to Libya in the 1970s, and appeared to attach tremendous gravity to the situation since Mr Brower characterised it as one of the most pressing issues in arbitration. Mr Brower was deemed to lack the necessary impartiality under the IBA Guidelines.

F ICS Inspection and Control Services Limited v. Republic of Argentina

ICS Inspection and Control Services Limited v. *Republic of Argentina* was an UNCITRAL arbitration in which the challenge was brought by Argentina against one of the arbitrators, Mr Alexandrov, who was a Sidley Austin partner.[36] In his statement accepting appointment, Mr Alexandrov had disclosed his law firm's past representation of an entity with potential ties to the claimant, and both his personal and his law firm's current representation of Vivendi, who were claimants in a long-standing and already existent dispute with Argentina.[37] Argentina challenged the arbitrator's impartiality, an issue that went before Mr Sekolec, the individual designated by the Secretary-General of the Permanent Court of Arbitration to hear the challenge. Mr Sekolec applied

---

[36] *ICS Inspection and Control Services Limited* v. *Republic of Argentina* (Decision on Challenge to Mr Stanimir A. Alexandrov of 17 December 2009).

[37] See *Compañía de Aguas del Aconquija SA and Vivendi Universal SA* v. *Argentine Republic* (ICSID Case No. ARB/97/3, Award of 21 November 2000); (Decision on the Challenge to the President of the Committee of 3 October 2001); (Decision on Annulment of 3 July 2002); (Decision of the ad hoc Committee on the Request for Supplementation and Rectification of its Decision Concerning Annulment of the Award of 28 May 2003).

the UNCITRAL rules for arbitrator challenge, but also noted the existence of the non-binding IBA Guidelines which list two issues implicated
in the case at hand in its 'orange list'.[38] These two issues are the situation
where an arbitrator's law firm is currently adverse to a party, and where an
arbitrator has acted as counsel against the party in the prior three years.
Mr Sekolec concluded that there was an appearance of bias in situations
where an arbitrator and his law firm concurrently act as counsel against
one of the parties, particularly where the cases are not dissimilar in that
they were both investment treaty disputes against the same respondent
State, creating a situation of adversity towards Argentina. The fact that the
Vivendi case may have been coming to an end did not resolve the appearance of bias as the possibility of continued representation remained.

G   Vito G Gallo *v.* Government of Canada

In *Vito G Gallo* v. *Government of Canada*,[39] Gallo brought a claim under
the North American Free Trade Agreement (NAFTA),[40] to be resolved
pursuant to the rules in Chapter 11 of NAFTA, as well as UNCITRAL
rules. The claimant sought the disqualification of one of the arbitrators,
Christopher Thomas, because he also served on an ongoing basis as legal
adviser to Mexico on investment treaty matters; and under NAFTA rules,
Mexico was entitled as a State Party to make submissions to the tribunal
on questions of treaty interpretation. Although the Deputy Secretary-
General of ICSID rejected the claimant's application to disqualify the
arbitrator, Mr Thomas was directed to choose, within seven days,
whether he wished to continue in his capacity as an arbitrator in the
case or whether he wished to continue serving as Mexico's legal adviser.

---

[38] See International Bar Association, 'IBA Guidelines on Conflicts of Interest in International Arbitration' (22 May 2004). The IBA divides conflicts into three categories:
(1) Red (which constitutes a definite conflict of interest for the arbitrator, such that she
cannot preside over the arbitration, although parties may waive some conflicts through
an informed and explicit waiver); (2) Green (which comprises situations that are not
actual or perceived conflicts of interests); and (3) Orange (situations that may give rise to
justifiable doubts as to the arbitrator's independence and impartiality, and must therefore be disclosed to the parties; parties are generally deemed to have waived such
conflicts if they do not object within 30 days of receiving the written disclosure). 'Issue
bias' falls in the orange category, and the parties must explicitly or implicitly waive the
conflict of interest before the arbitrator may continue serving in that capacity.

[39] *Vito G Gallo* v. *Government of Canada* (Decision of 14 October 2009 on the Challenge to
Mr J. Christopher Thomas QC).

[40] North American Free Trade Agreement, signed 17 December 1992, 32 ILM 289, 605
(entered into force 1 January 1995).

Simultaneously performing the two roles, the Deputy Secretary-General held, would raise in the mind of a reasonable and informed third party justifiable doubts regarding the arbitrator's impartiality and independence. This case is interesting both because of the application of the IBA Guidelines on Conflicts of Interest, as well as for illustrating the approach that may be taken in UNCITRAL arbitrations which are rarely published.

H   Rompetrol Group NV *v.* Romania

Another ICSID arbitration case is *Rompetrol Group NV* v. *Romania*,[41] concerning a challenge to the lead counsel for Rompetrol who was replaced subsequent to the prior counsel leaving employment with the law firm representing the petitioner, the Salans law firm. The new lead counsel was a former member of the same law firm as a member of the arbitral tribunal. The respondent promptly challenged the propriety of the new attorney acting as lead counsel for Rompetrol, although stressed that it did not seek to challenge any of the arbitrators, an option that the tribunal noted was, at any rate, not available to the parties at that point in time. The tribunal examined the *Hrvatska* case and the IBA Guidelines, noting that they were not binding on the tribunal, and further stating that the irregularity complained of would need to constitute a threat to the essential integrity of the arbitral process before the tribunal would exercise any inherent powers to remove counsel, a situation not explicitly addressed by the ICSID rules. The tribunal would only consider doing so in rare and compelling circumstances as determined by the tribunal itself on the facts of each case. Unlike in *Hrvatska*, where the challenged party engaged in wrongful lack of disclosure, the challenge here was promptly raised and dealt with, and the arbitral tribunal also differentiated the present case on other grounds. The tribunal concluded that an arbitrator who meets ICSID requirements of 'possessing high moral character and recognized competence' does not appear biased to a reasonable third party when one of the parties secures new counsel who was previously employed by the same law firm that currently employs one of the arbitrators. The tribunal referred to the jurisprudence of the European Court of Human Rights, indicating that the test for arbitrator bias was 'whether a fair-minded and informed observer,

---

[41] *Rompetrol Group NV* v. *Romania* (ICSID Case No. ARB/06/3, Decision of 14 January 2010 on the Participation of Counsel).

having considered the facts, would conclude that there was a real possibility that the tribunal was biased', a test applied by the United Kingdom House of Lords in the context of ECHR Article 6, the right to a fair trial. The tribunal further stated that parties are able to retain counsel of their choosing in accordance with ECHR Article 6, and the situation brought to the tribunal's attention did not affect the integrity of the proceedings.

These cases – and no doubt there are others not reported or yet to emerge – concern similar issues relating to the relationship between an individual who serves as counsel and one of the arbitrators, or to the same person serving in the capacity of arbitrator or counsel in a different proceeding. Examining the body of jurisprudence created by such cases leaves observers struggling to find common themes or approaches, in terms of the standards that are applied and the tests to be used in determining impartiality and independence in investment treaty arbitration. Yet one theme that does emerge is that the standard to be applied is an objective one, in which the perceptions of reasonable and independent observers will play a decisive role: as the House of Lords put it, would 'a fair-minded and informed observer' believe that the circumstances were such that there was a 'real possibility of subconscious bias'?

In ICSID and UNCITRAL arbitration the subjects of 'issue conflict' and 'role confusion' are in the ether, discernible but not yet fully defined. Given the range of cases, and the stakes at issue, it is not unreasonable to conclude that this subject is an accident that is waiting to happen, and one that gives rise to concerns in certain quarters about the legitimacy of the investment treaty dispute-settlement process.

V   Other international courts and tribunals: The ICJ and CAS

In this regard, it should be noted that the subjects of 'issue conflict' and 'role confusion' are not germane to investment treaty arbitration alone, and other institutional fora have addressed them. In October 2001, for example, the International Court of Justice (ICJ) adopted one of its early Practice Directions.[42] Before then – perhaps surprisingly – there was no bar to an individual acting as counsel at the ICJ whilst, simultaneously, serving as an ad hoc judge at the same court. The Practice Directions changed that, making clear the view of the Court that it is not considered to be appropriate for a person to wear the two hats at the same time. The

---

[42] International Court of Justice, 'Practice Directions' (2001, last amended 2009), www.icj-cij.org (last accessed 13 February 2011).

underlying rationale, which is not articulated in the ICJ Practice Directions, is that the judge might obtain special insights into the inner
workings of the Court, as well as developing relationships with other
judges. Having sat as an ICSID arbitrator, my experience confirms that
once you cross the threshold – and find yourself on the 'bench' rather
than facing it – you enter a world that makes you privy to insights and
contacts that may not be unhelpful to your role as counsel. It seems
reasonable to conclude that this must also have been the case at the ICJ.
The Court is to be commended for taking a decisive and early lead on
this issue, which is now reflected in other guidelines that have been
recently adopted.[43] Its actions gave rise to a certain number of complaints, to the effect that there was only a small pool of individuals who
could act as ad hoc judges, and that imposing new limitations would
effectively cripple the ICJ's ability to appoint such judges. However, in
the decade since the Practice Direction was adopted it cannot be said
that the ICJ system has come to a grinding halt in the appointment of ad
hoc judges having the necessary qualities, or that the pool of counsel has
diminished in any material sense. The same arguments are heard in the
field of investment treaty arbitration, to the effect that limiting the dual
role would diminish the pool of individuals who would be able to serve
as arbitrator. It is not an argument that seems particularly persuasive,
given the large and growing number of individuals with considerable
expertise in this field of international law.

The same issue has arisen in another forum, perhaps not as well
known to the community of public international lawyers as it should
be – namely the Court of Arbitration for Sport (CAS), a body that is
based in Lausanne, Switzerland, dealing with sports-related disputes.
The CAS used to operate a 'revolving door' policy whereby arbitrators
could also act as counsel, and vice versa, and over the years this created

---

[43] See e.g. the 2004 ILA Burgh House Principles on the Independence of the International
Judiciary, at section 13.3 ('Former judges shall not act as agent, counsel, adviser or
advocate in any proceedings before the court on which they previously served for a
period of three years after they have left office or such other period as the court may
establish and publish'). The flip side of this principle, implying requirements for counsel,
are reflected in the ILA 2010 Hague Principles on Ethical Standards for Counsel
Appearing before International Courts and Tribunals, section 4.3.4 of which states:
'The personal interests of counsel create an impermissible conflict where he or she . . .
has served as a judge or other officer of the international court or tribunal within the
previous three years or such other period as the court or tribunal may establish by its
rules' (section 1.2 states that 'international court or tribunal' refers 'as appropriate, to an
international arbitral tribunal in a proceeding in which one or more of the parties is a
state').

significant challenges. Following some controversies, in 2010 the Court became the first standing arbitration institution to prohibit individuals from wearing both hats.[44] The CAS Statute previously provided that:

> The personalities who appear on the list of arbitrators may be called upon to serve on Panels constituted by either of the CAS Divisions. Upon their appointment, the CAS arbitrators and mediators sign a declaration undertaking to exercise their functions personally with total objectivity and independence, and in conformity with the provisions of this Code.

The CAS has now added an additional line to that provision, which is of mandatory effect: 'CAS arbitrators and mediators may not act as counsel for a party before the CAS.'[45] In my attempts to find out what caused this change, I have communicated with a number of individuals, including the Secretary-General of the CAS, but have not been able to ascertain what precisely caused this amendment to be passed. However, it appears that a final catalyst for change was in the context of a CAS arbitration case brought by cyclist Floyd Landis, who challenged an arbitral award that upheld a doping disqualification imposed by the US Anti-Doping Agency for alleged use of synthetic testosterone in the 2006 Tour de France.[46] Landis also challenged the decision in the Central District Court of California on the grounds that the arbitrators lacked independence and impartiality.[47] The motion alleged that: 'These arbitrators constantly find themselves changing hats, arbitrator one day, litigant the next.'[48] Since the arbitrators and the counsel involved in arbitrations not only come from a small community where they know each other well, but also change roles among themselves quite frequently, Landis argued that such individuals were inclined to craft arbitral awards in each other's favour. The motion referred to several specific links between the arbitrators who had presided over the proceedings in his case, arguing that the arbitral award was tainted by the arbitrators' conflicts of interest. Eventually, the case was settled, so the California courts were not required to express a view on the matters raised. However, the

---

[44] Court of Arbitration for Sport, Statutes of the Bodies Working for the Settlement of Sports-Related Disputes (2004, last amended 2010).

[45] Ibid., s. 18.

[46] See Landis v. United States Anti-Doping Agency, CAS 2007/A/1394 (Court of Arbitration for Sport, 2008), www.wada-ama.org/Documents/Anti-Doping_Community/Court_of_Arbitration_for_Sport/CAS_Decisions/Landis.pdf (last accessed 28 January 2011).

[47] Landis v. US Anti-Doping Agency (No. CV 08–06330, Motion to Vacate Arbitration Award and Demand for Jury Trial, Central District of California of 25 September 2008).

[48] Ibid., p. 27.

timing of the change in CAS rules suggests that the issues raised in the *Landis* case may have been the final straw for the Court of Arbitration for Sport, prompting it to change its rules.

VI Going forward

If the CAS felt the need to make this change in circumstances that are familiar to anyone working in the field of investment treaty arbitration, the question arises as to what steps might be taken by ICSID, UNCITRAL and other arbitral arrangements for the resolution of investment disputes. One way of addressing the issue, which was discussed during the IBA meeting in Madrid, might be by increasing the disclosure requirements when arbitrators are appointed. It is striking that ICSID and other disclosures of arbitrators are quite limited, and do not refer to cases where one has acted as counsel. This is often for understandable reasons, where the case or the representation is confidential, so it is not a simple problem to resolve. Another approach is for individuals to elect whether to serve as counsel or arbitrator, which is the course taken by an increasing number of individuals. I am doubtful that disclosure alone is enough to address the concerns as to 'role confusion', but recognise that if full disclosure has occurred, and both parties accept individuals with knowledge of the two hats they might wear, then there would be no problem (at least for those parties).

At the IBA meting in Madrid in October 2009, two fundamental objections were raised with regard to the imposition of the same restrictions upon investment treaty arbitration as are in place at the ICJ and the CAS. The first argument was one made in the context of the ICJ: it is said that the pool of individuals who are capable of serving as high-class international arbitrators is small, and the system could not sustain a change. I do not buy this argument as being dispositive: there are many individuals who are capable of acting as arbitrators – and just as the ICJ was able to carry on with its work unaffected by the change in rules, so will investment treaty arbitrations. In this respect, it may be helpful to have another look at the book by Yves Dezalay – *Dealing in Virtue* – which describes a community of able lawyers driven by a particular perception of what is in the public good that appears to be closely connected to perception of what is in the interest of the members of the community.[49]

---

[49] Y. Dezalay and B. G. Garth, *Dealing in Virtue: International commercial arbitration and the construction of a transnational legal order* (University of Chicago Press, 1998).

The second objection is that not everyone is in a financial position such as to be able to opt to be arbitrator rather than counsel. This argument is essentially an economic one, recognising that appointments as arbitrator are not guaranteed and, having elected to discard appointments as counsel, the individual exposes himself to a risk of economic uncertainty. The argument is not an attractive one, in the sense that it might be seen by some as giving greater weight to economic interests than to an issue of principle. Moreover, I am not persuaded that the pool of possible candidates is as small as some would suggest; it is an expanding group, and over time it will grow even more, which must be a good thing in enriching the pool of lawyers who make the arguments. Beyond that, it seems inappropriate to allow what should be an issue of principle underpinning the legitimacy and effectiveness of the system to be driven by the particular economic considerations of individuals or law firms: given the parties involved, investment treaty arbitration has of necessity a public component and, relatedly, a public-service component: it is not a purely commercial activity (even if it is the case that this field has become an enormously lucrative area of international law, in which the costs of litigation have now risen very significantly). We need to keep our eye on the big picture: the system exists to protect the interests of investors and of States and to provide for efficient and effective means for resolving disputes when they arise.

In short, I believe there is a large and able pool of men and women from jurisdictions around the world who are perfectly well qualified to serve as arbitrators in investment treaty arbitrations, and who do not feel impelled to act both as counsel and arbitrator in investment treaty disputes. Future decision-making should be driven by principle and not by other factors. Such a principled approach is reflected in the approach taken by Lord Bingham in the decision of the House of Lords in *Lawal*: 'What the public was content to accept many years ago', he wrote, 'is not necessarily acceptable in the world of today. The indispensable requirement of public confidence in the administration of justice requires higher standards today than was the case even a decade or two ago.'[50] These words apply equally in relation to the emerging system of investment disputes, and are reflected in the words of Tom Buergenthal, the former ICJ judge, upon which I cannot improve:

> I believe that insufficient attention is being paid to some conflict of interest issues that can arise in the selection of those who are called upon

---

[50] *Lawal*, para. 23.

to settle disputes. Let me illustrate my point by reference to ICSID, since it is the arbitration facility I am most familiar with. I have long believed that the practice of allowing arbitrators to serve as counsel, and counsel to serve as arbitrators, raises due process of law issues. In my view, arbitrators and counsel should be required to decide to be one or the other, and be held to the choice they have made, at least for a specific period of time. That is necessary, in my opinion, in order to ensure that an arbitrator will not be tempted, consciously or unconsciously, to seek to obtain a result in an arbitral decision that might advance the interests of a client in a case he or she is handling as counsel. ICSID is particularly vulnerable to this problem because the interpretation and application of the same or similar legal instruments (the bilateral investment treaties, for example) are regularly at issue in different cases before it.

I also believe that repeated designations by counsel of the same arbitrator should be avoided. These revolving-door problems – counsel selecting an arbitrator who, the next time around when the arbitrator is counsel, selects the previous counsel as arbitrator – should be avoided. *Manus manum lavat*, in other words 'you scratch my back and I'll scratch yours', does not advance the rule of law.[51]

---

[51] T. Buergenthal, 'The proliferation of disputes, dispute settlement procedures and respect for the rule of law', *Arbitration International*, 22(4) (2006), 495–9.

3

Recent developments in the approach to identifying an 'investment' pursuant to Article 25(1) of the ICSID Convention

DAVID A. R. WILLIAMS QC AND SIMON FOOTE

I   Introduction

It is trite to say that:

> The jurisdiction of the tribunal is fundamental to the authority and decision making of the arbitrators. Awards rendered without jurisdiction have no legitimacy. The absence of jurisdiction is one of the few recognized reasons for a court to set aside or refuse recognition and enforcement of an award.[1]

The appealing possibility of a private investor litigating directly with a foreign State, the unique feature of the Convention for the Settlement of Investment Disputes between States and Nationals of other States (the ICSID Convention),[2] was balanced by carefully defining the jurisdiction of the International Centre for Settlement of Investment Disputes (ICSID or the 'Centre').[3] Article 25(1) of the ICSID Convention states that 'the jurisdiction of the Centre shall extend to *any legal dispute arising directly out of an investment*'.[4] The four requirements of subject matter jurisdiction, which were articulated in a similar form in *Mihaly* v. *Sri Lanka*,[5]

---

[1] J. D. M. Lew, L. A. Mistelis and S. M. Kröll, *Comparative International Commercial Arbitration* (The Hague: Kluwer, 2003), p. 329, citing J. Y. Gotanda, 'An efficient method for determining jurisdiction in international arbitrations', *Columbia Journal of Transnational Law*, 40 (2001), 15.

[2] Convention for the Settlement of Investment Disputes between States and Nationals of other States, opened for signature 18 March 1965, 575 UNTS 159 (entered into force 14 October 1966) (ICSID Convention).

[3] P. C. Szasz, 'The investment disputes convention: Opportunities and pitfalls' (How to Submit Disputes to ICSID), *Journal of Law and Economic Development*, 5 (1970), 23, 24.

[4] ICSID Convention, Art. 25(1) (emphasis added).

[5] *Mihaly International Corporation* v. *Democratic Socialist Republic of Sri Lanka* (ICSID Case No. ARB/00/2, Award of 15 March 2002), para. 31.

are, first, that there is a dispute; secondly that the dispute is of a legal nature; thirdly, that there is an investment; and finally, that the dispute arises directly out of that investment. This chapter focuses on the third requirement – that there is an 'investment'.

The interpretation of Article 25 plays a large part in establishing whether or not jurisdiction is to be granted in any particular case. It has been suggested that a liberal and purposive approach should be adopted.[6] The approach adopted by a tribunal is especially important given the undefined nature of the term 'investment' in Article 25(1).

This chapter addresses recent developments in the approach to identifying an 'investment' as required by Article 25(1), in particular the decisions of the tribunal and ad hoc Annulment Committee in *Malaysian Historical Salvors* v. *Malaysia*[7] and the tribunal in *Inmaris Perestroika Sailing Maritime Services GmbH* v. *Ukraine*.[8]

Before moving onto the substantive issues concerning the scope of Article 25(1) investments, it is perhaps fitting to bear in mind the words of the philosopher Stephen Toulmin who said:

> Definitions are like belts. The shorter they are, the more elastic they need to be. A short belt reveals nothing about its wearer, by stretching it, it can be made to fit almost anybody.[9]

II   Historical context of the definition of 'investment' in Article 25(1)

As has often been pointed out, this issue engendered considerable debate among the drafters of the ICSID Convention,[10] and it continues to attract the attention of tribunals, ad hoc committees and academics. By way of introduction, it is interesting briefly to place the notion of 'investment' in an historic context.

---

[6] C. F. Amerasinghe, 'Jurisdiction *ratione personae* under the Convention on the settlement of investment disputes between States and nationals of other States', *British Yearbook of International Law*, 47 (1974–1975), 227, 231.

[7] *Malaysian Historical Salvors SDN, BHD* v. *The Government of Malaysia* (ICSID Case No. ARB/05/10, Decision on the Application for Annulment of 16 April 2009).

[8] *Inmaris Perestroika Sailing Maritime Services GmbH* v. *Ukraine* (ICSID Case No. ARB/08/8, Decision on Jurisdiction of 8 March 2010).

[9] S. Toulmin, *Foresight and Understanding: An inquiry into the aims of science* (Indiana University Press, 1961), p. 18.

[10] The debate among the drafters as to whether, and if so, how, 'investment' should be defined in the Convention is succinctly traced by C. Schreuer *et al.* (eds.), *The ICSID Convention: A commentary*, 2nd edn (Cambridge University Press, 2009), pp. 114–17.

Until the mid twentieth century, with the emergence of the General Agreement on Tariffs and Trade (GATT), no distinction was made between investments and other forms of property and economic activity. In relation to dispute resolution, GATT exclusively governed trade differences whilst investment disputes were initially left by the wayside, picked up by the emergence of bilateral investment treaties (BITs) and ICSID Convention in the 1960s.

Various analytical reasons have been proposed for the distinction. However, the general perception tends to be that certain 'investment' is a 'catalyst for development and prosperity', which it helps by 'expanding welfare around the world'.[11] It is in this context that investment protection treaties are concluded and provide for a conscious derogation of State sovereignty. However, certain capital flows, usually of a transient nature, do not promote welfare or economic development; indeed those involving speculation in debt or currency may cause economic instability. In those circumstances, the derogation from State sovereignty provided for in the relevant treaty is not worth undertaking.[12] It is the concept of 'investment' that seeks to delineate between the constructive capital flow that a State wishes to attract (and therefore protect) and the transient transactions that it does not.

Professor Ian Brownlie's separate opinion in *CME Czech Republic BV (The Netherlands)* v. *The Czech Republic* noted the nature of investment from a State sovereignty perspective. Professor Brownlie stated that 'investment' does not include all kinds of property, and that the benefits of investment protection treaties should be conferred only on property rights that qualify as an 'investment'.[13] To do otherwise would be to betray the intent and the consent of the parties to arbitrate their disputes with aliens operating in their territory.

The notion of whether or not there is an investment for the purposes of the ICSID Convention is undoubtedly fundamental. The first draft of the Convention defined 'investment' to mean 'any contribution of money or other asset of economic value for an indefinite period or, if the period be defined, for not less than five years'.[14] In the end, the drafters

---

[11] N. Rubins, 'The notion of "investment" in international investment arbitration' in N. Horn (ed.), *Arbitrating Foreign Investment Disputes: Procedural and substantive legal aspects* (The Hague: Kluwer, 2004), pp. 283–6.

[12] *Ibid.*, p. 287.

[13] *CME Czech Republic BV (The Netherlands)* v. *The Czech Republic* (Separate Opinion to the Final Award of 14 March 2003), para. 73.

[14] *Analysis of Documents Concerning the Origin and the Formulation of the ICSID Convention* (1970), 116, extracted in Schreuer *et al.* (eds.), *The ICSID Convention*, p. 115.

of the Convention left the term 'investment' undefined. The Report of the Executive Directors explained:

> No attempt was made to define the term 'investment' given the essential requirement of consent by the parties, and the mechanism through which Contracting States can make known in advance, if they so desire, the classes of disputes which they would or would not consider submitting to the Centre (Article 25(4)).[15]

Despite the 'essential requirement of consent' of the parties, consent does not override the jurisdictional thresholds inherent in Article 25, including the requirement for the requisite investment to be viewed objectively. In other words, parties are not free to expand the jurisdiction of ICSID by consent. The Tribunal in *Joy Mining Machinery Limited v. Arab Republic of Egypt* put the point well:

> The parties to a dispute cannot by contract or treaty define as investment, for the purpose of ICSID jurisdiction, something which does not satisfy the objective requirements of Article 25 of the Convention. Otherwise Article 25 and its reliance on the concept of investment, even if not specifically defined, would be turned into a meaningless provision.[16]

Therefore, one of the issues addressed below is just where the boundaries of ICSID jurisdiction lie insofar as they are circumscribed by the term 'investment' in Article 25.[17] Tribunals have sought to determine whether the investment from which the dispute arises (a) falls within the terms of the parties' consent (usually the relevant BIT); and (b) is an investment objectively contemplated by Article 25. This two-stage test (not necessarily approached in that order) has been called a 'dual test',[18] the 'jurisdictional keyhole' approach[19] or a 'double-barrelled' test.[20]

---

[15] *Report of the Executive Directors on the Convention on the Settlement of Investment Disputes between States and Nationals of other States* (18 March 1965), reproduced in ICSID, *ICSID Convention, Regulation and Rules* (ICSID/15/Rev.1, January 2003), 35, para. 27.

[16] *Joy Mining Machinery Limited* v. *Arab Republic of Egypt* (ICSID Case No. ARB/03/11 Award of 6 August 2004), para. 50.

[17] See Schreuer *et al.* (eds.), *The ICSID Convention*, p. 122.   [18] *Ibid.*, p. 117.

[19] *Aguas del Tunari SA* v. *Republic of Bolivia* (ICSID Case No. ARB/02/3, Decision on Respondent's Objection to Jurisdiction of 21 October 2005), para. 278.

[20] *Malaysian Historical Salvors, Sdn, Bhd v. Malaysia* (ICSID Case No. ARB/05/10, Award on Jurisdiction of 17 May 2007), para. 55.

III   Investments: Relevance of types of economic activity

One commentator has suggested that the term 'investment' in the ICSID Convention encompasses:

> capital contributions, joint ventures, loans, as well as modern kinds of investment resulting from new forms of association between States and foreign investors, such as profit-sharing, service and management contracts, turn-key contracts, international leasing arrangements and agreements for the transfer of know-how and technology.[21]

The statement that an investment includes modern forms of association between foreign partners and host States is supported by Delaume.[22] Delaume further points out that transnational loans are clearly included in the definition of investment, referring both to the first draft of the Convention and the fact that the parties involved in transnational loan agreements specifically state that their loan is an investment for the purposes of the Convention.[23]

The areas of economic activity over which ICSID tribunals have exercised jurisdiction are diverse. They include construction and/or operation of hotels, hospital wards, fertiliser factories, housing units, cotton mills, aluminium smelters, cable TV systems, the production of plastic bottles and weapons, the exploration and distribution of natural resources, agricultural projects and banking activities including loans.[24]

Yet, as McLachlan, Shore and Weiniger point out, it is the form and nature of the investment activity, not simply the area of economic activity covered, that is the key issue in terms of the reach of ICSID's jurisdiction under Article 25.[25] For example, provision of a guarantee amounted to an investment in *Ceskoslovenska Obchodni Banka (CSOB) v. The Slovak*

---

[21] C. M. Koa, 'The International Bank for Reconstruction and Development and Dispute Resolution: Conciliation and arbitrating with China through the International Centre for Settlement of Investment Disputes', *New York University Journal of International Law and Politics*, 24 (1991), 439, 452.

[22] G. R. Delaume, 'ICSID and the transnational financial community', *ICSID Review – Foreign Investment Law Journal*, 1 (1986), 237, 242.

[23] *Ibid.*

[24] Schreuer *et al.* (eds.), *The ICSID Convention*, pp. 125–8. A survey of the subject matter involved in ICSID cases can be found on ICSID's website at www.worldbank.org/icsid/cases/cases.htm (last accessed on 13 May 2011).

[25] C. McLachlan, L. Shore and M. Weiniger, *International Investment Arbitration: Substantive principles* (Oxford University Press, 2007), paras. 6.06–07.

Republic[26] while it did not in *Joy Mining*, the difference being the nature of the underlying transaction: in *Joy Mining* the guarantee supported a one-off contract for sale and purchase.

IV 'Knowing one when you see it': Can this be a test for identifying an investment?

A piecemeal approach

During the debate over the draft of the Report of the Executive Directors, General Counsel Mr Broches suggested that while it may be difficult to define 'investment', an investment in fact was readily recognisable:[27] essentially a 'know one when you see one' approach.[28] Notwithstanding the uncertainty that arises from the lack of a clear definition, there is an inherent flexibility in leaving the term undefined. Indeed, leaving investment undefined has been described as 'preserving its integrity and flexibility and allowing for future progressive development of international law on the topic of investment'.[29]

However, the progressive development of international law on the topic of investment has led, perhaps inevitably, to piecemeal and sometimes inconsistent approaches to determining whether there is an investment as the term is used in Article 25(1). Speaking generally, some tribunals have taken a holistic and broad approach while others have propounded various criteria for identifying investments and opined on the relative importance of each criterion. Most recently, the trend towards a prescriptive definition based on immutable criteria has been reversed and a broad approach that places primacy on the consent of the parties

---

[26] *Ceskoslovenska Obchodni Banka (CSOB)* v. *The Slovak Republic* (ICSID Case No. ARB/97/4, Decision on Jurisdiction of 24 May 1999). See also the tribunal's comments in *Fedax NV* v. *Venezuela* (ICSID Case No. ARB/96/3, Award on Jurisdiction of 11 July 1997).

[27] *Documents Concerning the Origin and the Formulation of the ICSID Convention* (1968), pp. 957, 972; cited in Schreuer *et al.* (eds.), *The ICSID Convention*, p. 116.

[28] See Justice Stewart's concurring judgment in *Jacobellis* v. *Ohio* 378 US 184 (1984) regarding obscenity: 'I shall not today attempt further to define the kinds of material I understand to be embraced within that shorthand description ["hard-core pornography"]; and perhaps I could never succeed in intelligibly doing so. But I know it when I see it, and the motion picture involved in this case is not that.' This expression became one of the most famous phrases in the entire history of the US Supreme Court: see P. Gerwitz, 'I know it when I see it', *Yale Law Journal*, 105 (1996), 1023–47.

[29] *Mihaly International Corporation* (Award), para. 33.

to ICSID jurisdiction has asserted (or reasserted) itself. These developments and the relevant authorities are traced below.

Attempts by tribunals to achieve what the drafters of the Convention deliberately avoided – to define the outer limits of ICSID investment – began in 1997 with *Fedax NV* v. *Republic of Venezuela*.[30] The tribunal in *Fedax* had to decide whether the holding of promissory notes issued by the respondent was an investment under Article 25(1). The tribunal examined Article 25(1) and its application in previous arbitrations and adopted the approach propounded by Schreuer:

> The basic features of an investment have been described as involving a certain duration, a certain regularity of profit and return, assumption of risk, a substantial commitment and a significance for the host State's development.[31]

It concluded that the broad scope of Article 25 and previous decisions were sufficient to find that there was jurisdiction over such a transaction.[32] The tribunal further noted that because loans were clearly within the meaning of investment, and promissory notes were 'evidence of a loan and a rather typical financial and credit instrument' there was no reason that the purchase of promissory notes could not come within the scope of the Convention.[33]

The *Fedax* criteria have been applied by numerous ICSID tribunals, most notably in *Salini* v. *Morocco*.[34] In that case (which concerned the construction of a road in Morocco), the tribunal noted that the requirement for an investment under Article 25(1) was to be assessed objectively and said:

> The doctrine generally considers that investment infers: contributions, a certain duration of performance of the contract and a participation in the risks of the transaction . . . In reading the Convention's preamble, one may add the contribution to the economic development of the host State of the investment as an additional condition.[35]

---

[30] *Fedax NV* v. *Venezuela* (ICSID Case No. ARB/96/03, Award on Jurisdiction of 11 February 1997).

[31] *Ibid.*, para 43, as adapted from the preliminary publication of C. Schreuer, 'The ICSID Convention: A commentary', *ICSID Review – Foreign Investment Law Journal*, 11 (2001), 372.

[32] *Fedax* (Award), paras. 21–3, 25–9.   [33] *Ibid.*, para 29.

[34] *Salini Costruttori SpA and Italstrade SpA* v. *Morocco* (ICSID Case No. ARB/00/4, Decision on Jurisdiction of 23 July 2001).

[35] *Ibid.*, para. 52.

Similarly in *Joy Mining*, the tribunal said as regards the definition of investment in Article 25:

> The project in question should have a certain duration, a regularity of profit and return, an element of risk, a substantial commitment and that it should constitute a significant contribution to the host State's development.[36]

In their review of ICSID awards and decisions between 2003 and 2007, Happ and Rubins observe that: 'These [*Salini*] criteria have been used frequently during the 2003–2007 period as an indicator that an investment exists for ICSID Convention purposes.' They comment that most tribunals have taken a flexible approach to the criteria, incorporating a review of the totality of the alleged investment, but others have taken a stricter view whereby jurisdiction was declined despite the existence of a number of 'broadly investment-like characteristics'.[37]

Professor Schreuer opines that the repeated application of these criteria has strengthened the perception that they are mandatory standards as opposed to features indicative of investments.[38]

However, some tribunals, while referring to the *Fedax/Salini* criteria, emphasise the importance of viewing the instant transaction holistically and, while maintaining an objective viewpoint as to the requirement for an investment pursuant to Article 25(1), place considerable weight on whether the parties had consented to the ICSID jurisdiction by way of the relevant BIT or otherwise.

In *Ceskoslovenska Obchodni Banka (CSOB)* v. *The Slovak Republic* the tribunal had to deal with whether loans made by CSOB to a 'collection company', established by the Slovak Republic pursuant to a consolidation agreement, was an investment under Article 25(1).[39] The tribunal accepted that the mere description of a transaction as an 'investment' in the parties' consolidation agreement was insufficient to find that the

---

[36] *Joy Mining*, para. 53. See also, *LESI SpA et ASTALDI SpA v. Algeria* (ICSID Case No. ARB/05/3, Decision on Jurisdiction of 12 July 2006), para. 72; *Jan de Nul NV v. Arab Republic of Egypt* (ICSID Case No. ARB/04/13, Decision on Jurisdiction of 16 June 2006), para. 91; *Bayindir v. Pakistan* (ICSID Case No. ARB/03/29, Decision on Jurisdiction of 14 November 2005), paras. 130–8.

[37] R. Happ and N. Rubins, *Digest of ICSID Awards and Decisions 2003–2007* (Oxford University Press, 2009), pp. 341–2. Examples given of the 'stricter view' are the Award in *Malaysian Historical Salvors* (see discussion below) and *Mitchell* v. *Democratic Republic of Congo* (ICSID Case No. ARB/99/7, Decision on Annulment of 1 November 2006).

[38] Schreuer *et al.* (eds.), *The ICSID Convention*, p. 159.

[39] *Ceskoslovenska obchodni banka, a.s. v. Slovak Republic* (Case No. ARB/97/4, Decision on Jurisdiction of 24 May 1999).

transaction satisfied Article 25(1) – the transaction had to be considered objectively.[40] However, the tribunal further held that as the parties had consented to the Centre's jurisdiction a 'strong presumption that they considered their transaction to be an investment within the meaning of the ICSID Convention' had been created.[41] Turning to consider the instant loan, the tribunal found:

> it would seem that the resources provided through CSOB's banking activities in the Slovak Republic were designed to produce a benefit and to offer CSOB a return in the future, subject to an element of risk that is implicit in most economic activities. The Tribunal notes, however, that these elements of the suggested definition, while they tend as a rule to be present in most investments, are not a formal prerequisite for the finding that a transaction constitutes an investment as that concept is understood under the Convention.[42]

In *MCI* v. *Republic of Ecuador,* a case which concerned intangible assets such as accounts receivable and the existence of an operating permit, the tribunal referred to *Fedax/Salini*-type criteria as 'mere examples':

> The Tribunal states that the requirements that were taken into account in some arbitral precedents for purposes of denoting the existence of an investment protected by a treaty (such as the duration and risk of the alleged investment) must be considered as mere examples and not necessarily as elements that are required for its existence. Nevertheless, the Tribunal considers that the very elements of the Seacoast project and the consequences thereof fall within the characterizations required in order to determine the existence of protected investments.[43]

V   *Malaysian Historical Salvors*

The tension between a broad approach that focuses on the holistic nature of the transaction and emphasises the parties' consent to ICSID jurisdiction on the one hand, and a more prescriptive approach adhering closely to the existence of the *Fedax/Salini* criteria on the other, was evident in the award and subsequent annulment committee decision in *Malaysian Historical Salvors* v. *Malaysia*.[44]

---

[40] *Ibid.*, para. 68.   [41] *Ibid.*, para. 66.   [42] *Ibid.*, para. 90.
[43] *MCI* v. *Republic of Ecuador* (ICSID Case No. ARB/03/6, Award of 31 July 2007), para. 165.
[44] *Malaysian Historical Salvors* v. *Malaysia* (ICSID Case No. ARB/05/10, Award on Jurisdiction of 17 May 2007); *Malaysian Historical Salvors* v. *Malaysia* (ICSID Case No. ARB/05/10, Decision on the Application for Annulment of 16 April 2009).

The case concerned a contract for salvage of a cargo of porcelain from an ancient shipwreck. The proceeds from the sale of any recovered artefacts were to be shared between the claimant salvors and the respondent Malaysia (or a certain portion of their assessed value to be paid to the salvors should Malaysia choose to retain any artefact). The salvors claimed for a shortfall in payment of their share of the proceeds. Malaysia objected that there had been no 'investment' for the purposes of the ICSID Convention.

The tribunal recognised the two-stage or dual approach to investment jurisdiction and addressed first the objective assessment required by Article 25(1). The tribunal's starting point was the 'typical characteristics' of an investment identified by Schreuer: duration, regularity of profit and return, assumption of risk (usually by both sides), a substantial commitment, and a significant contribution to the host State's development. It noted Schreuer's view that these features should not necessarily be understood as jurisdictional requirements, but rather as typical characteristics of a qualifying investment.[45]

The tribunal then assessed the spirit and objectives of the ICSID Convention with reference to its preamble and the Report of the Executive Directors, both of which, it pointed out, referred to promotion of economic development of the host State. It concluded that an investment should be interpreted as 'an activity which promotes some form of positive economic development for the host State'.[46]

The tribunal identified what it termed 'seven decided cases of importance' on the issue as to whether the salvage contract was an Article 25(1) investment to assist in determining the correct approach to this question including *Salini, Joy Mining*, and *CSOB*.[47] From these cases, the tribunal divined two approaches to the defining features of an investment – the 'typical characteristics approach' and the 'jurisdictional approach'. The tribunal said:

> the Jurisdictional Approach, strictly defined, requires that all the established [*Salini*] hallmarks of 'investment' must be present before a contract can even be considered as an 'investment', [while] the Typical Characteristics Approach does not necessarily mean that a tribunal would find that there is an 'investment', even if one or more of the established hallmarks of 'investment' were missing.[48]

---

[45] *Malaysian Historical Salvors* (Award on Jurisdiction), para. 44, citing Schreuer *et al.* (eds.), *The ICSID Convention*, p. 140.

[46] *Malaysian Historical Salvors* (Award on Jurisdiction), paras. 65–8.

[47] *Ibid.*, para. 56.   [48] *Ibid.*, para. 70.

Having examined the approach and analysis of the tribunals in the seven relevant cases so as to 'discern a broad trend which emerges from ICSID jurisprudence on the "investment" requirement under the ICSID Convention',[49] the tribunal concluded that the difference between the two approaches was likely to be academic and that:

> The classical *Salini* hallmarks are not a punch list of items which, if completely checked off, will automatically lead to a conclusion that there is an 'investment'. *If any of these hallmarks are absent, the tribunal will hesitate (and probably decline) to make a finding of 'investment'.* However, even if they are all present, a tribunal will still examine the nature and degree of their presence in order to determine whether, on a holistic assessment, it is satisfied that there is an ICSID 'investment'.[50]

The *Malaysian Salvors* tribunal's approach arguably stopped short of the so-called jurisdictional approach (although it equated the two approaches). At the least, however, it appears to elevate the *Fedax/Salini* criteria to a presumption: if any criterion is absent, then jurisdiction will probably be declined. It is questionable whether such a prescriptive approach is appropriate where the possible features of financial commitments by claimants are as infinite as the fields of human endeavour: no one prospective investment is likely to be exactly as another.

Professor Schreuer considers the *Malaysian Salvors* award on Jurisdiction to be evidence of an 'unfortunate' development 'from a descriptive list of typical features to a set of mandatory legal requirements'.[51] He opines:

> To the extent that the '*Salini* test' is applied to determine the existence of an investment, its criteria should not be seen as distinct jurisdictional requirements each of which must be met separately. In fact, tribunals have pointed out repeatedly that the criteria that they applied were interrelated and should be looked at not in isolation but in conjunction.[52]

Schreuer points out that the tribunal in *Salini* emphasised that:

> In reality, these various elements may be interdependent. Thus, the risks of the transaction may depend on the contributions and the duration of performance of the contract. As a result, these various criteria should be assessed globally even if for the sake of reasoning, the Tribunal considers them individually here.[53]

[49] *Ibid.*, para. 104.   [50] *Ibid.*, para. 106(e) (emphasis added).
[51] Schreuer *et al.* (eds.), *The ICSID Convention*, p. 133.   [52] *Ibid.*   [53] *Ibid.*

He concludes:

> A rigid list of criteria that must be met in every case is not likely to facilitate the task of tribunals or to make decisions more predictable. The individual criteria carry a considerable margin of appreciation that may be applied at the tribunal's discretion.[54]

In reaching the conclusion that the salvage contract was not an 'investment' for the purposes of Article 25(1), the tribunal in *Malaysian Salvors* placed particular emphasis on the criterion of contribution to the host State's development, this criterion being of particular relevance to the spirit and objective of the ICSID Convention according to the tribunal. It found that, 'the weight of the authorities . . . swings in favour of requiring a *significant* contribution to be made to the host State's economy'.[55]

The tribunal found that the salvage contract did not benefit the Malaysian public interest in a material way and that so far as the recovery of historical artefacts was of cultural and historical value: 'These benefits, and any other direct financial benefits to [Malaysia], have not been shown to have led to significant contributions to the [Malaysian] economy in the sense envisaged in ICSID jurisprudence.'[56] Indeed it found that the benefits from the salvage contract were no different from benefits flowing to the place of performance of any normal service contract – they were not lasting benefits such as those imparted by public or banking infrastructure projects.[57]

Professor Schreuer points out that the reference to economic development of the host State in the preamble to the Convention supports the proposition that a transaction which is designed to promote such development may be presumed to be an investment, but it does not necessarily follow that activities that do not obviously benefit a host State are thereby excluded from the protection of the Convention.[58] He further cautions:

> A test that turns on the contribution to the host State's development should be treated with particular care . . . Any concept of economic development, if it were to serve as a yardstick for the existence of an investment and hence for protection under ICSID, should be treated with some flexibility. It should not be restricted to measurable contributions to GDP but should include development of human potential, political and social development and the protection of the local and the global environment.[59]

---

[54] *Ibid.*, p. 172.
[55] *Malaysian Historical Salvors* (Award on Jurisdiction), para. 123 (emphasis added).
[56] *Ibid.*, para. 132.   [57] *Ibid.*, para. 144.
[58] Schreuer *et al.* (eds.), *The ICSID Convention*, p. 134.   [59] *Ibid.*

The Tribunals in *LESI SpA et ASTALDI SpA* v. *Algeria*,[60] *Pey Casado* v. *Chile*,[61] and *Saba Fakes* v. *Turkey*[62] similarly dismissed the need for a specific contribution to the host State, let alone a significant one. The *Pey Casado* tribunal put its reasons firmly and, with respect, persuasively:

> The requirement of a contribution to the development of the host State, which is difficult to establish, appears to allude to the merits of the dispute rather than to the Centre's jurisdiction. An investment may or may not prove to be useful to the host State without losing its status as such. It is true that the preamble of the ICSID Convention makes reference to the contribution to the economic development of the host State. This reference is nevertheless presented as a consequence, and not a condition, of the investment: by protecting investments, the Convention foments the development of the host State. That does not mean that the development of the host State is a constitutive element of the notion of investment. This is why, as has been pointed out by certain arbitral tribunals, this fourth condition is in reality covered by the first three.[63]

The *Malaysian Salvors* tribunal, having determined that the salvage contract was not an ICSID investment in accordance with the criteria, found it unnecessary to discuss whether the contract was an investment as defined in the relevant BIT (in this case the UK–Malaysia BIT).[64]

The claimant applied for annulment of the tribunal's award on Jurisdiction. The decision of the Annulment Committee (Judge Stephen M. Schwebel (President), Judge M. Shahabuddeen and Judge P. Tomka) in *Malaysian Salvors*,[65] delivered in April 2009, annulled the award on

[60] *LESI SpA et ASTALDI SpA* v. *Algeria* (ICSID Case No. ARB/05/3, Decision on Jurisdiction of 12 July 2006), para. 72.
[61] *Pey Casado* v. *Chile* (ICSID Case No. ARB/98/2, Award of 8 May 2008).
[62] *Saba Fakes* v. *Turkey* (ICSID Case No. ARB/07/20, Award of 14 July 2010), paras. 107–11.
[63] *Ibid.* para. 232 (original in French):

> L'exigence d'une contribution au développement de l'Etat d'accueil, difficile à établir, lui paraît en effet relever davantage du fond du litige que de la compétence du Centre. Un investissement peut s'avérer utile ou non pour l'Etat d'accueil sans perdre cette qualité. Il est exact que le préambule de la Convention CIRDI évoque la contribution au développement économique de l'Etat d'accueil. Cette référence est cependant présentée comme une conséquence, non comme une condition de l'investissement: en protégeant les investissements, la Convention favorise le développement de l'Etat d'accueil. Cela ne signifie pas que le développement de l'Etat d'accueil soit un élément constitutif de la notion d'investissement. C'est la raison pour laquelle, comme l'ont relevé certains tribunaux arbitraux, cette quatrième condition est en réalité englobée dans les trois premières.

[64] *Malaysian Historical Salvors* (Award on Jurisdiction), para. 148.
[65] *Malaysian Historical Salvors* (Decision on the Application for Annulment).

Jurisdiction on the basis that the tribunal manifestly exceeded its powers by failing to exercise the jurisdiction with which it was endowed by the relevant BIT and the ICSID Convention. A dissent was filed by Judge Shahabuddeen. The majority of the Committee found that the tribunal failed to take account of the BIT, in particular failing to accord great weight to the definition of investment in that agreement; the tribunal's analysis of the *Salini* criteria wrongly elevated them to jurisdictional conditions and wrongly excluded ICSID protection from small contributions including contributions of a cultural and historical nature.[66]

The Committee began by establishing that the salvage contract was without doubt an investment as defined in the UK–Malaysia BIT. The salvage contract was 'one of a kind of asset', and additionally was 'a claim to money and performance under a contract having financial value'; it involved 'intellectual property rights' and was a 'business concession': all of which were alternative descriptions of an investment for which ICSID Convention protection was available according to the terms of the relevant BIT.[67]

As noted above, the tribunal had determined that the terms of the BIT were irrelevant to the issue of whether an investment recognised under the Convention existed. However, the Committee was of the view that what the parties had agreed to submit to ICSID's jurisdiction was fundamental and the appropriate starting point for jurisdictional issues. It found the tribunal's view to be incompatible with the intentions of the parties to the BIT:

> It cannot be accepted that the Governments of Malaysia and the United Kingdom concluded a treaty providing for arbitration of disputes arising under it in respect of investments so comprehensively described, with the intention that the only arbitral recourse provided . . . could be rendered nugatory by a restrictive definition of a deliberately undefined term of the ICSID Convention, namely, 'investment', as it is found in the provision of Article 25(1).[68]

The primacy of the parties' consent to ICSID jurisdiction in the BIT was supported, in the Committee's judgment, by the *travaux préparatoires* and the Report of the Executive Directors. The Committee pointed out that suggested definitions of investment including precise minima of quantum and duration were rejected by the drafters of the Convention.[69] Rather, the Committee said, the history of the Convention makes clear that it was decided that the consent of the parties should be the

---

[66] *Ibid.*, para. 80.   [67] *Ibid.*, paras. 60–1.   [68] *Ibid.*, para. 62.   [69] *Ibid.*, paras. 63–8.

cornerstone of ICSID jurisdiction and that investment would be left undefined given the essential requirement of consent of the parties.[70]

The Committee acknowledged that consent alone will not suffice to accord jurisdiction: there are limits in terms of the nature of the dispute and the parties thereto. However, the Centre's jurisdiction was not intended to be unduly constrained by reference to narrow ad hoc definitions of the deliberately undefined term 'investment' in Article 25(1):

> It appears to have been assumed by the Convention's drafters that use of the term 'investment' excluded a simple sale and like transient commercial transactions from the jurisdiction of the Centre. Judicial or arbitral construction going further in interpretation of the meaning of 'investment' by the establishment of criteria or hallmarks may or may not be regarded as plausible, but the intentions of the draftsmen of the ICSID Convention, as the *travaux* show them to have been, lend those criteria (and still less, conditions) scant support.[71]

The Committee found that the 'outer limits' of jurisdiction which consent could not broach were: the existence of a legal dispute; the parties must be a Contracting State and the national of another Contracting State; and the transaction cannot be a mere sale.[72] Otherwise:

> It is those bilateral and multilateral treaties which today are the engine of ICSID's effective jurisdiction. To ignore or depreciate the importance of the jurisdiction they bestow upon ICSID, and rather to embroider upon questionable interpretations of the term 'investment' as found in Article 25(1) of the Convention, risks crippling the institution.[73]

The Committee noted the decisions in *Salini* and *Joy Mining* as well as the typical investment criteria as propounded by Schreuer (it notes that Schreuer expressly does not raise these criteria to jurisdictional requirements), but preferred awards and analyses consistent with the approach outlined above. It referred to the 'persuasive' 2008 award in *Biwater v. Tanzania*,[74] where the tribunal held that:

> In the Tribunal's view, there is no basis for a rote, or overly strict, application of the five *Salini* criteria in every case. These criteria are not fixed or mandatory as a matter of law. They do not appear in the ICSID Convention . . . Further, the *Salini* test is problematic if, as some tribunals have found, the 'typical characteristics' of an investment as identified are elevated into a fixed and inflexible test, and if transactions are to be

---

[70] *Ibid.*, paras. 67–8, 70–2.   [71] *Ibid.*, para. 69.   [72] *Ibid.*, para. 72.   [73] *Ibid.*, para. 73.
[74] *Biwater Gauff* v. *United Republic of Tanzania* (ICSID Case No. ARB/05/22, Award of 24 July 2008), paras. 310, 312–18.

presumed excluded from the ICSID Convention unless each of the five criteria are satisfied . . . The Arbitral Tribunal therefore considers that a more flexible and pragmatic approach to the meaning of 'investment' is appropriate, which takes into account the features identified in *Salini*, but along with all the circumstances of the case, including the nature of the instrument containing the relevant consent to ICSID.[75]

Judge Shahabuddeen's dissenting opinion asserted that the boundaries to the outer limits of ICSID's objective jurisdiction include a requirement for a substantial contribution to the host State's economic development (in his view the salvage contract did not meet this criterion) and that it is a reversal of the logical process to begin with the parties' subjective agreement before considering the objective jurisdictional requirements of the Convention. Judge Shahabuddeen argued that the Contracting States did not agree that the burdens of ICSID jurisdiction would apply to transactions that did not significantly promote the economic development of the host State. The support of economic development of host States is, Judge Shahabuddeen said, ICSID's 'original mission'[76] to which it should be recalled by way of interpreting a qualifying investment to meet this criterion.

VI *Inmaris* v. *Ukraine*

The development of rigid criteria, and the need for a significant contribution to economic development in particular, have been met by the reservations of Schreuer cited above and were disregarded in the recent decision on jurisdiction in *Inmaris Perestroika Sailing Maritime Services GmbH* v. *Ukraine*.[77] The claimants in this case were a group of German companies collectively called the 'Inmaris Companies'. The dispute concerned various contracts to renovate and operate a ship owned by the Ukrainian government for the dual purpose of a tourist venture and to train Ukrainian merchant marine sailors.

The *Inmaris* tribunal recognised that the Germany–Ukraine BIT and Article 25(1) constituted the applicable law for deciding questions of

---

[75] *Ibid.*, paras. 312–16, extracted in *Malaysian Historical Salvors* (Decision on the Application for Annulment), para. 79.

[76] *Malaysian Historical Salvors* (Decision on the Application for Annulment, Dissenting Opinion of Judge Shahabuddeen), paras. 21–4. See also *Phoenix Action* v. *Czech Republic* (ICSID Case No. ARB/06/5, Award of 15 April 2009), paras. 114–15, where the tribunal adopted a 'supplemented' *Salini* test, including that the assets had to be invested in good faith.

[77] *Inmaris Perestroika Sailing Maritime Services GmbH* v. *Ukraine* (ICSID Case No. ARB/08/8, Decision on Jurisdiction of 8 March 2010).

the tribunal's jurisdiction. The tribunal then approached the issue of the existence of a protected investment in similar terms to those of the majority of the ad hoc Annulment Committee decision in *Malaysian Salvors*. The tribunal observed that Ukraine relied on a definition of investment 'established in the ICSID case law' which was sometimes referred to as the '*Salini* test'.[78] It further observed that: 'Various tribunals have adopted some or all of the typical characteristics of an investment identified by the tribunal in *Salini* v. *Morocco*, and have applied them as a compulsory, limiting definition of investment under the ICSID Convention'.[79] It disagreed with that approach, and set out its view as follows:

> in most cases – including, in the Tribunal's view, this one – it will be appropriate to defer to the State Parties' articulation in the instrument of consent (e.g. the BIT) of what constitutes an investment. The State Parties to a BIT agree to protect certain kinds of economic activity, and when they provide that disputes between investors and States relating to that activity may be resolved through, *inter alia*, ICSID arbitration, that means that they believe that that activity constitutes an 'investment' within the meaning of the ICSID Convention as well. That judgment, by States that are both Parties to the BIT and Contracting States to the ICSID Convention, should be given considerable weight and deference. A tribunal would have to have compelling reasons to disregard such a mutually agreed definition of investment.[80]

The tribunal considered that the *Salini* test 'may be useful in the event that a tribunal were concerned that a BIT or contract definition of investment was so broad that it might appear to capture a transaction that would not normally be characterized as an investment under any reasonable definition'.[81] In such a case, in the view of the tribunal, the *Salini* elements 'could be useful in identifying such aberrations'. It further noted that a number of tribunals and ad hoc committees had recently 'expressed the view that these elements should be viewed as non-binding, non-exclusive means of identifying (rather than defining) investments that are consistent with the ICSID Convention'.[82] The tribunals and ad hoc committees referred to are footnoted in the tribunal's decision on Jurisdiction, and they include the tribunals in *Biwater* v. *Tanzania* and *MCI* v. *Ecuador*, and the Annulment Committee in *Malaysian Salvors*.

---

[78] *Ibid.*, para. 129 (footnotes omitted).   [79] *Ibid.* (footnotes omitted).
[80] *Ibid.*, para. 130.   [81] *Ibid.*, para. 131.   [82] *Ibid.*

VII   To what effect is this apparent change of emphasis?

It is interesting to reflect on the potential effect on ICSID jurisdiction, if the parties' consent to ICSID jurisdiction is the critical or primary factor in determining the scope of investments covered by the Convention. On the one hand, some past cases may have been decided differently. On the other, it may be that the battleground has merely shifted to whether a certain transaction qualifies as an 'investment' under the relevant treaty; the argument being that save for explicit wording, general definitions of an investment under BITs or MITs still implicitly require the transaction to be in the nature of an investment as opposed to an ordinary commercial transaction. Attempts to distinguish between these two categories brings one back to the issue and relevance of *Salini*-type criteria – contribution, duration and risk.

An example of a case that may have been decided differently by focusing on the terms of the relevant BIT, is *Mihaly International Corporation* v. *Government of the Democratic Socialist Republic of Sri Lanka*[83] which concerned Build, Own, Operate and Transfer (BOOT) projects.[84] *Mihaly* dealt with a thermal electric power generating plant, the largest foreign investment at the time in Sri Lanka.[85] Sri Lanka, having studied extensively the various possibilities of infrastructure development, sent out a request for proposal for its BOOT project. Mihaly, a partnership between a Canadian and a US developer, was chosen in 1992 to carry out the project. In February 1993 Sri Lanka issued a letter of intent containing its agreement to negotiate in good faith to settle in a timely manner the necessary formal contracts. During the following three years of negotiations, which were stalled by both parties for various political and commercial reasons, Mihaly received an 'Award of Contract' and a renewal of the award. The renewal set out a detailed schedule of various

---

[83] *Mihaly International Corporation* (Award). Another borderline decision that may have been viewed differently is *Mitchell* v. *Democratic Republic of Congo* (ICSID Case No. ARB 99/7, Decision on Annulment of 1 November 2006).

[84] BOOT projects are being used by developing States, notably Asian States, for large infrastructure projects. The projects include the buildings of highways, ports, dams, mass transit systems, power generation plants, water supply systems and industrial estates. Their identifying feature is their connection with the economic development functions of the State, assigned to various ministries. Furthermore, legislation is usually passed to control the use of the projects. See M. Sornarajah, *The Settlement of Foreign Investment Disputes* (The Hague: Kluwer, 2000), pp. 46–8.

[85] J. M. Robinson, 'ICSID cases on its jurisdiction: A serious problem for public/private partnerships for infrastructure in developing countries', *International Business Lawyer*, (2004), 263.

obligations to be met in order to get the negotiations back on track. Mihaly met all its obligations, Sri Lanka none. The issue put before the ICSID tribunal was whether the significant expenditures by the Mihaly consortium (which amounted to almost US$6 million) to prepare for construction of the power plant (including plant engineering, financial advice, legal fees, etc.) expended in reliance on the letter of intent and its two renewals constituted an 'investment' sufficient to engage the jurisdiction of ICSID.

In support of its claim, Mihaly submitted an affidavit of a retired 'very senior official' of the World Bank. The official's expert opinion was that such expenditures would constitute investments in the host country.[86] Nevertheless, the tribunal refused to extend the definition of 'investment' to include expenditures in a project where neither a formal contract had been signed nor construction commenced. The tribunal concluded that Mihaly's expenditures did not amount to an 'investment' for the purposes of Article 25(1) and declined jurisdiction.[87]

Academic concern over such an approach has been summarised as follows:

> It is clear from most bilateral investment treaties, which contain defini-
> tions of 'investment', and from the jurisprudence, including leading
> arbitral decisions at ICSID and elsewhere, that the word investment is
> intended to be construed expansively, to suit current needs and practices.
> This decision by an ICSID Tribunal erects a barrier to that construction,
> and also to achieving the major purpose of ICSID: encouragement of
> private investment in developing countries.[88]

The tribunal in *Mihaly* did not examine the definition of investment in the relevant BIT (USA–Sri Lanka) in detail. It is fair to assume that letters of intent and the like that commit parties to a certain period of exclusivity, negotiation in good faith, and a build up of expenditure pending finalisation of contractual arrangements (such as in *Mihaly*) fall

---

[86] *Mihaly International Corporation* (Concurring Opinion of David Suratgar of 7 March 2002), para. 6.

[87] *Ibid.*, para. 61.

[88] J. M. Robinson, 'ICSID cases on its jurisdiction', p. 265. Indeed in his Concurring Opinion in *Mihaly*, Mr Suratgar allowed that he agreed with the conclusions of the Award 'reluctantly' in the absence of evidence of 'international legal and utility prece-dents and practice' with regard to BOOT projects (paras. 6, 9). Mr Suratgar opined that: 'Expenditure incurred by successful bidders do indeed produce "economic value" as specified by Article 1 of the US–Sri Lanka BIT and the protection mechanism developed under the aegis of the World Bank in the form of the ICSID Convention should be available to those who are encouraged to embark on such expensive exercises' (para. 10).

within the definition of 'investment' in most BITs. Rights arising from such arrangements are likely to be 'one of a kind of asset', 'a claim to money and performance under a contract having financial value' or possibly a 'business concession', for example. If so, a tribunal following the approach of the Committee in *Malaysian Salvors* and the tribunals in *Biwater* v. *Tanzania* and *Inmaris* v. *Ukraine* may well conclude that ICSID jurisdiction indeed extends to this type of investment.

The continued relevance of *Salini*-type criteria when identifying an investment pursuant to the relevant definition in a BIT was discussed in the recent award in *Romak* v. *Uzbekistan*.[89] While not an ICSID case, Uzbekistan challenged the jurisdiction of the tribunal on the basis that a claim for unpaid money for consignments of wheat supplied to an Uzbekistan government authority by Romak (and an arbitral award ordering payment) were not investments pursuant to the relevant BIT (Switzerland/Uzbekistan).

The BIT definition of investment (Article 1(2)) was typically broad and was expressed to 'include every kind of assets', particularly 'claims to money or to any performance having an economic value' and 'all other rights given by law, by contract or by decision of the authority in accordance with the law'.[90] Romak argued that its rights to payment for the wheat supplied to Uzbekistan fell within the ordinary meaning of these phrases. However, the tribunal found that:

> Based on the above considerations, Romak's proposed literal construction of Article 1(2) of the BIT is untenable as a matter of international law. The Arbitral Tribunal must therefore explore the meaning of the word 'investments' contained in the introductory paragraph of that Article. As stated above at paragraph 180, the categories enumerated in Article 1(2) are not exhaustive and are clearly intended as *illustrations*. Thus, for example, while many 'claims to money' will qualify as 'investments', it does not follow that *all* such assets necessarily so qualify. The term 'investments' has an intrinsic meaning, independent of the categories enumerated in Article 1(2). This meaning cannot be ignored.[91]

The *Romak* tribunal went on to consider ICSID jurisprudence including *Salini*, *CSOB*, and *Joy Mining*. It distinguished between the two approaches to identifying an investment discussed above as 'conceptualist' (the *Salini* approach) and 'pragmatic' (the *CSOB* approach).[92] The tribunal concluded:

---

[89] *Romak* v. *Uzbekistan* (PCA Case No. AA280, Award of 26 November 2009).
[90] *Ibid.*, para. 174.   [91] *Ibid.*, para. 188 (emphasis in original).
[92] *Ibid.*, paras. 197–204.

> The Arbitral Tribunal therefore considers that the term 'investments' under the BIT has an inherent meaning (irrespective of whether the investor resorts to ICSID or UNCITRAL arbitral proceedings) entailing a *contribution* that extends over a *certain period of time* and that involves some *risk*. The Arbitral Tribunal is further comforted in its analysis by the reasoning adopted by other arbitral tribunals . . . which consistently incorporates contribution, duration and risk as hallmarks of an 'investment'. By their nature, asset types enumerated in the BIT's non-exhaustive list may exhibit these hallmarks. But if an asset does not correspond to the inherent definition of 'investment', the fact that it falls within one of the categories listed in Article 1 does not transform it into an 'investment'.[93]

The *Romak* tribunal found on the facts before it that there was no evidence of contribution – the supply of wheat with an expectation of immediate payment was insufficient.[94] As far as duration was concerned, while 'short-term projects are not deprived of "investment" status solely by virtue of their limited duration', the five months over which wheat was delivered did not reflect a commitment greater than an ordinary commercial transaction in the absence of any intended ongoing relationship.[95] The tribunal also made some insightful comments about the nature of investment risk:

> All economic activity entails a certain degree of risk. As such, all con-tracts – including contracts that do not constitute an investment – carry the risk of non-performance. However, this kind of risk is pure commer-cial, counterparty risk, or, otherwise stated, the risk of doing business generally. It is therefore not an element that is useful for the purpose of distinguishing between an investment and a commercial transaction.
>
> An 'investment risk' entails a different kind of *alea*, a situation in which the investor cannot be sure of a return on his investment, and may not know the amount he will end up spending, even if all relevant counterparties discharge their contractual obligations. Where there is 'risk' of this sort, the investor simply cannot predict the outcome of the transaction.[96]

The risk of non-payment for the wheat supplied was pure commercial risk and did not indicate an investment as contemplated by the BIT. The *Romak* tribunal considered that its approach to the investment issue did not detract from the freedom of the contracting parties to the BIT to define investment, but rather was of the view that the inclusion of a pure sales contract as a qualifying investment would require specific and unambiguous wording.[97]

---

[93] *Ibid.*, para. 207 (emphasis in original). See also *Phoenix Action* v. *Czech Republic* (ICSID Case No. ARB/06/5, Award of 15 April 2009), paras. 74 and 82.
[94] *Ibid.*, paras. 214–15.   [95] *Ibid.*, paras. 225–7.   [96] *Ibid.*, paras. 229–30.
[97] *Ibid.*, para. 205.

On the *Romak* reasoning, the basic *Fedax/Salini* criteria – contribution, duration, risk – remain relevant to distinguishing between an ordinary commercial transaction and an investment, even if the apparently more permissive approach taken by the Annulment Committee in *Malaysian Salvors*, and the tribunals in *Biwater* and *Inmaris* is followed, depending ultimately, of course, on the exact wording of the relevant treaty.[98]

VIII   Conclusion

The pendulum that had swung toward a prescriptive list of criteria, which were raised as high as mandatory jurisdictional thresholds in some cases, has been rejected in large degree by the Annulment Committee in *Malaysian Salvors* and the tribunals in *Biwater* v. *Tanzania* and *Inmaris* v. *Ukraine*. The approach taken in these recent decisions reflects that of earlier decisions in *CSOB* and *MCI* v. *Ecuador*. The highly respected commentary of Professor Schreuer also resists attempts to impose a formulaic definition on a term deliberately left undefined by the drafters of the Convention following thorough debate.

The primacy of the parties' consent to ICSID jurisdiction is in the ascendancy. This approach determines first whether the parties have agreed that the instant transaction qualifies as an ICSID-protected investment. If so, it is presumed to be so, subject to the broad objective 'outer limit' imposed by Article 25(1) that an investment must be more than a transient sale and purchase. The Fedax/Salini criteria have been reduced to a non-binding, non-mandatory and non-exhaustive list of characteristics that may assist in the identification of an investment, as compared with a transient transaction, in borderline cases.

Notably, the requirement that an investment constitute a significant contribution to the economy of the host State has been severely diluted if not eliminated. The contribution may be modest and may be financial, cultural or environmental in nature. This will invariably be present in any transaction which the parties have agreed should have the benefit of the protection of the ICSID Convention.

[98] An interesting and, with respect, insightful, view as to how and where to draw the line between ordinary commercial transactions and ICSID protected investments is set out by V. Heiskanen, *Of Capital Import: The definition of investment in international investment law* (ASA Special Series No. 34 of May 2010), 51. Heiskanen proposes focusing on the owner's capital investment or equity. This delineates the nature of the business activity; activities unsupported by any equity investment or capital contribution shown in the owner's accounts cannot conceptually be considered as investments – rather they are businesses engaged in the ongoing sale of goods or services.

This permissive approach may broaden the scope and increase the number of transactions within ICSID jurisdiction, and, if generally accepted by tribunals and committees over the medium term, may result in fewer challenges to jurisdiction on the grounds of absence of a qualifying investment pursuant to Article 25(1). However, the *Romak* award suggests that the investment criteria debate may well shift to a different part of the reasoning process. In any event, focus on the exact terms of each relevant treaty will become the key consideration.

In the authors' opinion this is the proper approach. If one returns to the historical context of the definition of investment outlined above, it is for each Contracting State to decide on the balance of the bargain as between derogation of sovereignty and nature of investments the State is willing to protect in order to promote economic growth and welfare in its territory. This balance, as recorded in the terms of the relevant treaty, is therefore the natural starting point for any tribunal in determining whether a particular transaction should enjoy the benefits of treaty protection.

4

Investment treaty interpretation and customary investment law: Preliminary remarks

MARTINS PAPARINSKIS[*]

I Introduction

The historical development of investment protection law has resulted in a somewhat peculiar interplay of different treaty and customary law strata. As has been suggested elsewhere:

> the shift has been away from vague and crude substantive rules (set out in customary law, general principles and evocations of equity) discretionarily enforced by the home State, and in the direction of 'treatified' law of investment protection, implemented by means of investor–State arbitration . . . The results of the more recent efforts of [treaty] law-making sometimes accept and incorporate the classic [customary] rules; sometimes clarify the classic ambiguities or replace the unsatisfactory solutions; sometimes permit different approaches in parallel; and quite often maintain constructive ambiguity regarding the precise relationship between different rules.[1]

Particularly during the last decade, States, investment treaty tribunals and legal writers have grappled with perhaps not entirely foreseen theoretical and practical implications of the relationship between investment rules set out in treaty and customary law. Different facets of the

[*] I wrote this chapter while I was a Hauser Research Scholar at the New York University. I am grateful to Professors José Alvarez and Robert Howse for sharing with me their thoughts about treaties and customary law during my stay at the NYU. Earlier versions of this chapter have been presented at the NYU Global Fellows Forum, the Sydney Conference and the Society of International Economic Law Second Global Biennial Conference in Barcelona. I greatly appreciate the comments and criticism of the participants, particularly Sir Frank Berman and Professor Campbell McLachlan. I thank the organisers of the conference held at the University of Sydney for the financial support for my attendance of the conference. The views expressed and the errors or omissions made are the responsibility of the author alone.
[1] M. Paparinskis, 'Investment arbitration and the law of countermeasures', *British Yearbook of International Law*, 79 (2008), 264, 265.

relationship raise different legal questions, ranging from the more trad-itional inquiries about lawmaking (and the contribution of treaties to custom)[2] to perspectives of conflict (and the exclusion of custom by treaties)[3] and interpretation (of treaties by reference to custom).[4] This chapter engages in the latter exercise, relying on the practice and case law of the last decade to suggest an approach that an interpreter of an investment treaty should take regarding customary investment protec-tion law.

The limits of the permissible and required interpretative reference to customary law seem formulated with some ambiguity, raising important theoretical questions with considerable practical relevance. To consider some of the best-known examples, was the tribunal in *Loewen Group Inc. and Raymond L. Loewen* v. *US* right to interpret the temporal aspect of the investor's procedural rights in the North American Free Trade Agreement (NAFTA) by reference to the rule of continuous nationality from the customary law of diplomatic protection?[5] Conversely, was the Annulment Committee in *Sempra Energy International* v. *Argentina* correct in criticising the *Sempra* tribunal's reliance on the criteria of customary law of necessity in interpreting a so-called non-precluded-measures (NPM) clause in a US-Argentina bilateral investment treaty (BIT)?[6] The *Loewen* and *Sempra* cases show the practical importance of the interpretative relevance of customary law: in the former case, criteria

---

[2] A. F. Lowenfeld, 'Investment agreements and international law', *Columbia Journal of Transnational Law*, 42 (2003), 123; S. M. Schwebel, 'The influence of bilateral investment treaties on customary international law', *Proceedings of the American Society of Inter-national Law*, 98 (2004), 27; J. E. Alvarez, 'A BIT on custom', *New York University Journal of International Law and Politics*, 42 (2010), 17.

[3] Z. Douglas, 'The hybrid foundations of investment treaty arbitration', *British Yearbook of International Law*, 74 (2003), 151, 190–1; B. Juratowitch, 'The relationship between diplomatic protection and investment treaties', *ICSID Review – Foreign Investment Law Journal*, 23 (2008), 10, 14–27; Paparinskis, 'Countermeasures', pp. 281–97; Z. Douglas, *The International Law of Investment Claims* (Cambridge University Press, 2009), p. 95; Z. Douglas, 'Other specific regimes of responsibility: Investment treaty arbitration and ICSID' in J. Crawford and others (eds.), *The Law of International Responsibility* (Oxford University Press, 2010), pp. 816–17.

[4] C. McLachlan, 'Investment treaties and general international law', *International and Comparative Law Quarterly*, 57 (2008), 361.

[5] *Loewen Group Inc. and Raymond L. Loewen* v. *US* (ICSID Case No. ARB(AF)/98/3, Award of 26 June 2003), paras. 226–39 (*Loewen*).

[6] *Sempra Energy International* v. *Argentine Republic* (ICSID Case No. ARB/02/16, Decision on Annulment of 29 June 2010), paras. 186–209 (*Sempra*); see also *CMS Gas Transmission Company* v. *Argentina* (ICSID Case No. ARB 01/08, Decision on Annulment of 25 September 2007), paras. 129–35.

provided by customary law provided one of two grounds for rejecting the claim,[7] while in the latter case impermissible reliance on criteria provided by customary law was the ground for annulment.[8]

The methodology for distinguishing required interpretative reliance on custom from impermissible often seems at best unclear. For example, the tribunal in *Saluka Investment BV* v. *Czech Republic* accepted as uncontroversial an argument that a treaty rule of 'deprivation' made a reference to customary law of expropriation (that was in its turn explained in a draft text using the term of art of 'taking'). Forty paragraphs later, the same tribunal summarily rejected a proposition that the treaty rule of 'fair and equitable treatment' made a reference to the customary minimum standard.[9] Why was reliance on customary law appropriate in the former case but not in the latter one? Disputes about the scope of treaty rules of full protection and security[10] and umbrella clauses may also be traced to different views about the relevance of analogous customary rules.[11]

The purpose of this chapter is not to answer particular controversies but rather to identify the right questions, perspectives and criteria that require or preclude reliance on customary law in the interpretative process. This approach permits adopting a convenient intermediate position between general international law rules on sources and interpretation and the practice and case law of investment protection law. From the former perspective, the rules on interpretation from the Vienna Convention on the Law of Treaties (VCLT),[12] and the International Law Commission's (ILC) Study Group's work on fragmentation suggest the contours of the interpretative framework in investment protection law.[13] At the same time, the relationship is importantly symbiotic. From the perspective of investment protection law, the case

---

[7] *Loewen* (Award), para. 239.   [8] *Sempra*, paras. 211–23.

[9] *Saluka Investments BV* v. *Czech Republic* (UNCITRAL Partial Award of 17 March 2006), paras. 254–94 (*Saluka*).

[10] *Ibid.*, paras. 483–4.

[11] *SGS Société Générale de Surveillance SA* v. *Pakistan* (ICSID Case No. ARB/01/13, Decision on Jurisdiction of 6 August 2003), para. 167.

[12] Vienna Convention on the Law of Treaties, opened for signature 23 May 1969, 1155 UNTS 311 (entered into force 27 January 1980), Arts. 31–2 (VCLT).

[13] Report of the Study Group of the ILC, 'Fragmentation of international law: difficulties arising from diversification and expansion of international law', UN Doc. A/CN.4/L.682 206–43 (Report of the Study Group); Conclusions of the Work of the Study Group, 'Fragmentation of international law: Difficulties arising from diversification and expansion of international law', UN Doc. A/CN.4/L.682 Add 1, paras. 17–23 (Conclusions of the Work of the Study Group).

law of the investment treaty tribunals is perhaps the most convenient laboratory at the moment for identifying, refining and contributing to the development of general rules on interpretation by reference to custom.

The scope of this chapter is consciously narrow, dealing with the interpretation of investment treaties only by reference to *general customary investment protection law*. It does not deal with interpretation of investment treaties by reference to non-binding soft law, general principles, special customary law,[14] other treaties or model treaties,[15] rules not binding all parties or rules that in descriptive terms relate to non-investment law (like human rights law, environmental law or trade law).[16] The chosen focus should not be read to suggest that issues not addressed are less important: they obviously are, especially the latter ones. It simply makes methodological sense to first identify the position in the relatively easier situation where the *ratione personae* and broad *ratione materiae* overlap of binding rules may be *prima facie* taken as a given, and only then add other complicating factors to the normative mix.

The broad contours of the analysis are set by the historical continuities and discontinuities.[17] The questions about the relationship between treaty and customary rules on the protection of property interests of foreigners have an impressive pedigree. In the first half of the last

---

[14] The reliance on special custom is subject to the traditional caveat that it is not opposable to States that have not opted out from the general customary law, M. Paparinskis, 'Regulatory expropriation and sustainable development' in M. W. Gehring, M.-C. Cordonnier-Segger and A. Newcombe (eds.), *Sustainable Development in International Investment Law* (The Hague: Kluwer, 2011), pp. 295, 325.

[15] M. Paparinskis, 'Investment protection law and sources of law: A critical look', *Proceedings of the American Society of International Law*, 103 (2009), 76; M. Paparinskis, 'Sources of law and arbitral interpretation of *Pari Materia* investment protection rules' in O. K. Fauchald and A. Nollkaemper (eds.), *Unity or Fragmentation of International Law: The role of international and national tribunals* (Hart Publishing, forthcoming).

[16] A. van Aaken, 'Fragmentation of international law: The case of international investment law', *Finnish Yearbook of International Law*, 17 (2008), 91; M. Hirsch, 'Interactions between investment and non-investment obligations in international investment law' in C. Schreuer *et al.* (eds.), *Oxford Handbook of International Investment Law* (Oxford University Press, 2008); B. Simma and T. Kill, 'Harmonizing investment protection and international human rights: first Steps towards a Methodology' in C. Binder *et al.* (eds.), *International Investment Law for the 21st Century: Essays in honour of Christoph Schreuer* (Oxford University Press, 2009), p. 678.

[17] J. Crawford, 'Continuity and discontinuity in international dispute settlement' in C. Binder *et al.* (eds.), *International Investment Law for the 21st Century: Essays in honour of Christoph Schreuer* (Oxford University Press, 2009), p. 801; more generally P. Weil, 'Le droit international en quête de son identité', *Recueil des Cours de l'Académie de Droit International*, 236 (1992), 9, 25–39.

century, parties before the Permanent Court of International Justice (PCIJ) both expressed indignation about allegations of denial of justice in relation to rights of aliens acquired under a treaty[18] and successfully appealed for systemic integration of customary rules on the treatment of aliens because '*Aucune disposition du droit écrit n'est placée dans l'espace vide*.'[19] Indeed, already the 1837–42 *Sicilian Sulphur* dispute, that related to 'promulgation of unjust and impolitic edicts . . . interfering with the legitimate industry of individuals',[20] dealt with 'interpret[ation of] the words of the Commercial Treaty in the light of general principles of international law'.[21] There is a strong conceptual continuity with contemporary debates that can and should be usefully employed.

The argument will be made in two steps. First of all, the general international law rules of interpretation of treaties by reference to customary law will be dealt with, considering their application in the investment treaty context (section II). It will be suggested that not one but two different legal techniques are at play here: on the one hand, 'any relevant rules' of Article 31(3)(c) of the VCLT that in accordance with the *chapeau* of Article 31(3)(c) contextualise the ordinary meaning; on the other hand, a treaty rule that brings in a rule of customary law as its ordinary or special meaning. The second part of the chapter will illustrate the application of the suggested approaches on the basis of case studies (section III). In particular, the possible integration of investor–State arbitration and diplomatic protection (section III.A), primary rules of investment protection (section III.B) and NPM treaty clauses and customary circumstances precluding wrongfulness will be addressed (section III.C). It will be suggested that despite the complex interplay of treaty and customary strata in investment law, the concise formulae of the VCLT still provide the interpreter with the best framework for resolving interpretative queries. Even though the VCLT provides the interpreter

---

[18] *Phosphates in Morocco (Italy v. France)*, PCIJ Rep, Series C (No 85), 1039 (French pleadings by Basdevant).

[19] *Case Concerning Certain German Interests in Polish Upper Silesia (Germany v. Poland)* PCIJ Rep, Series C (No. 11), vol. I, 167 (German pleadings by Kaufmann). The Court agreed, *Case Concerning Certain German Interests in Polish Upper Silesia (Germany v. Poland)*, PCIJ Rep, Series A (No. 7), 21.

[20] *Sicilian Sulphur* (1839–1840) 28 British and Foreign State Papers 1163 (Correspondence between Great Britain and Sicily, relative to the Sulphur Monopoly in Sicily, 1837–1839), 1218 (letter No. 28 from Viscount Palmerston to Count Ludoff of 12 October 1838).

[21] *Oscar Chinn (UK v. Belgium)*, PCIJ Rep, Series C (No 75), 284–7 (British written pleadings).

with considerable flexibility, it still imposes certain structural restraints within which the artful interpretative exercise has to be carried out.

II Treaty interpretation and customary law: General issues

Interpretation of treaties by reference to other rules of international law has been subject to considerable attention in the last few years.[22] A common starting point of analysis is Article 31(3)(c) of the VCLT and analogous customary law[23] that provide that: 'There shall be taken into account, together with the context: . . . (c) any relevant rules of international law applicable in the relations between the parties.'[24] Each word and concept of Article 31(3)(c) – 'any', 'relevant', 'rules of international law', 'applicable', 'in the relations', 'between the parties' – has raised further interpretative questions relating to the scope of permissible reference. However, the narrow focus of this chapter seems to leave aside most of these controversies since general customary law rules are likely to be 'any . . . rules of international law applicable between the parties'.[25] The only explicit qualification for distinguishing appropriate from inappropriate interpretative references is that customary law has to be 'relevant'. The general issues of investment treaty interpretation by reference to customary law will be analysed in three steps: first of all, the admissibility of customary law as interpretative materials under Article 31(3)(c) will be considered; secondly, the interpretative weight

---

[22] Report of the Study Group, pp. 206–44; J. Pauwelyn, *Conflict of Norms in Public International Law: How WTO law relates to other rules of international law* (Cambridge University Press, 2003), pp. 253–74; C. McLachlan, 'The principle of systemic integration and Article 31(3)(c) of the Vienna Convention', *International and Comparative Law Quarterly*, 54 (2005), 279; D. French, 'Treaty interpretation and the incorporation of extraneous legal rules', *International and Comparative Law Quarterly*, 55 (2006), 281; J.-Mc. Sorel, 'Article 31: Convention de 1969' in O. Cortien and P. Klein (eds.), *Les Conventions de Vienne sur le droit des traités: Commentaires article par article* (Bruxelles: Bruylant, 2006), p. 1323; R. Gardiner, *Treaty Interpretation* (Oxford University Press, 2008), ch. 7; McLachlan, 'Investment treaties', pp. 369–401; I. van Damme, *Treaty Interpretation by the WTO Appellate Body* (Oxford University Press, 2009), ch. 9; M. E. Villiger, *Commentary on the 1969 Vienna Convention on the Law of Treaties* (Martinus Nijhoff Publishers, Leiden/Boston 2009), pp. 432–4.

[23] *Certain Questions of Mutual Assistance in Criminal Matters (Djibouti v. France)* [2008] ICJ Rep 177, para. 112.

[24] VCLT, Art. 31(3)(c).

[25] G. Abi-Saab, 'The appellate body and treaty interpretation' in G. Sacerdoti *et al.* (eds.), *The WTO at Ten: The contribution of the dispute settlement system* (Cambridge University Press, 2006), p. 463.

of admissible customary law will be addressed; thirdly, other approaches for dealing with custom suggested by the ILC will be dealt with.

First of all, the scope of 'relevance' in Article 31(3)(c) may be subject to different readings. At the narrower end of the spectrum, Judge Villiger has suggested that relevant rules 'concern the subject-matter of the treaty term at issue. In the case of customary rules, these may even be identical with, and run parallel to, the treaty rule.'[26] A number of authors explain relevance primarily by reference to the subject matter of the rules.[27] At the other end of the spectrum, Judge Simma and Theodore Kill have argued for a broad reading under which 'Almost any rule of international law will be "relevant" when considered with the proper degree of abstraction.'[28] The broader reading is supported by reference to Article 30 of the VCLT that explicitly uses the concept of 'the same subject-matter', with the ordinary meaning of 'relevant' *a contrario* suggesting a broader scope.[29] The International Court's judgment in the *Certain Questions of Mutual Assistance in Criminal Matters (Djibouti)* case seems closer to the latter reading of relevance, finding aspirational rules from a Friendship and Co-operation Treaty 'relevant' for interpreting rules on mutual criminal assistance in another treaty.[30] At the same time, the explicit reference to context in the *chapeau* of Article 31(3) and to 'applicable [rules]' in subparagraph (c) could narrow back the broader reading of relevance.[31]

The different readings of 'relevance' could have a significant impact on the interpretation of investment treaties that may be illustrated by reference to the *Loewen* and *Sempra* cases. If 'relevant' rules have to 'run parallel', then in the *Loewen* case the interpreter of treaty rules on

---

[26] Villiger continues by saying that: 'Non-identical customary rules on the same subject-matter may lead to a modification of the treaty term as a result of subsequent practice counter to the treaty provision.' This possibly implies that subpara. (c) applies only to identical customary rules, with non-identical rules and their effects properly falling to be considered under subpara. (b): Villiger, *Commentary on the 1969 Vienna Convention on the Law of Treaties*, p. 433.

[27] G. Marceau, 'Conflict of norms and conflict of jurisdictions: The relationship between WTO law and agreements and other treaties', *World Trade Journal*, 35 (2001), 1081, 1087; Pauwelyn, *Conflict of Norms in Public International Law*, p. 260.

[28] Simma and Kill, 'Harmonizing investment protection and international human rights', p. 696.

[29] *Ibid.*, p. 695.   [30] *Djibouti*, para. 113.

[31] *Oil Platforms (Iran v. US)* (Judgment) [2003] ICJ Rep 161, (Separate Opinion of Judge Higgins) 225, para. 46; F. Berman, 'Treaty interpretation in a judicial context', *Yale Journal of International Law*, 29 (2004), 315, 320; Gardiner, *Treaty Interpretation*, pp. 278–80.

investor–State arbitration could refer to customary law of diplomatic protection dealing with invocation of responsibility by States only if investor–State arbitration (despite appearance to the contrary) was also invocation of responsibility by States. Similarly, in the *Sempra* case the interpreter could refer to customary law of circumstances precluding wrongfulness only if the treaty rules on NPM clauses were secondary rules of State responsibility. An interpreter adopting this approach has to diligently identify the nature of treaty and customary law, and the absence of relevance directly leads to *ab initio* inadmissibility of custom as an interpretative material. Conversely, an interpreter for whom almost any rule of international law is relevant would probably be less concerned about the exact normative parallelism and admissibility of interpretative materials: even if *arguendo* investor–State arbitration is not exactly diplomatic protection or NPM clauses are not precisely secondary rules, with the proper degree of abstraction similar issues of invocation of responsibility or conduct in emergency situations may be identified.

Different (and changing) approaches to relevance raise the challenge for constructing a coherent interpretative methodology. For example, the Iran–United States Claims Tribunal's (IUSCT) practice of interpreting treaty rules on individual–State arbitration by reference to the customary law of diplomatic protection regarding (double) nationality[32] is considered to be a positive example of systemic integration.[33] Conversely, the *Loewen* tribunal's decision to interpret treaty rules on individual–State arbitration by reference to customary law of diplomatic protection regarding (continuous) nationality[34] is treated as a negative example where the tribunal borrowed inappropriately from customary law.[35] This is not to suggest that the broader positions cannot be

---

[32] *Nasser Esphahanian* v. *Bank Tejarat* (1983) 2 Iran–USCTR 157, 161; *Iran–United States*, Case No. A/18 (1984) 5 Iran–USCTR 251, 260.

[33] Report of the Study Group, paras. 434, 467; McLachlan 'Systemic integration', pp. 293–4, 312.

[34] *Loewen* (Award), paras. 226–39.

[35] M. Mendelson, 'Runaway train: The "continuous nationality" rule from the *Panavezys-Saldutiskis Railway* case to *Loewen*' in T. Weiler (ed.), *International Investment Law and Arbitration: Leading cases from the ICSID, NAFTA, bilateral treaties and customary international law* (Cameron May, 2005), pp. 97–8, 141; C. McLachlan, L. Shore and M. Weiniger, *International Investment Arbitration: Substantive principles* (Oxford University Press, 2007), pp. 151–5; *Waguih Elie George Siag and Clorinda Vecchi* v. *Egypt* (ICSID Case No. ARB/05/15, Award of 1 June 2009), para. 498 (*Siag*); *Yukos Universal Ltd* v. *Russian Federation*, PCA Case No. AA 227, Interim Award on Jurisdiction and Admissibility of 30 November 2009, para. 562 ('*Yukos*').

reconciled: as a starting point, the IUSCT was probably right in its reading of customary law[36] while the *Loewen* tribunal was probably not.[37] It is not implausible to suggest that the respectively accurate and erroneous identification of the content of custom could have influenced the perceived appropriateness of reliance on custom in the first place.[38] Still, when considering the proper methodology of interpreting treaties by reference to customary law, it is puzzling that the differences between individual-State and State–State proceedings have come to be accepted as determining relevance in investment cases but not regarding the IUSCT.

Secondly, even if customary rules have been recognised as admissible interpretative materials, their weight in the interpretative process still needs to be considered. The discussion of the role of customary law often focuses on the former aspect of admissibility, implicitly assuming that 'relevant' customary law would necessarily dictate the result of the interpretative exercise. However, the mere fact that customary law is 'relevant' does not on its own mean that it carries significant interpretative weight or even replaces the ordinary meaning of the treaty term. The criteria of Article 31(3)(c) only determine the admissibility of interpretative materials. It is the *chapeau* of Article 31(3) that explains the role and weight of admissible interpretative materials in the interpretative process by placing them 'together with the context'. The *chapeau* suggests that materials introduced in the interpretative process through Article 31(3)(c) play the same role and carry (only) the same interpretative weight as the context. To paraphrase the ILC Commentary, 'the ordinary meaning of a term is not to be determined in the abstract but in the context of the treaty [and relevant customary law] and in light of its object and purpose'.[39]

---

[36] ILC, 'Draft articles on diplomatic protection with commentaries' in *Report of the International Law Commission on the Work of its 61st Session*, UN Doc. A/61/10, Art. 7 Commentary 3, n. 81.

[37] *Ibid.*, Art. 5 Commentary, para. 5; J. Paulsson, 'Note – *Loewen* v. *United States*, ICSID Additional Facility Case No. ARB/AF/98/3 – Continuous Nationality in Loewen', *Arbitration International*, 20 (2004), 213, 213–15; Mendelson, 'Runaway train', pp. 99–123; *Siag*, paras. 498–9; *Yukos Universal Ltd* v. *Russian Federation*, para. 562.

[38] C. Leben, 'La Responsabilité internationale de l'état sur le fondement des traités de promotion et de protection des investissements', *Annuaire Française de Droit International*, 50 (2004), 683, 696.

[39] ILC, 'Draft Articles on the law of treaties with commentaries' in *Yearbook of the International Law Commission*, UN Doc. A/CN.4/SER.A/1966/Add.1, 112, 221 (vol. 2, 1966), para. 12.

In the *Djibouti* case, the ICJ found that the 'relevant' rules only 'have a certain bearing on interpretation' and 'cannot possibly stand in the way' of particular rules in the treaty under interpretation.[40] Simma and Kill have explained *Djibouti* as supporting a de facto sliding scale accompanying the broader approach to relevance – when the relevance appears only with a high degree of abstraction:

> the impact of the rule on the interpretation of the treaty in dispute should be low. If, however, the rule does provide 'operational guidance' for the determination of the meaning of a treaty's terms as argued by either party, then it is appropriate for that rule to play a greater role in informing the interpreters understanding of the treaty.[41]

Minimising the interpretative weight is a greater concern under the broader approach to relevance (where more interpretative materials would be admissible), but finding the appropriate role and weight for customary law is important under any reading of relevance. In fact, the methodology suggested by Simma and Kill may be anchored within the VCLT as explaining the application of the *chapeau* of Article 31(3). It seems fairly commonsensical that context (and rules considered 'together with context') should have greater bearing on the framing of the ordinary meaning if they deal with the same or similar issues and *vice versa*. Since a certain degree of 'sameness' of customary law may be assumed due to the scope-oriented admissibility criterion of relevance, customary law would play the same role as similar treaty rules would *qua* context, providing material for comparing and contrasting different approaches.[42]

For example, a customary rule 'no expropriation without full compensation' would be admissible for the interpretation of a treaty rule 'expropriation in North Arcadia can take place without full compensation' because it is 'relevant' even under the strictest possible reading. However, that is only the start of the interpretative exercise: the interpretative weight and role will be determined by 'taking [customary law] into account, together with the context', treating it in precisely the same way as one would an identically worded treaty rule providing context. Most likely, the interpreter would compare the ordinary meaning of the treaty term with the contextualising customary rule. The scope of

---

[40] *Djibouti*, para. 114.

[41] Simma and Kill, 'Harmonizing investment protection and international human rights', p. 696.

[42] Gardiner, *Treaty Interpretation*, pp. 185–6.

'expropriation' could be explained in light of customary law but the customary requirement of compensation would be contrasted with the ordinary meaning and rejected, precisely in the same way as if it had been expressed in another treaty rule. (The process of opting out of custom by treaty and lawmaking by *lex specialis* more generally may be described in these terms, with the customary law being a relevant interpretative material, contextualising and contrasting the differences in the treaty rule.) The criticism of excessive reliance on the customary *jus ad bellum* in the *Oil Platforms* case may be read in this light,[43] as directed at the inappropriate interpretative weight given to a particular interpretative material (precisely in the same way as excessive emphasis on subsequent practice or an element of context would have been criticised).

Thirdly, even though the textual expression of Article 31(3)(c) and the *chapeau* of Article 31(3) provides an adequate framework for dealing with customary law, most of the recent authorities have used a different vernacular without explicit pedigree in the VCLT. Campbell McLachlan's landmark article on systemic integration[44] and the ILC Study Group's Report[45] and Conclusions all suggest a number of considerations that support reference to customary law. To adopt the terminology of the ILC Study Group's Conclusions, in general terms there is a positive presumption that 'parties are taken to refer to customary international law and general principles of law for all questions which the treaty does not itself resolve in express terms'. More particularly, customary law is of particular relevance where 'The treaty rule is unclear or open-textured'; 'The terms used in the treaty have a recognized meaning in customary international law'; or the treaty is silent on applicable law and the general presumption is applied.[46]

This exposition is problematic on two levels: it both unnecessarily distances itself from the VCLT by creating new terminology of interpretation and seems to conflate two distinct legal arguments. First of all, the 'positive presumption' and the 'unclear or open-textured . . . rule' tests seem to be a somewhat roundabout way of expressing the reading of Article 31(3)(c) suggested in the previous paragraphs. The previous example of customary law of expropriation and treaty law permitting some expropriation without compensation in North Arcadia can be used

[43] *Oil Platforms (Iran v. US).*
[44] McLachlan, 'Systemic integration', pp. 311–13.
[45] Report of the Study Group, para. 467.
[46] Conclusions of the Work of the Study Group, para. 19.a, 20.a–c.

to illustrate this proposition. One can certainly justify the interpretative result suggested above by saying that parties had referred to customary law on all issues (the definition of expropriation) that had not been resolved in express terms (no compensation). One could also say that the 'treaty rule [on the definition of expropriation] is unclear [and] open-textured' and therefore customary law is 'of particular relevance' in clarifying the texture. McLachlan's later article supports the view that the technique of the ILC conclusions is simply another way of expressing Article 31(3)(c). In applying his methodology to particular case studies, McLachlan suggested that interpretation of treaty rules on fair and equitable treatment could draw upon the customary international minimum standard because:

> the legal protection afforded by the guarantee of fair and equitable treatment cannot be understood without a conception of the proper *function* of international law in assessing the standards of justice achieved by national systems of law and administration. It is this function which the protection shares with the minimum standard . . . The fair and equitable standard gives modern expression to a *general principle of due process* in its application to the treatment of investors.[47]

The criterion of similarity of functions between treaty and customary rules can be restated as a VCLT-compliant inquiry into 'relevance' under Article 31(3)(c). However, there is no obvious added value from introducing these new terms and criteria instead of the tests provided already by Article 31(3)(c).

As a starting point, introduction of a content-sensitive criterion ('does not resolve itself in express terms') as a matter of admissibility ('parties are taken to refer to customary international law') is problematic because it goes against the explicitly scope-focused and content-neutral test of the VCLT ('relevant', not 'relevant and not resolved differently in the treaty'). As a formal point, to the extent that these tests suggest something different from the VCLT, as a matter of sources one should probably prefer the customary law rules of interpretation established from 1960s onwards to a single quotation from one pre-World War II case.[48] As a practical point, even if the ILC only attempted to explain the application of the VCLT, the 'positive presumption' seems

---

[47] McLachlan, 'Investment treaties', p. 381 (emphasis in the original), more generally, pp. 380–3.

[48] Conclusions of the Work of the Study Group, para. 19(a), basing the 'positive presumption' on the *Georges Pinson* case (*France v. Mexico*) [1928] 5 RIAA 327, 422.

to merge the logical two-step process of separately establishing admissibility and weight of interpretative materials into one single exercise. This calls for a rather blunt technique of finding admissible only those materials that are important for the result of the interpretive process rather than accepting all relevant materials as admissible and using them for subtle contextualisation. In fact, much of the concern about overly excessive reliance on custom may be traced to the almost total focus on admissibility of interpretative materials, leaving aside the issues of interpretative weight and seemingly implying that any custom introduced replaces the ordinary meaning.

The implications of the technique are simultaneously too broad and too narrow. The technique may be too broad in suggesting a strong implicit presumption for custom filling every aspect within the scope of the treaty. As Sir Michael Wood noted in a different context, it is just as plausible that the treaty drafters created gaps between rules in a purposeful manner.[49] The technique may also be too narrow in lending some intellectual legitimacy to those who call for the 'clinical isolation'[50] of investment law, arguing in particular that treaty rules on fair and equitable treatment should be treated as 'autonomous' *qua* not referring to customary law.[51] Of course, the argument fails on its own terms since every 'treaty' rule inevitably has to be interpreted in accordance with international law rules of interpretation and *inter alia* by taking into account relevant customary law (to the extent that States have not explicitly provided for non-VCLT rules of interpretation). Still, to suggest that customary law may be brought in the interpretative process (only) in the absence of explicit language of the issue may *a contrario* lend some support to the isolationist point that the *presence* of particular language precludes reliance on custom.

Saying that a 'treaty rule . . . is unclear' is not that different from the concept of 'ambiguous or obscure' that Article 32 of the VCLT provides as one of the alternative preconditions for relying on supplementary means of interpretation. If a criterion for application of a part of the primary rule of interpretation is substantially the same as the condition for having resource to supplementary means, then the fundamental distinction between Articles 31 and 32 is close to disappearing, with

---

[49] M. Wood, 'The International Tribunal for Law of the Sea and General International Law', *International Journal of Marine and Coastal Law*, 22 (2007), 351, 361.

[50] *US – Standards for Reformulated and Conventional Gasoline*, WT/DS2/AB/R 17 (29 April 1996), p. 17.

[51] I. Tudor, *The Fair and Equitable Treatment Standard in the International Law of Foreign Investment* (Oxford University Press, 2008), pp. 54–68.

Article 31(3)(c) effectively collapsing into Article 32. Overall, to the extent that these tests only restate Article 31(3)(c), they are unnecessary, misleading and potentially dangerous; to the extent that they provide for a different approach, their supporters bear the burden of demonstrating the lawmaking processes through which the VCLT and analogous customary law have been displaced.

Secondly, reliance on 'recognized meaning in customary international law' is better treated as a different legal technique not falling under Article 31(3)(c) at all. As was suggested above, the application of Article 31(3)(c) may be analytically separated into finding 'relevant' customary rules admissible and then 'taking [them] into account, together with the context'. In other words, the treaty rule under interpretation sets the limits of admissible custom not by its content but by the scope of coverage, with the content of treaty and customary rules becoming important only during the interpretative exercise when custom serves the contextualising role. However, customary law may also be brought into the interpretative process directly when the treaty rule under interpretation makes a reference to customary law. Rather than engaging in a content-neutral exercise in order to place custom at the level of context, this is a content-focused exercise to place custom at the level of ordinary or special meaning. In other words, if a treaty term has a 'recognised meaning' in customary law, it seems better to say that reference to customary law simply *is* the 'ordinary meaning' under Article 31(1) or 'special meaning' under Article 31(4) of the particular term.[52]

There are at least two ways of making the reference. The easiest technique is to describe the process of reference. In *Military and Paramilitary Activities in and against Nicaragua,* the ICJ explained how the Charter of the United Nations:

> itself refers to pre-existing customary international law; this reference to customary law is contained in the actual text of Article 51, which mentions the 'inherent right' (in the French text the '*droit naturel*') of individual or collective self-defence, which 'nothing in the present Charter shall impair'. Article 51 of the Charter is only meaningful on the basis that there is a 'natural' or 'inherent' right of self-defence, and it is hard to see how this can be other than of a customary nature.[53]

---

[52] J. E. Alvarez, 'The factors driving and constraining the incorporation of international law in WTO adjudication' in M. E. Janow *et al.* (eds.), *The WTO: Governance, dispute settlement & developing countries* (New York: Juris Publishing Inc., 2008), p. 622.

[53] *Military and Paramilitary Activities in and against Nicaragua (Nicaragua v. US)* (Merits) [1986] ICJ Rep 14, para. 176 (*Nicaragua*).

The other technique mentioned in the Conclusions is to describe the result of the reference by using a term of art recognised in customary law. While the *Aegean Sea Continental Shelf* case is usually dealt with in the context of generic terms, it also shows how the use of a customary law term of art results in a reference to custom:

> the expression 'relating to the territorial status of Greece' in reservation *(b)* is to be understood as a generic term denoting any matters properly to be considered as comprised within the concept of territorial status under general international law, and therefore includes not only the particular legal régime but the territorial integrity and the boundaries of a State.[54]

The two ways of bringing customary law into the interpretative process have importantly different effects. In the first type of argument by Article 31(3)(c), the benchmark of admissibility is the subject matter of the treaty rule and the interpretative weight is limited to context. In the second type of argument by Article 31(1) or Article 31(4), the benchmark is the content of (the reference in) the treaty rule and the interpretative weight directly affects ordinary or special meaning. Sometimes, the result would be broadly similar under both techniques. To recall the North Arcadian example, an interpreter of the definition of 'expropriation' may treat customary law as 'relevant' under Article 31(3)(c) (and use it together with the context to explain the treaty definition) or read the term 'expropriation' as making a reference to custom (and use it to establish the ordinary or special meaning of the treaty definition). In other cases, the difference of approaches may be important, in particular where the precise difference between treaty and customary law may be unclear. An even more complex situation is where both techniques seem simultaneously at play, raising the question whether the treaty term operates only *qua* reference to the source of its meaning or also has some residual ordinary meaning that may be contextualised but not replaced by customary law.[55] The different techniques used in

---

[54] *Aegean Sea Continental Shelf (Greece v. Turkey)* (Judgment) [1978] ICJ Rep 3, para. 76 (*Aegean Sea*).

[55] In practice, the issue is particularly important regarding the interpretation of treaty rules on fair and equitable treatment, sometimes approached as not raising issues of customary law at all: *Saluka Investments BV v. Czech Republic*, paras. 294–5; sometimes as exclusively making a reference to customary law: *Glamis Gold v. United States of America* (Award of 8 June 2009), paras. 605–6; and sometimes as both making a reference and having a (non-reference) meaning: *Joseph Charles Lemire v. Ukraine* (ICSID Case No. ARB/06/18, Decision on Jurisdiction and Liability of 14 January 2010), para. 253.

investment treaty practice raise questions of considerable complexity, and the suggested methodology will not necessarily provide obvious answers to all cases. Still, a clear taxonomy of different legal arguments and different criteria is indispensable for creating a systemically coherent framework.

III   Investment treaty interpretation: Case studies

A   Investor–State treaty arbitration and diplomatic protection

The investment treaty rules on investor–State arbitration and the customary law rules on diplomatic protection both deal with the invocation of responsibility of the host States. They also raise at least *prima facie* similar issues, in particular relating to nationality but also to exhaustion of local remedies. The sometimes sparse wording of investment treaties has raised the question about the *ab initio* appropriateness of drawing upon the customary law of diplomatic protection. The decision of the *Loewen* tribunal to apply the customary law of continuous nationality of diplomatic protection to the interpretation of the NAFTA will be used as a case study for considering different methodological approaches.[56]

The dominant approach to *Loewen*, adopted both by the tribunal and most of its critics, has been to proceed in terms of a strict reading of relevance in Article 31(3)(c). The tribunal justified its reliance on public international law rules by pointing out that this was 'a field of international law where claimants are permitted for convenience to enforce what are in origin the rights of Party states'.[57] While disagreeing with the decision to refer to customary law, Zachary Douglas accepted the methodological premise of the tribunal: 'The direct consequence of this theoretical approach in *Loewen* was the application of a (controversial) rule governing the presentation of an international claim by one state to

---

[56] This part of the chapter only deals with the Art. 31(3)(c) argument. Clearly, investor–State arbitration is not a term of art for the customary law of diplomatic protection and therefore the second type of argument is not relevant here.

[57] *Loewen* (Award), para. 233. Another tribunal, chaired by the Fifth Special Rapporteur on State Responsibility James Crawford, offered some support for this reading when it justified non-reference to rules on continuous nationality by the fact that: 'NAFTA's apparent co-mingling of diplomatic protection concepts with investor–State claims (see, for example, Article 1136(5)), is not reflected in the BIT applicable to this arbitration': *EnCana Corporation* v. *Ecuador* (LCIA Case No. UN3481, Award of 3 February 2006), para. 128.

another through the mechanism of diplomatic protection.'[58] An interpreter following this approach has to start the analysis by determining whether the law of diplomatic protection 'run[s] parallel' to or at least addresses the same subject matter as the law of investor–State arbitration.

It is reasonably clear that diplomatic protection is a rule of admissibility in the invocation of State responsibility, operating to the extent that primary rules in question deal with injury to aliens.[59] The nature of investor–State arbitration is a more complex question. The Fifth Special Rapporteur on State Responsibility, James Crawford, has explained that investor–State arbitration may be perceived in two ways:

> It is a matter of interpretation whether the primary obligations (e.g., of fair and equitable treatment) created by such [investment] treaties are owed to the qualified investors directly, or only to the other contracting state(s) . . . an interstate treaty may create individual rights, whether or not they are classified as 'human rights'. . . on the other hand, one might argue that bilateral investment treaties in some sense institutionalise and reinforce (rather than replace) the system of diplomatic protection, and that in accordance with the *Mavrommatis* formula, the rights concerned are those of the state, not the investor.[60]

In his landmark article, Douglas elaborated on the distinction in terms of direct and derivative rights.[61] It is perhaps terminologically more convenient to use the terms of beneficiary and agency rights.[62] In the

---

[58] Douglas, 'Hybrid foundations', p. 163; see also Douglas, 'Other specific regimes', pp. 821–8.

[59] ILC, '2001 Draft Articles on responsibility of States for internationally wrongful acts with commentaries' in *Official Records of the General Assembly, Fifty-Sixth Session*, Supplement No. 10, UN Doc. A/56/10 20 Art. 44; 2006 ILC Articles on Diplomatic Protection.

[60] J. Crawford, 'ILC's Articles on responsibility of States for internationally wrongful acts: A retrospect', *American Journal of International Law*, 96 (2002), 874, 887–8 (internal footnote omitted).

[61] Douglas, 'Hybrid foundations', pp. 162–93.

[62] A. K. Bjorklund, 'Private rights and public international law: Why competition among international economic law tribunals is not working', *Hastings International Law Journal*, 59 (2007–2008), 241, 261–73. The terminological convenience is both normative and descriptive. In normative terms, the concepts of 'direct rights' and 'derivative rights' are not generally accepted terms of art in international law. By contrast, if investor–State arbitration is considered from the perspective of beneficiaries and agency, one may (*mutatis mutandis* with all due caution for the functional differences) draw upon the law of treaties rules on third-party rights, *RosInvestCo UK Ltd* v. *Russia* (SCC V 79/2005, Award on Jurisdiction of October 2007), para. 153; *Wintershall Aktiengesellschaft* v. *Argentina* (ICSID Case No. ARB/04/14, Award of 8 December 2008), para. 114; and the State practice of agency of diplomatic protection, E. Borchard, *Diplomatic Protection of Citizens Abroad* (New York: The Banks Law Publishing Co., 1915), pp. 471–5; A. P. Sereni, 'La Représentation en droit international', *Recueil des Cours de l'Académie de Droit International*, 73 (1948), 69, 112–17. In descriptive terms, 'derivative'

former case, the primary obligations are owed (also) to the investor and investor–State arbitration is an invocation of the host State's responsibility for the breach of this obligation. In the latter case, the primary obligations are owed only to the home State and investor–State arbitration is a modified agency of the home State's invocation of the host State's responsibility.[63]

Douglas has persuasively demonstrated that investor–State arbitration is very different from diplomatic protection on a number of levels, in particular relating to the functional control of the claim by the individual.[64] However, it does not necessarily follow that because investor–State arbitration is different in its important characteristics from diplomatic protection it is not an agency of diplomatic protection. To conclude otherwise suggests an assumption that States can modify only the *ratione personae* aspect of diplomatic protection (by agreeing that the investor invokes responsibility as an agent) but not other characteristics (like functional control and exhaustion of local remedies). In principle, these

---

rights may misleadingly suggest that the investor eventually comes to hold the rights (e.g. as in subrogated claims regarding insurers, Borchard, *Diplomatic Protection of Citizens Abroad*, p. 627; C. Schreuer *et al.*, *The ICSID Convention: A commentary*, 2nd edn (Cambridge University Press, 2009), p. 186). However, Crawford's and Douglas's point is precisely that in this case responsibility would be invoked on behalf of the home State to which the obligations are exclusively owed. For an argument that the alternative to direct rights actually is subrogated rights, somewhat leaving aside the distinction between primary and secondary rules that is crucial for Crawford and Douglas, see Juratowitch, 'The relationship between diplomatic protection and investment treaties', pp. 22–7.

[63] Crawford's dichotomy between beneficiary and agency rights is still the best explanation of possible approaches and has yet to be improved upon. Douglas has suggested another version of direct rights where the investor only has procedural rights, with the substantive obligations owed only to the home State and operating 'as the applicable adjudicative standards for the investor's cause of action rather than binding obligations owed directly to the investor', Douglas, 'Hybrid foundations', p. 184. However, if the investor is invoking responsibility on its own behalf, and the primary obligations are owed only to the home State, then either there is no responsibility to invoke by the investor in the first place because the host State has committed no wrongful act in its regard, or this direct model is actually a derivative model *sub silentio* and the investor invokes responsibility on the home State's behalf. Moreover, this view seems to go against Douglas' further argument that under the direct rights approach 'the injury is caused exclusively to the investor', p. 190. Roberts has suggested a third approach where investors have no rights at all, and enforce their home State's rights 'for the sake of convenience', A. Roberts, 'Power and persuasion in investment treaty interpretation: The dual role of States', *American Journal of International Law*, 104 (2010), 179, 184. The passage of the *Loewen* tribunal from which this language is probably taken is better read as addressing the motivation underlying the lawmaking process and not the legal nature of its result: an explicit procedural entitlement to independently bring a claim could hardly be described as conduct by convenience.

[64] Douglas, 'Hybrid foundations', pp. 167–84.

characteristics may either reflect the qualitatively different nature of investor–State arbitration or simply *lex specialis* modifications to the original rules of diplomatic protection.

Of course, it is more natural to read the factual autonomy of investors in most investment treaties as reflecting their legal autonomy,[65] rather than implying a somewhat counter-intuitive arrangement of modified agency.[66] Under this reading, the State would take up the case of its national to espouse it through diplomatic protection and then delegate the procedure of State–State espousal back to the same national who was injured in the first place. Since the same result may be achieved in the simpler terms of individual rights, the common-sense suspicion of unnecessarily complex intellectual constructs could support the explanation of investors as treaty beneficiaries. The ICJ may have already approved the individual nature of treaty-based rights in *Barcelona Traction Light and Power Company Limited* by talking about 'treaty stipulations', 'multilateral or bilateral treaties between States' and 'companies . . . themselves vested with a direct right to defend their interests against States through prescribed procedures'.[67] This proposition could plausibly exercise some indirect influence on the interpretative background against which post-1970 investment treaties have been made.[68]

---

[65] *Ibid.*; *Corn Products International Inc.* v. *Mexico* (ICSID AF Case No. ARB/(AF)/04/1, Decision on Responsibility of 15 January 2008), para. 169; Juratowitch, 'The relationship between diplomatic protection and investment treaties', pp. 22–7.

[66] Douglas, 'Hybrid foundations', p. 163; *Archer Daniels Midland Company and Tate & Lyle Ingredients Americas Inc.* v. *Mexico* (ICSID AF Case No. ARB/(AF)/04/5, Award of 21 November 2007), para. 176.

[67] *Barcelona Traction, Light and Power Company Limited (Belgium* v. *Spain)* [1970] ICJ Rep 3, para. 90; M. Paparinskis, '*Barcelona Traction*: A friend of investment protection law', *Baltic Yearbook of International Law*, 8 (2008), 105, 128–33; *CMS* (Annulment), para. 69; *RomPetrol Group NV* v. *Romania* (ICSID Case No. ARB/06/03, Decision on Jurisdiction and Admissibility of 18 April 2008), para. 91; *Azurix Corp.* v. *Argentina* (ICSID Case No. ARB/01/12, Decision on Annulment of 1 September 2009), para. 87.

[68] While the jurisdictional decision in the *Diallo* case has been described as 'do[ing] much to dispel the fallacy' of the 'morphed form of diplomatic protection' model (K. Parlett, 'Role of diplomatic protection in the protection of foreign investments', *Cambridge Law Journal*, 66 (2007), 533, 535), it is better read as leaving the question open. When describing the investment treaty regimes, the Court does not mention direct rights once – incidentally, unlike in *Barcelona Traction* (para. 90) – referring only to 'the protection of the rights of companies and the rights of their shareholders', 'benefit of an international treaty' and 'no other remedy available', *Ahmadou Sadio Diallo (Republic of Guinea* v. *Democratic Republic of Congo)* (Preliminary Objections) [2007] ICJ Rep, para. 88. This language may plausibly fit both the beneficiary and agency models. The rejection of investment treaty practice as contributing to customary law is also not determinative because investment treaties arguably provide also for diplomatic protection (Paparinskis,

However, a more fruitful perspective would consider the implications if the agency approach was to be spelled out explicitly in a treaty—for instance, as follows:

> Agency of diplomatic protection
>
> i. Parties agree to delegate the right of diplomatic protection for the breach of the Agreement to their investors who have suffered injury as a result.
> ii. Parties agree to the following modifications to the right of diplomatic protection:
>> (a) The exercise of diplomatic protection by the investor shall be limited to the submission of dispute to arbitration in accordance with Article ____.
>> (b) The investor shall be entitled to the full functional control of the claim.
>> (c) The requirement of exhaustion of domestic remedies is hereby waived . . .

The immediate question raised by this rule (but also by similar allegedly implied arrangement) is whether such a claim could be brought before a tribunal constituted under the International Centre for Settlement of Investment Disputes (ICSID). The ICSID Convention limits the jurisdiction of tribunals to investor–State disputes and explicitly suspends diplomatic protection during arbitration,[69] excluding State–State disputes in general and diplomatic protection in particular. If the agency model is adopted, it seems likely that investor–State treaty arbitration would be incompatible with the ICSID Convention on both grounds. No respondent State seems to have raised this objection in investment treaty

---

'Countermeasures', pp. 281–302), and in any event State–State treaties and cases are found irrelevant for precisely the same reason of being too 'special': *Diallo*, para. 90; cf. *Barcelona Traction*, paras. 62–3. In its judgment on the merits, the Court did not address the investment aspect at all: *Ahmadou Sadio Diallo (Republic of Guinea v. Democratic Republic of Congo)* (Merits) (Judgment of 30 November 2010), www.icj-cij. org (last accessed 13 January 2010). Judges Al-Khasawneh and Yusuf were the only ones to consider the investment treaty aspect in detail, and the language used may again plausibly fit both approaches. Their portrayal of treaty law as removing the limiting factors of customary law and in turn potentially contributing to customary law may be read as logically depending upon certain sameness of treaty and customary rules and therefore rather supporting the agency model: Dissenting Opinion of Judges Al-Khasawneh and Yusuf, pp. 2, 5, 7, 8.

[69] Convention on the Settlement of Investment Disputes between States and Nationals of other States, 18 March 1965, 575 UNTS 160 (entered into force 14 October 1966) Arts. 25, 27(1).

ICSID arbitrations.[70] The widespread and consistent failure of States to make an argument inescapably following from the agency model, particularly against the background of usually exhaustive jurisdictional objections, may signify an unchallenged consensus (or perhaps even *opinio juris*) that (at least ICSID) investor–State arbitration *is* something conceptually different.[71] The interpreter following the strict approach to relevance may conclude at this point that due to the difference of subject matter customary law of diplomatic protection is *ab initio* inadmissible.

Of course, the interpreter may also adopt a more relaxed approached to relevance and place the analytical perspective at a higher degree of abstraction.[72] In the absence of treaty rules to the contrary,[73] it may be possible to 'provide for a residual role for at least some aspects of the law of diplomatic protection'.[74] Another type of legal technique was employed by arbitrator Riphagen in the *A/18* case, noting that even though the IUSCT was not faced with the question of 'diplomatic protection' in the classic public international law sense of that notion, 'it is certainly relevant that even there where international courts and tribunals were faced with the question of the *persona standi* of a state, rather than of an individual, before such international court or tribunal, there is a clear tendency [supporting effective nationality]'.[75]

Whether the interpreter employs a *Djibouti*-style argument minimising the effect in light of the differences, or Riphagen's approach of

---

[70] According to one list (italaw.com/alphabetical_list_respondant.htm), 40 States have so far been respondents in ICSID investment treaty arbitrations reaching at least the jurisdictional stage where one would expect to find such objections (Albania, Algeria, Argentina, Bangladesh, Bolivia, Bulgaria, Burundi, Chile, Congo, Czech Republic, Ecuador, El Salvador, Egypt, Estonia, Georgia, Guatemala, Hungary, Jordan, Kazakhstan, Lebanon, Lithuania, Malaysia, Mexico, Morocco, Myanmar, Pakistan, Paraguay, Philippines, Romania, Slovak Republic, Spain, Sri Lanka, Tanzania, Trinidad and Tobago, Turkey, Ukraine, UAE, Venezuela, Yemen and Zimbabwe).

[71] Even though this argument seems more persuasive than the others, it only raises further questions about whether the appropriate benchmark for judging a State's attitude is the accession to the ICSID Convention, inclusion of an ICSID clause in (any or particular) treaty or failure to make a jurisdictional objection. More broadly, 'the nature of the rights is not an abstract and irrebutable *a priori* proposition, and as a rule of *jus dispositivum* is open to amendment or reinterpretation, in particular through subsequent agreement and practice', Paparinskis, 'Countermeasures', p. 335.

[72] Simma and Kill, 'Harmonizing investment protection and international human rights', pp. 695–6.

[73] Leben, 'La Responsabilité internationale de l'état', pp. 696–7.

[74] *Société Générale* v. *Dominican Republic* (LCIA Case No. UN 7927, Award on Preliminary Objections to Jurisdiction of 19 September 2008), para. 108.

[75] *Iran–United States, Case No. A/18*, 5 Ir-USCTR 273, Concurring Opinion of Arbitrator Riphagen, para. 2.

drawing upon similarities and tendencies, the result is likely to be similar. Both of these techniques can be anchored in the VCLT by treating them as explanations of how 'together with the context' may be approached, using the 'relevant' rules to contextualise the ordinary meaning. Unsurprisingly, 'relevant' rules would carry greater interpretative weight if they are closer related to the particular issue (or are at a lower degree of abstraction as per Simma and Kill or when the tendency is clearer as per Riphagen) and vice versa.

From this perspective, while the interpreter need not conclusively ascertain the legal nature of investor–State arbitration, the similarities and dissimilarities of the chief characteristics are likely to be important. One issue to consider would be the degree of functional similarity of rules on nationality and exhaustion of local remedies where they operate 'between' a State invoking responsibility and its nationals factually injured by the breach and where the invoking entity is also the injured entity. Another issue would relate to possibly different procedural roles that descriptively similar rules may play: while law of diplomatic protection relates to admissibility, at least nationality in investor–State arbitration is an issue of jurisdiction. While the weight of authority supports the stricter approach to relevance, an interpreter diligently following it is likely be sidetracked from the particular legal issue into complex and lengthy inquiries into the nature of investor–State arbitration sketched above. Conversely, even though a functional comparison of treaty and customary rules would not necessarily provide straightforward answers, it would provide a meaningful engagement with the actual issue, using VCLT rules to identify admissibility of interpretative materials and their appropriate weight.

B   Primary investment obligations in treaty and customary law

The interpretation of primary investment obligations raises different questions from those considered before in relation to invocation of State responsibility. In the latter case, the interpretative process had to focus on the structural relationship of treaty and custom, whether determining the *ab initio* admissibility of customary law (under the stricter reading of relevance) or setting the contours of the contextualising framework (under the broader reading). In the case of primary obligations, the issue of relevance of custom is relatively uncontroversial and the *ratione materiae* overlap of the subject matter is usually not challenged. The sameness of the subject matter of the treaty rules (on expropriation, full protection and security and fair and equitable treatment) and customary rules (on expropriation, full protection and security and international minimum standard) seems to be accepted, despite possible disagreement about the content. However, even though the closeness of subject matter resolves the issue of relevance, it raises the equally complex problem of possible presence of either or even both types of customary law arguments.

First of all, treaty rules may make a reference to customary law for the purpose of establishing their content. Investment treaties sometimes employ the *Nicaragua* technique of describing the process of reference. For example, the 2004 US Model BIT makes such a reference in relation to fair and equitable treatment, full protection and security[76] and expropriation,[77] and explicit references to customary law have become more common in recent practice.[78] In other instances, States have adopted the *Aegean Sea* technique, *ex abundanti cautela* using a number of terms in parallel that all are recognised as having customary law significance. Treaty practice in relation to expropriation and indirect expropriation often follow this pattern. In these cases, customary law would carry considerable interpretative weight since it would directly establish the ordinary meaning of treaty terms. In yet other cases, States merge different techniques together, describing the process of reference, using customary law terms of art and even explicitly explaining their understanding of customary law in treaty terms.[79]

Secondly, sometimes it is not clear whether the term used is a term of art in customary law. The identification of what a term of art may require the interpreter to trace the historical origins of different terms. In the *Case Concerning Certain German Interests in Polish Upper Silesia*, the PCIJ relied on 'the régime of liquidation instituted by peace treaties of 1919' to support the reference to customary law in the particular treaty.[80] The German pleadings emphasised that, even in the absence of express reference, the treaty rules were based on customary rules[81] and that only the customary rules could assist in interpreting the gaps and limitations of the treaty rules.[82] To consider a more contemporary

---

[76] 2004 US Model BIT Art. 5(1)–(2), Annex A.

[77] *Ibid.*, Annex A, Annex B(1).

[78] For an overview of treaty practice on fair and equitable treatment, see *AWG Group Ltd v. Argentina* (UNCITRAL Case, Decision on Liability of 30 July 2010), Separate Opinion of Arbitrator Nikken, paras. 6–8.

[79] 2004 US Model BIT, Annex A, Annex B(1).

[80] *Certain German Interests* (Judgment), para. 21.

[81] *Certain German Interests* (Pleadings), para. 261 (Kaufmann).　　[82] *Ibid.*, para. 167.

example, it has been suggested that 'it is inherently implausible that a treaty would use an expression such as "fair and equitable treatment" to denote a well-known concept like the "minimum standard of treatment in customary international law"'.[83] The rejection of the reference rests on two assumptions: that 'fair and equitable treatment' did not refer to customary law on the treatment of aliens, and that 'minimum standard of treatment' exclusively did.

State practice and legal writings of eighteenth, nineteenth and early twentieth centuries shows that 'fair and equitable treatment' and similar concepts were used in relation to international dispute settlement in cases about the treatment of aliens.[84] Indeed, already mid-seventeenth-century British treaties (concluded by Cromwell's Commonwealth and remade by Charles II) included obligations such as the Article 24 of the 1670 Treaty with Denmark to 'cause justice and equity to be administered to the subjects and people of each other according to the laws and statutes of either country'.[85] Similarly, while the grand narrative of the debate of the international standard with Calvo doctrine has retrospectively imposed the appearance of terminological consistency, the practice and writings of 1920s and 1930s were more chaotic, with 'justice due', 'denial of justice', 'fairness of treatment' and 'international minimum standard' being used interchangeably.[86] Consequently, even if a contemporary treaty drafter proceeding *de novo* would use different language to indicate a reference to customary law, the particular terms originated

---

[83] C. H. Schreuer, 'Fair and equitable treatment (FET): Interactions with other standards', *Transnational Dispute Management*, 4(5) (2007), 10; *AWG Group Ltd* v. *Argentina* (UNCITRAL Case, Decision on Liability of 30 July 2010), para. 184.

[84] Opinion of Lord Justice Loughborough (1798) 1 Moore International Arbitrations 326, 327 ('there might exist a fair and equitable treatment claim upon the King's treasury, under the provisions of the treaty'); note of C. F. Adams to Earl Russell of 23 October 1863 (1863) 1 Moore International Arbitrations 496 ('there is no fair and equitable form of international arbitrament or reference to which they (the United States) will not be willing to submit'); A. V. Freeman, *The International Responsibility of States for Denial of Justice* (London: Longmans, Green and Co., 1938) ('Wherever some irregular aspects of the proceedings is condemned as wrongful, an arbitral commission must inevitably have resource to some concept such as "fairness"').

[85] *Ambatielos case (Greece* v. *UK)* ICJ Pleadings 484, see generally, 412–13, 483–4 (British pleadings by Fitzmaurice).

[86] W. E. Beckett, 'Diplomatic claims in respect of injuries to companies', *Transactions of the Grotius Society*, 17 (1931), 175, 179, n. 1; Freeman, *The International Responsibility of States for Denial of Justice*, pp. 104, 181.

in the post-World War II treaty practice conducted against the background of the pre-war debate where such language may have been sufficient.

Thirdly, even when treaty rules do not make a reference to customary law, customary law can be brought into the interpretative process by the default operation of Article 31(3)(c). To consider again the example of fair and equitable treatment, the customary minimum standard is clearly 'relevant' and therefore is an admissible interpretative material. However, assuming that the argument is made only in terms of Article 31(3)(c), the customary rule would not provide the ordinary meaning of the treaty term but would only contextualise it. If there is a perceptible difference between the treaty rule and the customary rule, the treaty rule could be explained by the customary rule to the extent that they are similar and contrasted with the customary rule to the extent that they are not. The suspicion about the eroding effect of the customary rules can be taken care of by distinguishing between admissibility and interpretative weight.

The distinction may be illustrated by two cases. The *Saluka* tribunal accepted an argument that a treaty rule of 'deprivation' made a reference to customary law of expropriation explained in a draft text discussing 'taking'.[87] The customary law of expropriation was relied on to bring in a police powers exception (no expropriation for *bona fide* regulation despite substantial interference with the investment). If this is an instance of application of Article 31(3)(c) (as the tribunal suggested itself),[88] then the award may be criticised as confusing admissibility with interpretative weight. The ordinary meaning of 'deprivation' could suggest a rule under which the only criterion of compensation is the loss of the investor. While the customary rule (no compensation in some cases) would contextualise the treaty rule (compensation in all cases), it would not replace its ordinary meaning but only *a contrario* strengthen it. However, if this was rather an instance of a reference ('in using the concept of deprivation, Article 5 imports into the Treaty the customary international law notion'),[89] the tribunal was right to fully follow the *renvoi*. It is an open question whether a reference had actually taken place: unlike in other instances, the particular treaty did not use the multiplicity of parallel terms and 'deprivation' is probably not the most common term (although not unknown) for designating

---

[87] *Saluka*, para. 254.   [88] *Ibid.*   [89] *Ibid.*

expropriation. As the *Saluka* case suggests, making a clearer distinction between arguments under Article 31(3)(c) and Article 31(1) or (4) would not necessarily lead to a different result – the result is not indefensible in the latter terms – but would provide a coherent methodology that would enable a further systematisation and clarification of the law on the issue.

More recently, a tribunal in the *Chevron Corporation (USA) and Texaco Corporation (USA) v. Ecuador* case had to address the impact of customary law of denial of justice on the treaty obligation to 'provide effective means of asserting claims and enforcing rights'. The tribunal first dealt with the relationship of treaty and custom:

> The obligations created by Article II(7) overlap significantly with the prohibition of denial of justice under customary international law. The provision appears to be directed at many of the same potential wrongs as denial of justice. The Tribunal thus agrees with the idea, expressed in *Duke Energy v. Ecuador*, that Article II(7), to some extent, 'seeks to implement and form part of the more general guarantee against denial of justice.' Article II(7), however, appears in the BIT as an independent, specific treaty obligation and does not make any explicit reference to denial of justice or customary international law. The Tribunal thus finds that Article II(7), setting out an 'effective means' standard, constitutes a *lex specialis* and not a mere restatement of the law on denial of justice. Indeed, the latter intent could have been easily expressed through the inclusion of explicit language to that effect or by using language corresponding to the prevailing standard for denial of justice at the time of drafting.[90]

The tribunal did not employ the language of the VCLT but its methodology was VCLT-consistent. The absence of explicit language and language corresponding to the customary standard paralleled the *Nicaragua* and *Aegean Sea* techniques of introducing customary law in terms of Article 31(1) or (4). For reference to take place, the treaty would have had to refer to, for example, 'obligations in accordance with customary law' or the customary term of art 'denial of justice'. The degree of overlap and the similarity of wrongs relate to the question whether custom is 'relevant' in terms of Article 31(3)(c). The tribunal introduced customary law into the interpretative process because it was 'relevant' rather than directly referred to.

---

[90] *Chevron Corporation (USA) and Texaco Corporation (USA) v. Ecuador* (UNCITRAL Case, Partial Award on Merits of 30 March 2010), para. 242.

At the second stage of analysis, the tribunal accurately captured the subtle contextualising role that admissible 'relevant' international law may play, simultaneously explaining similarities and contrasting differences:

> the interpretation and application of Article II(7) is informed by the law on denial of justice. However, the Tribunal emphasizes that its role is to interpret and apply Article II(7) as it appears in the present BIT.[91]

On the one hand, customary law of denial of justice could be employed to elaborate the treaty term. The considerations relevant for the determination of delay of justice as denial of justice could also be applied to the treaty obligation.[92] Similarly, the general approach to burden of proof regarding the exhaustion of remedies could be relied on.[93] On the other hand, the formulation of the term itself was such as to require a lesser degree of severity for finding a breach.[94] In particular, the customary law requirement to fully exhaust the domestic remedies for denial of justice to take place applied only in a qualified manner.[95]

A purist may certainly object to the absence of the VCLT from this analysis as well as to certain terminological choices. In particular, the description of a reference to customary law as a 'restatement' may not be very fortunate: to restate a certain proposition is to repeat (codify) it rather than to refer to its original form. Still, one should applaud the VCLT-consistency of the methodology that was de facto applied. The tribunal distinguished between the issues of admissibility and weight of customary law in the interpretative process. At the first level of analysis, a further distinction was made between a reference to custom (that had not taken place) and introduction of 'relevant' custom because of the substantive and functional overlap. At the second level of analysis, custom operated in subtle contextualising terms, illuminating the methodology and criteria of the treaty obligation to the extent that treaty terms did not call for something different.

C Non-precluded-measure clauses and circumstances precluding wrongfulness

The relationship of the NPM clause in Article XI of the US–Argentina BIT and necessity as a circumstance precluding wrongfulness is perhaps the most visible example of the practical importance of customary law in interpretation. Indeed, the *Sempra* award was annulled precisely because

[91] *Ibid.*, para. 244. [92] *Ibid.*, paras. 250, 264. [93] *Ibid.*, paras. 328, 331.
[94] *Ibid.*, para. 244. [95] *Ibid.*, paras. 321, 323, 326.

the ad hoc committee perceived its reliance on customary criteria to have been excessive.[96] The awards have been discussed in greater detail in leading legal writings,[97] therefore it may be sufficient to summarise the different approaches in the following terms:

> According to the first approach, '[t]he question arising . . . is not . . . whether such measures are . . . justified counter-measures in general international law; the question is whether the measures in question are, or are not, in breach of the Treaty.'[98] The NPM clauses are then part of the particular primary rules, and the secondary rules of State responsibility regarding circumstances precluding wrongfulness have no direct relevance.
>
> The second approach would treat the NPM clause as a secondary rule, implicitly situating the treaty in a relationship of a *lex specialis* secondary rule towards customary law. It would seem to follow from this argument that the *lex specialis* excludes the *lex generalis*, thus the law of necessity would be replaced between the Contracting Parties by the NPM clause.[99]
>
> The third approach would treat the NPM clauses as 'inseparable from the customary law standard insofar as the definition of necessity and the conditions for its operation are concerned'.[100] While the Tribunals do not

---

[96] *Sempra* (Annulment), para. 186–223.

[97] See e.g. W. W. Burke-White and A. von Staden, 'Investment protection in extraordinary times: The interpretation and application of non-precluded measures provisions in bilateral investment treaties', *Virginia Journal of International Law*, 48 (2008), 307; J. E. Alvarez and K. Khamsi, 'The Argentine crisis and foreign investors: A glimpse into the heart of the investment regime', *Yearbook of International Investment Law Policy*, 1 (2008–2009), 379; C. Binder, 'Changed circumstances in investment law: Interfaces between the law of treaties and the law of State responsibility with a special focus on the Argentine crisis' in C. Binder and others (eds.), *International Investment Law for the 21st Century: Essays in honour of Christoph Schreuer* (Oxford University Press, 2009), 608; J. E. Alvarez and T. Brink, 'Revisiting the necessity defence: *Continental Casualty v. Argentina*', *Institute of International Law and Justice Working Paper*, March 2010), www.iilj.org/publications/2010-3.Alvarez-Brink.asp; J. Kurtz, 'Adjudging the exceptional at international law: Security, public order and financial crisis', *International and Comparative Law Quarterly*, 59 (2010), 325.

[98] *Military and Paramilitary Activities in and Against Nicaragua (Nicaragua v. US)* (Merits) [1986] ICJ Rep 14, (Dissenting Opinion of Sir Robert Jennings), 528, 541; *CMS Gas Transmission Company v. Argentina* (ICSID Case No. ARB 01/08, Decision on Annulment of 25 September 2007), paras. 129–233; *Continental Casualty v. Argentina* (ICSID Case No. ARB/03/9, Award of 5 September 2008), paras. 162–8.

[99] *LG&E v. Argentina* (ICSID Case No. ARB/02/1, Decision on Liability of 3 October 2006), paras. 245–61; *Patrick Mitchell v. DRC* (ICSID Case No. ARB 99/7, Decision on Annulment of 1 November 2006), para. 55.

[100] *Sempra Energy International v. Argentina* (ICSID Case No. ARB/02/16, Award of 28 September 2007), paras. 376, 378; *CMS Gas Transmission Company v. Argentina* (ICSID Case No. ARB 01/08, Final Award of 12 May 2005), paras. 315–82; *Enron Corporation & Ponderosa Assets LP v. Argentina* (ICSID Case No. ARB/01/3, Award of 22 May 2007), para. 334.

fully explain their argumentative process, it seems that in a somewhat circular manner they first of all accept the NPM clause to be a *lex specialis* secondary rule replacing the customary law rule, and then use VCLT Article 31(3)(c) to incorporate the customary law criteria from *lex generalis*.[101]

The first approach follows Article 31(3)(c) and probably the stricter reading of relevance: since customary law does not 'run parallel' to treaty law, it is *ab initio* inadmissible in terms of interpretative materials. It is slightly more complicated to say what the position of tribunals following the second and third approaches is. Perhaps they accept the stricter approach to Article 31(3)(c) but take the view that treaty rules are secondary rules (or that the distinction between primary and secondary rules is not useful for establishing relevance). Alternatively, perhaps they take the broader view of relevance suggested by Simma and Kill and consider that at a proper degree of abstraction similar issues relating to conduct in emergency situations may be identified. The second approach is defensible under either of these readings, implicitly finding customary rules admissible but their contextualising role having little effect on the interpretation of treaty rules.

The third approach is more problematic under Article 31(3)(c) since even under the stricter reading of relevance it seems to accord excessive interpretative weight to customary law. If a treaty rule permits 'necessary' conduct and customary rule permits 'necessary (with additional qualifications)', the proper *a contrario* lesson from the contextualising customary law could very well be that the treaty rule operates unqualified. However, the methodology of the third approach may be defended in terms of a reference to customary law. José Alvarez and Kathryn Khamsi have suggested that: 'Article XI appears to be the United States' attempt to include a general cross-reference to customary international law defences, particularly necessity.'[102] The debate about the existence of a reference to customary law in the particular instance raises further interesting questions, in particular relating to the inter-temporal aspects of the law of State responsibility.[103] It is not the purpose of this chapter to add to the commentaries of the Argentinean cases. Still, the

---

[101] Paparinskis, 'Countermeasures', pp. 349–50.
[102] Alvarez and Khamsi, 'The Argentine crisis and foreign investors', p. 427, see more generally, pp. 427–40.
[103] M. Paparinskis, 'Equivalent primary rules and differential secondary rules: Countermeasures in WTO and investment protection law' in T. Broude and Y. Shany (eds.), *Multi-Sourced Equivalent Norms* (Oxford: Hart Publishing, 2011), pp. 274–6.

argument of Alvarez and Khamsi about reference to customary law, unlike an argument about Article 31(3)(c), is defensible in methodological terms. Its substantive correctness, just as that of any other interpretative question, has to be resolved by reference to the traditional rules of interpretation.

IV Conclusion

The different historical strands of investment lawmaking make a systemically coherent framework for dealing with customary law indispensible. While treaty and custom may run parallel, the perspectives, techniques and teleological underpinnings are sometimes importantly different. The history of lawmaking in the area shows a battle of imagination against the constraints of a limited vocabulary[104] that almost completely ignored the protection of investments and corporate investors,[105] concentrating instead on outrageous behaviour towards the life and liberty of the physical person.[106] The theoretical perceptions of the law of State responsibility have been reappraised in the meantime,[107] possibly calling for a reconsideration of classic authorities in light of the modern vernacular.[108] The classic use of forcible reprisals that coloured the perception of primary rules as a rationalisation of Western policies at a period of their dominance[109] has been replaced by peaceful and avowedly depoliticised dispute settlement.[110] Finally, the alien has evolved from an object of international law[111] to

---

[104] In the sense of P. Allot, *Eunomia: A new order for a new world* (Oxford University Press, 1990), pp. 5–13; P. Allot, *The Health of Nations* (Cambridge University Press, 2002), pp. 415–16.

[105] P. Juillard, 'L'Évolution des sources du droit des investissements', *Recueil des Cours de l'Académie de Droit International*, 250 (1994), 9, 22.

[106] R. Y. Jennings, 'State contracts in international law', *British Yearbook of International Law*, 37 (1961), 156, 180.

[107] J. Crawford and T. Grant, 'Responsibility of States for injuries to foreigners' in J. P. Grant and J. C. Barker (eds.), *The Harvard Research in International Law: Contemporary analysis and appraisal* (W. S. Hein & Co., New York 2007), pp. 77–114.

[108] C. Greenwood, 'State responsibility for the decisions of national courts' in M. Fitzmaurice and D. Sarooshi (eds.), *Issues of State Responsibility before International Judicial Institutions* (Hart Publishing, Oxford 2004), pp. 57–8.

[109] Jennings, 'State contracts in international law', p. 159.

[110] A. Broches, 'The Convention on the Settlement of Investment Disputes between States and Nationals of other States', *Recueil des Cours de l'Académie de Droit International*, 136 (1972), 331, 344.

[111] L. Oppenheim, *International Law* (Longmans, Green, and Co., London 1905), I, p. 341.

a confident participant of the international legal process,[112] invoking State responsibility *qua* (usually corporate) investor before investment treaty tribunals.[113] A systemically coherent methodology for managing the interpretative relationship between treaty and custom is therefore indispensable.

This chapter has addressed the role of customary law in the interpretation of investment treaties from two perspectives. From the perspective of the broader debates about interpretation, it has been suggested that not one but two legal techniques are at play here: on the one hand, 'any relevant rules' of Article 31(3)(c) of the VCLT that in accordance with the *chapeau* of Article 31(3)(c) contextualise the ordinary meaning; on the other hand, a treaty rule that brings in a rule of customary law as its ordinary or special meaning. While being to some extent similar (and sometimes simultaneously employed in practice), the criteria for bringing in customary law and the weight it carries in the interpretative process are importantly different. When Article 31(3)(c) is applied, the criterion of admissibility is explicitly scope-focused and content-neutral ('relevant'), and the interpretative weight is less significant ('together with the context'). When a reference to custom is made, the criterion of admissibility is content-focused, describing either the process of reference or its target, and the interpretative weight directly affects the ordinary or special meaning of the term.

The second part of the chapter has illustrated the application of the suggested approach on a basis of three case studies. The interpretation of the treaty rules of investor–State arbitration by reference to customary law of diplomatic protection focuses on relevance in Article 31(3)(c). Conversely, in the interpretation of primary obligations relevance can usually be taken as a given, and different (often parallel) techniques of relying on custom have to be considered. Finally, the different interplay of NPM treaty clauses and customary circumstances precluding wrongfulness illustrate all possible positions on the analytical spectrum.

The purpose of this chapter has been consciously narrow and limited: to make certain preliminary observations about the way customary law can be introduced into the interpretative process and the effect that it may have. Detailed application of the methodology to particular case

---

[112] R Higgins, 'Conceptual thinking about the individual in international law', *New York Law School Law Review*, 24 (1978–1979), 11.

[113] Crawford, 'The ILC's Articles on responsibility of States for internationally wrongful acts', pp. 887–8.

studies is a matter for future research. The State practice and case law of the last decade suggest a great potential for investment protection law in contributing to greater clarification and elaboration of rules on interpretation. The point that this chapter has attempted to make is that the concise formulae of the VCLT still provide the interpreter with the best framework for resolving interpretative queries.

5

The public–private dualities of international investment law and arbitration

ALEX MILLS

And so these men of Indostan
Disputed loud and long,
Each in his own opinion
Exceeding stiff and strong,
Though each was partly in the right,
And all were in the wrong![1]

I Introduction

In recent years the thousands of international investment treaties in existence[2] have given rise to hundreds of investor–State arbitrations.[3] International investment law has thus become a topic of great practical importance, and one which has received significant attention in both arbitral awards and academic literature. The quotation of poetically undistinguished verse above is intended to imply, somewhat mischievously, that

---

This chapter is based on research conducted with the warm hospitality and generous support of an International Visiting Research Fellowship at the University of Sydney, and benefited from comments made by participants in the International Investment Treaty Law and Arbitration Conference: Evolution and Revolution in Substance and Procedure, February 2010, Sydney Law School, University of Sydney and the Society of International Economic Law Biennial Global Conference, July 2010, University of Barcelona.

[1] John Godfrey Saxe, *The Blind Men and the Elephant* (*c*.1873).
[2] See e.g. United Nations Conference on Trade and Development (UNCTAD), *Recent Developments in International Investment Agreements (2008-June 2009): IIA Monitor No. 3* (2009), UNCTAD Doc. No. UNCTAD/WEB/DIAE/IA/2009/8, www.unctad.org/en/docs/webdiaeia20098_en.pdf (last accessed 18 January 2011), p. 2 (noting 2,676 known international investment agreements).
[3] See e.g. UNCTAD, *Latest Developments in Investor–State Dispute Settlement: IIA Issues Note No. 1* (2010), UNCTAD Doc. No. UNCTAD/WEB/DIAE/IA/2010/3, www.unctad.org/en/docs/iteiia20083_en.pdf (last accessed 18 January 2011), p. 2 (noting 357 known disputes).

some of this attention has been not entirely dissimilar to the observations of the fabled (blind) 'men of Indostan' concerning the nature of an elephant – each perceiving different aspects of the subject at hand (for example, a tusk, the trunk, or a knee of the elephant), but insufficiently embracing the complexity of the whole (determining that an elephant is like a spear, a snake, or a tree, respectively). The complexity of international investment law is, however, not that of a whole made of variable parts (like an elephant), but of a whole which is itself open to different interpretations, which possesses inherent 'dualities' – a closer analogy might be with an optical illusion, a single image or object which may appear strikingly different to different viewers or from different perspectives.

The dualities of international investment law are presented in some of the most fundamental questions concerning its nature and purpose. This chapter explores the ideas or influences which lead analysis of the subject in conflicting directions and invite these seemingly contradictory viewpoints, by focusing on the 'public–private' distinctions or conceptions which lie at its contested foundations. These public–private dualities thus form a kind of conceptual lens through which international investment law may be viewed, and through which its different appearances or representations can be examined.

The use of the 'public–private' distinction as a lens for the purposes of the analysis in this chapter is not intended to imply a claim that the concepts of 'public' and 'private' are, or can ever be, entirely distinguishable, and certainly not that such distinctions can be made objectively or without normative implications. The problematic character of traditional public–private distinctions has long been recognised by legal theorists, including international legal theorists,[4] and the ambiguous status of international investment law is itself perhaps evidence of this breakdown in practice.[5] The distinction is, however, still useful for the purposes of the analysis in this chapter, because it offers a way of characterising the competing perspectives on the legal issues in this area – without entailing a normative claim that either perspective, or both, should be adopted. The argument is not that a public or private

---

[4] See e.g. C. Chinkin, 'A critique of the public/private dimension', *European Journal of International Law*, 10 (1999), 387 and H. Charlesworth, 'Worlds apart: Public/private distinctions in international law' in M. Thornton (ed.), *Public and Private: Feminist legal debates* (Oxford University Press, 1995).

[5] See e.g. A. Mills, *The Confluence of Public and Private International Law: Justice, pluralism and subsidiarity in the international constitutional ordering of private law* (Cambridge University Press, 2009), p. 94.

perspective has to be 'chosen', or that a decision has to be made as to which one is 'correct', but rather that international investment law inherently brings together these apparently contradictory perspectives, and that it is the amalgamation of these oppositions which gives it such uncertain foundations.

II The characterisation of international investment law

The first public–private duality is the question of how to describe or analyse the type of law which constitutes the subject of international investment law – whether it should be approached as part of general international law, or as an aspect of the particular relationships between specific States. Under this duality, the 'public' is the international community as a whole, and this is contrasted with 'private', quasi-contractual arrangements between particular States or between States and investors.

From one perspective, international investment law may appear to be a growing global consensus on collective standards of treatment which States must observe when dealing with foreign investors. This suggests, as it appears to have become increasingly fashionable to assert in academic writing, an emerging 'regime' of international investment law, a set of rules applicable to all States, regulating their exercise of power against the interests of foreign investors. This in turn suggests a process of treaty interpretation informed by the broader context of international investment agreements and arbitral awards. It invites arguments that inspiration should be drawn from equivalent rules of domestic public law, like administrative law – perhaps even that international investment law, as some have argued, is part of a new development of global administrative law.[6] Viewed from this angle, international investment law appears as a specialised subject of public international law – an evolving combination of interconnected treaties, customary international law standards and general principles, striving for (and perhaps achieving) universality.

Yet viewed from a different perspective, international investment law may appear as a series of disparate and isolated international agreements, largely in the form of bilateral investment treaties (BITs), under

---

[6] See generally S. Schill, *The Multilateralization of International Investment Law* (Cambridge University Press, 2009), p. 375; S. Montt, *State Liability in Investment Treaty Arbitration: Global constitutional and administrative law in the BIT generation* (Oxford: Hart Publishing, 2009); G. van Harten, *Investment Treaty Arbitration and Public Law* (Oxford University Press, 2007); G. van Harten and M. Loughlin, 'Investment treaty arbitration as a species of global administrative law', *European Journal of International Law*, 17 (2006), 121.

which individual States strike particular bargains in the hope that they will gain competitive advantages over other States in attracting or retaining foreign investment.[7] This suggests that there is no coherent regime, but only numerous individual international investment agreements. It invites arguments that inspiration should instead be drawn from the rules and techniques applied by courts and arbitrators in interpreting and enforcing private contractual agreements, with greater focus on the intentions of the particular State Parties to the treaty, as well as the commercial content and context of any actual contractual agreements which might operate between the investor and the host State, and any negotiating history of the texts under examination. Viewed from this angle, international investment law appears as a specialised subject of international commercial dispute resolution – it presents a series of individual private business disputes based on particular, usually bilateral, treaty and contractual arrangements.

This fundamental ambiguity in the characterisation of modern international investment law is clearly reflected in, and a product of, different accounts of its historical genesis. On the one hand, emphasis could be placed on the failure of attempts to multilateralise international investment law, most prominently through the abandoned Multilateral Agreement on Investment project of the 1990s, which suggests a fragmentation of regulation into individual treaty relationships. The tribunal in *UPS* v. *Canada*,[8] for example, found that:

> the many bilateral treaties for the protection of investments . . . vary in their substantive obligations; while they are large in number their coverage is limited; and . . . in terms of opinio juris there is no indication that they reflect a general sense of obligation. The failure of efforts to establish a multilateral agreement on investment provides further evidence of that lack of a sense of obligation.[9]

---

[7] Thus 'each BIT reflects the promotion and protection of each country's interest and the principles of law that are distilled into each treaty are essentially a by-product of an exchange of quid pro quo between the negotiating parties': B. Kishoiyian, 'The utility of bilateral investment treaties in the formulation of customary international law', *Northwestern Journal of International Law and Business*, 14 (1994), 327, 373. The efficacy of these agreements in attracting foreign investment is, as is well known, still unproven: see e.g. J. W. Yackee, 'Bilateral investment treaties, credible commitment, and the rule of (international) law: Do BITs promote foreign direct investment?', *Law and Society Review*, 42 (2008), 815.

[8] *United Parcel Service of America Inc.* v. *Canada* (Award on Jurisdiction of 22 November 2002).

[9] *Ibid.*, para. 97.

On the other hand, the numerous investment treaties share (at least superficially) a number of key features, and may be viewed as drawing (at least implicitly) on collective conceptions of their basic provisions. The tribunal in *CME* v. *Czech Republic*,[10] for example, discussing the international standard of compensation for expropriated property, examined the history of disagreement over the rules which are or should be applicable in this context, but concluded that 'in the end, the international community put aside this controversy, surmounting it by the conclusion of more than 2200 bilateral (and a few multilateral) investment treaties. Today these treaties are truly universal in their reach and essential provisions.'[11]

The large number of BITs which have been entered into by States around the world clearly have both common features and points of distinction. The extent to which writing on international investment law emphasises those commonalities (coming from or leading to a sense of coherence) or those differences (coming from or leading to a sense of fragmentation) may thus ultimately say more about the perspective adopted by the person conducting the analysis than it does about international investment law itself.

III The function of international investment arbitration

The different perspectives explored above on the question of the characterisation of international investment law may, although need not necessarily, correspond with two fundamentally contrasting perspectives on the function of investment arbitration, which may be adopted by different participants in the discipline.[12] On the one hand, there is the perspective of a public international lawyer, with a tendency to systematise, to look for coherence and universality, to identify and advocate the progressive development of international law in general, and international investment law in particular, as a global 'public' legal order. On the other, there is the perspective of an international commercial arbitrator, with a tendency to fragment by focusing not on questions of general principle but on the arbitrator's role as a 'private' dispute-resolution 'service provider', reflecting only the specific facts, arguments

---

[10] *CME Czech Republic BV* v. *Czech Republic* (Final Award of 14 March 2003).

[11] *Ibid.*, para. 497.

[12] See e.g. T. Wälde, 'Interpreting investment treaties: Experiences and examples' in C. Binder, U. Kriebaum, A. Reinisch and S. Wittich (eds.), *International Investment Law for the 21st Century: Essays in honour of Christoph Schreuer* (Oxford University Press, 2009), p. 724.

and sources presented by the parties.[13] International investment arbitration, situated in the disputed territory at the boundary of the two 'communities' of public international law and international commercial arbitration, has long been pervasively torn between these two identities.

An important part of the history of international investment law is, of course, the technical and sociological process of its establishment as its own distinct professional specialisation, a new 'field' of study and work. It has emerged in recent years as not merely a particular application of general rules of public international law or procedures for commercial dispute settlement, but as a new discipline requiring specialist (and expensive) knowledge and expertise, provided and supported by an 'epistemic community',[14] with its own networks, conferences, journals, newsletters, mailing lists etc. Nevertheless, participants in the practice (or study) of international investment law are likely to come from more generalist training as part of either the world of public international law or international commercial arbitration, bringing with them a perspective and technical skills shaped by that experience.

The more that an arbitrator characterises their role as 'quasi-judicial', as part of an evolving legal system of international investment law, the more they are likely to identify the content of the legal obligations applicable to the parties, even if this is not strictly necessary to resolve the specific dispute, in order to provide guidance for future cases – potentially extending to cases not based on the same treaty, depending on the way the applicable standards may be construed. This is related to the question of how extensive the reasons provided by an arbitrator need to be,[15] and whether they should focus on legal or factual analysis, which is itself related to the broader issue of whether a doctrine of precedent does or should operate in international investment arbitration. Underlying this is the (much debated) question of whether consistency is

---

[13] See discussion in S. Wilske and M. Raible, 'The arbitrator as guardian of international public policy? Should arbitrators go beyond solving legal issues?' in C. A. Rogers and R. P. Alford (eds.), *The Future of Investment Arbitration* (Oxford University Press, 2009), p. 249.

[14] The term is borrowed from international relations scholarship: see e.g. P. M. Haas, 'Introduction: Epistemic communities and international policy coordination', *International Organization*, 46 (1992), 1, 3 (defining an epistemic community as 'a network of professionals with recognized expertise and competence in a particular domain and an authoritative claim to policy-relevant knowledge within that domain or issue-area').

[15] See e.g. S. Schill, 'Crafting the international economic order: The public function of investment treaty arbitration and its significance for the role of the arbitrator', *Leiden Journal of International Law*, 23 (2010), 401, 424ff.

a virtue to which investment law should aspire – or even, perhaps through the often-mooted idea of some type of appellate mechanism or 'International Investment Court', whether consistency should be enforced.[16]

Viewing international investment law as a process of lawmaking, rather than bilateral dispute resolution, implies a commitment to systemic goals in substantive international investment law. A 'public'-minded arbitrator seeking universal rules and a coherent regime may seek to explain away apparent differences in the way that previous authorities have identified substantive obligations in international investment law by identifying underlying principles, finding that: 'To the extent that the case law reveals different formulations of the relevant thresholds, an in-depth analysis may well demonstrate that they could be explained by the contextual and factual differences of the cases to which the standards have been applied.'[17] Such an approach may also have implications for contemporary debates over arbitral procedure, supporting arguments that arbitrations should be open and 'public', with third-party involvement (including through *amicus* briefs), because national or even international 'community' interests are at stake.[18]

---

[16] See e.g. Schill, *The Multilateralization of International Investment Law*, pp. 278ff.; C. Kessedjian, 'To give or not to give precedential value to investment arbitration awards?' in C. A. Rogers and R. P. Alford (eds.), *The Future of Investment Arbitration* (Oxford University Press, 2009), p. 43; M. Weiniger (ed.), 'Symposium: Precedent in investment arbitration', *Transnational Dispute Management*, 5(3) (2008); van Harten, *Investment Treaty Arbitration and Public Law*, pp. 180ff.; T.-H. Cheng, 'Precedent and control in investment treaty arbitration', *Fordham International Law Journal*, 30 (2007), 1014; S. D. Franck, 'The legitimacy crisis in investment arbitration: Privatizing public international law through inconsistent decisions', *Fordham Law Review*, 73 (2005), 1521.

[17] *Saluka Investments BV (The Netherlands)* v. *Czech Republic* (Partial Award of 17 March 2006) (*Saluka*), para. 291; see also Schill, *The Multilateralization of International Investment Law*, pp. 347ff.

[18] See e.g. International Centre for Settlement of Investment Disputes Rules of Procedure for Arbitration Proceedings (ICSID Arbitration Rules), Rule 37(2); *Biwater Gauff (Tanzania) Ltd* v. *United Republic of Tanzania* (ICSID Case No. ARB/05/22, Award of 24 July 2008), paras. 356 *et seq.*; T. Ishikawa, 'Third party participation in investment arbitration', *International and Comparative Law Quarterly*, 59 (2010), 373; A. Asteriti and C. J. Tams, 'Transparency and representation of the public interest in investment treaty arbitration' in S. Schill (ed.), *International Investment Law and Comparative Public Law* (Oxford University Press, 2010), p. 787; Schill, 'Crafting the international economic order'; G. Born and E. Shenkman, 'Confidentiality and transparency in commercial and investor–State international arbitration' in C. A. Rogers and R. P. Alford (eds.), *The Future of Investment Arbitration* (Oxford University Press, 2009), p. 5.

By contrast, if decisions of investment tribunals are viewed as more like private arbitrations, then this supports arguments that they should be closed and 'private', as the facts and issues concerned may be commercially sensitive or confidential. The more that the arbitrator's role is identified in this way, the more they may be satisfied with limiting themselves to the minimum analysis necessary to resolve the particular dispute, based on the facts and arguments presented by the particular parties, with less focus on questions of public interest or policy. Such an arbitrator may prefer to take a looser approach to characterising the obligations which are applicable to States, making questions of fact more decisive, presenting the applicable standard as one which is 'subjective and depends heavily on a factual context',[19] or identifying it as 'a flexible one which must be adapted to the circumstances of each case',[20] perhaps focusing on the expectations of the particular investor, or on considerations of 'equity'. They may be wary of defining the law between States in a forum in which only one is represented,[21] conscious of their own lack of lawmaking legitimacy, or simply cautious of reducing their own value in the market in which arbitrators themselves compete for work by appearing to commit themselves to particular principles or approaches. From such a perspective, consistency cannot be aspired to as a goal (except perhaps in decisions of fact), but is instead only something to be found where the practice of States happens to be unvarying.

IV   The economic policy underlying international investment law

Contrasting perspectives on the question of the public or private character of international investment law are also offered by the different economic approaches to the policy interests served by the subject. One perspective may view the objective of international investment law as the construction of a global 'law market',[22] in which States constantly compete to attract capital from foreign investors (particular in times of scarcity of global capital flows, as under the financial crisis which began

[19] *Lauder* v. *Czech Republic* (Final Award of 3 September 2001), para. 292.
[20] *Waste Management Inc.* v. *United Mexican States (Number 2)* (ICSID Case No. ARB(AF)/00/3, Final Award of 30 April 2004), para. 99.
[21] But see also van Harten, *Investment Treaty Arbitration and Public Law*, p. 167.
[22] See generally E. A. O'Hara and L. Ribstein, *The Law Market* (Oxford University Press, 2009); Z. Elkins, A. T. Guzman and B. A. Simmons, 'Competing for capital: The diffusion of bilateral investment treaties, 1960–2000', *International Organisation*, 60 (2006), 811; P. B. Stephan, 'The futility of unification and harmonization in international commercial law', *Virginia Journal of International Law*, 39 (1999), 743.

in 2007), leading to improvements in national legal systems. For such a market to function effectively, the obligations on each State must be viewed as essentially bilateral (or at least non-universal), otherwise no competitive advantages can be gained and thus no incentives are generated for law reform. A functional market requires a 'private', quasi-contractual conception of international investment law in which individual States competitively trade regulatory capacity for capital – the emergence of a coherent 'public' system might even, under this approach, be considered a 'monopolistic' market failure.

From this perspective, a BIT is viewed as a way to encourage growth for the benefit of the particular States which enter into it, particularly but not exclusively for developing States without secure and independent domestic legal systems. It resolves the basic problem that a State cannot make a commitment to an investor under national law, because sovereign States are (generally) unable to bind themselves domestically – any contract or statute purporting to promise a standard of protection could be overturned by a later change in national law and, in any case, domestic courts may not enforce the law fairly and objectively.[23] This regulatory risk is greatest in the unstable political systems which often blight developing economies, and thus are perhaps most in need of foreign investment. By entering into a treaty commitment (with or without a contract governed by national law),[24] the government of the capital-importing State is able essentially to bind its successor

---

[23] See e.g. Yackee, 'Bilateral investment treaties', p. 807; A. T. Guzman, 'Why LDCs sign treaties that hurt them: Explaining the popularity of bilateral investment treaties', *Virginia Journal of International Law*, 38 (1998), 639, 658ff.

[24] The existence of two sources of obligation in such cases has long caused difficulties, as treaty obligations can be defined in such terms that a breach of the contract may also constitute a parallel breach of the treaty, particularly through an 'umbrella clause' in the investment treaty (in which a State may undertake to abide by its contractual obligations). On the relationship between international and national law in investment arbitration, and the effect of umbrella clauses, see e.g. M. Sasson, *Substantive Law in Investment Treaty Arbitration: The unsettled relationship between international law and municipal law* (The Hague: Kluwer, 2010); S. Schill, 'Enabling private ordering: Function, scope and effect of umbrella clauses in international investment treaties', *Minnesota Journal of International Law*, 18 (2009), 1; R. Dolzer and C. Schreuer, *Principles of International Investment Law* (Oxford University Press, 2008), pp. 153ff.; J. Crawford, 'Treaty and contract in investment arbitration', *Arbitration International*, 24 (2008), 351; C. McLachlan, L. Shore and M. Weiniger, *International Investment Arbitration: Substantive principles* (Oxford University Press, 2007), pp. 92ff.; T. Wälde, 'The "umbrella" clause in investment arbitration', *Journal of World Investment and Trade*, 6 (2005), 183; Z. Douglas, 'The hybrid foundations of investment treaty arbitration', *British Yearbook of International Law*, 74 (2003), 151.

governments to obligations through international law, backed up by independent arbitration. This elegant (albeit controversial) circumvention of internal constitutional and even democratic principles,[25] may, it is argued, ultimately lead to improvements in the domestic rule of law, as States subdue their institutions of government through the adoption of strict and (internationally) binding commitments. While it is possible that a government may do this in order to entrench particular domestic policies, ordinarily the intention is that, through this commitment, it hopes to encourage and facilitate investments to contribute to the local economy, bringing in not only capital, but potentially technology and expertise. The capital-exporting State receives protection for its national companies, which should lead to increased profits for them and ultimately increased economic growth and tax revenue when some or all of those profits are repatriated. The capital-exporting State may even attract further international capital, which it could incorporate there to take advantage of the special benefits which investors from this State receive. The same applies, of course, even if each State both imports capital from the other State and exports capital to it – both States receive the same mutual benefit of receiving priority treatment. Each BIT may thus be viewed as representing a negotiated competitive advantage for two particular States. This suggests that the correct analysis of international investment law does not reveal the emergence of international standards, but instead highlights the importance of differentiating between the positions adopted and the bargains struck by different States in their particular private 'contracts' in the global law market.

Another economic perspective may, by contrast, view the objective of international investment law as a gradual process of global harmonisation and systematisation, in which greater uniformity will lead to efficiency gains for States and investors. Under this perspective, the goal is that foreign investors should be able to rely on universal standards for the treatment of their investment, reducing transaction costs and allowing investors to choose the most efficient or mutually profitable location for their investment, rather than the 'safest'. Differences between States, in this analysis, do not reflect healthy market competition, but rather inefficiencies which are the product of inadequate standardisation – distorting and undermining the market for foreign investment. For international investment law to function effectively under this conception,

---

[25] See e.g. D. Schneiderman, *Constitutionalizing Economic Globalization: Investment rules and democracy's promise* (Cambridge University Press, 2008).

the obligations on each State must be viewed as essentially universal, as at least tending toward a coherent 'public' global regime, rather than a set of distinctive 'private' arrangements.

These two economic perspectives are at least *prima facie* contradictory, and yet they co-exist in international investment law. By way of illustration, the tension between them is present in the US Model BIT 2004,[26] which claims that reaching 'agreement on the treatment to be accorded such investment will stimulate the flow of private capital and the economic development of the Parties',[27] but then provides (among other obligations) that: 'Each Party shall accord to covered investments treatment in accordance with customary international law, including fair and equitable treatment and full protection and security.'[28] This obligation purports to recognise what is claimed as an existing global ('public') standard of treatment for investment law. But if each party accepts that it is already subject to customary international law obligations in the terms established under the treaty, then it is unclear what a further agreement to comply with these (already agreed) legal obligations really adds, beyond perhaps providing for an institutional framework of enforcement. The importance of such a framework should, however, not be overestimated. Enforcing any arbitral award which is made pursuant to a BIT obligation is likely to rely largely on the concerns of the host State that non-compliance would damage their reputation in the commercial world – the obligation to enforce an arbitral award domestically will itself only be (at most) another treaty obligation,[29] and assets of the host State located outside its territory will often attract immunity from civil claims before foreign courts.[30] The reputational risk associated with breaching a treaty may not be

---

[26] Treaty between the Government of the United States of America and the Government of [Country] Concerning the Encouragement and Reciprocal Protection of Investment, 2004.

[27] *Ibid.*, Preamble.   [28] *Ibid.*, Art. 5(1).

[29] See e.g. Convention on the Settlement of Investment Disputes between States and Nationals of other States, opened for signature 18 March 1965, 575 UNTS 159, (entered into force 14 October 1966), Art. 54, which requires States to recognise an arbitral award 'as if it were a final judgment of a court in that State'. Note, however, that the ICSID Convention also includes, in Art. 64, an (as yet unused) compromissory clause conferring jurisdiction on the International Court of Justice (ICJ) in respect of disputes concerning the interpretation or application of the Convention. But even the enforceability of an ICJ judgment is likely, in many cases, to depend on reputational considerations.

[30] The general scope of this immunity is the subject of proceedings presently before the ICJ: *Jurisdictional Immunities of the State (Germany v. Italy)*, instituted 23 December 2008.

significantly greater than that associated with a perceived improper treatment of foreign investment under customary international law standards. Although, absent a BIT, no court or arbitral tribunal may be available to make an 'objective' determination of whether international law has been breached, that is not likely to seriously diminish the reputational damage to a State among potential global investors if it treats foreign investment unfairly.

It is thus unclear how an agreement to perform existing international obligations can significantly 'stimulate the flow of private capital and the economic development of the Parties'.[31] On the other hand, if the treaty goes beyond what is generally accepted as customary international law, clarifying or extending the obligations applicable between the State Parties, then it might serve to promote investment between the two States. In such a case, however, the obligations under the treaty are particular to it as a 'private' quasi-contractual agreement, and not the universal 'public' obligations they may purport to be.

V   The interests served by international investment law

A further duality at the heart of international investment law, both in general and in terms of obligations under particular investment treaties, is the interests which it serves. International investment law can be viewed as essentially about empowering States, a mechanism for them to promote their economic development and administrative sophistication. Yet at the same time it can equally be viewed as essentially about disciplining States, a means of protecting investors from unfair regulatory excess. From the former 'public' perspective, international investment law is simply a device used by States to achieve regulatory goals, and should not obviously have any priority over other regulatory techniques or objectives. From the latter 'private' perspective, international investment law is a device to protect the functioning of a global marketplace of capital, which requires fundamental constraints on the regulatory powers of States, and thus a hierarchy of obligations. Within international investment law, there is thus a foundational tension between the public regulatory interests of States, and the private interests of investors.

The presence of this tension in international investment law is exacerbated by the fact that, although formally international investment law is created between States, the imposition of obligations on States with

---

[31] US Model BIT 2004, Preamble.

respect to private investors, together with the creation of arbitral mechanisms to enforce those obligations, means that international investment
law in reality creates internationalised private rights which are opposable
to the State, 'conferring or creating direct rights in international law in
favour of investors'.[32] The scope of those rights is determined, *inter alia*,
by how strictly the standards of treatment applicable to host States are
defined – how much regulatory space is retained for the State, and how
much freedom *from* regulation is guaranteed to the investor. The greater
the standards of protection which are applied under international investment obligations, the more the balance is shifted from public to private
interests. Under this 'public/private' duality, the 'public' is the collective
interests of the host State, and the 'private' is the individual interest of
the investor company in protecting, and profiting from, its capital.

This tension between opposing public and private interests is reflected
in the different perspectives which are taken on the standards of treatment
in international investment law – particularly in respect of the obligation
on the host State, included in many BITs, to give 'fair and equitable
treatment' (FET) to a foreign investment. One analysis may focus on
the private interests or expectations of the investor, the need to ensure a
predictable and secure regulatory environment – on the grounds that:

> A foreign investor expects the host State to act in a consistent manner,
> free from ambiguity and totally transparently in its relations with the
> foreign investor, so that it may know beforehand any and all rules and
> regulations that will govern its investments, as well as the goals of the
> relevant policies and administrative practices or directives, to be able to
> plan its investment and comply with such regulations.[33]

In perhaps its strongest form, it may even be asserted that there is, in
international law, 'an obligation not to alter the legal and business
environment in which the investment has been made'.[34] This analysis

---

[32] *Occidental Exploration & Production Company* v. *Republic of Ecuador* [2005] EWCA Civ
1116 (UK), para. 18.

[33] *Técnicas Medioambientales Tecmed SA* v. *United Mexican States* (ICSID Case No. ARB
(AF)/00/2), Award of 29 May 2003) (*Tecmed*), para. 154. See also the reference to the
'stability and predictability of the business environment, founded on solemn legal and
contractual commitments' in *CMS Gas Transmission Company* v. *The Argentine Republic*
(ICSID Case No. ARB/01/8, Award of 12 May 2005) (*CMS*), para. 284, and to 'the
obligation to grant and maintain a stable and predictable legal framework necessary to
fulfill the justified expectations of the foreign investor', in *LG&E* v. *Argentina* (ICSID
Case No. ARB/02/1, Decision on Liability of 3 October 2006), para. 131.

[34] *Occidental Exploration and Production Company* v. *The Republic of Ecuador* (Final Award
of 1 July 2004) (*Occidental*), para. 191.

may therefore approach the substantive obligations in an investment treaty on the basis that a tribunal should 'resolve uncertainties in its interpretation so as to favour the protection of covered investments'.[35]

Another analysis may, however, start with a presumption that States have the right to regulate freely in their territory, and that thus investors face a natural degree of regulatory risk, provided regulation is used in good faith – that:

> the fair expectations of [an investor are] that the . . . laws applicable to such investment, as well as the supervision, control, prevention and punitive powers granted to the authorities in charge of managing such system, [will] be used for the purpose of assuring compliance with environmental protection, human health and ecological balance goals underlying such laws.[36]

Those who follow this approach may thus hold that restrictions on the sovereignty of States should only be found where there is clear evidence that this was the intention of the State Parties – thus interpreting substantive obligations in treaties narrowly in the case of uncertainty,[37] and tending to defer to States where difficult questions of fact or policy arise.

The former approach suggests a greater influence for doctrines adapted from private law (such as contract, property law or estoppel), while the latter suggests a greater influence for public law doctrines which more obviously balance private rights against public interests (such as administrative law or human rights jurisprudence).[38] The tension is perhaps most obvious in arbitral awards which expressly seek a balanced approach, such as the award in *EDF Services* v. *Romania*,[39] which held that:

> The idea that legitimate expectations, and therefore FET, imply the stability of the legal and business framework, may not be correct if stated in an overly-broad and unqualified formulation. The FET might then mean the virtual freezing of the legal regulation of economic activities, in contrast with the State's normal regulatory power and the evolutionary character of economic life. Except where specific promises or representations are made

---

[35] *SGS Société Générale de Surveillance SA* v. *Republic of the Philippines* (ICSID Case No. ARB/02/6, Decision on Jurisdiction of 29 January 2004), para. 116.

[36] *Tecmed*, para. 157.

[37] *SGS Société Générale de Surveillance SA* v. *Islamic Republic of Pakistan* (ICSID Case No. ARB/01/13, Decision on Jurisdiction of 6 August 2003), para. 167.

[38] See e.g. Schill, (ed.), *International Investment Law and Comparative Public Law*.

[39] *EDF (Services) Limited* v. *Romania* (Award and Dissenting Opinion of 8 October 2009).

by the State to the investor, the latter may not rely on a bilateral investment treaty as a kind of insurance policy against the risk of any changes in the host State's legal and economic framework. Such expectation would be neither legitimate nor reasonable.[40]

Similarly, in *Saluka* v. *Czech Republic*, the tribunal held that:

No investor may reasonably expect that the circumstances prevailing at the time the investment is made remain totally unchanged. In order to determine whether frustration of the foreign investor's expectations was justified and reasonable, the host State's legitimate right subsequently to regulate domestic matters in the public interest must be taken into consideration as well.[41]

There is, however, in practice relatively little guidance provided in arbitral awards on how exactly these public and private interests are to be balanced. Reference to the underlying policies of investment agreements offers little interpretative assistance, because they are themselves so heavily contested. From one perspective, it might be argued that the overall objective of a BIT – the maximisation of economic development – can only be achieved by maximising the protection of investors, liberating them from State control and freeing up the international flow of capital, thus ensuring that capital goes where it can grow the most. From another perspective, economic development may be conceived of as the ability of States to pursue and protect public goods, including but not limited to wealth, which may require State regulation to ensure their maximisation. Foreign investment may thus be viewed as a necessary pathway to development, enhanced through maximising the protection of private interests, or as a crippling of a perhaps newly emergent sovereignty which must be overcome to establish a fully independent State able to pursue its own public interests.[42]

VI   The economic analysis of international investment agreements

This duality of public and private interests may also be identified and explicated through an economic analysis of the way these interests are balanced in international investment agreements. One factor which strongly affects this balance is the extent to which negotiating power

---

[40] *Ibid.*, para. 217.   [41] *Saluka*, para. 305.
[42] See e.g. M. Sornarajah, *The International Law on Foreign Investment*, 3rd edn (Cambridge University Press, 2010), p. 50.

and capital flows are symmetrical in an investment agreement. Assuming that investment obligations in a treaty are formally symmetrical (applicable equally to both States – something which is, however, not always the case), an agreement between a wealthy capital-exporting State and a poor capital-importing State is likely to favour private investor interests. This is because the State with greater negotiating strength will at least predominantly be interested in maximising the protection of its national investors. For the capital-exporting State, the duality of public and private interests is obscured, and replaced by an apparent congruence of interests between the State and investors from that State. This is part of the explanation for the emergence of investment arbitration to replace diplomatic protection – the State effectively 'delegates' its right of diplomatic protection to its nationals (or perhaps agrees to create for its nationals a new individual right to replace or augment it),[43] which can pursue a claim directly against the host State. In these circumstances, the tension between public and private interests will operate predominantly in the host State, which by contrast will readily perceive their conflict – investment treaties are likely to reflect concessions made by poor capital-importing States which perhaps frustratingly limit their public regulatory capacities.

As capital flows have become increasingly dynamic and complex in the modern global economy, the traditional categorisation of States as capital-importing or capital-exporting has, however, become less clear-cut, at least to some degree. In negotiations between States whose bilateral capital flows are more bi-directional, both States will be in the position of a host State as well as a capital exporter, and thus both face a balancing exercise between public and private interests. Conscious of the potential impact a BIT may have on their domestic regulatory powers, they may both thus favour weaker obligations which prioritise (public) State interests over (private) investor interests.[44] The point is well illustrated by the relaxation of standards in the US Model BIT 2004 in comparison with its predecessors, which reflects the fact that the United States has increasingly become a capital importer as well as

---

[43] Note that the 'delegated authority' approach has been rejected as a legal analysis of investment arbitration: see e.g. the decision of the England and Wales Court of Appeal in *Occidental Exploration & Production Company* v. *Republic of Ecuador* [2005] EWCA Civ 1116, para. 17.

[44] Alternatively, where capital flows are bi-directional but one State has a more powerful negotiating position, this may lead in practice to asymmetrical treaty obligations.

exporter. This will, of course, also depend on the extent to which the governments negotiating the agreement are interested in protecting domestic regulatory space, or to advancing the freedom of global capital – those ideologically committed to 'small government' may trade away regulatory capacity more readily, at least to the extent that they are not also 'protectionist'. In general, however, in such circumstances the congruence between the interests of investors and their State of nationality which is likely to exist in a BIT between States with asymmetrical capital flows is replaced by a tension between public and private interests which is felt within both States.

The fact that international investment law 'internationalises' the interests of private parties is, however, critical to the capacity of States to control the articulation and development of these standards of treatment, and thus of the balance of public and private interests. Even if two States intend to agree to relatively unrestrictive standards of treatment in a BIT, balancing public above private interests, in any investment arbitration subsequently held under the treaty, the interpretation of the State obligations may be skewed back toward private interests. This is because the investor, but not the investor's home State, will be a party to the arbitration. It has even been suggested that structural factors in international investment law incentivise arbitrators to take such an approach, as it could encourage future investment claims (which are of course always initiated by investors), which would in turn increase the value of their professional expertise.[45] Less conspiratorially, some arbitrators may naturally seek to conciliate or compromise between the competing positions which are argued before them, leading to a re-equilibration of public and private values to replace the balancing which has already taken place in treaty negotiations.

This procedural loss of State control over the interpretation of treaty obligations, and thus over their embedded weighing of public and private interests, is an important part of the explanation for the Interpretive Note issued by the North American Free Trade Agreement (NAFTA) Federal Trade Commission in 2001. In response to an evident trend toward the articulation of stricter standards by NAFTA investment tribunals, the note clarified that 'The concepts of "fair and equitable treatment" and "full protection and security" do not require treatment in addition to or beyond that which is required by the customary

---

[45] van Harten, *Investment Treaty Arbitration and Public Law*, pp. 167ff.

international law minimum standard of treatment of aliens',[46] thus shifting these standards back toward the (public) interests of the NAFTA States. Such a formal mechanism of interpretative guidance will, however, seldom be available in the context of bilateral investment obligations.[47] In the absence of such a mechanism, the carefully negotiated balancing of public and private interests in a BIT may become vulnerable to an irreversible rebalancing through the dispute-resolution process under which the treaty obligations are interpreted and applied.

VII Conclusions: The impact of the dualities in practice

The range of public–private distinctions and policy perspectives explored in this chapter are not points of purely academic interest – they have very real and practical consequences which are reflected in many of the major issues which are matters of contention in international investment law.

One impact, for example, is on the ongoing debate about the meaning of the obligation on a host State to give 'fair and equitable treatment' to a foreign investment, both generally, and as a matter of interpretation of any specific treaty. An important aspect of this debate is the question of whether an FET obligation is an autonomous treaty standard or the same as the customary international law minimum standard of treatment.[48] Those who view international investment law as a regime of emerging universal international standards are more likely to view an FET obligation as invoking the general standards of customary international law – characterising the object and purpose of the BIT as part of a public multilateral 'standard setting' process. By contrast, those who view international investment law as a series of negotiated bilateral agreements through which States define their mutual obligations in order to seek a competitive advantage are more likely to view an FET obligation as particular to the specific treaty under consideration – characterising the object and purpose of the BIT as defining the terms of a private 'contractual' bargain.

---

[46] NAFTA Free Trade Commission, *Statement on NAFTA Article 1105 and the Availability of Arbitration Documents*, 31 July 2001, www.naftalaw.org/files/NAFTA_Comm_1105_ Transparency.pdf (last accessed 19 January 2011).

[47] But see *CME*, paras. 87 *et seq.*; US Model BIT 2004, Arts. 28(2), 30(3) and 31.

[48] See e.g. Dolzer and Schreuer, *Principles of International Investment Law*, pp. 124ff.; K. Yannaca-Small, 'Fair and equitable treatment standard: Recent developments' in A. Reinisch (ed.), *Standards of Investment Protection* (Oxford University Press, 2008), pp. 111ff.; I. Tudor, *The Fair and Equitable Treatment Standard in the International Law of Foreign Investment* (Oxford University Press, 2008).

The identification of what type of FET obligation is present in a treaty may, thus, reflect different pre-existing policy perspectives on international investment law. This will in turn affect the methodology for establishing the content of the FET obligation – as the tribunal in *Glamis Gold* v. *United States* observed,[49] 'those treaties with fair and equitable treatment clauses that expand upon, or move beyond, customary international law, lead their reviewing tribunals into an analysis of the treaty language and its meaning, as guided by Article 31(1) of the Vienna Convention'.[50] By contrast, 'those treaties and free trade agreements, like the NAFTA, that are to be understood by reference to the customary international law minimum standard of treatment necessarily lead their tribunals to analyze custom'.[51]

In a number of cases, arbitrators have sought to avoid this issue by holding that it is unnecessary to resolve the question of the content of an FET obligation, because the facts of the case establish that there is (or is not) a breach, regardless of how the standard is characterised.[52] This in itself raises questions about what the role of the arbitrator is in an investment dispute, as explored above – whether it is to serve as a quasi-judicial public lawmaker (who ought to clarify the law in the general interest), or as a private dispute-resolution service provider (who should resolve the particular dispute as efficiently as possible). These debates and difficulties are a product of the contested status of international investment arbitrations, as both (public) tribunals of international law, contributing to the clarification and development of global standards, and arbiters of isolated (private) international commercial disputes.

In a range of ways, the practical methodology followed by an arbitrator will thus be at least partly a consequence of their policy perspectives, and, in particular, their approach to the foundational public–private dualities explored in this chapter. Among other things, this underlying conflict of policies highlights the critical importance, well understood among practitioners in the field, of the process of selection of arbitrators, and may also suggest the importance of supporting technical arguments about particular precedents, or rules of treaty interpretation or

---

[49] *Glamis Gold Ltd* v. *The United States of America* (Award of 8 June 2009).

[50] *Ibid.*, para. 606.   [51] *Ibid.*

[52] See e.g. *Occidental*, para. 192; *CMS*, para. 284; *Saluka*, para. 291; *Azurix* v. *Argentine Republic* (ICSID Case No. ARB/01/12, Award of 14 July 2006), para. 364; *Duke Energy Electroquil Partners & Electroquil SA* v. *Ecuador* (ICSID Case No. ARB/04/19, Award of 18 August 2008), para. 333.

customary international law formation, with more basic policy arguments about what international investment law is for and how it is supposed to work.

The explosion in popularity of international investment law in recent years, both academically and in practice, should not mask these underlying foundational conflicts and uncertainties – the fault lines on which the thriving investment arbitral community is building its village. Many of the important debates, issues and inconsistencies which characterise this dynamic area of international law are products of these underlying public–private dualities, and thus will not be susceptible to technical or doctrinal solutions.

6

Outline of a normative framework for evaluating interpretations of investment treaty protections

JONATHAN BONNITCHA*

I Introduction

There are at least two ways in which legal scholarship might be approached. One might ask what the law on a particular subject *is*. This question invites doctrinal inquiry through an examination of authoritative sources internal to a legal system. Alternately, one might ask whether the law on a particular subject matter is *desirable* or *just*. This normative inquiry typically begins with a characterisation of what the law on a given subject is, but its primary objective is the evaluation of law by external, normative criteria.[1]

Arbitral tribunals charged with interpreting and applying international investment treaties (IITs) continue to grapple with legal concepts such as 'fair and equitable treatment' and 'indirect expropriation'. Different tribunals have interpreted common treaty language in distinct ways; for example, in an earlier work I argue that tribunals have used six, identifiably distinct approaches to distinguish indirect expropriation from legitimate non-compensable regulation.[2] It would be useful to be able to examine which interpretations were more desirable – in a normative sense – and which were inadvisable. This chapter presents a

---

* Due to space constraints, this chapter is a significantly abbreviated presentation of a framework developed in the course of the author's doctoral research. Readers interested in a fuller statement of the argument, and those with comments or criticisms, are invited to contact the author at jonathan.bonnitcha@magd.ox.ac.uk.
[1] For a sophisticated discussion of the distinction between internal and external perspectives on law see H. L. A. Hart, *The Concept of Law*, 2nd edn (Oxford University Press, 1994).
[2] J. Bonnitcha, *The Implications of the Structure of the Regulatory Expropriation Enquiry in International Investment Law* (M.Phil. Dissertation, University of Oxford, 2008), http://ora.ouls.ox.ac.uk/objects/uuid:1ad79a6c-c86f-469c-b53c-90d842a70cf4 (last accessed 6 December 2010).

framework for normative evaluation of interpretations of the substantive protections of foreign investment contained in IITs.

This chapter adopts the methodology of consequential evaluation, as developed in Sen's work.[3] The methodology implies that a normative (as opposed to doctrinal) preference for one interpretation over another should be based on a comparison of the consequences that would be likely to follow from each interpretation. This chapter proposes that the consequences of a given interpretation of an IIT protection can be divided into five categories, its effects on:

1. the distribution of wealth
2. efficiency
3. flows of foreign direct investment (FDI) into host States
4. the realisation of human rights and environmental conservation in host States
5. respect for the rule of law in host States.

Within this framework, the chapter provides a synthesis of evidence and theory, on the basis of which conclusions about the likely consequences of different interpretations can be drawn.

The framework also specifies the normative criteria by which the identified consequences should be evaluated. Three of the identified consequences are normatively desirable in themselves – economic efficiency, the realisation of human rights and environmental conservation, and respect for the rule of law. Furthermore, the attraction of FDI is accepted as a proxy for other desirable consequences. This chapter recognises considerable disagreement about the normative criteria by which redistribution of wealth should be evaluated. Three independent normative criteria are proposed, against each of which the consequences of an interpretation should be evaluated.

That three of these consequences focus explicitly on the host States does not reflect a pre-judgement that the impact of IITs on host States are more important than those on home States. Rather, it reflects the fact that IIT protections govern the legal relationship between host States and foreign investors present in host States. A comprehensive mapping of the consequences of IIT protections inevitably leads to the conclusion that most consequences are geographically located in host States. That said, the five-part framework is capable of fully identifying the consequences

---

[3] See A. Sen, 'Consequential evaluation and practical reason', *The Journal of Philosophy*, 97(9) (2000), 477.

of alternate interpretations for home States – for example, global improvements in economic efficiency and redistribution of wealth between host States and foreign investors are both consequences of IITs that may affect home States (or, at least, companies and individuals present in home States).

II   Distributive impacts of IITs: The allocation of losses

A   The nature and extent of the distributive consequences of IIT protections

The protections for investment contained in IITs allocate losses between host States and foreign investors. If a State causes loss to a foreign investor in a manner that breaches an IIT protection, the State must compensate the investor; if a State causes loss to a foreign investor in a manner that does not breach an IIT the loss will lie with the investor (subject to domestic law and any relevant contractual arrangements). From an *ex post* perspective, the payment of compensation is a simple transfer of wealth.[4] To be sure, it is the honouring of a treaty obligation to compensate, rather than the obligation itself, which has an effect on the distribution of wealth. However, with respect to IITs containing compulsory investor–State arbitration, it is reasonable to assume that investors have some capacity to enforce their rights and will choose to do so.

The general distributive consequence of IIT protections can be stated simply: to the extent that IITs cause host States to make compensation payments – either as a result of arbitral awards or through settlements negotiated in the shadow of IITs – their effect is to redistribute wealth from host States to foreign investors. Two qualifications should be added to this statement. First, IITs only redistribute wealth to foreign investors to the extent they go beyond a State's obligation to compensate for loss under domestic law. Secondly, different interpretations of IIT provisions may cause different patterns of wealth transfers.

B   Evaluating the distributive consequences of IITs

Different theories of distributive justice suggest different normative criteria by which redistributions should be evaluated. This section does not attempt to resolve debates about distributive justice that have filled

---

[4] L. Blume and D. Rubinfeld, 'Compensation for takings: An economic analysis', *California Law Review*, 72 (1984), 569, 580.

many libraries worth of books. Instead, it examines three of the most influential schools of thinking on distributive justice: libertarian, egalitarian and utilitarian. It then explores the implications of each school for a normative evaluation of transfers between foreign investors and host States.

C   Libertarian theories of distributive justice

The libertarian conception of distributive justice is based on entitlement to existing, validly acquired, property rights.[5] This school of thought is most associated with the theoretical work of Robert Nozick. However, Richard Epstein has done more than any other scholar to apply Nozickian libertarian principles to the law of property protection. Epstein observes that a full commitment to the protection of property would imply a *minimal State* unable to supply even the most basic public goods.[6] In such a State, every individual could be worse off than in a State with a limited system of public good provision.[7] Epstein argues that the appropriate theoretical response for a libertarian is to allow the State to interfere with property rights, provided that affected individuals are left no worse off.[8]

Libertarian theory, based on Nozick and developed by Epstein, provides a clear normative criterion by which to evaluate the distributive effects of IIT protection: justice requires a host State to compensate a foreign investor for loss caused by interference with the investor's property rights. However, this principle applies only to compensation for interferences with an investor's *rights* of ownership – its legal entitlements relating to the possession, use and disposition of the property in question.[9] The libertarian claim is for the protection of legal entitlements, rather than insurance of the value of those entitlements.[10] Economic loss only comes into the analysis as the measure of compensation

---

[5] R. Nozick, *Anarchy, State and Utopia* (Basil Blackwell, Oxford 1974), p. 151.

[6] R. Epstein, 'One step beyond Nozick's minimal state: The role of forced exchanges in political theory', *Social Philosophy and Policy*, 21(1) (2005), 286, 290.

[7] *Ibid.*   [8] *Ibid.*, 293.

[9] R. Epstein, *Takings: Private property and the power of eminent domain* (Harvard University Press, 1985), p. 100.

[10] e.g. 'While property "rights" are claims with respect to things, property "values" are assumptions regarding the market price of those claims': S. Eagle, *Regulatory Takings* (Charlottesville: Michie, 1996), p. 62.

once a deprivation of rights has been established.[11] The distinction between rights and value is crucial when it comes to evaluating the distributive consequences of an IIT provision in libertarian terms. When an investor acquires an investment in a foreign country, it validly acquires a bundle of property rights that are defined by domestic law at the time of purchase.[12] A libertarian theory of justice implies that a State should compensate an investor if it alters the scope of those rights; it does not imply that a State should compensate an investor for losses flowing from changes in policy that do not affect an investor's rights.

D   Egalitarian theories of distributive justice

Virtually all theories of justice argue for equality of something, whether it is equal protection of rights, equal weighting of each individual's utility or equality of income and wealth.[13] Egalitarianism, in the sense used in this chapter, refers to the latter form of equality: equality in the distribution of income, wealth and resources.

The work of John Rawls occupies a central position in egalitarian thought. Although different theorists incorporate egalitarian norms into their theories in different ways, the conclusions of many thinkers – among them Pogge, Cohen and Sen – are developed through criticism and extension of Rawls's ideas.[14] This chapter's characterisation of the norms of egalitarianism is based on the difference principle in Rawls's *A Theory of Justice*.[15] Rawls's difference principle can be expressed in two simple normative propositions: that primary goods, which include wealth and income, should be distributed equally; and that any inequality in the distribution can be justified only to the extent it improves the position of the worst off.[16]

It is possible to imagine a compensatory transfer to a foreign investor that would lead to a more egalitarian distribution of wealth. Such a situation could occur if the shareholders of a foreign investor were a large

---

[11] Epstein, *Takings: Private property and the power of eminent domain*, p. 103.
[12] Z. Douglas, 'The hybrid foundations of investment treaty arbitration', *British Yearbook of International Law*, 74 (2003), 151, 197.
[13] A. Sen, *Inequality Reexamined* (Clarendon Press, 1992), p. ix.
[14] T. Pogge, *Realizing Rawls* (Ithaca: Cornell University Press, 1989), p. 1; G. A. Cohen, *Rescuing Justice and Equality* (Harvard University Press, 2008), p. 1; A. Sen, *The Idea of Justice* (London: Allen Lane, 2009), p. 1.
[15] J. Rawls, *A Theory of Justice*, rev. edn (Cambridge, MA: Belknap Press, 1999), p. 53.
[16] *Ibid.*, p. 67.

number of relatively poor individuals in circumstances where the compensation paid by the State would otherwise have been siphoned off by a wealthy elite. Nevertheless, four facts suggest that the distributive consequences of compensating foreign investors are unlikely to be desirable on egalitarian grounds. First, the investors whose claims have come to international investment arbitration are predominantly medium-large corporations from the developed world.[17] Secondly, in developed countries shares are more commonly owned, and owned in greater proportion, by the wealthy than the poor.[18] Thirdly, the respondent States in investment claims are predominantly developing countries.[19] Fourthly, regardless of whether a State is corrupt or beset by cronyism, fiscal shortfalls are likely to be at least part-funded through general taxation, transferring any gains or losses of the State onto the general population.

E   Utilitarian theories of distributive justice

Classical utilitarianism is based on the norm of seeking 'the greatest happiness for the greatest number'.[20] Happiness, in this sense, is conventionally described as 'utility', a concept that posits a single metric capable of fully describing an individual's subjective well-being. Evaluating distributive transfers in utilitarian terms requires a comparison of the loss of utility of those who bear the burden of a compensatory transfer with the gain in utility of those who benefit from it. As the amount of money lost in a transfer by those who pay is, by definition, equal to the amount gained by those who benefit, a change in aggregate utility can only arise if people derive different levels of subjective well-being from the same amount of money.

Those who have invoked utilitarian norms to evaluate distributive consequences rely on the assumption that the utility of additional wealth is higher for the poor than the rich, as the poor lack for more of the things that might dramatically improve the quality of their lives.[21] Under

---

[17] S. Franck, 'Empirically evaluating claims about investment treaty arbitration', *North Carolina Law Review*, 86 (2007), 1, 29.

[18] e.g. in the United Kingdom 'wealth is considerably less evenly distributed than income' with the wealthiest half of the population owning 99% of non-dwelling, marketable wealth: Office for National Statistics, 'Share of the wealth' (2006), www.statistics.gov.uk/cci/nugget.asp?id=2 (last accessed 6 December 2010).

[19] Franck, 'Empirically evaluating claims', p. 32.

[20] This quote is customarily attributed to Bentham. B. J. H. Burns, 'Happiness and utility: Jeremy Bentham's equation', *Utilitas*, 17 (1) (2005), 46, 46.

[21] A. C. Pigou, *The Economics of Welfare* (Macmillan, London 1932), 1.VIII.3.

this assumption, a utilitarian analysis roughly follows an egalitarian analysis,[22] although without the same insistence that attention focus specifically on the interests of the worst off: compensatory transfers would be desirable to the extent that they transfer money from wealthy to less-wealthy individuals. It is difficult to see how the distributive effect of IIT protections – the transfer of wealth from host States to foreign investors – could be justified on utilitarian grounds.

Neo-classical economics is based on ethical premises similar to classical utilitarianism, with one crucial difference. Normative applications of neo-classical economics call for the maximisation of economic welfare, rather than individuals' subjective utility.[23] While one might expect economic welfare to correspond to happiness, the accounting of welfare in dollar terms excludes the possibility that differently situated individuals might derive different levels of happiness from the same amount of money. Distributive transfers have no net impact on economic welfare by this standard – the losses to some from any transfer necessarily cancel out the gains of others. Legal rules may affect investors' and States' behaviour, which in turn may affect net economic welfare, but these are not *distributive* consequences. These consequences are identified and evaluated in section C, which addresses efficiency.

F   Summary of distributive consequences of IITs

The identification and evaluation of the distributive consequences of IIT protections can be summarised in the following six propositions:

1. One important consequence of IIT protections is that they alter the distribution of wealth between host States and foreign investors. To the extent that IIT protections provide investors with rights to compensation for losses that go beyond the investors' rights in the law of the host State, their effect is to redistribute wealth from host States to foreign investors.
2. The scope and extent of the transfer of wealth from host States to foreign investors is a purely empirical question. An evaluation of whether these distributive consequences are desirable relies on the articulation of underlying normative premises about distributive justice.

---

[22] This argument is developed in A. Lerner, *The Economics of Control: Principles of welfare economics* (Macmillan, New York 1944), p. 35.
[23] R. Posner, *The Economics of Justice* (Harvard University Press, 1981), p. 49.

3. Libertarian theories of justice suggest that validly acquired property rights should be protected. This provides a justification for transfers of wealth to foreign investors that serve to compensate investors for interferences with their property rights by the host State. However, libertarian theories do not justify compensatory transfers for losses that do not result from a deprivation of property rights.
4. Egalitarian theories of distributive justice suggest that transfers of wealth are desirable to the extent they improve the position of the worst off. There is no plausible argument that distributive consequences of IIT protections are desirable on egalitarian grounds.
5. Utilitarian theories of distributive justice suggest that transfers of wealth are desirable to the extent they increase aggregate subjective utility. There is no plausible argument that the *distributive* consequences of IIT protections are desirable on utilitarian grounds.

III   Efficiency

This section examines the likely consequences of treaty protection in terms of economic efficiency. Efficiency is not a directly observable consequence of an action in a way that other consequences might be observed. It is a conceptual construct that allows for the aggregation of a variety of different economic effects. However, in principle, efficiency has an empirical basis; with enough information it would be possible to make a definitive statement about the relative efficiency of two alternate states of affairs, given current (observed) market prices.

A   The concept of efficiency

The concept of efficiency is central to economic analysis of public policy, including economic analysis of legal rules. A state of affairs is Pareto-efficient if commodities are allocated so that no person can be made better off without making someone else worse off. The notion of Hicks-Kaldor efficiency, which is derived from Pareto efficiency, is more useful. A policy change improves Hicks-Kaldor efficiency if the gains of those who are better off as a result of the change would be sufficient to compensate those made worse off, demonstrating the potential for Pareto improvement.[24] In this chapter, 'efficiency' refers to Hicks-Kaldor

---

[24] R. Cooter and T. Uren, *Law and Economics* (Boston: Pearson Addison-Wesley, 2008), p. 47.

efficiency. Examination of questions of efficiency is conducted from a global (as opposed to national) perspective.

B   Free markets and competitive equality: A basic efficiency analysis

The theoretical foundation for examining the effect of IIT protections on efficiency is the neo-classical model of markets. This model is based on a number of simplifying assumptions, including perfect information about investment opportunities, zero transaction costs and no external-ities to production that are not reflected in prices. In a simplified world of this sort, competitive equality among producers – within and between industries – will lead to the most efficient organisation of production. This is because more efficient firms will be able to produce more profitably than less efficient firms under conditions of competitive equality. Greater potential profitability – all other things being equal – means that efficient firms will win investment contracts and expand their production at the expense of less efficient firms. The outcome is a more efficient organisation of production (from a global perspective).

The application of this model to investment treaties is relatively straightforward. Legal rights that entitle firms to compensation for certain classes of loss are valuable. If all firms are granted the same legal rights, a situation of competitive equality prevails. If some firms are granted legal rights beyond those of their competitors, the privileged firms will be able to expand their market share at the expense of their more efficient competitors.[25] On this basis, interpretations of investment treaties that confer equal legal status to domestic and foreign investors will tend to increase efficiency. Interpretations of investment treaties that confer legal rights on foreign investors that go beyond the legal rights of domestic investors will tend to reduce efficiency.

One objection to this simplified treatment of efficiency is that foreign firms, despite being entitled to equal treatment as a matter of law, may face practical obstacles in their regulatory relationships with government that similarly situated domestic firms do not face. Given the difficulties of reforming national bureaucracies, it might be argued that conferring additional legal rights on foreign firms is a simple and effective way to

---

[25] K. Vandevelde, 'The economics of bilateral investment treaties', *Harvard International Law Journal*, 41 (2000), 469, 478; J. Stiglitz, 'Regulating multinational corporations: Towards principles of cross-border legal frameworks in a globalized world balancing rights with responsibilities', *American University International Law Review*, 23 (2008), 451, 468.

redress foreigners' initial disadvantage. This argument is implicit in many of the justifications for IITs asserted by lawyers – for example, the suggestion that the international legal rights of foreign investors are a counterbalance to the political influence of domestic firms,[26] or systemic bias in domestic courts.[27] The underlying structure of argument has been formalised in the economic theory of the second best. The theory shows that if there is a departure from conditions of competitive equality then a further, compensating departure may increase efficiency (while still resulting in a less efficient outcome than the removal of the original obstacle to competitive equality).[28]

On closer examination, there are theoretical weaknesses in the argument that IIT protections are an efficiency-improving counterbalance for domestic firms' political influence. Administrative discrimination against foreigners might provide an efficiency justification for strong national treatment protections, even if domestic firms are not protected by reciprocal legal rights to be treated no worse than foreign investors. Similarly, discrimination against foreigners in domestic courts could, plausibly, justify foreign investors' entitlement to initiate investor–State arbitration, which domestic investors are unable to utilise. However, it is difficult to see how the objective of redressing either form of discrimination is advanced by substantive standards of protection that are defined without reference to the way in which similarly situated domestic investors are treated.

There are further empirical objections to the applicability of 'second best' arguments to investment treaties. To the extent that evidence exists, it suggests that foreign investors are not at a disadvantage in their dealings with host governments compared to domestic firms.[29] The conclusion must be that, in the absence of externalities, interpretations that put foreign investors in a better position than domestic investors are less efficient than interpretations that put foreign and domestic investors in an equivalent legal position.

---

[26] S. Ratner, 'Regulatory takings in institutional context: Beyond the fear of fragmented international law', *American Journal of International Law*, 102 (2008), 475, 483; J. Paulsson, 'Indirect expropriation: Is the right to regulate at risk?' (2005), www.oecd. org/dataoecd/5/52/36055332.pdf (last accessed 6 December 2010), p. 4.

[27] T. Wälde and T. Weiler, 'Investment arbitration under the Energy Charter Treaty in the light of new NAFTA precedents: Towards a global code of conduct for economic regulation', *Transnational Dispute Management*, 1(1) (2004), text following n. 119; W.-M. Choi, 'The present and future of the investor–State dispute settlement paradigm', *Journal of International Economic Law*, 10(3) (2007), 725, 735.

[28] R. Lipsey and K. Lancaster, 'The general theory of the second best', *The Review of Economic Studies*, 24(1) (1956), 11, 16.

[29] See, e.g., R. Desbordes and J. Vanday, 'The political influence of foreign firms in developing countries', *Economics and Politics*, 19 (2007), 421, 447.

C   Efficient government and investor conduct

One of the most common justifications for laws requiring governments to compensate property-owners for expropriation of their property is that such laws encourage *governments* to make more efficient decisions.[30] A closely related issue is whether such laws encourage *investors* to make more efficient investment decisions.

The argument that compensation requirements induce more efficient government decision-making is premised on the assumption that public decision-makers tend to undervalue the economic costs of a decision that fall on private actors.[31] A compensation requirement might assist in redressing this bias by forcing government decision-makers to consider the costs that the measure under consideration would impose on affected individuals, and factor these costs into the overall evaluation of that measure.[32] The extent to which government decisions are likely to be influenced by the IIT protections owed to foreign investors – and whether this influence is likely to lead to more efficient decisions – is difficult to assess in general terms. A whole range of legislative and executive decisions, made by different tiers of government, could potentially become the subject of a claim made by a foreign investor. The associated processes of decision-making, and their sensitivity to a national government's obligations to compensate foreign investors, can be expected to vary both within and between countries. Ultimately, governments decision-making processes' sensitivity to compensation rules raises empirical questions on which, in the IIT context, there is little evidence available.

In the absence of empirical evidence, there are conceptual flaws in the argument that providing legal protection to foreign investment is likely to encourage more efficient government decision-making. On the argument's own premises, decision-makers are more sensitive to the costs and benefits of a decision if the government is forced to bear the costs of the decision directly. The assumption of sensitivity implies that decision-makers underestimate any economic benefits of a decision unless they are able to be captured by the government. On this basis, requiring decision-makers to bear the costs of a policy when they cannot capture its benefits would lead to inefficient reluctance to alter the status

---

[30] L. Blume, D. Rubinfeld and P. Shapiro, 'The taking of land: When should compensation be paid?', *The Quarterly Journal of Economics*, 99(1) (1984), 71, 88.

[31] *Ibid.*

[32] Blume and Rubinfeld, 'Compensation for takings: An economic analysis', p. 621.

quo.[33] Moreover, the assumption of sensitivity implies that decision-makers are more sensitive to the private costs that the government is forced to bear. Requiring governments to compensate foreign investors for their losses, while not extending equivalent protection to other private actors, is likely to lead decision-makers to over-value the interests of foreign investors. This distortion could only be justified if it corrected a systematic bias in government decision-making, which caused government to value foreign investors' losses less than other private losses.[34] There is little evidence that a bias of this sort exists.

The likely effect of compensation rules on investors' decisions also raises empirical questions. However, the assumption that investors' behaviour is driven by profitability – a plausible first approximation – means that investors' likely response to legal rules can be modelled with greater confidence. This discussion proceeds on the assumption of investor risk neutrality. Given that the investments in question are commercial ventures owned by international actors, in contrast to family homes owned by private individuals, it is reasonable to assume risk neutrality.[35]

To the extent that compensation rules insure investors from the cost of efficiency-improving government measures they are likely to result in inefficiently high levels of investment.[36] This is because such rules encourage moral hazard – a situation in which investors fail to allow for the risk posed to contemplated investments by efficiency-improving measures.[37] This scenario is easier to illustrate with an example. It would be inefficient for an investor to sink capital into building a factory which would operate at a profit of $1,000 a year by dumping pollutants in a river that cause $2,000 a year's worth of damage to a downstream oyster industry. Nevertheless, an investor would be more likely to build such a factory if it knew that the government would be required to compensate it for introducing a future regulation that prohibited such dumping.

---

[33] V. Been and J. Beauvais, 'The global Fifth Amendment? NAFTA's investment protections and the misguided quest for an international "regulatory takings" doctrine', *New York University Law Review*, 78 (2003), 30, 96.

[34] In a domestic context, the argument is that certain forms of government – particularly local government – institutionally undervalue the costs of decisions on politically weak minorities. This argument is developed at length in W. Fischel, *Regulatory Takings: Law, economics and politics* (Harvard University Press, 1995).

[35] For a more complex examination that allows for investor risk aversion, see Blume, Rubinfeld and Shapiro, 'The taking of land: When should compensation be paid?', p. 86.

[36] *Ibid.*, p. 81.

[37] E. Aisbett, L. Karp and C. McAusland, 'Police powers, regulatory taking and the efficient compensation of domestic and foreign investors', *Economic Record*, 86 (2010), 367; Stiglitz, 'Regulating multinational corporations', p. 529.

The corollary is also true: to the extent that compensation rules insure investors from the cost of efficiency-reducing measures, such rules are likely to encourage more efficient investment decisions. This is because such compensation entitlements ensure that investors are not dissuaded from undertaking efficient investments by the risk of efficiency-reducing measures; the investor's decision function factors in only the efficient probability of loss due to a government measure.[38] The hold-up problem – that without guarantees of compensation for any future expropriation an investor may be reluctant to incur the sunk costs associated with an investment – can be understood as a special case of this more general result.[39]

In principle, the distinction between efficient and inefficient measures is clear. In practice, determining whether a government measure is inefficient, and therefore whether compensation is likely to encourage efficient investment decisions, is likely to pose considerable evidentiary problems. These practical difficulties invite a consideration of alternative institutional arrangements that might be able to provide a compensation structure that encourages efficient investment.

If an IIT does not provide compensation to investors for inefficient regulation, investors are in a strong position to protect themselves by pre-contracting with government.[40] On the other hand, if an IIT does provide compensation to investors for efficient regulation there is no countervailing penalty that can be levied on investors.[41] This analysis of substitutes suggests that, from the narrow perspective of encouraging efficient investment decisions, it is preferable to err by refusing compensation for an inefficient government measure than by awarding compensation for loss caused by an efficient measure.

D   Summary of efficiency

The examination of the impact of investment protection on efficiency can be summarised in the following three propositions:

---

[38] T. Miceli and K. Segerson, 'Regulatory takings: When should compensation be paid?', *Journal of Legal Studies*, 23 (1994), 749, 762.

[39] E. Aisbett, L. Karp and C. McAusland, 'Compensation for indirect expropriation in international investment agreements: Implications of national treatment and rights to invest', *Journal of Globalization and Development* (forthcoming, 2011), pt 3.2.

[40] J. Yackee, 'Do we really need BITs? Toward a return to contract in international investment law', *Asian Journal of WTO and Health Law*, 3 (2008), 121, 129.

[41] E. Aisbett, L. Karp and C. McAusland, 'Police powers, regulatory taking and the efficient compensation of domestic and foreign investors', *Economic Record*, 86 (2010), 367, 370.

1. Interpretations of IIT protections that place investors in a position of competitive equality are likely to lead to more efficient outcomes. Interpretations that give foreign investors greater or lesser legal rights than domestic investors are likely to decrease efficiency.
2. Determining whether IIT protections improve the efficiency of government decisions raises difficult empirical questions about the influences on public sector decision-making. From a theoretical perspective, it seems unlikely that legal protection of foreign investment will increase the efficiency of government decisions, regardless of how these protections are interpreted.
3. Interpretations of IIT protections that compensate investors for loss caused by inefficient government measures are likely to increase the efficiency of investment decisions. Interpretations of investment protections that compensate investors for loss caused by efficient government measures are likely to decrease the efficiency of investment decisions. In a situation of *ex post* uncertainty about the efficiency of an impugned government measure, the efficiency loss due to incorrectly compensating an investor is likely to be greater than efficiency loss due to incorrectly denying an investor compensation.

IV   Attraction of foreign direct investment

A   *Is additional FDI normatively desirable?*

The desire to attract FDI is widely cited as an explanation for States' decisions to sign investment treaties.[42] This is not because FDI has any intrinsic normative value. Rather, FDI is sought for its supposed instrumental value in promoting positive economic externalities – 'spillover' benefits that accrue to a host State beyond those associated with other forms of investment. This raises a threshold question of whether there is any evidence to support a correlation between FDI and identifiable externalities. There is some evidence that FDI is associated with higher wages, faster productivity growth and greater diffusion of knowledge than domestic investment, particularly in developing countries.[43]

---

[42] See UNCTAD, *South–south Cooperation in International Investment Agreements* (United Nations, Geneva 2007), p. 47.

[43] See the overview of empirical studies in T. H. Moran, E. M. Graham and M. Blomström, 'Introduction and overview' in T. H. Moran, E. M. Graham and M. Blomström (eds.), *Does Foreign Direct Investment Promote Development?* (Institute for International Economics, Washington 2005), p. 4. Although, contrast J. Robbins, 'The emergence of

For the purposes of argument, this chapter accepts the simplifying assumption that increases in FDI correlate with positive economic externalities. There are several pragmatic justifications for adopting this assumption: it seems to be accepted by States;[44] it is accepted in most of the existing literature;[45] and attempting to disaggregate the extent to which different types of investment are associated with different externalities would complicate the analysis enormously. As the following examination casts doubt on the hypothesis that IITs affect FDI flows, this simplifying assumption has little influence on the final analysis.

B   The relationship between BITs and FDI

A survey of scholarship examining the connection between bilateral investment treaties (BITs) and FDI reveals fourteen studies that claim statistically significant findings to support the hypothesis that signing BITs increases FDI.[46] This count includes: studies that find that only

positive obligations in bilateral investment treaties', *University of Miami International and Comparative Law Review*, 13 (2006), 403, 408.

[44] 'One uncontroversial truth is that virtually all countries value FDI as a means to advance their economic development.' L. Sachs and K. Sauvant, 'BITs, DTTs and FDI flows: An overview' in K. Sauvant and L. Sachs (eds.), *The Effect of Treaties on Foreign Direct Investment: Bilateral investment treaties, double taxation treaties and investment flows* (Oxford University Press, 2009), p. lx.

[45] J. Yackee, 'Are BITs such a bright idea? Exploring the ideational basis of investment treaty enthusiasm', *University of California Davis Journal of International Law and Policy*, 12 (2005), 195, 219.

[46] In K. Sauvant and L. Sachs (eds.), *The Effect of Treaties on Foreign Direct Investment: Bilateral investment treaties, double taxation treaties and investment flows* (Oxford University Press, 2009): J. Salacuse and N. Sullivan, 'Do BITs really work?: An evaluation of bilateral investment treaties and their grand bargain', p. 149; T. Buthe and H. V. Milner, 'Bilateral investment treaties and foreign direct investment: A political analysis', p. 213; E. Neumayer and L. Spess, 'Do bilateral investment treaties increase foreign direct investment to developing countries', p. 247; D. Swenson, 'Why do developing countries sign BITs?', p. 455; P. Egger and M. Pfaffermayr, 'The impact of bilateral investment treaties on foreign direct investment', p. 262; R. Grosse and L. Trevino, 'New institutional economics and FDI location in Central and Eastern Europe', p. 288; K. Gallagher and M. Birch, 'Do investment agreements attract investment? Evidence from Latin America', p. 305; UNCTAD, 'The impact on foreign direct investment of BITs', p. 347; T. Coupé, I. Orlova and A. Skiba, 'The effect of tax and investment treaties on bilateral FDI flows to transition economies', p. 709. Also, R. Banga, 'Impact of government policies and investment agreements on FDI inflows' (Working Paper No. 116, India Council for Research on International Economic Relations, November 2003), www.icrier.org/pdf/WP116.PDF (last accessed 6 December 2010), p. 34; K. Sokchea, 'Bilateral investment treaties, political risk and foreign direct investment', *Asia Pacific Journal of Economics & Business*, 11 (2007), 6, 22; P. Egger and V. Merlo, 'The impact of bilateral investment

some types of BITs increase FDI;[47] two studies reporting apparently contradictory findings – one that only US BITs increase co-signatories' FDI and another that most BITs increase FDI but US BITs do not increase co-signatories' FDI from the US;[48] a study that finds only a 'minor and secondary' relationship between BITs and FDI;[49] and a study that finds that BITs increase FDI but with diminishing returns of FDI to each additional BIT a country signs.[50] A further five studies reject the hypothesis that BITs increase FDI.[51]

There are several obstacles to reliable testing of the causal relationship between FDI and BITs. They include: measurement problems – finding data on financial flows and determining which financial flows should count as FDI; coding issues – for example, determining whether all BITs or only those with certain characteristics (such as compulsory investor–State arbitration) constitute the independent variable;[52] and, most significantly, endogeneity problems – disentangling reverse-causality effects and controlling for policy shifts made concurrently with the signing of BITs.[53]

treaties on FDI dynamics', *The World Economy*, 30 (2007), 1536, 1546; C. H. Oh and M. Fratianni, 'Do additional bilateral investment treaties boost foreign direct investment?' (2010), http://mofir.univpm.it/files/working%20paper/Mofir_43.pdf (last accessed 6 December 2010), p. 17; M. Busse, J. Königer and P. Nunnenkamp, 'FDI promotion through bilateral investment treaties: More than a bit?' (2008), www.econstor.eu/bitstream/10419/4227/1/kap1403.pdf (last accessed 6 December 2010), p. 27.

[47] Banga, 'Impact of government policies and investment agreements', p. 34; Sokchea, 'Bilateral investment treaties, political risk and foreign direct investment', p. 22.

[48] Salacuse and Sullivan, 'Do BITs really work?', p. 148; Gallagher and Birch, 'Do investment agreements attract investment?', p. 305.

[49] UNCTAD, 'The impact on foreign direct investment of BITs', p. 347.

[50] Oh and Fratianni, 'Do additional bilateral investment treaties boost foreign direct investment?', p. 17.

[51] In K. Sauvant and L. Sachs (eds.), *The Effect of Treaties on Foreign Direct Investment: Bilateral investment treaties, double taxation treaties and investment flows* (Oxford University Press, 2009): M. Hallward-Driemeier, 'Do bilateral investment treaties attract FDI? Only a Bit . . . And They Could Bite', p. 374; J. Yackee, 'Do BITs really work? Revisiting the empirical link between investment treaties and foreign direct investment', p. 390; E. Aisbett, 'Bilateral investment treaties and foreign direct investment: Correlation versus causation', p. 414. Also, J. Tobin and S. Rose-Ackerman, 'Foreign direct investment and the business environment in developing countries: The impact of bilateral investment treaties', *Yale Law and Economics Research Paper*, No. 293 (2005), 31; W. Mina, 'External commitment mechanisms, institutions, and FDI in GCC countries', *International Financial Markets, Institutions and Money*, 19 (2009), 371, 383.

[52] J. Yackee, 'Conceptual difficulties in the empirical study of bilateral investment treaties', *Brooklyn Journal of International Law*, 33(2) (2008), 405, 441.

[53] Aisbett, 'Bilateral investment treaties and foreign direct investment', p. 396.

Overall, the studies that better control for endogeneity appear less likely to find a causal relationship between BITs and FDI.[54] Indeed, in an important article, Aisbett shows that the results of two of the studies supporting a causal link between BITs and FDI are not robust once endogeneity effects are controlled for.[55] That the findings of studies which support a relationship between BIT–FDI are not consistent with one another casts further doubt on their reliability. Together, the issues of endogeneity effects and consistency cast serious doubts on the hypothesis that BITs increase FDI. The tentative conclusion must be that the relationship between BITs and FDI is unclear.

C   Conclusion

The examination of the impact of investment protection on FDI can be summarised in the following propositions:

1. Current evidence casts doubt on the hypothesis that BITs increase FDI.
2. If entering IITs does not increase FDI, then different interpretations of individual IIT protections are highly unlikely to have any consequences for FDI flows.

V   Regulatory chill: The consequences of IIT protections for the realisation of human rights and for environmental conservation

This section examines the consequences of IIT protections for the realisation of human rights and the protection of the environment in host States. Any impact of IIT protections stems from their effect on the way in which host States exercise their regulatory powers – an effect sometimes described as 'regulatory chill'.[56] This section examines the extent to which IIT protections are likely to cause regulatory chill, and

---

[54] Hallward-Driemeier, 'Do bilateral investment treaties attract FDI?', p. 358; Yackee, 'Do BITs really work?', p. 389; Aisbett, 'Bilateral investment treaties and foreign direct investment', p. 414.

[55] Aisbett, 'Bilateral investment treaties and foreign direct investment', pp. 395, 410.

[56] High Commissioner for Human Rights, 'Economic, social and cultural rights: Human rights, trade and investment', UN Doc. E/CN.4/Sub.2/2003/9 (2 July 2003), p. 21; Been and Beauvais, 'The global Fifth Amendment?', p. 132; S. Schill, 'Do investment treaties chill unilateral State regulation to mitigate climate change?', *Journal of International Arbitration*, 24(5) (2007), 469, 470; K. Tienhaara, *The Expropriation of Environmental Governance: Protecting foreign investors at the expense of public policy* (Cambridge University Press, 2009), p. 262.

the consequences of regulatory chill for the realisation of human rights and the protection of the environment.

A Conceptual issues in an inquiry into regulatory chill

Chilling effects are difficult to identify because they require counter-factual evidence about the regulations that would have existed in the absence of the purported chilling.[57] Regulatory chill due to IIT protections is particularly difficult to isolate because, in addition to identifying a chilling effect, one must be able to exclude the possibility that it was attributable to some other cause.

One starting point of existing discussions of 'chilling' effects is doctrinal inquiry – inquiry that examines whether certain types of governmental measures would give rise to liability under IIT protections. Schill, for example, argues that IIT protections will not chill unilateral State regulation to mitigate climate change because proportionate and reasonable mitigation measures would not breach IITs.[58] The twin assumptions which underpin this methodology are that States will be dissuaded from adopting measures that entail liability but will not be dissuaded from adopting measures that do not. Other scholars contest the second assumption, while implicitly accepting the first. They argue that uncertainty about the implications of IIT protections for specific regulatory proposals will discourage decision-makers from adopting measures that would have been permissible regulation.[59]

---

[57] E. Neumayer, *Greening Trade and Investment* (Earthscan, London 2001), p. 78.

[58] Schill, 'Do investment treaties chill unilateral State regulation to mitigate climate change?', p. 477. Similarly, K. Vandevelde, *Bilateral Investment Treaties: History, Policy and Interpretation* (Oxford University Press, 2010), p. 107.

[59] S. Louthan, 'A brave new Lochner era? The constitutionality of NAFTA Chapter 11', *Vanderbilt Journal of Transnational Law*, 34 (2001), 1443, 1446; Been and Beauvais, 'The global Fifth Amendment?', p. 134; R. Bachand and S. Rousseau, 'International investment and human rights: Political and legal issues' (Background Paper for the Think Tank Rights and Democracy, 11 June 2003), www.ichrdd.ca/site/_PDF/publications/globalization/bachandRousseauEng.pdf (last accessed 6 December 2010), p. 21; H. Mann, 'Investment agreements and the regulatory State: Can exceptions clauses create a safe haven for governments?' (International Institute for Sustainable Development, 2007), www.iisd.org/pdf/2007/inv_agreements_reg_state.pdf (last accessed 6 December 2010), p. 5; R. Suda, 'The effect of bilateral investment treaties on human rights enforcement and realization', Global Law Working Paper 01/05 (Hauser Global Law Program, New York University), n. 103; J. Waincymer, 'Balancing property rights and human rights in expropriation' in P.-M. Dupuy, F. Francioni and E.-U. Petersmann (eds.), *Human Rights in International Investment Law and Arbitration* (Oxford University Press, 2009), p. 306.

The division among existing contributions illustrates a useful conceptual distinction between two types of regulatory chill that might be caused by IIT protections: the chilling of measures that would clearly give rise to liability; and the chilling of measures that may not give rise to liability. For the former type of regulatory chill to occur, at least two empirical conditions would need to be present: decision-makers would need to be aware of the existence of IITs;[60] and concerned (as opposed to indifferent) about the possibility of the State being required to compensate foreign investors.[61] For the latter type of regulatory chill to occur a third, additional, condition must be present: there must be uncertainty regarding the application of IIT protections to specific proposals under consideration.

There is a further empirical distinction, within both types of regulatory chill, between the effect of IITs in dissuading decision-makers from *adopting* regulatory measures and their effect in dissuading States from *maintaining* or *enforcing* regulatory measures. When the adoption of new regulations is being contemplated, decision-makers would need independent knowledge of IITs for the existence of IIT protections to have any influence on their decision-making.[62] In contrast, once a measure has been introduced (or, at least, once it has been proposed in a public consultation), affected foreign investors are more likely to be aware of the measure. If affected investors threaten legal action or lobby against the measure on the basis of an IIT, the relevant decision-maker will be alerted to the existence of the IIT.[63] The empirical question that follows is: whether such threats of litigation have any influence on decisions to maintain or enforce existing regulation?

B   What sort of evidence would be needed to test hypotheses about regulatory chill?

To empirically test the extent of 'adoption' and 'maintenance' regulatory chill effects, different types of case studies would be needed. Investigation

[60] S. Franck, 'The legitimacy crisis in investment treaty arbitration: Privatizing public international law through inconsistent decisions', *Fordham Law Review*, 73 (2005), 1521, 1592.
[61] J. Coe and N. Rubins, 'Regulatory expropriation and the *Tecmed* case: Context and contributions' in T. Weiler (ed.), *International Investment Law and Arbitration: Leading cases from the ICSID, NAFTA, bilateral treaties and customary international law* (Cameron May, London 2005), p. 599. Most scholars accept as self-evident that States will be concerned about the risk of liability, e.g. Mann, 'Investment agreements and the regulatory State', p. 5.
[62] Coe and Rubins, 'Regulatory expropriation and the *Tecmed* case', p. 599.
[63] Tienhaara, *The Expropriation of Environmental Governance*, p. 262.

of cases in which foreign investors have publicly cited IIT protections in opposing regulations, including cases where the investor commences international arbitration, would be useful in identifying 'maintenance' chill. In contrast, a systematic examination of 'adoption' chill would need to focus on cases of governmental decision-making when there was no public opposition to a measure by foreign investors. To my knowledge, no such research has been published.

An additional complexity in the study of regulatory chill is that variation in the characteristics of decision-making bodies, both within and between countries, is likely to lead to variation in the extent of regulatory chill. Within countries, national governments – which bear initial responsibility for paying any adverse award in international arbitration – may be more sensitive to the risk of liability under IITs than decision-makers with a high degree of autonomy from national government.[64] Between countries, one might expect that decision-makers in developing countries, which are less able to finance adverse arbitral awards, would be more concerned about avoiding liability under IITs than decision-makers in developed countries.[65] These hypotheses are both plausible, yet they raise essentially empirical questions.

C Regulatory chill 1: Liability and chilling

This section examines the assumption that States are dissuaded from adopting or maintaining measures that would give rise to liability under IITs. A brief survey of decided cases reveals a number in which States maintained measures that purported to pursue environmental benefits, notwithstanding the ultimate expense of compensating foreign investors, among them: *Metalclad* v. *Mexico*; *Tecmed* v. *Mexico*; and *Santa Elena* v. *Costa Rica*.[66] Similarly, in two cases involving water privatisation – *Aguas del Tunari* v. *Bolivia* and *Biwater* v. *Tanzania* – the States in question cancelled water concession contracts, purporting to protect the right to water.[67] The arbitration in *Aguas del Tunari* ultimately

---

[64] Been and Beauvais, 'The global Fifth Amendment?', p. 90.

[65] Mann, 'Investment agreements and the regulatory State', p. 5.

[66] *Metalclad* v. *Mexico* (ICSID Case No. ARB(AF)/97/1, Award of 30 August 2000); *Técnicas Medioambientales Tecmed SA* v. *Mexico* (ICSID Case No. ARB(AF)/00/02, Award of 29 May 2003); *Compañía del Desarrollo de Santa Elena SA* v. *Republic of Costa Rica* (ICSID Case No. ARB(AF)/00/01, Final Award of 17 February 2000).

[67] *Compañia de Aguas del Aconquija SA and Vivendi Universal SA* v. *Argentine Republic* (ICSID Case No. ARB/97/3, Award of 20 August 2007); *Biwater Gauff (Tanzania) Ltd* v. *United Republic of Tanzania* (ICSID Case No. ARB/05/22, Award of 24 July 2008).

settled.[68] In *Biwater* the Tanzanian government was found liable for breaching the BIT in question, although no economic loss to the foreign investor flowed from the breach.

This survey is unlikely to be representative of the effect of liability under IIT protections on regulatory decisions. Arbitration normally involves cases in which States have not been dissuaded from maintaining measures, and brings such cases to public attention. In contrast, situations where a State has been dissuaded from maintaining measures do not have an equivalent mechanism by which they are publicised. Care should be taken not to overestimate the extent to which States maintain measures that will clearly give rise to liability.

There is a dearth of evidence relating to the effect of IIT protections on the adoption of regulatory measures. In the absence of specific evidence to the contrary, a reasonable hypothesis is that administrative decision-makers that do not have direct and ongoing dealings with foreign investors are not aware of IITs.[69] On this basis, it is likely that most decision-makers do not internalise the constraints of IIT protections when evaluating the adoption of new governmental measures.[70] However, this hypothesis must be open to revision in light of future evidence if and when it comes to light.

D   Regulatory chill 2: Uncertainty and chilling

This section examines the assumption that States are not dissuaded from adopting or maintaining measures that would not have given rise to liability under IITs. It is more difficult to find evidence to test this assumption. Among Tienhaara's fourteen detailed case studies, there are only two cases in which States abandoned arguably permissible measures due to the threat of litigation under IITs: the notorious *Ethyl Corp.* v. *Canada* and the less well-known events surrounding Vannessa Ventures dealings with the Costa Rican environmental authorities.[71]

---

[68] D. Vis-Dunbar and L. E. Peterson, 'Bolivian water dispute settled, Bechtel forgoes compensation', *Investment Treaty News* (22 January 2006), www.iisd.org/pdf/2006/itn_jan20_2006.pdf (last accessed 6 December 2010).

[69] Coe and Rubins, 'Regulatory expropriation and the *Tecmed* case', p. 599.

[70] Contrast with, D. Schneiderman, *Constitutionalizing Economic Globalization: Investment Rules and Democracy's Promise* (Cambridge University Press, 2008), p. 114.

[71] Tienhaara, *The Expropriation of Environmental Governance*, p. 157.

Gross describes a further case in Indonesia – a remarkably similar constellation of facts to the case of Vannessa Ventures.[72]

In all three cases there seems to have been some chilling effect. The more difficult question is whether the abandoned measures were likely to have been permissible. In each it seems that the State had an arguable case on the merits, suggesting that either uncertainty about the implications of IIT protections, or concern about the costs of arbitration, played a role. The facts of *Ethyl* bear some similarity to a later case, *Methanex* v. *US*, in which the US successfully defended a ban on a gasoline additive on environmental grounds.[73] This suggests that the abandoned measure may have been permissible. The Costa Rican and Indonesian cases raise more difficult legal issues. Both essentially involved a government agency refusing to issue a foreign investor the necessary permits to commence open-pit mining on a concession owned by the investor. Other tribunals appear to have accepted that States are entitled to refuse permission for land to be used in a certain way, so long as fair administrative processes are followed and the State has not made any assurances to the contrary to the investor.[74] This suggests that the strength of both Costa Rica's and Indonesia's defences would have depended on the scope of permission held by and the assurances made to mining companies before the changes in policy.

In contrast, there are examples in which decision-makers have maintained permissible environmental and human rights measures, despite opposition from foreign investors. In *Methanex* v. *US*, *Glamis Gold* v. *US* and *Lucchetti* v. *Peru* the respective respondent States maintained the impugned measures throughout arbitration proceedings and ultimately avoided liability.[75] Similarly, the South African government has maintained its affirmative action policies in the mining sector, which were the subject of arbitration in *Piero Foresti* v. *South Africa*.[76]

---

[72] S. Gross, 'Inordinate chill: BITs non-NAFTA MITs and host State regulatory freedom: An Indonesian case study', *Michigan Journal of International Law*, 24 (2003), 893, 895.

[73] D. Gantz, 'Potential conflict between investor rights and environmental regulation under NAFTA's Chapter 11', *George Washington International Law Review*, 33 (2001), 651, 665.

[74] *MTD* v. *Chile* (ICSID Case No. ARB/01/7, Award of 21 May 2004), para. 163; *Tecmed*, para. 173; *Metalclad*, para. 97.

[75] *Methanex* v. *United States of America* (Award on Jurisdiction and Merits of 7 September 2005); *Glamis Gold* v. *United States of America* (Award of 8 June 2009); *Lucchetti* v. *Peru* (ICSID Case No. ARB/03/4, Award of 7 February 2005).

[76] *Piero Foresti, Laura de Carli and ors* v. *Republic of South Africa* (ICSID Case No. ARB (AF)/07/1).

Overall, it is clear that foreign investors' invocation of IIT protections does not always lead to the chilling of the governmental measure subject to challenge. That said, there is some evidence to suggest that IIT protections do, on occasion, dissuade States from maintaining measures that may not have given rise to liability – enough evidence to throw serious doubt on the hypothesis that any chilling is limited only to measures that would breach IIT protections. This is all the more so given that there is likely to be a bias in available evidence, with cases in which regulation is not chilled being more likely to come to public attention. While the evidence is complex and inconclusive, the implications of the theory that uncertainty increases regulatory chill are relatively clear: interpretations that provide decision-makers with greater certainty about how IIT protections would apply to governmental measures will reduce the chilling of permissible measures.

E   The consequence of regulatory chill for human rights and environmental conservation

Finally, there is the key issue of the impact of chilling effects on the realisation of human rights and the protection of the environment. Assessing this impact requires comparison of the consequences of regulation that was not adopted (or not maintained) with the consequences of regulation actually introduced. This assessment raises complex empirical questions. Chilling is unlikely to lead to improvements in the realisation of human rights or environmental conservation. The effectiveness of measures to realise human rights is a function of their consequences for a wide range of individuals; the effectiveness of measures to protect the environment is a function of their achievement of non-economic conservation objectives. While the economic interests of foreign investors may occasionally coincide with these objectives,[77] they are not representative of them. As a result, reluctance on the part of decision-makers to interfere with the interests of foreign investors is unlikely to inadvertently lead to the realisation of these objectives.

---

[77] e.g. in late 2009 Graeme Hall Sanctuary filed a notice of dispute under the Canada–Barbados BIT against Barbados. The prospective claimant alleged that Barbados had violated the BIT by failing to enforce its own environmental laws. E. Whitsitt, 'Claimant seeks enforcement of environmental laws in notice of dispute alleging expropriation of Barbadian nature sanctuary', *Investment Treaty News* (14 February 2010), www.iisd.org/itn/2010/02/10/claimant-seeks-enforcement-of-environmental-laws-in-notice-of-dispute-alleging-expropriation-of-barbadian-nature-sanctuary/ (last accessed 6 December 2010), p. 4.

The extent of negative consequence for the realisation of human rights and environmental conservation will depend on the particular interpretation of an IIT protection under consideration. This difference in consequences stems from variation in the risk of decision-makers being discouraged from enacting measure that are effective in realising these objectives because they impose costs on foreign investors. For example, an interpretation in which the effectiveness of a measure in realising human rights weighs against an ultimate finding of liability under an IIT is less likely to chill effective human rights measures than an otherwise identical interpretation in which the human rights impacts of a measure are deemed irrelevant.

F   Summary of regulatory chill

The examination of regulatory chill can be summarised in the following propositions:

1. The extent of regulatory chill is likely to vary between decision-makers within and between countries.
2. There is little evidence to suggest that concern about liability under IIT protections is internalised in decision-making processes, thereby chilling the adoption of governmental measures. Evidence of chilling consists primarily of cases in which States have not maintained measures in the face of opposition from foreign investors based on IITs protections.
3. States are less likely to maintain measures that give rise to liability under IIT protections than to maintain measures that do not.
4. In theory, one would expect interpretations of IIT protections that provide greater certainty to decision-makers to reduce the chilling of measures that would not have given rise to liability.
5. Chilling effects are highly unlikely to have positive consequences for the realisation of human rights and environmental conservation. The extent of any negative consequences will depend on the interpretation of the IIT protection in question.

VI   Consequences for the rule of law

The protections contained in IITs may also affect host States' legal institutions and the formal characteristics of the laws promulgated and enforced by them. Raz's seminal work on the rule of law proposes three desirable characteristics of laws and a further five desirable characteristics of the legal institutions that enforce them.[78] The formal characteristics that law should possess are that it be: prospective, open and clear; relatively stable; and that the making of particular (subsidiary) laws should be guided by open clear and stable general rules.[79] The principles governing legal institutions include that: the judiciary should be independent; the courts should be accessible; and natural justice should be observed.[80] This chapter adopts the Razian conception of the rule of law and takes as given that the qualities he identifies are intrinsically normatively desirable.

Other scholars have argued for broader conceptions of the rule of law that address the substantive content, as well as the formal characteristics, of law.[81] For the purpose of this chapter, it is unnecessary to resolve debates about whether the Razian conception is unduly narrow. The consequences of IIT protections for the substantive content of host-governmental regulations are examined above, in terms of efficiency and the realisation of human rights and environmental conservation. The purpose of this section is to identify the consequences of IIT protections on the formal and institutional qualities of host States' legal systems – their Razian characteristics – that are not assessed in previous sections.

A   Distinguishing debate about international arbitration and the rule of law

Most discussion of the relationship between IITs and the rule of law centres on the institutions and procedures of investor–State arbitration. Many of the references to the rule of law are somewhat opaque, but they seem to reflect a belief that the resolution of investment disputes by legal adjudication, rather than by negotiation or political pressure, is more consistent with the rule of law.[82] Van Harten rejects this view, arguing

---

[78] J. Raz, 'The rule of law and its virtue', *The Law Quarterly Review*, 93 (1977), 195, 202.

[79] *Ibid.*, p. 198.   [80] *Ibid.*, p. 200.

[81] P. Craig, 'Formal and substantive conceptions of the rule of law: An analytical framework', *Public Law*, (1997), 467.

[82] G. Sampliner, 'Arbitration of expropriation cases under U.S. investment treaties: A threat to democracy of the dog that didn't bark', *ICSID Review – Foreign Investment Law Journal*, 18 (2003), 41; UNCTAD, 'Development implications of international investment agreements', *IIA Monitor No. 2 (2007): International Investment Agreements*, UN Doc. No. UNCTAD/WEB/ITE/IAA/2007/2 (2007), p. 5; Paulsson, 'Indirect expropriation', p. 2; Vandevelde, *Bilateral Investment Treaties*, p. 119; C. Brower and L. Steven,

that arbitration is inconsistent with the rule of law because 'There can be no rule of law without an independent judiciary.'[83] For present purposes, however, it is not necessary to determine the extent to which the resolution of international investment disputes through compulsory investor–State arbitration is consistent with the rule of law. This chapter presents a framework to evaluate interpretations of the substantive protections contained in IITs, taking as given that these protections can be enforced through investor–State arbitration.

B   Consequences of IIT protections for the rule of law in host States

Only a handful of scholars have reflected on the relationship between IITs and improvements in the rule of law in host States. These contributions fall into two opposing camps. One view is that IITs, and international arbitration under them, complement domestic legal systems. According to this theory, arbitration under IITs demonstrates the benefits of impartial legal institutions, thereby engendering domestic support in host States for reforms that promote the rule of law.[84] The alternate view is that IITs entrench weakness in domestic legal systems.[85] This theory runs that, by allowing foreign investors to exit the domestic legal regime, international investment arbitration removes an important constituency that might advocate for greater respect for the law and stronger legal institutions at the domestic level. Determining which view is correct raises a complex set of empirical questions, which have not yet been investigated in great detail. The only existing empirical treatment, Ginsburg's regression analysis, suggests that signing IITs has a minor negative impact on the rule of law in signatory States.[86]

In any case, both theories are based on the argument that the ability of foreign investors to access compulsory investor–State arbitration will have consequences for the respect for the rule of law in host States. As such, both theories suggest that the extent of any impact on the rule

'Who then should judge? Developing the international rule of law under NAFTA Chapter 11', *Chicago Journal of International Law*, 2(1) (2001), 193, 202.

[83] G. van Harten, *Investment Treaty Arbitration and Public Law* (Oxford University Press, 2007), p. 174.

[84] S. Franck, 'Foreign direct investment, investment treaty arbitration, and the rule of law', *Global Business and Development Law Journal*, 19 (2007), 337, 367. Similarly, Walde and Weiler, 'Investment arbitration under the Energy Charter Treaty', n. 22.

[85] T. Ginsburg, 'International substitutes for domestic institutions: Bilateral investment treaties and governance', *International Review of Law and Economics*, 25 (2005), 107, 119.

[86] *Ibid.*, p. 121.

of law in particular States would vary with the presence (absence) of provisions in IITs that govern the ability of investors to exit the domestic legal system and access arbitration: exhaustion of local remedies requirements, fork-in-the-road clauses, umbrella clauses and the like. Neither theory implies an obvious relationship between the interpretation of the substantive protections of IITs and consequences for the rule of law.

In the abstract, only tentative hypotheses are possible about the relationship between different interpretations of substantive IIT protections and the improvements in the rule of law in domestic legal systems. Reasoning from first principles, the most that can be said is: interpretations that impose liability when a measure does not comply with the requirements of the rule of law but do not impose liability when a measure does meet the requirements of the rule of law are more likely to create an incentive structure that encourages respect for the rule of law in host States. Interpretations in which the determination of liability for a measure is independent of whether the measure meets the requirements of the rule of law are unlikely to create such incentives. This hypothesis must be open to revision in light of future evidence if and when it comes to light. The hypothesis, as stated, provides a consequence-based rationale for deference to host States' substantive judgments.

C   Summary of rule of law

The examination of the rule of law can be summarised in the following two propositions:

1. Little is known about the impact of the substantive protections of IITs on the respect for the rule of law in host States.
2. In theory, interpretations where a State's liability depends on a measure's non-compliance with Razian rule of law norms are more likely to create an incentive structure that encourages respect for the rule of law.

VII   Conclusion

This chapter presents a framework for identifying and evaluating the consequences of different interpretations of IIT protections. These consequences can be divided into five categories – the effect of IIT protections on: the distribution of wealth; efficiency; flows of FDI into host States; the realisation of human rights and environmental conservation in host States; and respect for the rule of law in host States. I hope that others will find this framework to be a constructive contribution to ongoing normative debate about IITs. In my view, it is also a useful basis for further normative research.[87] While this chapter does not attempt to apply the evaluative framework, it is worth drawing attention to three general insights that emerge from it.

First, the economic justifications for IIT protections are weaker than might be assumed. Evidence on the relationship between BITs and FDI flows suggests that broader (pro-investor) interpretations of individual IIT protections are unlikely to increase FDI flows. The analysis of economic efficiency is more nuanced; however, interpretations that are more favourable to the interests of foreign investors are not, self-evidently, associated with greater efficiency.

Secondly, a lack of evidence inhibits a full understanding of the consequences of IIT protections for the realisation of human rights, environmental conservation and respect for the rule of law in host States. Any generalisations relating to the realisation of these objectives must be cautious, relying on evidence to the extent it exists, and with theoretical arguments complementing evidence where possible. On this basis, interpretations of IIT protections in which liability turns on an examination of whether the exercise of governmental power in question is consistent with the realisation of human rights, environmental conservation and the rule of law are more likely to lead to the realisation of these objectives than interpretations in which liability turns on the degree of interference with the interests of the investor. This tentative conclusion gives partial support to the argument that IIT protections should be interpreted in conformity with public law values, albeit for different reasons.

Thirdly, IIT protections have significant distributive consequences that are clearly demonstrated by existing evidence. Evaluation of distributive consequences should be more central to normative debate about the interpretation of IIT protections than the existing literature acknowledges.

---

[87] In my doctoral research, I apply the framework to evaluate alternate interpretations of the indirect expropriation, fair and equitable treatment and national treatment protections contained in IITs.

7

Investment treaty arbitration as global administrative law: What this might mean in practice

DANIEL KALDERIMIS*

I Introduction

In 2008, Professor Jan Paulsson gave an address in Montreal in which he declared dramatically that 'international arbitration is not arbitration'.[1] It is not the aim of the present chapter to contend that investment treaty arbitration is not arbitration. That is a feat of debating for which only Professor Paulsson would be qualified. However, the premise advanced does have more than a whiff of paradox about it: that bilateral investment treaties (BITs) are not international investment agreements; they are instruments of global administrative law. The purpose of this chapter is to consider what this might mean in practice.

My premise is nothing new. It was the central thesis of Gus van Harten's seminal 2007 book, *Investment Treaty Arbitration and Public Law*. In that book, he neatly summarised his case as follows:

> Investment treaty arbitration is often viewed as a form of reciprocally consensual adjudication between an investor and a state. The argument of this chapter is that it should be viewed as a mechanism of adjudicative review in public law. That is the case for two reasons: first, the system is established by a sovereign act of the state; second, it is predominantly used to resolve disputes arising from the exercise of sovereign authority . . . As a public law system, investment treaty arbitration engages the regulatory relationship between state and individual, rather than a reciprocal relationship between juridical equals.

---

* This chapter is based on a presentation given by the author at the International Investment Treaty Law and Arbitration Conference, University of Sydney, 19–20 February 2010.
[1] J. Paulsson, 'International arbitration is not arbitration' (Paper presented at the John E. C. Brierley Memorial Lecture, McGill University, Montreal, 28 May 2008).

> Indeed, unlike any other form of international arbitration, it gives private arbitrators a comprehensive jurisdiction over disputes in the regulatory sphere.[2]

I consider van Harten's thesis to be the single most profound observation about investment treaty arbitration made in the last ten years. But I think its implications have yet to be grasped by participants and practitioners in the system.

Consider, for example, a simple BIT such as that between Australia and Argentina.[3] This does not look particularly like a public law document. It is written in anodyne, technical language; it does not refer to regulatory principle; it does not in any obvious way seek to balance investor rights against State functions. At first glance, it is simply an international treaty between two consenting countries, which accords limited and defined rights to private investors to be vindicated in a private forum – a hybrid of international law and private law.[4] Is it unduly presumptuous to consider that it contains public law implications?

I do not consider that it is. Even though the form of the Australia–Argentina BIT is unprepossessing, woven into the DNA of that instrument are precisely the very same intractable issues which arise in

---

[2] G. van Harten, *Investment Treaty Arbitration and Public Law* (Oxford University Press, 2007), p. 45. See also G. van Harten and M. Loughlin, 'Investment treaty arbitration as a species of global administrative law', *European Journal of International Law*, 17 (2006), 121.

[3] Agreement between the Government of Australia and the Government of the Argentine Republic on the Promotion and Protection of Investments, signed on 23 August 1995 (entered into force 11 January 1997).

[4] For the well-known account of the hybrid and *sui generis* nature of investment treaties – as being simultaneously international law and commercial instruments, but importantly different from both – see Z. Douglas, 'The hybrid foundations of investment treaty arbitration', *British Yearbook of International Law*, 74 (2003), 151 at 153 in which Douglas points out:

> the present tendency is for States to see elements of diplomatic protection lurking in the shadows cast by investment treaties, whereas investors are often convinced of a striking resemblance to international commercial arbitration. The *lex arbitri* created by the investment treaty regime, as this study will demonstrate, is a long way from both these legal institutions for the resolution of disputes.

Whilst recognising the uniqueness of investment treaties, Douglas did not in that article focus on their public law dimension. See, more recently, Z. Douglas, *The International Law of Investment Claims* (Cambridge University Press, 2010), pp. 6–12.

domestic administrative law. Two immediate and basic questions hint at the swirling depths within:

1. What is the true meaning of Article 4(1), which provides that: 'each Contracting Party shall at all times ensure fair and equitable treatment ('FET') to investments'? The FET standard is fast becoming the international investment law equivalent of a legitimate expectations doctrine – and, unlike its domestic law equivalents, has been rapidly applied to expectations of result as well as of due process. But precisely when, how and to what extent does a published policy of a government effectively bind it to a course of action? By what jurisprudential yardstick does one define the meaning and nuances of this standard?

2. What are the limits of Article 7(1), which provides that: 'Neither Contracting Party shall nationalise, expropriate or subject to measures having effect equivalent to expropriation the instruments of investors of the other Contracting Party', unless the expropriation is for a public purpose, non-discriminatory and accompanied by the payment of prompt, adequate and effective compensation? What is the precise meaning of 'measures having effect equivalent to expropriation'? Is a measure with this effect forbidden if it is a reasonable exercise of state regulatory powers?

Many more such questions exist; consider, for example, the comparison exercise required for national treatment, the extension of most-favoured nation (MFN) clauses to procedural rights, the role of *bona fides* for investors seeking relief and the umbrella clause debates. Where an investment treaty dispute arises in connection with a contractual dispute there are also familiar questions about when it is appropriate for, in effect, commercial State entities to be made subject – directly or indirectly – to more stringent disciplines than purely private parties.

Van Harten's insight was that the procedural innovation allowing an investor to prosecute international treaty rights directly against a State has created a whole new area of substantive law. That area of law is neither international commercial arbitration, nor is it public international law; although it is the offspring of, and has considerable elements of, both. Properly understood, investment treaty arbitration is part of what Benedict Kingsbury called the 'efflorescent' – unfolding as if coming into flower – field of global administrative law. This insight is important for those who practice in the area; and especially for those who adjudicate it.

II   Global administrative law

The origins of global administrative law as a discrete concept can be traced in large part to the work done by, and in association with, NYU Law School's Global Administrative Law Project.[5] In the same essay in which he coined his superb adjectival label, Kingsbury offered a desultory definition of global administrative law, which I gratefully adopt:

> The idea of the emerging global administrative law is animated in part by the view that much of global governance (particularly global regulatory governance) can usefully be analysed as administration. Instead of neatly separated levels of regulation (private, local, national, inter-state) a congeries of different actors and different layers together form a variegated 'global administrative space' that includes international institutions and transnational networks, as well as domestic administrative bodies that operate within international regimes or cause transboundary regulatory effects. The idea of a 'global administrative space' marks a departure from those orthodox understandings of international law in which the international is largely inter-governmental, and there is a reasonably sharp separation of the domestic and the international. In the practice of global governance, transnational networks of rule-generators, interpreters and appliers cause such strict boundaries to break down.[6]

Investment treaty arbitration is one such transnational network of interpreters, appliers and – some would contend – rule-generators. But it is by no means the only one. Another obvious example is the World Trade Organization (WTO), which has long been recognised as an institution of global governance, and has more recently been contextualised as a vehicle for the making of global administrative law.[7]

---

[5] The Project's website is at www.iilj.org/GAL. For a sample of some of the articles in this field, see: B. Kingsbury, N. Krisch and R. Stewart, 'The emergence of global administrative law', *Law and Contemporary Problems*, 68 (2005), 15; C. Marian, 'Balancing transparency: The value of administrative law and mathews-balancing to investment treaty arbitrations', *Pepperdine Dispute Resolution Law Journal*, 10 (2010), 275; T. Wuertenberger and M. Karacz, 'Using an evaluative comparative law analysis to develop global administrative law principles', *Michigan State Journal of International Law*, 17 (2008), 567; A. Somek, 'The concept of "law" in global administrative law: A reply to Benedict Kingsbury', *European Journal of International Law*, 20 (2010), 985; and M. S. Kuo, 'The concept of "law" in global administrative law: A reply to Benedict Kingsbury', *European Journal of International Law*, 20 (2010), 997.

[6] B. Kingsbury, 'The concept of "law" in global administrative law', *European Journal of International Law*, 20 (2009), 23, 24.

[7] See e.g. R. Stewart, 'The World Trade Organization: Multiple dimensions of global administrative law' (Discussion Draft, New York University Paper, January 2009).

III   Neither international commercial arbitration nor public international law are appropriate paradigms

This chapter contends that neither of the two paradigms which gave birth to investment treaty law – international commercial arbitration and public international law – themselves contain the necessary concepts for constructively developing this new field. Yet, largely because of familiarity with one or both of these paradigms, many arbitrators still approach investment treaty decisions as if they can manfully wrestle the square peg into the round hole.

Let us consider first international commercial arbitration. Arbitrators with a strong background in this field are professional contractual dispute-resolvers. Their skill lies in procedural fairness, forensic and witness skills, effective case management and, above all else, producing a timely and enforceable decision. For them, interpreting an investment treaty is a matter of sensible construction based on the words of the treaty, in light of the submissions of the parties. Although some regard may be had to previous decisions on a point, these are dismissed with the (entirely correct) observation that those decisions are not binding and often arise under differently worded instruments. One will often find extensive recounting of the procedural history of the arbitration, contrasted with concise legal reasoning unburdened by exegesis, express reliance on extrinsic material or controversial conceptual baggage. This approach is simple, effective and difficult to challenge. But – in the result – it is not very helpful. For whether we like it or not, the phrase 'fair and equitable treatment' in a BIT is simply too large to be construed as if it were a troublesome contractual indemnity. That provision carries within it deep questions about the relation of the individual and the State which in other contexts have vexed some of the world's greatest jurists. It cannot sensibly be dismissed in two paragraphs of prose.

Next, let us consider public international law. There is no doubt that investment treaties are treaties and that investment treaty arbitration takes place on the plane of public international law. But just because investment treaties are a modern incarnation of public international law does not entail that traditional public international law concepts are adequate to resolve all investment treaty arbitration questions. Interpretation debates carried out in the name of the 1969 Vienna Convention on the Law of Treaties (VCLT)[8] have a slightly arid ring.

---

[8] Vienna Convention on the Law of Treaties, opened for signature 23 May 1969, 1155 UNTS 331 (entered into force 27 January 1980).

That is, Articles 31 and 32 of the VCLT do lay down the appropriate interpretative rules, but these are not usually very helpful in practice.

I am aware that this last point is potentially at odds with Professor Paulsson's blistering dissent in *Hrvatska Elektropriveda d.d. (HEP) (Croatia) v. Republic of Slovenia.*[9] That case arose out of a dispute between the national energy company of Croatia and Slovenia over the ownership and operation of a nuclear power plant located in Slovenia near the Croatian border, which was jointly constructed by both republics (then regions within Yugoslavia) and remains a significant resource for both countries post-independence.

Paulsson disagreed with the interpretation reached by the majority and memorably wrote:

> I have no concern whatever that my colleagues, any more than I, harbour some *a priori* preference for either party. My confidence in the majority's impartiality is total. Our difference is purely a matter of principle, but that does not make it less acute. It is my view that the majority have engaged in a remarkable rewriting of history, as though the epic battles that led to the VCLT had gone the other way. To disregard the VCLT's vindication of Gerald Fitzmaurice's view of treaty interpretation is the jurisprudential equivalent of pretending that Octavian lost at Actium. . . . The general rule of the VCLT is to the effect (Article 31) that a treaty:
>
> > shall be interpreted in good faith in accordance with the meaning to be given to the terms of the treaty in their context and in the light of their object and purpose.
>
> The majority appear simply to have erased the words 'in accordance with the meaning to be given to the terms of the treaty in their context' and gone on to determine the outcome that commends itself to them.[10]

Despite these rhetorical flourishes, it is apparent that *both* the majority *and* Professor Paulsson took great pains to apply Article 31.[11] They just had different views as to the meaning of the text in light of its object

---

[9] *Hrvatska Elektropriveda d.d. (HEP) (Croatia) v. Republic of Slovenia* (ICSID Case No. ARB/05/24, Decision on the Treaty Interpretation Issue of 8 June 2009).

[10] *Ibid.* (Individual Opinion of Jan Paulsson of 8 June 2009), paras. 40–3.

[11] *Hrvatska Elektropriveda d.d. (HEP) (Croatia) v. Republic of Slovenia* (ICSID Case No. ARB/05/24, Decision on the Treaty Interpretation Issue of 12 June 2009), paras. 157–60, 176. The following quote is from para. 176:

> It is important to note that the above view is reached as a result of construing the words of the 2001 Agreement as prescribed by Articles 31 and 32 of the VCLT. Nothing more and nothing less . . . The Tribunal's construction of Article 17 and Exhibit 3 becomes clearer still when, as the VCLT requires, one considers their wording 'in light of the [the 2001 Agreement's] object and purpose' and 'in their context'.

and purpose. Though we might wish it were otherwise, the requirement that one interpret text in context and in light of its object and purpose is not revelatory and does not guarantee that all minds will come to the same answer. As Sir Franklin Berman QC wrote in 2005:

> For treaties, the process of interpretation is far less technical [than the traditional approach to interpreting British statutes]. Huge doctrinal debates raged as the Vienna Convention was in gestation, but they died away almost immediately afterwards. [Aside from the ECJ,] [o]ther international courts don't waste time analysing any theory of interpretation; they just do it, applying in a rational way the Golden Rule in Article 31(1) of the Vienna Convention . . . To be sure, there are other rules defining what the context is (but nothing similar for object or purpose!) . . . But the rules are untechnical, and reflect good common sense; maxims of interpretation are quite out of fashion.[12]

This view accords with the International Law Commission's (ILC) 1966 commentary on its then-Draft Articles on the Law of Treaties (which became VCLT Articles 31 and 32), which stated:

> Most cases submitted to international adjudication involve the interpretation of treaties, and the jurisprudence of international tribunals is rich in reference to principles and maxims of interpretation. In fact, statements can be found in the decisions of international tribunals to support the use of almost every principle or maxim of which use is made in national systems of law in the interpretation of statutes and contracts . . . [These principles] are, for the most part, principles of logic and good sense valuable only as guides to assist in appreciating the meaning which the parties may have intended to attach to the expressions that they employed in a document . . . In other words, recourse to many of these principles is discretionary rather than obligatory and the interpretation of documents is to some extent an art, not an exact science . . . Accordingly the Commission confined itself to trying to isolate and codify the comparatively few general principles which appear to constitute general rules for the interpretation of treaties.[13]

In a masterly study in 2009 for the New Zealand Centre for Public Law,[14] International Court of Justice (ICJ) judge Sir Kenneth Keith quoted Professor Jennings who added his own twist on the ILC's words in

---

[12] F. Berman, 'International treaties and British statutes', *Statute Law Review*, 26(1) (2005), 1–12.

[13] International Law Commission, 'Reports of the Commission to the General Assembly', *Yearbook of the International Law Commission*, 2 (1996), 218–19.

[14] K. J. Keith, 'Interpreting treaties, statutes and contracts', Occasional Paper No. 19, (Wellington: New Zealand Centre for Public Law, 2009).

stating that 'the rules and principles [of interpretation] are elusive in the extreme. Certainly the interpretation of treaties is an art rather than a science, though it is part of the art that it should have an appearance of a science'.[15] As Sir Kenneth concluded, after surveying a range of approaches in national and international law, 'The common positions tend to emphasise the finding of meaning on the basis of the text read in context and in light of its purpose.'[16]

The VCLT is helpful and it is no doubt correct: it is just not terribly illuminating in elucidating the dense concepts as reflected in the text of a particular investment treaty. Thus, I do not agree with those who consider that the true meaning of 'fair and equitable treatment' will be revealed merely by following the correct rules.

Furthermore, it is clear that attempting to parse investment treaties through broader concepts of traditional public international law does not completely resolve these difficulties either. A recent example comes from the 2006 *Thunderbird* NAFTA[17] decision seeking to explain how NAFTA Article 1105 protects legitimate expectations:

> Having considered recent investment case law and the good faith principle of international customary law, the concept of 'legitimate expectations' relates, within the context of the NAFTA framework, to a situation where a Contracting Party's conduct creates reasonable and justifiable expectations on the part of an investor (or investment) to act in reliance on such conduct, such that a failure by the NAFTA Party to honour those expectations could cause the investor (or investment) to suffer damages.[18]

Whilst no doubt comforting, it is difficult to see that the generalised 'good faith principle of international customary law' had any genuine role in developing the specific principle of legitimate expectations fashioned and applied in that case.[19] Free-standing public international law concepts are appealing to litigants and arbitrators alike. But the practical assistance they provide is often limited or confined. Another example is the use of the customary international law 'necessity' defence[20] in the Argentina cases which, though invoked in numerous cases, was decisive

---

[15] *Ibid.*, p. 25.   [16] *Ibid.*, p. 54.

[17] North American Free Trade Agreement, signed 17 December 1992, 32 ILM 289 (entered into force 1 January 1994).

[18] *International Thunderbird Gaming Corp.* v. *Mexico* (NAFTA Award of 26 January 2006), para. 147.

[19] The same might be said for the reasoning of the tribunal in *Tecmed* v. *Mexico* (ICSID Case No. ARB/00/2, Award of 29 May 2003), para. 154.

[20] Based on Art. 25 of the International Law Commission Articles on Responsibility of States for Internationally Wrongful Acts (ILC Articles), adopted in 2001.

in none.[21] Indeed, the key criticism of the International Centre for Settlement of Investment Disputes (ICSID) Annulment Committee in disagreeing with the reasoning of the *CMS* tribunal was that the latter had conflated the customary international law necessity defence with the requirements of the non-precluded measures provision in Article IX of the US–Argentina BIT.[22]

In short, public international law assistance – whether through inter-pretation of treaty text, or through the invocation of broader principles – certainly adds an important layer of context, sophistication and nuance. But it is relatively rarely decisive to the resolution of a thorny interpre-tative issue. As Sir Franklin Berman QC said of recourse to *travaux préparatoires*:

> No interpreter worth his salt would dream of committing himself to a definitive view on a disputed point of interpretation without first checking whether there are any relevant *travaux préparatoires* and, if there are, what they say . . . Nor would any international judge worth his salt do any different. But in 99 cases out of 100 the result (as it appears in the judgment) is along the following lines: 'I have been invited to take into account the negotiating history of this provision; I have looked into

---

[21] See e.g. *CMS Gas Transmission Company* v. *Argentine Republic* (ICSID Case No. ARB/01/8, Award of 12 May 2005), paras. 304–94; *Enron Corporation Ponderosa Assets, L.P* v. *Argentine Republic* (ICSID Case No. ARB/01/3, Award of 22 May 2007), paras. 288–345 (now annulled, see below); *Sempra Energy International* v. *Argentine Republic* (ICSID Case No. ARB/02/16, Award of 28 September 2007), paras. 325–97 (now annulled, see below); *LG&E Energy Corp., LG&E Capital Corp., LG&E International Inc.* v. *Argentine Republic* (ICSID Case No. ARB/02/1, Award of 3 October 2006), paras. 201–61; *Continental Casualty* v. *Argentine Republic* (ICSID Case No. ARB/03/9, Award of 5 September 2008), paras. 162–6, 233.

[22] *CMS Gas Transmission Company* v. *Argentine Republic* (ICSID Case No. ARB/01/8, Decision of the Ad Hoc Committee on the Application for Annulment of the Argentine Republic of 25 September 2007). This essential reasoning was also applied in two recent successful annulment applications: *Sempra Energy International* v. *Argentina* (ICSID Case No. ARB 02/16, Decision on Annulment of 29 June 2010), paras. 208–9 (finding that the tribunal erred in applying Art. 25 of the ILC Articles to the exclusion of Article XI of the US–Argentina BIT and accordingly manifestly exceeded its powers by depriv-ing Argentina of its entitlement to have its right of preclusion in Art. XI subjected to legal scrutiny); and *Enron Creditors Recovery Corp.* v. *Argentina* (ICSID Case No. ARB/01/3, Decision on Annulment of 30 July 2010), paras. 400–5 (finding that the inter-relationship of Arts. XI and 25 of the ILC Articles fell for decision by the tribunal, but were not properly addressed). The *CMS* and *Sempra Annulment* decisions in particular tend to confirm conventional wisdom that the treaty text, and not public international law exegesis, is of paramount importance (although the *Enron Annulment* decision expressly found that the tribunal failed to properly apply Art. 25 of the ILC Articles (see paras. 392–5)).

the papers, without prejudice to whether they are relevant to the issue before me, but I find that – to the extent they illuminate the issue at all – they simply reconfirm the interpretation I had already arrived at.'[23]

It would certainly be going too far to call public international law citations mere garnishing or window-dressing of a tribunal's decisive reasoning. Cases such as *Saluka* (relying on *Methanex*) have, for instance, relied upon customary international law for the proposition that regulation within police powers does not comprise an unlawful taking.[24] In doing so, however, the *Saluka* tribunal acknowledged:

> international law has yet to identify in a comprehensive and definitive fashion precisely what regulations are considered 'permissible' and 'commonly accepted' as falling within the police or regulatory power of States and, thus, noncompensable. In other words, it has yet to draw a bright and easily distinguishable line between non-compensable regulations on the one hand and, on the other, measures that have the effect of depriving foreign investors of their investment and are thus unlawful and compensable in international law. It thus inevitably falls to the *adjudicator* to determine whether particular conduct by a state 'crosses the line' that separates valid regulatory activity from expropriation. Faced with the question of *when, how and at what point an otherwise valid regulation becomes, in fact and effect, an unlawful expropriation*, international tribunals must consider the circumstances in which the question arises.[25]

This case demonstrates the difficulty of weighing the investor's legitimate and reasonable expectations on the one hand and the State's legitimate regulatory interests on the other, using nothing more than the principles provided by public international law.

This is not, when one thinks about it, surprising. Public international law is inherently about the rights of States against States, not about the rights of individuals against States. The investment treaty framework – whilst in one sense itself a form of public international law – is, in a more fundamental sense, a new development which requires new thinking. Whilst public international law provides an important historical and conceptual backdrop to interpreting and applying investment treaties, only limited practical assistance will usually be derived from public international law principles developed for that different paradigm.

---

[23] Berman, 'International treaties and British statutes', p. 10.

[24] *Saluka Investments BV* v. *Czech Republic* (Partial Award of 17 March 2006), paras. 259–63 (on expropriation) and paras. 307–8 (on fair and equitable treatment). See generally, A. Newcombe and L. Paradell, *Law and Practice of Investment Treaties: Standards of treatment* (The Hague: Kluwer, 2009), pp. 288–9, 359.

[25] *Saluka Investments BV* v. *Czech Republic*, paras. 263–4 (emphasis added).

IV   The public law paradigm

One can discern from reading many investment treaty decisions that the real debate is beneath the surface. Public law is intrinsically about the rights of the few against the many – the great concepts of exit and voice, social ordering and the rule of law. On a more practical level, the scenario faced by an investment treaty tribunal is familiar all over the world: a State entity – representing the combined will of the people – acts in a way which causes hardship to a particular person or group. The question in each case is whether the State has acted properly so that its actions are lawful, or whether it has acted improperly, in which case its actions are unlawful. The closest parallel to investment treaty arbitration is, in fact, national administrative law.

National law shows us that there are several 'rule of law' principles which arise when decision-makers are called on to adjudicate administrative questions. Professor Kingsbury has sought to extend these to global administrative law, contending for procedural norms including the need for arrangements for review, publicity/transparency, reason-giving, participation, legal accountability and liability.[26]

We are by now used to the refrain that investment treaty arbitration needs to become more transparent – and we have seen initiatives through NAFTA, ICSID and UNCITRAL to increase public access to hearings and materials, and to permit *amicus curiae* briefs. Yet it may well be asked whether the implications do not go deeper still; whether the very process of interpreting and applying codified administrative law is different from the process of interpreting and applying an ordinary contract, statute or treaty. It may well be that for public law questions, as with constitutional law questions, a purely textual answer just does not exist.

This was the insight – in an admittedly different context – of the 1819 US Supreme Court case of *McCulloch* v. *Maryland* concerning whether there was any federal power to incorporate a bank.[27] In deciding there was, Chief Justice Marshall famously wrote:

> [The federal government] is acknowledged by all to be one of enumerated powers. The principle that it can exercise only the powers granted to it [is] now universally admitted. But the question respecting the extent of the powers actually granted, is perpetually arising, and will probably

[26]   B Kingsbury, 'The concept of "law" in global administrative law', p. 41.
[27]   19 US (4 Wheat) 316 (1819).

> continue to arise, as long as our system shall exist . . . A constitution, to
> contain an accurate detail by which all of the subdivisions of which its
> great powers will admit, and of all the means by which they may be
> carried into execution, would partake of the prolixity of a legal code, and
> could scarcely be embraced by the human mind. It would probably never
> be understood by the public. Its nature, therefore, requires, that only its
> great outlines should be marked, its important objects designated, and
> the minor ingredients which compose those objects be deduced from
> the nature of the objects themselves. That this idea was entertained by the
> framers of the American constitution, is not only to be inferred from the
> nature of the objects themselves, but from the language . . . In considering
> this question, then, we must never forget, that it is a *constitution* we are
> expounding.[28]

This rhetoric, called by Justice Frankfurter 'the single most important
utterance in the literature of constitutional law – most important
because most comprehensive and most comprehending',[29] may seem
too extravagant for the investment treaty arbitration practitioner. It is
also a controversial passage, which some have identified as an inevitable
precursor to the court 'throwing the constitutional text, its structure and
its history to the winds in reaching its conclusion'.[30]

But whilst investment treaties are not constitutions, they are public
law documents which trespass on some of the same territory. The
most obvious constitutional overlap is between expropriation provisions in investment treaties and, say, the Fifth Amendment of the
United States Constitution.[31] The first NAFTA expropriation decisions
under Article 1110 encouraged outrage from some US academics for
their failure to apply the principles of the Fifth Amendment, and
applying instead entirely new principles to regulatory takings jurisprudence.[32] Whilst I cannot see why NAFTA Article 1110 ought to
have been interpreted in precisely the same way as the Fifth Amendment,

---

[28] *Ibid.* (emphasis in original).
[29] Mr Justice Frankfurter, 'John Marshall and the judicial function', *Harvard Law Review*,
      69 (1955), 217–19.
[30] P. B. Kurland, 'Curia regis: Some comments on the divine right of kings and courts to say
      what the law is', *Arizona Law Review*, 23 (1981), 582–91.
[31] It is widely understood that the principles in Annex B of the US Model BIT (which have
      found their way into other documents, such as Chapter 11 of the NZ–China FTA) are
      heavily influenced by Fifth Amendment jurisprudence.
[32] V. Bean and J. Beauvais, 'Global Fifth Amendment: NAFTA's investment protection
      and the misguided quest for an international regulatory takings doctrine', *New York
      University Law Review*, 78 (2003), 30.

I do agree that its interpretation should be approached with the same seriousness of thought and broadness of mind.

Professor Sornarajah has explored some of these issues in his book, *The International Law of Foreign Investment*, now in its third edition.[33] There he has written on the philosophical underpinnings of takings jurisprudence as this is expressed in investment treaty law. He argues, provocatively, that:

> there is a clear project to foster in the international regime, as the centrepiece of foreign investment protection, a theory of absolute protection of foreign investment which sits uneasily with the constitutional systems that are recognised in different parts of the world. In each age of globalisation, the hegemonic power has sought to project its own vision of property onto the world.[34]

He goes on to critique the *Metalclad* decision, and counsels' arguments in the *Ethyl* and *Methanex* cases, as illustrating the expansive scope of expropriation in NAFTA.[35] Whilst this is a deliberately provocative – and not necessarily representative – view, there can be no doubt that the meaning of phrases 'tantamount to a taking' or 'equivalent to a taking' require careful consideration which goes beyond the aid of an Oxford English Dictionary and a well-thumbed copy of *Chorzów Factory.*[36]

V   Conclusion and further thoughts

Ultimately, investment treaty arbitrators need to create the principles which govern this new area. They cannot do this pretending that they are presiding over a private commercial dispute. They cannot do it simply by borrowing from established principles of public international law, which are not well-developed enough to provide the answers. And, practically speaking, they cannot do this by starting anew in each case and reinventing the wheel. Some investment treaties are of course fairly clear and can be applied to specific cases without the need for exegesis – particularly later models with detailed rights and exception clauses. But many are vague, terse and leave much to be refined and clarified through the adjudicative process.

---

[33] M. Sornarajah, *The International Law of Foreign Investment*, 3rd edn (Cambridge University Press, 2010).

[34] *Ibid.*, p. 371.   [35] *Ibid.*, pp. 372–3.

[36] *Factory at Chorzów (Germany v. Poland)* (Jurisdiction), Ser. A, No. 13 (PCIJ, 1928); *Chorzów Factory* (Merits), Ser. A, No. 17 (PCIJ, 1928).

There are undoubtedly many aspects of investment treaty arbitration that might be improved, and constraints of space prevent an exhaustive exploration. Nevertheless, I suggest five broad points of guidance:

1. The staple discussion of whether or not there is precedent in investment treaty arbitration has become a distraction.[37] Clearly, there is no strictly binding doctrine of precedent. Equally clearly, one cannot create administrative law principles in a vacuum. It is both legitimate and necessary to consider what other tribunals have said and thought on the relevant issues – even when they are interpreting a different treaty. This does not make prior decisions determinative, but they may well be relevant. Thus, the cliché that such decisions have been read but were of no assistance to the question at hand should be replaced by more honest and open formulations.

2. Whilst all interpretative decisions must be made in accordance with Article 31 of the VCLT and justified by the text of the specific treaty at issue, a realist will admit that the text will only get you so far. By its very nature, public law interpretation demands a certain degree of systemic and conceptual thinking, which continually polishes and delimits the meaning of a few, very important, words. Investment treaty arbitrators should understand the implications of their decisions for governmental decision-making, and seek over time to build a coherent and credible jurisprudence.

3. Arbitrators must be serious about resolving the dispute according to law – that is obviously their role. But they must also be serious about taking account of, and making room for, the public dimension. This means accepting *amicus* briefs where appropriate – and not only as documents to be received with reluctance and never read. Just as interveners are common in administrative law cases – for instance to emphasise the importance of a decision taken to protect waterways, but which impacts adversely upon industrial users – so too interveners

---

[37] See G. Kaufmann-Kohler, 'Arbitral precedent: Dream, necessity or excuse?', *Arbitration International*, 23(3) (2007), 357; J. P. Commission, 'Precedent in investment treaty arbitration: The empirical backing', *Trans'l Dispute Management*, 4(5) (2007), 6; and A. Christie, 'The evolution of a precedential system in mandatory arbitration: Domain names' (presentation at the AMINZ Conference held from 5 to 7 August 2010 in Christchurch, New Zealand), in which the values of fairness, efficiency and integrity – combined with mandatory jurisdiction and on-line structured access to past decisions – were suggested as reasons why some forms of arbitration appear to have embraced an informal precedential citation practice.

have a potentially important role to play in bringing a wider perspective to investment treaty arbitration.

4. Arbitrators must be very careful about avoiding becoming classed as 'claimant' or 'respondent' arbitrators. Indeed, they must be very careful about conflicts, apparent bias and probity in general. It is especially inappropriate to have administrative law questions decided by those who are perceived to be anything other than objective and impartial.

5. Finally, arbitrators should be alive to cross-fertilisation from other areas of international law,[38] for the field of global administrative law is flowering. Guidance and inspiration is available with respect to a wide variety of other institutions, be it the WTO, the European Court of Justice or the work of UN bodies. The writings of leading jurists, academics and national court judges also offer valuable insight. A comparative approach must not be unbridled, and may often be inappropriate if used explicitly in reasoning, but it can do much to help inform the philosophical compass of the decision-makers who are required to fashion a new administrative law out of a few short words.

In essence, it is critical not to underestimate the extent of the paradigmatic shift which investment treaty arbitration represents. International commercial arbitration teaches one to look straight ahead – at the parties, their pleadings and their evidence. Public international law teaches one to look behind – at States' practices and principles which have evolved and crystallised over time. Global administrative law, like so much else in our globalised age, requires that one look sideways and take note of the converging strands in global governance, of which investment treaty arbitration is an important part.

If my premise is right, and investment treaty arbitration is not arbitration, but global administrative law, then arbitrators must be pioneers as well as practitioners and scholars. As well as resolving the dispute before them, and applying public international law rules where relevant and appropriate, arbitrators must demonstrate that they understand and can contribute to the development of sound and legitimate international regulatory principles. It is a difficult challenge, but one to which I am sure the investment treaty arbitration community will rise.

---

[38] See e.g. C. Brown, *A Common Law of International Adjudication* (Oxford University Press, 2007).

PART III

Actors in international investment law

8

Sovereign wealth funds and international investment law

MARKUS BURGSTALLER*

I Introduction

Sovereign wealth funds (SWFs) have increasingly come under scrutiny in recent years because of both their size and their investment strategies. States and international organisations have attempted to react to the surge of SWFs by enacting barriers to these investments. Yet, it is questionable whether these measures, in particular national laws, comply with the obligations of States under international investment law.[1]

This chapter aims to analyse whether SWFs may have recourse against national protectionist measures under international investment agreements. It is structured as follows. Section II describes the growth in SWF cross-border activity and resulting national security and economic concerns of the host States in which SWFs have invested. Section III considers conflicting approaches to regulating SWF activity. The tension between the need to maintain capital inflows from SWFs, on the one hand, and to address legitimate national security concerns of host States, on the other hand, has led to a mix of 'hard law' and 'soft law' regulatory approaches. Soft law initiatives developed by the Organisation for Economic Cooperation and Development (OECD) and the International Monetary Fund (IMF) have been intended to counter protectionist measures taken

---

* The author wishes to thank Chester Brown for comments on an earlier draft and Marisa Orr for research assistance. The views expressed herein are the views of the author and do not necessarily represent those of Hogan Lovells or its clients. The author may be reached at markus.burgstaller@hoganlovells.com.

[1] International investment law consists of general international law, international economic law, and of distinct rules peculiar to its domain, in particular bilateral investment treaties (BITs) and laws of the host State. See R. Dolzer and C. Schreuer, *Principles of International Investment Law* (Oxford University Press, 2008), p. 3.

by States against SWFs. Section IV analyses whether SWFs may have recourse against such protectionist measures under international investment agreements, in particular bilateral investment treaties (BITs). The analysis will focus on three main issues. The first issue is whether SWFs and their investments are covered by the terms 'investor' and 'investment' under typical BIT definitions. The second issue is whether the temporal dimension of BITs provides coverage for SWFs against protectionist measures. Since most BITs provide protection only after the establishment of an investment, it may be that State measures against SWFs, aimed at the pre-establishment phase, fall outside the scope of most BITs. The third issue is whether a host State may invoke 'essential security' or similar exceptions in BITs or customary international law to defend its protectionist measures. Section V concludes.

II   The rise of SWFs

The number of SWFs has increased exponentially in recent years, with the establishment of twenty new SWFs since 2000 including twelve new SWFs since 2005.[2] As commented by the OECD Investment Committee, 'SWFs have much to offer. SWFs' recent injections of capital into several OECD financial institutions were stabilising because they came at a critical time when risk-taking capital was scarce and market sentiment was pessimistic.'[3] This was accentuated by many financial institutions' drive to de-leverage, which reduced the availability of debt finance. Examples of significant investments of SWFs include the US$5 billion investment by China's SWF, China Investment Corporation (CIC), in Morgan Stanley in December 2007 in return for a 9.9 per cent stake,[4] and the provision of much of a US$21 billion investment in Citigroup and Merrill Lynch by Singapore's

---

[2] See M. Audit, 'Is the erecting of barriers against sovereign wealth funds compatible with international investment law?', *Journal of World Investment and Trade*, 10 (2009), 617; G. Lyons, 'State capitalism: The rise of sovereign wealth funds', *Law and Business Review of the Americas*, 14 (2008), 179.

[3] OECD Investment Committee Report, 'Report on sovereign wealth funds and recipient country policies', 4 April 2008, www.oecd.org/dataoecd/34/9/40408735.pdf (last accessed 20 September 2010).

[4] See e.g. C. Harper, 'Morgan Stanley posts loss, sells stake to China (Update 5)', *Bloomberg*, 19 December 2007, www.bloomberg.com/apps/news?pid=newsarchive&sid=a61Th6IcsbsU (last accessed 20 September 2010).

Temasek Holdings (Temasek), the Kuwait Investment Authority and Korean Investment Corporation in January 2008.[5]

While 2009 saw a greater tendency to invest at home, the overall value of the 113 publicly reported transactions made by SWFs worldwide in 2009 was US$68.8 billion.[6] Eighty-five per cent of this figure is attributable to the third and fourth financial quarters of 2009.[7] This spike in growth has led to a 9 per cent increase from 2009 to 2010 in the aggregate total assets managed by SWFs worldwide, with the figure in March 2010 standing at US$3.51 trillion.[8]

A   SWF activity and the role of governments in the global economy

The heavy reliance by developed-country governments on capital infusions from relatively new sources – in essence, wealthy investing arms of foreign, emerging market governments – has brought into sharper focus the commercial–political ratio in the investment decisions of SWFs. Any analysis of SWFs must take into account the changing role of governments in the global economy.

The decline of the post-Second World War social-democratic model from the early 1980s resulted in a less significant role for developed-country governments in their domestic economies. What ensued was a transfer of power from governments to the private sector, as multinational corporations and denationalised enterprises penetrated the markets to provide services, which had been provided by State enterprises since the Second World War. This left governments only a limited regulatory role.

More recently, however, the growth of budget surpluses in some countries due to large foreign exchange reserves and a commodities boom has encouraged some governments to establish their own SWFs to maximise their wealth and project economic power in the world market. The strict traditional view that States regulate the market and

---

[5] See e.g. Y. Onaran, 'Citigroup, Merrill receive $21 billion from investors (Update 3)', *Bloomberg*, 15 January 2008, www.bloomberg.com/apps/news?pid=newsarchive&sid=aevafxG9n_ls (last accessed 20 September 2010).

[6] Monitor, 'Back on course: Sovereign wealth fund activity in 2009', 17 May 2010, www.monitor.com/Expertise/BusinessIssues/EconomicDevelopmentandSecurity/tabid/69/ctl/ArticleDetail/mid/705/CID/20101305154110429/CTID/1/L/en-US/Default.aspx (last accessed 20 September 2010).

[7] *Ibid.*

[8] Preqin, 'Sovereign wealth funds total assets grow to $3.51 trillion', 10 March 2010, www.preqin.com/docs/reports/Preqin_PR_Sovereign_Wealth_Funds_2010.pdf (last accessed 20 September 2010).

non-State actors participate in it has, therefore, come under scrutiny: whether a State regulates or participates in the global economy fluctuates depending on whether it acts in its sovereign or corporate capacity. As a result of this new form of State engagement in the global economy, 'some States seem to have become pools of national economic wealth, the power of which matches or exceeds their traditional sovereign power'.[9]

B   Shift in investment strategies of SWFs

The substantial increase in the number of SWFs is in itself not a concern. Concerns have been raised, however, in relation to the change in their investment strategies. Historically, SWFs invested in their own countries and mainly in conservative assets. The use by States of SWFs as vehicles through which they hold reserves and protect their financial security has generally been regarded as a limited extension of governmental power.[10] A government's decision to take direct ownership of certain sectors of its national economy has similarly been viewed as an acceptable assertion of regulatory power.[11] Recently, however, the activities of certain SWFs have targeted investments in foreign markets – particularly in Europe and North America – and in a diverse portfolio of assets such as hedge funds, private equity funds and in foreign companies.[12]

The commercial-driven nature of such investment strategies is questionable. Certain SWFs appear to target more sensitive sectors of a host State's economy such as the financial or energy sectors. Examples include the investment of US$400 million by the Qatar Investment Authority in PME Infrastructure Management Limited Fund, set up to invest in African transportation, communication and energy sectors,[13] and CIC's acquisition of a 15 per cent stake in US-based electrical power company AES in November 2009.[14] Given that new SWF owners such as China or

---

[9] L. Backer, 'Sovereign investing in times of crisis: Global regulation of sovereign wealth funds, State-owned enterprises and the Chinese experience', *Transnational Law and Contemporary Problems*, 19(1) (2010), 3, 11.

[10] *Ibid.*, p. 16.   [11] *Ibid.*

[12] Audit, 'Is the erecting of barriers against sovereign wealth funds compatible with international investment law?', p. 617.

[13] SWF Institute, 'South Africa and Qatar to hold bilateral consultations', 3 February 2009, www.swfinstitute.org/tag/qatar-investment-authority/ (last accessed 20 September 2010).

[14] China Investment Corporation, 'China Investment Corporation invests in AES Corporation', 6 November 2009, www.china-inv.cn/cicen/resources/resources_news16.html (last accessed 20 September 2010).

Russia emanate from regimes with wider geopolitical goals than those of traditional SWF owners like the Gulf countries,[15] it is unsurprising that recipient countries have begun to query the legitimacy of their investment decisions.

However, even some traditional SWF owners (namely, some Middle Eastern States) have been viewed with suspicion as a result of heightened fears about national security.[16] The forced sale in 2006 of US ports owned by P&O after the acquisition of the British operator by Dubai Ports World illustrates this point, the forced sale having arisen amid fears that allowing key US infrastructure to come under the control of the United Arab Emirates would pose a fundamental national security risk.[17] An early example is the forced sale by the Kuwaiti Investment Authority of more than half of its investment in BP in 1988.[18]

When investing in foreign markets SWFs typically make minority investments in foreign business enterprises. This strategy draws less attention, at least at the initial point of investment, to potential geopolitical reasons underpinning a SWF's investment choices than would be the case if that SWF targeted majority stakes in the relevant foreign entities. For example, in May 2007 CIC invested US$3 billion for a 10 per cent stake without voting rights in US hedge fund Blackstone.[19] Also, a recent Securities and Exchange Commission filing shows that CIC's

---

[15] Audit, 'Is the erecting of barriers against sovereign wealth funds compatible with international investment law?', p. 617.

[16] L. Hsu, 'Sovereign wealth funds, recent US legislative changes, and treaty obligations', *Journal of World Trade*, 43 (2010), 451, 455; Deutsche Bank, 'Sovereign wealth funds: State investments on the rise', 10 September 2007, www.dbresearch.com/PROD/CIB_INTERNET_EN-PROD/PROD0000000000215270.pdf (last accessed 20 September 2010).

[17] Hsu, 'Sovereign wealth funds, recent US legislative changes, and treaty obligations', p. 453. See also Council on Foreign Relations, 'Foreign ownership of U.S. infrastructure', 13 February 2007, www.cfr.org/publication/10092/foreign_ownership_of_us_infrastructure.html (last accessed 20 September 2010); E. Chalamish, 'Protectionism and sovereign investment post global recession' (OECD Global Forum VIII on International Investment, 7–8 December 2009), www.oecd.org/dataoecd/31/22/44231385.pdf (last accessed 20 September 2010), p. 9.

[18] Los Angeles Times, 'British tell Kuwait to cut BP stake: Arab oil producer could lose $593 million in selloff', 5 October 1988, http://articles.latimes.com/1988–10–05/business/fi-2758_1_arab-oil (last accessed 20 September 2010). See also D. Gaukrodger, 'Foreign State immunity and foreign government controlled investors' (OECD Working Papers on International Investment, 2010), www.oecd.org/dataoecd/21/32/45036449.pdf (last accessed 20 September 2010), pp. 48–50.

[19] BBC, 'China buys $3 billion Blackstone stake', 21 May 2007, http://news.bbc.co.uk/1/hi/business/6675453.stm (last accessed 20 September 2010).

holdings in US companies consist of relatively small stakes.[20] Indeed, CIC's President Gao Xiqing stated that long-term financial return is CIC's top priority.[21]

The more cynical view, however, is that China is attempting to negate the perceptible spike in Chinese acquisitions of US assets so that it can continue its expansive foreign investment policies. Although Mr Gao stated that none of CIC's recent investments in developed countries comprised more than a 20 per cent stake, he also made it clear that CIC would not cap its stakes in overseas companies at that level.[22] Given that CIC's assets have grown to around US$300 billion and so far only half of the US$110 billion reportedly allocated to overseas investments has been spent,[23] this cap is not surprising. According to the US Treasury, China's US equity portfolio holdings have swollen from US$4 billion in 2006 to US$93 billion in early 2010.[24] If the global economic recovery continues, we may expect to see a revival of hostility towards Chinese business interests as the accumulative effect of its more discreet acquisitions gain broader recognition.[25]

From the perspective of the host State, this method of discreetly squeezing into its economy – especially if the SWF's overarching objective is the achievement of geopolitical rather than economic goals – can be troubling. Once a SWF has gained access to a foreign economy, the task of manoeuvring into a position where it can influence and manipulate that economy becomes easier. In addition, investment protections afforded in international investment agreements may restrict the way in which the host State can handle the SWF's investment.

C   Concerns of home States over investment strategies of SWFs

SWFs have also received criticism from their own States for being over-diversified and investing extensively in Western markets, especially in Europe.[26] For example, the Government Pension Fund of Norway, the largest SWF in Europe, compounded losses of around US$500 million in

---

[20] Council on Foreign Affairs, 'China goes to Wall Street', 29 April 2010, www.foreignaffairs.com/articles/66398/jc-de-swaan/china-goes-to-wall-street (last accessed 20 September 2010).
[21] China Daily, 'Long-term financial returns top priority for CIC, says Gao', 19 December 2009, www.china.org.cn/business/2009–12/19/content_19095856.htm (last accessed 20 September 2010).
[22] Ibid.   [23] Council on Foreign Affairs, 'China goes to Wall Street'.   [24] Ibid.
[25] Ibid.
[26] Chalamish, 'Protectionism and sovereign investment post global recession', p. 4.

2008 through its injection of US$1 billion to refinance six US and European banks.[27] As a result, home States have called for investments to be limited to the geographical region of the fund.

On one hand, such criticisms underline the increased outreach of SWFs' investment activities in the global economy and concomitant concern over a lack of transparency in their activities. On the other hand, the home States' criticisms point to a healthy divide between the activities of SWFs and the relevant State that owns its funds. This reinforces the view that when SWFs make their investments in foreign markets, States – acting in their corporate capacity – are 'participators' in the world economy in much the same way as private entities.[28]

III   Conflicting approaches to regulating SWF activity

Facing the increased activity and criticism of SWFs lawmakers have attempted to regulate SWFs. There are two types of legal answers to SWFs. First, there have been 'hard law' answers consisting of national measures against SWFs' investments in strategic economic sectors. Secondly, there have also been 'soft law' answers consisting of various international soft law measures, primarily adopted by the IMF and the OECD.[29] As will be shown, these two answers are not, at least not always, in line with each other.

A   The 'hard law' answer

Some governments have responded to increasing SWF activity in foreign markets by introducing new domestic legislation which either blocks the entry of foreign investment into their domestic economies or limits foreign investment in strategic economic sectors. The key protectionist measures taken can be split into three categories.

The first category consists of regulation that blocks foreign investment in certain entities based on their classification as government-owned

---

[27] R. Tomlinson and V. Laroi, 'Norway oil fund Lehman losses exacerbate Kingdom's worst return', *Bloomberg*, 2 February 2009, www.bloomberg.com/apps/news?pid=newsarchive&sid=aBMkhtkUBEds&refer=home (last accessed 20 September 2010).

[28] Backer, 'Sovereign investing in times of crisis', p. 13.

[29] This terminology is meant to indicate that the instrument or provision in question is not of itself 'law', but its importance within the general framework of international legal development is such that particular attention requires to be paid to it. See M. Shaw, *International Law*, 6th edn (Cambridge University Press, 2008), p. 117; H. Hilgenberg, 'A fresh look at soft law', *European Journal of International Law*, 10 (1999), 499.

entities. France, for example, established SWF Fonds Stratégique d'Investissement (FSI) in November 2008 to help key domestic companies survive the financial crisis.[30] It is clear from President Sarkozy's statements in the month preceding its establishment that the FSI serves as a 'white knight' when a foreign government-owned entity bids on a local champion, intended to block hostile takeovers.[31]

The second type of protective measure consists of prohibiting foreign investment in select industries. The US, for example, prevents foreign acquisitions of sensitive technology and defence companies and maintains exclusions to this effect as schedules to international investment agreements or as specific national laws.[32] Similarly, Russia enacted domestic legislation in 2008 to prevent foreign investment in, among other industries, the aviation, defence and gas and oil sectors.[33]

The third category consists of screening proposed foreign investments in sensitive industries to ensure that the SWF is driven by commercial motives.[34] The result of such screening is either to block or approve the investment, including taking any necessary protective measures to ensure a separation between the ownership and management of the invested company. There are many such measures to which reference can be made, but in the interests of brevity, just two examples of national measures, in the United States and in Germany, will be mentioned.

In the US, the main body charged with screening foreign investment is the Committee on Foreign Investment in the United States (CFIUS).[35]

---

[30] Reuters, 'Update 1: French investment fund ups stake in Technip to 5 percent', 9 September 2009, www.reuters.com/article/idUSL911784320090909 (last accessed 20 September 2010). See also SWF Institute, 'France's FSI raises its Carbone Lorraine stake above 10 percent', www.swfinstitute.org/fund/france.php (last accessed 20 September 2010).

[31] Chalamish, 'Protectionism and sovereign investment post global recession', p. 5.

[32] Foreign Investment and National Security Act of 2007 (FINSA 2007), Pub L No. 110–149, 121 Stat 246 (2007), www.treasury.gov/resource-center/international/foreign-investment/Pages/cfius-legislation.aspx (last accessed 20 September 2010). The Act amends the Defense Production Act of 1950, 50 USC App. 2170.

[33] Procedures for Foreign Investment in Companies Strategically Important for the Defense and National Security of the Russian Federation, 2008 Fed L No. 52-FZ.

[34] For an overview of investment laws of Canada, China, France, Germany, India, Japan, the Netherlands, Russia, United Arab Emirates and the United Kingdom, see United States Government Accountability Office, *Foreign Investment: Laws and policies regulating foreign investment in 10 countries*, February 2008, www.gao.gov/new.items/d08320.pdf (last accessed 20 September 2010).

[35] For details on CFIUS see e.g. Hsu, 'Sovereign wealth funds, recent US legislative changes, and treaty obligations'; B. J. Farrar, 'To legislate or to arbitrate: An analysis of US foreign investment policy after FINSA and the benefits of international arbitration', *Journal of International Business & Law*, 7 (2008), 167.

While CFIUS and CFIUS-like models have been in existence for a long time,[36] many of them have been adjusted as a result of the new wave of global SWF investors. Thus, in July 2007 then President George W. Bush signed into law the Foreign Investment and National Security Act of 2007 (FINSA 2007). Its preamble states that it aims:

> to ensure national security while promoting foreign investment and the creation and maintenance of jobs, to reform the process by which such investments are examined for any effect they may have on national security, to establish the Committee on Foreign Investment in the United States, and for other purposes.[37]

As a result of these legislative changes, there is expanded Executive oversight on foreign investments.

Similar to the CFIUS, in Germany, as of 24 April 2009, an inter-ministerial commission has the power to review proposed acquisitions by State-backed investment funds in any industry sector where the stake to be acquired in the German company is more than 25 per cent. Further, the amendments to the Foreign Trade and Payments Act and the Foreign Trade and Payments Regulation introduced increased powers of review over foreign investments that may jeopardise German public policy or security.[38]

B   The 'soft law' answer

In an effort to head off a counterproductive reaction to SWFs, in October 2007 the US Treasury tasked the Group of Seven (the US, UK, Japan, Canada, Germany, France and Italy) together with the leaders of

---

[36] CFIUS was introduced by Executive Order 11858, 40 FR 20263 by President Ford in 1975.

[37] FINSA 2007.

[38] See Thirteenth Act amending the Foreign Trade and Payments Act and the Foreign Trade and Payments Regulation of 18 April 2009, www.bmwi.de/BMWi/Redaktion/PDF/Gesetz/englischer-gesetzestext-eines-dreizehnten-gesetzes-zur-aenderung-aussenwirtschaft, property=pdf,bereich=bmwi,sprache=de,rwb=true.pdf (last accessed 20 September 2010). It may be added that also at the European Union (EU) level, there has been talk about setting up a CFIUS equivalent. The European Commission has put forward a proposal arguing for the need for a common approach to SWFs in the EU. The need to maintain a clear and predictable legal environment is emphasised while at the same time acknowledging the right of EU Member States to protect their national interests without falling into the trap of protectionism. See e.g. http://ec.europa.eu/internal_market/finances/docs/sovereign_en.pdf (last accessed 20 September 2010).

eight SWF nations to draft voluntary codes of 'best practices'.[39] One year later, in October 2008, the OECD and the IMF have published guidelines for recipient countries and SWFs alike in an attempt to provide the international community with a robust framework for promoting mutual trust and confidence and reaping the full benefits of SWFs for home and host countries.[40]

The OECD has focused its efforts on recipient countries' policies towards investments from SWFs. Its general investment policy principles are enshrined in the OECD Code of Liberalisation of Capital Movements, adopted by the OECD members in 1961, and the OECD Guidelines for Multinational Enterprises of 1976 (as revised in 2000),[41] adopted by forty-one OECD and non-OECD members.[42] The OECD has also published several guidelines against the backdrop of the broader Freedom of Investment process, which was launched in 2006.[43] This process provides a multilateral forum for investment policy dialogue among SWFs, home governments and recipient governments, and includes a process of peer surveillance to ensure that commitments to an open international investment environment are respected.[44] The OECD has also invited SWFs of non-OECD members to contribute to the process. The recent attendance of speakers on behalf of SWFs from China and Russia at the OECD Forum 2010 is an example.[45] The OECD promotes five key principles:

1. non-discrimination (foreign investors to be treated no less favourably than domestic investors in like situations)

---

[39] See for details T. E. Crocker, 'What banks need to know about the coming debate over CFIUS, foreign direct investment, and sovereign wealth funds', *Banking Law Journal*, 125 (2008), 457, 464.

[40] OECD Investment Division – Secretariat of the OECD Investment Committee, 'Sovereign wealth funds and recipient countries: Working together to maintain and expand freedom of investment', 11 October 2008, www.oecd.org/dataoecd/0/23/41456730.pdf (last accessed 20 September 2010), pp. 1–2; International Working Group of Sovereign Wealth Funds, 'Generally Accepted Principles and Practices (GAPP): Santiago Principles', October 2008, www.iwg-swf.org/pubs/gapplist.htm (last accessed 20 September 2010), pp. 4–5.

[41] OECD, 'OECD guidelines for multinational enterprises', 27 June 2000, www.oecd.org/dataoecd/56/36/1922428.pdf (last accessed 20 September 2010).

[42] OECD Investment Division – Secretariat of the OECD Investment Committee, 'Sovereign wealth funds and recipient countries', p. 3.

[43] *Ibid.*, p. 1.   [44] *Ibid.*

[45] OECD, 'OECD Forum 2010: Speakers', 26–7 May 2010, www.oecd.org/document/3/0,3343,en_21571361_44354303_44907267_1_1_1_1,00.html (last accessed 20 September 2010).

2. transparency (comprehensive and publicly accessible information on restrictions on foreign investment)
3. progressive liberalisation (gradual elimination of restrictions on capital movements)
4. 'standstill' (no new restrictions on foreign investment)
5. unilateral liberalisation (liberalisation measures taken not to be conditioned on liberalisation measures being taken by other countries).[46]

In contrast to the OECD's approach, the IMF focuses instead on the behaviour of SWFs themselves. For this purpose, it set up the International Working Group of Sovereign Wealth Funds, which produced a voluntary code of conduct called the Generally Accepted Principles and Practices (GAPP), commonly referred to as the 'Santiago Principles', in October 2008.[47] The code comprises twenty-four voluntary principles aimed at improving the governance, transparency and investment conduct of SWFs.[48] While such principles do not restrict the purpose for which SWFs can be used, the policies in relation to a SWF's approach to funding and its spending operations should be clear and publicly disclosed.[49] Ultimately, the Santiago Principles are designed to help SWFs operate more professionally like private investment funds.[50]

C Co-operation of host States, home States and SWFs with OECD and IMF measures

There has been a mixed response from host States, home States and SWFs to the combined efforts of the OECD and the IMF. A positive example is the OECD's recognition of the Norwegian Government Pension Fund's compliance with the OECD Principles of Corporate

---

[46] OECD Investment Division – Secretariat of the OECD Investment Committee, 'Sovereign wealth funds and recipient countries', p. 3. These principles have been reaffirmed by the OECD Ministers' adoption of the OECD Declaration on SWFs and Recipient Country Policies in June 2008. See OECD, Investment Division of the OECD Directorate for Financial and Enterprise Affairs, 'OECD investment news: Results of the work of the OECD Committee', June 2008, www.oecd.org/dataoecd/18/28/40887916.pdf (last accessed 20 September 2010), p. 5.

[47] International Working Group of Sovereign Wealth Funds, 'Generally Accepted Principles and Practices (GAPP): Santiago Principles', pp. 7–9.

[48] For a discussion of the legal framework and objectives of the Santiago Principles, see ibid., pp. 11–25.

[49] Ibid., pp. 14, 21.   [50] Ibid. See e.g. pp. 12, 15, 19, 25–6, 31.

Governance and the OECD Guidelines for Multinational Enterprises.[51] However, OECD members such as the US, France and Germany – which have also declared adherence to the OECD Guidelines for Multinational Enterprises[52] – continue to take a protectionist stance against SWFs through their national laws. The absence of any indication to reverse such measures offends the progressive liberalisation principle underpinning OECD initiatives. This, in turn, casts doubt over the level of genuine commitment by OECD members.

Transparency is key to the international soft law answer. Indeed, some SWFs have taken steps to abate concern about the lack of transparency over their investment activities. For example, Singapore's SWFs – Temasek and the Government of Singapore Investment Corporation (GIC) – have expanded the level of information that is publicly available to include details on their size, source of funding, governance structure, asset mix, geographical investment allocation and investment strategy.[53] These funds have also made concerted efforts to emphasise their autonomy from their State shareholder.[54] Furthermore, these Singaporean SWFs have also stressed that they operate independently of each other in making their commercial decisions to maximise long-term returns.[55] Similar statements by the Abu Dhabi Investment Authority provide a further example.[56]

---

[51] OECD, 'Investment newsletter: The reach of OECD investment instruments expand', October 2007, www.oecd.org/dataoecd/0/57/39534401.pdf (last accessed 20 September 2010), p. 5.

[52] OECD Investment Division – Secretariat of the OECD Investment Committee, 'Sovereign wealth funds and recipient countries', p. 3.

[53] See e.g. Temasek's website, www.temasekholdings.com.sg/about_us.htm (last accessed 20 September 2010); GIC's website, www.gic.com.sg/ (last accessed 20 September 2010). See also GIC, 'GIC report on the management of the government's portfolio for the year 2008/09', September 2009, www.gic.com.sg/PDF/GIC_Report_2009.pdf (last accessed 20 September 2010).

[54] Temasek's website states that Temasek is 'Guided by an independent board . . . Neither the President of Singapore nor the Singapore Government is involved in [its] investment, divestment or other business decisions': www.temasekholdings.com.sg/about_us_corporate_governace.htm (last accessed 20 September 2010). Likewise, according to GIC's website, the Government of Singapore 'owns the funds that [GIC] manages': www.gic.com.sg/ (last accessed 20 September 2010).

[55] Channel NewsAsia, 'Circumstances make Singapore's two wealth funds different from most', 29 January 2008, www.channelnewsasia.com/stories/singaporebusinessnews/view/325683/1/.html (last accessed 20 September 2010).

[56] See e.g. Abu Dhabi Investment Authority, 'Relationship with government', www.adia.ae/En/Governance/Abudhabi_Government.aspx (last accessed 20 September 2010): 'ADIA carries out its investment programme independently and without reference to the Government of Abu Dhabi or other entities that also invest funds on the Government's behalf'; Abu Dhabi Investment Authority, 'Guiding principles', www.adia.ae/En/About/

However, the contrasting operation of China's CIC highlights real differences between SWFs. CIC's inclusion of the Chinese Communist Party on its board of directors as well as its direct accountability to China's State Council[57] mean that its investment decisions can only be understood in the wider context of the national and geopolitical objectives of Chinese State policy.

Positive behaviour in response to soft law instruments indicate a growing awareness of the need of SWFs to win the trust of foreign States in order to continue making extensive international investments. Further, such reactions show that States need to relax protectionist measures if they want to attract and benefit from SWFs' investments. However, proper adherence to voluntary codes of conduct has commonly arisen in response to global pressure and has, as a result, been rather piecemeal. The failure by the newly established Libyan SWF to disclose detailed information on its investment strategy despite an announcement in early 2009 to do so is a case in point.[58] This highlights an inherent problem with compliance with and effectiveness of 'soft law': that sets of principles have to be observed widely enough to be seen by all participants as a necessary part of doing business.[59]

IV   Protection of investments of SWFs under international investment law

It is important to note that under public international law generally, States are not obliged to admit foreign investments into their national economies. But this does not mean that SWFs do not have any possibility to have recourse against protectionist State measures in the international legal system. It has been suggested that the World Trade Organization (WTO) is the appropriate forum to address SWF issues on the basis that SWFs' investments are already covered by WTO agreements and any grievances are best dealt with in the context of the WTO's multilateral framework.[60] In particular, one agreement that may be applicable to SWFs is the General Agreement on Trade in Services

Guiding_Principles.aspx (last accessed 20 September 2010): 'ADIA does not seek active management of the companies in which it invests.'

[57] Backer, 'Sovereign investing in times of crisis', pp. 112–14.   [58] *Ibid.*, p. 36.

[59] On the different concepts of compliance and effectiveness generally see M. Burgstaller, *Theories of Compliance with International Law* (Martinus Nijhoff, 2005), pp. 3–5.

[60] Peterson Institute for International Economics, 'Currency undervaluation and sovereign wealth funds: A new role for the World Trade Organization', 16 January 2008, www.iie.com/publications/interstitial.cfm?ResearchID=871 (last accessed 20 September 2010).

(GATS).[61] Nevertheless, several obstacles to applying the GATS to SWF investments and to monitoring relevant protective measures against them need to be mentioned. First, the GATS rules only apply where the foreign entity has control over the acquired company,[62] thereby not covering SWF minority investments, which have become the rule rather than the exception. Secondly, the GATS includes general and specific exceptions that can frequently be applied to SWF investments.[63] Thirdly, the WTO's dispute-resolution mechanism is not ideally suited to SWF investments.[64] For these reasons, it may be that international investment law is a more suitable tool for SWFs to look for remedies against protectionist measures.

To date, however, SWFs do not appear to have commenced any investment arbitrations against host States, either before the International Centre for Settlement of Investment Disputes (ICSID) or under any other arbitration mechanism. Temasek's recent threat to pursue an international arbitration claim against Indonesia illustrates that SWFs are at least considering such options.[65] On 5 May 2010 the Indonesian Supreme Court upheld a decision to fine Temasek for breach of Indonesian anti-trust laws and ordered it to divest its indirect stake in either Indosat or Telkomsel, Indonesia's largest two mobile telecommunications companies.[66] We are yet to see

---

[61] See in particular, Arts. II, V and VI GATS. In addition, WTO Member States are bound by the Agreement on Trade-Related Investment Measures (TRIMs). TRIMs is relatively limited in scope, covering 'investment measures related to trade in goods only', and contains a relatively small number of obligations such as national treatment and quantitative restrictions, especially insofar as they may relate to performance requirements.

[62] Art. XXVIII(m)(ii) GATS indicates that a 'commercial presence' by a 'juridical person of another Member' is a juridical person that is 'owned or controlled by' a (natural or legal) person of that Member.

[63] For details see e.g. B. De Meester, 'International legal aspects of sovereign wealth funds: Reconciling international economic law and the law of State immunities with a new role of the State', *European Businesses Law Review*, (2009), 779.

[64] See B. J. Reed, 'Sovereign wealth funds: The new barbarians at the gate? An analysis of the legal and business implications of their ascendancy', *Virginia Law & Business Review*, 4 (2009), 97, 122.

[65] See e.g. W. Utami and A. Sukarosono, 'Temasek loses final appeal against Indonesian antitrust law breach ruling', *Bloomberg*, 24 May 2010, www.bloomberg.com/news/2010–05–24/temasek-loses-final-appeal-against-indonesian-antitrust-law-breach-ruling.html (last accessed 20 September 2010).

[66] KPPU Commission for the Supervision of Business Competition, 'KPPU's decisions on Temasek case strengthened by the Supreme Court', http://eng.kppu.go.id/jppu%e2%80%99s-decisions-on-temasek-case-strengthened-by-the-supreme-court/ (last accessed 20 September 2010). See also *The Strait Times*, 'Antitrust case: Temasek loses final appeal; Indonesian Supreme Court ruling ends Singapore investment firm's long battle to clear its name', 25 May 2010.

whether Temasek will commence international arbitration against Indonesia. In any case, it is noteworthy that Temasek's concern about the impact of an adverse court ruling on its foreign investment operations was what drove it to contest the decision all the way up to the Indonesian Supreme Court. It may be that as a result of worldwide increasing SWF investments and State protectionist measures against these investments SWFs increasingly turn to international investment arbitration to seek protection. But are SWF investments covered by the ICSID Convention and/or typical BITs?

A   Protection of SWF investments under the ICSID Convention and BITs

The preamble to the ICSID Convention reads in relevant parts as follows: 'Considering the need for international cooperation for economic development, and the role of private international investment therein.' This indicates that the investor must be a private individual or corporation and that States acting as investors may not commence ICSID arbitration.[67] The idea of permitting States to have standing as investors before ICSID was raised at one point during the Convention's preparation, but was quickly put to rest and was not pursued.[68] The situation is less clear when it comes to wholly or partly government-owned entities such as SWFs. The Comment to the Preliminary Draft stated: 'It will be noted that the term "national" is not restricted to privately-owned companies, thus permitting a wholly or partially owned company to be a party to proceedings brought by or against a foreign State.'[69] This statement was never contradicted in the course of the subsequent deliberations on the Convention. But neither is it repeated in the Executive Director's Report.[70] Instructive guidance on this question can be found by Broches, who said:

> There are many companies which combine capital from private and governmental sources and corporations all of whose shares are owned by the government, but who are practically indistinguishable from the completely privately owned enterprise both in their legal characteristics and in their activities. It would seem, therefore, that for purposes of the Convention a mixed economy company or government-owned

---

[67] C. Schreuer *et al.*, *The ICSID Convention: A commentary*, 2nd edn (Cambridge University Press, 2009), p. 161.
[68] *Ibid.*   [69] *Ibid.*   [70] *Ibid.*

corporation should not be disqualified as a 'national of another Contracting State' unless it is acting as an agent for the government or is
discharging an essentially governmental function.[71]

Consequently, it would seem that SWFs have access to ICSID regardless
of them being government-owned.

As for BITs, it would seem that there are no BITs which specifically
exclude SWFs from the definition of 'investor'. Some BITs, such as those
concluded by Saudi Arabia, expressly state that public institutions and
government agencies are covered.[72] For example, the term 'investor'
under the Saudi Arabia–Germany BIT includes 'the Government of the
Kingdom of Saudi Arabia and its financial institutions and authorities
such as the Saudi Arabian Monetary Agency, public funds and other
similar governmental institutions existing in Saudi Arabia'.[73] A similar
formulation appears in the Saudi Arabia–France BIT.[74] Nevertheless, the
majority of BITs are silent on whether SWFs qualify for protection.

Case law confirms that significant State ownership interest does not
prevent investors from seeking protection under the ICSID Convention
and applicable BITs. Four cases are on point.

First, in *CSOB v. Slovakia* the respondent objected to the tribunal's
jurisdiction on the basis that the claimant was a State agency of the
Czech Republic rather than an independent commercial entity and that
it was discharging essentially governmental activities. The tribunal did
not accept the objection, relying on the ICSID Convention's legislative
history and on the passage by Broches cited above. The tribunal in *CSOB
v. Slovakia* also noted that, notwithstanding the fact that the Czech

---

[71] A. Broches, 'The Convention on the Settlement of Investment Disputes between States
and Nationals of other States', *Recueil des Cours*, 136 (1972), 331, 354–5. By referring to a
'mixed economy company', Broches appears to have referred to a company which
combines capital from private and governmental sources.

[72] United Nations Conference on Trade and Development, 'The protection of national
security in IIAs', 2009, www.unctad.org/en/docs/diaeia20085_en.pdf (last accessed 20
September 2010), pp. 43–4.

[73] Abkommen zwischen der Bundesrepublik Deutschland und dem Königreich Saudi-
Arabien über die Förderung und den gegenseitigen Schutz von Kapitalanlagen (Agreement between the Federal Republic of Germany and the Kingdom of Saudi Arabia on the
Promotion and Reciprocal Protection of Investments), signed 29 October 1996 (entered
into force 9 January 1999) (Saudi Arabia–Germany BIT), Art. 1(3)(a)(III).

[74] Accord entre le Gouvernement de la République Française et le Gouvernement du
Royaume d'Arabie Saoudite sur l'Encouragement et la Protection Réciproques des
Investissements (Agreement between the Government of the Republic of France and
the Government of the Kingdom of Saudi Arabia on the Reciprocal Encouragement and
Protection of Investments), signed 26 June 2002 (entered into force 18 March 2004)
(Saudi Arabia–France BIT), Art. 1(2).

Republic owned 65 per cent of CSOB's shares and supported CSOB's investment operations in Slovakia, 'the focus must be on the nature of these activities and not their purpose'[75] when assessing whether or not CSOB qualifies as an 'investor' under the BIT. The tribunal stated that, 'While it cannot be doubted that in performing the above-mentioned activities, CSOB promoting the governmental policies or purposes of the State, the activities themselves were essentially commercial rather than governmental in nature.'[76] Accordingly, the tribunal decided that it had jurisdiction to hear CSOB's claim.

Secondly, in *CDC* v. *Seychelles* the claimant was wholly owned by the United Kingdom government, but acted on a day-to-day basis without any government instruction or involvement. The respondent initially objected to ICSID's jurisdiction on the basis that the claimant was not a 'national of another Contracting State'. As the objection was withdrawn, the tribunal did not have to comment on this objection.[77]

Thirdly, in *Telenor* v. *Hungary* the claimant was 75 per cent owned by the State of Norway. The respondent did not even attempt to object to ICSID's jurisdiction on that basis.[78]

Fourthly, in *Rumeli* v. *Kazakhstan* the tribunal held that the claimants were independent commercial entities and rejected the respondent's argument that Turkey was actually the interested party. The tribunal held that the extent of any control over the claimants by the Turkish government and the possibility that the proceeds of any award might be remitted to the Turkish Treasury did not deprive them of this status.[79]

Therefore, international arbitral practice confirms that wholly or partially government-owned entities such as SWFs may seek protection under both the ICSID Convention and typical BITs.

B   The temporal dimension of protection of SWF investments under BITs

Having concluded that the ICSID Convention and typical BITs provide jurisdiction *ratione personae* for SWFs, it is important to consider whether SWFs fall within the temporal protection of BITs. In this regard,

---

[75] *Ceskoslovenska Obchodni Banka, a.s.* v. *The Slovak Republic* (ICSID Case No. ARB/97/4, Decision of the Tribunal on Objections to Jurisdiction of 24 May 1999), para. 20.

[76] *Ibid.*

[77] *CDC* v. *Seychelles* (ICSID Case No. ARB/02/14, Award of 17 December 2003), para. 12.

[78] *Telenor* v. *Hungary* (ICSID Case No. ARB/04/15, Award of 13 September 2006), para. 20.

[79] *Rumeli Telekom AS and Telsim Mobil Telekomikasyon Hizmetleri AS* v. *Kazakhstan* (ICSID Case No. ARB/05/16, Award of 29 July 2008), paras. 325–8.

investment treaties reveal a distinction between what UNCTAD has labelled a 'post-entry model' and a 'pre-entry model'.[80] The vast majority of BITs do not include binding provisions concerning the admission of foreign investment. In particular, treaties concluded by European countries do not grant a right of admission but limit themselves to standards and guarantees for those investments which the host State has unilaterally decided to admit. A typical clause of this kind reads: 'Each Contracting Party shall in its territory promote as far as possible investments by investors of the other Contracting State and admit such investments in accordance with its legislation.'[81] Although these BITs encourage foreign investment, national protectionist measures taken by a contracting party against a foreign SWF to prevent that SWF from investing in the contracting party's economy are not reviewable by a tribunal.

The United States, followed by Canada and Japan, have pursued a different admission policy from European countries. They have negotiated BITs which, to some extent, grant market access. Under these BITs a right of admission, although in limited scope, is typically based on a national treatment clause.[82] For example, the 2004 US Model BIT provides in Article 3(1):

> Each Party shall accord to investors of the other Party treatment no less favourable than that it accords, in like circumstances, to its own investors *with respect to the establishment*, expansion, management, conduct, operation, and sale or other disposition of investments in its territory.[83]

Even where treaty protection is available in the pre-establishment phase, the usefulness of this protection is questionable. In fact, there have been no published instances of disputes arising under the few BITs based on the 'pre-entry model'.[84] SWFs, just like other investors, are more likely to have recourse under BITs against national protectionist measures which are adopted in the post-establishment phase. Arguably, since most concerns about SWF investments arise when they aim to access the host

---

[80] UNCTAD, 'Most-favoured nation treatment' in *Series on Issues in International Investment Agreements* (1999), 8.

[81] Germany Model BIT (2005), Art. 2(1). See also UK Model BIT (2005 with 2006 amendments), Art. 2(1); China Model BIT, Art. 2(1).

[82] R. Dolzer and C. Schreuer, *Principles of International Investment Law* (Oxford University Press, 2008), p. 81.

[83] US Model BIT, Art. 3(1) (emphasis added).

[84] Z. Douglas, *The International Law of Investment Claims* (Cambridge University Press, 2009), p. 141.

economy, the limited applicability of most BITs to the pre-establishment phase leaves SWFs unprotected against protectionist measures.

C   Host State defences

If a SWF is covered against a State measure under a BIT or under another investment instrument, a host State may have recourse to essential security or necessity exceptions enshrined in the relevant BIT and/or under customary international law. If protectionist measures fall within these exceptions, the host State would, as a result, be released from its obligations under the relevant BIT.

A preliminary question is whether such a clause is self-judging or not. In other words, the question is whether or not the language of a BIT would allow a tribunal to review a State's assessment of the necessity of its action. The International Court of Justice (ICJ) in *Nicaragua* v. *United States of America* considered this question. In that case, the ICJ held that the omission of the words 'it considers necessary' from the security exception in the applicable Friendship, Commerce and Navigation (FCN) Treaty[85] was crucial to its finding that the actions taken by the US were non-self-judging and, consequently, subject to the scrutiny of the ICJ.[86]

Following the ICJ decision, the US Model BIT was drafted to contain self-judging language.[87] Recent BITs and Free Trade Agreements (FTAs) also use this formulation.[88] However, the US remains party to several older BITs – for example, the US–Argentina BIT – which do not contain self-judging language. The non-self-judging character of the clause in

---

[85] In some respects, FCN treaties may be said to be predecessors of BITs. While FCN treaties commonly contained investment protection provisions, their chief weakness as compared to BITs was the absence of an investor–State dispute-resolution provision. See, C. McLachlan, L. Shore and M. Weiniger, *International Investment Arbitration: Substantive Principles* (Oxford University Press, 2007), p. 26.

[86] *Case concerning Military and Paramilitary Activities in and against Nicaragua (Nicaragua* v. *United States of America) (Jurisdiction and Admissibility)* [1984] ICJ Rep 14, 392.

[87] US Model BIT (2004), Art. 18.

[88] See e.g. United States–Singapore Free Trade Agreement, signed 6 May 2003 (entered into force 1 January 2004), Art. 21.2, www.ustr.gov (last accessed 20 September 2010); Treaty between the United States of America and the Oriental Republic of Uruguay concerning the Encouragement and Reciprocal Protection of Investment, signed 4 November 2005 (entered into force 1 November 2006) (US–Uruguay BIT), Art. 18(2); Treaty between the Government of the United States of America and the Government of the Republic of Rwanda concerning the Encouragement and Reciprocal Protection of Investment, signed 19 February 2008 (not yet in force) (US–Rwanda BIT), Art. 18(2).

this particular BIT was confirmed in a series of ICSID cases.[89] Nevertheless, variations in individual treaty language which may affect interpretation could lead future tribunals to differ on the 'self-judging' issue.[90]

In the mentioned Argentine cases under the US–Argentina BIT the
tribunals were charged not only with interpreting the essential security
defence in Article XI of the BIT, but also Article 25 of the Articles on
State Responsibility. This Article, which is reflective of customary international law,[91] entitled 'Necessity', reads as follows:

1. Necessity may not be invoked by a State as a ground for precluding the
   wrongfulness of an act not in conformity with an international obligation of that State unless the act:
   (a) is the only way for the State to safeguard an essential interest
       against a grave and imminent peril; and
   (b) does not seriously impair an essential interest of the State or
       States towards which the obligation exists, or of the international
       community as a whole.
2. In any case, necessity may not be invoked by a State as a ground for
   precluding wrongfulness if:
   (a) the international obligation in question excludes the possibility of
       invoking necessity; or
   (b) the State has contributed to the situation of necessity.[92]

---

[89] Art. XI of the Treaty between the United States of America and the Argentine Republic
concerning the Encouragement and Reciprocal Protection of Investment, signed 14
November 1991 (entered into force 20 October 1994) (US–Argentina BIT) reads as
follows: 'This Treaty shall not preclude the application by either Party of measures
necessary for the maintenance of public order, the fulfilment of its obligations with
respect to the maintenance or restoration of international peace or security, or the
protection of its own essential security interests.' The non-self-judging character of this
clause was confirmed in *CMS Gas Transmission Company* v. *Argentine Republic* (ICSID
Case No. ARB/01/8, Award of 12 May 2005), para. 373; *LG&E Energy Corp., LG&E
Capital Corp., LG&E International Inc.* v. *Argentine Republic* (ICSID Case No. ARB/02/1,
Award of 3 October 2006), para. 212; *Enron Corporation Ponderosa Assets, L.P* v.
Argentine Republic (ICSID Case No. ARB/01/3, Award of 22 May 2007), para. 339;
Sempra Energy International v. *Argentine Republic* (ICSID Case No. ARB/02/16, Award
of 28 September 2007), para. 374; *Continental Casualty* v. *Argentine Republic* (ICSID
Case No. ARB/03/9, Award of 5 September 2008), para. 187.

[90] Hsu, 'Sovereign wealth funds, recent US legislative changes, and treaty obligations', p. 472.

[91] The ICJ has acknowledged that 'the state of necessity is a ground recognized by
customary international law, for precluding the wrongfulness of a fact not in conformity
with an international obligation': *Case Concerning the Gabcikovo-Nagymaros Project
(Hungary/Slovakia)* [1997] ICJ Rep 7, 40, para. 51.

[92] ILC Articles on State Responsibility, Art. 25, reproduced in James Crawford, *The
International Law Commission's Articles on State Responsibility: Introduction, Text and
Commentaries* (Cambridge University Press, 2002), p. 61.

Argentina regularly invoked both Article XI of the US–Argentina BIT and Article 25 of the Articles on State Responsibility.[93] The underlying facts were in all cases the same. In brief, between 1998 and 2001 Argentina's currency collapsed and its economy went through a deep recession. From January 2002 onwards, the government enacted a series of emergency laws. The laws permitted renegotiation of contracts with public service providers and obliged the transfer of US dollar obligations into Argentine pesos on a 1:1 exchange rate. Several public service providers found their investments to have been massively devalued as a result of these laws and commenced arbitration against Argentina.[94]

The tribunals concurred in holding that the 'essential security' exception is not confined to military or defence-related threats. For example, the tribunal in *Sempra* considered that 'essential security interests can eventually encompass situations other than the traditional military threats for which the institution found its origins in customary law'.[95] In *LG&E*, the tribunal stated that:

---

[93] For a more detailed discussion on the application of Argentina's defence in these cases see e.g. A. Reinisch, 'Necessity in international investment arbitration: An unnecessary split of opinions in recent ICSID cases? Comments on *CMS v. Argentina* and *LG&E v. Argentina*', *Journal of World Investment & Trade*, 8 (2007), 191–214; S. Schill, 'International investment law and the host State's power to handle economic crises: Comment on the ICSID decision in *LG&E v. Argentina*', *Journal of International Arbitration*, 24 (2007), pp. 265–86; M. Waibel, 'Two worlds of necessity in ICSID arbitration: *CMS* and *LG&E*', *Leiden Journal of International Law*, 20 (2007), 637–48; A. Martinez, 'Invoking State defences in investment treaty arbitration' in M. Waibel *et al.* (eds.), *The Backlash against Investment Arbitration* (The Hague: Kluwer, 2010), pp. 315–37; W. W. Burke-White, 'The Argentine financial crisis: State liability under BITs and the legitimacy of the ICSID system' in M. Waibel *et al.* (eds.), *The Backlash against Investment Arbitration* (The Hague: Kluwer, 2010), pp. 407–32.

[94] It may be added that in addition to the cases mentioned under the US–Argentina BIT, there were several other cases under other BITs, including under Argentina's BITs with the United Kingdom, Spain and France. However, these BITs do not include a provision similar to Art. XI of the US–Argentina BIT. Therefore, in these cases, Argentina only relied on Art. 25 of the Articles on State Responsibility. See *National Grid* v. *Argentine Republic* (UNCITRAL, Award of 3 November 2008); *BG Group Plc* v. *Argentine Republic* (UNCITRAL, Award of 24 December 2007); *Suez, Sociedad General de Aguas de Barcelona and Vivendi Universal* v. *Argentine Republic* (ICSID Case No. ARB/03/19, Decision on Liability of 30 July 2010) and *AWG Group* v. *Argentine Republic* (UNCITRAL, Decision on Liability of 30 July 2010).

[95] *Sempra v. Argentina* (ICSID Case No. ARB/02/16, Award of 28 September 2007), para. 374. See also *LG&E v. Argentina* (ICSID Case No. ARB/02/1, Decision on Liability of 3 October 2006), para. 238: 'The Tribunal rejects the notion that Article XI is only applicable in circumstances amounting to military action and war.'

> what qualifies as an 'essential' interest is not limited to those interests referring to the State's existence . . . economic, financial or those interests related to the protection of the State against any danger seriously compromising its internal or external situation, are also considered essential interests.[96]

In *Continental Casualty*, the tribunal reiterated that 'international law is not blind to the requirement that States should be able to exercise their sovereignty in the interest of their population free from internal as well as external threats to their security'[97] and 'a severe economic crisis may thus qualify under Article XI [of the US–Argentina BIT] as affecting an essential security interest'.[98]

There have only been two cases in which Argentina has successfully been able to invoke the defence of 'essential security' under the BIT and the defence of 'necessity' under customary international law before tribunals: *LG&E* and *Continental Casualty*. In *LG&E*, the tribunal exonerated Argentina for a certain period under Article XI of the US–Argentina BIT and then essentially came to the same conclusion under Article 25 of the Articles on State Responsibility.[99] Contrarily, in *Continental Casualty*, the tribunal found that there were differences between the situation regulated under Article 25 of the Articles on State Responsibility and Article XI of the BIT. The tribunal concluded that invocation of Article XI of the BIT, as a specific provision bilaterally agreed by the Contracting Parties, is not necessarily subject to the same conditions of application as the plea of necessity under customary international law. The tribunal found, however, a 'link' between the two types of regulation and decided to apply customary international law as a specific bilateral regulation of necessity for purposes of the BIT insofar as the concept there used 'assisted' the tribunal in the interpretation of Article XI itself.[100]

In the majority of cases, however, the tribunals have not accepted Argentina's defence. To give but one example, the tribunal in *Suez,*

---

[96] *LG&E v. Argentina* (ICSID Case No. ARB/02/1, Decision on Liability of 3 October 2006), para. 251. See also *CMS v. Argentina* (ICSID Case No. ARB/01/8, Award of 12 May 2005), paras. 319–31.

[97] *Continental Casualty v. Argentina* (ICSID Case No. ARB/03/9, Award of 5 September 2008) para. 175.

[98] *Ibid.*, para. 178.

[99] *LG&E v. Argentina* (ICSID Case No. ARB/02/1, Decision on Liability of 3 October 2006), paras. 258–66.

[100] *Continental Casualty v. Argentina* (ICSID Case No. ARB/03/9, Award of 5 September 2008), paras. 167–8.

Sociedad General de Aguas de Barcelona, and *InterAgua Servicios Integrales del Agua,* deciding the case merely on the basis of the necessity defence under customary international law,[101] concluded that (1) the Argentine measures were not the only way to safeguard an essential interest; (2) Argentina's measures did not impair an essential interest of the investors' home States or the international community; and (3) government policies and their shortcomings significantly contributed to the crisis and the emergency, and while exogenous factors did fuel additional difficulties they did not exempt Argentina from its responsibility.[102]

Unsatisfied with the outcome, Argentina has moved to have these awards annulled. Amongst other reasons, Argentina argued that the respective tribunals applied customary international law as enshrined in Article 25 of the Articles on State Responsibility before and without considering separately Article XI of the US–Argentina BIT. Here, again, the outcomes in the annulment proceedings were different. The *CMS* Annulment Committee, while identifying 'errors and lacunas' in the award, said that the tribunal applied Article XI of the treaty, although applying it 'cryptically and defectively'. Thus, the Committee did not find a manifest excess of powers.[103] Conversely, the *Enron* Annulment Committee found that the tribunal's decision that the requirements of Article 25 of the Articles on State Responsibility were not met was 'tainted by annullable error'.[104] As this finding formed the basis of the tribunal's decision that Article XI of the BIT was inapplicable in the case, the *Enron* Annulment Committee concluded that the latter finding of the tribunal must also be annulled.[105] Finally, the *Sempra* Annulment Committee found that the tribunal in this case adopted Article 25 of the Articles on State Responsibility as the primary law to be applied, rather

---

[101] The applicable BITs in this case did not have a provision similar to Art. XI of the US–Argentina BIT: at n. 94.

[102] *Suez* v. *Argentina* (ICSID Case No. ARB/03/19, Decision on Liability of 30 July 2010), paras. 238–42. See also *CMS* v. *Argentina* (ICSID Case No. ARB/01/8, Award of 12 May 2005), paras. 354–8; *Enron* v. *Argentina* (ICSID Case No. ARB/01/3, Award of 22 May 2007), paras. 305–13; *Sempra* v. *Argentina* (ICSID Case No. ARB/02/16, Award of 28 September 2007), paras. 346–55.

[103] *CMS* v. *Argentina* (ICSID Case No. ARB/01/8, Decision on Annulment of 25 September 2007), para. 136.

[104] *Enron* v. *Argentina* (ICSID Case No. ARB/01/3, Decision on Annulment of 30 July 2010), para. 395. The Annulment Committee appears to have been of the view that the tribunal had manifestly exceeded its powers (Art. 52(1)(b) of the ICSID Convention).

[105] *Ibid.,* para. 405.

than Article XI of the BIT, and in so doing made a fundamental error in identifying and applying the applicable law. This failure constituted an excess of powers within the meaning of the ICSID Convention.[106]

These cases show that tribunals seem to be ready to interpret the 'necessity' or 'essential security' defence as going beyond purely military threats to security. This opens the possibility for States, in possible investment claims brought by SWFs against typical measures against these investors, to invoke such a defence. However, the grounds on which States may base this defence tend to be interpreted restrictively and will not be easily available. In particular, if an applicable BIT does not provide for a broadly worded essential security defence provision, the criteria of the necessity defence under customary international law are very restrictive. It would seem that the only secure way for a State to rely on a defence of this kind is if the applicable clause in a BIT is a self-judging clause. In this way, States will have substantial leeway in applying measures against SWFs. It is thus unsurprising that the most recent US Model BIT contains a self-judging clause to this effect. It remains to be seen whether other States follow suit.

V Conclusion

National protectionist measures targeted at SWF investments may increasingly come under the scrutiny of investment tribunals. As confirmed by international arbitral practice, significant State ownership does not prevent investors from seeking protection under the ICSID Convention and typical BITs. Because of the limited applicability of most BITs to the pre-establishment phase, SWFs typically cannot seek protection against protectionist measures before the establishment of an investment. Once an investment is lawfully established in the host State, the latter may have recourse to essential security or similar exceptions in BITs and/or customary international law. Notwithstanding mixed outcomes of the application of such a host State defence in cases arising out of the Argentine crisis, this defence will not be easily available under customary international law. Certainly, it should not discourage SWFs from commencing international arbitration against protectionist measures.

---

[106] *Sempra* v. *Argentina* (ICSID Case No. ARB/02/16, Decision on Annulment of 29 June 2010), paras. 208–9.

9

Investor misconduct: Jurisdiction, admissibility or merits?

ANDREW NEWCOMBE*

I Introduction

In *Quantum of Solace*, the latest film in the James Bond series, the ruthless Dominic Greene, frontman for the evil international organisation, Quantum, forges a deal with exiled Bolivian General Medrano. In return for some large briefcases of euros and the new title of president, Medrano signs over a vast tract of desert, which, unbeknownst to him, contains most of his country's fresh water. Having acquired rights to the country's water, Greene then forces Medrano to provide his organisation an exclusive concession for provision of water services, under threat of forceful removal. The fictional events in *Quantum of Solace* play on a popular theme in contemporary film – that of the nefarious multinational corporation acquiring rights to natural resources in a poor, developing State through illegitimate means, often with the connivance of a rich, developed State.

In Ian Fleming's original story by the same name, the term 'quantum of solace' refers to the common humanity required between two people for a relationship to survive. As James Bond says in the story: 'When the other person not only makes you feel insecure but actually seems to want to destroy you, it's obviously the end. The Quantum of Solace stands at zero. You've got to get away to save yourself.'[1] This

---

* This chapter is based on the author's presentation at the Sydney Law School Conference 'International investment treaty law and arbitration: Evolution and revolution in substance and procedure', Sydney, Australia, 19–20 February 2010. The author can be contacted at newcombe@uvic.ca.
[1] I. Fleming, 'Quantum of Solace' in *For Your Eyes Only* (New York: Penguin Books, 2003), pp. 77, 93.

view is likely shared at times by both States and foreign investors when the conduct of either party erodes the trust and confidence between them that is necessary for a successful and mutually beneficial foreign investment relationship.

'Quantum of Solace' is my name for an ongoing research project on investor misconduct in investment treaty law and arbitration. The sometimes 'stormy relationship'[2] between foreign investors and host States requires a quantum of solace. If the host State is intent on destroying the investor, then the relationship is likely at an end. The ability of host States to misuse sovereign powers and harm foreign investment is, of course, one of the primary purposes of international investment treaty law and arbitration. Modern investment treaties allow foreign investors to hold the host State accountable for breaching commitments to foreign investors and, more generally, for misuse of sovereign powers. International investment law serves as a commitment mechanism that deals with the problem of the 'obsolescing bargain' – the fact that once the investor has made its investment in the host State, its bargaining power can rapidly diminish.[3] In other words, international investment law provides a measure of comfort through binding standards and investor–State arbitration. The quantum of solace in any relationship, however, is reciprocal. What about the investor that has engaged in some form of serious misconduct, such as fraud, corruption or illegality? Does this investor have any measure of comfort that it is entitled to the benefits of investment treaty protection or does it, as a result of its misconduct, forfeit the protection afforded by the treaty?[4]

---

[2] For the reference to the 'stormy relationship', although in a different context, see P. Weil, 'The State, the foreign investor, and international law: The no longer stormy relationship of a ménage à trois', *ICSID Review – Foreign Investment Law Journal*, 15 (2000), 401.

[3] See R. Vernon, *Sovereignty at Bay: The multinational spread of U.S. enterprises* (New York: Basic Books, 1971), p. 46.

[4] Where serious misconduct is present, there will likely be a breach of the domestic laws of the host and home States; e.g. Siemens AG has been the subject of corruption and bribery investigations by numerous domestic authorities, pleaded guilty to a series of offences, and agreed to pay massive fines. See report on 'Legal proceedings' dated 3 December 2009, http://w1.siemens.com/press/pool/de/events/corporate/2009-q4/2009-q4-legal-proceedings-e.pdf (last accessed 8 July 2010).

A number of recent articles have discussed the issues of corruption[5] and illegality[6] in investment treaty arbitration. Other studies have addressed the issues of crime,[7] corruption[8] and contractual illegality[9] in international commercial arbitration. This chapter focuses on a narrow but important procedural issue – do investment treaty tribunals have a general power to dismiss an investor's claim as inadmissible where serious investor misconduct is present? It questions the approach of a number of awards, which treats investor misconduct as a jurisdictional impediment. This chapter suggests that serious misconduct might also be addressed either by dismissing the investor's claim (or part of it) as inadmissible or by finding that the investor is precluded from the substantive protections of the investment treaty. In less serious cases, investor misconduct might provide a defence to the host State on the merits or have remedial implications with respect to the amount of damages and the ordering of costs. Returning to the theme of 'Quantum of Solace', the foreign investor that engages in serious misconduct might have the comfort of knowing that an investment treaty tribunal has the

[5] See B. Cremades, 'Corruption and investment arbitration' in G. Aksen *et al.* (eds.), *Reflections on International Law, Commerce and Dispute Resolution: Liber amicorum in honour of Robert Briner* (Paris: International Chamber of Commerce, 2005), p. 203; H. Raeschke-Kessler and Dorothee Gottwald, 'Corruption' in P. Muchlinski, F. Ortino and C. Schreuer (eds.), *The Oxford Handbook of International Investment Law* (Oxford University Press, 2008), p. 584; and F. Haugeneder, 'Corruption in investor–State arbitration', *Journal of World Investment and Trade*, 10(3) (2009), 319.

[6] See C. Knahr, 'Investments "in accordance with host State law"', *Transnational Dispute Management*, 4 (2007), 5; U. Kriebaum, 'Illegal investments', *Austrian Yearbook on International Arbitration* (2010), 307.

[7] M. S. Kurkela, 'Criminal laws in international arbitration: The may, the must, the should and the should not', *ASA Bulletin*, 26(2) (2008), 280; D. Hiber and V. Pavić, 'Arbitration and crime', *Journal of International Arbitration*, 25(4) (2008), 461.

[8] M. Scherer, 'International arbitration and corruption: Synopsis of selected arbitral awards', *ASA Bulletin*, 19(4) (2001), 710; K. Karsten and A. Berkely (eds.), *Arbitration: Money laundering, corruption and fraud* (Paris, 2003); A. Court de Fontmichel, *L'Arbitre, le juge et les practiques illicites du commerce international* (Paris: Editions Panthéon Assas, 2004); A. Syed, *Corruption in International Trade and Commercial Arbitration* (The Hague: Kluwer, 2004); A. Mourre, 'Arbitration and criminal law: Reflections on the duties of the arbitrator', *Arbitration International*, 22(1) (2006), 95.

[9] R. H. Kreindler, 'Aspects of illegality in the formation and performance of contracts', *ICCA Congress Series No. 11* (The Hague: Kluwer, 2003), p. 209; K. Mills, 'Corruption and other illegality in the formation and performance of contracts and in the conduct of arbitration relating thereto', *ICCA Congress Series, No. 11* (The Hague: Kluwer, 2003), p. 288; and H. Raeschke-Kessler, 'Corrupt practice in the foreign investment context: Contractual and procedural aspects' in N. Horn (ed.), *Arbitrating Foreign Investment Disputes: Procedural and substantive aspects* (The Hague: Kluwer, 2004), p. 471.

jurisdiction to hear its claim, but serious misconduct may well render this claim inadmissible.

The chapter proceeds in four parts. The first part provides an overview of the various ways that misconduct arises at different phases of the investment and arbitration proceedings. The second discusses the distinction between jurisdiction and admissibility. Part three turns to whether an investment treaty tribunal has the power to dismiss claims as inadmissible. The final part of the chapter offers some concluding thoughts on why treating misconduct as a question of admissibility might be a preferable approach.

II   Mapping investor misconduct by phase of investment and arbitration proceedings

The issue of investor misconduct arises in investment treaty cases in myriad ways and circumstances. Accordingly, general statements about the effect of investor misconduct on investment treaty protection should be treated with care. First, there are significant differences between various types of misconduct.[10] Each form of misconduct – be it corruption of public officials, non-compliance with regulatory requirements (illegality), fraud, lack of due diligence or human rights violations – raises different issues and may well require a different response based on the type and severity of the misconduct in question. Secondly, investor misconduct can arise at different phases of the investment process. Misconduct can arise at the time of initiation of the investment, as exemplified in *Inceysa* v. *El Salvador* and *Fraport* v. *Philippines*.[11] Misconduct can arise during the operation of the investment, such as instances of non-compliance with regulatory requirements or bribery in order to obtain operational permits. Investor misconduct can also arise in the dispute-resolution process, such as where the investor

---

[10] It should be noted that 'misconduct' is not a legal term of art and has no defined meaning. Misconduct is used in this Article in a very general way to refer to investor conduct that might have a bearing on whether the investor is entitled to obtain treaty protection or that might have consequences for the merits of a claim or reparation. Misconduct might range from a lack of due diligence and business judgment to serious illegality. Further, I am referring to cases where the investor misconduct is proven and the issue is the legal significance of this misconduct.

[11] *Inceysa Vallisoletana S.L.* v. *Republic of El Salvador* (ICSID Case No. ARB/03/26, Award of 2 August 2006); *Fraport AG Frankfurt Airport Services Worldwide* v. *Philippines* (ICSID Case No. ARB/03/25, Award of 16 August 2007) (*Fraport*).

engages in sham transactions in order to obtain the benefit of investment treaty protection – a form of abusive forum shopping after a dispute has arisen.[12] Different legal consequences to an investor's claim under an investment treaty may ensue depending on the timing, type and severity of the misconduct.

In the context of investment treaty arbitrations, investor conduct can have legally relevant consequences at various stages in the arbitration proceedings. First, the tribunal might treat investor conduct as a jurisdictional issue. In *Fraport*, the majority of the tribunal treated illegality as a jurisdictional impediment.[13] Likewise, in *Inceysa*, the tribunal found that the State's consent to arbitrate was limited to investments made in accordance with host State laws.[14] In *Phoenix Action Ltd v. Czech Republic*, the tribunal found that investments 'not made in good faith, obtained . . . through misrepresentations, concealments or corruption, or amounting to an abuse of the international ICSID arbitration system'[15] were not protected and that, as a result, the tribunal lacked jurisdiction. Secondly, investor conduct might provide the State with a defence on the merits of the case. In a number of cases, tribunals have found the investor's lack of due diligence to be relevant in assessing State obligations to the investor.[16] Investor conduct may provide a State with a defence on the merits, as in *Genin* v. *Estonia*, where a banking license was revoked.[17] Thirdly, investor conduct may be relevant in assessing damages. In *MTD Equity Sdn. Bhd. & MTD Chile SA* v. *Chile*, the tribunal found the investor responsible for 50 per cent of damages

---

[12] *Cementownia 'Nowa Huta' SA* v. *Turkey* (UNCITRAL (NAFTA), Award of 13 August 2009 (not public)); *Europe Cement Investment & Trade SA* v. *Turkey* (ICSID Case No. ARB(AF)/07/2, Award of 13 August 2009) (*Europe Cement*).

[13] *Fraport*, paras. 396–404. The tribunal in *Alasdair Ross Anderson and ors* v. *Costa Rica* (ICSID Case No. ARB(AF)/07/3, Award of 19 May 2010) made a similar finding.

[14] *Inceysa*, para. 207.

[15] *Phoenix Action Ltd* v. *Czech Republic* (ICDIS Case No. ARB/06/5, Decision of 15 April 2009), para. 100.

[16] In *Genin* v. *Estonia*, the tribunal considered the investor's unreasonable reluctance to divulge information relevant in assessing whether the State breached treaty obligations in revoking a banking licence: *Genin and ors* v. *Estonia* (ICSID Case No. ARB/99/2, Award of 25 June 2001), paras. 348–73. Likewise in *Joseph Charles Lemire* v. *Ukraine* (ICSID Case No. ARB/06/18, Decision on Jurisdiction and Liability of 14 January 2010), para. 285, the tribunal noted that the investor's duty to perform an investigation before effecting the investment is relevant in assessing a breach of fair and equitable treatment.

[17] P. Muchlinski, '"Caveat investor"? The relevance of the conduct of the investor under the fair and equitable treatment standard', *International and Comparative Law Quarterly*, 55 (2006), 27.

because its conduct increased business risks.[18] Fourthly, investor conduct may be relevant to apportionment of the costs of the arbitration and the parties' legal fees. In *Cementownia*, the tribunal, because of the investor's abuse of process, ordered the investor to bear all the costs of the arbitration and the State's legal fees and expenses.[19] More generally, where the misconduct arises during the course of the arbitration proceedings, the tribunal might impose various sanctions such as granting interim measures, refusing to admit evidence or drawing adverse inferences.[20] In addition to these stages of the arbitration proceedings, a tribunal can find that even though it has jurisdiction, the claim before it is inadmissible and cannot proceed to a merits determination.

III   Distinguishing between jurisdiction and admissibility

Distinguishing between jurisdiction and admissibility is very difficult. In his article 'Jurisdiction and admissibility', Jan Paulsson wrote that although the two concepts are as different as night and day, 'There is a twilight zone.'[21] In *The Law and Procedure of the International Court of Justice*, Judge Fitzmaurice distinguished the concepts as follows: an objection to jurisdiction 'is a plea that the tribunal itself is incompetent to give any ruling at all whether as to the merits or as to the admissibility of the claim', while an objection to substantive admissibility is 'a plea that the tribunal should rule the claim to be inadmissible on some ground other than its ultimate merits'.[22]

The jurisdiction of an investment treaty tribunal generally depends on whether the claimant satisfies four necessary jurisdictional requirements for establishing the existence of adjudicative power – is there jurisdiction:

---

[18]   *MTD Equity Sdn. Bhd. & MTD Chile SA v. Chile* (ICSID Case No. ARB/01/7, Award of 25 May 2004), paras. 242–3.

[19]   *Cementownia*, para. 177. For a discussion of abuse of process in investment treaty arbitration, see J. Gaffney, '"Abuse of process" in investment treaty arbitration', *Journal of World Investment and Trade*, 11(4) (2010), 515.

[20]   See A. Kolo, 'Witness intimidation, tampering and other related abuses of process in investment arbitration: Possible remedies available to the arbitral tribunal', *Arbitration International*, 26(1) (2010), 43.

[21]   J. Paulsson, 'Jurisdiction and admissibility' in G. Aksen *et al.* (eds.), *Reflections on International Law, Commerce and Dispute Resolution: Liber amicorum in honour of Robert Briner* (Paris: International Chamber of Commerce, 2005), p. 603.

[22]   G. Fitzmaurice, *The Law and Procedure of the International Court of Justice* (Cambridge: Grotius Publications Limited, 1986), pp. 438–9.

1. *ratione voluntatis* (is there unqualified consent to arbitrate the claim in question?)
2. *ratione personae* (is the claimant a covered investor under the treaty?)
3. *ratione materiae* (is the subject matter of the claim within the scope of the treaty?; is there a covered investment?)
4. *ratione temporis* (was the treaty in force when the dispute arose?).

In contrast, admissibility is a question of the exercise of the tribunal's adjudicative power, an issue that only arises *after* the tribunal has established the existence of such power (jurisdiction).[23] Admissibility goes to the nature of the claim and whether there are impediments to a properly constituted tribunal hearing the claim.

Jan Paulsson suggests that the question can be framed as whether the objecting party is taking aim at the tribunal or the claim. If the challenge succeeds because the 'claim could not be brought to the particular forum seized, the issue is ordinarily one of jurisdiction and subject to further recourse.'[24] If the reason for the successful challenge is 'that the claim should not be heard at all (or at least not yet), the issue is ordinarily one of admissibility and the tribunal's decision is final'.[25] The distinction has important consequences. If a tribunal improperly asserts jurisdiction, its award might be reviewed for excess of jurisdiction. If the issue goes to the admissibility of the claim, the tribunal's decision is generally final.[26] In the case of admissibility, the tribunal exercises its adjudicative power to make a determination about the claim before it.

IV Can an investment treaty claim be dismissed as inadmissible?

There are conflicting statements in investment treaty cases on the power of a tribunal to dismiss a claim as inadmissible. It is important to note that, unlike the Rules of Court of the International Court of Justice[27] or the European Convention on Human Rights,[28] the ICSID Convention,

---

[23] See Z. Douglas, *The International Law of Investment Claims* (Cambridge, 2009), paras. 301–12. In *Waste Management Inc.* v. *Mexico* (ICSID Case No. ARB(AF)/00/3, Dissenting Opinion of 2 June 2000), para. 58, Keith Highet made the distinction as follows: 'Jurisdiction is the power of the tribunal to hear the case; admissibility is whether the case itself is defective – whether it is appropriate for the tribunal to hear it.'
[24] Paulsson, 'Jurisdiction and admissibility', p. 617.   [25] *Ibid.*   [26] *Ibid.*, p. 603.
[27] Art. 79 of the Rules of Court refers to objections to the admissibility of the claim.
[28] Art. 35 establishes admissibility criteria. Art. 35(3) states that the Court shall declare as inadmissible any individual application that it considers manifestly ill-founded or an abuse of the right of application.

the ICSID Arbitration Rules and the UNCITRAL Arbitration Rules do
not expressly refer to admissibility or preclusion of claims. Further, the
indices of the major treatises on international commercial arbitration do
not refer to 'admissibility' as a separate topic. The general approach in
international arbitration appears to be that if the tribunal has jurisdiction based on the consent of the parties, then the tribunal should, *indeed
must*, rule on the merits of the claim.

Notwithstanding the absence of an express reference to the concept
of admissibility in arbitration rules, investment treaty tribunals, as
creatures of public international law, should be viewed as having
inherent or incidental jurisdiction to find that claims are inadmissible
for abuses of process or other serious forms of misconduct.[29] Some
authority for this proposition might be drawn from the decision on
preliminary issues in *Libananco* v. *Turkey*, which stated that 'like any
other international tribunal, it must be regarded as endowed with the
inherent powers required to preserve the integrity of its own process'.[30] Other investment treaty cases have recognised a general power
to control the admissibility of claims. For example, in *SGS Société
Générale de Surveillance SA* v. *Philippines*, the tribunal, having confirmed that it had jurisdiction, found that the investor's claim was

---

[29] In 1961, in his separate ICJ opinion in *Northern Cameroons*, Sir Gerald Fitzmaurice
stated:

> In the general international legal field there is nothing corresponding to
> the procedures found under most national systems of law, for eliminating
> at a relatively early stage . . . claims that are considered to be objectionable
> or not entertainable on some a priori ground. The absence of any corres-
> ponding 'filter' procedures in the [ICJ's] jurisdictional field makes it
> necessary to regard a right to take similar action, on similar grounds, as
> being *part of the inherent powers or jurisdiction of the Court as an inter-
> national tribunal. [Case Concerning Northern Cameroons (Cameroon v.
> United Kingdom)* [1963] ICJ Rep 15, paras. 106–07 (emphasis added)]

For a summary of the power of international courts to dismiss a claim as an abuse of
process, see Professor Vaughan Lowe's submissions in *Request for Interpretation of the
Judgment of 31 March 2004 in Avena and Other Mexican Nationals (Mexico v. United
States), (Provisional Measures)* (CR 2008/15, 19 June 2008, Vaughan Lowe), paras. 45–52;
C. Brown, *A Common Law of International Adjudication* (Oxford Universtiy Press, 2007),
pp. 45–52.
[30] *Libananco Holdings Co. Limited* v. *Turkey* (ICSID Case No. ARB/06/8, Decision on
Preliminary Issues of 23 June 2008), para. 78. It should be noted that this statement
was in reference to its finding that parties have an obligation to arbitrate fairly and in
good faith in the context of allegations of interception of privileged communications –
and not with respect to the admissibility of claims.

inadmissible due to an exclusive jurisdiction clause in the investment contract. As a result, the majority of the tribunal issued a stay of the arbitration proceedings.[31] Although a number of tribunals have suggested that there is no general power to dismiss claims as inadmissible,[32] a growing number of cases appear to recognise the distinction between admissibility and jurisdiction.[33] For example, in the decision on jurisdiction in *Burlington Resources Inc.* v. *Ecuador,* the tribunal found that the claimant had failed to comply with the six-month

---

[31] *SGS Société Générale de Surveillance SA* v. *Pakistan* (ICSID Case No. ARB/01/13, Decision on Jurisdiction of 6 August 2003), para. 154.

[32] In *Methanex* v. *United States of America* (UNCITRAL (NAFTA), Partial Award of 7 August 2002), a NAFTA tribunal operating under the UNCITRAL Arbitration Rules stated at para. 124: 'There is here no express power to dismiss a claim on the grounds of "inadmissibility", as invoked by the USA; and where the UNCITRAL Arbitration Rules are silent, it would be still more inappropriate to imply any such power from Chapter 11.' However, as Paulsson highlights (Paulsson, 'Jurisdiction and admissibility', p. 607), the US objection was that Methanex's claim was legally meritless. It was not an objection to admissibility. It was an application for summary dismissal or strike out on the merits. In *CMS Gas Transmission Company* v. *Argentine Republic* (ICSID Case No. ARB/01/8, Decision on Jurisdiction of 17 July 2003), para. 41, the tribunal expressed doubt as to the distinction between admissibility and jurisdiction, stating that this distinction 'does not appear quite appropriate in the context of ICSID as the Convention deals only with jurisdiction and competence'. Compare with *Rompetrol Group NV* v. *Romania* (ICSID Case No. ARB/06/3, Decision on Jurisdiction of 18 April 2008) where the tribunal notes that the applicable ICSID arbitration rule contemplates not merely objections that a dispute is not within the jurisdiction of the Centre, but also any objection that the dispute is 'for other reasons, not within the competence of the Tribunal'. According to the tribunal, this appears to permit objections of a preliminary character whether they go strictly to jurisdiction, or to questions of competence or admissibility (para. 112).

[33] A series of tribunal decisions has recognised the distinction between jurisdiction and admissibility: *Ioan Micula, Viorel Micula, SC European Food SA SC Starmill SRL and SC Multipack SRL* v. *Romania* (ICSID Case No. ARB/05/20, Decision on Jurisdiction and Admissibility of 24 September 2008) found that an objection to jurisdiction goes to the ability of a tribunal to hear a case while an objection to admissibility aims at the claim itself and presupposes that the tribunal has jurisdiction (paras. 63–4); *Técnicas Medioambientales Tecmed SA* v. *Mexico* (ICSID Case No. ARB(AF)/00/02, Award of 29 May 2003) distinguished between objections to jurisdiction and non-compliance with requirements governing the admissibility of the foreign investor's claims (para. 73–4); *Generation Ukraine Inc* v. *Ukraine* (ICSID Case No. ARB/00/9, Award of 16 September 2003) found that a denial of benefits clause is not a jurisdictional hurdle but a potential filter on the admissibility of claims that can be invoked by the respondent State (para. 15.7); and *Bureau Veritas, Inspection, Valuation, Assessment and Control, BIVAC BV* v. *Paraguay* (ICSID Case No. ARB/07/9, Decision on Jurisdiction of 29 May 2009) distinguishes between jurisdiction and admissibility issues in discussing a claim under an umbrella clause (para. 132).

waiting period for a particular claim and, as a result, its claims were inadmissible under the treaty.[34]

A number of issues are generally recognised as giving rise to questions of admissibility. In Jan Paulsson's article, he identifies timeliness,[35] extinctive prescription, waiver of claims and mootness as admissibility issues.[36] Another example, from investment treaty practice, is a 'denial of benefits' provision that deprives an investor of the benefit of investment protection.[37] Even though a tribunal may have jurisdiction, where a denial of benefits provision is operative, the claim must be dismissed as inadmissible.[38] And, as noted above, *SGS* v. *Phillipines* suggests that a contractual choice of forum clause may give rise to a question of admissibility.[39]

If it is accepted that, as a general principle, investment treaty tribunals in the exercise of their jurisdiction have the power to dismiss claims as inadmissible in certain limited circumstances, the next question is whether those circumstances include cases of serious investor misconduct. For example, where an investor's conduct is contrary to international public policy, such as involvement in bribery and corruption, can a tribunal find that, despite having jurisdiction, it can dismiss the claim as inadmissible? A number of cases suggest this avenue may be open.

In *World Duty Free* v. *Kenya*,[40] the tribunal stated that claims based on contracts of corruption or on contracts obtained by corruption could not be upheld by the tribunal. In its conclusion, the tribunal, having already stated that as a result of the illegality Kenya avoided any contractual liability, found that: 'The Claimant is not legally entitled to

---

[34] *Burlington Resources Inc. and ors* v. *Republic of Ecuador and Empresa Estatal Petróleos del Ecuador (PetroEcuador)* (ICSID Case No. ARB/08/5, Decision on Jurisdiction of 2 June 2010), para. 336.

[35] Further, traditionally in diplomatic protection claims, international law has treated exhaustion and undue delay (laches) as a question of inadmissibility.

[36] Paulsson, 'Jurisdiction and admissibility', p. 616.

[37] See Art. 17, Energy Charter Treaty.

[38] See Douglas, *The International Law of Investment Claims*, ch. 13, 'Admissibility: Denial of benefits', referring to *Generation Ukraine* v. *Ukraine* where the tribunal found at para. 15.7 that the denial of benefits provision in Art. 1(2) of the Ukraine–US BIT was not 'a jurisdictional hurdle for the Claimant to overcome in the presentation of its case; instead it is a potential filter on the admissibility of claims which can be invoked by the respondent State'.

[39] See Douglas, *The International Law of Investment Claims*, ch. 10 'Admissibility: Contractual choice of forum'.

[40] *World Duty Free* v. *Kenya* is not an investment treaty case. Jurisdiction was based on a contract, which had been obtained as a result of the bribe.

maintain any of its pleaded claims in these proceedings as a matter of *ordre public international* and public policy under the contract's applicable laws.'[41] The reference to being not 'legally entitled to maintain' a claim might be interpreted on the one hand as there being no legal cause of action or claim (because the contract was illegal), a conclusion on the merits. On the other hand, the reference could be interpreted as confirming the principle that, as the claimant had admitted the bribery, it was not entitled to maintain its claim as a matter of *ordre public international*. In other words the claim was inadmissible because of a breach of international public policy.

In *Plama* v. *Bulgaria*, a case under the Energy Charter Treaty, the tribunal concluded that there had been deliberate concealment of the true identity of the investor amounting to fraud[42] and that the investor's conduct was illegal under Bulgarian law.[43] The tribunal concluded that 'the substantive protections of the ECT cannot apply to investments that are made contrary to law'[44] and that the 'Claimant is not entitled to any of the substantive protections afforded by the ECT'.[45] The tribunal stated that granting the protection of the ECT would be contrary to the principle of *nemo auditur propriam turpitudinem allegans* – no one is *heard* when alleging one's own wrong.[46] Further, the tribunal found that allowing the claim would be contrary to basic notions of international public policy and the principle of good faith, which encompass 'the obligation for the investor to provide the host State with relevant and material information concerning the investor and the investment'.[47] In *Plama*, the *nemo auditor* principle ('no one is heard') appears to be used as a reason for the inadmissibility of the claim. Unlike in *Inceysa, Fraport* or *Phoenix*, the investor misconduct was not viewed as a jurisdictional issue, but an issue that affected the substantive inadmissibility of the claim.[48]

---

[41] *World Duty Free Company Limited* v. *Kenya* (ICSID Case No. ARB/00/7, Award of 4 October 2006), para. 188.

[42] In *Plama Consortium Limited* v. *Bulgaria* (ICSID Case No. ARB/03/24, Award of 27 August 2008), the tribunal concluded that Vautrin (the indirect controlling shareholder) deliberately misrepresented the true identity of the investor to Bulgarian authorities (para. 129) and that the investment was the result of deliberate concealment amounting to fraud (para. 135).

[43] *Ibid.*, para. 137.   [44] *Ibid.*, para. 139.   [45] *Ibid.*, para. 325.

[46] *Ibid.*, para. 143. *Inceysa*, para. 240, in contrast, translates the expression into Spanish as '*nadie puede beneficiarse*', or 'no one can benefit'.

[47] *Ibid.*, para. 144.

[48] *Plama* might also be read as suggesting that the substantive protections of the ECT are applicable only if the investment is legal, which is a question of the merits of the claim.

V Concluding thoughts

On the one hand, serious misconduct on the part of foreign investors should not be condoned. On the other hand, serious misconduct is not necessarily always a jurisdictional issue.[49] Rather than reading in a good faith requirement as a precondition to jurisdiction as the tribunal did in *Phoenix*, the same substantive result might be achieved by applying the principle of substantive admissibility. Where an investor meets the technical conditions for jurisdiction (as the investor did in *Phoenix*), the tribunal should proceed to exercise its adjudicative power, rather than imply additional jurisdictional requirements.[50] The question in *Phoenix* was not jurisdictional. It was properly a question of admissibility and merits: should the claim be heard at all? The better response would have been to find that there was an abuse of process or, alternatively, that the claim was manifestly without legal merit.[51]

The distinction between jurisdiction and admissibility might be viewed as contrived. Although it is true that the immediate result might well be the same – the investor's claim is dismissed in a final award – approaching investor misconduct as a question of admissibility is preferable for a number of reasons.

First, as a matter of principle, I am drawn to Dr Bernardo Cremades' dissent in *Fraport* where he noted that:

> If the legality of the Claimant's conduct is a jurisdictional issue, and the legality of the Respondent's conduct a merits issue, then the Respondent Host State is placed in a powerful position. In the Biblical phrase, the Tribunal must first examine the speck in the eye of the investor and defer, and maybe never address, a beam in the eye of the Host State.[52]

---

[49] I should not be understood as saying that illegality, corruption or other serious misconduct can never be a jurisdictional issue. If there is illegal conduct in the acquisition of an investment, there might have been no property rights acquired under host State law in the first place. In this case, there might be no investment for the purposes of the investment treaty. In such a case, a tribunal would lack jurisdiction *ratione materiae*.

[50] In *Saba Fakes v. Turkey* (ICSID Case No. ARB/07/20, Award of 14 July 2010), paras. 112–14, the tribunal rejected the *Phoenix* approach of reading the principles of good faith and legality into the definition of investment in the ICSID Convention.

[51] The claimant in *Phoenix* informed the Czech Republic of the existence of an investment dispute a little more than 2 months after acquiring the investment. See *Phoenix*, para. 2. In light of the short time between the acquisition of the investment and the notification of the investment dispute and the other facts in the case, serious doubts can be raised whether there was any State conduct that breached the treaty after the acquisition of the investment.

[52] Dissenting Opinion of Mr Bernardo Cremades, 19 July 2007 at para. 37. With respect to investor misconduct, Dr Cremades states, at para. 40, that in cases of 'gross illegality'

Jurisdiction is binary – there is or there is not jurisdiction. Jurisdictional decisions are a very imperfect tool where there is misconduct of various shades on both sides.

Secondly, where there is serious misconduct that violates general principles of public international law or applicable customary or treaty rules, tribunals in the exercise of adjudicative power can have a role in denouncing misconduct by finding a claim inadmissible. For example, a strong case can be made that corruption of public officials is contrary to customary international law. In cases where the investment was obtained through corruption, an investment treaty tribunal that had jurisdiction could declare an investor's claim inadmissible.

Thirdly, if a claim is dismissed on jurisdictional grounds, it might be easier for the claimant to challenge the award under the New York Convention or before an ad hoc annulment committee for failure to exercise jurisdiction.[53] In contrast, a decision on admissibility, as an exercise of adjudicative power, would not generally be subject to review.

The central argument of this chapter is that investor misconduct can be addressed at various stages of the arbitration process and that there are a range of procedural responses available to a tribunal. Although recent decisions have focused on jurisdiction as the 'control mechanism' for addressing investor misconduct, given its binary function, jurisdiction is a blunt tool for dealing with the complexity and variety of issues that arise in investor misconduct cases, particularly where State misconduct is also a live issue. Admissibility is another tool available to tribunals to address cases of misconduct.

Using an admissibility approach appears to be particularly suited for egregious cases where the misconduct at issue should be explicitly denounced. The tribunal in the exercise of its jurisdiction sends a very strong message when it says that, despite having jurisdiction, we are unwilling to allow the claim to proceed. Dismissing a claim as inadmissible, however, is a very powerful tool and could be misused, which might explain tribunals' reluctance to use it. Finding that a claim is inadmissible is a decision as important as one on jurisdiction or the merits and deserves clear analysis and legal reasoning based on established principles of public international law. Caution must be exercised

---

there may be other reasons for the inadmissibility of the claim, referring to *Inceysa* and *World Duty Free*.

[53] See e.g. *Malaysian Historical Salvors SDN, BHD* v. *Malaysia* (ICSID Case No. ARB/05/10, Decision on Annulment of 16 April 2009), where the ICSID ad hoc Committee found at para. 80 that the tribunal exceeded its powers by failing to exercise jurisdiction.

and a tribunal should not proceed with a rote recitation of a series of high-minded principles and dismiss the claim. In this respect, general references to international public policy should be avoided in favour of reliance on established rules of public international law. Finally, as the exact scope and extent of the power to dismiss claims as inadmissible is unclear, further legal analysis on this issue is warranted.

10

The European Union as a global investment partner: Law, policy and rhetoric in the attainment of development assistance and market liberalisation?

PAUL JAMES CARDWELL AND DUNCAN FRENCH[*]

I Introduction

The European Union's (EU) interest and involvement in foreign direct investment (FDI) is by no means new.[1] However, it has only been comparatively recently that one has been able to begin to distinguish the particularities of a specific EU approach to FDI, especially when placed within a broader developmental context. The approach has been most visible during the ongoing negotiations of Economic Partnership Agreements (EPAs) with the African, Caribbean and Pacific (ACP) grouping of States. Though the EU–ACP relationship is often promoted (by the EU) as a model of mutual and benign co-operation between economically divergent States, the relationship highlights, in fact, political and normative challenges for both sides. In particular, whereas the EU has sought to utilise its links with the ACP countries to fashion a uniquely global role for itself, practice suggests this relationship is much

[*] Duncan French wishes to thank the British Academy for its financial support, thus allowing him to attend the 'International investment treaty law and arbitration: Evolution and revolution in substance and procedure' conference at the University of Sydney, February 2010. This chapter is a revised version of P. J. Cardwell and D. French, 'Liberalising investment in the CARIFORUM–EU Economic Partnership Agreement: EU priorities, regional agendas and developmental hegemony' in M.-C. Cordonier Segger, M. Gehring and A. Newcombe (eds.), *Sustainable Development in World Investment Law* (The Hague: Kluwer, 2011), p. 433. Both authors are grateful to Agnieszka Paszcza for research assistance undertaken through an internship with the Sheffield Centre for International and European Law ('SCIEL') at the University of Sheffield.
[1] This chapter does not deal with intra-EU bilateral investment treaties and the controversy surrounding their compatibility within the fundamental freedoms of the internal market, on which see H. Wehland, 'Intra-EU investment agreements and arbitration: Is European Community law an obstacle?', *International and Comparative Law Quarterly*, 58 (2009), 297–320.

more problematic for both. And what has in the past proved true for trade, is proving equally true in relation to FDI.

This chapter seeks to critically address the role of the EU as a global investment actor, with particular focus on the supposed synergies between FDI as a development assistance tool and FDI as a means to promote market liberalisation. This is especially significant as the entry into force of the Treaty of Lisbon in December 2009 has, for the first time, introduced the first explicit reference to foreign investment in the EU's treaty arrangements. While the grant of competence to the EU in this area will provide a clearer mandate for action, it fails to resolve the overarching question as to its purpose. The chapter thus focuses on one particular aspect of this broader debate, namely, the negotiation of investment provisions within EPAs, with particular comment on the investment provisions of the 2008 EPA negotiated between the EU and the Caribbean States.[2] In devising the rules on investment, the final text is innovative in numerous respects, though whether the investment liberalisation attained will also provide the stated developmental benefits is more contested. The chapter concludes by noting the unique range of pressures exerted on the EU in framing co-ordinated policies in the areas of FDI and development; thus, while the EU's rhetoric is often extremely positive on such issues, its capacity to implement them – and implement them fully and in an integrated manner – is invariably subject to the risk of incoherence and fragmentation.

II   Foreign direct investment as a matter of EU law and practice

One of the defining aspects of the EU – right from the establishment of the European Economic Community (EEC) in 1957 – has been its common commercial policy.[3] The policy represents an area in which the Member States have pooled sovereignty in external trade from the earliest days of the European integration project, granting the EU exclusive competence to act.[4] Through its supranational institutions, most

---

[2] Economic Partnership Agreement between the CARIFORUM States of the one part, and the European Community and its Member States, of the other part, 15 October 2008, [2008] OJ L289/I/3 (CARIFORUM–EU EPA).

[3] The legal basis for the common commercial policy is found in Art. 207 of the Treaty on the Functioning of the European Union (TFEU) (formerly Art. 133 of the EC Treaty). Art. 218 TFEU provides the legal basis for agreements with third countries or international organisations.

[4] For a detailed analysis of the common commercial policy see, inter alia, P. Koutrakos, *EU International Relations Law* (Hart, 2006), chs. 1–2.

prominently the Commission,[5] the EU has thus been able to present a unified policy agenda on matters of external trade. This has had enormous implications both for the development of the regional organisation itself, but also for the international trading system.[6] But it has always been accepted that this exclusive competence did not include investment policy; that the Commission could not negotiate – at least not without the express permission of the Member States – on matters of FDI.[7] Moreover, even when it did so, this was restricted to issues of market access, certain aspects of post-establishment liberalisation (notably national treatment) and investment promotion, almost always within the context of negotiating preferential *trade* agreements with third countries. Thus, the emphasis has clearly been on market liberalisation and not investment protection. In addition, the Commission has very conspicuously sought to place its FDI approach within a pro-development framework.[8] On the other hand, Member States have eagerly negotiated bilateral investment treaties (BITs) with third States,[9] with particular emphasis on ensuring post-establishment protection of their investors, often premised upon the implicit view that investment protection is a *sine qua non* for investor confidence, which will in turn generate developmental benefits. This bipartite division – between market liberalisation and investor protection – reflects a clear distinction between international trade agreements and international investment agreements in international economic law.[10] Though one can oversimplify this distinction, there is significant truth in portraying how these two areas of international economic law have been perceived and

---

[5] In matters of international trade, the European Commission acts as the principal negotiator on behalf of the European Union (TFEU, Art. 207(3)).

[6] See generally G. de Búrca and J. Scott, *The EU and the WTO: Legal and constitutional issues* (Hart, 2002).

[7] There are, of course, a number of multilateral treaties to which the EU – technically the European Communities – and its Member States are parties, which traverses the trade–investment interface, including the 1994 Agreement on Trade-related Aspects of Investment Measures, the 1994 Agreement on Trade-related Aspects of Intellectual Property Rights and 1994 General Agreement on Trade in Services, all supervised by the World Trade Organization. See S. Subedi, *International Investment Law: Reconciling policy and principle* (Hart, 2008), pp. 37–9.

[8] See http://ec.europa.eu/trade/creating-opportunities/trade-topics/investment/ (last accessed 15 October 2010).

[9] Indeed, the first-ever BIT was signed by West Germany and Pakistan in 1959, on the relevance of which see n. 28 below.

[10] F. Viale, 'External trade policy and the Lisbon Treaty: An enforcement of liberalisation of European commercial policy', www.s2bnetwork.org/download/LisbonTreaty&Trade (last accessed 15 October 2010).

regulated over the last fifty years. And while there is evidence of increased synergy between them, the links between them remain tentative and not fully explored.[11]

Moreover, despite the negotiation of international rules on investment by the EU (together with its Member States) for some time, it is the entry into force of the Treaty of Lisbon in December 2009 that is likely to have the most profound impact upon the capacity of the EU to act proactively in this area. The inclusion in (what has now become) Article 207 of (what is now) the Treaty on the Functioning of the European Union (TFEU) of explicit reference to FDI in the common commercial policy is of great significance. The full text of Article 207(1) is as follows:

> The common commercial policy shall be based on uniform principles, particularly with regard to changes in tariff rates, the conclusion of tariff and trade agreements relating to trade in goods and services, and the commercial aspects of intellectual property, foreign direct investment, the achievement of uniformity in measures of liberalisation, export policy and measures to protect trade such as those to be taken in the event of dumping or subsidies. The common commercial policy shall be conducted in the context of the principles and objectives of the Union's external action.

The TFEU also stipulates in Article 207(4) that foreign direct investment is one of the areas (alongside trade in services and the commercial aspects of intellectual property) where the principle of qualified majority voting amongst the Member States in the Council does not apply. This is due to the fact that the Member States are required to vote on the basis of unanimity 'where such agreements include provisions for which unanimity is required for the adoption of internal rules'.

Not only is this the first express reference to FDI in EU treaty law,[12] but its incorporation within the common commercial policy thus transforms it into a matter for which the EU has exclusive competence. Moreover, the provision within the common commercial policy that the right of the Member States to 'maintain and conclude agreements with third countries . . . in so far as such agreements comply with

---

[11] A. Qureshi and A. Ziegler, *International Economic Law*, 2nd edn (Sweet and Maxwell, 2007), p. 401.

[12] The Treaty Establishing a Constitution for Europe 2003 had included this provision, but the treaty was not ratified by all Member States having been rejected in referenda in France and the Netherlands in 2005. The Treaty of Lisbon 'rescued' key provisions from the dropped Constitutional Treaty, including what became Art. 207.

Community law'[13] has been dropped in favour of the more ambiguous provision stating that the competences of the common commercial policy 'shall not affect the delimitation of competences between the Union and the Member States, and shall not lead to harmonisation of legislative or regulatory provisions of the Member States in so far as the Treaties exclude such harmonisation'.[14] The Commission had long claimed that the EU's powers could not be exercised effectively whilst Member States were still able to create investment treaties of their own accord.[15] Judgments of the European Court of Justice in 2009 on BITs concluded by three Member States – Austria, Sweden and Finland with third countries – before their entry into the EU in 1994 found that some clauses contained in their BITs were incompatible with EU obligations and the Member States were therefore required to seek to amend them.[16] One might also note, however, that other non-EU-based dispute-resolution mechanisms may not share the same view.[17] Nevertheless, against this background, the inclusion of FDI within the common commercial policy raises the prospect of much more concerted – and centralised – activity at the European level.

In July 2010, the Commission followed up on the entry into force of the Treaty of Lisbon by bringing forward a proposal for a regulation establishing transitional arrangements for BITs between Member States and third countries.[18] The proposal was accompanied by a policy paper situating the proposed regulation within the goal of creating a

---

[13] Former Art. 133(5) EC.   [14] Art. 207(6) TFEU.

[15] J. Wouters, D. Coppens and B. De Meester, 'The European Union's external relations after the Lisbon Treaty' in S. Griller and J. Ziller (eds.), *The Lisbon Treaty: EU constitutionalism without a constitutional treaty?* (Springer-Verlag, 2008), p. 171.

[16] Case C-249/06 *Commission* v. *Sweden* [2009] ECR I-1335; Case C-205/06 *Commission* v. *Austria* [2009] ECR I-1301; Case C-118/07 *Commission* v. *Finland* [2009] not yet reported. For further comment on these cases, see E. Denza, 'Bilateral investment treaties and EU rules on Free Transfer: Comment on *Commission* v. *Austria*, *Commission* v. *Sweden* and *Commission* v. *Finland*', *European Law Review*, 35(2) (2010), 263–74.

[17] In *Eureko* v. *Slovakia* [2010] PCA Case No. 2008–13 (Award on Jurisdiction, Arbitrability and Suspension of 26 October 2010), which concerned the interpretation of the investment agreement between the Netherlands and the Czech and Slovak Republics, the arbitral tribunal found that it had jurisdiction to hear the case, despite Slovakia's argument that the agreement had been effectively superseded by EU law following Slovakia's accession in 2004.

[18] Proposal for a Regulation of the European Parliament and of the Council establishing transitional arrangements for bilateral investment agreements between Member States and third countries (COM (2010) 344 final, 7 July 2010) (Regulation Proposal).

'comprehensive European international investment policy'.[19] The aim of the regulation is to set out more clearly, and with more legal certainty, the terms, conditions and procedures by which Member States may conclude or retains BITs and to oblige the Commission to review all current agreements in force in order to assess compliance with Union law. Member States will be required to notify the Commission of their intention to enter BIT negotiations with a third State,[20] and it would be for the Commission to authorise the opening of negotiations.[21]

More concerted and centralised activity at the EU level, however, is not without either its problems or its ambiguities. First, FDI is not defined by the treaty, and though many would expect that the use of this terminology clearly indicates the EU's competence is limited to a traditional understanding of FDI, and thus does not include short-term portfolio investments, there are many instances in international invest-ment agreements (IIAs) where investment is defined much more broadly.[22] Doubts were raised, for instance, of the reach of the invest-ment provisions during both referenda held in Ireland on the Lisbon Treaty.[23] While the absence of a definitive understanding is unlikely to prove problematic per se, it invariably leaves open the future possibility of a more flexible approach to investment, especially if Member States either accept – or resign themselves – to the EU utilising its competence on a more generalised basis. Although the scope of the proposed regulation refers only to 'bilateral agreements with third countries relating to investment',[24] the Commission's paper (whilst taking a generally expansive view of what FDI entails) suggests that foreign *direct* investment differs from foreign investment, the latter including

---

[19] Communication from the Commission to the Council, the European Parliament, the European Economic and Social Committee and the Committee of the Regions: Towards a Comprehensive European International Investment Policy (COM (2010) 343 final, 7 July 2010) (Commission Communication).

[20] Regulation Proposal, Art. 8.   [21] *Ibid.*, Art. 9.

[22] Subedi, *International Investment Law*, pp. 58–62. Portfolio investments have been seen by the European Court of Justice as 'the acquisition of shares on the capital market solely with the intention of making a financial investment without any intention to influence the management and control of the undertaking: Case C-282/04 *Commission v. Netherlands* (2008) ECR I-9141, para. 19.

[23] See e.g. J. Kennedy, 'Why Lisbon Treaty vote has mobilised Ireland's tech multinational leaders', *Irish Independent*, 27 August 2009, www.independent.ie/business/technology/why-lisbon-treaty-vote-has-mobilised-irelands-tech-multinational-leaders-1870952.html (last accessed 15 October 2010). It is worth noting at this point that Ireland is the only EU Member State not to have signed any BITs.

[24] Regulation Proposal, Art. 1.

short-term portfolio investments.[25] For the time being at least, it appears that the Commission's view of the nature of the competence now included with the common commercial policy follows the generally understood meaning of FDI.

Secondly, and much more significantly, there is the question as to the scope of the EU's exclusive competence in this area. Does it refer only to issues of market access, investment promotion and certain aspects of post-establishment liberalisation (as seen, for instance, in the CARIFORUM-EU EPA, discussed below)? Or might it go further and take a comprehensive approach to FDI and include, in addition to the above, the traditional post-establishment protections currently only found within States' BITs, such as requiring the payment of appropriate compensation for expropriation, demanding 'fair and equitable treatment' and establishing binding international arbitration in the event of disputes? This is clearly not just a matter of legal interpretation, but has huge political and economic significance, both in terms of future negotiations but also – controversially – for those hundreds of BITS already negotiated by the Member States.[26] Though the finer details of the scope of the competence may ultimately have to be determined by recourse to the European Court of Justice,[27] the lack of detail within the final text at least implies the postponement of controversial debates yet to be had both between Member States and between Member States and the institutions, especially the Commission. Much may also depend on the negotiations to be undertaken in relation to the proposed regulation in the Council, where the Member States may try to water down the provisions.[28] The Council, in October 2010, welcomed the Commission's proposals and supported a broad scope for new EU policy in this area, though with the apparent condition that it is 'to be further elaborated in full respect of the respective competences of the Union and its

[25] Commission Communication, pp. 2–3.

[26] D. Vis-Dunbar, 'The Lisbon Treaty: Implications for Europe's international investment agreements', *Trade Negotiations Insights*, 8(9) (November 2009), http://ictsd.org/i/news/tni/59585/ (last accessed 15 October 2010): 'Not only could the Lisbon Treaty impact on future investment negotiations with the European Commission, it could also affect the more than two hundred BITs that currently exist between European and ACP Member States.'

[27] The general competences of the Court of Justice are found in Art. 19(3) of the Treaty on European Union (TEU).

[28] It has not gone unnoticed that Germany signed a replacement BIT with Pakistan on 1 December 2009, on the same day that the Treaty of Lisbon entered into force, and without recourse to, or consultation with, the Commission.

Member States as defined by the Treaties'[29] and that the action of the Commission should act 'on the basis of the experience and the best practices of the Member States'.[30]

Nevertheless, despite this ambiguity some are clear that a narrower interpretation is *a priori* the more preferable:

> the extension of the common commercial policy to foreign direct investment could and should be read more narrowly . . . The inclusion of foreign direct investment . . . should therefore be understood to refer only to those aspects of foreign direct investment which have a direct link to international trade agreements.[31]

While not necessarily disagreeing with this analysis, this chapter also accepts that the pull towards a more centralised – and comprehensive – understanding cannot be ignored. The political temptation and economic necessity of being able to negotiate wide-sweeping IIAs, mirroring the capacity of other major trading blocs to do so, may be too large to pass over. Certainly, it would seem to be the case that the Commission, perhaps not unsurprisingly, believes the new competence is worded to allow this broader interpretation – a 2008 communication from the Commission had already linked the importance of investment with the EU's internal strive for 'growth and jobs'.[32] As Woolcock has noted, 'The EU has already developed a common platform on investment rules and one must expect pressure to develop further a common EU policy on FDI.'[33] Though it is far too early to speculate precisely how the new competence will be exercised, it is surely not inappropriate to note that the inclusion of FDI within the treaty framework is an important

---

[29] Council of the European Union, 'Conclusions on a comprehensive European international investment policy', 3041st Foreign Affairs Council Meeting, Luxembourg, 25 October 2010, para. 7.

[30] *Ibid.*, para. 15.

[31] Viale, 'External trade policy and the Lisbon Treaty', pp. 2–3.

[32] Communication from the Commission to the European Parliament, the Council, the European Economic and Social Committee and the Committee of the Regions on the External Dimension of the Lisbon Strategy for Growth and Jobs: Reporting on market access and setting the framework for more effective international regulatory cooperation (COM (2008) 874 final, 16 December 2008), 5: 'As the world's largest exporter of commercial services and a major source of outward direct investment, the EU has an obvious interest to improve its access to foreign markets and to free the full potential of the EU's internal strength in services and establishment.'

[33] S. Woolcock, 'The potential impact of the Lisbon Treaty on European Union external trade policy', www.kommers.se/upload/Analysarkiv/In%20English/Analyses/Woolcock%20paper%20on%20impact%20of%20Lisbontreaty%20on%20tradepolicy.pdf (last accessed 15 October 2010), p. 4.

milestone, and that it would not be unexpected if the EU, certainly the Commission, were to utilise this competence to promote itself as a global investment actor. This approach is certainly apparent within its 2010 paper, which links the promotion of investment by the Member States in their bilateral agreements with the liberalisation agenda promoted by the Commission.[34] In recognising the economic significance of investment liberalisation, the chapter now turns to consider the EU's development policy (with particular reference to EU–ACP relations), which will then be followed by an analysis of the investment provisions of the CARIFORUM–EU EPA, which is at the forefront of EU attempts to converge these respective policy objectives.

III   EU–ACP relations: Situating investment in the development context

The EU's relationships with States in Africa, the Caribbean and the Pacific have been an inherent part of the external dimension of the European integration process. At the time of the signature of the Treaty of Rome in 1957, some of the original Member States of the EEC, principally Belgium and France, were yet to embark on a comprehensive decolonisation programme. Pre-independence territories in Africa and elsewhere were accorded the status of 'associated territories' in the EEC Treaty with preferential access to the markets of other EEC Member States.[35] Member States were obliged to apply the same rules to commercial exchanges with the associated territories as to other Member States.[36] The EEC Treaty also laid down the requirement for Member States to 'contribute to the investments required by the progressive development of these countries and territories'.[37]

Following the independence of most French and Belgian sub-Saharan African States in 1960, the 1963 Yaoundé Convention between the EEC, its Member States and nineteen newly independent States was signed. This association agreement, concluded for five years and renewed in 1969, continued the preferential and reciprocal trade access between the EEC and associated States. It also created the European Development Fund (EDF) as a supplementary source of finance,[38] and it established common institutions: an Association Council, a Parliamentary Conference

---

[34] Commission Communication, p. 11.   [35] Arts. 131–6 EEC (original text).
[36] Art. 132(2) EEC (original text).   [37] Art. 132(3) EEC (original text).
[38] Yaoundé Convention, 20 July 1963, [1964] OJ 93/1431, Arts. 16–17.

and an Arbitration Court.[39] The Yaoundé Convention set the template for EU–ACP relations to this day.[40] In 1974, following UK accession to the EEC and the expiry of the second Yaoundé Convention, the first Lomé Convention came into being, substantially enlarging the participating States to include former British colonies. The ACP group was thus born, and the Lomé Convention was renewed on four successive occasions in 1979, 1984, 1990 and 1995.

The Lomé Conventions, granting preferential trade relations on a non-reciprocal basis, were designed to be more beneficial to the ACP States than the Generalised System of Preferences (GSP) which, alongside access to the EDF, was intended to promote a more rounded development model for – and within – ACP States. Evidence suggests, however, that such mechanisms did little to increase actual trade between the EU and the ACP States.[41] It was only in the post-Cold War global context that the content of the EU–ACP agreements began to diversify. Against the background of the creation of the EU in the 1992 Treaty of Maastricht, which included provisions on foreign policy so as to improve the EU's presence on the world stage, the content of the final Lomé Convention (1995)[42] and Cotonou Agreement (2000)[43] was adapted to include provisions on, inter alia, human rights and good governance.[44]

[39] *Ibid.*, Arts. 39–53.
[40] Cf. E. Koeb, 'The Lisbon Treaty: Implications for ACP–EU relations', *Trade Negotiations Insights*, 8(8) (October 2009), http://ictsd.org/i/news/tni/57537/ (last accessed 15 October 2010):

> it is noteworthy that the reference to the ACP – in place since the Treaty of Maastricht of 1992 that safeguarded the intergovernmental nature of EU–ACP relations – has been removed from the Lisbon Treaty. The 'Declaration on the European Development Fund', part of the Treaty of the EU under the Final Act since the Maastricht Treaty, stipulating that the EDF should be outside the budget, has also been removed. These two changes are politically significant and give some indication that the ACP may be sliding from the EU agenda.

[41] J. Mayall, 'The shadow of empire: The EU and the former colonial world' in C. Hill and M. Smith (eds.), *International Relations and the European Union* (Oxford, 2005), p. 307.
[42] Revised Fourth Lomé Convention, 4 November 1995, [1998] OJ L156/3.
[43] Partnership Agreement between the Members of the African, Caribbean and Pacific Group of States of the one part, and the European Community and its Member States, of the other part, 23 June 2000, [2000] OJ L317/3 (Cotonou Agreement).
[44] Art. 9(4) of the Cotonou Agreement states that: 'The Partnership shall actively support the promotion of human rights, processes of democratisation, consolidation of the rule of law, and good governance.' This is also reflected in the 2005 European Consensus on Development – Joint Statement by the Council and the representatives of the

In any event, the need to reform the content of the EU–ACP agreement was prompted by adverse decisions in the General Agreement on Tariffs and Trade (GATT) and the WTO during the 1990s, which related to disputes over fundamental differences in the manner of EU treatment of banana imports from ACP and non-ACP developing countries.[45] The Cotonou Agreement therefore represented a significant break from the past, most notably in mandating that, because the preferential trade relations were incompatible with the same States' obligations under WTO rules,[46] they were to be replaced with EPAs premised upon reciprocity of treatment. The original date foreseen for their replacement was 1 January 2008.[47] The EPAs were to be negotiated with the ACP States organised largely through six regional blocs: the Economic Community of West African States (ECOWAS), the Communauté Economique et Monétaire de l'Afrique Centrale (CEMAC), Eastern and Southern Africa (ESA), the Southern African Development Community (SADC), the Caribbean (CARIFORUM), and the Pacific group. Critics, however, point out that where these regional negotiations have stalled, the EU has sought to undertake subregional and even individual negotiations, in direct contradiction to its assertion of the importance of regional integration.[48] This arguably reflects more general concerns about the rather aggressive handling of the negotiations by the Commission.[49]

governments of the Member States meeting within the Council, the European Parliament and the Commission on European Union Development Policy, 24 February 2006, [2006] OJ C46/01), para. 13.

[45] For a comprehensive account of the challenges to the EU banana regime, see P. Eeckhout, *External Relations of the European Union* (Oxford, 2004), pp. 381–94.

[46] Art. 36(1) Cotonou Agreement: 'In view of the objectives and principles set out above, the Parties agree to conclude new World Trade Organization ("WTO") compatible trading arrangements, removing progressively barriers to trade between them and enhancing cooperation in all areas relevant to trade.'

[47] This was the first day after the end of the WTO waiver (Decision of 14 November 2001) which temporarily legitimised the EU–ACP preferential trade relationship.

[48] EU–ACP Economic Partnership Agreements: Tearfund's provisional assessment of outcomes (January 2008), www.tearfund.org/webdocs/Website/Campaigning/Tearfund%20policy%20brief%20-%20provisional%20assessment%20of%20outcomes%20of%20EU-ACP%20EPAs.pdf (last accessed 15 October 2010): 'One of the key objectives of EPAs – increased regional integration – has been seriously undermined by the Commission's strategy to strike deals with individual governments or a regional sub-group, inevitably leading to increased trade barriers between neighbouring countries.'

[49] As a 2005 British Parliamentary report on EPA negotiations commented, 'The relationship between the EU and the ACP has never been an equal one. This has not changed in the negotiations for the Economic Partnership Agreements' (UK House of Commons, International Development Committee, 'Fair trade? The European Union's trade agreements with African, Caribbean and Pacific Countries' (HC 68, 6 April 2005, para. 6).

The EU has asserted that, notwithstanding the removal of trade preferences and, more generally, the move towards reciprocity, such EPAs would continue to incorporate a significant developmental focus. As the Cotonou Agreement stated, 'Negotiations shall take account of the level of development and the socio-economic impact of trade measures on ACP countries, and their capacity to adapt and adjust their economies to the liberalization process.'[50] This flexibility is to be achieved in numerous ways, though the principal device is the entrenchment of 'asymmetrical reciprocity' within the legal texts. In other words, though EPAs are to be premised upon ACP States opening up their markets to the EU, this will be done incrementally and more gradually than the EU will open its own markets to ACP States.[51]

This approach is rooted in the notion that market liberalisation is a key aspect in promoting development, despite the fact that the benefits of opening up developing country markets are rarely automatic but dependent upon endogenous capacity-building, developmental assistance (particularly in areas such as infrastructure and other supply-side constraints) and flexibility in implementation. Moreover, one can point to the rather blunt nature of asymmetrical reciprocity; longer run-in times and variable geometry in the scope of binding commitments will not necessarily, in themselves, be sufficient to accommodate the special concerns and considerations of developing countries. While the EU would seem to recognise the importance of such matters (such as endorsing aid-for-trade financial packages),[52] its preferred method is to consider these issues 'off table' and certainly, as far as possible, not within the text of the EPAs themselves.

The concern is that the economically and politically weaker ACP States have little choice but to accept the EU's negotiating stance. This point is particularly acute considering the lack of financial and technical

---

[50] Cotonou Agreement, Art. 37(7).

[51] Whether such asymmetrical reciprocity is compatible with WTO rules, specifically Art. XXIV GATT on regional trade agreements (RTAs), remains uncertain. The Cotonou Agreement itself recognises that the EU and ACP Parties will have to collaborate in the WTO 'with a view to defending the arrangements reached, in particular with regard to the degree of flexibility available' (Cotonou Agreement, Art. 37(8)).

[52] See Communication from the Commission to the Council and the European Parliament: Economic Partnership Agreements (COM (2007) 635 final, 23 October 2007), para. 5: 'Full EPAs will allow EDF funding to be directed towards the range of adjustment needs arising from commitments taken by ACP countries and will help establish priorities for additional funding from Member States.'

support specified in the EPA. A study by the European Parliament reported in March 2009 that:

> Although EU donors have made commitments that appear to be adequate there is no guarantee that they will be applied in an appropriate and timely way – and there is complete uncertainty over the funds for EPA support that will be committed by the European Commission and EU Member States beyond 2013.[53]

Of particular controversy is the extent to which EPAs should include rules on the so-called 'Singapore issues', namely foreign direct investment, competition, government procurement and trade facilitation. Developing countries have successfully removed these issues (apart from trade facilitation) from negotiation at the global-trade level within the Doha Development Round.[54] The EU has however been keen to ensure that these topics are negotiated within the context of EPAs. Most ACP States, on the other hand, have been singularly more reticent and defensive about their inclusion.[55] Particular controversy has surrounded the issue of investment, and whilst FDI is not an entirely novel feature of contemporary EU–ACP relations,[56] it has attained a new intensity with the negotiation of the EPAs. The wording of the Cotonou Agreement simply required that 'general principles on protection and promotion of investments' be 'introduce[d]' within EPAs.[57] In any event, if the underlying purpose of EPAs is primarily to ensure compatibility with WTO *trade* commitments, then clearly such negotiations are additional to the core requirements.

More fundamentally, many ACP States are concerned that the inclusion of Singapore issues within EPAs jeopardises their overall developmental focus. As one commentator noted in evidence to a British Parliamentary investigation on EPAs, 'what [ACP States] fear is that the EU will twist their

---

[53] European Parliament, Directorate-General for External Policies, *The CARIFORUM-EU Economic Partnership Agreement (EPA): The development component (Study)* ((2009) EXPO/B/DEVE/2008/60), p. 10.

[54] Though included in the initial 2001 Doha Declaration, due to the absence of consensus within the WTO membership, these issues were jettisoned in the so-called July 2004 package.

[55] See e.g. S. Woolcock, *Government Procurement Provisions in CARIFORUM EPA and Lessons for Other ACP States*, www2.lse.ac.uk/internationalRelations/centresandunits/ITPU/ITPUindexdocs.aspx (last accessed on 25 May 2011).

[56] S. Bilal and D. te Velde, 'Foreign direct investment in the ACP–EU development cooperation: From Lomé to Cotonou' (UNCTAD Expert Meeting, The Development Dimension of FDI, Geneva 6–8 November 2002).

[57] Cotonou Agreement, Art. 78(3).

arm to accept with the EPAs things they would never have to accept on a more level playing field'.[58] Moreover, the ongoing negotiation and conclusion of interim EPAs with a number of regional groupings and individual States is entirely due to the fact that these ACP States have so far refused to agree rules on, amongst other things, the Singapore issues. Nevertheless, the incorporation of so-called *rendez-vous* provisions within these interim agreements, setting forth areas (such as investment liberalisation) to be included in the subsequent negotiations towards the conclusion of comprehensive EPAs, against the general wishes of ACP negotiators, again indicates both the general wariness of ACP States to negotiate on these issues as well as the unequal bargaining strength of the EU.

The debate over the inclusion of investment within the EPAs is therefore not unsurprising. If there is a general debate about how far and how quickly developing countries can, and should, be integrated into the global economy on a level of *reasonable* parity, differences in viewpoint become ever more acute when viewed from the perspective of the regulation and liberalisation of FDI. From a developmental perspective, investment policy inevitably polarises an already strained debate. As a report for one non-governmental organisation has noted,

> The EU and ACP countries agree on the potential value of investment and of sound, well-functioning regulatory regimes for development. What is in dispute is the added value of a rules-based investment agreement between the regions. Many ACP states already have ongoing domestic reforms relating to their investment regimes. The added value of an ACP–EC agreement could only be the EC's belief that it would ensure implementation and 'locking in' of reforms – thus increasing attractiveness to EU investors – or that it would act as an additional impetus for this reform agenda.[59]

The same report is however sceptical of such value:

> Developing countries want to attract inward investment, and manage such investment through regulation to minimise costs and maximise benefits. The usefulness of binding international rules on investment for developing countries is controversial, as they tend to limit these policy choices and do little to attract new investment.[60]

---

[58] UK House of Commons, International Development Committee, 'Fair trade?', para. 25 (evidence submitted by Dr Christopher Stevens, Research Fellow, Institute of Development Studies).

[59] M. Masiiwa *et al.*, *EPAs and Investment*, www.christianaid.org.uk/Images/epas_and_investment.pdf (last accessed, December 2009), p. 6.

[60] *Ibid.*, 9.

Others, however, view investment as pivotal to developmental opportunities; 'the approach proposed by the EU demonstrates a strong development component . . . creating an open, transparent and predictable environment that delivers enhanced legal certainty would reduce the current perceived risk to invest in many of the ACP economies'.[61] Thus, the remainder of this chapter focuses on the first (and, at the time of writing, the only) full EPA that has so far been signed – between the EU and the CARIFORUM States – and specifically on its rules on FDI.

A   Investment provisions in the CARIFORUM–EU EPA: A meeting of minds?

Unlike many ACP States, the CARIFORUM States[62] were, as a whole, more willing to engage in comprehensive negotiations, in particular on investment and cross-border services.[63] To that extent, the very process of regional EPA negotiations has fragmented any semblance of ACP global policy coherence; those more cynical would note the EU's ability to strengthen its own position by undertaking disparate negotiations with different regional groupings.[64]

---

[61] F. Gehl, 'Services and EPA: A difficult but vital relationship', *Trade Negotiations Insights*, 8(8) (October 2009), http://ictsd.org/i/news/tni/57522/ (last accessed 15 October 2010).

[62] CARIFORUM covers members of the Caribbean Community (CARICOM) (Antigua and Barbuda, Bahamas, Barbados, Belize, Dominica, Grenada, Guyana, Haiti, Jamaica, Saint Kitts and Nevis, Saint Lucia, Saint Vincent and the Grenadines, Suriname and Trinidad and Tobago) and the Dominican Republic.

[63] Cf. Traidcraft, 'First economic partnership agreement (EPA) is signed amid confusion' (21 October 2008), www.traidcraft.co.uk/news_and_events/news/first_deal_signed.htm (last accessed 15 October 2010):

> The first EPA was signed between the EU and 13 Caribbean countries on 15th October 2008. The disarray surrounding the signing shows the extent of their unpopularity in the region and the pressure that the EU had to resort to in order to secure agreement. The signing was postponed several times after parliamentarians, leading academics and civil society organisations across the Caribbean voiced their concerns over the effects the deals would have on development.

[64] South Centre, *EPAs and Development Assistance: Rebalancing rights and obligations* (September 2008), www.southcentre.org/index.php?option=com_content&task=view&id=902 (last accessed 15 October 2010), para. 103:

> The European Union's Commission must recognize that the problems that have arisen as a result of the negotiations – the internal splintering of ACP regions, the lack of ACP countries signing before the deadline, and the concerns continually brought up by ACP negotiators – as indications of the problematic issues inherent within the EPAs.

As regards the provisions on investment in the CARIFORUM–EU EPA, it is important to note certain background factors that undoubtedly influenced the negotiations. First, as already noted, unlike many ACP States, there was a willingness amongst many of the CARIFORUM governments to negotiate on investment issues. In fact, as an analysis of the EPA notes, 'CARIFORUM is by far the most service-centric partner of all those the EU is currently negotiating with.'[65] More specifically, it seems that these States 'were in fact highly comfortable in negotiating on investment issues and exploiting the potential "signalling" properties of negotiating advances in this area'.[66] This is perhaps an overly generous assessment of the situation; certainly, a number of CARIFORUM States had (and continue to have) significant reservations over the entire EPA process.[67]

Secondly, and building upon the previous point, CARIFORUM States had in fact sought to take investment negotiations further to include not only matters of market access and liberalisation – the topics that were eventually to form the core of the final investment commitments – but also issues on investment protection and promotion. As noted above, these topics were beyond the current competence of the EU. Thus, it was for any BIT agreed between individual Caribbean and European States to determine matters such as expropriation and compensation, and the possibility of recourse to international arbitration.[68] To that extent, existing and future BITs will remain extremely relevant to many aspects of FDI between these (and other) parties.[69] Moreover, the EPA contains no minimum standard of treatment rules; as will be noted below, the EPA's provisions on post-establishment regulatory conduct are both limited and potentially qualified in nature. The EPA's focus is investment

---

[65] P. Sauvé and N. Ward, 'The EC–CARIFORUM economic partnership agreement: Assessing the outcome on services and investment' (Brussels: European Centre for International Political Economy, 2009), www.ecipe.org/publications/ecipe-working-papers/the-ec-cariform-economic-partnership-agreement-assessing-the-outcome-on-services-and-investment/PDF (last accessed 15 October 2010), p. 14.

[66] *Ibid.*, 15.

[67] See e.g. CARIFORUM-EU EPA, Art. 63, concerning the application of the investment and service provisions to the Bahamas and Haiti (cf. Bahamas initials trade in services and investment commitments, January 2010, http://trade.ec.europa.eu/doclib/docs/2010/january/tradoc_145746.pdf (last accessed 15 October 2010)).

[68] Footnote to CARIFORUM–EU EPA, Art. 66.

[69] Indeed, in the Commission's 2010 paper on European international investment policy, it is notable that the ACP countries are not mentioned at all: the investment focus is placed squarely within seeking wide-ranging agreements with China, India and Russia (Commission Communication, p. 7).

liberalisation: through market access, national treatment, and the application of the most-favoured-nation (MFN) concept.

Thirdly, as with trade obligations within the EPA, investment and service commitments are asymmetrical in nature.[70] In summarising the level of these commitments, the Commission notes that: 'the EU opens up for investment to a much wider extent than Cariforum countries do towards the EU. Cariforum applies many more conditions and limitations to a more limited sectoral coverage.'[71] And in relation to cross-border services, the Commission calculates that the EU 'makes commitments in 94% of sectors while CARIFORUM does so, on average, in 75% of sectors'.[72] As an aside, it should be noted that unlike the 1994 General Agreement on Trade in Services (GATS), but like the 1992 North American Free Trade Agreement (NAFTA), the investment rules cover both service and non-service economic activities (referred to as 'commercial presence'); cross-border services are regulated separately, though many of the basic precepts remain the same.

Though it is not possible to discuss all the investment provisions of the CARIFORUM–EU EPA, certain aspects are clearly worth highlighting.[73] First, the EPA does not adopt a comprehensive definition of investment, but rather is based upon the notion of 'commercial presence',[74] which is either the 'constitution, acquisition or maintenance of a juridical person'[75] (which itself requires the establishment or maintenance of 'lasting economic links'[76]) or 'the creation or maintenance of a branch or representative office . . . for the purpose of performing an economic activity'[77] (which itself is defined as having 'the appearance of permanency'[78]). Highly volatile share dealings – sometimes considered

---

[70] The commitments made are set out in Annex IV to the CARIFORUM–EU EPA.

[71] EC, *CARIFORUM-EC EPA: Investment*, http://trade.ec.europa.eu/doclib/docs/2008/october/tradoc_140979.pdf (last accessed 15 October 2010).

[72] EC, *CARIFORUM-EC EPA: Trade in Services*, http://trade.ec.europa.eu/doclib/docs/2008/october/tradoc_140974.pdf (last accessed 15 October 2010).

[73] Other important provisions include Articles on investment promotion (Art. 121), the maintenance of national standards (Art. 73) and a general exemption (Art. 184(3)). See generally, A. Dimopoulos, 'The common commercial policy after Lisbon: Establishing parallelism between internal and external economic relations?', *Croatian Yearbook of European Law and Policy*, 4 (2008), 101–29.

[74] CARIFORUM–EU EPA, Art. 65(a): '"commercial presence" means any type of business or professional establishment. The definition of "investor" is equally tied to the notion as an "investor" is "any natural or juridical person that performs an economic activity *through* setting up a commercial presence"' (Art. 65(b), emphasis added).

[75] *Ibid.*, Art. 65(a)(i).   [76] *Ibid.*, footnote to Art. 65(a)(i).   [77] *Ibid.*, Art. 65(a)(ii).

[78] *Ibid.*, Art. 65(f).

as FDI in certain contexts but which would be unlikely to support the host country's long-term development – would fall outside this definition.

Secondly, the contracting parties agree to open up only those sectors listed in their schedules of commitments – and this after taking into account those sectors which are *ex ante* excluded.[79] Within those schedules, parties may set out limitations and qualifications, both in relation to market access and the obligation of national treatment. Moreover, these qualifications may be not just those current non-conforming measures which States wish to retain but also where States wish to post a reservation as to the possibility of enacting future non-conforming regulations. Thus the view expressed in one review – that 'Liberalisation will therefore principally be achieved through the binding of existing regulatory practice and the resulting limitations on future attempts to close the door further to foreign investors'[80] – though indeed correct, must be further qualified by recognising the role of speculative reservations as to future regulatory conduct, which are also permitted in the schedules.

However, in those sectors where market access commitments are agreed, parties commit themselves to a range of obligations, subject to whatever qualifications they have included.[81] These obligations are to 'not maintain or adopt' (i) limitations on the number of commercial presences, (ii) limitations on the total value of transactions or assets, (iii) limitations on the total number of operations or on the total quantity of output, (iv) limitations on the participation of foreign capital and (v) measures which restrict or require specific types of commercial presence.[82] As regards national treatment, subject to the scheduling of non-conforming measures, parties guarantee to each other 'treatment no less favourable than that they accord to their own like commercial presences and investors'.[83]

Thirdly, and often viewed as one of the most controversial provisions, is the inclusion of an MFN obligation. Despite the controversy, the

---

[79] *Ibid.*, Art. 66. Exceptions include the 'mining, manufacturing and processing of nuclear materials' and the 'production of or trade in arms, munitions and war material'.

[80] T. Westcott, 'Investment provisions and commitments in the CARIFORUM–EU EPA', *Trade Negotiations Insights*, 7(9) (November 2008), http://ictsd.net/i/news/tni/32972 (last accessed 15 October 2010).

[81] CARIFORUM–EU EPA, Art. 67(1): '[the respective States] shall accord to commercial presences and investors of the other Party a treatment no less favourable than that provided for in the specific commitments contained in Annex IV'.

[82] *Ibid.*, Art. 67(2).   [83] *Ibid.*, Art. 68.

CARIFORUM–EU EPA highlights that it is possible to negotiate a highly asymmetrical commitment in this regard. In particular, while the EU commits to providing CARIFORUM States the same rights and privileges as it gives to any third country with which it negotiates a future economic integration agreement with improved terms,[84] the MFN obligations on CARIFORUM States is significantly less extensive. First, CARIFORUM States are not obliged to give the EU MFN status unless they negotiate a future economic integration agreement with a 'major trading economy' (rather than simply with any third party).[85] Moreover, the grant of MFN to EU Member States in this situation is not automatic but will be subject to 'consultations' between the EU and CARIFORUM parties.[86] And secondly, CARIFORUM States are not required to grant MFN status to EU Member States where the increased liberalisation is the result of greater regional integration amongst the CARIFORUM States themselves.[87] In short, the asymmetry has led some to wonder whether the EPA 'reduces the MFN commitment to almost zero'.[88] Others, however, still remain concerned that the very existence of the inclusion of an MFN provision exacerbates the economic disparity between the parties still further.[89] Moreover, as it is possible that the larger developing country economies, such as Brazil, may fall within the definition of 'major trading economy', such an MFN provision might also undermine South–South liberalisation if the EU sought to take advantage of greater rights given to other countries in the region.[90]

---

[84] *Ibid.*, Art. 70(1)(a).   [85] *Ibid.*, Art. 70(1)(b).

[86] *Ibid.*, Art. 70(5): 'The Parties may decide whether the concerned Signatory CARIFORUM State may deny the more favourable treatment contained in the economic integration agreement to the EC Party.'

[87] *Ibid.*, Art. 70(2).

[88] Westcott, 'Investment provisions and commitments in the CARIFORUM–EU EPA', para. 11.

[89] M. Stichele, *ACP Regionalism: Thwarted by EPAs and interim agreements on services and investments* (SOMO, 2007), http://somo.nl/publications-en/Publication_2530/view (last accessed 15 October 2010), p. 2: 'The EC's proposed definition of regional integration is extremely narrow. It limits the potential for ACP regions to derogate from "most favoured nation" treatment *vis-à-vis* the EU – as proposed by the EC.'

[90] See Sauvé and Ward, 'The EC–CARIFORUM economic partnership agreement', pp. 14–15:

> Brazil, in particular, has expressed concern in the WTO General Council that the insertion of such a provision into the CARIFORUM EPA and the interim EPAs may have the effect of discouraging countries from concluding [preferential trade agreements] with EPA partners . . . Neither CARIFORUM nor EC officials appear to find Brazil's arguments persuasive. CARIFORUM officials contend that major developing trading partners are unlikely to match the terms of the EPA.

Fourthly, in what was clearly a 'win' for CARIFORUM States, the EPA includes a singularly important provision on investor behaviour. Though the EU had been prepared to consider general wording, perhaps of a more preambular kind, the final result was a legally binding provision. The provision is worth quoting extensively: 'The EC Party and the Signatory CARIFORUM States shall cooperate and take, within their own respective territories, such measures as may be necessary, *inter alia*, through domestic legislation, to ensure that:' (a) investors 'are forbidden from, and held liable for, offering, promising or giving any undue pecuniary or other advantage' for the purposes of bribing or corrupting public officials; (b) investors 'act in accordance with [International Labour Organization] core labour standards'; (c) investors act in a way that does not 'circumvent . . . international environmental or labour obligations'; and (d) investors 'establish and maintain, where appropriate, local community liaison processes, especially in projects involving extensive natural resource-based activities'.[91] As one review of the EPA notes, 'It bears noting that the above provisions were inserted into the EPA at the behest of CARIFORUM'.[92] This is itself telling both as to the EU's own negotiating priorities and its regard for the values inherent within the preamble of the EPA itself.[93] Moreover, it is still unclear whether, and how far, the EU will adopt legal measures to regulate *extraterritorially* the activities of its private investors in the CARIFORUM region, or whether responsibility for the behaviour of EU investors will be left as purely a matter for the Caribbean States. Though the wording of the provision might seem to exclude an extraterritorial extension of 'home' law, a reasonable argument can at least be made that the objectives contained therein can only be fully assured through a co-ordinated approach between all parties.

Assessing the long-term developmental impact of the CARIFORUM–EU EPA is, of course, decidedly premature. Other ACP States, certainly those which have less experience in the service sector and a different history towards FDI, are likely to be less willing to adopt such a rule-based

---

[91] CARIFORUM–EU EPA, Art. 72.
[92] Sauvé and Ward, 'The EC–CARIFORUM economic partnership agreement', p. 15.
[93] CARIFORUM–EU EPA, preamble:

> Considering the need to promote economic and social progress for their people in a manner consistent with sustainable development by respecting basic labour rights in line with the commitments they have undertaken within the International Labour Organisation and by protecting the environment in line with the 2002 Johannesburg Declaration.

liberalisation approach. Many developing countries are likely to want to endorse a much more co-operative framework, first building up local capacity and governance capability. If legal rules are to be negotiated, they would wish for their principal focus to be upon technical assistance, as well as (where appropriate) much greater asymmetry in commitments and significant flexibility in implementation. In fact, investment liberalisation in an EPA may be simply premature if it has not yet been grounded at the regional or subregional level.

IV   Conclusion: Accommodating divergences in EU development and FDI policies

Whatever its perceived weaknesses, the CARIFORUM–EU EPA undoubtedly signals a new phase in both EU development and FDI policy. But in taking this process forward, one needs to appreciate the pressures upon the EU, as a political and economic entity, to act coherently both internally and at the global level. Of course, the EU is subject to many of the same pressures as any other major trading power, be that Japan, the United States or China; however the collective nature of the EU also means that it is also subject to a unique range of factors. These pressures reflect, in particular, the institutional and political nature of the EU in framing co-ordinated policies, developing legislative responses and negotiating international treaties. One approach to identifying such pressures – admittedly rather crude in many respects – is to differentiate between those that are internal to the EU qua regional economic integration organisation from those that are external thereto. For internal pressures, mention might be made of the differing priorities of the Member States on matters of development and FDI policy, the autonomous agenda of the European Commission on these issues and the deliberative, and indeed decision-making, role of the European Parliament. Such tensions are of course systemic to the EU-project as a whole, including in matters of general external relations, and thus it is unsurprising that the institutionalised tensions within these general relationships will play a significant role in how EU policy in this area will evolve, particularly now with the entry into force of the Treaty of Lisbon and its express extension of Union competence.

But in addition to these internal pressures are those that might be better described as 'external' – the influence of civil society, the views of business interests, the negotiating positions of other major trading blocs, as well as the general norms of the international economic system – in framing the EU's approach to these issues. And while such pressures are not unique to the EU, it is arguable that when combined with, and filtered through, the internal pressures identified above, it creates a curious array of policy drivers that might help throw some light on – if not explain – the challenges in accommodating divergent, but notionally equally foundational, objectives within the same policy-space. Thus, while the EU's rhetoric is often good – if not exemplary – the potential for fragmentation between the EU's goal of supporting global development and expanding its own global investment opportunities is not only arguably an inevitable tension in-built within its own institutional framework but it is also representative of the EU, more generally, trying to continually (re-)position itself within the global order. However, in seeking to become a global *investment* partner, the EU must be forever mindful of the plethora of its other identities, both within and without the European region.

The 'fair and equitable treatment' standard and the circumstances of the host State

NICK GALLUS[*]

I Introduction

Investment treaties oblige the parties to provide a certain level of protection to investments and investors from the other parties to the treaty. For example, most investment treaties oblige the State to pay compensation if it expropriates the investment, as well as to provide 'fair and equitable treatment'. The treaties generally also give foreign investors the right to claim before a tribunal that the State has failed to provide that level of protection.

Some States have responded to these claims by arguing that their circumstances affect the standard of fair and equitable treatment that they are obliged to provide. The States have argued that, while their treatment of the foreign investor was fair and equitable, similar treatment by another State not facing similar circumstances would fall short of the standard.[1]

The response of tribunals to these arguments has been inconsistent. For example, the tribunal in *Sempra* held that Argentina's financial crisis affected the fair and equitable treatment standard which it was obliged

---

[*] The views expressed in this chapter are the author's and do not necessarily reflect the views of the Government of Canada.

[1] See e.g. *CMS Gas Transmission Company* v. *Argentina* (ICSID Case No. ARB/01/8, Argentine Republic's Application for Annulment of 8 September 2005) (*CMS*), para. 58:

> The Tribunal had no authority to determine what was fair and equitable or a breach of an investment-related obligation in a vacuum. Nowhere in its decision is there any explanation of what is fair and equitable treatment of foreign investors in the midst of a severe economic crisis . . . The Tribunal's authority was limited to determining what was fair and equitable during the actual crisis ravaging Argentina, not during a period of idyllic stability which did not exist during the relevant time period.

to provide.[2] By contrast, the tribunal in *National Grid* held that the same crisis did not affect the standard.[3] This inconsistency generates uncertainty over the application of the fair and equitable treatment standard.

   Section II of this chapter describes the obligation in investment treaties to provide fair and equitable treatment. Sections III and IV address the decisions which have considered the relationship between the standard and the circumstances of the host State and the uncertainty generated by those decisions. Part V attempts to help resolve this uncertainty by identifying key factors which determine the influence of the circumstances of the host State on the fair and equitable treatment standard.

II   The obligation in investment treaties to provide fair and equitable treatment

Investment treaties require the parties to provide a certain level of protection to investors and investments from the other party. This level of protection is partly expressed through several specific obligations. For example, almost every investment treaty requires the host State to pay compensation if it expropriates an investment from the other party.[4] Similarly, many treaties require the host State to provide national and most-favoured nation treatment; that is, the treaties require the host State to treat investors and investments from the other party no less favourably than the host State treats its own investors and investments, or investors and investments from third parties, which are in like circumstances.[5]

---

[2] *Sempra Energy International* v. *The Argentine Republic* (ICSID Case No. ARB/02/16) (*Sempra*).

[3] *National Grid plc* v. *The Argentine Republic* (Award of 3 November 2008) (*National Grid*).

[4] See e.g. Art. IV(1) of the Treaty Between United States of America and the Argentine Republic Concerning the Reciprocal Encouragement and Protection of Investment (US–Argentina BIT), signed 14 November 1991 (entered into force 20 October 1994): 'Investments shall not be expropriated or nationalized either directly or indirectly through measures tantamount to expropriation or nationalization ("expropriation") except for a public purpose; in a non-discriminatory manner; upon payment of prompt, adequate and effective compensation; and in accordance with due process of law and the general principles of treatment provided for in Article II(2) . . .'

[5] See e.g. Art. II(1) of the US–Argentina BIT: 'Each Party shall permit and treat investment, and activities associated therewith, on a basis no less favorable than that accorded in like situations to investment or associated activities of its own nationals or companies, or of nationals or companies of any third country, whichever is the more favorable . . .'

In addition to these specific obligations, most investment treaties also impose a more general obligation of 'fair and equitable treatment'. For example, Article 2(2) of the United Kingdom–Albania bilateral investment treaty (BIT) states that 'investments of nationals or companies of each Contracting Party shall at all times be accorded fair and equitable treatment . . . in the territory of the other Contracting Party'.[6]

According to Dolzer and Schreuer, 'the purpose of the [fair and equitable treatment] clause as used in [investment treaty] practice is to fill gaps that may be left by the more specific standards, in order to obtain the level of investor protection intended by the treaties'.[7] Another explanation, offered by McLachlan, Shore and Weiniger, is that the clause 'affords a basis by which international law judges the adequacy of treatment meted out to a foreign investor by the judicial and administrative agencies of the host State. It reflects treatment which all civilized nations should accord to their citizens as well as to aliens.'[8]

Tribunals have attempted to identify in abstract terms which State actions breach the obligation to provide fair and equitable treatment. For example, in a passage which has been repeatedly quoted by subsequent tribunals,[9] the tribunal in *Tecmed* v. *Mexico* said that the fair and equitable treatment standard 'requires the Contracting Parties to provide to international investments treatment that does not affect the basic expectations that were taken into account by the foreign investor to make the investment'.[10] The tribunal went on to say that:

> The foreign investor expects the host State to act in a consistent manner, free from ambiguity and totally transparently in its relations with the foreign investor . . . The foreign investor also expects the host State to act

---

[6] Agreement between the Government of the United Kingdom of Great Britain and Northern Ireland and the Government of the Republic of Albania, signed 30 March 1994 (entered into force 30 August 1995).

[7] R. Dolzer and C. Schreuer, *Principles of International Investment Law* (Oxford University Press, 2008), p. 122.

[8] C. McLachlan, L. Shore and M. Weiniger, *International Investment Arbitration: Substantive principles* (Oxford University Press, 2007), para. 7.178. For a general discussion of the fair and equitable treatment standard in investment treaties, see S. Schill, 'Fair and equitable treatment under investment treaties as an embodiment of the rule of law', Institute for International Law and Justice Working Paper 2006/6; C. Schreuer, 'Fair and equitable treatment in arbitral practice', *Journal of World Investment and Trade*, 6 (2005), 357; I. Tudor, *The Fair and Equitable Treatment Standard in the International Law of Foreign Investment* (Oxford University Press, 2008).

[9] See e.g. *Sempra* (Award of 28 September 2007), para. 298.

[10] *Técnicas Medioambientales Tecmed SA* v. *United Mexican States* (ICSID Case No. ARB (AF)/00/2, Award of 29 May 2003) (*Tecmed*), para. 154.

consistently . . . The investor also expects the State to use the legal instruments that govern the actions of the investor or the investment in conformity with the function usually assigned to such instruments . . .[11]

More recently, the tribunal in *Bayindir* v. *Pakistan* stated that:

> the different factors which emerge from decisions of investment tribunals as forming part of the [fair and equitable treatment] standard . . . comprise the obligation to act transparently and grant due process, to refrain from taking arbitrary or discriminatory measures, from exercising coercion or from frustrating the investor's reasonable expectations with respect to the legal framework affecting the investment.[12]

Commentators have also attempted to identify in abstract terms which State actions breach the obligation to provide fair and equitable treatment. For example, McLachlan, Shore and Weiniger state that: 'The standard is concerned with the *process* of decision-making as it affects the rights of the investor . . .'[13] Thus: 'In assessing the adequacy of administrative decision-making, tribunals have been primarily concerned with either (a) the protection of legitimate expectations or (b) the application of a fair decision-making process.'[14] Similarly, 'When applied to judicial decisions, the standard provides a protection against denials of justice, being a failure to accord due process to the investor.'[15]

The various interpretations of the standard of fair and equitable treatment have been applied by tribunals in various situations, where they have found that States have failed to meet the standard. For example, tribunals have found a breach of the fair and equitable treatment standard by:

- Mexico failing to fulfil representations to the investor that an investment permit would be renewed[16]
- Chile issuing an investment permit for an urban renewal project that was inconsistent with local planning laws[17]

---

[11] *Ibid.*
[12] *Bayindir Insaat Turizm Ticaret Ve Sanayi AS* v. *Islamic Republic of Pakistan* (ICSID Case No. ARB/03/29, Award of 27 August 2009) (*Bayindir*), para. 178.
[13] McLachlan, Shore and Weiniger, *International Investment Arbitration*, para. 7.182 (emphasis in original).
[14] *Ibid.*   [15] *Ibid.*   [16] *Tecmed*, paras. 154 and 174.
[17] *MTD Equity Sdn. Bhd. & MTD Chile SA* v. *Chile* (ICSID Case No. ARB/01/7, Award of 25 May 2004) (*MTD*), para. 188.

- Poland reneging on a commitment to sell shares to an investor[18]
- the Czech Republic designing a sugar production quota formula to minimise the investor's quota[19]
- Yemen forcing an investor to sign a settlement agreement[20]
- Kazakhstan terminating a contract without following the procedure agreed to in the contract[21]
- Argentina responding to a financial crisis by reneging on a commitment to allow utility providers to charge tariffs in US dollars and to adjust those tariffs with inflation[22]
- Spain permitting money to be transferred from an investor's bank account without consulting the investor on the terms of that transfer.[23]

The examples above illustrate that countries in very different circumstances have been found to breach the fair and equitable standard. For example, Spain's gross national income per capita (GNIPC) is over thirty times that of Yemen.[24] Moreover, while Spain enjoys relative economic stability, Argentina was found to breach the fair and equitable treatment standard while responding to a crisis, during which, according to one tribunal, 'All of the major economic indicators reached catastrophic proportions' and which 'threaten[ed] total collapse of the Government and the Argentine State'.[25]

Does the obligation to provide fair and equitable treatment require countries facing such different circumstances to provide the same level of treatment? Recent decisions do not provide a clear answer.

---

[18] *Eureko BV* v. *Republic of Poland* (Partial Award of 19 August 2005), para. 233.

[19] *Eastern Sugar BV* v. *Czech Republic* (SCC Case No. 088/2004, Partial Award of 27 March 2007) (*Eastern Sugar*).

[20] *Desert Line Projects LLC* v. *Yemen* (ICSID Case No. ARB/05/17, Award of 6 February 2008), para. 179.

[21] *Rumeli Telekom AS and Telsim Mobil Telekomunikasyon Hizmetleri AS* v. *Kazakhstan* (ICSID Case No. ARB/05/16, Award of 29 July 2008), paras. 615–8.

[22] *CMS* (ICSID Case No. ARB/01/8, Award of 25 April 2005), para. 275–81.

[23] *Maffezini* v. *Spain* (ICSID Case No. ARB/97/7, Award of 13 November 2000), para. 83.

[24] According to the World Bank, Spain's GNIPC in 2009 was US$32,120, while Yemen's was just US$1,060: see World Bank, World Development Indicators Database (15 December 2010), http://siteresources.worldbank.org/DATASTATISTICS/REsources/GNIPC.pdf (last accessed 5 January 2011).

[25] *LG&E Energy Corp., LG&E Capital Corp. and LG&E International Inc.* v. *Argentine Republic* (ICSID Case No. ARB/02/1, Decision on Liability of 3 October 2006), paras. 231–2.

III Decisions concerning the relationship between the host State's circumstances and the fair and equitable treatment standard

A Decisions arising from Argentina's financial crisis

In the 1980s Argentina privatised many of its assets, including the companies responsible for providing its electricity and gas. To encourage foreign companies to purchase these assets, Argentina passed a number of laws, including laws which pegged the Argentine peso to the US dollar and gave utility companies the right to calculate prices in US dollars as well as the right to increase those prices consistent with US inflation.

Two of the many foreign companies which were attracted to Argentina were the British company, National Grid, and the US company, Sempra. They purchased stakes in Argentine companies which held the concessions to transmit electricity, and distribute natural gas, respectively.

In 1999, Argentina's economy began to rapidly deteriorate. By December 2001, the main Argentine share index had fallen by 60 per cent,[26] unemployment had reached almost 25 per cent,[27] and close to half of the Argentine population was living in poverty.[28]

In response to the deteriorating economy, Argentines and foreigners exchanged their pesos for US dollars. The government was unable to maintain the parity between the currencies and, in January 2002, it was abandoned. The government also froze utility prices, abolished the right of utility companies to increase those prices consistent with US inflation, and forced the companies to charge in pesos, at the rate of one peso to one US dollar.[29] Since the peso eventually fell to less than a third of a dollar, the income of National Grid and Sempra fell by more than two-thirds.

National Grid and Sempra responded by initiating arbitration against Argentina, arguing that Argentina had breached its investment treaty obligation to provide fair and equitable treatment. The *Sempra* tribunal agreed that Argentina breached its obligation to provide fair and equitable treatment by substantially changing the legal and business framework under which the investment was made. According to the tribunal:

> The measures in question in this case have beyond any doubt substantially changed the legal and business framework under which the investment was decided and implemented. Where there was business certainty

[26] *Ibid.*, para. 232.   [27] *Ibid.*, para. 234.   [28] *Ibid.*
[29] Law 25,561, Public Emergency and Exchange Rate Reform Law, passed 6 January 2002.

and stability, there is now the opposite. The tariff regime speaks for itself in this respect. A long-term business outlook has been transformed into a day-to-day discussion about what is next to come.[30]

In reaching this decision, the *Sempra* tribunal rejected an argument that Argentina's financial crisis affected the fair and equitable treatment standard. The tribunal noted the parties' 'extensive' discussion of the 'issue of whether crisis conditions should result in the lowering of standards set under treaties and investment law, to the benefit of the State'.[31] The *Sempra* tribunal quoted Professor W. Michael Reisman, the claimant's expert, who argued that:

> of course governments in these circumstances must take measures to restore public order, but from the investment *law* standpoint – and this is for the future of all investments – international investment law says you may do it, but you must pay compensations. If exceptions are made for like these or other circumstances, the entire purpose of modern investment law, which is to accelerate the movement of private funds into developing countries for development purposes, will be frustrated.[32]

While the precise language used by the tribunal slightly confuses the issue, the tribunal appeared to follow Professor Reisman's view and refused to lower the standard for Argentina when assessing its liability:

> The Tribunal does not believe that the issue here is one of lowering the standards of protection set under the Treaty or the law. This being said, however, the manner in which the law has to be applied cannot ignore the realities resulting from a crisis situation, including how a crisis affects the normal functioning of any given society. This is the measure of justice that the Tribunal is bound to respect. The Tribunal will accordingly take into account the crisis conditions affecting Argentina when determining the compensation due for the liability found in connection with the breach of the Treaty standards.[33]

Consequently, the tribunal took into account Argentina's crisis when awarding compensation, rather than when determining if Argentina had breached the fair and equitable treatment standard.[34]

---

[30] *Sempra* (Award of 28 September 2007), para. 303.   [31] *Ibid.*, para. 396.
[32] Quoted in *ibid.*, para. 396 (emphasis in original).   [33] *Ibid.*, para. 397.
[34] See also *CMS* (Argentine Republic's Application for Annulment of 8 September 2005), para. 356: 'Just as the Tribunal concluded when the situation under domestic law was considered, there were certain consequences stemming from the crisis. And while not excusing liability or precluding wrongfulness from the legal point of view they ought nevertheless to be considered when determining compensation.'

Shortly after the decision in *Sempra*, the *National Grid* tribunal issued its award. The tribunal began by stating that Argentina had failed to provide fair and equitable treatment because it fundamentally changed the legal framework on which the claimant had relied.[35] However, the tribunal went on to reverse this conclusion:

> The Tribunal's conclusion that the Respondent has been in breach of the Treaty cannot ignore the context in which the Measures were taken. The determination of the Tribunal must take into account all the circumstances and in so doing cannot be oblivious to the crisis that the Argentine Republic endured at that time. What is fair and equitable is not an absolute parameter. What would be unfair and inequitable in normal circumstances may not be so in a situation of an economic and social crisis.[36]

This principle was applied by the tribunal to find that there was no breach of the obligation to provide fair and equitable treatment until Argentina forced National Grid's Argentine subsidiary to renounce its legal remedies as a precondition to renegotiation of the concession. Thus, the tribunal ultimately held that, in the circumstances of Argentina's economic crisis, the change in the legal framework on which the claimant had relied was insufficient to breach the fair and equitable treatment standard. The tribunal held that it was only after Argentina subsequently required the renunciation of legal remedies that its conduct fell below the fair and equitable treatment standard.[37]

Hence, in contrast to the outcome in *Sempra*, the tribunal in *National Grid* held that Argentina's economic crisis *did* affect the standard of fair and equitable treatment that it was obliged to provide. Moreover, the tribunal in *National Grid* applied this principle to hold that the same measure which breached the obligation in *Sempra* – the change in the legal framework on which the claimant had relied – did not breach the obligation.[38]

---

[35] *National Grid* (Award of 3 November 2008), para. 179: 'It is the conclusion of the Tribunal that the Respondent breached the standard of fair and equitable treatment because: (a) it fundamentally changed the legal framework on the basis of which the Respondent itself had solicited investments and the Claimant had made them.'

[36] *Ibid.*, para. 180.

[37] For further discussion of *National Grid* and the relationship between the host State's circumstances and the fair and equitable treatment standard, see N. Gallus, '*National Grid v. Argentina* case note', *American Journal of International Law*, 103 (2009), 722.

[38] Argentina challenged both the award in *Sempra* and that in *National Grid*. The United States District Court for the District of Columbia held that the challenge to *National Grid* was time-barred: *Argentine Republic* v. *National Grid* (Civil Action No. 09–248,

B Decisions applying elements of the fair and equitable treatment standard

Sempra and *National Grid* are not the only decisions which have addressed the relationship between the circumstances of the host State and the fair and equitable treatment standard. There are several decisions which have addressed the relationship between those circumstances and *elements* of the fair and equitable treatment standard, which were described in section II above. Just like *Sempra* and *National Grid*, those decisions do not clearly explain the influence of the circumstances of the host State on the fair and equitable treatment standard.

1 Denial of justice

As explained in section II above, the obligation to provide fair and equitable treatment has been described as obliging the State to provide a certain level of treatment concerning judicial proceedings. When a State fails to provide that level of treatment concerning judicial proceedings, the State commits a 'denial of justice'. Two tribunals recently addressed the influence of the circumstances of the host State on denial of justice and reached different conclusions.

The tribunal in *Pantechniki* v. *Albania* concluded that the standard concerning judicial proceedings does not vary with the circumstances of the host State.[39] The claimant in that case was a Greek company which was awarded a contract to repair roads and bridges in Albania. In March 1997, the site at which the company was operating was invaded by locals rioting in the aftermath of the collapse of Ponzi schemes allegedly supported by the government. The rioting Albanians destroyed or stole much of the claimant's equipment. The Greek company claimed that Albania failed to provide full protection and security, in breach of the Albania–Greece bilateral investment treaty.[40] The obligation to provide

---

Order of 7 June 2010). An ICSID Annulment Committee agreed that the *Sempra* tribunal manifestly exceeded its powers by failing to apply the defence of necessity contained in Art. XI of the US–Argentina BIT and annulled the entire award: *Sempra* (ICSID Case No. ARB/02/16, Decision on the Argentine Republic's Application for Annulment of the Award of 29 June 2010).

[39] *Pantechniki SA Contractors & Engineers* v. *Republic of Albania* (ICSID Case No. ARB/07/21, Award of 30 July 2009) (*Pantechniki*).

[40] Agreement between the Government of the Hellenic Republic and the Government of the Republic of Albania for the Encouragement and Reciprocal Protection of Investments, signed 1 August 1991, entered into force 4 January 1995.

full protection and security often appears in the same investment treaty provision which requires States to provide fair and equitable treatment.

When assessing the claim, Jan Paulsson, acting as sole arbitrator, posed questions central to this chapter. Paulsson asked:

> Should a State's international responsibility bear some proportion to its resources? Should a poor country be held accountable to a minimum standard which it could attain only at great sacrifice while a rich country would have little difficulty in doing so?[41]

Paulsson did not answer these questions with an absolute 'yes' or a 'no'. Instead, his answer depended on the particular aspect of the standard allegedly breached. Thus, he began his answer by addressing the issue of denial of justice. Paulsson stated that: 'No such proportionality factor has been generally accepted with respect to denial of justice.'[42] He went on to explain that two reasons 'appear salient'.[43] According to Paulsson:

> The first is that international responsibility does not relate to physical infrastructure; States are not liable for denial of justice because they cannot afford to put at the public's disposal spacious buildings or computerised information banks. What matters is rather the human factor of obedience to the rule of law. Foreigners who enter a poor country are not entitled to assume that they will be given things like verbatim transcripts of all judicial proceedings – but they are entitled to decision-making which is neither xenophobic nor arbitrary.[44]

Paulsson went on to explain the second reason that the standard for a denial of justice does not vary with the circumstances of the host State:

> The second is that a relativistic standard would be none at all. International courts or tribunals would have to make ad hoc assessments based on their evaluation of the capacity of each State at a given moment of its development. International law would thus provide no incentive for a State to improve. It would in fact operate to the opposite effect: a State which devoted more resources to its judiciary would run the risk of graduating into a more exacting category.[45]

Having decided that the circumstances of the host State should not influence the standard of treatment with regard to judicial proceedings, Paulsson turned to the standard of full protection and security:

> To apply the same reasoning with respect to the duty of protection and security would be parlous. There is an important distinction between the two in terms of the *consciousness* of State behaviour in each case. A legal

---

[41] *Pantechniki* (Award of 30 July 2009), para. 76.   [42] *Ibid.*
[43] *Ibid.*   [44] *Ibid.*   [45] *Ibid.*

system and the dispositions it generates are the products of deliberate choices and conduct developed or neglected over long periods. The minimum requirement is not high in light of the great value placed on the rule of law. There is warrant for its consistent application. A failure of protection and security is to the contrary likely to arise in an unpredictable instance of civic disorder which could have been readily controlled by a powerful State but which overwhelms the limited capacities of one which is poor and fragile. There is no issue of incentives or disincentives with regard to unforeseen breakdowns of public order; it seems difficult to maintain that a government incurs international responsibility for failure to plan for unprecedented trouble of unprecedented magnitude in unprecedented places. The case for an element of proportionality in applying the international standard is stronger than with respect to claims of denial of justice.[46]

Hence, for Jan Paulsson, actions which amount to a denial of justice are consistent across countries but the standard of full protection and security can change depending on the circumstances of the host State.

This decision in *Pantechniki* contrasts with that in *Toto* v. *Lebanon*.[47] The claimant in *Toto* was an Italian company which was awarded the contract to construct part of a highway between Beirut and Damascus. In August 2001, Toto filed two claims before the Lebanese Administrative Court seeking indemnification for unforeseen works it had to carry out because the nature of the soil did not meet the specifications set out in the contract and because the design specified in the contract had been substantially changed. By March 2007, the court had still not decided the claims. Toto initiated arbitration under the Italy–Lebanon bilateral investment treaty,[48] arguing that the delay was a denial of justice which breached Lebanon's obligation to provide fair and equitable treatment.

The tribunal held that it had no jurisdiction to hear the claim because Toto had failed to demonstrate that the delays could amount to failure to provide fair and equitable treatment.[49] In reaching this decision, the tribunal partly relied on the circumstances in Lebanon during the period of delay. As noted by the tribunal:

---

[46] *Ibid.*, para. 77.
[47] *Toto Costruzioni Generali SpA* v. *Republic of Lebanon* (ICSID Case No. ARB/07/12, Decision on Jurisdiction of 11 September 2009).
[48] Agreement between the Italian Republic and the Lebanese Republic on the Promotion and Reciprocal Protection of Investments, signed 7 November 1997 (entered into force 9 February 2000).
[49] *Toto*, para. 168.

In February 2005, Lebanon's former Prime Minister, Rafic Hariri, was assassinated. This was followed by several terrorist bombings and assassinations that disrupted normal life in Lebanon. In summer 2006, a destructive war took place between Lebanon and Israel. In Mid-2007 there was severe internal fighting between the organization Fatah al-Islam and the Lebanese Army. In May 2008, another internal armed conflict exploded following a 17-month political crisis.[50]

The tribunal concluded that: 'These circumstances undoubtedly were not conductive to the functioning of Lebanon's judicial system and affected the proper functioning of Lebanese courts between 2002 and 2008.'[51]

Hence, the tribunal in *Toto* held that Lebanon's war with Israel and internal conflicts affected the standard with regard to judicial proceedings. The decision contrasts with the statements in *Pantechniki* that the standard concerning judicial proceedings is rigid.

2 Protection of legitimate expectations

The protection of legitimate expectations is also often described as an element of the obligation to provide fair and equitable treatment. Tribunals have addressed the influence of the host State's circumstances on this element of the fair and equitable treatment standard, just as they have addressed the influence of those circumstances on denial of justice.

The majority of tribunals have taken into account the host State's circumstances when considering if there has been a failure to protect legitimate expectations. The award in *Bayindir* provides an example. In that case, Bayindir alleged that the termination of its concession to construct a highway breached Pakistan's obligation to provide fair and equitable treatment. Specifically, Bayindir alleged that Pakistan frustrated its legitimate expectations.

When assessing this claim, the tribunal began by acknowledging that it had to take into account the circumstances of Pakistan at the time that Bayindir's concession was revived:

> A second question concerns the circumstances that the Tribunal must take into account in analyzing the reasonableness or legitimacy of Bayindir's expectations at the time of the revival of the Contract. In so doing, it finds guidance in prior decisions including *Saluka*, *Generation Ukraine* and *Duke Energy* quoted above, which relied on 'all circumstances, including not only the facts surrounding the investment, but also the political, socioeconomic, cultural and historical conditions prevailing in the host State'.[52]

[50] *Ibid.*, para. 165.   [51] *Ibid.*   [52] *Bayindir*, para. 192.

The tribunal applied this principle to find that Pakistan had not frustrated the claimant's legitimate expectations. It found that 'the Claimant could not reasonably have ignored the volatility of the political conditions prevailing in Pakistan at the time it agreed to the revival of the Contract'.[53]

Hence, the tribunal in *Bayindir* examined the circumstances of the host State when deciding if that State had breached its obligation to provide fair and equitable treatment through a failure to fulfil the investor's legitimate expectations. The approach in *Bayindir* is consistent with *Generation Ukraine* v. *Ukraine,*[54] *Parkerings* v. *Lithuania,*[55] *Duke* v. *Ecuador,*[56] and *Biwater* v. *Tanzania.*[57]

---

[53] *Ibid.,* para. 193.
[54] *Generation Ukraine Inc.* v. *Ukraine* (ICSID Case No. ARB/00/9, Award of 16 September 2003), para. 20.37:

> it is relevant to consider the vicissitudes of the economy of the State that is host to the investment in determining the investor's legitimate expectations, the protection of which is a major concern of the minimum standards of treatment contained in bilateral investment treaties. The Claimant was attracted to the Ukraine because of the possibility of earning a rate of return on its capital in significant excess to the other investment opportunities in more developed economies. The Claimant thus invested in the Ukraine on notice of both the prospects and the potential pitfalls.

[55] *Parkerings-Compagniet AS* v. *Lithuania* (ICSID Case No. ARB/05/8, Award of 11 September 2007), paras. 278, 306 and 335:

> In 1998, at the time of the Agreement, the political environment in Lithuania was characteristic of a country in transition from its past being part of the Soviet Union to candidate for the European Union membership. Thus, legislative changes, far from being unpredictable, were in fact to be regarded as likely. As any businessman would, the Claimant was aware of the risk that changes of laws would probably occur after the conclusion of the Agreement. The circumstances surrounding the decision to invest in Lithuania were certainly not an indication of stability of the legal environment. Therefore, in such a situation, no expectation that the laws would remain unchanged was legitimate.

[56] *Duke Energy Electroquil Partners & Electroquil SA* v. *Ecuador* (ICSID Case No. ARB/04/19, Award of 18 August 2008), para. 347: 'To identify [the investor's] expectations and to assess their reasonableness, it may be useful to recall that the investment was made in the political and economic context of Ecuador's energy crisis and national shortage.'
[57] *Biwater Gauff (Tanzania) Ltd* v. *United Republic of Tanzania* (ICSID Case No. ARB/05/22, Award of 24 July 2008), para. 601: 'the Arbitral Tribunal has also taken into account the submissions of the Petitioners, as summarized earlier, which emphasize . . . the limit to legitimate expectations in circumstances where an investor itself takes on risks in entering a particular investment environment'.

While several tribunals have taken into account the circumstances of the host State when deciding if that State has failed to fulfil the investor's legitimate expectations, these circumstances were not taken into account by arbitrator Robert Volterra in *Eastern Sugar* v. *Czech Republic*. The claimant in that case was a Dutch company which purchased Czech sugar mills as part of the widespread privatisation of Czech industry in the late 1990s. The Czech Republic subsequently passed three sugar decrees which reduced the claimant's sugar production quota. The tribunal held that the formula for deciding sugar quotas contained in the third decree was designed specifically to minimise Eastern Sugar's quota. By targeting the foreign investor, the tribunal held that the third decree breached the Czech Republic's obligation to provide fair and equitable treatment.

One of the arbitrators, Robert Volterra, dissented from the majority and also found that the first two decrees breached the obligation to provide fair and equitable treatment.[58] Unlike the majority, Volterra addressed the consequence of the first two decrees for the claimant's legitimate expectations. He held that the claimant had a legitimate expectation that it would retain its production quota and the reduction of that quota in the two decrees frustrated that legitimate expectation, thereby breaching the obligation to provide fair and equitable treatment.[59]

In concluding that the Czech Republic had frustrated the claimant's legitimate expectations, Volterra did not take into consideration the Czech Republic's recent transition from communism to a market system. Indeed, he stated (in the part of the award with which he agreed with the other arbitrators) that he 'does not believe that for historical reasons the Czech Republic should be held to a less stringent [fair and equitable treatment] standard than other countries, say the Netherlands'.[60]

IV   The uncertainty over the relationship between the host State's circumstances and the fair and equitable treatment standard

The decisions described above demonstrate that the relationship between the host State's circumstances and the fair and equitable treatment standard is uncertain. Moreover, they highlight arguments both for and against adjusting the standard.

---

[58] *Eastern Sugar* (Partial Dissenting Opinion of Robert Volterra of 27 March 2007).
[59] *Ibid.*, para. 27.
[60] *Eastern Sugar* (Partial Award of 27 March 2007), para. 273.

The award in *National Grid* highlights the argument that the wording of the standard supports taking into account the host State's circumstances. As explained by the tribunal, 'What would be *unfair* and *inequitable* in normal circumstances may not be so in a situation of an economic and social crisis.'[61] Indeed, commentators have relied on the wording of the standard to endorse the view that the host State's circumstances should be taken into account. When the fair and equitable treatment formula first emerged, Professor Schwarzenberger praised the insertion of the word 'equitable' for this very reason. He said that the formula:

> presents an imaginative attempt to combine the minimum standard with the standard of equitable treatment. This decision is well justified [because] . . . in relations between heterogeneous communities – in varying stages of technological advancement, social structure and political organization – and in an age of rapid change, the standard of equitable treatment provides equality on a footing of commendable elasticity.[62]

In their recent treatise, McLachlan, Shore and Weiniger draw from this passage to conclude that:

> The inclusion of the reference to equitable treatment also provides a means by which an appropriate balance may be struck between the protection of the investor and the public interest which the host State may properly seek to protect in the light of the particular circumstances then prevailing.[63]

Yet, just as the decisions discussed in section III above highlight arguments for taking into account the circumstances of the host State, they also highlight arguments against it. In the passage quoted in *Sempra*, Professor Reisman argued that, by lowering the standard to take into account the circumstances of the host State, tribunals will discourage investment into those States and, thereby, prevent those circumstances from improving.[64] The sole arbitrator in *Pantechniki* added that taking into account the host State's circumstances not only discourages foreign investment but also discourages States from addressing those circumstances.[65]

---

[61] *Ibid.*, para. 180 (emphasis added).
[62] G. Schwarzenberger, 'The Abs-Shawcross Draft Convention on Investments Abroad: A critical commentary', *Public Law Journal*, 9 (1960), 147, 152.
[63] McLachlan, Shore and Weiniger, *International Investment Arbitration*, para. 7.17.
[64] *Sempra*, paras. 396–7.   [65] *Pantechniki*, para. 76.

V   Resolving the uncertainty over the relationship between the host State's circumstances and the fair and equitable treatment standard

Properly weighing the arguments for and against taking into account the circumstances of the host State is difficult. It is beyond the scope of this short chapter. Instead, the remainder of this chapter identifies four factors which recent decisions indicate are important to deciding the proper relationship between the host State's circumstances and the fair and equitable treatment standard. Those four factors are:

1. the element of the fair and equitable treatment standard which is being considered
2. the standard of treatment required by the element which is being considered
3. the relationship between the fair and equitable treatment standard and the customary international law standard of treatment
4. the damages awarded by the tribunal.

A   The element of the fair and equitable treatment standard which is being considered

On their face, the awards in *Sempra* and *National Grid* may give the impression that the tribunals in those cases considered whether the *entire* fair and equitable treatment standard should move up or down depending on the circumstances of the host State. Tudor's book on fair and equitable treatment may give the same impression.[66] She states that: 'The general situation of the State is indeed taken into account by the arbitrator in order to set the threshold at which the standard would operate in a specific case; thus, the standard of treatment is set at different levels, depending on the situation of the State.'[67]

However, the award in *Pantechniki* highlights that the relationship between the fair and equitable treatment standard and the circumstances of the host State does not need to be addressed in absolute terms. *Pantechniki* highlights that the fair and equitable treatment obligation may be distilled into several elements and different elements may be influenced differently by the circumstances of the host State.

---

[66] Tudor, *The Fair and Equitable Treatment Standard.*   [67] *Ibid.*, p. 235.

B   The standard of treatment required by the element
which is being considered

Just as the precise element of the fair and equitable treatment standard being applied is important, so too is the standard of treatment required by that element. The higher the standard to which a country is held, the more persuasive the argument to adjust that standard for a particular country's circumstances. The point can be illustrated by considering the obligation to protect legitimate expectations.

As explained above, some tribunals have held that the obligation to provide fair and equitable treatment includes an obligation to protect the legitimate expectations of an investor. The tribunal in *Tecmed* said that: 'The foreign investor expects the host State to act in a consistent manner, free from ambiguity and totally transparently in its relations with the foreign investor.'[68] According to *Tecmed*, failure to fulfil these expectations is a breach of the fair and equitable treatment standard. However, Zachary Douglas has argued that the *Tecmed* standard is difficult for any country to fulfil.[69] He says that: 'The Tecmed "standard" is actually not a standard at all; it is rather a description of perfect public regulation in a perfect world, to which all States should aspire but very few (if any) will ever attain.'[70] If the *Tecmed* standard is one which is impossible for any State to obtain, it is difficult to argue that every State should be held to it, regardless of that State's circumstances.

Perhaps in response to criticism of the *Tecmed* standard, some tribunals have described the legitimate expectations of an investor more narrowly. They have explained that a State's obligation to fulfil legitimate expectations only requires the State to fulfil direct representations made to the foreign investor.[71] It is easier to argue that States facing different circumstances should fulfil their representations, rather than all meet a standard which 'very few (if any) will ever attain'.

---

[68] *Tecmed*, para. 154.
[69] Z. Douglas, 'Nothing if not critical for investment treaty arbitration: *Occidental, Eureko* and *Methanex*', *Arbitration International*, 22(1) (2006), 27.
[70] *Ibid.*, 28.
[71] See e.g. *EDF (Services) Limited* v. *Romania* (ICSID Case No. ARB/05/13, Award of 8 October 2009), para. 219: 'Except where specific promises or representations are made by the State to the investor, the latter may not rely on a bilateral investment treaty as a kind of insurance policy against the risk of any changes in the host State's legal and economic framework. Such expectation would be neither legitimate or reasonable.'

C   The relationship between the fair and equitable treatment
standard and the customary international law standard of treatment

If the actual standard of fair and equitable treatment is important in deciding the influence of the circumstances of the host State, then the relationship between that standard and the customary international law minimum standard of treatment is also important.

Customary international law is 'the general and consistent practice of States that they follow from a sense of legal obligation'.[72] The customary international law minimum standard of treatment is, therefore, the general and consistent treatment of foreigners performed out of a sense of legal obligation. The 1910 description of the standard given by the then US Secretary of State, Elihu Root, is often repeated:

> There is a standard of justice, very simple, very fundamental, and of such general acceptance by all civilized countries as to form a part of the world . . . If any country's system of law and administration does not conform to that standard, although the people of the country may be content or compelled to live under it, no other country can be compelled to accept it as furnishing a satisfactory measure of treatment of aliens.[73]

The relationship between the customary international law standard of treatment and the fair and equitable treatment standard is unclear. Some tribunals have held that the customary international law standard of treatment has evolved to the point where it is the equivalent to the obligation to provide fair and equitable treatment.[74] Other tribunals have rejected this view.[75]

If the standards are equivalent, then the decisions which have considered the influence of the circumstances of the host State on the customary international law minimum standard of treatment become relevant. A key part of that jurisprudence is the recent decision in *Glamis Gold Ltd* v. *US*. In that case, the Canadian investor argued that the US breached its obligation in the *North American Free Trade Agreement* (NAFTA) to provide the customary international law standard of treatment through legislation which required the investor to 'back-fill' pits it

---

[72] Agreement between the Government of the United States of America and the Government of [Country] Concerning the Encouragement and Reciprocal Protection of Investment, 2004 (US Model BIT), Annex A.

[73] E. Root, 'The basis of protection to citizens residing abroad', *American Journal of International Law*, 4(3) (1910), 517, 521–2.

[74] See e.g. *Biwater*, para. 592.

[75] See e.g. *Glamis Gold Ltd* v. *United States of America* (*Glamis*) (Award of 8 June 2009), para. 614.

had dug while mining for gold. The investor argued that the US should be held to a higher standard of treatment because it was a rich country with plenty of resources to devote to meeting a higher standard.[76] The tribunal rejected this argument:

> The customary international law minimum standard of treatment is just that, a minimum standard. It is meant to serve as a floor, an absolute bottom, below which conduct is not accepted by the international community . . . it cannot vary between nations as thus the protection afforded would have no minimum.[77]

Thus, if the fair and equitable treatment standard is equivalent to the customary international law standard of treatment, any argument to take into account the circumstances of the host State must confront the decision in *Glamis*.

D   The compensation awarded by the tribunal

The final key factor to deciding the influence of the circumstances of the host State on the fair and equitable treatment standard which will be addressed in this chapter is the relationship between that standard and the compensation awarded by the tribunal.

Recent decisions demonstrate that tribunals have the ability to take into account the circumstances of the host State when awarding compensation. The award in *Sempra*, described in section III above,

---

[76] *Glamis* (Memorial of Claimant of 5 May 2006), para. 519:

> the particular resources and levels of development of the host State play a role in the application of the standard to the particular circumstances . . . For a highly developed legal system with relatively extensive resources and institutional stability, such as the United States, the [fair and equitable treatment] standard thus, requires better conduct than what may be required for a less-developed country.

See also *Glamis* (Reply Memorial of Claimant), paras. 220–1: 'Although the fair and equitable treatment is a non-contingent standard, its exact meaning is to be determined "by reference to specific circumstances of application". The specific circumstances of application necessarily involves a consideration of the host State's level of development.' Note that the claimant made a similar argument in *Chemtura v. Canada*: 'As a general matter, the level of development of the host State, including the quality, strength and resources available to support a system of "rule of law", plays an important role in the application of the standard to the particular circumstances of a case': *Chemtura Corporation* v. *Government of Canada* (Memorial of 2 June 2008), para. 353. The tribunal did not address this argument in its award: *Chemtura Corporation* v. *Canada* (Award of 2 August 2010).

[77] *Glamis* (Award of 8 June 2009), para. 615.

illustrates how a tribunal can take into account the host State's circumstances when valuing property that has been damaged through a breach
of an investment treaty obligation.[78] Similar to *Sempra*, the tribunal in
CMS stated that: 'there were certain consequences stemming from the
[Argentine financial] crisis. And while not excusing liability or precluding wrongfulness from the legal point of view they ought nevertheless to
be considered by the Tribunal when determining compensation.'[79] The
tribunal went on to apply this principle when calculating the future
profits that the claimant's gas distribution company would have made
in Argentina but for the actions in breach of the treaty. The tribunal
considered the effects of the crisis in its analysis of the demand for gas,[80]
revenues,[81] and the discount rate.[82]

---

[78] *Sempra*, paras. 397, 422, 429, 441–2 and 448. See e.g. para. 448:

> There is little doubt in the Tribunal's mind that gas consumption, at such
> but-for scenario prices, would have been likely to decrease in the residen-
> tial, commercial and industrial sectors during the first years following 2001
> or CGP and CGS would have been faced with a serious increase in
> defaulting payments.

[79] *CMS*, para. 356. See also para. 406: 'the crisis cannot be ignored and it has specific
consequences on the question of reparation'.

[80] See e.g. *ibid.*, para. 444: 'it would be inappropriate to assume that the demand for gas
would have remained stable . . . despite the economic crisis'; see also para. 445: 'It is
difficult to believe that, with a tripling of the gas transportation costs . . . there would not
have been a further reduction in demand and/or a significant rise in delinquent accounts,
with its consequent impact upon TGN's cash flows.'

[81] *Ibid.*, para. 446: 'it is reasonable to assume that sales revenue would have decreased by
5% in each of 2002 and 2003 and by 1% in 2004'.

[82] *Ibid.*, paras. 450 and 453. The discount rate refers to the percent by which the compensation
of the claimant's lost future profits is reduced because the claimant receives money now
rather than the future. The more unstable the country, the less likelihood of receiving money
in the future, the less money an investor is willing to accept now to avoid having to wait and,
therefore, the higher the discount rate. See also *American Manufacturing and Trading Inc.* v.
Zaire (ICSID Case No. ARB/93/1, Award of 21 February 1997), paras. 63–4; *Siemens* v.
Argentina (ICSID Case No. ARB/02/8, Award of 6 February 2007), para. 382: 'the discount
rate to be applied to the estimated profits should reflect the cost of money and the country
and business risks'; *Enron Corporation and Ponderosa Assets LP* v. *Argentine Republic* (ICSID
Case No. ARB/01/3, Award of 22 May 2007), paras. 411–3: 'The Tribunal's expert considers it
appropriate to use a higher premium for risk than those used by [the claimant's valuation
expert] . . . the Tribunal considers that the figure proposed by the Tribunal's expert is
reasonable'; *Patrick Mitchell* v. *Democratic Republic of the Congo* (ICSID Case No. ARB/99/7,
Annulment Decision of 1 November 2006), para. 65: 'The Arbitral Tribunal adopted a lower
capitalization rate than the one adopted by the expert, duly taking into account "the economic
and political environment of the Congo"'; *CME Czech Republic BV* v. *Czech Republic* (*CME*)
(Final Award of 14 March 2003), para. 561:

When awarding compensation to a successful claimant, the valuation of property may not be the only means through which a tribunal can take into account the circumstances of the host State. Several investment treaty tribunals have found that, regardless of the actual damage to the claimant, they can adjust the compensation to ensure that it is equitable.

For example, the tribunal in *Tecmed* said that an 'Arbitral Tribunal may consider general equitable principles when setting the compensation owed to the Claimant'.[83] The tribunals in both *MTD*[84] and *Bogdanov*[85] may have

> The valuation of CNTS at USD 400 million is largely driven by the application of the multiple 8.0, which was selected by SBS . . . in reference to Eastern European operators risks in contrast to other countries. . . . The Tribunal's position is that it is not the Respondent's duty to make good this general risk, which may have many reasons outside of the control of the parties to this arbitration.

[83] *Tecmed*, para. 190. It is unclear whether the tribunal applied this principle in awarding Tecmed compensation. The tribunal merely identified the compensation awarded to the claimant and said, at para. 195, 'In such calculation, the Arbitral Tribunal has further considered . . . the circumstances explained in' several paragraphs, which included the paragraph in which the tribunal recognised it could apply equitable principles when awarding compensation.

[84] *MTD*, paras. 242–3. However, as Hobér notes, the tribunal may have taken 'the view that the Claimants had not established a causal link between the violation of the fair and equitable treatment standard going beyond 50 per cent of the expenditures': K. Hobér, 'Fair and equitable treatment: Determining compensation', *Transnational Dispute Management*, 4(6) (2007), 9.

[85] *Iurii Bogdanov, Agurdino-Invest Ltd and Agurdino-Chimia JSC v. Republic of Moldova* (Arbitral Award of 22 September 2005), section 5.2. See the discussion of this aspect of the decision in I. Tudor, 'Balancing the breach of the FET standard', *Transnational Dispute Management*, 4(6) (2007). See also the separate opinion of Ian Brownlie in *CME* (Separate Opinion on Final Award of 14 March 2003), para. 117, noting that the treaty required 'just compensation' and holding that just compensation 'is incompatible with profit levels derived from a dominant position in the media market'. Professor Brownlie applied this principle to reduce the claimant's damages for foreseeable profits by 10%. See also *Sapphire International Petroleums Ltd v. National Iranian Oil Company* (1963) 35 *International Law Reports* 136, 189: 'It is the arbitrator's task to decide [compensation] *ex aequo et bono* by considering all the circumstances'; *Himpurna California Energy Ltd v. PT. PLN (Persero)* (Final Award of 4 May 1999), para. 237: 'considerations of fairness enter into the picture, to be assessed – inevitably – by reference to particular circumstances. The fact that the Arbitral Tribunal is influenced in this respect by equitable factors does not mean that it shirks the discipline of deciding on the basis of legal obligations'; *Compañía del Desarrollo de Santa Elena SA v. The Republic of Costa Rica* (ICSID Case No. ARB/96/1, Award of 17 February 2000), para. 95; *Phillips Petroleum Company Iran v. The Islamic Republic of Iran, The National Iranian Oil Company* (Award No. 425–39–2 of 29 June 1989), 21 Iran–US Claims Tribunal Reports 79, 123: 'the determination of value by a tribunal must take into account all relevant circumstances, including equitable considerations'; *Kuwait v. American Independent Oil Co. (Aminoil)* (Final

applied equitable principles when reducing the compensation they awarded to the claimant because of the claimant's conduct.

Commentary supports the view that investment treaty tribunals can apply equity to adjust compensation. Thomas Wälde and Borzu Sabahi have observed: 'Tribunals ultimately, when choosing between competing and equally plausible and legitimate valuation methods . . . cannot avoid exercising discretion. This is where they will be influenced by equitable considerations.'[86]

Commentary has also recognised that, when applying equity to adjust compensation, a tribunal can consider the circumstances of the host State. As long ago as 1949, Roth stated that:

> Nobody would deny that a colonial territory, for example, and a highly organized metropolitan territory, should not be put on the same footing. The standard is always the same, but it is for the judges to take the particular circumstances into consideration which may call for special leniency. An analogy to penal law may be useful in this connection. A murder is a murder, but the appreciation of the circumstances alone enable the judge to fix a penalty in conformity with civilized justice.[87]

Thus, there is support for the view that investment treaty tribunals can take into account the circumstances of the host State when valuing damaged property and when awarding compensation. However, no tribunal has yet considered how an ability to adjust compensation to take into account the circumstances of the host State affects the application of the fair and equitable treatment standard. Thus, no tribunal has yet considered whether the ability undermines the arguments for taking into account those circumstances when applying the fair and equitable treatment standard.[88]

Award of 24 March 1982), 21 ILM 976, para. 78: 'It is well known that any estimate in purely monetary terms of amounts intended to express the value of an asset, of an undertaking, of a contract, or of services rendered, must take equitable principles into account.'

[86] T. Wälde and B. Sabahi, 'Compensation, damages and valuation in international investment law' in P. Muchlinski, F. Ortino and C. Schreuer (eds.), *The Oxford Handbook of International Investment Law* (Oxford University Press, 2008), pp. 1049, 1105.

[87] A. H. Roth, *The Minimum Standard of International Law Applied to Aliens* (Leiden: A.W. Sijthoff, 1949), pp. 120–1.

[88] For further discussion of the issue, see N. Gallus, 'The influence of the host State's level of development on international investment treaty standards of protection', *Journal of World Investment and Trade*, 6(5) (2005), 711.

VI Summary

Recent decisions highlight that the relationship between the fair and equitable treatment standard and the circumstances of the host State is uncertain. While the tribunal in *National Grid* took into account Argentina's financial crisis when applying the standard, the tribunal in *Sempra* refused; while the sole arbitrator in *Pantechniki* stated that the standard concerning judicial proceedings is rigid, the tribunal in *Toto* subsequently took into account Lebanon's wars; while several tribunals have held that the investor's legitimate expectations must take into account the circumstances of the host State, Robert Volterra did not consider those circumstances when finding that the Czech Republic frustrated a Dutch investor's legitimate expectations.

Although recent decisions highlight this uncertainty, they also reveal some key factors which will need to be addressed to resolve that uncertainty. These factors include:

• the element of the fair and equitable treatment standard which is being considered – the sole arbitrator in *Pantechniki* observed that different elements of the standard may be influenced differently by the circumstances of the host State

• the actual level of conduct required by the fair and equitable treatment standard – the higher the level of host State conduct that is required, the more persuasive the arguments that the standard should adjust to the circumstances of the host State

• the relationship between the fair and equitable treatment standard and the customary international law minimum standard of treatment – if the standards are equivalent then the argument for adjusting the standard to take into account the circumstances of the host State must confront the decision in *Glamis* that a standard which varies is not a minimum standard at all

• the ability of tribunals to take into account the circumstances of the host State when awarding compensation – this ability may affect arguments to take those circumstances into account when applying the standard of fair and equitable treatment, itself.

12

The plea of necessity under customary international law: A critical review in light of the Argentine cases

AVIDAN KENT AND ALEXANDRA R. HARRINGTON

I Introduction

Necessity, it is often said, is the mother of invention. However, in the context of international law, and the tribunals which apply and interpret it, perhaps it is more appropriate to say that necessity is the source of an exception, one that is meant to preclude the wrongfulness of conduct by States in times of crisis, when the conduct in question results in a breach of international law. Indeed, the invocation of the necessity doctrine as a defence has linked such diverse governmental interests as fur seal trading,[1] food supplies,[2] provisions for troops[3] and government bonds. Over its history, the necessity doctrine – and its legal antecedents – has encompassed a variety of emergencies giving rise to the necessity designation, key among them being the environmental and financial needs of the State.

The necessity doctrine has been analysed by the United Nations International Law Commission (ILC) and several international tribunals. Recently, it has also been the subject of several investment cases regarding emergency measures taken by the Argentine government earlier this decade

---

[1] 'Articles on responsibility of states for internationally wrongful acts, with commentaries', UN Doc. A/56/10 (2001), pp. 80–3, http://untreaty.un.org/ilc/texts/instruments/english/commentaries/9_6_2001.pdf (last accessed 26 January 2011) (ILC Articles).

[2] In 1795, Great Britain seized an American vessel carrying food supplies. It argued that its conduct was justified by the doctrine of necessity: according to Great Britain, hunger in Great Britain (due to the war with France) had given rise to the circumstances which justified the expropriation of that cargo: ILC, *Yearbook of the International Law Commission*, 2(1) (1980), 34 (*ILC Yearbook 1980*).

[3] In 1832, Portugal violated its agreement with the United Kingdom requiring it to respect the property of British subjects, while expropriating such property under the justification of having a pressing necessity for providing for its troops: *ibid.*, p. 30.

(the Argentine cases).[4] The cases against Argentina constitute a significant part of the International Centre for Settlement of Investment Dispute (ICSID) arbitral work today – as of August 2010, out of a total of 125 cases pending before the ICSID, 27 were filed against Argentina; the majority of which relate to the Argentine financial crisis and involve the necessity doctrine at some level.[5] Despite the many instances in which the doctrine has been invoked in the Argentine context, the 'Argentine tribunals' have been inconsistent in their interpretation and application of the necessity doctrine. This inconsistency has been described as potentially damaging as such conflicting results may lead to credibility loss and instability within the investment arbitration system.[6] Furthermore, conflicting results also generate uncertainty regarding the right use of the necessity doctrine during crises.

At the same time, the understanding of environmental, financial, health and security risks is becoming increasingly more global and less domestic in nature. Thus, the measures which a State may apply for counteracting an evolving crisis may be of relevance to the entire global community. For this reason, the interests examined in any legal analysis of the invocation of the necessity doctrine should not only be those of the conflicting parties, but should also include a wider investigation and understanding of the facts and interests involved in claims of necessity.

Lastly, following the recent global financial crisis, many States enacted economic 'rescue plans'. It has been argued by some that the implementation of these plans is likely to violate investment treaties (mainly non-discrimination obligations) and trigger investment disputes.[7] While the

---

[4] *Continental Casualty* v. *Argentine Republic* (ICSID Case No. ARB/03/9, Award of 5 September 2008) (*Continental Casualty*); *CMS Gas Transmission Company* v. *Argentine Republic* (ICSID Case No. ARB/01/8, Award of 12 May 2005) (*CMS*); *Enron Corporation Ponderosa Assets, L.P* v. *Argentine Republic* (ICSID Case No. ARB/01/3, Award of 22 May 2007) (*Enron*); *Sempra Energy International* v. *Argentine Republic* (ICSID Case No. ARB/02/16, Award of 28 September 2007) (*Sempra*); *LG&E Energy Corp., LG&E Capital Corp., LG&E International Inc.* v. *Argentine Republic* (ICSID Case No. ARB/02/1, Award of 3 October 2006) (*LG&E*); *National Grid* v. *Argentine Republic* (Award of 3 November 2008) (*National Grid*).

[5] See at the ICSID web site, http://icsid.worldbank.org/ICSID/FrontServlet?requestType=GenCaseDtlsRH&actionVal=ListPending (last accessed 26 January 2011).

[6] A. Reinisch, 'Necessity in international investment arbitration: An unnecessary split of opinions in recent ICSID cases? Comments on *CMS* v. *Argentina* and *LG&E* v. *Argentina*', *Journal of World Investment and Trade*, 8(2) (2007), 191, 212–13; J. E. Alvarez and K. Khamsi, 'The Argentine crisis and foreign investors: A glimpse into the heart of the investment regime', *Yearbook of International Investment Law and Policy*, 1 (2008–2009), 379, 385.

[7] J. Kurtz and A. van Aaken, 'The global financial crisis: Will States' emergency measures trigger international investment disputes?', *Transnational Dispute Management*, 7(1) (2010), www.transnational-dispute-management.com/members/articles/welcome.asp (last accessed 25 January 2011).

economic crisis affected many countries, in certain countries, it has had catastrophic impacts. Given the investor response to the Argentine financial crisis, it would, therefore, be interesting to examine the possibility of future invocation of the necessity plea in such situations and to consider whether States such as Iceland, for example, could make use of this doctrine in order to excuse themselves from violations of any applicable investment treaty obligations.

An understanding of the necessity doctrine is, therefore, important in the current international investment environment, and, in particular, in light of its evolving formulation in investment disputes. The arguments presented in this chapter speak to this emerging issue and are set out in three sections. First, it is asserted that the necessity doctrine is an important tool for States in times of crisis and is crucial for their recovery trajectories. Secondly, it is argued that the necessity doctrine as it is currently applied at the international arbitral level is outdated and not suitable for dealing with many types of crisis. Thirdly, it is asserted that, through an 'evolutive' approach to treaty interpretation,[8] several of the doctrine's conditions should be modified. In this way, it is argued that a more appropriate use of the doctrine, one that takes better account of the needs of the State in crisis, could emerge within investor–State arbitration.

II   The plea of necessity: Basic parameters

Article 25 of the ILC articles is widely accepted as the representative expression of the necessity doctrine in customary international law. The Article provides:

> 1. Necessity may not be invoked by a State as a ground for precluding the wrongfulness of an act not in conformity with an international obligation of that State unless the act:
>   (a) is the only way for the State to safeguard an essential interest against a grave and imminent peril;
>   and
>   (b) does not seriously impair an essential interest of the State or States towards which the obligation exists, or of the international community as a whole.

---

[8] i.e. recognising that the meanings of certain terms may change with time; see C. Brown, 'Bringing sustainable development issues before investment treaty tribunals' in M.-C. Cordonnier-Segger, M. Gehring and A. Newcombe (eds.), *Sustainable Development in International Investment Law* (The Hague: Kluwer, 2011), p. 171.

2. In any case, necessity may not be invoked by a State as a ground for precluding wrongfulness if:
   (a) the international obligation in question excludes the possibility of invoking necessity;
   or
   (b) the State has contributed to the situation of necessity.

As is clearly enunciated in Article 25, the necessity doctrine may only be used under exceptional circumstances, and thus there are strict conditions which must be met for a successful invocation of the necessity doctrine. The language of Article 25 also establishes that the conditions are cumulative,[9] which, in practice, makes the threshold for the necessity doctrine harder to fulfil since failure to meet even one condition can bar the application of the necessity doctrine.[10] Each of these elements is discussed in more detail below.

A   Protected interest must be an essential interest

This condition relates to the interest which the invoking State wishes to protect and explicitly requires that this interest must be 'essential'. As described by Roberto Ago, 'essential interests' are 'those interests which are of exceptional importance to the State seeking to assert it'.[11] The ILC considers environmental concerns, the preservation of the existence of a State, and ensuring the safety of the civilian population[12] to be examples of 'essential interests'.

Twenty years before promulgating its definition of necessity, the ILC offered a more comprehensive definition of 'essential' as 'represent[ing] a grave danger to the existence of the State itself, its political or economic survival, the continued functioning of its essential services, the maintenance of internal peace, the survival of a sector of its population, the preservation of the environment of its territory or a part thereof'.[13] A similar definition has been used recently by some tribunals.[14] The list of 'essential interests' recognised by tribunals to date includes

---

[9] A. K. Bjorklund, 'Emergency exceptions: State of necessity and *force majeure*' in P. Muchlinski, F. Ortino and C. Schreuer (eds.), *Oxford Handbook of International Investment Law* (Oxford University Press, 2008), p. 459.
[10] *Ibid.*, p. 475.   [11] *ILC Yearbook 1980*, p. 19.
[12] ILC Articles, Art. 25 (Commentaries paras. 4–16), *Yearbook of International Law Commission*, 2(2) (2001), 81–3.
[13] *ILC Yearbook 1980*, p. 14.   [14] *Continental Casualty*, para. 166; *LG&E*, para. 251.

environmental interests,[15] economic interests[16] and security interests.[17] This list is not exhaustive, however, and ultimately the decision as to whether a State's claim represents an 'essential interest' is left to the tribunal.[18]

B   The potential peril should be grave and imminent

Roberto Ago has described a qualifying peril under this element of the necessity doctrine as *'extremely* grave and imminent'.[19] As discussed below, the Argentine cases before investment tribunals demonstrate that the threshold for this element is exceedingly high.

With regard to the degree of certitude required to establish a claim for such peril, the International Court of Justice (ICJ) commented in the *Gabčíkovo-Nagymaros* case:

> The word 'Peril' certainly evokes the idea of 'risk': that is precisely what distinguishes 'peril' from material damage. But a state of necessity could not exist without a 'Peril' duly established at the relevant point in time: the mere apprehension of a possible 'peril' could not suffice in that respect.[20]

Therefore, according to the ICJ, it is possible that a claim of future peril can meet the requisite threshold under the necessity doctrine without establishing that the future peril will occur with absolute certitude, provided that the existence of a future peril can be established. In this respect, 'a measure of uncertainty' is acceptable.[21]

The Argentine tribunals have shown that the threshold for this condition is extremely high, as even Argentina's financial crisis of the early 2000s was not considered by most of these tribunals as sufficiently grave to reach the threshold of Article 25. In this regard, Argentina has argued that the economic crisis it faced was believed to be a severe national crisis, where 'the very existence of the Argentine State was threatened by

---

[15] *Gabčíkovo-Nagymaros Project (Hungary* v. *Slovakia) (Judgment)* [1997] ICJ Rep 3, para. 53 (*Gabčíkovo-Nagymaros*).

[16] See e.g. *CMS*, para. 319.

[17] *Legal Consequences of the Construction of a Wall in the Occupied Palestinian Territory* [2004] ICJ Rep. 136 (*Israeli Wall Advisory Opinion*), p. 195. The Israeli wall did not satisfy the third condition of Art. 25 though, as it did not prove the chosen route of the wall was the only available means for the protection of its interests.

[18] *ILC Yearbook 1980*, p. 19, see also ILC Articles, p. 83; *Gabčíkovo-Nagymaros*, para. 53.

[19] *ILC Yearbook 1980*, p. 20 (emphasis added).

[20] *Gabčíkovo-Nagymaros*, para. 42.   [21] See also ILC Articles, p. 83.

the events'.[22] The situation was described as 'chaotic' and as such could have been followed by economic and social collapse.[23] The *CMS* tribunal seemed to agree at one point with this depiction by describing the situation as of 'catastrophic proportions'.[24] Eventually, however, the tribunal determined that the situation had been severe, but not severe enough for the purposes of Article 25.[25] The tribunal justified this finding by arguing that 'compared to other contemporary crises affecting countries in different regions of the world it may be noted that such crises have not led to the derogation of international contractual or treaty obligations'.[26]

The *LG&E* tribunal reached contrary conclusions. Instead of comparing Argentina's crisis to 'other contemporary crises' in the world, it looked at the situation itself, and performed an examination of the economic and social factors which existed in Argentina at the time, reviewing: the deterioration of Argentina's gross domestic product (GDP), the drop in private consumption, the decline in prices and value of assets of companies in Argentina, the country's risk premium (which was the highest in the world at the time, and which made the option of borrowing money from foreign markets impossible for Argentina) and the liquidity of the Central Bank of Argentina's reserves.[27] The tribunal also reviewed poverty data (almost half of the Argentine population lived below the poverty line at the time), unemployment data from the relevant period, prices of pharmaceutical products (which were very high, and thus unavailable to the local population) and the health crisis the State faced at the time (due to poor alimentation and lack of medications). The tribunal described the widespread violent protests, looting and rioting, and the curfews which followed in order to control the situation. Taking into account all of these considerations, the tribunal concluded that:

> Evidence has been put before the Tribunal that the conditions as of December 2001 constituted the highest degree of public disorder and threatened Argentina's essential security interests. This was not merely a period of 'economic problems' or 'business cycle fluctuation' as Claimants described (Claimants' Post-Hearing Brief, p. 14). Extremely severe crises in the economic, political and social sectors reached their apex and converged in December 2001, threatening total collapse of the Government and the Argentine State.[28]

---

[22] *CMS*, para. 305.   [23] *Ibid.*, para. 306.   [24] *Ibid.*, para. 320.
[25] The situation 'did not result in total economic and social collapse', *CMS*, para. 355.
[26] *Ibid.*, para. 355.   [27] *LG&E*, paras. 232–5.   [28] *Ibid.*, para. 231.

The *Continental Casualty* tribunal agreed with the *LG&E* tribunal's conclusions as to the circumstances in Argentina at the relevant time, and reviewed at length the 'powerful evidence of its [the crisis'] gravity such as that could not be addressed by ordinary measures'.[29] The *Enron* tribunal considered the facts of the Argentine crisis as well, but unlike the *LG&E* and the *Continental Casualty* tribunals, was not convinced that the described circumstances were severe enough to be considered as a 'grave and imminent peril', since 'the very existence of the State and its independence' were not compromised,[30] and since it was not sufficiently proved by Argentina's experts 'that the events were out of control or had become unmanageable'.[31]

C   The course of action taken in order to protect an essential interest must be the only available means for resolving the peril

As Ago explained, 'it must be impossible for the peril to be averted by any other means, even one which is much more onerous but which can be adopted without a breach of international obligations'.[32] A more accurate description of this condition is that, once another solution – one which is lawful or will have a lesser effect on the claimant's injury – is available, the State's claim of necessity will not be upheld. The logic of this condition is obvious – there is no necessity to excuse certain conduct once an alternative means of conduct exists. The ILC Articles refined this analysis, establishing that the existence of alternatives will exclude the use of the necessity doctrine 'even if they may be more costly or less convenient'.[33] The ICJ, in its Advisory Opinion concerning the *Legal Consequences of the Construction of a Wall in the Occupied Palestinian Territory*, applied the same interpretation of this condition, stating that other ways were probably available for Israel to safeguard its security interests, and thus the necessity defence could not be sustained.[34]

The Argentine tribunals were divided as to whether Argentina's contested acts were the only available means by which its essential interests could be secured. The *Sempra* and the *Enron* tribunals compared the Argentine crisis to other crises, and decided that other means were indeed available since other governments used different means under similar circumstances.[35] The *Sempra* tribunal also stated that the

---

[29] *Continental Casualty*, para. 180.   [30] *Enron*, para. 306.   [31] *Ibid.*, para. 307.
[32] *ILC Yearbook 1980*, p. 20. See also ILC Articles, p. 80.   [33] ILC Articles, p. 83.
[34] *Israeli Wall Advisory Opinion*, para. 140.
[35] *Sempra*, para. 350; *Enron*, para. 308.

question of whether other means were recommendable should not be considered, but rather that it should only consider whether other means for resolving the crisis actually existed.[36]

The *LG&E* tribunal, on the other hand, examined the facts of the case and found that Argentina's conduct was indeed the only available means of action.[37] The *CMS* tribunal acknowledged that the question of whether Argentina's actions were the only available solution was 'indeed debatable',[38] but eventually found that there were other means available to Argentina and, thus, Argentina's plea of necessity could not be justified.[39]

The above raises two problems regarding this condition. The first difficulty relates to the 'aftermath nature' of the examination of alternatives available to the State claiming protection under the necessity doctrine. As Bjorklund argues, 'it is easy to overlook the sense of urgency that animates decision makers in times of crisis once the immediate emergency has passed'.[40] When the claiming State acts, it acts under pressure and severe time and information limitations. However, the tribunal usually adjudicates the matter without any of these pressures, with the privilege of comfortably listening to a variety of experts and opinions, and with the advantage of possessing significantly more information on the crisis, as the information available to a tribunal usually provides a hindsight perspective of the crisis and the State's actions in response to it. The 'other available way of action' may therefore truly exist, but becomes known (and thus available) to the acting State only in the aftermath of the crisis.

The second problem relates to the interpretation of this condition and its requirements. This third condition, as interpreted by the tribunals, does not require the tribunal to assess the merits of any 'other means', but only their availability.[41] However, it is almost always possible to find experts who will argue that there were other alternatives available to the State. This may be especially true concerning economic policies[42] (where

[36] *Sempra*, para. 351.   [37] *LG&E*, para. 257.

[38] *CMS*, para. 323; see also *Enron*, para. 305.   [39] *CMS*, para. 324.

[40] A. Bjorklund, 'The necessity of sustainable development?' in M.-C. Segger, M. Gehring, and A. Newcombe (eds.), *Sustainable Development in World Investment Law* (The Hague: Kluwer, 2011), p. 371.

[41] See e.g. *Enron*, paras. 308–9.

[42] M. Waibel, 'Two worlds of necessity in ICSID arbitration: *CMS* and *LG&E*', *Leiden Journal of International Law*, 20 (2007), 636, 646; see also *Enron Corporation and Ponderosa Assets LP* v. *Argentine Republic* (ICSID Case No. ARB/01/3, Decision on Annulment of 30 July 2010), para. 369.

it was said that 'divergence of views lies in the nature of economic policy'[43]) and security policies,[44] but may be true of other fields as well. Reflecting on this matter, the *Enron* tribunal stated:

> A rather sad world comparative experience in the handling of economic crises, *shows that there are always many approaches to address and correct such critical events* . . . While one or other party would like the Tribunal to point out which alternative was recommendable, it is not the task of the Tribunal to substitute for the governmental determination of economic choices, only to determine whether the choice made was the only way available, and this does not appear to be the case.[45]

The ILC also commented that:

> There will often be issues of scientific uncertainty and different views may be taken by informed experts on whether there is a peril, how grave or imminent it is and whether the means proposed are the only ones available in the circumstances.[46]

An interpretation of this clause should not, therefore, simply take into account the availability of different experts' opinions, as this interpretation would almost automatically exclude the use of the plea for necessity.[47] Furthermore, arguing that other means would have been sufficient for dealing with a certain crisis is highly speculative, as the 'other means' are usually suggested by the claimants in the aftermath of the events, and are not tested under the actual circumstances.[48]

The authors take the view that Article 25's strict demand for the measure to be the 'only way for a State to safeguard an essential interest' should be interpreted in a more lenient manner, or, indeed, should be revised altogether. While examining the 'only way', a tribunal should not be satisfied with the existence of any other means presented by the parties'

---

[43] *Ibid.* The *Enron* tribunal had noted in this connection that the issue 'is also a question on which the parties and their experts are profoundly divided': *Enron*, para. 308.

[44] *Israeli Wall Advisory Opinion*, paras. 138–41.   [45] *Enron*, para. 308 (emphasis added).

[46] ILC Articles, Art. 25 (Commentaries, para. 16), *Yearbook of the International Law Commission*, 2(2) (2001), 83.

[47] *Enron* (Annulment), paras. 376–7; see also Waibel, 'Two worlds of necessity', p. 646; Bjorklund, 'Emergency exceptions'; G. Mayeda, 'International investment agreements between developed and developing countries: Dancing with the devil? Case comment on the *Vivendi*, *Sempra* and *Enron* awards', *McGill International Journal of Sustainable Development Law and Policy*, 4(2) (2009), 119, 227; W. W. Burke-White, 'The Argentine financial crisis: State liability under BITs and the legitimacy of the ICSID system' in M. Waibel *et al.* (eds.), *The Backlash against Investment Arbitration* (The Hague: Kluwer, 2010), pp. 407–32.

[48] *Enron* (Annulment), para. 371.

experts. As mentioned above, most policies taken by States cannot possibly pass such a threshold. Tribunals should instead ask whether the used means were reasonable, according to the common and accepted knowledge that existed at the time when the State faced the crisis, in light of the potential damage third parties might suffer, together with a consideration of the known available alternatives. A similar approach was applied by the *Continental Casualty* tribunal.[49] It is important to note, however, that the *Continental Casualty* tribunal expressly mentioned that it was not applying the conditions of Article 25 and the necessity doctrine, but rather the legal tests of Article XX of the General Agreement on Tariffs and Trade (GATT), from which Article XI of the US–Argentina BIT is derived.[50]

As mentioned above, the current criterion could potentially defeat almost any plea of necessity, and may not capture the true nature of the situation facing a State in the midst of a crisis. A shift to the 'reasonableness'-based criterion may lead the arbitrators to a more appropriate assessment of the wrongfulness of the State's conduct, and, consequently, to a fairer judgment of its actions.

D   The measures taken by the State must not seriously impair an essential interest of another State toward which the obligation exists

The ILC has refined this rule, and explained that the essential interest (the one the State has safeguarded) must be of more importance than any other interest, whether of another State or of the international community as a whole.[51] Essentially, there is a 'proportionality' requirement that prohibits a State from defending its own interests through the violation of other States' interests.[52] Neither the Argentine tribunals nor the ICJ in the *Gabčíkovo-Nagymaros* case dedicated much attention to this condition, although the question of whether investors' interests may be counted as a form of 'essential interest of another State toward which the obligation exists' has been raised both in academic writings and investment law jurisprudence.[53] It is hard to see how investors' interests could be left outside of the State's interests domain, as clearly one of the BITs' main objectives is the protection of the State's investors. The

---

[49] *Continental Casualty*, paras. 193–4.   [50] *Ibid.*, para. 192.
[51] ILC Articles, Art. 25 (Commentaries, para. 17), *Yearbook of the International Law Commission*, 2(2) (2001), 84.
[52] *ILC Yearbook 1980*, p. 20; see also *LG&E*, para. 254.
[53] *CMS*, paras. 356–8; Bjorklund, 'Emergency exceptions', p. 487.

question of how essential these interests are, however, especially in light of the host State's interests in times of crisis, remains an issue.

E Necessity may not be claimed if the violated obligation in question specifically prohibits the possibility of invoking necessity

This fifth condition has been described by Bjorklund as an 'exception'[54] (as opposed to a 'positive condition'). The commentary to the ILC Articles explains that the fifth condition (or the first exception) is meant to prohibit the use of the necessity doctrine in cases where certain conventions specifically exclude the use of it.[55] The ILC mentions 'humanitarian conventions applicable to armed conflict [which] expressly exclude reliance on military necessity'. The ILC also mentions that, even when the application of the necessity doctrine is not specifically prohibited by a convention, a tribunal may still exclude it if 'the non-availability of the plea of necessity emerges clearly from the object and the purpose of the rule',[56] or in other words, where it is implicitly excluded.

Some claim that when it comes to BITs, the 'obligation in question' indeed implicitly prohibits the use of the necessity doctrine.[57] This possibility is likely, so it is argued, in light of the main rationale for BITs, being the protection of foreign investments from measures taken by States.[58] It is argued that 'if this rationale is accepted it is hard to see why it should be abandoned once the economic difficulties grow even worse and thus the risk of investor–adverse measures is even increased'.[59]

Although the logic of this position is clear, the authors consider that, for several reasons, it would be wrong to consider BITs as implicitly prohibiting the use of the necessity doctrine. First, according to customary international law, the necessity doctrine is designed to exonerate a State for the wrongfulness of actions taken under extreme circumstances. It should be noted, therefore, that the above-presented approach would have dramatic outcomes as it attributes wrongfulness to conduct taken in order to face a severe crisis. States, in all likelihood, would not easily

---

[54] Bjorklund, 'Emergency exceptions', p. 487.   [55] ILC Articles, p. 84.   [56] *Ibid.*
[57] Reinisch, 'Necessity in international investment', pp. 204–5.
[58] See also review as for the objectives of the US BIT in Alvarez and Khamsi, 'The Argentine crisis', pp. 411–12: 'U.S. negotiators were quite clear that the U.S. BIT was not designed to promote economic development or employment as such but was intended to achieve one clear purpose: to protect foreign investment.'
[59] Reinisch, 'Necessity in international investment', p. 205.

forego the necessity doctrine and the assumption of implicit concession of this important safeguard by a State Party, especially when it comes to extreme crises, is simply unrealistic.

Secondly, as the *CMS* tribunal argued, it is wrong to assume that the rationale of BITs represents only the protection of investors. Rather, 'it must also be kept in mind that the scope of a given bilateral treaty, such as this, should normally be understood and interpreted as attending to the concerns of both parties'.[60] The tension between the private interests of investors and the public interests of the host State is the focus of several contemporary studies[61] and the view that once considered BITs main objective as 'promoting of investments' is increasingly shifting into a more balanced approach, one that may be expressed as 'promoting investment so as to foster the development of host States'.[62] Assuming this, relinquishment of a safeguard with the importance of the necessity doctrine by a State without having its explicit consent is thus overreaching, inconsistent with contemporary views of investment law, and ignores the State Party's important interests, such as acting justifiably in times of crises.

Lastly, we would argue that as the necessity doctrine is of a paternalist nature, it should not be easily interpreted as implicitly excluded from treaties. This paternalism does not necessarily refer to the signatory States, but instead can apply to international interests as well. In the era of globalisation, crises may influence more than just the signatory States and, accordingly, third parties may also have interests in the application of the necessity doctrine. It is within the international community's interest to exonerate a State for the wrongfulness of preventive measures under extreme circumstances, which could, if unaddressed, lead to domestic and global economic damage, and thus the necessity doctrine should not be assumed to be excluded in the interpretation of BITs.

F   Necessity may not be claimed if the State claiming it has contributed to the creation of the crisis

A second exception (or a sixth condition) which precludes a successful appeal to necessity deals with the State's own contribution to the

---

[60] *CMS*, para. 360.
[61] See e.g. Cordonnier-Segger, Gehring and Newcombe (eds.), *Sustainable Development in World Investment Law*.
[62] Jan Wouters and Nicolas Hachez, 'The institutionalization of investment arbitration and sustainable development' in Cordonnier-Segger, Gehring and Newcombe (eds.), *Sustainable Development in World Investment Law*, p. 611.

creation of the crisis. The justification for this exception is relatively clear, as the *Enron* tribunal states: 'This is of course the expression of a general principle of law devised to prevent a party taking legal advantage of its own fault.'[63] The ILC has explained that a contribution may be either by act or by omission, and must rise to a level which is 'sufficiently substantial and not merely incidental or peripheral'.[64]

An important issue with regard to the gravity of a 'contribution' is the role of the former administration in the occurrence or exacerbation of the crisis. Should the administration at the time of the crisis be prevented from claiming necessity where former administrations have failed in their duties or are seen as being at fault? According to several tribunals,[65] the 'contribution' does not necessarily have to be made by the current administration and may be attributed to former administrations as well.

The *LG&E* tribunal, on the other hand, reviewed the actions of current administrations alone, and did not attribute significance to past administration policies.[66] The *LG&E* tribunal avoided the need to elaborate substantively on this issue, as it held that the burden of proof for qualifying contribution is on the claimants, and that the burden was not met in that case.[67] This approach may be problematic for the additional reason that the policies of current administrations may, in some instances, be seen as continuing the practices of the former administration, and the fact that recent administrations did not reform previous policies may be seen as a 'contribution' in itself.[68]

Another important question regarding contribution is the impact of international factors on the creation of the crisis. Several tribunals[69] have agreed that the Argentine crisis had international causes as well as domestic.[70] According to the *CMS* tribunal, '[such] is the case in most crises of this kind, the roots extend both ways and include a number of

---

[63] *Enron*, para. 311.   [64] *ILC Yearbook 2001*, p. 84.
[65] *Enron*, para. 312; *CMS*, para. 329; *Sempra*, para. 354.
[66] *LG&E*, paras. 256–7.   [67] *Ibid.*, para. 256.
[68] Contribution may be either by act or by omission: *Gabčíkovo-Nagymaros*, para. 205.
[69] *CMS*, para. 328; *Enron*, para. 311; *Sempra*, para. 353; *National Grid*, para. 260.
[70] Various international elements are mentioned:

> the slowdown of capital flows to emerging markets after the Asian and Russian crises; the ensuing economic weakness of commercial partners of the Argentine Republic, in particular Brazil; the devaluation of the Brazilian currency early in 1999; the strengthening of the dollar between 1998 and 2001; and the restrictive monetary policy of the US from mid 1999 to mid 2000.

See e.g. *National Grid*, para. 259.

domestic as well as international dimensions'.[71] This statement raises the question of the appropriate weight to be attributed to the contribution exception when the necessity doctrine is invoked with regard to an economic crisis with international causes. We live in the era of globalisation, and, as the *CMS* tribunal recognised, fault in an economic crisis cannot always be clearly attributed to domestic policies. Moreover, it has been argued that the disentanglement of domestic and international causes in financial crises is practically impossible.[72] Indeed, the effects of globalisation have been demonstrated recently as a domestic US economic crisis has driven many foreign economies into recession. The authors argue that this example vividly illustrates the reason why these considerations should not be ignored under this analysis.

Another problem with regard to the sixth condition is the hindsight nature of its approach. Most tribunals have held that Argentina's financial policies contributed to the creation of its crisis, and thus Argentina has been blamed for not correcting or changing these failing policies. However, as was mentioned by the *Continental Casualty* tribunal, Argentina's former financial policies were considered for many years by the international financial community as an accepted and beneficial economic policy.[73] Indeed, these policies were recommended by the IMF and supported by the US.[74] Under these circumstances, how can Argentina be faulted for not revising such policies? Should the non-amendment of a successful policy be counted as a 'faulted' action? It seems that these determinations were affected by a retrospective, rather than contemporary, analysis of the events which assumed knowledge and insights that were not at all clear at the time.

The *Continental Casualty* tribunal presented another approach regarding this condition. The tribunal first points to the fact that economic crises inherently involve some form of contribution of the State:

> It cannot be denied that a country is always ultimately responsible of its economic policy and of its consequences, at least politically and economically. The conduct of economic affairs, as any other affairs, pertains to the Government, so that the State bears the ultimate responsibility for any failure.[75]

The *Continental Casualty* tribunal emphasises, however, that the legal test in this condition is based on different parameters – not whether

---

[71] *CMS*, para. 328.   [72] Waibel, 'Two worlds of necessity', p. 643.
[73] *Continental Casualty*, para. 235.   [74] *Ibid.*, para. 235.
[75] *Continental Casualty*, para. 235.

Argentina's policies have led to the creation of the crises, but, rather, whether these policies were reasonable at the time. The tribunal states that what is regarded retrospectively as 'contribution', was regarded beforehand as reasonable and thus should not be counted as 'contribution'.[76] The focus of this approach is on 'reasonableness', rather than on the determination of contribution as a 'clear-cut' decision. This approach indeed provides some solutions for the above-discussed problems, especially concerning the 'hindsight nature' of the analysis and in adopting a more appropriate attribution of 'fault'. It should be noted, however, that neither the ILC nor the ICJ have applied such an approach concerning a State's 'contribution', and that the *Continental Casualty* tribunal's approach, although appealing, may not correspond with the common interpretation of this condition.

The accepted rationale of the sixth condition is that the wrongdoer should not benefit when it causes a crisis to occur. However, when assessing the contribution of policies and actions of current and former administrations and the effects that international and domestic causes had on the creation of a crisis – or even whether it was reasonable to expect the invoking State to change such policies – the picture remains vague with regard to the actual contribution and 'guilt' of the State, or whether it can be considered a 'wrongdoer'. Furthermore, the attribution of former administrations' erroneous policies as a conclusive factor under this condition excludes the use of the doctrine when it comes to financial crises. We would, therefore, suggest that such a contribution alone should not preclude a plea of necessity, unless the negative effects of the contribution are clear and straightforward to detect. In other cases, a contribution should either impact on the compensation due from the hosting State,[77] or serve as a supportive indicator for any of the other conditions in Article 25. We consider that this approach is more complimentary to the idea of excluding the wrongfulness of State conduct under extreme circumstances as it recognises the problematic aspects of such a determination on the one hand, but, on the other, does not exclude such a contribution from the final decision.

---

[76] *Ibid.*

[77] Assuming the debate over the issue of compensation under the necessity doctrine would be settled (see further below).

III   Compensation

There is wide-ranging disagreement as to whether the State is obliged to pay compensation for damages created by conduct which has been excused through a claim of necessity. The *CMS* tribunal argued that the successful invocation of the necessity doctrine 'does not exclude the duty to compensate'.[78] This holding is derived from the rationale of avoiding the imposition of an economic burden on an innocent party (the investor). This rationale has been supported by the ICJ in the *Gabčíkovo-Nagymaros* case.[79] On the other hand, the *LG&E* tribunal determined that the State should not be liable for any damages suffered while the state of necessity existed.[80] This approach is also somewhat supported by the decision of the *Metalpar* tribunal,[81] which stated:

> Claimants did not prove that their investments in the Argentine Republic were adversely affected by the actions taken by the Argentine Government, which would make it pointless to decide whether the measures taken by Argentina and challenged by Claimants, were executed due to there being a 'state of necessity,' which would extinguish the liability that could be attributed to Respondent.

The issue of compensation for justified actions – actions which have been acknowledged as not wrongful due to the existence of a 'state of necessity' – is, therefore, still in dispute. Bjorklund has proposed two possibilities for the direction which future tribunals may take in deciding the issue of compensation for justified actions.[82] The first approach is that, once the necessity doctrine has been successfully invoked, the invoking State will be exempted from paying any compensation.[83] Burke-White argues in favour of this course, stating that such a possibility would 'serve the purpose of guaranteeing greater freedom of action to States in cases of emergency'.[84] Under this scenario, an innocent third party would have to bear the burden of the damages resulting from the State's act.[85] The ILC commentaries do not support this approach, as

---

[78]   *CMS*, paras. 388–90.   [79]   *Gabčíkovo-Nagymaros*, paras. 42, 48.

[80]   *LG&E*, para. 264.

[81]   *Metalplar SA and Buen Aire SA* v. *Argentine Republic* (ICSID Case No. ARB/03/5, Award of 6 June 2008), para. 211.

[82]   Bjorklund, 'Emergency exceptions', p. 514.

[83]   Such approach was taken by the *LG&E* tribunal: *LG&E*, para. 266.

[84]   It should be noted that these words were said concerning Art. XI of the Argentina–US BIT and not directly concerning the necessity doctrine: see further Burke-White, 'The Argentine financial crisis', pp. 214–15.

[85]   Bjorklund, 'Emergency exceptions', p. 515; see also ILC Articles, p. 86.

they specifically acknowledge the possibility of compensation,[86] and an overview of international cases which have dealt with emergency situations and the demand for compensation indicates a tendency to award compensation despite the existence of an emergency.[87] Earlier work of the ILC has been even more vigorous in rejecting this approach.[88]

A second possible direction is that the right to compensation will only be suspended, and, therefore will remain actionable at some point in the future.[89] It is important to mention that this approach does not conform to the accepted rationale behind Chapter V of the ILC Articles – after all, once an action is not regarded as 'wrongful', why should it lead to compensation?[90] This approach, as mentioned above, was supported by the *LG&E* tribunal.[91]

A   Necessity: A 'defence' or an 'excuse'?

An important question regarding this issue is whether necessity indeed precludes wrongfulness of actions or only excuses actions which are considered as wrong. Professor Vaughan Lowe describes the first option as a 'defence' and the second as an 'excuse',[92] defining the distinction as follows: 'There is behaviour that is right; and there is behaviour that, though wrong, is understandable and excusable.'[93] Interpreting the doctrine of necessity as a 'defence', therefore, means that the action is not counted as wrongful by nature, and, thus, it could be argued, should not

---

[86] *Ibid.*

[87] See in S. W. Schill, 'International investment law and the host State's power to handle economic crisis: Comment on the ICSID decision in *LG&E v. Argentina*', *Journal of International Arbitration*, 24(3) (2007), 265, 282–4. It should be observed, however, that these cases did not involve the necessity doctrine, and thus the comparison may not be completely accurate.

[88] *ILC Yearbook 1980*, p. 21, n. 35.

[89] Bjorklund, 'Emergency exceptions', p. 515; see also C. Foster, 'Necessity and precaution in international law: Responding to oblique forms of urgency', *New Zealand Universities Law Review*, 23(2) (2008), 265, 268–72.

[90] V. Lowe, 'Precluding wrongfulness or responsibility: A plea for excuses', *European Journal of International Law*, 10(2) (1999), 405, 410.

[91] *LG&E*, para. 259.

[92] Lowe, 'Precluding wrongfulness', pp. 405–6; see also I. Johnstone, 'The plea of "necessity" in international legal discourse: Humanitarian intervention and counter-terrorism', *Colombia Journal of Transnational Law*, 43 (2004–2005), 337, 350; see also Lowe, 'Precluding wrongfulness', pp. 405–6.

[93] Lowe, 'Precluding wrongfulness', pp. 406–10. However it should be noted that it has been argued before that the possibility of compensation for lawful acts indeed exist, see *ILC Yearbook 1980*, p. 21, n. 35.

lead to compensation. Indeed, why should one compensate a party if one did nothing wrong?[94]

Under the 'excuse interpretation', on the other hand, the actions taken by a State are considered wrongful, but under the circumstances are excused. Under this interpretation, compensation may be justified, as once the 'state of necessity' is over, the 'excuse' is no longer valid and no real reason for avoiding compensation is left.

It seems, at first glance, that Article 25 regards necessity as a 'defence' since it uses the phrasing 'precluding the wrongfulness of an act' and, thus, if, to use Lowe's words, it 'is behaviour that is right'. On the other hand, however, the ILC has also stated:

> Chapter V, on the other hand, said that a range of circumstances, e.g. distress, *force majeure* and necessity, precluded wrongfulness. In those circumstances, the State's conduct would therefore not be wrongful. But it was very difficult to say that the State was acting in conformity with the obligation when it was acting in a situation of distress or necessity. It would be more appropriate to say that the State was not acting in conformity with the obligation but that, in the circumstances, it was excused – possibly conditionally – for its failure to do so.[95]

This current situation creates confusion concerning the outcomes of the necessity doctrine. On the one hand, it seems that at least for now the more accepted position regarding necessity is that it constitutes a defence,[96] since it is more generally regarded as precluding wrongfulness rather than just excusing conduct. Several tribunals regarded this as a basis for determining that compensation should not be granted once the plea of necessity has been successful.[97] On the other hand, the ILC's above-mentioned quote and the interpretation of the *CMS* tribunal regarding compensation certainly represent a different, although well-accepted approach.[98] It remains, however, to ask the purpose for which a State should use the necessity doctrine if the 'excuse' approach is accepted, as compensation would be due regardless of success or failure in the invocation of the necessity doctrine.

---

[94] See the approach adopted by the tribunals in *LG&E* and *Metalpar*.

[95] ILC, 'Report of the International Law Commission on the work of its fifty-first session, 3 May–23 July 1999' in *Official Records of the General Assembly, fifty-fourth session*, Supplement No. 10 (1999), UN Doc. A/54/10, p. 51.

[96] Johnstone, 'The plea of "necessity"', pp. 352–3.

[97] It should also be added that other tribunals did not consider the lack of wrongfulness as a sufficient reason to rule out compensation.

[98] See also Lowe's opinion on the matter: Lowe, 'Precluding wrongfulness', p. 411.

IV   Recent economic crisis and the future
of the necessity doctrine

In reviewing the outcomes of the Argentine cases, the future direction of the necessity doctrine within investment disputes is unclear. What can one, therefore, conclude about any future invocation of this plea? The recent economic crises that have engulfed many States may produce some answers to this question in the near future. The global financial crisis that emerged in 2007, triggered by the collapse of the United States mortgage market, developed into the most severe economic crisis the world has seen since the early 1930s.[99]

As part of their efforts to combat the adverse effects of the financial crisis, many States have enacted domestic 'rescue plans'.[100] It has been suggested that these measures can have discriminatory effects and are likely to trigger investment disputes.[101] It is thus possible that the necessity doctrine will again be raised in the future as a defence to investor claims. Interestingly, to the best of the authors' knowledge, no investment dispute has yet been initiated in the wake of these emergency plans.[102] This lack of legal activity, however, could be associated with the fact that the majority of these financial plans are currently still in early stages of their implementation and the potential for future investor–State arbitration should not be readily dismissed.

The 'Icesave' dispute is an interesting case study through which the necessity defence could be evaluated in light of the recent economic crisis. This case emphasises both the difficulties that States may endure during this recent crisis and the tensions these difficulties may have vis-à-vis the property of foreign nationals.

A   The Icesave dispute

Although the impact of this currant global economic crisis has been felt across borders and markets,[103] a number of States have been particularly

---

[99] C. Rude, 'The world economic crisis and the federal reserve's response to it: August 2007–December 2008', *Studies in Political Economy*, 85 (2010), 125; G. G. Kaufman, 'The financial turmoil of 2007–09: Sinners and their sins', (Networks Financial Institute Policy Brief No. 2010-PB-01, 2010), http://papers.ssrn.com/sol3/papers.cfm?abstract_id=1577264&rec=1&srcabs=1574296 (last accessed 25 January 2011).

[100] See review in Kurtz and van Aaken, 'The global financial crisis'.   [101] *Ibid.*

[102] UNCTAD, *Latest Developments in Investor State Dispute Settlement* (IIA Issues Note No. 1 2010), www.unctad.org/en/docs/webdiaeia20103_en.pdf, pp. 11–12 (last accessed 14 February 2011).

[103] Rude, 'The world economic crisis'.

affected. Inarguably, the financial crisis produced devastating conditions within Iceland. For example, in less than two weeks during October 2008, Iceland's three leading banks, which represented 85 per cent of the State's entire banking system collapsed;[104] trading on Iceland's stock market exchange was suspended; the average exchange value of the Icelandic krona declined by 50 per cent; and financial relations between Iceland and foreign countries practically ceased.[105] According to an OECD survey, a comparison of five other large financial crises which occurred in developed countries in recent decades ('the big five') shows that Iceland's crisis was remarkably long and deep.[106]

On 6 October 2008, Iceland's prime minister, Geir Haarde, announced that the State was at risk of 'national bankruptcy'.[107] Together, these events led to riots in Iceland and to the collapse of the coalition government, including Haarde's resignation as prime minister.[108] Describing the sense of chaos existing in Iceland during the height of the crisis, Icelandic musician Björk has noted:

> And then the economic crisis hit. Young families are threatened with losing their houses and elderly people their pensions. This is catastrophic. There is also a lot of anger.[109]

One of the Icelandic banks which collapsed in 2008, 'Landsbanki', had an online division, 'Icesave', which operated in several European countries. Following the collapse of the Icelandic banks, the Icelandic government announced that it would fully cover all 'deposits in domestic commercial and savings banks and their branches in Iceland',

---

[104] 'Iceland halts trading, seizes bank', *The Wall Street Journal* (10 October 2008); 'Report on Iceland's banking collapse blasts ex-officials', *The Wall Street Journal* (13 April 2010); 'Key dates of Iceland's crisis', *The Wall Street Journal* (28 January 2009); OECD, 'Economic survey of Iceland 2009: The financial and economic crisis', www.oecd.org/document/20/0,3343,en_33873108_33873476_43576468_1_1_1_1,00.html (last accessed 26 January 2011).

[105] OECD, 'Economic survey of Iceland'; T. Eggertsson and T. Herbertsson, 'System failure in Iceland and the 2008 global financial crisis' (Paper presented at the 13th Annual Conference of the International Society for New Institutional Economics, 2009), http://extranet.isnie.org/uploads/isnie2009/eggertsson_herbertsson.doc (last accessed 26 January 2011).

[106] OECD, 'Economic survey of Iceland', pp. 51–2.

[107] 'Key dates of Iceland's crisis', *The Wall Street Journal* (28 January 2009).

[108] 'Crisis claims Icelandic Cabinet', *BBC News* (26 January 2009), http://news.bbc.co.uk/1/hi/world/europe/7851415.stm (last accessed 26 January 2011).

[109] Björk, 'After financial meltdown, now it's meltdown', *The Sunday Times* (28 October 2008), www.timesonline.co.uk/tol/comment/columnists/guest_contributors/article 5026175.ece (last accessed 26 January 2011).

including domestic clients of Landsbanki.[110] However, under this announced plan, Iceland would not cover the deposits of Icesave's customers who had accounts outside of Iceland, thus clearly discriminating against foreign creditors of the bank. As a result, roughly 400,000 account holders from the United Kingdom and the Netherlands were left unsecured. In order to ensure the protection of their citizens and assets, these clients were eventually paid by the British and Dutch deposit insurance schemes.[111] Following this payment, the United Kingdom and the Netherlands turned to Iceland, demanding the sum of €20,887 per depositor, basing their claims on the EC Deposit-Guarantee directive.[112]

Given its dire economic situation, Iceland was, unsurprisingly, less than willing to accede to these demands. On 30 October 2008, Iceland's prime minister issued the following statement: 'We hope that a joint solution can be found, but the Icelandic authorities have been quite clear on the point that we will never agree to conditions that would ruin our economy. This, the British must understand.'[113] In a letter dated 23 October 2008, Solrun Gisladottir, Iceland's foreign minister, wrote in regard to these demands: 'Total possible liabilities, if pushed to their maximum, could impose on Iceland reparations on a similar economic scale to the Treaty of Versailles.'[114] These claims found support in a number of corners, including, for example, in commentary by Thráinn Eggertsson, in the Financial Times: 'The burden is unrealistic. The most likely consequences are: extremely high inflation, economic decline, mass emigration and political disorder. I am reminded of the situation facing Germany in 1919 following the

[110] Announcement of the Icelandic Prime Minister's Office (6 October 2008), http://eng. forsaetisraduneyti.is/news-and-articles/nr/3033 (last accessed 26 January 2011); see also Reuters, http://uk.reuters.com/article/idUKTRE61P3LC20100226 (last accessed 26 January 2011).

[111] M. Waibel, 'Iceland's financial crisis: Quo vadis', ASIL Insights, 14(5) (2010), www.asil. org/insights100301.cfm (last accessed 26 January 2011).

[112] EC, Directive 94/19/EC of the European Parliament and of the Council of 30 May 1994 on deposit-guarantee schemes, http://eurlex.europa.eu/LexUriServ/LexUriServ.do? uri=CELEX:31994L0019:EN:HTML (last accessed 26 January 2011); Waibel, 'Iceland's financial crisis'.

[113] Address of Prime Minister Geir H. Haarde to the Althngi (30 October 2008), http://eng. forsaetisraduneyti.is/news-and-articles/nr/3190 (last accessed 26 January 2011).

[114] R. Mason, 'UK freezing of Landsbanki assets "As damaging to Iceland as Treaty of Versailles"', Daily Telegraph (6 July 2009), www.telegraph.co.uk/finance/newsbysector/ banksandfinance/5761176/UK-freezing-of-Landsbanki-assets-as-damaging-to-Iceland-as-Treaty-of-Versailles.html (last accessed 26 January 2011).

Versailles Peace Treaty.'[115] Iceland, in short, rejected its international obligations as a means to protect its own collapsing economy. Put in legal terms, Iceland implicitly turned to the necessity defence.

B The 'Icesave' dispute and the doctrine of necessity

Can Iceland raise the necessity doctrine in its defence against the claims of the UK and the Netherlands? In light of the analysis conducted above, it would seem that the chances for a successful invocation of the necessity defence are very low. First of all, following the Argentine cases, it is not at all clear whether the Icelandic crisis could be considered as 'grave enough' to satisfy the second condition of Article 25. Given that the *CMS* and *Enron* tribunals rejected the Argentine crisis as 'not grave enough', it is difficult to see how the Icelandic crisis could pass such a threshold.

Secondly, regarding the third condition for invoking necessity, an alternative available means for resolving this peril is not only perceivable, but was practically supplied by the parties in the form of an agreement for settlement of the disputed claims which was negotiated and agreed upon by the parties themselves.[116] It is true that the citizens of Iceland rejected this agreement in a referendum that was held on 6 March 2010.[117] However, the fact that an acceptable alternative existed (that is, the rejected agreement) remains. Interestingly, the rejected agreement included, inter alia, a 'grace period' of seven years in which Iceland could have sold the assets of its banks, helping to ensure the recovery of its economy and placing itself financially in a position to compensate the United Kingdom and Netherlands governments. In other words, the parties agreed on a solution similar to that achieved through a successful plea of necessity, where the necessity doctrine is regarded as an 'excuse' and thus compensation is only delayed, not done away with altogether.

Lastly, regarding the sixth condition of the necessity doctrine, Iceland will have to convince any future tribunal that it made no substantial contribution to the creation of this crisis. Iceland could argue in this respect that the crisis was global in nature caused mainly by

---

[115] T. Eggertsson, 'Long-term consequences may be ruinous for Iceland', *Financial Times Online* (27 October 2008), www.ft.com/cms/s/0/f24b1540-a3c6–11dd-942c-000077b07658.html (last accessed 26 January 2011).

[116] 'Iceland to reimburse UK for 2.3 bn GBP paid to Icesave customers', *The Guardian* (6 June 2009), www.guardian.co.uk/business/2009/jun/06/iceland-icesave-bank-compensation (last accessed 26 January 2011).

[117] 'Iceland reject plan to repay Icesave debts', *BBC News* (7 March 2010), http://news.bbc.co.uk/1/hi/business/8553979.stm (last accessed 26 January 2011).

international causes. Militating against this argument, however, claims would probably be raised regarding Iceland's inadequate economic policies in the years before the financial crisis. Indeed, an OECD survey of Iceland's economy stated that:

> While Iceland is in part a victim of the international crisis, its severe plight largely results from a recent history of ineffective bank supervision, exceptionally aggressive banks and inadequate macroeconomic policies.[118]

Considering the fact that financial crises are almost always the result of failing financial policies, attributing the State's contribution to the financial crisis is self-evident. It can, therefore, be predicted that according to the conditions set by Article 25 and the previous interpretation of these conditions by international tribunals, Iceland's potential claim of necessity would be destined to fail.

C   Lessons from the Icesave dispute

From the discussion above, it can be surmised that countries that are currently struggling with financial difficulties would most probably not be able to raise successfully the necessity doctrine in their defence. The 'Icesave' dispute has shown, however, that some claimants are willing to accept the existence of state of necessity, when these claims are presented as an 'excuse' – that is, where compensation is only delayed, not disputed.

The agreement achieved by the parties (and rejected by the Icelandic people) demonstrates that the claimants in this case acknowledged Iceland's state of necessity and agreed to a result which is similar to a successful invocation of the necessity doctrine (if considered as an 'excuse'). The fact that the claimants agreed to what probably would have been rejected by international tribunals only emphasises how unsuitable the necessity defence in its current formulation is with regard to certain types of disputes.

V   Conclusion

With regard to the factual aspects of crises, the *CMS* tribunal remarked:[119] 'As is many times the case in international affairs and international law, situations of this kind are not given in black and white

---

[118] OECD, 'Economic survey of Iceland', p. 24.   [119] *CMS*, para. 320.

but in many shades of grey.' This statement is true not only concerning financial crises but also in relation to security, environmental and health risks in cases where no clear scientific answers are available. Nevertheless, the application of the necessity doctrine's conditions is generally made in 'black and white' terms. There is almost no recognition of the 'many shades of grey' that usually represent the reality of such cases and the divergence of opinions concerning possible means of action and the level of 'guilt' the invoking State bears.

This application of the necessity doctrine portends the unjust failure of the necessity doctrine in many future cases. This is particularly so as tribunals may feel they must decide issues in definitive terms, especially concerning the third condition (only available means) and sixth condition (State's contribution), rather than in a manner that represents the reality of these circumstances, being typically that of 'many shades of grey'. Indeed, a more appropriate approach would be to regard some conditions in the same conclusive manner (such as the first and the second conditions, possibly the fourth and the fifth), while the failure to meet the terms of other conditions (the third and the sixth conditions) could affect the amount of compensation due, or serve as a factor which may support the fulfilment of other conditions.

It is widely agreed that financial crises should represent an 'essential interest' of the State and that, when the circumstances embody a financial 'catastrophe', a State should be allowed to claim 'necessity'.[120] Under prevailing treatments of this subject, however, this recognition would most likely not be applied by tribunals. The necessity doctrine is an important legal tool that enables the international community to assess the actions taken by a State under exceptional circumstances. It represents an appreciation that States' priorities in times of trouble can shift. Nevertheless, the possibility of using this doctrine in the future seems doubtful as the strict application by tribunals of the conditions set out in Article 25 is overly restrictive and the threshold one must pass in order to successfully invoke the doctrine is too high.[121]

There are, of course, indications that a more appropriate application of the doctrine to bring about a less unjust outcome for the host State could emerge, as pointed to in the *Continental* award. However, even in this case, the tribunal applied the specific provisions of the relevant bilateral investment treaty rather than relying on the customary law

---

[120] See e.g. *ILC Yearbook 1980*, p. 14; *CMS*, para. 319.
[121] Bjorklund, 'Emergency exceptions', p. 521.

doctrine of necessity. As discussed in this chapter, the Argentine cases, in particular, highlight the need for a re-articulation of this doctrine. It is hoped that tribunals in investor–State disputes will respond to this need and promote the evolution of the necessity doctrine to assist host States in the modern globalised environment. In this regard, we would do well to recall the words of Ago, who wrote, almost thirty years ago, that 'if [the necessity doctrine is] driven out of the door it would return through the window, if need be in other forms'.[122] We consider that 'other forms' are indeed necessary in order to preserve the use of this doctrine and have argued for a reshaping of its conceptual formulation and a revisiting of its accepted application. In this way, a fairer balance could be struck as between the interests of investors and the needs of host States during times of crisis.

[122] *ILC Yearbook 1980*, p. 51.

13

Making way for the public interest in international investment agreements

SUZANNE A. SPEARS[*]

I Introduction

One of the crucial questions posed by the expanding application of international investment agreements (IIAs) over the last two decades is the extent to which they regulate host States' ability to enact and enforce regulation intended to protect society and the environment.[1] That question is now on the agenda of the international community and has been taken up by a prominent figure at the United Nations, the Special-Representative of the Secretary-General (SRSG) on the Issue of Human Rights, Transnational Corporations and Other Business Enterprises, Harvard political science professor John Gerald Ruggie.[2] In his 2009 report to the Human Rights Council, the SRSG expressed concern that 'recent experience suggests that some [investment] treaty guarantees

---

[*] This chapter was presented at the Investment Treaty Law and Arbitration Conference held at the University of Sydney on 19–20 February 2010. The views expressed do not necessarily reflect the views of the author's firm or any of its clients.

[1] By the end of 2009, there were nearly 2,750 bilateral investment treaties (BITs) and 295 other international economic agreements with investment provisions (collectively international investment agreements or 'IIAs'). UNCTAD, *World Investment Report 2010*, p. 81 (2010). By the end of 2009, the total number of known investor–State dispute settlement cases filed under IIAs was 357. *Ibid.*, p. 83.

[2] See e.g. James Zhan, 'UNCTAD's 2010 World Investment Forum: High-level experts discuss investment policies for sustainable development', *Investment Treaty News* (16 December 2010), http://www.iisd.org/itn/2010/12/16/unctads-2010-world-investment-forum-high-level-experts-discuss-investment-policies-for-sustainable-development/ (last accessed 17 January 2011); Doha Declaration: Outcome Document of the Follow-up International Conference on Financing for Development to Review the Implementation of the Monterrey Consensus, para. 14 (2009); SRSG, 'Business and human rights: Towards operationalizing the "protect, respect and remedy" framework' (A/HRC/11/13, 2009), paras. 29–31; SRSG, 'Business and human rights: Further steps towards the operationalization of the "protect, respect and remedy" framework' (A/HRC/14/27, 2010), paras. 20–3.

and contract provisions may unduly constrain the host Government's
ability to achieve its legitimate policy objectives, including its international
human rights obligations'.[3] Undue constraints may emerge, the SRSG
explained, because 'under threat of binding international arbitration, a
foreign investor may be able to insulate its business venture from new laws
and regulations, or seek compensation from the Government for the cost
of compliance'.[4] A number of non-governmental organisations (NGOs)
and other analysts have expressed similar concerns and warned that IIAs
and investor–State arbitration may have a chilling effect on host State
regulatory initiatives that are needed to address non-investment policy
objectives.[5]

The SRSG and others cite as the basis for their concern a growing
number of investor–State cases in which investors have challenged sensitive domestic legislative and administrative measures.[6] These include
cases under the North American Free Trade Agreement (NAFTA) in
which investors have challenged environmental and social regulation;[7]

---

[3] SRSG, 'Protect, respect and remedy' (2009), para. 30.   [4] Ibid.

[5] See e.g. V. Bean and J. Beauvais, 'Global Fifth Amendment: NAFTA's investment
protection and the misguided quest for an international regulatory takings doctrine',
New York University Law Review, 78 (2003), 30; UNCTAD, 'World investment Report'
(2003), p. xvii; Public Citizen, 'NAFTA's threat to sovereignty and democracy: The record
of NAFTA Chapter 11 investor–State cases 1994–2005' (2005); J. W. Salacuse and
N. P. Sullivan, 'Do BITs really work? An evaluation of BITs and their grand bargain',
Harvard International Law Journal, 67 (2005), 46, 77; G. van Harten, Investment Treaty
Arbitration and Public Law (Oxford University Press, 2007), p. 67; K. Miles, 'International
investment law and climate change' (Society of International Economic Law, Working
Paper No. 27/08, 2008), pp. 22–6; ILA, 'Report of the Rio de Janeiro Conference on
International Law on Sustainable Development' (2008).

[6] The SRSG has expressed particular concern about the case Piero Foresti, Laura de Carli
and ors v. Republic of South Africa (ICSID Case No. ARB(AF)/07/1, Award and Concurring Statement of Arbitrator Matthews of 4 August 2010), in which Italian investors
challenged a South African law intended to address the legacy of apartheid-era discrimination in the mining sector. See SRSG, 'Protect, respect and remedy' (2009); SRSG,
'Protect, respect and remedy' (2010), para. 21.

[7] See e.g. Ethyl Corp. v. Canada (Decision on Jurisdiction of 24 June 1998) (proposed
ban on ethyl as a carcinogenic substance); Metalclad v. Mexico (ICSID Case No. ARB(AF)/
97/1, Award of 30 August 2000) (refusal to issue a waste disposal permit and an order
establishing an ecological park); SD Myers Inc. v. Canada (First Partial Award of
13 November 2000) (ban on hazardous waste exports); Methanex v. United States of
America (Final Award of 3 August 2005) (measures to protect public water supplies);
Grand River Enterprises Six Nations Ltd and ors v. United States (Decision on Jurisdiction
of 20 July 2006) (tobacco settlement legislation); Glamis Gold v. United States of America
(Award of 8 June 2009) (measures to protect indigenous peoples' culture and health);
Chemtura Corporation v. Canada (Award of 2 August 2010) (ban on pesticide as environ-
mental contaminant, and threat to human and animal health).

cases brought by investors from the US and UK in which Argentina has been held liable as a result of measures that it took in response to a serious economic crisis in 2001;[8] and cases under a range of IIAs in which investors have challenged regulatory measures that host States have defended as designed to achieve legitimate domestic policy objectives.[9]

States have responded to concerns about the potential for investment law to place undue constraints on sovereign regulatory power in a variety of ways in recent years. At one extreme, a number of countries in Latin America have responded by denouncing or insisting on the renegotiation of some of their IIAs, and by withdrawing from the Convention on the Settlement of Investment Disputes between States and Nationals of other States (ICSID Convention) or seeking to limit the jurisdiction of the Centre established by the Convention (ICSID).[10] Countries in Southern and Eastern Africa have been more moderate in their response – rather than rejecting the IIA and investor–State dispute-resolution regime, they have adopted a comprehensive investment promotion treaty among themselves, with different provisions from traditional IIAs.[11] Other States have issued joint interpretations clarifying the substantive provisions of their existing IIAs or adopted new IIAs with language that seeks to address the tension between the principles of investment protection and host States' need for regulatory

---

[8] On cases involving claims by US investors in Argentina's gas transportation and distribution utilities, see J. E. Alvarez and K. Khamsi, 'The Argentine crisis and foreign investors: A glimpse into the heart of the investment regime', *Yearbook on International Investment Law and Policy*, 1 (2008–2009), 379.

[9] See e.g. *Occidental* v. *Ecuador* (LCIA Case No. UN 3467, Final Award of 1 July 2004) (value-added tax on oil profits); *Aguas del Tunari SA* v. *Republic of Bolivia* (ICSID Case No. ARB/02/3, Decision on Jurisdiction of 21 October 2005) (measures to protect water services); *Azurix Corp.* v. *Argentina* (ICSID Case No. ARB/01/12, Award of 14 July 2006) (measures to protect water services); *Biwater Gauff* v. *United Republic of Tanzania* (ICSID Case No. ARB/05/22, Award of 24 July 2008) (measures to protect water services); *Vattenfall and ors* v. *Federal Republic of Germany* (ICSID Case No. ARB/09/6) (environmental measures).

[10] See *Investment Treaty News*, 'Bolivia notifies World Bank of withdrawal from ICSID, pursues BIT revisions' (9 May 2007); Alvarez and Khamsi, 'The Argentine crisis', p. 386; F. C. Diaz, 'Ecuador continues exit from ICSID', *Investment Treaty News* (8 June 2009); Global Arbitration Review (GAR), 'Ecuador to denounce remaining BITs', 30 October 2009, www.globalarbitrationreview.com/news/article/19251/ (last accessed 29 September 2010).

[11] See e.g. Agreement Establishing the Common Market for Eastern and Southern Africa Common Investment Area (22–3 May 2007) (COMESA CIAA); P. Muchlinski, 'Trends in international investment agreements: Balancing investor rights and the right to regulate: The issue of national security', *Yearbook on International Investment Law and Policy*, 1 (2008–2009), 37–45.

discretion.[12] Over the last two years, the United States,[13] Norway[14] and South Africa[15] have undertaken official reviews of their IIAs to determine whether they now strike an appropriate balance between these competing principles or whether additional changes are needed. Although each of these reappraisals has taken place within a specific national or regional context and has addressed a range of issues, each has criticised the investment law regime for failing to afford States sufficient space to choose between legitimate public-policy objectives and has called into question the regime's social legitimacy.[16]

[12] See below Sections II and III. See also K. Vandevelde, 'A comparison of the 2004 and 1994 US Model BITs: Rebalancing investor and host country interests', *Yearbook on International Investment Law and Policy*, 1 (2008–2009), 288–9; S. M. Schwebel, 'The United States 2004 model bilateral investment treaty and denial of justice' in C. Binder *et al.* (eds.), *International Investment Law for the 21st Century: Essays in honour of Christoph Schreuer* (Oxford University Press, 2009).

[13] The review of the US Model BIT follows on President Obama's campaign pledge: 'I will ensure that foreign investor rights are strictly limited and will fully exempt any law or regulation written to protect public safety or promote the public interest': Barack Obama, Pennsylvania Fair Trade Coalition 2008 Presidential Candidate Questionnaire (2 April 2008). See also US Department of State, Office of the United States Trade Representative, Public Notice 6693, 74 Fed. Reg., 14 July 2009; D. Vis-Dunbar, 'United States reviews its model bilateral investment treaty', *Investment Treaty News* (5 June 2009).

[14] Norway's review responded to the government's desire to conclude future IIAs that give security to investors while safeguarding the ability of governments to regulate in the public interest. See L. E. Peterson, 'Norway proposes significant reforms to its investment treaty practices', *Investment Treaty News* (27 March 2008). Norway's very progressive draft Model BIT was withdrawn in 2009 when it failed to gain parliamentary approval. See D. Vis-Dunbar, 'Norway shelves its draft model bilateral investment treaty', *Investment Treaty News* (8 June 2009); Draft Agreement between the Kingdom of Norway and [Country] for the Promotion and Protection of Investments (Draft Norway Model BIT), http://ita.law.uvic.ca/investmenttreaties.htm (last accessed 1 November 2010).

[15] The South African Department of Trade and Industry explained that it is undertaking an official policy review of the country's BITs because 'the Executive had not been fully apprised of all the possible consequences of BITs', including for human rights, when the young post-apartheid government began entering into them in 1994. South African Department of Trade and Industry, *Bilateral Investment Treaty Policy Framework Review* (June 2009).

[16] See e.g. M. Waibel *et al.*, 'The backlash against investment arbitration: Perceptions and reality' in M. Waibel *et al.* (eds.), *The Backlash against Investment Arbitration: Perceptions and reality* (The Hague: Kluwer, 2010), p. xxxvii; J. Crawford, 'Foreword' in Z. Douglas, *The International Law of Investment Claims* (Cambridge University Press, 2009), p. xxi; C. Brower, M. Ottolenghi and P. Prows, 'The saga of CMS: Res Judicata, precedent, and legitimacy of ICSID arbitration' in C. Binder *et al.* (eds.), *International Investment Law for the 21st Century: Essays in honour of Christoph Schreuer* (Oxford University Press, 2009), p. 519; Alvarez and Khamsi, 'The Argentine crisis', p. 472; C. H. Brower II, 'Obstacles and pathways to consideration of the public interest in investment treaty disputes', *Yearbook on International Investment Law and Policy*, 1 (2008–2009), 356. Some foresaw the possibility of a backlash against the investment law regime even before the

This chapter examines how some States are responding to this criticism by drafting and entering into a new generation of IIAs that possess one or a combination of several new features. Section II below introduces the interpretive language that has been added to some new treaties to clarify the principal investment disciplines in an effort to ensure that they allow States space to pursue competing policy objectives. Section III describes the general exceptions clauses that some States have added to their treaties to provide escapes from investment disciplines when certain competing policy objectives are at stake. Section IV surveys the language that has been added to the preambles of some new IIAs to expand the object and purpose of these treaties beyond investment protection and promotion to non-economic policy objectives. Section V offers some concluding observations.

II Legal disciplines in new-generation IIAs

Some claim that investors have been able to challenge legislative and administrative measures that ordinarily would fall well within the purview of sovereign States because arbitrators have interpreted the most commonly invoked standards of treatment for investors under IIAs – expropriation, fair and equitable treatment, and non-discrimination – in an overly expansive manner.[17] In response to this claim a number of States have sought to reel in the principal standards of treatment by including interpretive language in their IIAs that reformulates or clarifies the standards. This interpretive language instructs arbitrators to conduct a balancing exercise to determine whether government actions taken in response to legitimate regulatory concerns have violated investors' rights.[18] The inclusion of the language is based on the premise that the

---

recent reappraisals began. See e.g. J. Paulsson, 'Arbitration without privity', *ICSID Review – Foreign Investment Law Journal*, 10 (1995), 232, 257.

[17] See e.g. M. Sornarajah, 'A coming crisis: Expansionary trends in investment treaty arbitration' in K. Sauvant (ed.), *Appeals Mechanism in International Disputes* (2008); van Harten, *Investment Treaty Arbitration*.

[18] Arbitrators may have already been obligated to engage in such an exercise by the customary rules on State responsibility to aliens, which anticipate that weighing the respective interests of sovereign and investor is part of determining whether a substantive guarantee has been breached. See Alvarez and Khamsi, 'The Argentine crisis', p. 449, citing L. B. Sohn and R. R. Baxter, 'Responsibility of States for injuries to the economic interests of aliens', *American Journal of International Law*, 55 (1961), 561; American Law Institute, *Restatement (Third) Foreign Relations Law of the United States* (1986), section 712, comment (g).

competing objectives of investor protection and social or environmental protection can be resolved within the substantive IIA standards.

A   Expropriation

Expropriation was the first treatment standard to raise serious concerns about its potential to limit host States' right to regulate in pursuit of legitimate non-investment policy objectives.[19] IIAs prohibit States from expropriating or nationalising a covered investment except for a public purpose, in a non-discriminatory manner, on payment of prompt, adequate and effective compensation, and in accordance with due process of law. Although certain governments, commentators and legal texts reject the position that regulatory activity can constitute expropriation,[20] several arbitral decisions have decisively held that regulatory activity is not, per se, outside the scope of expropriation.

Following on its finding that 'expropriation need not involve the transfer of title to a given property, which was the distinctive feature of traditional expropriation under international law', the tribunal in *Occidental* v. *Ecuador*, for example, found that regulatory measures that 'affect the economic value of an investment' can constitute a compensable, albeit indirect, expropriation.[21] Several tribunals have also held that because 'regulations can indeed be exercised in a way that would constitute creeping expropriation . . . a blanket exception for regulatory measures would create a gaping loophole in international protection against expropriation'.[22] Yet, few recent decisions have actually found

---

[19]   See Been and Beauvais, 'Global Fifth Amendment'; Miles, 'International investment law', pp. 11–19; M. Sornarajah, 'The retreat of neo-liberalism in investment treaty arbitration' in C. A. Rogers and R. P. Alford (eds.), *The Future of Investment Arbitration* (2009), pp. 199, 283–7; van Harten, *Investment Treaty Arbitration*, pp. 90–3; OECD, 'International investment law: A changing landscape' (2005), pp. 43–71.

[20]   C. McLachlan, L. Shore and M. Weiniger, *International Investment Arbitration: Substantive Principles* (Oxford University Press, 2007), p. 306; See also OECD, 'International investment law', pp. 50–3, citing European Convention for the Protection of Human Rights and Fundamental Freedoms, opened for signature 4 November 1950, 213 UNTS 221 (entered into force 3 September 1953), Art. 1 of Protocol 1; Harvard Draft Convention on the International Responsibility of States for Injury to Aliens, Art. 10(5) (1961); OECD Draft Convention on the Protection of Foreign Property, Commentary to Art. 3 (1967); Restatement (Third) of the Foreign Relations Law of the United States, section 712, comment (g).

[21]   *Occidental* v. *Ecuador*, paras. 85, 92.

[22]   *Pope & Talbot Inc.* v. *Canada* (Interim Award of 26 June 2000), para. 99; followed by *Feldman* v. *Mexico* (ICSID Case No. ARB(AF)/99/1, Award of 16 December 2002), para. 110.

regulatory measures to constitute expropriation,[23] and it would appear that, as one arbitrator has stated, 'in the vast run of cases, regulatory conduct by public authorities is not remotely the subject of legitimate complaints' under the expropriation provisions of IIAs.[24]

Arbitral practice has been inconsistent in this area, however, with a number of decisions raising concerns about the methods that arbitrators have employed to determine whether specific regulatory conduct amounted to expropriation. On the one hand, several awards have been criticised as encroaching too far on States' rights under customary international law to exercise their police powers by failing to consider the purpose of a challenged measure when determining whether it constituted an indirect expropriation.[25] The NAFTA tribunal in *Metalclad* v. *Mexico*, for example, held that it 'need not decide or consider the motivation or intent of the adoption of the Ecological Decree', but only whether it had the effect of depriving the foreign investor 'of the use or reasonably-to-be-expected economic benefit of property'.[26] Similarly, for the tribunal in *Azurix* v. *Argentina*, the issue was 'not so much whether the measure concerned is legitimate and serves a public purpose, but whether it is a measure that, being legitimate and serving a public purpose, should give rise to a compensation claim'.[27]

On the other hand, other awards are said to have exaggerated the distinction between a State's exercise of its police powers and an indirect expropriation under international law by failing to consider whether an individual investor should have to bear the full costs of certain regulations that might be borne more appropriately, at least in part, by society as a whole.[28] The NAFTA tribunal in *Methanex* v. *United States*, for example, found that, in determining whether a regulation had resulted in an indirect expropriation, the primary issue was whether the measure concerned was legitimate and served a public purpose. In support of the

---

[23] See Sornarajah, 'The retreat of neo-liberalism', p. 287.

[24] *SD Myers Inc.* v. *Canada* (13 November 2000) (Separate Opinion of Schwarz).

[25] See OECD, 'International investment law', pp. 62–4; H. Mann, 'International investment agreements, business and human rights: Key issues and opportunities' (IISD Report for the UN SRSG, 2008), p. 22.

[26] *Metalclad Corp.* v. *Mexico*, paras. 103, 111.

[27] *Azurix Corp.* v. *Argentina*, para. 310. See also, *Técnicas Medioambientales Tecmed SA* v. *Mexico* (ICSID Case No. ARB(AF)/00/02, Award of 29 May 2003), paras. 115–17; *Siemens Corp.* v. *Argentina* (ICSID Case No. ARB/02/8, Award of 6 February 2007), para. 270; *Compañía del Desarrollo de Santa Elena SA* v. *Costa Rica* (ICSID Case No. ARB(AF)/00/01, Final Award of 17 February 2000), para. 72.

[28] See Brower, 'Obstacles and pathways', pp. 363–4.

customary international law police-powers concept, the tribunal held that, 'as a matter of general international law, a non-discriminatory regulation for a public purpose, which is enacted in accordance with due process and, which affects, inter alios, a foreign investor or invest-ment is not deemed expropriatory and compensable'.[29] The tribunal did not consider the economic impact of the regulation at issue or the degree of interference with the investor's legitimate expectations.

In 2004, the US and Canada responded to the controversy surrounding the content of the indirect expropriation standard by revising their model BITs to provide some guidance to tribunals. Each added an interpretive annex to their model BITs subjecting claims of indirect expropriation to a 'case-by-case', fact-specific inquiry that requires the balancing of at least three factors.[30] The three factors that must be considered – the economic impact of the government measure, the extent to which the measure interferes with distinct, reasonable investment-backed expectations and the character of the government measure – are drawn from a leading takings case decided by the US Supreme Court.[31] The annexes also provide that, except 'in rare circumstances', non-discriminatory regulatory actions that are 'designed and applied to protect legitimate public welfare objectives, such as public health, safety, and the environment, do not constitute indirect expropriations'.[32] A number of other States, including Singapore and India in their 2005 FTA,[33] and China and India in their 2006 BIT,[34] have followed the approach of the US and Canada and incorporated similar interpretive statements in their IIAs.

Not satisfied, some NGOs and academics have proposed that the 'except in rare circumstances' caveat should be removed from the

---

[29] *Methanex* v. *United States of America*, para. 278.

[30] See Treaty between the Government of the United States of America and the Government of [Country] Concerning the Reciprocal Protection of Investment (US Model BIT), Art. 6(1) and Annex B(4), (2004); Agreement between Canada and [Country] for the Promo-tion and Protection of Investments (Canada Model BIT), Art. 13 and Annex B.13(1) (2004).

[31] *Penn Central Transp. Co.* v. *City of New York*, 438 US 104, 123–25 (1978).

[32] US Model BIT, Art. 6 and Annex B (4)(b) (2004); Canadian Model BIT, Art. 13 and Annex B(13)(1)(c) (2004).

[33] See Comprehensive Economic Cooperation Agreement between the Republic of India and the Republic of Singapore, signed 29 June 2005, Annex 3 (India–Singapore CECA).

[34] See J. E. Alvarez, 'The evolving BIT' (Address at Juris Conference on Investment Treaty Arbitration: Interpretation in Investment Arbitration, 30 April 2009), p. 11, n. 30, citing C. Congyan, 'China–U.S. BIT negotiations and the future of investment treaty regime: A grand bilateral bargain with multinational implications', *Journal of International Economic Law*, 1 (forthcoming 2009), 22.

interpretive statement in the US model BIT to provide that non-discriminatory regulation can never be indirect expropriation and to effectively codify the tribunal's holding in *Methanex*.[35] Others have resisted such a change, arguing that it would be inconsistent with international and US domestic law on indirect takings and would create too much of a 'safe harbour' for government regulation.[36] While the latter view appears likely to prevail in the US, other States have already adopted the former view. Eastern and Southern African countries, for example, included the following language in their 2007 COMESA CIAA:

> Consistent with the right of States to regulate and the customary international law principles on police powers, bona fide regulatory measures taken by a Member State that are designed and applied to protect or enhance legitimate public welfare objectives, such as public health, safety and the environment, shall not constitute an indirect expropriation under this Article.[37]

The 2009 ASEAN Comprehensive Investment Agreement takes the same absolute approach.[38] Alongside these new agreements, the vast majority of BITs contain no such interpretive language, raising the question of whether they will be interpreted according to the approach set forth in *Metalclad*, the 2004 US and Canadian Model BITs, or *Methanex*.

B Fair and equitable treatment

The second standard of treatment that has caused considerable controversy in relation to public policy measures is the fair and equitable treatment (FET) standard.[39] The FET standard is found in most IIAs and has become the most common standard for the resolution of investment disputes in recent years, particularly those involving tensions between an investor's rights and the State's legitimate interest in

---

[35] See e.g. R. Stumberg, Professor of Law (Georgetown University Law Center, Testimony before the US House of Representatives Committee on Ways and Means, Subcommittee on Trade, 14 May 2009).

[36] See e.g. L. Menghetti, Vice President (Emergency Committee for American Trade, Testimony before the US House of Representatives Committee on Ways and Means, Subcommittee on Trade, Statement, 6, 14 May 2009).

[37] COMESA CIAA, Art. 20(8).

[38] *ASEAN Comprehensive Investment Agreement*, signed 26 February 2009, Annex 2 (ASEAN CIA).

[39] See Miles, 'International investment law', pp. 19–22; van Harten, *Investment Treaty Arbitration*, pp. 86–90; Sornarajah, 'The retreat of neo-liberalism', pp. 289–90; OECD Draft, 'Foreign property', pp. 73–125.

regulating in the public interest.[40] The FET standard has provoked three persistent questions that may not yet be resolved.

The first question poised by the FET standard relates to its content. Many tribunals have given the standard content by reference to general principles of law falling under the rubric of good faith, transparency, consistency of government action and stability of the legal and business framework relevant to the affected investment.[41] Some of these tribunals are said to have expanded the content of the FET standard so far as to imperil any new environmental or social regulation that a government may wish to impose.[42] Thus, for example, in a frequently cited case, the tribunal in *Tecmed SA* v. *Mexico* held that:

> the foreign investor expects the host State to act in a consistent manner, free from ambiguity and totally transparently in its relations with the foreign investor, *so that it may know beforehand any and all rules and regulations that will govern its investments*, as well as the goals of the relevant policies and administrative practices or directives, to be able to plan its investment and comply with such regulations.[43]

By contrast, several more-recent decisions that have given the FET standard content by reference to general principles of law have lent greater support to the sovereign right to regulate. The tribunal in *Parkerings* v. *Lithuania*, for example, observed that, while it is prohibited 'for a State to act unfairly, unreasonably or inequitably in the exercise of its legislative power . . . there is nothing objectionable about [an] amendment brought to the regulatory framework existing at the time an investor made its investment'.[44] An investor's right to have legitimate

---

[40] Different IIAs formulate the FET differently. The standard US and Canadian FET provisions mention customary international law, while the standard European FET provisions (Dutch, German, Swedish, among others) do not.

[41] A. H. Ali and K. Tallent, 'The effect of BITs on the international body of investment law: The significance of fair and equitable treatment provisions' in C. A. Rogers and R. P. Alford (eds.), *The Future of Investment Arbitration* (Oxford University Press, 2009), pp. 199, 213.

[42] Miles, 'International investment law', pp. 21–2.

[43] *Técnicas Medioambientales Tecmed SA* v. *United Mexican States*, para. 154 (emphasis added). See also *MTD Equity Sdn. Bhd. & MTD Chile SA* v. *Chile* (ICSID Case No. ARB/01/7, Award of 25 May 2004), para. 114; *Occidental* v. *Ecuador*, para. 185; *PSEG Global Inc.* v. *Republic of Turkey* (ICSID Case No. ARB/02/5, Award of 19 January 2007), para. 240; *CME Czech Republic BV* v. *Czech Republic* (UNCITRAL, Partial Award of 13 September 2001), para. 611; *Enron Corporation Ponderosa Assets LP* v. *Argentine Republic* (ICSID Case No. ARB/01/3, Award of 22 May 2007), para. 254.

[44] *Parkerings-Compagniet AS* v. *Lithuania* (ICSID Case No. ARB/05/8, Award of 11 September 2007), para. 332.

expectations protected is contingent on those expectations being reasonable in light of the circumstances and on the investor having exercised due diligence.[45]

To give the FET standard content by reference to something more specific than the full range of general principles of law, a few States have included language in their more recent IIAs referring to the obligations of States not to 'deny justice' to foreign investors. The 2004 US Model BIT, for example, specifies that the concept of '"fair and equitable treatment" includes the obligation not to deny justice . . . in accordance with due process'.[46] Similarly, the 2009 ASEAN Comprehensive Investment Agreement provides that: 'For greater certainty . . . fair and equitable treatment requires each Member State not to deny justice.'[47] There is some debate as to whether the use of the term 'includes' in the US BIT and 'requires' in the ASEAN agreement is intended to indicate that denial of justice is the only form of government action that violates the FET standard or that it is just one example.[48]

A second question that persists in relation to FET is whether it is an autonomous treaty standard or reflects the international minimum standard of treatment (MST) for aliens under customary international law.[49] In 2001, the tribunal in *Pope and Talbot* v. *Canada* interpreted the FET provision in NAFTA to mean that FET was 'additive' to the MST.[50] A few months later, the NAFTA Free Trade Commission (FTC) issued a Note of Interpretation rejecting that assertion and clarifying that the reference to FET in Article 1105 of NAFTA is equivalent to the 'customary international law minimum standard of treatment of aliens'.[51] The US and Canada have also included interpretive statements in their respective 2004 Model BITs and subsequent IIAs to the same effect.[52]

---

[45] *Ibid.*, para. 333. See also *Saluka Investments BV* v. *Czech Republic* (Partial Award of 17 March 2006), para. 305.

[46] US Model BIT, Art. 5(2)(a) (2004).   [47] ASEAN CIA, Art. 11.

[48] Compare Alvarez, 'The evolving BIT', p. 10 with Menghetti, 'Emergency committee', p. 4.

[49] Muchlinski, 'Trends in international investment', p. 42.

[50] *Pope & Talbot Inc.* v. *Canada* (Award on the Merits of Phase 2 of 10 April 2001), para. 110. See also *Sempra Energy International* v. *Argentina* (ICSID Case No. ARB/02/16, Award of 28 September 2007), para. 302; *PSEG Global Inc., The North American Coal Corporation, and Konya Ingin Electrik Uretim ve Ticaret Limited Sirketi* v. *Turkey*, para. 239; *Saluka Investments BV* v. *Czech Republic*, para. 309.

[51] NAFTA Communication, Notes of Interpretation (31 July 2001).

[52] See US Model BIT, Art. 5(2) (2004); Canada Model BIT, Art. 5(2) (2004).

Other States have also expressed their disagreement with arbitral awards holding that the FET standard is in addition to or higher than the MST. After the tribunal in *Tecmed SA* v. *Mexico* held that the scope of the FET provision in the 1995 Spain–Mexico BIT should result 'from an autonomous interpretation, taking into account the text of [the FET provision] according to its ordinary meaning',[53] Spain and Mexico adopted a new BIT in 2006 clarifying that the FET standard is included within the MST and is not a stand-alone provision.[54] Mexico also entered into a BIT with China in 2008 that closely approximates the US and Canada's articulation of the FET standard.[55] Southern and Eastern African countries also included language in the COMESA CIAA clarifying that the FET does not require treatment in addition to what is required by the MST,[56] while India and Singapore chose to omit all reference to both the FET and the MST standards in their 2005 FTA.[57] Despite these developments, there are still many IIAs in force that do not expressly link the FET standard to the MST and tribunals may continue to interpret FET as establishing an autonomous treaty standard in the context of such treaties.[58]

The third recurring question relating to the FET standard is whether its inclusion in the vast majority of IIAs and expositions on its scope under those IIAs by an array of arbitral tribunals have had any impact on the content of the MST under customary iternational law.[59] A number of tribunals have indicated that that might be the case, including the tribunal in *Mondev* v. *United States*, which observed:

> On a widespread basis, States have repeatedly obliged themselves to accord foreign investment [fair and equitable] treatment. In the Tribunal's view, such a body of concordant practice will necessarily have influenced the content of rules governing the treatment of foreign

---

[53] *Técnicas Medioambientales Tecmed SA* v. *Mexico*, para. 154.

[54] Contrast the Agreement between the Kingdom of Spain and the United Mexican States on the Reciprocal Promotion and Protection of Investments, signed 22 June 1995 (entered into force 18 December 1996) (Spain–Mexico BIT 1995), Art. IV(1), with the Agreement between the Kingdom of Spain and the United Mexican States for the Promotion and Reciprocal Protection of Investments, signed 10 October 2006 (Spain–Mexico BIT 2006), Art. IV(1).

[55] Alvarez, 'The evolving BIT', p. 11 and n. 29 (citing the Agreement between the Government of the United Mexican States and the Government of the People's Republic of China on the Promotion and Reciprocal Protection of Investments, signed 11 July 2008 (Mexico–China BIT), www.transnational-dispute-management.com (last accessed 1 November 2010)).

[56] COMESA CIAA, Art. 14(2).   [57] India–Singapore CECA.

[58] See *Glamis Gold* v. *United States of America* (Award of 8 June 2009), para. 260.

[59] Ali and Tallent, 'The effect of BITs'.

> investment in current international law . . . In these circumstances, the content of the minimum standard today cannot be limited to the content of customary international law as recognized in arbitral decisions in the 1920s.[60]

Following similar reasoning, a number of other tribunals have incorporated elements of the FET standard as developed in arbitral practice into their analysis of the requirements of the MST under customary international law.[61]

The past two years have seen NAFTA tribunals take opposing sides in the debate over whether the customary international law MST has evolved since the 1920s, particularly in light of arbitral practice under the FET provisions of IIAs. In 2009, the tribunal in *Glamis Gold* v. *United States* held that the claimant had not proved that the customary international law MST standard had evolved beyond that elucidated in the 1926 Mexico–United States Claims Commission award in *Neer* v. *Mexico*.[62] The tribunal in *Neer* held that:

> The treatment of an alien, in order to constitute an international delinquency, should amount to an outrage, to bad faith, to willful neglect of duty, or to an insufficiency of governmental action so far short of international standards that every reasonable and impartial man would readily recognize its insufficiency.[63]

In contrast, in 2010, two NAFTA tribunals stated that they could not overlook the evolution of customary international law since the *Neer* case, nor the impact of IIAs on this evolution. On that basis, the first tribunal, in *Merrill & Ring* v. *Canada*, held that today's MST is broader than that defined in the *Neer* case and provides for the fair and equitable treatment of alien investors within the confines of 'reasonableness' – rather than within the more narrow confines of 'outrageousness' as was

---

[60] *Mondev International Ltd* v. *United States* (ICSID Case No. ARB(AF)/99/2, Award of 11 October 2002), paras. 116, 125.

[61] See e.g. *ADF Group Inc.* v. *United States* (ICSID Case No. ARB (AF)/00/1, Award of 9 January 2003); *Waste Management Inc.* v. *Mexico (No. 2)* (ICSID Case No. ARB(AF)/00/3, Final Award of 30 April 2004), para. 98; *Occidental* v. *Ecuador*, paras. 188–90; *Azurix Corp.* v. *Argentina*.

[62] *Glamis Gold Ltd*, para. 627.

[63] *LFH Neer & Pauline Neer* v. *Mexico*, 4 UNRIAA 60 (15 October 1926), pp. 61–2. Applying this standard, the *Glamis* tribunal held that a breach of the NAFTA FET standard 'requires an act that is sufficiently egregious and shocking – a gross denial of justice, manifest arbitrariness, blatant unfairness, a complete lack of due process, evident discrimination, or a manifest lack of reasons': *Glamis Gold Ltd*, para. 268.

the case in the 1920s.[64] The second tribunal, in *Chemtura Corporation v. Canada*, also stated that the MST is not confined to the kind of outrageous treatment referred to in the *Neer* case,[65] but rather requires an analysis of the record as a whole to determine whether a government acted fairly, in keeping with due-process standards and in good faith when taking regulatory measures.[66]

During the ongoing review of the US Model BIT, some academics and NGOs have proposed that language be added to the model's FET provision to codify the view expressed by the US government in the *Glamis* case that the MST under customary international law has been established 'in only a few areas,' including with respect to 'denial of justice'.[67] Those who argue for this change claim that the US cited denial of justice in its submissions in *Glamis* and in the 2004 Model BIT as the only form of government action that violates the FET component of the MST.[68]

Those who oppose such a change claim that the US cited denial of justice as just one example of government action that violates the FET component of the MST and claim that other actions cited by arbitral tribunals, including the violation of an investor's legitimate expectations, have become or are becoming part of customary international law.[69] The US should not define the MST to include only the denial of justice, according to these observers, as it would thereby forego the benefits of customary international law's evolution.[70] It remains to be seen whether and how this debate will be resolved in the new US Model BIT. It also remains to be seen whether arbitral tribunals will begin to produce consistent answers to the three questions discussed above regarding the content of the FET standard, its relationship to the MST and its impact on customary international law.

---

[64] *Merrill & Ring* v. *Canada* (Award of 31 March 2010), para. 213.

[65] *Chemtura Corporation* v. *Canada* (Award of 2 August 2010), para. 215.

[66] *Ibid.*, paras. 123, 162, 179, 184, 215, 216, 219 and 224.

[67] See e.g. Stumberg, 'Testimony before the U.S. House', p. 3.

[68] *Ibid.* However, the *Glamis* tribunal's view of the scope of the MST went beyond the narrow US government position to include, not only a 'a gross denial of justice', but also 'manifest arbitrariness, blatant unfairness, a complete lack of due process, evident discrimination, or a manifest lack of reasons'. The tribunal also noted that a breach of the customary international law MST, as codified in NAFTA's FET provision, could also be exhibited by 'the creation by the State of objective expectations in order to induce investment and the subsequent repudiation of those expectations': *Glamis Gold Ltd*, para. 627.

[69] See e.g. Menghetti, 'Emergency Committee', p. 4.   [70] *Ibid.*

C   Non-discrimination

Finally, some have expressed concern that the application of the non-discrimination standard contained in most IIAs could result in the undue restriction of regulatory discretion.[71] The non-discrimination standard is by definition relative in the sense that it measures the State's treatment of foreign investors against the treatment of similarly situated domestic or other foreign investors. Thus, a tribunal must determine how to identify similarly situated or categories of 'like' investors. Concerns have arisen where tribunals have drawn such categories without regard to public policy objetives.[72]

Thus, for example, the tribunal in *Occidental* v. *Ecuador* provoked alarm when it adopted a very broad definition of 'like' investor, comparing the treatment accorded to a foreign oil company with the treatment accorded to exporters in general, rather than with the treatment of domestic oil companies.[73] Other tribunals have adopted more tailored definitions of 'like' investor, thereby sending reassuring signals that legitimate distinctions can be made between individuals and economic actors when these are justified by sound public-policy goals. In the case of *Parkerings* v. *Lithuania*, for example, the tribunal held that no discrimination had occurred when a foreign investor's car-parking project was treated differently from a domestic investor's project, because the foreign investor's project was within a section of Vilnius designated by UNESCO as a World Cultural Heritage site.[74]

Although IIA jurisprudence does not provide clear guidance on what amounts to a legitimate policy goal, it does provide some guidance on how tribunals should assess whether a measure undertaken in pursuit of such a goal constitutes a violation of the non-discrimination standard. In *Pope & Talbot* v. *Canada*, for example, the tribunal held that, to withstand a challenge on the grounds of discrimination, a measure must have a 'reasonable nexus to rational government policies that (1) do not distinguish, on their face or *de facto*, between foreign-owned and domestic companies, and (2) do not otherwise unduly undermine the investment liberalizing objectives of NAFTA'.[75]

---

[71] See van Harten, *Investment Treaty Arbitration*, pp. 83–6; Muchlinski, 'Trends in international investment', p. 43; Sornarajah, 'A coming crisis', pp. 62–3.

[72] *Ibid.*   [73] See e.g. *Occidental* v. *Ecuador*, paras. 173–6.

[74] *Parkerings-Compagniet*, section 8.3.

[75] *Pope & Talbot Inc.* (Award on the Merits of Phase 2 of 10 April 2001), para. 78. See also *GAMI Investments Inc.* v. *Mexico* (Final Award of 15 November 2004), para. 114.

To ensure that tribunals do not delineate categories of investors too narrowly, one new IIA includes a non-exhaustive list of possible factors to consider when determining whether investors are in 'like circumstances' for the purposes of the application of the national treatment or most-favoured nation non-discrimination standards. The COMESA CIAA provides that:

> For greater certainty, references to 'like circumstances' in [the National Treatment article] requires an overall examination on a case by case basis of all the circumstances of an investment including, inter alia:
>
> (a) its effects on third persons and the local community;
> (b) its effects on the local, regional or national environment, including the cumulative effects of all investments within a jurisdiction on the environment;
> (c) the sector the investor is in;
> (d) the aim of the measure concerned;
> (e) the regulatory process generally applied in relation to the measure concerned; and
> (f) other factors directly relating to the investment or investor in relation to the measure concerned; and the examination shall not be limited to or be biased towards any one factor.[76]

The draft Norwegian Model BIT took a different approach.[77] It included a footnote to its national treatment and most-favoured nation clauses acknowledging that the pursuit of some legitimate public-policy objectives may necessarily result in discrimination and indicating that such discrimination should not implicate the host State's treaty obligations.[78]

The COMESA CIAA and the draft Norwegian Model BIT appear to be unique in their inclusion of language clarifying the non-discrimination standards in IIAs. Some have proposed that language should be added to the US Model BIT indicating 'that national treatment requires evidence of either (1) intentional discrimination or (2) *de facto* discrimination against investors as a group'.[79] But neither this suggestion nor the idea of adding other language to clarify the scope of the non-discrimination standard has been under serious discussion during the US review.

---

[76] COMESA CIAA, Art. 17(2).

[77] As noted above, the draft was released for comment in 2007, but has since been withdrawn for failure to gain parliamentary approval. See n. 15 above.

[78] *Ibid.*

[79] See e.g. G. van Harten, *Testimony Before U.S. State Department Public Hearing on Bilateral Investment Treaty Reform* (Osgoode Hall Law School, 7 July 2009).

III General exceptions clauses in new-generation IIAs

Most older IIAs contain no exceptions or identify only a limited range of sectors or types of regulatory measures that are excluded from the coverage of the treaty, most notably taxation and essential security measures. A small but growing number of IIAs also now include one of several types of so-called 'general exceptions' clauses to ensure that investors' rights are balanced against the regulatory concerns of host States.

The rationale for a general exception clause is to exempt a contracting party from the obligations of the treaty in situations in which compliance would be incompatible with key policy objectives explicitly identified in the agreement.[80] Thus, rather than directing a tribunal to balance the competing objectives of investor protection against societal or environmental protection in determining whether the treaty has been breached, a general exception clause directs the tribunal to balance specified objectives in determining whether a given breach is excused on the basis of the general exception clause.

The first type of general exception clause included in some IIAs is based on GATT Article XX or GATS Article XIV.[81] This general exception method makes the exception conditional on the fulfilment of certain requirements aimed at preventing its abuse. In particular, it usually obliges the host State to apply the otherwise non-conforming measure in a manner that would not constitute arbitrary or unjustifiable discrimination and to avoid using it as a disguised restriction on investment. Depending on the exact language used, this method also requires the host State to show that the non-conforming measure was 'necessary', 'relating' or 'designed and applied' to further one of the policy objectives specified in the clause.

Canada began including general exceptions clauses of this type in its IIAs in the late 1990s.[82] It also incorporated such a clause into its 2004 Model BIT, Article 10 of which provides:

---

[80] See *United States – Measures Affecting the Cross-Border Supply of Gambling and Betting Services* (WT/DS285/AB/R, adopted 20 April 2005), para. 291.

[81] Unlike Art. XX of the General Agreement on Tariffs and Trade, opened for signature 15 April 1994, 1867 UNTS 190 (entered into force 1 January 1995) (GATT), Art. XIV of the General Agreement on Trade in Services, opened for signature 15 April 1994, 1869 UNTS 183 (entered into force 1 January 1995) (GATS) does not contain an exemption for measures relating to the conservation of exhaustible natural resources.

[82] See e.g. Agreement between the Government of Canada and the Government of the Republic of Armenia for the Promotion and Protection of Investments, signed 8 May 1997 (entered into force 29 March 1999) (Canada–Armenia BIT), Art. XVII.

Subject to the requirement that such measures are not applied in a manner
that would constitute arbitrary or unjustifiable discrimination between
investments or between investors, or a disguised restriction on international trade or investment, nothing in this Agreement shall be construed
to prevent a Party from adopting or enforcing measures necessary:

  (a) to protect human, animal or plant life or health;
  (b) to ensure compliance with laws and regulations that are not
      inconsistent with the provisions of this Agreement; or
  (c) for the conservation of living or non-living exhaustible natural
      resources.[83]

A number of other countries, particularly in Asia, also began incorporating
general exceptions provisions based on all or portions of GATT Article
XX[84] or the similar GATS Article XIV,[85] or both,[86] into their IIAs in the late

---

[83] Canada Model BIT, Art. 10 (2004). See also Agreement between Canada and the
Republic of Peru for the Promotion and Protection of Investments, signed 14 November
2006 (entered into force 20 June 2007) (Canada–Peru BIT), Art. 10(c); Canada–
Colombia Free Trade Agreement, signed 21 November 2008 (Canada–Colombia FTA),
Art. 2201.3(c); Canada–Peru Free Trade Agreement, signed 1 August 2009 (Canada–Peru
FTA), Art. 2201.3(c).

[84] See e.g. Singapore–Australia Free Trade Agreement, signed 17 February 2003 (entered
into force 28 July 2003) (Singapore–Australia FTA), Art. 19; Agreement between Japan
and the Republic of Singapore for a New-Age Economic Partnership Agreement, signed
13 January 2002 (entered into force 30 November 2002) (Japan–Singapore FTA), Art. 83;
Bilateral Investment Treaty between the Government of the Hashemite Kingdom of
Jordan and the Government of the Republic of Singapore, signed 29 April 2004 (entered
into force 22 August 2005) (Jordan–Singapore BIT), Art. 18; India–Singapore CECA,
Art. 6.11; Agreement between the Government of Japan and the Government of Malaysia
for an Economic Partnership, signed December 2005 (entered into force 13 July 2006)
(Japan–Malaysia EPA), Art. 10; ASEAN CIA, Art. 17; Agreement on Investment of the
Framework Agreement on Comprehensive Economic Cooperation between the Association of South-East Asian Nations and the People's Republic of China, signed 15 August
2009 (ASEAN–China Investment Agreement), Art. 16; Comprehensive Economic Partnership Agreement between Korea and India, signed 7 August 2009 (entered into force
1 January 2010) (Korea–India CEPA), Art. 10.18.

[85] Panama–Taiwan Free Trade Agreement, signed 21 August 2003 (entered into force 1 January
2004) (Panama–Taiwan FTA), Art. 20.02; Korea – Singapore Free Trade Agreement, signed
4 August 2005 (entered into force 2 March 2006) (Korea–Singapore FTA), Art. 21.2;
Agreement Establishing the Association of Southeast Asian Nations (ASEAN)–Australia–
New Zealand Free Trade Area, signed 27 February 2009, [2010] ATS 1 (entered into force
1 January 2010 for Australia, New Zealand, Brunei, Burma, Malaysia, the Philippines,
Singapore and Vietnam; 12 March 2010 for Thailand; 1 January 2011 for Laos; 4 January
2011 for Cambodia) (ASEAN–Australia–New Zealand FTA), Chapter 15, Arts. 1–5.

[86] New Zealand–China Free Trade Agreement, signed 7 April 2008 (entered into force
1 October 2008), Art. 200 (New Zealand–China FTA); Japan–Malaysia EPA, Art. 10;
Thailand–Australia Free Trade Agreement, signed 5 July 2004 (entered into force
1 January 2005) (Thailand–Australia FTA), Art. 1601.

1990s.[87] Southern and Eastern African countries also have incorporated a general exception clause based on Article XX of the GATT in their regional investment promotion agreement; although, unlike most other general exceptions clauses, the COMESA CIAA clause uses the term 'designed and applied' rather than 'necessary' to describe the non-conforming measures that may be used to further the specified policy objectives.[88]

A second general exception method indicates that the exceptions are conditional on the fulfilment of fewer substantive and more procedural requirements than the general exceptions clauses in the GATT and GATS. This method permits non-conforming measures that are necessary to protect certain policy objectives as long as the State invoking the exception is not seeking to avoid its obligations and has notified the other State Party to the IIA about the measure as soon as possible. The 2002 BIT between Japan and the Republic of Korea, which employs this method, provides:

1. Notwithstanding any other provisions in this Agreement . . . each Contracting Party may . . . take any measure necessary to protect human, animal or plant life or health.
2. In cases where a Contracting Party takes any measure, pursuant to paragraph 1 above, that does not conform with the obligations of the provisions of this Agreement . . . that Contracting Party shall not use such measure as a means of avoiding its obligations.
3. In cases where a Contracting Party takes any measure, pursuant to paragraph 1 above, that does not conform with the obligations of the provisions of this Agreement . . . that Contracting Party shall, prior to the entry into force of the measure or as soon thereafter as possible, notify the other Contracting Party of the following elements of the measure: (a) sector and sub-sector or matter; (b) obligation or article in respect of which the measure is taken; (c) legal source or authority of the measure; (d) succinct description of the measure; and (e) motivation or purpose of the measure.[89]

---

[87] The Agreement between the Government of the Argentine Republic and the Government of New Zealand for the Promotion and Reciprocal Protection of Investments, signed 27 August 1999 (Argentina–New Zealand BIT), Art. 5(3), incorporates a general exceptions clause of this type with somewhat different format and wording. The US also includes general exceptions clauses based on Art. XX of the GATT in its IIAs, but only in relation to performance requirements. See e.g. US Model BIT, Art. 8(3)(c) (2004).

[88] COMESA CIAA, Art. 22.

[89] Agreement between the Government of the Republic of Korea and the Government of Japan for the Liberalisation, Promotion and Protection of Investment, signed 22 March 2002 (entered into force 1 January 2003) (Korea–Japan BIT), Art. 16.1(c).

A third general exceptions method used in some IIAs is conditional on an even more limited range of requirements designed to prevent its abuse. The Mauritius–Switzerland BIT, for example, simply provides that: 'Nothing in this Agreement shall be construed to prevent a Contracting Party from taking any action necessary . . . for reasons of public health or the prevention of diseases in animals and plants.'[90] Some general exceptions clauses of this type impose even less stringent requirements on the invoking party. Rather than requiring that the State show that the particular measure was 'necessary', these clauses only require that the State show that the measure was 'proportional' to the objective sought (e.g. the Colombian Model BIT)[91] or that the State had determined in good faith that the measure was 'appropriate' with respect to the objective sought (e.g. the COMESA CIAA).[92]

IV   Non-economic policy objectives in the preambles of new-generation IIAs

Under the rules of treaty interpretation contained in the Vienna Convention on the Law of Treaties, tribunals must interpret treaty provisions 'in accordance with the ordinary meaning to be given to the terms of the treaty in their context and in the light of [the treaty's] object and purpose'.[93] Investor–State arbitral tribunals commonly use preambles and statements of objectives to identify the context of a treaty's terms and the treaty's overall object and purpose.[94] Thus, preambles and statements of objectives provide important interpretive tools in investor–State arbitration.

The preambles and objectives of IIAs have typically focused exclusively on the protection and promotion of investment. The preamble of the 1991 UK–Argentina BIT, for example, states that the governments agreed to the treaty because they 'desir[ed] to create favourable conditions for greater investment' and because they 'recogniz[ed] that the encouragement and reciprocal protection under international agreement

---

[90] Agreement between the Swiss Confederation and the Republic of Mauritius concerning the Promotion and Reciprocal Protection of Investments, signed 26 November 1998 (entered into force 21 April 2000) (Switzerland–Mauritius BIT), Art. 11.
[91] Colombia Model BIT, Art. 8 (2007).   [92] COMESA CIAA, Art. 22.
[93] Vienna Convention on the Law of Treaties, opened for signature 23 May 1969, 1155 UNTS 311 (entered into force 27 January 1980), Art. 31.
[94] See Brower, 'Obstacles and pathways', p. 375.

of such investments will be conducive to the stimulation of individual business initiative and will increase prosperity'.[95] In the rare instance that a non-economic policy objective – such as promoting the well-being of workers – is mentioned in the preamble of an 1990s-era IIA, it is – like the 'stimulation of individual business initiative' and the 'increase [in] prosperity' in the UK–Argentina BIT – assumed to be a natural outcome of achieving the investment protection and promotion objectives of the treaty.[96] Non-investment policy objectives are not stated as self-standing treaty objectives in older IIAs and nothing in those treaties implies that investor guarantees are conditional on the achievement of non-investment objectives.[97]

Given that the object and purpose of most older IIAs is narrowly focused on investment protection and promotion, many investor–State tribunals have, after applying the Vienna Convention's rules of treaty interpretation, determined that such treaties' provisions must be interpreted in favour of the protection of foreign investment.[98] For example, in a case against Argentina, a tribunal noted that, in interpreting the BIT's provisions, it must 'be guided by the purpose of the Treaty, as expressed in its title and preamble,' which was 'to create favourable conditions for investments'.[99] Similarly, another tribunal observed that

---

[95] Agreement between the Government of the United Kingdom of Great Britain and Northern Ireland and the Government of the Argentine Republic for the Promotion and Protection of Investments, signed 11 December 1990 (entered into force 19 February 1993) (United Kingdom–Argentina BIT), preamble. See also e.g. Treaty between the United States of America and the Argentine Republic concerning the Encouragement and Reciprocal Protection of Investment, signed 14 November 1991 (entered into force 20 October 1994) (US–Argentina BIT), preamble; Agreement between the Kingdom of the Netherlands and Ukraine on Promotion and Reciprocal Protection of Investments, signed 14 July 1994 (entered into force 1 June 1997) (Netherlands–Ukraine BIT), preamble.

[96] See e.g. US–Argentina BIT, preamble ('Recognizing that the development of economic and business ties *can contribute* to the well-being of workers in both Parties and promote respect for internationally recognized worker rights', emphasis added). See also, Alvarez and Khamsi, 'The Argentine crisis', p. 470.

[97] Alvarez and Khamsi, 'The Argentine crisis', pp. 470–1. The promotion of 'sustainable development' appears to be stated as an autonomous treaty objective in the preamble of NAFTA, but the treaty's objectives provision does not include it. See North American Free Trade Agreement, signed 17 December 1992), United States–Canada–Mexico (1993) 32 ILM 289, 605 (entered into force 1 January 1994), preamble and Art. 102(2).

[98] See D. Kalderimis, *Investment Treaties and Public Goods* (Paper presented at the Inaugural Asian International Economic Law Network Conference, Tokyo, 3 August 2009), pp. 13–14; Brower, 'Obstacles and pathways', p. 361; J. E. Alvarez, 'Book review of Gus van Harten, investment treaty arbitration and public law', *American Journal of International Law*, 102 (2008), 909.

[99] *Siemens* v. *Argentina*, para. 81.

it was obliged to interpret a treaty provision 'in the manner most conducive to fulfil the objective of the BIT to protect investments and create conditions favourable to investments'.[100] And, another tribunal found that, in light of a BIT's narrow preambular language, it was 'legitimate to resolve uncertainties in its interpretation so as to favor the protection of covered investments'.[101]

Even when tribunals have disavowed an intention to interpret an IIA presumptively in favour of investment protection, the narrow object and purpose set forth in most preambles has influenced decision-making. Thus, for example, the tribunal in *Azurix* v. *Argentina* maintained that it did 'not consider that the BIT should be interpreted in favour or against the investor'.[102] It nevertheless observed that, 'the Tribunal in interpreting the BIT must be mindful of the objective the parties intended to pursue by concluding it'.[103] In the instant case, that objective was to require 'certain treatment of investment' in order 'to stimulate the flow of private capital'.[104] Similarly, the tribunal in *Saluka* v. *The Czech Republic*, cautioned against presumptions in favour of investors, but only on the grounds that the preamble's references to both 'protection' and 'promotion' of investment allowed for some 'balancing' between those two objectives.[105] The tribunal found that it should not adopt 'an interpretation which exaggerates the protection to be accorded to foreign investments', as this 'may serve to dissuade host States from admitting foreign investments'.[106]

Tribunals have also interpreted the few exceptions that exist in some older IIAs restrictively in light of the narrow object and purpose of those treaties. Thus, for example, two tribunals interpreting the essential security clause in the US–Argentina BIT emphasised that the 'object and purpose of the Treaty is, as a general proposition, to apply in situations of economic difficulty and hardship that require the protection of the international guaranteed rights of its beneficiaries'.[107] It followed that 'any interpretation resulting in an escape route from the obligations defined cannot be easily reconciled with that object and purpose [and] a restrictive interpretation of any such alternative is mandatory'.[108] Similarly, the tribunal in *Canfor* v. *US* suggested that, even if there were exceptions

---

[100] *MTD Equity Sdn. Bhd. and MTD Chile SA*, para. 104.
[101] *SGS Société Générale de Surveillance SA* v. *Republic of the Philippines* (ICSID Case No. ARB/02/6, Decision on Jurisdiction of 29 January 2004), para. 116.
[102] *Azurix Corp.*, para. 307.   [103] *Ibid.*   [104] *Ibid.*
[105] *Saluka Investment BV*, para. 300.   [106] *Ibid.*
[107] *Enron Corp.*, para. 337; *Sempra Energy*, para. 373.   [108] *Ibid.*

clauses in IIAs like those in WTO agreements, investor–State tribunals would need to interpret them narrowly to be consistent with the investment promotion and protection purpose of IIAs.[109]

A number of governments have responded to cases in which tribunals have examined terse preambular language and determined that the object and purpose of a treaty is limited to investment protection and promotion, even when a dispute implicates other legitimate governmental objectives. Some governments have added new preambular language to their IIAs – language that reflects an awareness of the growing number of cases in which investors have challenged host State regulatory measures designed to protect legitimate domestic policy objectives, including social and environmental protection. New preambles contain three primary types of new language, with some preambles employing more than one type.

First, some new preambles indicate that, while investment protection and promotion remains the principal objective of the IIA, that objective is not an end in and of itself that must be achieved at all costs.[110] The preamble to the 2004 US Model BIT and agreements based on it, for example, indicates that the parties 'Desir[e] to achieve [investor protection] objectives in a manner consistent with the protection of health, safety, and the environment, and the promotion of internationally recognized labor rights'.[111] A growing number of IIAs expressly indicate

---

[109] See *Canfor and ors* v. *United States* (Decision on the Preliminary Question of 6 June 2006), citing *Canada–Import Restrictions on Ice Cream and Yoghurt*, Report of the Panel adopted at the Forty-fifth Session of the Contracting Parties on 5 December 1989 (L/6568 – 36S/68, 27 September 1989), para. 59; and *Tariffs Applied by Canada to Certain U.S.–Origin Agricultural Products*, CDA-95–2008–01, 2 December 1996), para. 122.

[110] The preambles of some new-generation IIAs still assume that investment protection will automatically lead to the achievement of certain social and environmental policy objectives. However, the inclusion of reformulated provisions or general exceptions clauses in these treaties implicitly acknowledges that this may not always be the case and that investment protection may sometimes need to give way to the protection of such other objectives. See e.g. preambles to the Korea–Japan BIT; Canada Model BIT (2004); Bilateral Investment Treaty between the Government of the Hashemite Kingdom of Jordan and the Government of the Republic of Singapore, signed 29 April 2004 (entered into force 22 August 2005) (Jordan–Singapore BIT); Canada–Peru BIT; COMESA CCIA; New Zealand–China FTA; ASEAN–Australia–New Zealand FTA; Australia–Chile Free Trade Agreement, signed 30 July 2008 (entered into force 6 March 2009) (Australia–Chile FTA); Korea–India CEPA.

[111] US Model BIT (2004), preamble. See also, preambles to the Treaty between the United States of America and the Oriental Republic of Uruguay concerning the Encouragement and Reciprocal Protection of Investment, signed 4 November 2005 (entered into force 1 November 2006) (US–Uruguay BIT); India–Singapore CECA; Draft Norway Model BIT (2007); Canada–Colombia FTA; Canada–Peru FTA; Korea–India CEPA; Australia–Chile FTA.

that treaty objectives must be pursued in a manner compatible with the principles of sustainable development in particular.[112]

Secondly, other relatively new preambles indicate that certain non-investment policy objectives constitute self-standing objectives of IIAs. According to the preamble to their agreement, the parties to the 2008 Canada–Colombia FTA, for example, entered into the agreement not only to promote investment, but also to protect the environment and workers' rights, 'promote sustainable development', 'encourage enterprises . . . to respect internationally recognized corporate social responsibility standards' and 'promote broad-based economic development in order to reduce poverty'.[113] Sustainable development is a specific treaty objective in a small but growing number of IIAs.[114]

Finally, the preambles of some new-generation IIAs also expressly provide that the parties do not intend to relinquish their right to regulate in the public interest. Thus, for example, in their 2005 FTA, India and Singapore reaffirmed 'their right to pursue economic philosophies suited to their development goals and their right to regulate activities to realize their national policy objectives'.[115] In similar fashion, the preambles of some IIAs simply reaffirm the parties' commitments to non-investment policy objectives – including their obligations under non-investment bodies of international law – that may require government intervention in the economy.[116]

---

[112] See e.g. Panama–Taiwan FTA; Australia–United States Free Trade Agreement, signed 18 May 2004 (entered into force 1 January 2005) (Australia–US FTA); India–Singapore CECA; United States–Peru Trade Promotion Agreement, signed 12 April 2006 (entered into force on 1 February 2009) (US–Peru FTA); Draft Norway Model BIT (2007); ASEAN–China Investment Agreement.

[113] Canada–Colombia FTA, preamble. See also, preambles to the Panama–Taiwan FTA; US–Peru FTA; Draft Norway Model BIT (2007); New Zealand–China FTA; Canada–Peru FTA.

[114] See e.g. Canada–Colombia FTA; Canada–Peru FTA. The promotion of 'sustainable development' appears to be stated as an autonomous treaty objective in the preambles of NAFTA and the United States–Dominican Republic–Central America Free Trade Agreement, signed 28 May 2004 (entered into force for the United States on 28 February 2006; El Salvador 1 March 2006; Honduras and Nicaragua 1 April 2006; Guatemala 1 July 2006; Dominican Republic 1 March 2007; Costa Rica 1 January 2009) (CAFTA–DR), but those treaties' 'objectives' provisions do not mention it. See NAFTA, preamble and Art. 102(2) (1994); CAFTA–DR, preamble and Art. 1.2 (2004). But see discussion of *SD Myers* (First Partial Award of 13 November 2000) and accompanying text.

[115] India–Singpore CECA, preamble. See also, preambles to the Canada–Colombia FTA; and the ASEAN–China Investment Agreement.

[116] See e.g. Draft Norway Model BIT (2007).

V   Concluding comments

New-generation IIAs have yet to produce a significant and consistent body of case law, so one can only speculate at this point about how the innovations they contain will affect international investment law in the long run. On the one hand, by directing tribunals to engage in balancing, new-generation IIAs are likely to embolden investor–State tribunals to consider non-investment policy objectives more often than they have in the past and to provide them a broad framework of analysis for doing so. Many new-generation IIAs also instruct tribunals not to resolve uncertainties in treaty interpretation presumptively in favour of investment protection, as tribunals have tended to do in the past. As a result, new-generation IIAs may produce revolutionary new interpretations of the substantive protections of investment law and rulings that expressly preserve social and environmental policy space for host State governments.

On the other hand, just because they direct tribunals to engage in balancing and place some non-investment policy objectives on the same normative plane as investment policy objectives, new-generation IIAs should not be seen as more analytically decisive than they actually are with regard to host States' regulatory interests.[117] Substantive standards are still stated in a highly indeterminate manner in new-generation IIAs, while general exceptions clauses and new preambular language refer to a wide range of non-economic policy objectives only in vague terms. Tribunals adjudicating disputes under new-generation IIAs will still be called upon to make determinations as to whether, in light of the circumstances, a State made a reasonable decision when allocating the costs associated with a challenged public-policy measure to a foreign investor rather than to a host society.[118] In other words, while balancing and emphasising non-investment policy objectives will enable the investment law regime to serve as an arena to contest decisions regarding allocation, they will not substitute for such decisions.[119]

---

[117] D. Kennedy, 'The rule of law, political choices, and development common-sense' in D. M. Trubek and A. Santos (eds.), *The New Law and Economic Development* (Cambridge, 2006), pp. 95, 166.

[118] Of the general exceptions discussed above, only Art. 22 of the COMESA CIAA, which permits a Member State to adopt 'any measure that it considers appropriate' without further qualification, appears to be subject to a good faith standard that would prevent an arbitral tribunal from second-guessing a host State's determination that a nonconforming measure was necessary or proportionate to a specified policy objective: COMESA CIAA, Art. 22.

[119] Kennedy, 'The rule of law', p. 169.

Vesting tribunals with the power to engage in a balancing exercise and to consider States' non-investment priorities also raises a wide array of important theoretical, procedural and substantive issues. While these are beyond the scope of this short chapter, some – such as the complex relationship between IIAs and customary international law, the emergence of new actors in investment treaty law and the growing importance of procedural issues, including challenges to arbitrators – are addressed elsewhere in this volume. Just a few of the many other questions that arise include: What legitimacy will international arbitrators be able to claim for performing a balancing exercise that can be equated with the administration of global administrative or constitutional law? What weight should arbitrators give to competing policy objectives and what degree of deference should they show to sovereign regulatory decisions? What types of evidence and what sources of law will be relevant to the adjudicative exercise? The ability of new-generation IIAs to restore legitimacy to the investment law regime may ultimately depend on finding satisfactory answers to these and other difficult questions.

Restoring legitimacy to the investment law regime should, however, be a crucial objective for the regime's proponents as well as for all but its most vehement opponents. In its current State, the investment law regime is producing some results that are the very opposite of what its proponents intend – the establishment of a more stable investment environment in host countries. As discussed above, a number of countries are withdrawing from the regime and some critics in places like the US, Norway and South Africa would like to see changes made to the regime that would effectively undermine it. Yet undermining the investment law regime would also defeat the principal objective of the regime's most significant critics – the promotion of sustainable development. There is widespread consensus in the international community that foreign direct investment is necessary for sustainable development[120] and a growing body of evidence indicating that participation in the investment law regime is one among a number of factors that increase a State's attractiveness to foreign investors.[121]

---

[120] See A. Newcombe, 'Sustainable development and investment treaty law', *Journal of World Investment and Trade*, 8 (2007), 357.

[121] See UNCTAD, 'The role of international investment agreements in attracting foreign direct investment to developing countries' (2009), p. 23; K. P. Sauvant and L. E. Sachs (eds.), *The Effect of Treaties on Foreign Direct Investment: Bilateral investment treaties, double taxation treaties, and investment flows* (Oxford University Press, 2009); K. Vandevelde, *Bilateral Investment Treaties: History, policy and interpretation* (Oxford University Press, 2010).

In conclusion, one of the most important challenges facing the international investment law regime today is how to reach a compromise between the forces of economic globalisation – represented at one extreme by those who would prefer to see the investment law regime remain as constructed during the 1990s – and the forces of social and environmental protection – represented at the other extreme by those who would prefer to see the regime dismantled. By adding interpretive provisions, general exceptions clauses and new preambular language to their treaties, States have taken important steps towards reaching such a compromise and thereby stem the ongoing backlash against the investment law regime while protecting the interests of investors. If the serious doctrinal questions they raise can be answered satisfactorily, these new-generation IIAs may be able to save the investment law regime from its most unabashed cheerleaders as well as its most virulent critics.

14

The participation of sub-national government units as *amici curiae* in international investment disputes

ANDREA K. BJORKLUND*

In 1937, the US Supreme Court stated, 'In respect of all international negotiations and compacts, and in respect of our foreign relations generally, state lines disappear. As to such purposes the State of New York does not exist.'[1] This memorable but oversimplified statement summarises the convention that federal governments are the actors who count in international law and international affairs. Consistent with this view, sub-national government units have played a limited role in the arbitration of international investment disputes. Their most common appearance has been as the governmental entity that has allegedly breached a nation's investment obligations, but their role has seldom involved 'a speaking part'. Is that likely to change? Should it change?

Three different activities prompted these questions. The first was a conversation with a staff member in the California Attorney General's

* I am grateful to Chester Brown and Kate Miles, and other participants at 'International investment treaty law and arbitration: Evolution and revolution in substance and procedure', a conference held at Sydney Law School, for insightful comments and suggestions. I also thank Deans Johnson and Amar, and the University of California, Davis, Academic Senate, for financial support.
[1] *United States* v. *Belmont*, 301 US 324, 331 (1937). The European Community effectively took over the rights and obligations under the General Agreement on Tariffs and Trade (GATT) of its Member States. The Community's ambassador to the GATT commented with respect to France's opposition to the establishment of a panel in the Community's 'Oilseeds' dispute with the United States, 'when France spoke as a contracting party, its views as to trade policies were null and void and could not be taken into account': see GATT, Council Minutes C/M/222 (June 1988), pp. 11–14, cited in E.-U. Petersmann, 'International activities of the European Union and sovereignty of Member States' in E. Cannizzaro (ed.), *The European Union as an Actor in International Relations* (The Hague: Kluwer, 2002), pp. 321, 333.

office who worked on the *Methanex* case.[2] She expressed both satisfaction and frustration about her position in the case: first, she was very pleased with the US government's handling of the case – as is not surprising since the United States won – but also frustrated that she and her colleagues could not represent themselves.[3] The second activity was my writing a paper on the development of the quasi-precedential norm whereby *amici curiae* can participate in investment arbitrations. I wrote that in future we would likely see provincial and local governments acting as *amici* in cases involving challenges to their measures.[4] My confidence in this prediction had been bolstered by the filing of an *amicus curiae* brief by the Quechan Indians in the North American Free Trade Agreement (NAFTA) dispute between Glamis Gold Ltd and the United States.[5] Third, I was reading several articles describing the resurgence of 'federalism' in the United States – which, contrary to what one might think, suggests a greater exercise of authority by state governments rather than an increase in the power of the federal government – and the concomitant increase in sub-national governments' engagement in foreign affairs.[6] One US scholar, Robert Ahdieh, advocates an embrace of this multi-jurisdictional approach to foreign affairs as a way to promote greater innovation in regulation and governance and even to achieve greater democratic representation as more people at different levels of government become involved.[7] Could such an approach be beneficial for investment law? What would be the pros and the cons?

---

[2] *Methanex Corporation* v. *United States* (Final Award of 3 August 2005).

[3] The Mexican states of Guadalcazar and San Luis Potosi were reportedly unhappy about their inability to influence the outcome of *Metalclad Corporation* v. *Mexico* (ICSID Case No. ARB(AF)/97/1, Award of 30 August 2000): see L. J. Dhooge, 'The North American Free Trade Agreement and the environment: The lessons of *Metalclad Corporation* v. *United Mexican States*', *Minnesota Journal of Global Trade*, 10 (2001), 209, 213 and n. 32.

[4] A. K. Bjorklund, 'The promise and peril of precedent: The case of *Amici Curiae*', *ASA Bulletin* (2010) (Special Series No. 34), 165, 186.

[5] *Glamis Gold Ltd* v. *The United States of America* (*Glamis Gold*) (Non-Party Submission of 19 August 2005).

[6] See e.g. R. B. Ahdieh, 'Foreign affairs, international law, and the new federalism: Lessons from-coordination', *Missouri Law Review*, 73 (2008), 1185; J. G. Ku, 'The state of New York does exist: How the states control compliance with international law', *North Carolina Law Review*, 82 (2003–4), 457; J. Resnik, 'The internationalism of American federalism: Missouri and Holland', *Missouri Law Review*, 73 (2008), 1105; J. Resnik and C. R. Sevilla, 'When subnational meets international: The politics and place of cities, states, and provinces in the world' in A. K. Bjorklund, M. Carlson and M. P. Scharf (eds.), *Proceedings of the 102nd Annual Meeting of the American Society of International Law: The politics of international law* (2008), p. 339.

[7] Ahdieh, 'Foreign affairs, international law, and the new federalism', pp. 1208–10. For a similar approach to complementary engagement in international affairs in the EU

First, let me be clear that I am discussing provincial and local governments – not State-owned enterprises that might or might not be viewed as independent of the government.[8] My starting point is that provincial and local governments are unquestionably State actors, and are subsumed within the federal government insofar as principles of State responsibility and State attribution are concerned.[9] Secondly, I am not proposing that it would be wise to change the well-established principle that a federal government is responsible for the acts of its constituent states. My question is whether the international investment regime would be strengthened by giving sub-national government units an enhanced role in investment disputes – and in particular the right to participate as *amici curiae* – without replacing or eliminating the role that federal governments play in securing the rights and obligations they have undertaken in international investment treaties or to which they may be subject under customary international law.[10] For ease of reference, I will

context, see J. Klabbers, 'Restraints on the treaty-making powers of Member States deriving from EU law: Towards a framework for analysis in E. Cannizzaro (ed.), *The European Union as an Actor in International Relations* (The Hague: Kluwer, 2002), pp. 151, 159–61.

[8] See H. Elsheshtawy, 'Issues of sovereign and State entities in international arbitration: A look into investor–State arbitration' (2010), www.ssrn.com/abstract=1581466 (last accessed 30 January 2011).

[9] Art. 4 of the of the International Law Commission's (ILC's) Articles on State Responsibility provides that:

1. The conduct of any State organ shall be considered an act of that State under international law, whether the organ exercises legislative, executive, judicial or any other functions, whatever position it holds in the organization of the state, and whatever its character as an organ of the central government or of a territorial unit of the State.

2. An organ includes any person or entity which has that status in accordance with the internal law of the State.

'Responsibility of States for internationally wrongful acts', GA Res 56/83, 6th Comm., 56th Session, 85th Plenary Mtg, UN Doc. No. A/RES/56/83 (12 December 2001).

[10] Another option that the international community might consider is whether and when sub-national government units could or should play a larger role in negotiating international agreements. Australia has established a consultation mechanism whereby the federal government is to seek and take into account the views of the states and territories in the formulation of negotiating policies on matters of interest to the states and territories: see Council of Australian Governments (COAG), *Principles and Procedures for Commonwealth–State Consultation on Treaties* (1996). While the Principles require consultation, they also provide that their operation should not be allowed 'to result in unreasonable delays in the negotiating, joining or implementing of treaties by Australia': see Part A.

refer to 'provincial governments', as opposed to 'states', to distinguish them from nation States.

Provincial and local governments can, and often do, participate in the federal government's defence of State measures alleged to be breaches of international investment agreements. On those occasions during which the governmental sub-unit is content to co-operate with the central government, with the central government wielding the pen and arguing for both entities, problems of independent voice do not arise. When the local or provincial government is dissatisfied with the arguments made by the federal government, however, or when it simply wants to air its views independently, it might want to participate in its own right in an investment arbitration.

The focus of this chapter is on investment treaty arbitration in situations where the provincial government is not a disputing party in its own right. In investment arbitrations arising from investment agreements (often in the form of State contracts) it is not out of the question that provincial governments could act as respondents. This is specifically permitted, albeit with certain requirements, by Article 25 of the Convention on the Settlement of Investment Disputes between States and Nationals of other States (ICSID Convention).[11] Article 25(1) provides that a federal State may 'designate' to the International Centre for Settlement of Investment Disputes (ICSID) a constituent subdivision or State agency to act as a party, while Article 25(3) permits sub-national government units to act as parties if they consent to the arbitration and if their status as a potential respondent is approved by the federal government of the State of which they are a part.[12] Article 25(3) is directed to arbitrations arising under concession contracts rather than under investment treaties in that provincial governments do not consent to treaty arbitration. The treaty is a *federal* State's offer to arbitrate investment disputes with investors of the other contracting party.[13] The provincial governments will not ordinarily have consented to arbitration under the treaty.

---

[11] Convention on the Settlement of Investment Disputes between States and Nationals of other States, opened for signature 18 March 1965, 575 UNTS 159 (entered into force 14 October 1966) (ICSID Convention).

[12] *Ibid.*, Art. 25(1) and (3); C. Schreuer, *The ICSID Convention: A commentary*, 1st edn (Cambridge University Press, 2001), paras. 199–205, 608–21. Designation might act as approval, but contracting parties would be well advised to obtain specific consent from the federal government with respect to a specific contract: see paras. 200–1, 610.

[13] J. Paulsson, 'Arbitration without privity', *ICSID Review – Foreign Investment Law Journal*, 10(2) (1995), 232.

Whether or not a federal State could implead the sub-national government unit as a full party in an investment treaty dispute, assuming the provincial government agrees or that municipal law in the respondent State authorises the federal government to compel the participation of the province, is an interesting question. They could not do so to evade liability themselves given the obligations they have undertaken in the treaty.[14] Investment treaties themselves do not contemplate the idea.[15] Adding co-respondents would presumably require the consent of both disputing parties and would have to be permitted by the applicable rules.[16] Practical considerations might impede that consent; the claimant would presumably want to face only one respondent, while the respondent might not wish to be required to co-ordinate with co-counsel. The provincial government might not be keen to participate if doing so meant it would be subject to sharing in the payment of the award.

---

[14] Federal States may not avoid their international obligations by pleading inconsistent local law, absent an explicit reservation in a treaty: Vienna Convention on the Law of Treaties, opened for signature 23 May 1969, 1155 UNTS 331 (entered into force 27 January 1980), Art. 27. Art. 105 of the North American Free Trade Agreement, opened for signature 17 December 1992, 32 ILM 289, 605 (entered into force 1 January 1994) (NAFTA) expresses the principle as follows: 'The Parties shall ensure that all necessary measures are taken in order to give effect to the provisions of this Agreement, including their observance, except as otherwise provided in this Agreement, by state and provincial governments.'

[15] The closest thing one finds is the idea of consolidation of related claims that have questions of law or fact in common, which some investment agreements – notably NAFTA Chapter 11 and the US and Canadian Model BITs – explicitly permit: see NAFTA Art. 1126. Multiparty disputes can also occur with the agreement of all involved; the consolidation provision in NAFTA and its successor agreements places the decision in the hands of an arbitral tribunal rather than in the hands of the parties. But even in those cases the assumption is of consolidation of claims against the respondent State Party to the treaty. Cf. NAFTA Art. 1117(3) (directing that claims by investors in their own right, and claims by investors on behalf of an enterprise be consolidated in a proceeding under Art. 1126).

[16] An award that recently became public addressed several of these issues: see *Government of the Province of East Kalimantan* v. *PT Kaltim Prima Coal and ors* (ICSID Case No. ARB/07/3, Award on Jurisdiction of 28 December 2009). In that case, a province of Indonesia, East Kalimantan, sought damages from PT Kaltim Prima Coal under a concession contract. One question was whether the Regency of East Kutai could be joined to the procedure as a claimant, even though the ICSID Rules do not permit joinder. The tribunal concluded that it need not resolve the question, as the requirements for joinder would not have been satisfied even if it were permitted: paras. 157–9. The tribunal also concluded that the Province of East Kalimantan had not been designated by Indonesia as a constituent subdivision entitled to participate in an ICSID Arbitration, as required by Art. 25(1) of the ICSID Convention: see paras. 186–202.

Moreover, elevating provincial governments to the status of disputing party might undermine the bedrock principle that the federal government is responsible for the acts of constituent states. One could imagine the federal government seeking to absolve itself of responsibility, including financial liability, by placing blame on the provincial government. Amending international agreements explicitly to provide for joint-and-several liability on the part of provincial and federal governments might have some advantages, but is unlikely to happen in the near future.[17]

Assuming that elevating a provincial government to the rank of respondent in an investment treaty arbitration is unlikely, would there be any impediment to its acting as *amicus curiae*? The biggest hurdle it would have to overcome is to show that it is not a disputing party. The agreements that explicitly address *amicus curiae* participation, as well as Article 37(2) of the ICSID Arbitration Rules (the Rules) and Article 41(3) of the ICSID Additional Facility Arbitration Rules (the Additional Facility Rules), permit *amicus* participation by a person or entity that is not a 'disputing party'.[18] Yet none of them explicitly bars participation by provincial governments. Could the sub-federal government be viewed as a 'disputing party' if its measure were at issue? From a formal standpoint, the answer appears to be 'no'. The federal government would be acting as the respondent, as the entity responsible for the treaty breach, and thus as the disputing party.[19] To my knowledge, in most investment

---

[17] Imposing financial liability on provincial governments for their treaty breaches might help to deter them from committing such breaches. It would also give investors the ability to seek provincial, as well as federal, assets in payment of arbitral awards. Yet obtaining the consent of provincial governments to be fully responsible parties in investment treaties seems unlikely, to say the least. Canada is in the process of ratifying the ICSID Convention, which it signed in December 2006. The federal government has enacted implementing legislation, but is waiting for the provincial and territorial governments to pass complementary implementing legislation. Though treaty making is generally a matter for federal law in Canada, the Convention affects matters traditionally entrusted to provincial or territorial legislation. Thus the Canadian government has determined that it is necessary, 'or at least desirable', to have provincial approval of the agreement: see A. de Lotbinière McDougall, 'Why has Canada not ratified the ICSID Convention?' (24 August 2010), www.kluwerarbitrationblog.com/blog/2010/08/24/why-has-canada-not-ratified-the-icsid-convention/ (last accessed 30 January 2011).

[18] e.g. Art. 10.20(3) of the Dominican Republic–Central America Free Trade Agreement, opened for signature 28 May 2004, 43 ILM 514 (entered into force in the United States on 2 August 2005) (DR–CAFTA) provides that: 'The tribunal shall have the authority to accept and consider *amicus curiae* submissions from a person or entity that is not a disputing party.'

[19] One could analogise to the diplomatic protection exercised in the pre-investor–State dispute-settlement era. An injury to a national was an injury to the State and the State could espouse the claim on behalf of the national. The claim effectively belonged to

arbitrations the federal government does not take 'instruction' from the provincial government whose measure is alleged to be a breach;[20] there is no attorney–client relationship between the two entities. From that perspective the provincial government is less like a disputing party. Even without occupying the position of client, however, the provincial government might well be co-operating with the federal government in building the defence. The more the provincial government co-operates with the federal government (assuming the co-operation is harmonious), the less likely it will want to play an independent role. Yet the provincial government's occupying a position akin to that of a co-operative witness would not elevate the provincial government to the level of disputing party. It would lack the authority to direct the defence or make final decisions about what arguments to make.

In the case of ICSID Convention arbitration specifically, the question arises whether permitting provincial governments to act as *amici* subverts the design of the Convention under which federal governments must authorise the provincial government to be a respondent in an ICSID arbitration. Acting as *amicus* would seem to fall short of serving as a disputing party, and would not give the *amicus* the same rights enjoyed by a disputing party as *amici* have fewer rights than disputing parties. The current version of the Rules give them no right to have access to pleadings, and they have no right to attend hearings.[21] Certain treaties, however, might give them greater access to documents.[22] An ICSID Additional Facility Tribunal recently concluded that non-disputing parties must have access to some of the submissions of the disputing parties in order for them to focus their submissions on issues not already covered.[23] In the absence of the agreement of the parties, their ability to

---

the State. For a description of the diplomatic protection process, see A. Bjorklund, 'Reconciling State sovereignty and investor protection in denial of justice claims', *Virginia Journal of International Law*, 45 (2005), 809, 821–5.

[20] I am indebted to Todd Weiler for raising this interesting point.

[21] See Bjorklund, 'The problem and peril of precedent', pp. 176–7; ICSID Arbitration Rule 32(2) (permitting non-disputing entities to attend hearings unless either disputing party objects) and ICSID Additional Facility Arbitration Rule 39(2) (same). Certain investment agreements provide for public access to documents. These include NAFTA and all post-NAFTA Canadian or US BITs.

[22] See M. Kinnear, A. K. Bjorklund and J. F. G. Hannaford, *Investment Disputes Under NAFTA: An annotated guide to NAFTA Chapter 11*, 2nd edn (The Hague: Kluwer, 2009), paras. 1120.50–1120.51.

[23] *Piero Foresti, Laura de Carli and ors v. The Republic of South Africa* (ICSID Case No. ARB (AF)/07/01, Letter Regarding Non-Disputing Parties of 5 October 2009).

see all of the materials will depend on the tribunal's decision in each individual case or on the Rules in the governing treaties.[24]

Provincial governments seem to occupy a position between that of a disputing party and a typical non-disputing party. They have fewer rights than the former, but more than the latter. How close they come to occupying the position of a disputing party will depend on the applicable treaty, the rules governing the dispute, and perhaps on the degree of co-ordination the federal government is willing to undertake in a given case. It is hard, therefore, to formulate a single rule about their status. In the absence of such a rule, tribunals will make case-by-case determinations. For the reasons offered below, it is unlikely they will routinely prevent participation as *amici* by provincial governments.

If a provincial government overcomes the 'disputing party' hurdle, the question remains whether it would satisfy the other criteria typically used by tribunals for determining whether *amicus* participation is warranted. The NAFTA Free Trade Commission has established criteria for the participation of *amici*.[25] I will use those criteria below, as they are reflected in the Rules and in the Additional Facility Rules, although the latter do not explicitly include a reference to the 'public interest' in the outcome of the dispute.[26]

---

[24] In *Biwater Gauff (Tanzania) Ltd v. United Republic of Tanzania* (ICSID Case No. ARB/05/22, Procedural Order No. 5 on *amicus curiae* of 2 February 2007) the tribunal declined to order access to the documents filed by the parties in the arbitration, although it noted that after the hearing had been concluded the concerns underlying the confidentiality order made by the tribunal might have diminished: see paras. 66–8.

[25] NAFTA Free Trade Commission, *Statement of the Free Trade Commission on Non-Disputing Party Participation*, www.naftaclaims.com/Papers/Nondisputing-en.pdf (last accessed 30 January 2011).

[26] Art. 37(2) of the Rules provides:

> In determining whether to allow such a filing, the Tribunal shall consider, among other things, the extent to which:
>
> (a) the non-disputing party submission would assist the Tribunal in the determination of a factual or legal issue related to the proceeding by bringing a perspective, particular knowledge or insight that is different from that of the disputing parties;
> (b) the non-disputing party submission would address a matter within the scope of the dispute;
> (c) the non-disputing party has a significant interest in the proceeding.
>
> The Tribunal shall ensure that the non-disputing party submission does not disrupt the proceeding or unduly burden or unfairly prejudice either party, and that both parties are given an opportunity to present their observations on the non-disputing party submission.

Art. 41(3) of the Additional Facility Rules is to similar effect.

Could sub-national government units assist the tribunal in determin-ing factual or legal issues relating to the dispute by bringing perspectives, particular knowledge, or insight different from that of the disputing parties? This is very likely to be the case. The provincial government will have special expertise regarding the measure at issue, including the reasons for its adoption. This will not necessarily be *exclusive* expertise, as much of the information regarding the measure might be publicly available, but the provincial government will have a perspective that differs from that of the federal government, and might well wish to emphasise different aspects of the measure.

Moreover, the defence mounted by the federal government will be formulated with reference to *national* government policies. The federal government will wish not only to protect itself in disputes in which it is the respondent but also to protect its citizens who invest abroad and who may be or become plaintiffs in investment disputes with other countries. It will choose to defend itself in such a way that the interests of its own investors are not unduly harmed by its arguments. There might also be estoppel and credibility issues; if a capital-exporting country has consistently taken strong pro-investor positions, it might be difficult to take what seem to be contrary positions when the country is acting as a respondent. Thus, provincial governments could very well wish to take more aggressive positions while defending their measures.[27]

The Quechan Indian submission in the *Glamis Gold* case is a good illustration of the different perspectives offered by a governmental entity other than the federal government. As *amici*, the Quechan tribe argued persuasively that their perspective was not altogether represented by the United States, especially with respect to the protection of cultural heri-tage sites and sacred places.[28]

It is true that Native American tribes do not occupy the same position as the constituent states of the United States.[29] The sad history of the US treatment of Native Americans makes the argument that the federal government cannot speak for them especially resonant. Native American tribes have been described as 'domestic dependent nations' that may not be taxed and that have entered into numerous treaties with the federal

---

[27] One might analogise to the relationship between a physician and her insurance company in a medical malpractice suit. Often the insurer settles contrary to the doctor's wishes. One party's interests are financial; the other's interests are reputational.

[28] *Glamis Gold* (Non-Party Submission of 19 August 2005).

[29] See generally P. P. Frickey, '(Native) American exceptionalism in federal public law', *Harvard Law Review*, 119 (2005), 431.

government.[30] Yet they are not treated as foreign sovereigns either, and have no ability to enter into treaties with foreign nations.[31] For purposes of foreign affairs, then, they play a role analogous to the US states.

Provincial government *amici* would almost always be addressing matters 'within the scope of the dispute', and would almost inevitably have a 'significant interest in the outcome of the dispute'. A provincial government would have the greatest incentive to intervene if one of its measures was at issue in the arbitration. In such a case both criteria would readily be satisfied. It might also want to play a role if another province's measure were at issue and that measure were similar to one of its own. Even though most investment tribunals have awarded monetary damages only, and some treaties preclude them from offering specific relief,[32] the possibility of repeated infringements could cause a federal government to put pressure on the states to repeal legislation. *Methanex* v. *United States* involved a challenge to California's ban on the gasoline additive methyl tertiary-butyl ether (MTBE). More than twenty other US states had also banned the use of MTBE as a gasoline oxygenate. Had the United States lost that case, it is possible that the federal government would have sought to pressure other states to reconsider their ban, whether by enacting pre-emptive legislation or engaging in 'regulatory bribery'.[33]

In most cases, too, there will be a 'public interest' in the outcome of the dispute.[34] It is useful to explore briefly what is meant by the public interest – this language is often used when the investment arbitration involves hot-button issues such as environmental regulation, human or

[30] *Ibid.*, pp. 437–8.

[31] See T. Miller, 'Easements on tribal sovereignty', *American Indian Law Review*, 26 (2001–2), 105, 107. This does not mean that American Indian tribes never participate in treaty negotiations; e.g. the Treaty Between the Government of the United States of America and the Government of Canada Concerning Pacific Salmon, signed 28 January 1985 (entered into force 18 March 1985) balanced the interests of 4 US states, 24 US Indian tribes, 1 Canadian province and 1 Canadian territory, and all affected parties participated in the negotiations: see J. A. Yanagida, 'The Pacific Salmon Treaty', *American Journal of International Law*, 81 (1987), 577.

[32] S. Ripinsky (with Kevin Williams), *Damages in International Investment Law* (London: British Institute of International and Comparative Law, 2008), pp. 51–9.

[33] See D. Halberstam and M. Reimann, 'Federalism and legal unification: A comparative empirical investigation of 20 systems', *University of Michigan Law School Public Law and Legal Theory Working Paper No. 186* (23 February 2010) (discussing ways in which federal governments seek to ensure legal uniformity).

[34] C. Knahr, 'Transparency, third party participation and access to documents in international investment arbitration', *Arbitration International*, 23 (2007), 327, 347–8 (noting the presence of a public interest in 'the vast majority' of international investment disputes).

animal health-and-safety regulation, or the regulation of land use in areas of cultural sensitivity, such as ancient Native American spiritual lands. But the public interest is also served by simply having access to the proceedings, whether or not any particular group cares much about the given case or not. Access permits 'the people' to assure themselves that their civil servants are representing them adequately, and might serve to dissipate concerns about secret proceedings in which unidentified arbitrators allegedly strip the respondent's citizens of their rights and strip the respondent government, as well as provincial officials, of their sovereign authority.

Finally comes the question of whether participation by provincial governments would lead to an unfair burden on one or both of the disputing parties, or whether it would prejudice those parties. In a typical case, permitting a sub-national government to file an *amicus* brief arguably tips the scale in favour of the respondent government. Assuming that the interests of the federal government and the provincial government are at least broadly aligned, one would potentially be giving the government two opportunities to make arguments – even those that contradict each other. For example, a federal government in a capital-exporting State might refrain from making aggressive arguments about the extent to which the doctrine of 'police powers' excuses any and all State regulation designed to protect human health and the environment but which is harmful to investors' financial interests, whereas the provincial government would have no such hesitation about making such an aggressive argument. Both positions would be placed before the tribunal, yet the federal government could preserve its official position on the topic.[35]

A federal government would not necessarily welcome these contributions. It might be forced by the tribunal to take a position either endorsing or rejecting the view put forth by the provincial government. Thus, it is at least arguable that a provincial government's submission could prejudice not only the claimants – who would face a double-barrelled

---

[35] Another example could be arguments relating to waiver of the exhaustion of local remedies rule; e.g. most agree that NAFTA Art. 1121 waived the exhaustion of local remedies rule, yet the US government in *Loewen Group Inc. and Raymond L. Loewen* v. *United States* (ICSID Case No. ARB(AF)/98/3, Award on Merits of 26 June 2003) took the somewhat equivocal position that NAFTA had 'relaxed the rule' to an undefined degree: see para. 146. One could imagine the state of Mississippi, whose court measures were impugned in the *Loewen* case, arguing that NAFTA had in fact *not* waived the exhaustion of local remedies rule. On exhaustion generally, see W. S. Dodge, 'National courts and international arbitration: Exhaustion of remedies and *res judicata* under Chapter Eleven of NAFTA', *Hastings International and Comparative Law Review*, 23 (2000), 357, 373–6.

defence – but also the respondent State, which would have de facto co-counsel who could undermine potentially carefully calibrated positions.

There could be some impediments to this kind of collaboration. First, the practicalities of arbitration could prevent it. The provincial government would be acting on its own behalf and would often write its memorial without necessarily seeing the pleadings of the respondent. Yet the pleadings and memorials in US and Canadian arbitrations are generally public, and the United States and Canada, at least, took the position that they had the right to share documents with sub-national government units even before the NAFTA Free Trade Commission mandated the publication of materials in investment cases.[36] While there is no universally followed timetable, in many cases an *amicus* might be able to see the disputing parties' submissions before finalising its own. Indeed, that result is desirable if an *amicus* is required to present its case without duplicating arguments made by the disputing parties.[37]

Secondly, the tribunal could itself impose a bar to co-operation in memorial writing. It could not limit all communication or information-sharing between the federal and provincial governments on the subject of the case given the necessity for the federal government to defend itself. But it could require that the memorials be written in isolation from each other. This would minimise the danger of strategic co-ordination; it might also maximise the danger of divergent positions between entities defending the same measure.

Thirdly, another impediment could be imposed by a tribunal's holding fast to the generally accepted requirement that *amici* make submissions only on those matters on which they have particular expertise or a different and valuable perspective. The provincial government would generally not have expertise on the appropriate interpretation of international law. This approach places the burden on the arbitral tribunal to grant *amicus* status only when an aspiring non-disputing party demonstrates in their petition for *amicus* status what contribution they intend to make. In the event the submission covers matters outside that area of expertise, the tribunal should reject it.

It would seem, then, that permitting sub-national government units to file *amicus* briefs faces several impediments under the general practices governing *amicus curiae* submissions. But there are countervailing trends that might belie this conclusion.

[36] Kinnear, Bjorklund and Hannaford, *Investment Disputes*, para. 1120.50.
[37] Bjorklund, 'The promise and peril', p. 179.

First, the extant rules do not explicitly ban or permit participation by provincial or local governments. This omission means that tribunals will have to make any decision on a case-by-case basis. There could well be political pressure on them to accept a filing from a provincial government unit. Indeed, it seems there have been very few cases in which *amicus* petitions have been rejected.[38] This might be due to the high quality of the organisations who have sought to participate as *amici*, but it might also suggest a general reluctance on the part of tribunals to inhibit participation and the airing of views. This pressure would be consistent with what seems to be an emerging trend towards openness in international investment arbitration.[39]

Secondly, tribunal practice on submissions by non-party governmental entities, although minimal, already appears to support such filings. First is the case of the Quechan Indians, to the extent that one considers the tribe to be a sub-national government unit. The *Glamis Gold* case involved questions of cultural heritage and indigenous peoples' rights, matters which the Quechan Indians are undeniably best qualified to explicate. In that respect, it might be distinguishable from a case in which the provincial government's position appears to be ably represented by the federal government. But the *Glamis Gold* tribunal did not explicitly consider the potential for duplicative or co-ordinated submissions when it decided to accept the Quechan Indians' memorial.[40]

The second example is the apparently obverse situation illustrated by the European Commission's participation as *amicus curiae* in several

---

[38] In *Aguas del Tunari SA v. Republic of Bolivia* (ICSID Case No. ARB/02/3, Letter from President of Tribunal Responding to Petition of 29 January 2003) the aspiring intervenors sought to participate as parties, to participate in the hearings and to have access to all relevant documents. The tribunal concluded that it lacked the authority to grant the requests absent acquiescence from the disputing parties, which was not forthcoming. It was not clear whether the tribunal viewed itself as having the authority (prior to the revision of the ICSID Arbitration Rules) to grant participation as *amicus*: see Bjorklund, 'The promise and peril', p. 172 (noting that reference to a Singaporean bilateral investment treaty (BIT) that specifically provides for *amicus* participation could be viewed as an oblique reference to a lack of authority in the absence of such a provision).

[39] See A. K. Bjorklund, 'The emerging civilization of investment arbitration', *Penn State Law Review*, 114 (2009), 1269, 1286–94.

[40] *Glamis Gold* (Decision on Application and Submission by Quechan Indian Nation of 16 September 2005). The decision is somewhat cursory, and states only that the tribunal was 'of the view that the submission satisfies the principles of the Free Trade Commission's Statement on non-disputing party participation': see para. 10. The tribunal discussed the question of burden on the parties with respect to procedural issues, such as delay in the proceedings: see para. 11.

investor–State claims.[41] Investment disputes involving Member States of the European Union have raised several different legal issues regarding the interplay between EU law, the laws of Member States, and the Member States' BITs. The two most concrete issues have been (1) whether in a particular case a Member State's law or regulation was compelled by its membership in the EU, and whether that compulsion should excuse the Member State from any violation under the BIT; and (2) whether a Member State's intra-EU BITs are superseded by membership in the European Union.

The Commission has successfully moved to participate in at least three cases involving whether State measures compelled by EU law could nonetheless violate the States' investment treaty obligations, though the decisions granting its request are not public.[42] The States involved will presumably raise in their defence the argument that the measures taken were required by EU law; the degree to which the Commission has expertise or a perspective different from that of the Member States is unclear. In those cases the States might argue as vociferously as the Commission that the measures taken were required by EU law. In *AES Summit* v. *Hungary*, the European Commission participated as *amicus curiae*.[43] The dispute concerned Hungary's decision to change the legal regime governing the price the government paid for electricity. One of Hungary's defences was that the Commission regarded the preferential pricing scheme granted in the 2001 settlement of a dispute regarding the fees payable under a power purchase agreement to be State aid incompatible with Commission competition laws, and that Hungary had changed its pricing mechanism in response to concerns expressed by the Commission.[44] The European Commission's

---

[41] L. E. Peterson, 'European Commission moves to intervene in another ICSID arbitration, *Micula v. Romania*: A dispute hinging on withdrawal of investment incentives by Romania', *Investment Arbitration Reporter*, 2(8) (11 May 2009); L. E. Peterson, 'European Commission seeks to intervene as *amicus curiae* in ICSID arbitrations to argue that long-term power purchase agreements between Hungary and foreign investors are contrary to European Community law', *Investment Arbitration Reporter*, 1(10) (17 September 2008).

[42] Peterson, 'European Commission moves to intervene'.

[43] *AES Summit Generation Limited and AES-Tisza Erömü Kft v. The Republic of Hungary* (ICSID Case No. ARB/07/22, Award of 23 September 2010), para. 3.22. The tribunal did not grant the Commission's request for copies of the parties' written submissions because the parties had not agreed to disclose them.

[44] *Ibid.*, paras. 10.13.15–10.13.19. A majority of the tribunal rejected this argument, finding that even though the Commission had expressed concern about the prices under the PPA, it had not yet sought to compel any response from Hungary and that Hungary was therefore under no legal obligation to change its electricity pricing regime: see para. 10.3.16.

memorial is not publicly available and the award does not summarise the Commission's arguments, although the award states that the tribunal took them into account.[45]

The Commission would presumably be willing to co-operate with the States in helping them construct their arguments. The Commission would in that way have its arguments aired, even if not directly by it, and even if their presentation might not be exactly as the Commission would choose. The situation would likely be analogous to the expertise a provincial government could offer with respect to *its* measures. Notwithstanding the likelihood that similar legal arguments would be made, entities wishing to present their views often feel strongly that they should be allowed to do so, and they do not seem likely to be satisfied by arguments that others could speak persuasively for them.

The second scenario – whether or not intra-EU BITs are pre-empted by EU law – more clearly demonstrates the potential for different views from the Commission and the Member States. A few investment cases have addressed whether or not accession to the EU has extinguished the rights investors had under intra-EU BITs.[46] EU Member States and the Commission have taken different views about the desirability of maintaining intra-EU BITs.[47] The European Commission's views are fairly thoroughly canvassed in the recent award *Eureko BV* v. *The Slovak Republic*.[48] The EU's concerns about intra-EU BITs 'relate to the

---

[45] *Ibid.*, para. 8.2. The claimants argued that 'all Community institutions, including the Commission, must, as a matter of Community law, respect any award issued by this Tribunal': see para. 7.3.13. One might infer that the European Commission questioned that authority of an ICSID tribunal to intervene in matters it regards as governed by Community law.

[46] L. E. Peterson, 'Details surface of jurisdictional holdings in *Binder* v. *Czech Republic*: UNCITRAL tribunal saw no conflict between BITs and European law; more recently, majority of EU Member-States have taken similar view', *Investment Arbitration Reporter*, 2(4) (28 February 2009).

[47] *Ibid.*; see also Council of the European Union, 'Report to the Commission and the Council on the movement of capital and freedom of payments', Doc. No. 17363/08 (17 December 2008), paras. 16–17.

[48] *Eureko BV* v. *The Slovak Republic* (PCA Case No. 2008–13, Award on Jurisdiction, Arbitrability and Suspension of 26 October 2010). The European Commission expressed its views on the issue in *Eastern Sugar BV* v. *Czech Republic* (SCC Case No. 088/2004), but it is not clear whether the Commission formally participated as *amicus* in that case: see para. 31 (noting that the *Eureko* tribunal invited the Commission to update the views it had expressed in the Eastern Sugar case).

compatibility of such BITs with mandatory provisions of EU law and with the EU's judicial system'.[49]

The *Eureko* decision does not shed any light on the question of *amicus* participation as such. The tribunal in *Eureko*, after consulting with the parties, invited the Commission and the Netherlands to submit their views on the validity of the BIT between the Netherlands and the Slovak Republic[50] in the light of the Slovak Republic's accession to the EU.[51] It does demonstrate, however, the possibility of stark differences in opinion between a federal-level entity and constituent government units. Given the facts of the case, it is hard to imagine the Commission would not satisfy the generally used criteria governing *amicus* participation.

With the entry into force of the Treaty of Lisbon,[52] the European Commission's interest in BIT arbitration will only become stronger. A recent report by the European Parliament's Committee on International Trade addresses regulations proposed to govern transitional arrangements for BITs between EU Member States and non-EU countries (extra-EU BITs). It recommends that no provision in existing BITs be permitted to impede the implementation of the Union's policies relating to investment, and in particular the formation of a common commercial policy.[53] The Report suggests that the EU should withhold authorisation from any BIT which does not grant the European Commission access to notices of arbitration and to all documents rendered by tribunals or which does not give the Commission the ability to participate '*at least as an amicus curiae*'.[54] The impediment would be grounds for withdrawal of the EU's authorisation for a BIT. Whether or not this

---

[49] *Eureko*, para. 177. The concerns expressed by the Commission include: infringement of the exclusive jurisdiction of the European Court of Justice to determine questions of EU law and the concern that EU law would not be recognised as trumping inconsistent municipal law or inconsistent BIT provisions; the discrimination inherent in permitting investors with rights under intra-EU BITs to seek dispute settlement in investor–State arbitration rather than limiting them to redress before national courts or the Commission; and the undesirability of suggesting that certain Member States' municipal courts are not trustworthy: see paras. 176–86.

[50] Agreement on Encouragement and Reciprocal Protection of Investments Between the Kingdom of the Netherlands and the Czech and Slovak Federal Republic, signed 29 April 1991 (entered into force 1 October 1992).

[51] *Eureko*, para. 154.

[52] Treaty of Lisbon, signed 13 December 2007 (entered into force 1 December 2009).

[53] C. Schlyter, 'Bilateral investment agreements between Member States and third countries: Transitional arrangements', European Parliament Doc. No. COD/2010/0197, www.europarl.europa.eu/oeil/FindByProcnum.do?lang=2&procnum=COD/2010/0197 (last accessed 6 February 2011), 8/26.

[54] *Ibid.*, 13/26 (emphasis added).

amendment to the regulation will be adopted is an open question, but if
it is (and perhaps even if it is not) it will likely put pressure on tribunals
to accept the European Commission's requests to participate in investment arbitrations.[55]

Thirdly, in the United States and elsewhere there is a trend towards
devolution, with local governments trying to gain more control over
issues important to them.[56] Certainly the power to protect citizens with
respect to matters threatening human health and the environment is
generally thought to be important.[57] And there are numerous issues that
have traditionally been entrusted to provincial and local governments,
notwithstanding the formal view of the primacy of federal control over
foreign affairs matters.[58] When devolutionary sentiments are combined
with free-speech ideals, the pressure to permit a provincial government
to air its views is likely to be strong.

Fourthly, as noted above, the European Commission has been considering whether, and to what extent, it is going to assert control over
investment.[59] Should the Commission actually assert competence over
investment, it would not be surprising to see the Member States seeking
to retain some right to air their views – perhaps via the submission of
amicus briefs. Moreover, because the EU is not a party to the ICSID
Convention or to the New York Convention, it might be that the EU and
individual Member States would exercise a shared competence.

The most convincing argument for preventing provincial and local
governments from acting as *amici curiae* in international investment
disputes is that their interests are subsumed in those of the federal

---

[55] See J. Kleinheisterkamp, 'The dawn of a new BIT generation? The new European investment policy', *Kluwer Arbitration Blog* (23 December 2010).

[56] See e.g. Ahdieh, 'Foreign affairs', pp. 1217–21; 'Bolivian breakup?', *Investor's Business
Daily* (18 December 2007), A12; I. White and J. Yonwin, 'Devolution in Scotland', UK
Parliament Standard Note No. SN/PC/3000 (5 April 2004). Of course, one could argue
that the adoption of the Treaty of Lisbon by the Member States of the European Union
evinces a countervailing trend in favour of a strong federal government. Yet it seems
there are differences of opinion between the Commission and the Member States about
just how far the EU's authority should reach.

[57] Dhooge, 'The North American Free Trade Agreement', p. 263.

[58] Ku, 'The state of New York', pp. 478–99.

[59] See e.g. A. de Mestral, 'The Lisbon Treaty and the expansion of EU competence
over foreign direct investment and the implications for investor–State arbitration'
in K. P. Sauvant (ed.), *Yearbook on International Investment Law & Policy 2009–2010*
(Oxford University Press, 2010), p. 365; N. Lavranos, 'Developments in the interaction
between international investment law and EU law', *The Law and Practice of International
Courts and Tribunals*, 9(3) (2010), 409.

government acting as respondent in the case. Yet non-governmental organisations (NGOs) have successfully argued that the public interest is not adequately represented by a federal government, even though such a government might be seen as the quintessential representative of the public interest.[60] Provincial and local governments might be expected to make similar arguments about *their* interests. It will be difficult to resist such arguments if others, even those less directly interested, are allowed to participate as *amici curiae*. Thus, it is reasonable to expect that more provincial and local governments will seek a voice in international investment law, continuing the trend of recognising the role played in international law by non-traditional actors such as NGOs, corporations, indigenous peoples, and individuals.

---

[60] C. H. Brower, II, 'Obstacles and pathways to consideration of the public interest in investment treaty disputes' in K. P. Sauvant (ed.), *Yearbook on International Investment Law and Policy 2008–2009* (Oxford University Press, 2009), pp. 347, 365–6 (citing statement by A. J. Menaker, the then-Chief of the NAFTA Arbitration Division in the US Department of State's Office of the Legal Adviser, that she and her colleagues represented the public interest).

PART IV

The new significance of procedure

15

The new rules on participation of non-disputing parties in ICSID arbitration: Blessing or curse?

CHRISTINA KNAHR

I Introduction

Over the last fifteen years, various substantive matters that have arisen in investor–State arbitration have attracted significant controversy. Recently, however, there has also been an increasing focus on procedural issues. Of particular note were the procedural changes introduced in 2006 by the International Centre for Settlement of Investment Disputes (ICSID). The ICSID amended its arbitration rules which now, inter alia, include an express provision allowing for non-disputing parties to make written submissions to investment tribunals (Rule 37(2)), an option that was not expressly provided for previously. This chapter will take stock of the first few years since the adoption of this new rule and examine the impact of this particular amendment on the conduct of proceedings. In what way has this new possibility affected the disputing parties and the conduct of the arbitral process? How frequently has this option even been used in practice? Do written submissions of non-disputing parties have an influence on the decision-making process and the findings of arbitral tribunals? How can this increased transparency during the proceedings be reconciled with the necessity to provide for confidentiality of sensitive information?

In answering these questions, this chapter will examine recent cases where this new provision has become applicable, starting with *Biwater Gauff (Tanzania) Ltd* v. *Tanzania*,[1] the first case where a number of non-governmental organisations (NGOs) submitted *amicus curiae* briefs to the tribunal on the basis of the new Rule 37(2). Interestingly, however, it is not just NGOs that have made use of this option. Recently, the

---

[1] *Biwater Gauff (Tanzania) Ltd* v. *United Republic of Tanzania* (ICSID Case No. ARB/05/22) (*Biwater Gauff*).

European Commission has also discovered this procedural tool, enabling its participation in investment arbitrations that have been instituted against new EU members. In these cases, investors have initiated arbitration against countries such as Romania and Hungary alleging violations of certain provisions of bilateral investment treaties (BITs) or the Energy Charter Treaty (ECT).[2] In these particular circumstances, an additional layer of controversy arises from the potential conflict between obligations under BITs and obligations under EU law. On account of this possible conflict, the European Commission, the 'Guardian of the Treaties', possesses a vested interest in becoming involved in such arbitrations. However, participation of this nature necessarily generates still further questions – how much influence can or should a highly influential political institution such as the European Commission exercise on investment tribunals? Is this a positive development or does increased participation of potent non-disputing parties cause more harm to the system of investment arbitration than it creates benefits? This chapter will explore these issues. It will assess the relevance of non-disputing party participation in arbitral practice thus far and weigh the benefits of this new option against any potential risks posed by this new mechanism.

II   The legal framework since 2006

It is not the purpose of this chapter, and would certainly exceed its scope, to describe in detail the developments leading up to the inclusion of an express provision on non-disputing party participation in the ICSID Arbitration Rules in 2006.[3] What should be mentioned at this point, however, is the fact that the amendments in 2006 came as a consequence of developments in arbitral practice.[4] Prior to 2006, the issue of non-disputing party participation was not addressed in the ICSID

---

[2] *Energy Charter Treaty*, signed 17 December 1994, (1995) 34 ILM 381 (entered into force 16 April 1998).

[3] For more details on this development, see e.g. A. Bjorklund, 'The promise and peril of arbitral precedent: The case of *amici curiae*', *ASA Bulletin* (2010) (Special Series No. 34), 165; C. Knahr, 'Transparency, third party participation and access to documents in international investment arbitration', *Arbitration International*, 23 (2007), 327.

[4] See Knahr, 'Transparency, third party participation and access to documents'; A. Mourre, 'Are *amici curiae* the proper response to the public's concern on transparency in investment arbitration?', *The Law and Practice of International Courts and Tribunals*, 5 (2006), 257.

Convention,[5] nor in the ICSID Arbitration Rules. Nonetheless, NGOs attempted to participate as *amicus curiae* in several cases.[6]

Furthermore, the tendency towards more transparency and increased involvement of non-disputing parties in investment arbitration is certainly not a development restricted to this particular field. It has been preceded by the *amicus curiae* debate in the World Trade Organization (WTO) in the 1990s.[7] Although there are no rules in place expressly providing for *amicus curiae* participation in the WTO agreements,[8] it is, by now, well-established practice that NGOs and other non-disputing parties may make written submissions to panels as well as the Appellate Body, which have the option, but are under no obligation, to accept and consider such briefs.[9]

Similarly, in Chapter 11 cases under the North American Free Trade Agreement (NAFTA),[10] non-disputing parties have tried to gain access

---

[5] Convention on the Settlement of Investment Disputes between States and Nationals of other States, opened for signature 18 March 1965, 575 UNTS 159 (entered into force 14 October 1966), 4 ILM 532 (1965).

[6] See e.g. *Aguas Provinciales de Santa Fe SA, Suez, Sociedad General de Aguas de Barcelona SA, and InterAguas Servicios Integrales del Agua SA* v. *Argentine Republic* (ICSID Case No. ARB/03/17, Order in Response to a Petition for Participation as *Amicus Curiae* of 17 March 2006); *Aguas Argentinas SA, Suez, Sociedad General de Aguas de Barcelona SA and Vivendi Universal SA* v. *Argentine Republic* (ICSID Case No. ARB/03/19, Order in Response to a Petition for Transparency and Participation as *Amicus Curiae* of 19 May 2005).

[7] For more on the discussions in the WTO context, see e.g. P. C. Mavroidis, '*Amicus curiae* briefs before the WTO: Much ado about nothing' in A. Von Bogdandy, P. C. Mavroidis and Y. Mény (eds.), *European Integration and International Co-ordination: Studies in transnational economic law in honour of Claus-Dieter Ehlermann* (The Hague: Kluwer, 2002); A. Reinisch and C. Irgel, 'The participation of non-governmental organisations (NGOs) in the WTO dispute settlement system', *Non-State Actors and International Law*, 1 (2001), 127; G. Marceau and M. Stillwell, 'Practical suggestions for *amicus curiae* briefs before WTO adjudicating bodies', *Journal of International Economic Law*, 4 (2001), 155; S. Charnovitz, 'Participation of non-governmental organizations in the World Trade Organization', *University of Pennsylvania Journal of International Economic Law*, 17 (1996), 331; C. Knahr, *Participation of Non-State Actors in the WTO Dispute Settlement System: Benefit or burden?* (Bern, Switzerland: Peter Lang, 2007).

[8] Marrakesh Agreement Establishing the World Trade Organization, signed 15 April 1994, 1867 UNTS 3 (entered into force 1 January 1995), Annex 2 (Understanding on Rules and Procedures Governing the Settlement of Disputes).

[9] *United States – Import Prohibition of Certain Shrimp and Shrimp Products*, WT/DS58/R (Report of the Panel of 15 May 1998); *United States – Import Prohibition of Certain Shrimp and Shrimp Products*, WT/DS58/AB/R (Report of the Appellate Body of 12 October 1998); *European Communities – Measures Affecting Asbestos and Asbestos-Containing Products*, WT/DS135/R (Report of the Panel of 18 September 2000); *European Communities – Measures Affecting Asbestos and Asbestos-Containing Products*, WT/DS135/AB/R (Report of the Appellate Body of 12 March 2001).

[10] 32 ILM 289 (1993).

to the proceedings, also in the absence of express provisions governing this issue. In the NAFTA context, the Free Trade Commission issued a statement clarifying that non-disputing parties may make written submissions to tribunals, stating that: 'No provision of the North American Free Trade Agreement ("NAFTA") limits a Tribunal's discretion to accept written submissions from a person or entity that is not a disputing party (a "non-disputing party").'[11]

Although the issue of transparency and participation of non-disputing parties is certainly not less relevant in investment arbitration under NAFTA or the United Nations Commission on International Trade Law Arbitration Rules (UNCITRAL Rules), this chapter focuses on arbitration under the auspices of ICSID in an effort to determine the impact of the new 2006 rules on participation. In the ICSID context, through amendments adopted in 2006,[12] a new paragraph was inserted in Rule 37 of the arbitration rules. Rule 37(2) now provides:

> After consulting both parties, the Tribunal may allow a person or entity that is not a party to the dispute (in this Rule called the 'non-disputing party') to file a written submission with the Tribunal regarding a matter within the scope of the dispute. In determining whether to allow such a filing, the Tribunal shall consider, among other things, the extent to which:
>
> (a) the non-disputing party submission would assist the Tribunal in the determination of a factual or legal issue related to the proceeding by bringing a perspective, particular knowledge or insight that is different from that of the disputing parties;
> (b) the non-disputing party submission would address a matter within the scope of the dispute;
> (c) the non-disputing party has a significant interest in the proceeding.
>
> The Tribunal shall ensure that the non-disputing party submission does not disrupt the proceeding or unduly burden or unfairly prejudice either party, and that both parties are given an opportunity to present their observations on the non-disputing party submission.

---

[11] NAFTA Free Trade Commission, *Statement of the Free Trade Commission on Non-Disputing Party Participation* (7 October 2003), para. A(1), www.naftaclaims.com/Papers/Nondisputing-en.pdf (last accessed 18 January 2011).
[12] *Amendments to the ICSID Rules and Regulations and the Additional Facility Rules, Effective 10 April 2006*, ICSID Reports, 15 (2006), 633.

Further, with regard to participation at hearings, Rule 32(2) provides:

> Unless either party objects, the Tribunal, after consultation with the Secretary-General, may allow other persons, besides the parties, their agents, counsel and advocates, witnesses and experts during their testimony, and officers of the Tribunal, to attend or observe all or part of the hearings, subject to appropriate logistical arrangements. The Tribunal shall for such cases establish procedures for the protection of proprietary or privileged information.

There are no rules governing the publication of documents during the arbitral proceedings. Only with regard to publishing the final award, Rule 48(4) provides that: 'The Centre shall not publish the award without the consent of the parties. The Centre shall, however, promptly include in its publications excerpts of the legal reasoning of the Tribunal.'

III Arbitral practice since 2006

Arguably, arbitral practice since the establishment of the new rules on participation and transparency demonstrates that these changes have had an impact on the conduct of investment disputes. There have been several cases where non-disputing parties have filed *amicus curiae* applications with tribunals based on Rule 37(2) of the ICSID Arbitration Rules. Of these, only two awards have been rendered; the remaining cases are still pending. It is, therefore, too early to determine conclusively the impact of *amicus curiae* briefs on the actual decision-making process of tribunals. Nonetheless, it is certainly possible to examine the cases available thus far and draw conclusions as to potential benefits or drawbacks of this new mechanism for participation by non-disputing parties.

A Biwater Gauff

Biwater Gauff is an ICSID case that attracted significant public interest from the very beginning of the arbitration.[13] It became well known early on in the proceedings when the issue of publication of documents arose and the tribunal for the first time addressed this question in a detailed fashion.[14] It is also the first case in which NGOs relied on

---

[13] *Biwater Gauff* (ICSID Case No. ARB/05/22, Award of 24 July 2008).

[14] *Biwater Gauff* (ICSID Case No. ARB/05/22, Procedural Order No. 3 of 29 September 2006); for more on the tribunal's reasoning and an analysis of this case, see C. Knahr and A. Reinisch, 'Transparency versus confidentiality in international investment arbitration:

the new provision in the ICSID Arbitration Rules when submitting written submissions to the tribunal.[15]

The arbitration was initiated on 2 August 2005 and led to a first session of the tribunal in March 2006 dealing with procedural issues and a request for provisional measures.[16] The Minutes of this First Meeting of the Tribunal were communicated to the parties in June 2006 and, together with Procedural Order No. 2,[17] subsequently published on the Internet by the respondent State, Tanzania.

The claimant, Biwater Gauff (Tanzania) Ltd (BGT), filed a request for provisional measures on confidentiality, complaining about unilateral disclosure of the abovementioned documents without an agreement of both parties to this effect. BGT requested that the tribunal order measures that the parties should discuss on a case-by-case basis the publication of all decisions other than the award produced in the course of the proceedings and if no agreement of the parties could be reached that the matter should be referred to the tribunal. In addition, BGT requested that the tribunal should also order that the parties refrain from disclosing to third parties any of the pleadings and any correspondence between the parties and/or the tribunal exchanged during the proceedings.

In reaction to the claimant's request, the tribunal issued Procedural Order No. 3 which, as indicated above, for the first time addressed the issue of publication of documents during the arbitral proceedings in detail. This order is noteworthy for two reasons: first, for the tribunal's thorough analysis, weighing transparency[18] against procedural integrity and non-aggravation of the dispute[19] and, secondly, for its separate examination of various kinds of documents produced during the proceedings with respect to their suitability for publication.[20]

The *Biwater Gauff* compromise', *The Law and Practice of International Courts and Tribunals*, 6(1) (2007), 97.

[15] *Biwater Gauff* (ICSID Case No. ARB/05/22, Petition for *Amicus Curiae* Status of 27 November 2006); *Biwater Gauff* (ICSID Case No. ARB/05/22, Procedural Order No. 5 on *Amicus Curiae* of 2 February 2007).

[16] *Biwater Gauff* (ICSID Case No. ARB/05/22, Minutes of the First Session of the Arbitral Tribunal of 23 March 2006).

[17] *Biwater Gauff* (ICSID Case No. ARB/05/22, Procedural Order No. 2 of 24 May 2006).

[18] *Biwater Gauff* (ICSID Case No. ARB/05/22, Procedural Order No. 3 of 29 September 2006), paras. 114–34.

[19] *Ibid.*, paras. 135–47.   [20] *Ibid.*, paras. 148–63.

The tribunal argued that 'its mandate and responsibility includes ensuring that the proceedings will be conducted in the future in a fair and orderly manner'.[21] It scrutinised the existing rules on confidentiality in international investment arbitration (ICSID, ICSID Additional Facility, NAFTA Chapter 11 and the UNCITRAL Rules), reaching the conclusion that none of these provisions contained a general duty of confidentiality.[22] On the other hand, the tribunal took into account potential risks to procedural integrity. As a media campaign had been fought by both disputing parties, the tribunal concluded that a sufficient risk of aggravation of the dispute existed to warrant some form of control by the tribunal.[23] Nonetheless, the tribunal also emphasised the significance of the public interest in the case, therefore determining that 'any restrictions must be carefully and narrowly delimited'.[24]

In its analysis, the *Biwater Gauff* tribunal made a distinction between various kinds of documents produced in the course of the proceedings – that is, minutes of a hearing, pleadings or written memorials of the parties, and decisions or orders of the tribunal – and reached different conclusions as to the permissibility of publication and distribution of these documents. The tribunal also differentiated between the disclosure of documents while proceedings were still pending as opposed to the publication of final awards. The tribunal argued that the tensions between increasing transparency and safeguarding procedural integrity are only pertinent as long as the proceedings are pending. Concerns regarding procedural integrity would no longer apply after the conclusion of the proceedings.[25] The tribunal therefore drew the conclusion that disclosure of documents produced during the proceedings is more problematic and should therefore be handled more restrictively than the publication of final awards rendered by a tribunal. This distinction between documents produced during the proceedings and final awards and their publication has already been addressed in scholarly literature,[26] and it has been noted that the provisions of the ICSID Convention

---

[21] *Ibid.*, para. 145.
[22] *Ibid.*, paras. 121 (with regard to ICSID), 128 (with regard to the ICSID Additional Facility Rules), 130 (with regard to NAFTA Chapter 11) and 132 (with regard to the UNCITRAL Arbitration Rules).
[23] *Ibid.*, para. 146. [24] *Ibid.*, para. 147. [25] *Ibid.*, paras. 140 and 142.
[26] C. Schreuer, *The ICSID Convention: A commentary* (Cambridge University Press, 2001), pp. 819–28.

and the Administrative and Financial Regulations only deal with publication of documents by the Centre itself,[27] an assessment that the *Biwater Gauff* tribunal also shared.[28]

The tribunal reached a rather restrictive conclusion, declaring permissible only that a party may publish its own documents,[29] and that the parties engage in a general discussion about the case in public, under the condition that such a discussion be 'restricted to what is necessary and not be used as an instrument to antagonise the parties [and] exacerbate their differences'.[30] Other documents produced during the proceedings should either not be published at all or their publication should be subject to certain restrictions. Minutes of the hearings should not be disclosed to the public, unless there was an agreement of the parties or the tribunal issued a direction to that effect, since the publication of these documents could at least potentially affect the procedural integrity and efficiency of the hearing.[31] Similarly, the tribunal argued that pleadings or written memorials should be restricted, because any uneven publication of these documents would be likely to give misleading information of the proceedings,[32] certainly undesirable for the conduct of the arbitral process. Correspondence between the parties and/or the tribunal was considered by the *Biwater Gauff* tribunal as 'a category in which the needs of transparency (if any) are outweighed by the requirements of procedural integrity'.[33] According to the tribunal, this correspondence would usually concern the conduct of the process itself rather than substantive issues, which would make it appropriate to restrict publication.[34] Also, the tribunal determined that any documents produced by the opposing party should not be disclosed to the public.[35] The tribunal argued that: 'The interests of transparency are here outweighed, since the threat of wider publication may well undermine the document production process itself, as well as the overall arbitration procedure.'[36] Finally, with regard to decisions, orders or directions of the tribunal, it concluded that a presumption should be made in favour of publication of these documents, arguing that such documents 'as a general matter, will be less likely to aggravate or exacerbate a dispute, or to exert undue

---

[27] *Ibid.*, p. 822.
[28] *Biwater Gauff* (ICSID Case No. ARB/07/22, Procedural Order No. 3 of 29 September 2006), paras. 123–4.
[29] *Ibid.*, para. 156.   [30] *Ibid.*, para. 163(d).   [31] *Ibid.*, para. 155.
[32] *Ibid.*, para. 158.   [33] *Ibid.*, para. 161.   [34] *Ibid.*   [35] *Ibid.*, para. 163(a).
[36] *Ibid.*, para. 157.

pressure on one party, than publication of parties' pleading or release of other documentary materials'.[37] Nonetheless, publication of such documents should still be subject to prior permission of the tribunal.[38]

In the context of the ongoing debate about transparency in international investment arbitration, this order is a valuable contribution, providing some clarity on appropriate ways in which to address the issue of publication of documents in arbitral proceedings. Its novelty lies in the differential treatment of various kinds of documents produced by the parties as well as the tribunal in the course of the proceedings and the tribunal's distinct conclusions regarding these documents. The tribunal's weighing of the competing interests of increasing transparency on the one hand and protecting the procedural integrity of the arbitration on the other hand provides a useful framework in which to consider the kinds of documents that should and should not be disclosed to a wider audience.

As indicated above, the issues surrounding the publication of documents were not the only significant aspects of the *Biwater Gauff* award. It was also the first time that NGOs based a petition to make written submissions to a tribunal on the new Rule 37(2) of the ICSID Arbitration Rules. Upon release of the decision, *Biwater Gauff* also became the first case in which an arbitral panel reached an award on the merits where a written submission by non-disputing parties based on Rule 37(2) had been made. It is thus interesting to look at whether, and if so, in the extent to which the tribunal took the points made in the non-disputing party submission into account in its decision-making process and whether they had any impact on the final outcome of the arbitration. Indeed, the final award contains one section addressing the *amicus curiae* brief submitted to the tribunal.[39] It recalls the procedural background relevant to their participation,[40] and provides a summary of the main points raised in this submission.[41] As for the relevance of the submission for its decision-making process, the tribunal stated that it 'has found the *Amici's* observations useful. Their submissions have informed the analysis of the claims . . . and where relevant, specific points arising from the *Amici's* submissions are returned to in that context.'[42]

---

[37] *Ibid.*, para. 152.   [38] *Ibid.*, para. 163(c).
[39] *Biwater Gauff* (ICSID Case No. ARB/05/22, Award of 24 July 2008), paras. 356–92.
[40] *Ibid.*, paras. 356–69.   [41] *Ibid.*, paras. 370–91.   [42] *Ibid.*, para. 392.

B   Piero Foresti, Laura de Carli and ors *v.* South Africa

Due to the subject matter of the dispute, this case has generated considerable public interest.[43] It was brought under the Additional Facility Rules, which were also amended in 2006, and now contain similarly worded provisions concerning submissions of non-disputing parties and attendance at hearings as the ICSID Arbitration Rules.[44]

In this case, two South African and two international NGOs jointly filed a petition to make a written submission to the tribunal.[45] In this

---

[43]   *Piero Foresti, Laura de Carli and ors* v. *The Republic of South Africa* (ICSID Case No. ARB (AF)/07/01)) (*Piero Foresti*).

[44]   Rule 41(3) of the Additional Facility Rules provides:

> After consulting both parties, the Tribunal may allow a person or entity that is not a party to the dispute (in this Article called the "non-disputing party") to file a written submission with the Tribunal regarding a matter within the scope of the dispute. In determining whether to allow such a filing, the Tribunal shall consider, among other things, the extent to which:
>
> (a) the non-disputing party submission would assist the Tribunal in the determination of a factual or legal issue related to the proceeding by bringing a perspective, particular knowledge or insight that is different from that of the disputing parties;
> (b) the non-disputing party submission would address a matter within the scope of the dispute;
> (c) the non-disputing party has a significant interest in the proceeding.

> The Tribunal shall ensure that the non-disputing party submission does not disrupt the proceeding or unduly burden or unfairly prejudice either party, and that both parties are given an opportunity to present their observations on the non-disputing party submission.

> Rule 39(2) of the Additional Facility Rules provides:

> Unless either party objects, the Tribunal, after consultation with the Secretary-General, may allow other persons, besides the parties, their agents, counsel and advocates, witnesses and experts during their testimony, and officers of the Tribunal, to attend or observe all or part of the hearings, subject to appropriate logistical arrangements. The Tribunal shall for such cases establish procedures for the protection of proprietary or privileged information.

[45]   *Piero Foresti* (ICSID Case No. ARB(AF)/07/01, Petition for Limited Participation as Non-disputing Parties in Terms of Articles 41(3), 27, 39, and 35 of the Additional Facility Rules of 17 July 2009); see also L. Peterson, 'NGOs seek leave to intervene in ICSID arbitration arising out of South Africa's treatment of foreign mining companies', *Investment Arbitration Reporter* (online), 2(12), 17 July 2009, www.iareporter.com/downloads/20100413_1 (last accessed 19 January 2011); L. Peterson, 'South Africa Mining Arbitration Sees Another *Amicus Curiae* Intervention', *Investment Arbitration Reporter* (online), 2(14), 2 September 2009, www.iareporter.com (last accessed 19 January 2011).

fairly lengthy submission (fifty-nine pages), the petitioners laid out in detail why they were interested in participating in this case and provided comprehensive information about their background and expertise. In addition, they also systematically address each of the requirements for participation laid down in the Additional Facility Rules and explained why these requirements are met. Their request sought to be permitted to make a written submission, be granted access to key documents and to attend oral hearings.

With regard to access to documents, the petitioners emphasised that this element was particularly important in order for them to obtain information necessary to make a meaningful submission. This is certainly a valid point as non-disputing parties are supposed to not simply repeat parties' submissions, but to supply additional information that is not contained in these documents and that might nonetheless be important for tribunals to take into consideration. On the other hand, it is exactly that point that might become problematic for the disputing parties since it bears the risk of having to disclose information they would rather keep confidential. Of course, confidentiality has always been a cornerstone of arbitration. However, due to the regular involvement of States and matters of public interest in investment arbitration, this form of dispute resolution is certainly in a different category to commercial arbitration. International commercial arbitration is an option employed where disputes exist between private parties and they do not tend to have an impact on the general public in the same way as investment arbitrations frequently do. Thus, it is validly argued that the level of confidentiality should be lower in investment arbitration than in commercial arbitration. As there are no rules in place for ICSID arbitrations determining explicitly which documents should be made public and those to remain confidential during the proceedings, it is within the discretion of tribunals to determine in each individual case which documents should be made accessible to non-disputing parties.

In the *Piero Foresti* case, the tribunal decided that the petitioners were allowed to participate in the arbitral proceedings in accordance with Additional Facility Rule 41(3).[46] The tribunal based its decision on two considerations:

---

[46] *Piero Foresti* (ICSID Case No. ARB(AF)/07/01, Letter Regarding Non-Disputing Parties of 5 October 2009). See also L. Peterson, 'NGOs permitted to intervene in South Africa mining case and – for second time at ICSID – tribunal orders would-be petitioners to be given access to case documents', *Investment Arbitration Reporter* (online), 2(16), 14 October 2009, www.iareporter.com/categories/20100326_1 (last accessed 21 January 2011).

> (1) NDP [Non-Disputing Parties] participation is intended to enable NDPs to give useful information and accompanying submissions to the Tribunal, but is not intended to be a mechanism for enabling NDPs to obtain information from the Parties.
> (2) Where there is NDP participation, the Tribunal must ensure that it is both effective and compatible with the rights of the Parties and the fairness and efficiency of the arbitral process.[47]

Further, the tribunal, recalling the scarcity of practice thus far on this issue, decided that:

> In view of the novelty of the NDP procedure, after all submissions, written and oral, have been made the Tribunal will invite the Parties and the NDPs to offer brief comments on the fairness and effectiveness of the procedures adopted for NDP participation in this case. The Tribunal will then include a section in the award, recording views (both concordant and divergent) on the fairness and efficacy of NDP participation in this case and on any lessons learned from it.[48]

This last point would have been particularly interesting had it been further developed. It could have potentially become relevant for future cases where non-disputing parties petitioned tribunals to participate in proceedings. Unfortunately, this arbitration did not get to that point. The proceedings were discontinued and the tribunal's decision on discontinuance and costs did not make any further reference to the issue of participation of non-disputing parties.[49]

C   AES Summit v. Hungary and Electrabel v. Hungary

In *AES Summit*,[50] a dispute arose out of power purchase agreements between the claimants and the Hungarian State-owned entity, Magyar Villamos Muvek (MVM). AES claimed violations by Hungary of protection granted to them under the Energy Charter Treaty when MVM allegedly changed prices paid for the electricity at the request of the Government of Hungary.[51] During the arbitration, an issue

---

[47] *Ibid.*   [48] *Ibid.*

[49] *Piero Foresti* (ICSID Case No. ARB(AF)/07/01, Award and Concurring Statement of Arbitrator Matthews of 4 August 2010).

[50] *AES Summit Generation Limited and AES-Tisza Erömü Kft v. The Republic of Hungary* (ICSID Case No. ARB/07/22).

[51] See L. Peterson, 'European Commission seeks to intervene as *amicus curiae* in ICSID arbitrations to argue that long-term power purchase agreements between Hungary and foreign investors are contrary to European Community law', *Investment Arbitration*

arose concerning the compatibility of the abovementioned power purchase agreements with European Community law. The European Commission wanted to intervene in the arbitration as a non-disputing party and make a written submission to the tribunal. Accordingly, in September 2008, it submitted a petition for *amicus curiae* participation to the tribunal.[52] In a procedural order issued in November 2008, the tribunal granted the petitioner permission to file a written submission pursuant to ICSID Arbitration Rule 37(2).[53] In January 2009, the tribunal then received the written submission from the European Commission.[54] Unfortunately, at the time of writing this chapter, the submission has not been made publicly available and thus its content cannot be analysed.

Electrabel is an arbitration instituted at ICSID parallel to *AES Summit*, also arising out of power purchase agreements and also alleging violations by Hungary of its obligations under the Energy Charter Treaty.[55] In much the same way as in *AES Summit*, the *Electrabel* tribunal received a petition for *amicus curiae* participation from the European Commission in September 2008.[56] The tribunal granted permission to file a submission in April 2009 and received the submission in June 2009.[57] Regrettably, this submission is also not publicly available.

As of .yet, only *AES Summit* has been decided on the merits; *Electrabel* is still pending. In its award the *AES* tribunal, however, only briefly referred to the submission of the European Commission, noting that it took it into consideration, without getting into detail in how far or what points specifically might have become relevant for its findings. It stated that it 'acknowledges the efforts made by the European Commission to explain its own position to the Tribunal and has duly considered the points developed in its *amicus curiae* brief in its deliberations'.[58]

Reporter (online), 1(10), 17 September 2008, www.iareporter.com/categories/20100326 (last accessed 21 January 2011).

[52] Information on the procedural steps in this case available at www.encharter.org/index.php?id=359&L=0#c1076 (last accessed 21 January 2011).

[53] *Ibid.*   [54] *Ibid.*

[55] *Electrabel SA* v. *Republic of Hungary* (ICSID Case No. ARB/07/19). Information on the procedural steps in this case is available at www.encharter.org/index.php?id=358&L=0#c1075 (last accessed 21 January 2011).

[56] *Ibid.*   [57] *Ibid.*

[58] *AES Summit* (ICSID Case No. ARB/07/22, Award of 23 September 2010), para. 8.2.

D   Micula v. Romania

The arbitration in *Micula* v. *Romania* has also become relevant for the present discussion due to the involvement of the European Commission as a non-disputing party.[59] The claimants in this case are two individuals, Ioan Micula and Viorel Micula, and three corporations under their control. The dispute arose after Romania had partially withdrawn or amended investment incentives that it had previously granted to investors, including exemption from customs duties and other specific taxes, together with the grant of preferential subsidies.[60] In connection with its accession to the European Union, Romania had made changes to its legal framework, amending legislation and thereby terminating the incentives. The present dispute resulted from those changes.[61]

Romania raised several objections to the tribunal's jurisdiction, most notably with regard to the claimants' nationality. The considerations of the tribunal in this respect are certainly not without interest, but are not especially relevant for purposes of this chapter.[62] What is important here, however, is the fact that the claimants requested restitution as relief, which is only rarely demanded by aggrieved investors. The question whether the tribunal could potentially order restitution is especially delicate in this case since it touches upon a possible conflict between obligations of EU Member States under BITs and their obligations under EU law. Thus, the European Commission has indicated its intention to present its own legal arguments in the arbitration.[63] The tribunal granted permission to file a written submission and the Commission submitted its brief in summer 2009.[64] Again, just as with *AES Summit* and *Electrabel*, the Commission's submission in *Micula* is not publicly available.

---

[59] *Ioan Micula, Viorel Micula, S.C. European Food SA, S.C. Starmill SRL and S.C. Multipack SRL* v. *Romania* (ICSID Case No. ARB/05/20, Decision on Jurisdiction and Admissibility of 24 September 2008).

[60] *Ibid.*, paras. 28 and 31.   [61] *Ibid.*, paras. 42–8.

[62] For more of the tribunal's reasoning and an analysis of the tribunal's findings, see C. Knahr, 'International decisions – *Ioan Micula, Viorel Micula, S.C. European Food SA, S.C. Starmill SRL, & S.C. Multipack SRL* v. *Romania*', *American Journal of International Law*, 104 (2010), 81.

[63] See L. Peterson, 'European Commission moves to intervene in another ICSID arbitration, *Micula* v. *Romania*: A dispute hinging on withdrawal of investment incentives by Romania', *Investment Arbitration Reporter*, 2(8) (11 May 2010), www.iareporter.com/downloads/20100107 (last accessed 18 January 2011).

[64] See the information on procedural steps in this case available at http://icsid.worldbank.org/ICSID/FrontServlet (last accessed 21 January 2011).

Recent years have increasingly seen investment claims brought against Central and Eastern European countries that became members of the European Union in 2004.[65] Although the briefs are not publicly available, the Commission's interest in *Micula*, *AES* and *Electrabel* is likely motivated by its concern over this growing number of cases and the possibility that other new members might be confronted with similar claims after having adjusted their legal frameworks to bring them into conformity with European law. As the 'Guardian of the Treaties', the Commission has to ensure that EU Member States observe their obligations under Community law even when facing arbitral proceedings.[66] In light of the cases instituted before ICSID in recent years, this concern does seem justified. The compatibility of new Member States' BITs with European law involves controversial legal questions that are now being discussed within both Member States and the academic community. With regard to the Lisbon Treaty in particular,[67] there remain unanswered questions concerning the fate of currently existing BITs of EU members and the exact scope of the EU's new competence on investment policy.

Currently, *Micula* is being heard on the merits, and no final award has yet been rendered. It is thus not possible to assess whether and, if so, to what degree the written submission by the European Commission indeed will have an influence on the tribunal. It will certainly be worth following this case in order to see how the tribunal deals with the submission of this powerful non-disputing party. Further, in a broader sense, as these issues are very much still unfolding, they reflect not only the new appreciation of the importance of procedural matters in investment arbitration, but also the evolving nature of procedural developments within the field.

---

[65] For examples of other cases, see L. Peterson, 'Path cleared for BIT arbitration by Swedish investors to challenge the withdrawal of investment incentives by Romania: Romania says withdrawal of incentives for investments in economically-depressed region was done in order to comply with European Union restrictions on State aid, *Investment Arbitration Reporter*, 1(11) (1 October 2008), www.iareporter.com/Archive/IAR-10-01-08.pdf (last accessed 18 January 2011).

[66] See e.g. Peterson, 'European Commission moves to intervene', p. 3.

[67] Treaty of Lisbon, signed 13 December 2007 (entered into force 1 December 2009), www.europa.eu/lisbon_treaty/full_text/index_en.htm (last accessed 21 January 2011).

IV Reasons to include non-disputing parties
in arbitral proceedings

1 Which perspective?

When trying to assess whether opening the arbitral process to non-disputing parties is beneficial, an important question to ask seems to be: what is the added value of including non-disputing parties in the proceedings? The answer might of course differ depending upon the perspective one takes. From the perspective of potential non-disputing parties – which not only refers to NGOs, but also to other non-State actors (NGOs are, as practice has shown, most likely to make use of the option to participate) – providing for more transparency and options to make their voices heard will most likely be welcomed. Like the WTO, investment arbitration has been criticised for lack of transparency and the absence of options for civil society to participate in the proceedings so as to alert tribunals to additional issues, such as human rights or environmental considerations. In many ways, the amendments to the ICSID Arbitration Rules concerning written submissions and attendance at hearings for non-disputing parties have met this demand.

From the perspective of the disputing parties, however, the situation might look somewhat different. There may not be unreserved support for non-disputing party participation at all. In particular, their interest in a confidential and swift resolution of their dispute may very well conflict with options available to non-disputing parties to file written submissions, have access to documents and be present at hearings. Such forms of participation certainly generate additional administrative issues. A key concern in this regard is that integrating the filing of *amicus curiae* briefs into the arbitral process and allowing sufficient time for the disputing parties to respond to these submissions could potentially prolong the arbitration. However, careful management by tribunals perhaps provides an answer to such concerns. A responsible weighing of interests by tribunals could ensure that participation of non-disputing parties adds value to the process also from the point of view of the disputing parties, rather than obstructing the efficient resolution of disputes.

Finally, from the institutional perspective of the ICSID dispute-resolution mechanism as a whole, it seems that the system could benefit from more transparency and openness. As this has become such a contentious issue, it could strengthen the trust in the system if arbitral proceedings – which, as mentioned above, regularly affect more than just the two disputing parties – are conducted not in an entirely confidential setting behind closed doors but, rather, with an option for outside stakeholders to become involved and to scrutinise the process.

2 Expertise of non-disputing parties

Further arguments in favour of allowing participation of non-disputing parties in investment arbitration concentrate on the expertise that specialised NGOs can bring to the table. As experts within their fields, NGOs often have extensive research capabilities, technical information and specialist knowledge on areas outside the competence of either of the parties in dispute. In particular, NGOs may bring information to the attention of tribunals with regard to, for example, human rights or environmental issues that may not be brought forth by the disputing parties, but which are nonetheless relevant for a tribunal's decision-making processes. Although tribunals are certainly under no obligation to follow the arguments presented in *amicus curiae* briefs, they may still take them into consideration and this could, potentially, lead to better-informed decisions.

V Dangers associated with allowing non-disputing parties to participate in arbitral proceedings

1 Politicisation of investment disputes?

Now that it is expressly permissible for non-disputing parties to make written submissions to tribunals, it is not just NGOs that have made use of this option. The political 'heavyweight' that is the European Commission has also filed *amicus curiae* briefs in some cases.[68] According to Rule 37(2), this is undoubtedly possible. This rule does not distinguish between more or less politically potent applicants. There is no exclusive list determining who may, and who may not, make written submissions. Thus, if the requirements of Rule 37(2) are met, potentially highly influential political actors, such as the European Commission, can participate in just the same way as a small, little-known NGO. Despite this equality in principle, it is questionable whether, and if so, to what extent, tribunals themselves would view such submissions in the same light. It is not unimaginable that arbitrators may feel more inclined to take the *amicus curiae* brief of

---

[68] See e.g. *AES Summit, Electrabel,* and *Micula.*

an actor such as the European Commission into consideration in their reasoning and decision-making processes to a greater extent than they would a brief submitted by an NGO. In principle, arbitrators would certainly be entitled to act in such a manner. The question still remains, however, whether political influence should be possible in an arbitral proceeding. After all, one of the major goals of investment arbitration under the ICSID Convention and its capacity to provide for direct investor–State dispute resolution was to have a de-politicised process.[69] The participation of entities such as the European Commission certainly raises the spectre of the politicisation of investment disputes. A central issue will be whether there is indeed a risk that arbitrators will bow to that political pressure to the detriment of the dispute-resolution process.

Practice thus far has shown that there are already several cases where the European Commission has made written submissions to tribunals.[70] To date, however, only one decision on the merits has been rendered in these disputes and it is therefore not yet possible to assess definitively what impact the participation of the Commission has had on the outcome of the proceedings. Nonetheless, the issue of a potential politicisation of investment disputes through written submissions by non-disputing parties is an emerging issue of some significance and demonstrates the evolving impact of procedural innovation on substantive outcomes.[71]

2   Overstraining of the arbitral process?

In principle, it lies within the discretion of tribunals to decide whether or not to take into account *amicus curiae* briefs. In light of the ever growing number of investment disputes that increasingly also concern issues of public interest,[72] and with the new rules in place – which now officially provide for the possibility of non-disputing party involvement – it is possible that the number of written submissions of non-disputing parties could also increase. This points to the potential overloading of

---

[69] I. F. I. Shihata, 'Towards a greater depoliticization of investment disputes: The roles of ICSID and MIGA', *ICSID Review – Foreign Investment Law Journal*, 1 (1986), 1.

[70] See above Part III (C)–(D).

[71] See also Bjorklund, 'The promise and peril of arbitral precedent'.

[72] See ICSID, *Caseload Statistics*, http://icsid.worldbank.org/ICSID/FrontServlet?requestType=CasesRH&actionVal=OpenPage&PageType=AnnouncementsFrame&FromPage=Announcements&pageName=Announcement24 (last accessed 21 January 2011).

the arbitral process. Arbitral practice thus far demonstrates, however, that this risk of overburdening the system has not materialised. Although it is certainly possible in each and every dispute for non-disputing parties to participate, so far this option has not been used to an extent that would overburden the system. In the vast majority of cases, although also concerned with issues of public interest, no non-disputing parties have filed petitions to submit written submissions to tribunals in the proceedings.

VI Concluding remarks

Arbitral practice has shown that the adoption of the new rules on participation of non-disputing parties in 2006 has not led to a situation where non-disputing parties have become 'regulars' in investment arbitrations. There have been comparatively few cases where NGOs or other non-State actors have petitioned tribunals to participate in the proceedings. Due to the scarcity of cases, and even fewer decisions on the merits, as of yet it is too soon to make a conclusive assessment of this new procedural option. Nonetheless, it is possible to discern certain trends. What can be seen already, for example, is that tribunals tend to grant permission if they receive petitions to make written submissions from non-disputing parties. Thus far, in the cases where this issue has become relevant, all tribunals have granted applicants the possibility to submit written briefs.

Whether a new development is positive or negative will, as always, depend upon the perspective one takes – this is no different with the question of participation of non-disputing parties in ICSID arbitration. It is one of the particularities distinguishing investment arbitration from commercial arbitration that in most instances it is more than just the disputing parties' interest at stake in the disputes. Thus, the demand for more transparency and possibilities for participation of non-disputing parties seems all the more justified in investment arbitration. Ultimately, however, increased participation and transparency should only be advocated so long as the interests of disputing parties in the efficient resolution of their dispute are not unduly compromised. In other words, it should still essentially remain the disputing parties' process. Those primarily responsible for ensuring this outcome are the arbitrators conducting the proceedings. Practice to date has demonstrated that the arbitrators concerned exercised their discretion in this regard conscientiously and responsibly. Accordingly, as yet, there seems to be no reason to view the establishment of the new rules concerning participation of non-disputing parties as having had a negative impact on ICSID arbitration, or that it has led to any undue burden on the parties in individual disputes or on the system as a whole. To the contrary, the new provisions have provided clarity on the permissibility of written submissions to tribunals by non-disputing parties and have answered the demand for increased transparency. Future practice will evidence how this new procedural tool will evolve and to what extent written submissions of non-disputing parties will, in fact, influence the decision-making processes of tribunals and have a substantive impact on awards.

16

The role of procedure in the development of investment law: The case of Section B of Chapter 11 of NAFTA

SERGIO PUIG[*]

I Introduction

Investment law, one of the fastest growing areas of international law, has emerged from the proliferation of bilateral and multilateral international investment agreements (IIAs).[1] More than 2,600 IIAs have been negotiated, involving almost all countries. Most of these agreements provide for international arbitration as the means to settle disputes between investors and the host country.[2]

Many scholars argue that the emergence of multiple and varied mechanisms for the settlement of economic disputes and of treaties providing for investment arbitration may be exacerbating what is called a 'fragmentation' process of international law.[3] Today, economic actors seeking relief under international law may be forced to go to different courts or tribunals in order to seek compliance (i.e. conformity to the rules of a particular regime, including dispute-resolution and interpretation provisions) and/or economic compensation for the State's breach of its obligations. This may be increasing the risk that tribunals will come to inconsistent, conflicting and incompatible

---

[*] The views expressed in this chapter do not represent the official views of any current or former employer of the author.

[1] K. Vandevelde, 'The political economy of a bilateral investment treaty', *American Journal of International Law*, 92 (1998), 621.

[2] See UNCTAD, 'Analysis of BITS', www.unctadxi.org/templates/Page____1007.aspx (last accessed 18 January 2011).

[3] International Law Commission, 'Report of the study group on fragmentation of international law: Difficulties arising from the diversification and expansion of international law', UN Doc. A/CN.4/L.682 of 4 April 2006 (ILC Fragmentation Report), prepared by Martti Koskenniemi, noting both positive and negative sides of the development of more mechanisms to apply international law.

decisions.[4] Faced with this danger, the question addressed in this chapter is as follows: in the absence of a homogeneous, hierarchical meta-system capable of doing away with problems derived from multiple and varied mechanisms for the settlement of economic disputes, can agreed procedural tools be a source of co-ordination?

This chapter explores this question in the context of the investment chapter of the North American Free Trade Agreement (NAFTA, or 'the Agreement').[5] It studies how the following procedural mechanisms included in Section B of the investment chapter of NAFTA (Chapter 11) may have helped to improve systemic coherence: (a) the 'no-U-turn' access model to arbitration; (b) the consolidation process of common claims; (c) the ability to consolidate claims brought on behalf of an enterprise and non-controlling shareholders; (d) the possibility of submissions by non-parties to the dispute; and (e) the Free Trade Commission's binding interpretation process.

This chapter discusses NAFTA's development and main contributions to investment law in its first fifteen years, with a particular focus on these distinctive procedural features. The chapter answers in the affirmative the question posed and concludes with some lessons learned for other investment protection systems based on the practice and evolution of NAFTA investment treaty law.

II   Systemic coherence in international investment law

A   Why is systemic coherence so elusive?

The difficulty in achieving coherence in investment law can be associated with the three features that define the process to resolve investment disputes: scope, standing and structure.

1   Scope

Many international tribunals were created to hear specialised disputes in what are essentially closed systems. The dispute-settlement mechanisms are tied to a treaty where jurisdiction is limited to disputes arising under

---

[4] See e.g. T. Buergenthal, 'The proliferation of disputes, dispute settlement procedures and respect for the rule of law', *Arbitration International*, 22 (2006), 495 (noting also two reasons for proliferation of dispute-settlement mechanisms: as more tribunals exist to hear more cases the predictability of outcomes increases; as tribunals are perceived to be successful, international organisations are inclined to emulate that success by imitation).

[5] North American Free Trade Agreement, signed 17 December 1992), United States–Canada–Mexico (1993) 32 ILM 289, 605 (entered intro force 1 January 1994) (NAFTA).

a specific treaty or chapter of a treaty.[6] However, parties often find law proxies (substantive bodies of law) in several jurisdictions, including domestic courts or other international *fora* to bring different claims based on the same series of facts.[7] Thus, different tribunals and courts tend to hear disputes arising under different treaties, even when those disputes arise from related or even identical facts.

The difference between jurisdictions and their respective standards of protection creates an incentive for businesses to pursue all available options under different specialised systems to seek compliance and/or compensation, including those options available in national courts. A litigation strategy of pursuing all available remedies may become not only possible, but necessary for transnational businesses to be made whole and re-establish the normal pre-breach situation.[8] If the corporate or other relationship between the claimants in investment cases involves different nationalities among the shareholders, the dispute may also involve different treaties as the source of jurisdiction.

2   Structure

Investment disputes are heard by ad hoc tribunals that lack a hierarchical structure and precedential value (*stare decisis*) to link tribunals and encouraging their interaction. Unlike national courts or domestic administrative agencies, limited competences and highly specialised mandates are not linked by a 'Supreme Court of Investment' with powers to confirm, correct or revoke a decision of a particular tribunal.[9]

---

[6] See e.g. *Mexico – Tax Measures on Soft Drinks and Other Beverages* (WT/DS308/R, 2005, adopted as modified by the Appellate Body on 24 March 2006).

[7] W. S. Dodge, 'National courts and international arbitration: Exhaustion of remedies and *res judicata* under Chapter 11 of NAFTA', *Hastings International and Comparative Law Review*, 23 (2000), 357.

[8] See further J. Crawford, *The International Law Commission's Articles on State Responsibility: Introduction, text and commentaries* (2002), pp. 58–60.

[9] *MTD Equity & MTD Chile* v. *Republic of Chile* (ICSID Case No. ARB/01/7, Decision on Annulment of 21 March 2007), para. 52. At the outset, in the ICSID system, annulment has a limited function. As stated in *MTD* v. *Chile* (Annulment):

> [a committee] . . . cannot substitute its determination on the merits for that of the Tribunal. Nor can it direct a Tribunal on a resubmission how it should resolve substantive issues in dispute. All it can do is annul the decision of the tribunal: it can extinguish a *res judicata* but on a question of merits it cannot create a new one. A more interventionist approach by committees on the merits of disputes would risk a renewed cycle of tribunal and annulment proceedings of the kind observed in *Klöckner* and *Amco*.

3 Standing

The rigid distinction between States and individuals reflected in many international institutions contrasts with the reality of modern international businesses and IIAs.[10] The early public international law was developed around inter-State relations.[11] However, IIAs have developed a 'hybrid' decentralised system which gives the prime role in enforcement to private investors, and leaves less room for inter-State actions.[12]

Achieving coherence is especially problematic in structures permitting less inter-State actions. States are generally reluctant to pursue theories regarding the obligation of other States to protect investment that are inconsistent with the type of protections they are willing to provide themselves.[13] By contrast, private parties may press for the adjudication of claims by advancing more sophisticated legal theories in their disputes and which may result in an increase of the obligations originally agreed in the treaty or over-legalisation.[14] The decision is then left to ad hoc tribunals with limited mandates, whose decisions can be only scrutinised under limited circumstances.

These characteristics are frequently found in IIAs that grant a remedy to qualifying investors for damages only (compensation), most of the time without any mechanism to appeal or to correct for errors of law, as reflected in Table 16.1.

---

[10] *Case concerning Ahmadou Sadio Diallo (Guinea v. Congo) (Preliminary Objections)* (Judgment of 24 May 2007), para. 88. In its judgment, the International Court of Justice noted that: 'in contemporary international law, the protection of the rights of companies and the rights of their shareholders, and the settlement of the associated disputes, are essentially governed by bilateral or multilateral agreements . . . In that context, the role of diplomatic protection has somewhat faded.'

[11] N. DiMascio and J. Pauwelyn, 'Nondiscrimination in trade and investment treaties: Worlds apart or two sides of the same coin?', *American Journal of International Law*, 102 (2008), 48.

[12] See, Z. Douglas, 'The hybrid foundations of investment treaty arbitration', *British Yearbook of International Law*, 74 (2004), 151.

[13] A. O. Sykes, 'Public versus private enforcement of international economic law: Standing and remedy', *Journal of Legal Studies*, 34 (2005), 631.

[14] According to Professor Helfer: 'Overlegalization' exists 'where a treaty's augmented legalization levels require more extensive changes to national laws and practices than was the case when the state first ratified the treaty, generating domestic opposition to compliance or pressure to revise or exit from the treaty': L. Helfer, 'Overlegalizing human rights and international relations theory and the Commonwealth Caribbean backlash against human rights regimes', *Columbia Law Review*, 102 (2002), 1832.

Table 16.1 *Scope, standing and structure under IIAs*

Scope	Standing	Structure
System to recover damages only for treaty breaches	System of private right of action for qualifying investors	System lacking hierarchical structures
1. System providing compensation only for non-compliance;	1. Private actors have more control over pace and extent of boundaries;	1. Ad hoc tribunals hear each specific dispute;
2. Limited number of disciplines based on specific treaty obligations;	2. State of nationality of investor may have interest but not rights;	2. No appeals mechanism and limited scrutiny;
3. Limited power of tribunals to order preservation of rights.	3. Corporate structures of investors may complicate the dispute.	3. Tribunals not bound by past decisions (*stare decisis*).

B   Consequences of the three S's that affect the development of investment law

The consequences of the main characteristics of the modern system for investment protection vary. For example, procedurally, the problem is mainly one of inefficiency. Multiple tribunals must educate themselves about the same facts underlying the claim at issue, while the parties bear the expense of arguing and co-ordinating multiple proceedings. From a procedural point of view, multiple proceedings may also give rise to a problem of real or perceived fairness by allowing abuses of process and forum-shopping, or the decision to choose a forum where the complainant's case can be most favourably presented. Indeed, as pointed out by Professor Andrea Bjorklund, 'Forum shopping can be corrosive . . . when it gives rise to the possibility of multiple bites at the apple – the chance of gaining relief in a second forum notwithstanding the first forum's dismissal of a suit, or even worse, duplicative relief if suits in both tribunals proceed successfully.'[15] Also, substantively these characteristics may 'threaten the coherence of the international legal system [and] create the danger of conflicting and incompatible rules, principles,

---

[15] A. K. Bjorklund, 'Private rights and public international law: Why competition among international economic law tribunals is not working', *Hastings Law Journal*, 59 (2007), 241.

rule-systems and institutional practices'.[16] From a substantive point of view the main characteristics of the modern system of investment protection affect, and sometimes even preclude, systemic coherence.

The dynamics described above are problematic because coherence is considered a core value of legal systems, including systems within international law. As stated by the International Law Commission (ILC): 'coherence is valued positively owing to the connection it has with predictability, certainty and legal security'.[17] Coherence is more than only deference to past decisions or treating the same legal subjects equally. Deciding like cases in the same unjust way is obviously wrong and negatively affects the credibility of investment arbitration. In such cases, the value of justice can be undermined by inconsistency in decision-making. Coherence in international decision-making should not necessarily presuppose consistency as inherently valuable. However, consistency is one among other elements that coherent legal systems should encourage.

Underlying the problem of fragmentation is the broader issue of the legalisation of international law and the consequent increase of international dispute-settlement mechanisms. And, underlying the legitimacy of an increasingly legalised international order is the problem of coherence and efficiency of systems that are no longer exclusively controlled by States. Thus, if we aspire to have coherent international investment law systems, a structure that generates problems of normative uncertainty and procedural inefficiency should be strengthened to prevent some of the negative consequences of the scope, the standing and the structure of investment arbitration.[18]

III   Systematic approach under NAFTA

Generally, IIAs include procedural provisions aimed at avoiding the duplication of proceedings, and maintaining procedural efficiency and substantive coherence in decision-making processes. Also, some procedural 'tools' can be derived from private international law as applied

---

[16] J. I. Charney, 'The impact on the international legal system of the growth of international courts and tribunals', New York University Journal of International Law and Politics, 31 (1999), 697.

[17] ILC Fragmentation Report, p. 240.

[18] See generally, R. Higgins, 'The reformation in international law' in R. Rawlings (ed.), Law, Society and Economy: Centenary essays for the London School of Economics and Political Science 1895–1995 (Oxford, 1997), p. 207.

by municipal courts to deal with disputes involving cross-border trans-actions.[19] This chapter focuses on describing the provisions explicitly provided for in Section B of Chapter 11 of NAFTA. After a brief explanation of how these procedural tools protect both the fair disposal of a claim in each specific case and the development of a treaty system, this chapter describes the experience during the first fifteen years (1994–2009) of NAFTA.

A Waiver or 'no-U-turn' access model to arbitration

1 Background

The first important provision can be found in Article 1121, drafted to manage jurisdictional conflicts, mainly between international and domestic decision-makers but also potential conflicts with decision-makers outside of a national jurisdiction.

Article 1121 requires as a condition precedent to bringing a claim under NAFTA that the investor and/or the investor on behalf of the enterprise that is owned or controlled by the investor, comply with certain procedural requirements.[20] This model is a departure from the 'fork-in-the-road' model included in the *travaux préparatoires* and other IIAs signed by the NAFTA parties.[21] Specifically, these provisions require the disputing party (investor and/or enterprise) to:

> waive their right to initiate or continue before any administrative tribunal or court under the law of any Party, or other dispute settlement procedures, any proceedings with respect to the measure of the disputing Party that is alleged to be a breach . . . except for proceedings for injunctive, declaratory or other extraordinary relief, not involving the

---

[19] For Professor Bjorklund, 'The two most commonly identified tools to resolve jurisdictional conflicts are the familiar doctrines of *res judicata* and *lis pendens*, or *litispendence*', and could be used where parallel or subsequent claims meet the conditions for the application of these doctrines. As Professor Bjorklund explains, '*Res judi*cata governs the effect to be given an award or judgment rendered by another tribunal, while *lis pendens* refers to the effect to be given concurrent proceedings.' In addition to their use in both common and civil law systems, these principles can apply to international proceedings: see Bjorklund, 'Private rights and public international law', pp. 157–8 (footnote omitted). See also Y. Shany, *The Competing Jurisdictions of International Courts and Tribunals* (Oxford University Press, 2003), p. 157; and *Certain German Interests in Polish Upper Silesia (Germany v. Poland) (Jurisdiction)*, Ser. A, (No. 6) (PCIJ, 1925).

[20] See NAFTA, Art. 1121(1)(b) and (2)(b).

[21] NAFTA, *travaux préparatoires* of December 1991.

payment of damages, before an administrative tribunal or court under the law of the disputing Party.[22]

The main rationale of this provision is to avoid simultaneous or concurrent remedies, including any type of dispute-settlement procedures (e.g. mediation, commercial arbitration etc.) that can lead to double redress for the same measure. The focus here is on the term measure, not only because the NAFTA obligations extend to measures,[23] but also because a single measure can give rise to domestic or international adjudication based on different causes of action that may or may not give raise to monetary damages. In other words: 'the same facts can give rise to different legal claims. The similarity of prayers for relief does not necessarily bespeak an identity of causes of action.'[24]

Since the waiver is applied to the same measure, it foresees that two causes of action may give rise to proceedings under different jurisdictions (domestic and international),[25] meaning that a domestic proceeding could co-exist with an arbitration proceeding under NAFTA, where the aim of both proceedings is to challenge exactly the same measure.[26] This provision therefore also co-ordinates potential jurisdictional conflicts, limiting Chapter 11 tribunals to hear treaty claims for damages.

2   Practice

In most Chapter 11 cases against the NAFTA parties, the same investor (or its local enterprise) has pursued domestic remedies

---

[22] See NAFTA, Art. 1121(1)(b) and (2)(b). The drafters anticipated one instance in which the waiver would not be required. 'Only where a disputing investor of control of an enterprise: (a) a waiver from the enterprise under paragraph 1(b) or 2(b) shall not be required; and (b) Annex 1120.1(b) shall not apply.'

[23] NAFTA, Art. 201 defines the term 'measure' to include any law, regulation, procedure, requirement or practice.

[24] *Pantechniki SA Contractors & Engineers* v. *Republic of Albania* (ICSID Case No. ARB/07/21 Award of 30 July 2009), para. 62.

[25] Art. 27 of the Vienna Convention of the Law of Treaties and Art. 32 of the Article on State Responsibility are both cemented in the idea that national and international adjudication is exercised under different mandates. Art. 27 states: 'A party may not invoke the provisions of its internal law as justification for its failure to perform a treaty.' Art. 32 states: 'The responsible State may not rely on the provisions of its internal law as justification for failure to comply with its obligations.' The ICJ in *Elettronica Sicula SpA (United States of America* v. *Italy)* [1989] ICJ Rep 15–121; ILM 28 (1989), 1109, reaffirmed this principle: 'It must be borne in mind that the fact that an act of a public authority may have been unlawful in municipal law does not necessarily mean that that act was unlawful in international law, as a breach of treaty or otherwise.'

[26] Cf. *Waste Management Inc.* v. *United Mexican States* (ICSID Case No. ARB(AF)/00/3, Final Award of 30 April 2004), para. 101.

before submitting an international claim without necessarily being required to do so. For example, in the case of the tax on soft drinks using 'high fructose corn syrup' (the HFCS Tax), which was the source of three different investment disputes against Mexico (*Corn Products International Inc.* v. *Mexico, Archer Daniels Midland/Tate & Lyle Ingredients Americas Inc.* and *Cargill Inc.* v. *Mexico*), there were simultaneous proceedings in national courts, the WTO and investment tribunals.[27]

While this situation may derive from contradictory decisions between national and international decision-makers, the inconsistencies mostly derive from the respective jurisdictions and mandates of each decision-maker. A positive aspect however is that the tribunals have benefited from the domestic court's development of the facts and some issues of law, particularly those domestic law issues on which the international tribunals lack expertise. Even when the domestic court's decision would not bind the tribunal, the court's analysis would improve the tribunal's understanding of the law and facts applicable to the case.[28]

The analysis of the Chapter 11 claims also shows that the use of both systems encouraged cross-fertilisation between national courts and tribunals in a manner that respects the jurisdiction of national courts and does not preclude coherence in international substantive law. For example, in *GAMI Investments Inc.* v. *Mexico*, the arbitral tribunal recognised Mexican courts as a source of congruent application of national law and the government agencies as guardians of the legitimate goals of policy.[29] Thus, while referring to the decision that ruled on the expropriation as a matter of Mexican law, the tribunal

---

[27] J. Pauwelyn, 'Adding sweeteners to softwood lumber: The WTO–NAFTA "spaghetti bowl" is cooking', *Journal of International Economic Law*, 9 (2006), 3, 4. For the NAFTA Chapter 11 cases, see *Corn Products International Inc.* v. *Mexico* (ICSID Case No. ARB (AF)/04/1) (*Corn Products*); *Archer Daniels Midland Company and Tate & Lyle Ingredients Americas Inc.* v. *Mexico* (ICSID Case No. ARB(AF)/04/5) (*ADM/TLIA*); *Cargill Inc.* v. *Mexico* (ICSID Case No. ARB(AF)/05/2) (*Cargill*).

[28] See e.g. *Metalclad* v. *Mexico* (ICSID Case No. ARB(AF)/97/1, Award of 30 August 2000). In such cases whether denial of a construction permit violated the NAFTA Art. 1105 depended in part on whether the municipality had authority under Mexican law over hazardous-waste matters. In *Azinian, Davitian, & Baca* v. *Mexico* (ICSID Case No. ARB (AF)/97/2, Award of 1 November 1999) (*Azinian*), by contrast, the question of whether a municipality had grounds under Mexican law to repudiate a concession contract had been adjudicated by the Mexican courts, and the tribunal was able to rely on their decisions in rejecting the investor's expropriation claim.

[29] *GAMI Investments Inc.* v. *United Mexican States* (Final Award of 15 November 2004).

348   SERGIO PUIG

deferred to the decision of the Mexican courts as an authoritative expression of national law.[30] In addition, in the *ADM/TLIA* v. *Mexico* case also arising out of the HFCS Tax, the tribunal relied on the Mexican Supreme Court's decision as evidence of the measure's protectionist intent.[31]

The NAFTA experience suggests that although the waiver model may constitute a pull against procedural efficiency, it also encourages cross-fertilisation and interactions between national courts and tribunals resulting in the domestic court's development of the facts and some issues of law. There is room for debate, however, concerning the extent to which the waiver model permits other prior or simultaneous proceedings, especially in domestic legal systems, which would assist in informing the decisions of investment tribunals under Chapter 11, and allow for more contextual and cohesive analysis.

B   Consolidation process of common claims

1   Background

NAFTA Article 1126 includes a process for consolidation of claims that have a question of law or fact in common. This provision puts the question of consolidation (which can be sought by any disputing party) at the discretion of a different tribunal (consolidation tribunal) when doing so is 'in the interest of fair and efficient resolution of the claims'.[32]

Notwithstanding the discretionary nature of the question, Article 1126 contemplates a two-step process: first, a consolidation tribunal should determine whether two or more claims contain a common question of law or fact. Only if the answer to this question is positive, the consolidation tribunal should then move to the second step by analysing whether the consolidation furthers the fair and efficient resolution of the claims.

The consolidation process attempts, on the one hand, to balance the interests of fair and efficient resolution of common claims and, on the other, the implications of having different investment tribunals dealing with cases that have questions of law or fact in common. The mechanism has to be understood in a context of investment arbitration where there

---

[30] *Ibid.*
[31] *ADM/TLIA* (ICSID Case No. ARB(AF)/04/5, Award of 21 November 2007), paras. 146–7.
[32] NAFTA, Art. 1126(2).

are limited mechanisms to correct for errors in the application of law,[33] or to deal with the contradictions in their findings.[34]

Having claims consolidated may result in cost savings and efficiencies in some cases, however, experienced practitioners have also noted that 'proceedings involving more than two parties can lead to a multitude of difficulties on a procedural level',[35] especially because most arbitration rules are tailored to two-party proceedings. Other complexities may include how to adequately protect confidential information when the combined proceeding involves competitors in the same sector. These are questions that the consolidation tribunal has to address within the second step of the process mostly related to the efficient resolution of common claims.

The second step of the consolidation process under NAFTA also protects fairness. The ability of foreign investors to vindicate their claims before international arbitral tribunals may result, as explained before, in problems of unfairness by treating similarly situated claimants differently, resulting in inconsistent decisions. In other words, when numerous claims arising out of common facts or shared questions of law are decided by different tribunals, different interpretations of the same legal issues or different understandings of the same facts are more probable. This should be considered an interest of the disputes as much as

---

[33] ICSID tribunals have sought to distinguish between failure to apply the law and error in its application. For instance the Committee in the *MINE* case stated that:

> a tribunal's disregard of the agreed rules of law would constitute a derogation from the terms of reference within which the tribunal has been authorized to function. Examples of such a derogation include the application of rules of law other that the ones agreed by the parties, or a decision not based on any law unless the parties had agreed on a decision *ex aequo et bono*. If the derogation is manifest, it entails a manifest excess of power. Disregard of the applicable rules of law must be distinguished from erroneous application of those rules which, even if manifestly unwarranted, furnishes no ground for annulment.

Maritime International Nominees Establishment v. *Republic of Guinea* (1989) 4 ICSID Reports 79, 87, para. 5.04. See also *Enron Creditors Recovery Corporation and Ponderosa Assets LP* v. *Argentine Republic* (ICSID Case No. ARB/01/3, Decision on Annulment of 30 July 2010), para. 68 (*Enron* (Annulment)).

[34] According to Professor Wälde, contradictions between two investment tribunals can be in the assessment of facts and in the definition of the legal obligations applicable to the particular situation. T. Wälde, 'Investment arbitration under the Energy Charter Treaty: An overview of key issues', *Transnational Dispute Management*, 1(2) (2004).

[35] E. Gaillard, 'The consolidation of arbitral proceedings and court proceedings', *ICC Court Bulletin: Complex arbitrations – special supplement* (2003), p. 8.

favouring the systemic functioning of the dispute-settlement mechanism under Chapter 11.

If it is true that a single tribunal may be better equipped to deal with multiple claims by a 'class' of investors based on the same or similar facts, it is also true that large-numbered class proceedings may create imbalances not originally contemplated by investment arbitration.[36] Indeed, in domestic court systems the process of consolidating class claims has evidenced tensions that may be also encountered in investment arbitration. For example, while the consolidation of mass claims ensures that similar or identical cases are decided in an efficient and consistent manner it may be the case that the consolidated group of claimants gains much greater bargaining power, even if the underlying claim is unmeritorious. This increase in bargaining power stems from the prospect that claims of a class of many claimants might result in large aggregate judgments. This change in bargaining power can be so extreme that unmeritorious claims settle rather than proceed to a final judgment, as some argue to be the experience of mass tort claims in the United States.[37]

This balance is important, because where disputes involve sensitive political questions or structural or economic policy changes which are common topics addressed by investment tribunals, consolidation tribunals have to be extremely careful in assessing both the systemic interest of having the claims consolidated, and the interest of the parties to the dispute. Under the NAFTA, these elements should be balanced by answering if consolidation is 'in the interests of fair and efficient resolution of the claims'.[38] This is a step that follows an affirmative answer to the question of commonality of law or fact.

2   Practice

In two instances under the NAFTA, States have relied on Article 1126 to attempt the consolidation of claims.[39] In the claims brought by *Canfor*,

---

[36] e.g. the consolidation agreed by the disputing parties in the claims that the Canadian cattle producers brought against the United States in connection with its import ban on Canadian beef. Outside of NAFTA, for example, the case of *Giovanna a Beccara and ors* v. *Argentine Republic* (ICSID Case No. ARB/07/5, Procedural Order No. 3, Confidentiality Order of 27 January 2010) consolidates under the same proceedings the claims brought by a class of Italian bondholders.

[37] G. L. Priest, 'Procedural versus Substantive controls of mass tort class actions', *The Journal of Legal Studies*, 26 (1997), 521–73.

[38] NAFTA, Art. 1126(2).

[39] In some cases the parties to a NAFTA dispute have agreed to consolidate cases: see e.g. *Azinian* (ICSID Case No. ARB(AF)/97/2, Award of 1 November 1999).

Tembec and *Terminal Forest Products* the United States successfully consolidated three related cases concerning the softwood lumber industry;[40] in the cases brought by *Corn Products* and *ADM/TLIA* the investors successfully opposed Mexico's move to consolidate two out of the three claims concerning the HFCS Tax.[41] Additionally, in the *Canadian Cattlemen Claims* the parties agreed to consolidate claims of a class of 107 investors located in Canada.[42] These three cases illustrate the usefulness and tensions of consolidating (or not) common claims.

In the *Canadian Cattlemen Claims*, consolidation permitted the efficient disposal of claims brought by 107 different claimants. The class, Canadian ranchers affected by a ban on imports of meat products into the United States following the discovery of bovine spongiform encephalopathy in Canada, claimed an estimate of US$225 million in damages. The same tribunal heard all claims in a single proceeding that lasted less than three years and presumably proceeded in a more cost-efficient manner than it would have if the claims had been heard separately. The tribunal dismissed all the claims at the jurisdiction stage in view of the fact that the physical location of the investment was not the United States.[43]

In the case concerning the HFCS Tax, four producers of HFCS in Mexico brought three different investment claims under NAFTA. Mexico

[40] *Canfor Corporation* v. *United States*, *Tembec and ors* v. *United States*, *Terminal Forest Products Ltd* v. *United States* (Order of the Consolidation Tribunal of 7 September 2005).

[41] *Corn Products* (ICSID Case No. ARB(AF)/04/1, Order of the Consolidation Tribunal of 20 May 2005); *ADM/TLIA* (ICSID Case No. ARB(AF)/04/5, Order of the Consolidation Tribunal of 20 May 2005).

[42] *Canadian Cattlemen for Fair Trade* v. *United States* (Procedural Order No. 1 of 20 October 2006) (*Canadian Cattlemen Claims*).

[43] *Canadian Cattlemen Claims* (Award on Jurisdiction of 28 January 2008), para. 112. The tribunal added (para. 193):

> Although this Tribunal concludes that it has no jurisdiction to hear Claimants' claims, its decision today does not leave them with no remedy under the NAFTA. Their remedy lies not in the investor–State dispute resolution mechanism of Chapter 11, but in the State-to-State dispute resolution mechanism of Chapter 20 of the NAFTA. As such, it is for the government of Canada to pursue against the United States. Nothing in this holding precludes the Canadian government from doing so. Indeed, taking Claimant's factual submissions at face value, Claimants would be wholly justified in pressing their government to seek recourse against the U.S. Government for the measure at issue. Although such a remedy may be less attractive to Claimants than a direct claim for damages, it is, in the Tribunal's view, the remedy provided by the NAFTA for a trade dispute of this nature.

tried unsuccessfully to consolidate the separate claims into a single proceeding,[44] resulting in significantly inconsistent decisions in the different cases. For instance, the three NAFTA tribunals held that Mexico had breached Article 1102 (National Treatment) and dismissed the claims under Article 1110 (Expropriation).[45] However, unlike the *Corn Products* tribunal, the *ADM/TLIA* and *Cargill* tribunals found the HFCS Tax to be in breach of Article 1106 (Performance Requirements).[46] The proceedings against the HFCS Tax resulted in three decisions that are difficult to reconcile. And on top of this, Mexico was required to defend the three cases separately. However, at the same time, the separate proceedings also gave the three claimants – which are fierce global competitors with little incentive to co-operate with each other – the opportunity to argue their cases separately.

Contrary to the HFCS Tax disputes, the softwood lumber proceedings against the United States were decided by a single consolidation tribunal. That tribunal concluded that it had jurisdiction to analyse the effects of the Byrd Amendment on the investors only,[47] and soon after the decision, the United States and Canada settled the larger conflict over softwood lumber.[48] The Chapter 11 proceedings were conducted in an efficient manner by the International Centre for Settlement of Investment Disputes but required exceptional effort to accommodate the multiparty proceeding within its Rules, which are of course tailored for two-party proceedings.[49]

---

[44] See discussion in Y. Andreeva, '*Corn Products v. Mexico*: First NAFTA (Non)-Consolidation Order', *International Arbitration Law Review*, No. 8 (2006), 78–81.

[45] *ADM/TLIA* (ICSID Case No. ARB(AF)/04/5, Final Award of 27 November 2007), para. 304 (*ADM/TLIA* (Final Award)); *Corn Products* (ICSID Case No. ARB(AF)/04/01, Decision on Responsibility of 15 January 2008), para. 193 (*Corn Products* (Decision on Responsibility)); *Cargill* (ICSID Case No. ARB(AF)/05/2, Award of 18 September 2009) (available as part of the Judgment of the Ontario Superior Court of Justice of 26 August 2010 on the Application to Set Aside the Award), paras. 554–560 (*Cargill* (Award)).

[46] *ADM/TLIA* (Final Award), para. 227; *Corn Products* (Decision on Responsibility), para. 80; *Cargill* (Award) at para. 319.

[47] On 28 October 2000, the United States enacted the Continued Dumping and Subsidy Offset Act of 2000, which amended the Tariff Act of 1930 (the Byrd Amendment). The Byrd Amendment was to the effect that duties assessed pursuant to countervailing duty or antidumping orders were to be distributed to affected domestic producers.

[48] Softwood Lumber Agreement between the Government of Canada and the Government of the United States of America, signed 12 September 2006 (entered into force 12 October 2006), http://www.international.gc.ca/controls-controles/softwood-bois_oeuvre/index.aspx?lang=eng (last accessed 18 January 2011).

[49] Interview with Gonzalo Flores, Senior Counsel ICSID, January 2010.

It is worth noting that in the HFCS Tax cases, the Consolidation Tribunal was 'satisfied that the risk of unfairness to Mexico from inconsistent awards resulting from separate proceedings [did not] outweigh the unfairness to the claimants of the procedural inefficiencies that would arise in consolidated proceedings'.[50] However, in the softwood lumber proceedings, the Consolidation Tribunal recalled that the factors to be considered in relation to the term 'in the interests of fair and efficient resolution of the claims'[51] include the avoidance of conflicting decisions.[52] Based on this factor, the consolidation tribunal disagreed with the proposition sustained by the HFCS consolidation tribunal and decided that the risk of inconsistent decisions was of greater concern than the risk of disclosure of confidential information among competitors leading to an inefficient arbitration process. As it turned out to be so in the HFCS Tax cases, the softwood lumber tribunal anticipated an important problem that could result from having different tribunals deciding claims that have questions of law or fact in common.

In one way, the consolidated claims permitted a more manageable disposal of the proceedings for the United States; however this may have played against the interest of the moving party (somewhat ironically, in this case, the United States). After the tribunal found jurisdiction, the claimants arguably earned some degree of leverage to include the potentially meritorious investment claims in the settlement agreement. In contrast, in the case of Mexico, a settlement over the related State-to-State dispute (i.e. access to sugar market) was also reached; however, the HFCS Tax claims were not included as part of that settlement. The reasons for this are unclear, and certainly it would be speculative to read too much into this outcome. Nevertheless, it is arguable that a consolidated group of claimants, acting together, might have been more effective in attempting to settle their claims arising out of the HFCS Tax cases.

C   Consolidation process of related parties claims

1   Background

NAFTA permits more than one claimant to submit claims arising out of the same events. In some instances, this measure may affect different

---

[50] See e.g. *ADM/TLIA* (ICSID Case No. ARB(AF)/04/5, Order of the Consolidation Tribunal of 20 May 2005), para. 17.

[51] NAFTA, Art. 1126.

[52] *Canfor and ors* v. *United States* (Order of the Consolidation Tribunal of 7 September 2005), para. 126.

qualifying investors in the same investment. For that purpose, Article 1117(3) caters for the consolidation of claims when different claims are brought on behalf of an enterprise under Article 1117 and, at the same time, a claim arising from the same events is submitted by one, or more than one, non-controlling shareholder.[53]

This 'mandatory' consolidation process applies to cases in which the corporate or other relationship between the claimants in the same investment may give rise to two or more different claims. Additionally, this provision helps to limit the possibilities of duplicative relief if suits in different tribunals proceed successfully. As put by the respondent in the *Loewen and ors* v. *United States* case, this provision attempts to limit the offering of 'divergent and possibly conflicting' theories on behalf of the same enterprise'.[54]

Article 1117(3) aligns cases that different shareholders in the same investment may bring, reducing the possibility that different tribunals decide inconsistently cases arising out of the very same events and affecting the same investment brought by claimants that are related by the corporate structure. In this case, and unlike the standard of Article 1126, the tribunal 'should' (not 'may') hear the cases together, unless it finds that the interests of a disputing party would be prejudiced. Therefore, it would be up to the disputing party that alleges prejudice as a consequence of this mandated consolidation to prove the prejudice suffered by the consolidation.

Also, this process attempts to limit instances of double recovery or problems of co-ordination when awarding damages for a breach in a case that will have a degree of connection. By aligning the cases of related corporate parties, the interests of the enterprise and of the investor may be managed in the same case and, if a breach is found, the losses or damages arising out of that breach would be more easily assessed and paid to the investor. In the words of the United States' Article 1128 submission in *GAMI* v. *Mexico*:

> the distinct functions of Articles 1116 and 1117 ensure that there will be no double recovery. When an investor that owns or controls an enterprise submits a claim under Article 1117 for loss or damage suffered by that enterprise, any award in the claimant investor's favor will make the enterprise whole and the value of the shares will be restored.[55]

---

[53] NAFTA, Art. 1117(3).

[54] *Loewen Group Inc. and Raymond L. Loewen* v. *United States* (ICSID Case No. ARB(AF)/98/3, Award of 26 June 2003).

[55] *GAMI Investments Inc.* v. *Mexico* (Article 1128 Submission of the United States), para. 18.

2   Practice

In at least three cases, claimants have brought consolidated claims under this provision.[56] Of particular interest is the decision in *Mondev International Ltd* v. *United States*, which did not deal with a consolidation issue. However, the tribunal held that Article 1117 applies where ownership or control of the investment enterprise is divided. In the proceedings, the three parties to the Agreement suggested that this article attempted to limit inconsistent outcomes, and the tribunal concluded that:

> a NAFTA tribunal should be careful not to allow any recovery, in a claim that should have been brought under Article 1117 [Claim by an Investor of a Party on Behalf of an Enterprise], to be paid directly to the investor. There are various ways of achieving this, most simply by treating such a claim as in truth brought under Article 1117.[57]

In other words, the tribunal confirmed that this provision attempts not only to encourage a cost-effective disposition of related claims, but also coherence in recovery matters. This means, primarily instances of double recovery as a consequence of claims derived from the same events and affecting an enterprise and its investors.

The consolidated claim brought jointly by *ADM* and *TLIA* versus Mexico is the only instance where this provision has been fully operative in a consolidated claim that has resulted in the obligation to compensate the claimants. The tribunal did not address the issue of how the compensation should be allocated between the claimants which were both shareholders in an enterprise. Arguably, given that the corporate structure of the joint venture enterprise ALMEX (the investment) was 50/50, the compensation should have been divided similarly. In this regard the tribunal concluded only that the compensation should be paid to 'the Claimants'.

D   Participation by a party to NAFTA and amicus curiae

1   Background

Article 1128 was included in NAFTA as a way to allow the State Parties to make submissions to a tribunal 'on a question of interpretation of th[e] Agreement' as third parties with interest but not a right in the specific

---

[56] These claims include *Azinian* (ICSID Case No. ARB(AF)/97/2), *ADM/TLIA* (ICSID Case No. ARB(AF)/04/5), and *The Loewen Group Inc. and Raymond L. Loewen* v. *United States* (ICSID Case No. ARB(AF)/98/3).

[57] *Mondev International Ltd* v. *United States* (ICSID Case No. ARB(AF)/99/2, Award of 11 October 2002), para. 86.

dispute.[58] Article 1128 serves to guide the process of interpretation of the Agreement during the adjudication process and to inform in general terms the States' position on a particular legal issue. Since NAFTA dispute documents are in the public domain, Article 1128 submissions become known by the general public.[59]

States may use this mechanism to inform the tribunals on their position regarding the meaning of specific standards of protection, and also to express and signal the State's position on specific legal questions. NAFTA tribunals can rely on the parties' positions on the relevant provision, and can inform their decision with such submissions. The submission might be of interest also to subsequent claimants to anticipate the position of a State on related legal issues in subsequent cases.

This procedural tool helps to maintain the balance between the systemic interests of the agreement and those interests that may be affected in each individual dispute. By helping to guide the interpretation process, this provision may help to maintain harmony, consistency and logic between different provisions of the Agreement. However, the systemic benefits cannot be obtained at the expense of changing the procedural balance of the parties to the specific dispute. Thus, the participation of the NAFTA parties is limited to matters of interpretation of the treaty.

As it is well known, in return for agreeing to investment arbitration, the host State of the investor is assured that the State of the investor's nationality will not intervene in the controversy between an investor and the host State. If the right of the parties to make a submission to the tribunal under Article 1128 were not limited to 'question[s] of interpretation', the participation of the State of nationality in support of the investor may be seen precisely as an unwelcome intervention. Accordingly, the limitation in Article 1128 to questions of treaty interpretation serves to reduce the possibilities of real or perceived intrusions that may affect diplomatic (or other) relationships between the States Parties to the Agreement. As recognised by Professors Clyde Pearce and Jack Coe:

---

[58] NAFTA, Art. 1128.

[59] The three NAFTA parties, moved by public-interest group pressure, joined in an interpretative note issued by the Free Trade Commission (FTC). The shared position establishes that 'Nothing in the NAFTA imposes a general duty of confidentiality on the disputing parties' and represents a commitment of the three States to grant free access to documents with limited exceptions: NAFTA Free Trade Commission, 'Interpretative notes to certain Chapter 11 provisions' (31 July 2001), para. A(1) (Notes of Interpretation).

A Party's right to intervene may be a mixed blessing for a claimant. NAFTA Parties are unlikely to endorse interpretations and theories of recovery that enlarge their own exposure to claims. Their involvement in the process is nonetheless to be welcomed. During the seminal stages of NAFTA investment jurisprudence, Party submissions that agree on an interpretative point will presumably be helpful to the tribunal. And such submission may provide an important check upon fanciful theories of recovery or treaty interpretations proffered by only one NAFTA Party.[60]

In addition to the informative nature of the submission, the parties to NAFTA have argued that the consistent view on the interpretation between the parties on specific areas of the Agreement in their different submissions should be considered a subsequent agreement between the three NAFTA parties. As discussed further, at the very least, the consistent view of the three States can be highly persuasive to a tribunal.

In addition to the participation of the State Parties to the Agreement, the Statement of the NAFTA Free Trade Commission (FTC) of 7 October 2003 confirmed that the language in NAFTA does not prevent tribunals from accepting written submissions from a non-disputing party. The FTC recommended procedures to follow with respect to the acceptance of submissions.[61] The FTC guidance provides that any non-disputing party (defined as any person of a party or who has significant presence in the territory of the party) that seeks to file a written submission must apply for leave from the tribunal, attaching the submission to the application. The non-disputing party submission will be circulated to all disputing parties and the tribunal will provide a timeframe for the parties to comment on the application for leave to file a non-disputing party submission. If the tribunal decides to grant leave to the application, it will then set a date for the disputing parties and NAFTA parties to submit a written reply on the submission.[62]

The FTC grants the tribunal discretion over the entire process. It explicitly states that in the event that a tribunal grants leave to a non-disputing party, the tribunal is 'not required to address that submission

---

[60] C. C. Pearce and J. Coe Jr, 'Arbitration under NAFTA Chapter Eleven: Some pragmatic reflections upon the first case filed against Mexico', *Hastings International and Comparative Law Review*, 23 (2000), 311, 338.

[61] FTC Statement on Non-Disputing Party Participation (7 October 2003), www.international. gc.ca/trade-agreements-accords-commerciaux/disp-diff/nafta_commission_aspx?lang=en (last accessed 18 January 2011).

[62] *Ibid.* The FTC Statement only addresses the written submission process, and cross-references the FTC's Note of Interpretation of 31 July 2001 with respect to non-disputing parties' access to documents.

at any point in the arbitration'.[63] This statement recognises the balance of the adjudication process and the character of these parties as non-disputing parties as well as the complexity of having to respond to every single allegation by an undefined group of potential participants. This view was supported by the tribunal in *Methanex* v. *United States* after the International Institute for Sustainable Development (IISD), an environmental non-governmental organisation, sought to present its views on the matter at issue in the arbitration. Methanex had objected to the submission of *amicus* submissions, arguing that:

> Equality and fairness in the proceedings will be compromised if the Claimant has to respond not only to the submissions of the Respondent, but also to the submissions and petitions of others not contemplated by NAFTA.[64]

The tribunal observed in its decision that:

> The Tribunal notes the argument raised by the Claimant to the effect that a burden will be added if *amicus* submissions are presented to the Tribunal and the Disputing Parties seek to make submissions in response. That burden is indeed a potential risk. It is inherent in any adversarial procedure which admits representations by a non-party third person.[65]

It concluded, however, that:

> Whilst there is a possible risk of unfair treatment as raised by the Claimant, the Tribunal is aware of that risk and considers that it must be addressed as and when it may arise. There is no immediate risk of unfair or unequal treatment for any Disputing Party or Party.[66]

More importantly, allowing non-disputing parties to participate recognises the relevance of having civil society and interest groups represented in matters that almost inevitably concern the public interest. However, the process of accepting and addressing *amici* submissions is left to the discretion of the tribunal, reflecting the inherent tension between the benefit *amici* bring to rendering a fully informed judgment and those concerns related to the specific dispute, such as economic efficiency of judicial administration.

---

[63] *Ibid.*, para. B(9).
[64] *Methanex* v. *United States* (Submission of the Claimant respecting Petition of the IISD of 31 August 2000), para. 17.
[65] *Methanex* v. *United States* (Decision on Petitions from Third Persons to Participate as *Amici* of 15 January 2001), para. 35.
[66] *Ibid.*, para. 37.

2   Practice

(a) **NAFTA party 1128 Submissions**   More than fifty Article 1128 submissions in at least eighteen cases, involving the interpretation of a number of questions, have guided NAFTA tribunals on different points of interpretation. While not binding on the tribunal, the influence of such participation can be seen in *Glamis Gold Ltd* v. *United States*, where the tribunal concluded that:

> It appears to this Tribunal that the NAFTA State Parties agree that, at a minimum, the fair and equitable treatment standard is that as articulated in *Neer*: 'the treatment of an alien, in order to constitute an international delinquency, should amount to an outrage, to bad faith, to willful neglect of duty, or to an insufficiency of governmental action so far short of international standards that every reasonable and impartial man would readily recognize its insufficiency.'[67]

In the *Canadian Cattlemen Claims*, the tribunal also relied on the parties' submissions. The parties to the NAFTA had expressed that the purpose of Chapter 11 was to protect those investors and investments with respect to another NAFTA party's territory. The tribunal did not agree with the respondent in that case that a subsequent agreement existed as a consequence of the US position and Mexico's Article 1128 submission in the arbitration and to Canada's statements on this issue in its counter-memorial in a different matter. The tribunal concluded however that such positions could be considered 'subsequent practice' within the meaning of Article 31(3)(b) of the Vienna Convention.[68]

There has not been any other clear instance in which a tribunal has directly referred to Article 1128 submissions to maintain a finding of law. However, in the process of shaping the meaning of Articles 1110 of NAFTA the governments of Mexico, Canada and the United States had an active role in the early cases. In particular, in *Metalclad* v. *Mexico* and *Pope & Talbot* v. *Canada*, the parties addressed the tribunals on the interpretation that should be given to 'measures tantamount to expropriation' rejecting that this term was intended to create a new category of expropriation not previously recognised in customary international law.

---

[67] *Glamis Gold Ltd* v. *United States* (Award of 6 June 2009) (*Glamis Gold* (Award)), para. 612, n. 1257 (citing *ADF Group* v. *United States* (Second Article 1128 Submission of the United Mexican States of 22 July 2002), p. 15, quoting *Pope & Talbot* v. *Canada*, Post-Hearing Article 1128 Submission of the United Mexican States of 3 December 2001 (Damages Phase)), para. 8, quoting *Pope & Talbot* v. *Canada* (Respondent's Counter-Memorial (Phase 2) of 18 August 2001), para. 309.

[68] *Canadian Cattlemen Claims* (Award on Jurisdiction of 28 January 2008), paras. 181–9.

(b) *Amicus curiae* **participation in Chapter 11 cases**   There have been *amici* submissions in at least three Chapter 11 cases concluded before 2010.

In *Methanex* v. *United States*, a dispute filed by a producer and supplier of methanol in California, several groups requested permission to file an *amicus* brief, to make oral submissions, and to have observer status at oral hearings. In the view of one of these groups, the tribunal's decision would have 'critical practical impact on environmental and other public welfare law-making at the federal, state and provincial levels throughout the NAFTA region . . . [and] . . . [t]he issues in this case are matters of public interest distinct from the commercial issues that arbitration processes normally handle'.[69]

The tribunal issued an order allowing *amici* submissions[70] and recognised that the subject matter of the arbitration was of great public interest and that the Chapter 11 arbitration could benefit from public perception of arbitration as a more transparent process.[71] In the award, the tribunal also cited one *amicus* submission and decided in a way consistent with the position of the civil-society groups.[72]

In *UPS* v. *Canada* the investor brought a Chapter 11 claim arguing that the Government of Canada engaged in unfair competition by exempting Canada Post from customs requirements – a benefit that was not extended to UPS, a courier service company. The Canadian Union of Postal Workers and the Council of Canadians[73] filed a joint *amicus* brief, urging that UPS's claim be dismissed.[74] The US Chamber of Commerce also filed an *amicus* brief, which the tribunal accepted. The

---

[69] *Methanex* v. *United States* (Petition for *Amicus* Standing of the International Institute for Sustainable Development of 25 August 2000), paras. 3.2–3.3.

[70] *Methanex* v. *United States* (Decision of the Tribunal on Petitions from Third Persons to Intervene as *Amici Curiae* of 15 January 2001).

[71] *Ibid.*, para. 49. Later in the proceedings, the International Institute for Sustainable Development, Bluewater Network, Communities for a Better Environment and the Center for International Environmental Law solicited the tribunal's permission to make another written submission but the tribunal declined to grant such request.

[72] *Methanex* v. *United States* (Final Award of 3 August 2005), Part IV, Chapter B, p. 17, para. 33; also Part IV, Chapter D, p. 4, para. 7, and Part IV, Chapter B, p. 13 para. 27 (citing *Amicus Curiae* Brief of International Institute for Sustainable Development of 9 March 2004, para. 34).

[73] See *UPS* v. *Canada* (*Amicus* Submission of the Canadian Union of Postal Workers and Council of Canadians of 20 October 2005, *Amicus* Submission of the US Chamber of Commerce of 20 October 2005, and *Amicus* Submission of the CUPE and Council of Canadians of 3 November 2005).

[74] *UPS* v. *Canada* (*Amicus* Submission of Canadian Union of Postal Workers and the Council of Canadians of 20 October 2005), para. 63.

tribunal rendered a decision dismissing all of the investor's claims.[75] However, the tribunal's discussion of interpretation of NAFTA provisions at issue did not reference the submissions it received from the *amici*.

Finally, in *Glamis Gold Ltd* v. *United States*, the Canadian investor was a corporation engaged in the extraction and exploration of precious metals in North America. The investor commenced mining operations in a location only after it received confirmation and approval from Bureau of Land Management (BLM) that the land was outside of the wilderness areas where mining was prohibited.[76] In response to complaints from the Quechan Tribe (and others), the US Solicitor of the Interior allowed BLM to reverse its decision and deny the mining permit.[77]

Several groups petitioned the tribunal to participate as *amici*. The Quechan Indian Nation, a United States-recognised American Indian tribe, filed an application[78] arguing that the arbitration processes 'could affect the integrity of the sacred area and the Tribe's relation to it', and 'the manner in which this sacred area and the Tribe's interest in it will be portrayed in this arbitral process is of great concern for native peoples worldwide, who are similarly attempting to protect their irreplaceable sacred places and ensure religious freedoms'.[79] The Tribe informed the tribunal that accepting the submission would 'assist the tribunal in the determination of factual and legal issues by bringing the perspective, particular knowledge and insight that is unique to American tribal sovereign governments'.[80]

After receiving replies to the Tribe's application from both disputing parties, the tribunal accepted the *amicus* submission.[81] The tribunal rendered its award, wherein it denied the claimant's claim for damages[82] and explained why it believed that it was not necessary to reference the *amici* submissions in its opinion:

> it is the Tribunal's view that it should address those filings explicitly in its Award to the degree that they bear on decisions that must be taken. In this case, the Tribunal appreciates the thoughtful submissions made by

---

[75] *UPS* v. *Canada* (Award on the Merits of 24 May 2007).

[76] *Glamis Gold Ltd* v. *United States* (Notice of Arbitration of 9 December 2003), p. 6.

[77] *Ibid.*, pp. 7–10.

[78] *Glamis Gold Ltd* v. *United States* (Quechan Indian Nation Application for Leave to File a Non-Party Submission of 19 August 2005).

[79] *Ibid.*, para. 2.   [80] *Ibid.*, para. 3.

[81] *Glamis Gold Ltd* v. *United States* (Decision Accepting Quechan *Amicus* Application of 16 September 2005).

[82] *Glamis Gold* (Award), para. 830.

a varied group of interested non-parties who, in all circumstances, acted with the utmost respect for the proceedings and [p]arties. Given the Tribunal's holdings, however, the Tribunal does not reach the particular issues addressed by these submissions.[83]

While the *Methanex* outcome was considered a landmark Chapter 11 case in the environmental and civil-society sectors because of the recognition of the importance of civil-society participation in investment arbitration,[84] the three cases demonstrate that the influence that *amici* have in the process is difficult to determine. Even though the tribunals did not actually cite the *amici* submissions in their decisions, the outcomes of the cases were consistent with the overall outcome most *amici* would have preferred. But the fact that *amici* positions are generally not cited in the awards suggests that investment arbitration remains, in the view of the tribunals, a relatively closed system.

E   *Free Trade Commission's binding interpretations*

1   Background

NAFTA has a procedural device to issue binding interpretation of the Agreement's provision, including the provisions of Chapter 11. Article 2001 creates the FTC and in accordance with Article 1131(2): 'An interpretation by the [FTC] of a provision for this Agreement shall be binding on a tribunal established under this Section.'[85]

The FTC is a 'political' and centralised body because the decision-making functions are not delegated to independent and impartial decision-makers. The parties to the Agreement control the outcomes and decisions of the FTC and any binding decision is adopted by consensus of the parties.

The FTC is a powerful mechanism to provide guidance to the interpretation of the NAFTA provision. It is also a useful mechanism when private parties have standing. In the context of investment arbitration it is likely that allegations of violations will be more frequently brought and it is likely that investors may advance more fanciful (and aggressive) legal theories in their disputes than when the access to international dispute-settlement procedures is controlled by the State itself through

---

[83] *Ibid.*, para. 8.
[84] S. E. Gaines, '*Methanex Corp. v. United States*', *American Journal of International Law*, 100 (2006), 683, 689.
[85] NAFTA, Art. 1131(2).

the exercise of diplomatic protection. The investor can pursue very expansive theories about State obligations to protect investment because investors do not have to live with the systemic consequences if these arguments are successful. In this scenario, as put by Professor Alan Sykes, bodies like the FTC 'can serve as *ex post* political filters, undoing the undesirable decisions while avoiding the costs of sorting the larger number of cases that arise *ex ante*'.[86]

As a way to maintain certainty and keep the power of the parties in a dispute under Chapter 11 of the Agreement undisturbed, the tribunal is only bound to follow 'interpretations' of the FTC. This prevents the possibility that, in the middle of a dispute, the parties to NAFTA agree to amend the Agreement for the benefit of the respondent parties. Certainly there is room for debate regarding how far a binding interpretation of the FTC can go before being considered an amendment. Nonetheless, the FTC is an effective mechanism to prevent an undesired evolution of the Agreement.

2 Practice

The FTC has been an effective mechanism to underline the public access of the documents submitted to, or issued by, a Chapter 11 tribunal and to allow the development of *amicus curiae* submissions in the NAFTA Chapter 11 process. The FTC has also issued statements to deal with the formalities required for the Notices of Intent. However, Article 1105 (Minimum Standard of Treatment) is the only substantive discipline that has benefited from an interpretation exercise.

Three decisions encouraged the FTC to clarify the meaning in Article 1105. First, in *Metalclad* v. *Mexico*, a case involving a US investor whose investment expectations were frustrated when local authorities announced that a local grant of permission was required, the arbitral tribunal concluded:

> Mexico failed to assure a transparent and predictable framework for [the investor's] business planning and investment. The totality of [the] circumstances demonstrates a lack of orderly process and timely disposition in relation to an investor of a party acting in the expectation that it would be treated fairly and justly in accordance with the NAFTA.[87]

---

[86] A. O. Sykes, 'Public versus private enforcement of international economic law: Standing and remedy', *Journal of Legal Studies*, 34 (2005), 631, 653.

[87] *Metalclad* v. *Mexico* (ICSID Case No. ARB(AF)/97/1, Award of 30 August 2000), para. 110.

Secondly, in *S. D. Myers* v. *Canada*, a case in which an Ohio corporation was affected by Canada's ban on the export of PCB wastes from Canada to the US, the tribunal concluded:

> Although . . . the Tribunal does not rule out the possibility that there could be circumstances in which a denial of the national treatment provisions of the NAFTA would not necessarily offend the minimum standard provisions, a majority of the Tribunal determines that on the facts of this particular case the breach of Article 1102 essentially establishes a breach of Article 1105 as well.[88]

Finally, in *Pope & Talbot* v. *Canada* the tribunal adopted the 'additive test' by concluding that a 'possible interpretation of the presence of the fairness elements in Article 1105 is that they are *additive* to the requirements of international law'.[89]

These three awards triggered the FTC's adoption of a binding interpretative statement, in which it stated that the concepts of 'fair and equitable treatment' and 'full protection and security' do not require treatment in addition to, or beyond, customary international law as a minimum standard of treatment. It also stated that a determination that there has been a breach of another provision of the NAFTA, or a separate international agreement, does not establish that there has been a breach of Article 1105.[90] The effect of the interpretive note was to freeze the minimum standard of treatment under NAFTA to the standard of customary international law, and to limit possible confusion derived from the so-called 'additive test'.

After the interpretative note was issued, most tribunals have applied directly the FTC interpretation. For example in *Glamis Gold Ltd* v. *United States* the tribunal concluded: 'Article 1105's fair and equitable treatment standard is, as Respondent phrases it, simply "a shorthand reference to customary international law"'.[91]

---

[88] *S. D. Myers Inc.* v. *Canada* (Second Partial Award (Damages) of 21 October 2002), para. 310.

[89] *Pope & Talbot Inc* v. *Canada* (Award on the Merits of Phase 2 of 10 April 2001), para. 110 (emphasis in original).

[90] FTC Notes of Interpretation of Certain Chapter 11 Provisions (31 July 2001).

[91] See *Glamis Gold* (Award), para. 608. See also *International Thunderbird Gaming Corporation* v. *Mexico* (Award of 26 January 2006): 'The tribunal shall accordingly measure the Article 1105(1) of the NAFTA minimum standard of treatment against the customary international law minimum standard, according to which foreign investors are entitled to a certain level of treatment, failing which the host State's international responsibility may be engaged.'

The FTC interpretative statement was an effective device to control the standard under Article 1105 to what the NAFTA parties had allegedly intended. This interpretation has Article 1105 serving as a floor, an absolute bottom, below which a government's conduct is not accepted by the international community. In the wake of this interpretation, the question has been to determine what this customary international law minimum standard actually means.

While most tribunals have adopted this interpretation as the basis to understand Article 1105, the FTC exercise was not free of costs for the NAFTA parties. Not only had some respected international lawyers such as Sir Robert Jennings cautioned about the 'suspicious ... timing and seeming purpose of the three-Party intervention',[92] but at least one tribunal qualified the note as an 'amendment'.[93] Many more criticised the seemingly impartial effects on those cases pending at the time of the issuance of the note. In part due to this criticism and the use of the other explained methods to assist tribunals, the three parties have not relied on this procedural tool to influence the meaning of the substantive standards of NAFTA since then.

IV   Conclusions

The development of international investment law has yielded many tensions which are derived from the scope, standing and structure of investment arbitration. As this chapter has sought to explain, the effects of the increasing pluralism permitted by investment arbitration on the one hand, and the demands for coherence and efficiency on the other, pull in different directions. Thus, concerns about the development of a coherent international investment law are not only of academic interest; they are real and have practical effects.

The majority of IIAs follow a model that makes it more difficult to protect coherence and efficiency than in the past. Therefore, States have adopted different approaches to deal with the tensions and difficulties that investment arbitration generates for the development of a coherent law of foreign investment.

NAFTA, its evolution and its related jurisprudence, serve as an example of how coherence and efficiency can be balanced by understanding the interests involved in a specific dispute and how they relate to the systemic interests involved. A summary of these provisions can be found in Table 16.2.

---

[92] *Methanex Corporation* v. *United States* (Fourth Opinion of Sir R. Jennings QC: 'The meaning of Article 1105(1) of the NAFTA agreement' of 6 September 2001).

[93] *Pope & Talbot Inc.* v. *Canada* (Award on Damages of 31 May 2002), para. 47.

Table 16.2 *Summary of NAFTA and its related jurisprudence*

Procedural feature	Dispute interests	Systemic interests	Effects on substance	Case law
1. Art. 1121 or waiver model of accession.	Establishes consent to arbitration by the claimant. Prevents double redress for the same breach.	Co-ordinates potential jurisdictional conflicts. Limits jurisdictional limits to 'claims for damages only'.	Cross-fertilisation between national and international decision-makers. Positive effects of domestic courts' development of the facts and issues of law.	*Waste Management v. Mexico*; *Fireman's Fund v. Mexico*; *Gami v. Mexico*; *International Thunderbird Gaming Corp. v. Mexico*; *HFCS Tax Disputes v. Mexico*; *Lumber Disputes v. US*
2. Art. 1126 or consolidation of common claims.	Permits efficient disposal of common claims. Maintains parties' procedural balance.	Contemplates the possibility of 'mass' claims. Maintains consistency in addressing common factual and legal questions.	Maintain consistency in addressing common factual and legal questions.	*HFCS Tax Disputes v. Mexico*; *Lumber Disputes v. US*; *Canadian Cattlemen Claims*
3. Art. 1117(3) or consolidation of related parties' claims.	Permits efficient disposal of common claims. Mandates co-ordination of related investors' claims.	Encourages co-ordinated disposal of related claims. Maintains consistency in addressing common factual and legal questions and compensation.	Avoid instances of double or unfair recovery.	*ADM/TLIA v. Mexico*

4. Art. 1128 or participation by party to NAFTA and *amicus curiae*.	Assists the tribunal on matters of treaty interpretation. Assists the tribunals on aspects affecting the public interest. Maintains parties' procedural balance.	Informs treaty interpretation. Permits State's signalling of position on matters of treaty interpretation. Assists NAFTA tribunals on aspect of public interest. Encourages the rendering of fully informed decisions.	'Agreement' of the parties. 'Subsequent practice' within the meaning of Art. 31(3)(b) of the Vienna Convention. Insightful as to the parties' object and purpose. *Amici*: adds a layer of transparency and public legitimacy.	*Glamis Gold Ltd v. US*; *Canadian Cattlemen Claims*; *Metalclad v. Mexico*; *Pope & Talbot v. Canada*; *Methanex v. US*
5. Art. 1131 or FTC binding interpretations.	Assists the tribunal on matters of treaty interpretation. Maintains parties' procedural balance.	Informs treaty interpretation. Controls effects of potential undesirable decisions.	Binding interpretation as 'a shorthand reference to customary international law'. Correct the undesired consequences of additive interpretation of Art. 1105.	*Gami v. Mexico*; *International Thunderbird Gaming Corp. v. Mexico*; *Glamis Gold Ltd v. US*

NAFTA's specific procedural provisions have encouraged a more coherent body of law by adding some procedural tools to co-ordinate specific disputes and the systemic interests involved. Various provisions in Chapter 11 show the importance of the active participation of States in maintaining coherence in international investment law. Indeed, like drops of water that shape stones, Article 1128 submissions may have a remarkable influence in maintaining coherence over time. The consolidation provisions at the request of a respondent encourage cost-effectiveness and promote coherence. Finally, the FTC interpretative powers can be effectively used to control undesired evolutions of the international investment treaty.

17

Navigating the parallel universe of investor–State arbitrations under the UNCITRAL Rules

JUDITH LEVINE[*]

I Introduction

Most investment treaties include a dispute-resolution clause presenting the parties with a range of options for arbitration, the two most common of which are (i) arbitration under the Convention on the Settlement of Investment Disputes between States and Nationals of other States, done at Washington on 18 March 1965 (ICSID Convention),[1] and (ii) arbitration under the United Nations Commission on International Trade Law Arbitration Rules (the UNCITRAL Rules).[2]

Much has been said about the practice and procedure of arbitrations conducted under the auspices of ICSID. ICSID decisions are published.[3] ICSID makes available on its website a list of pending and past cases.[4] There are detailed commentaries on the ICSID Convention and cases

---

[*] The views expressed herein are those of the author alone.

[1] Convention on the Settlement of Investment Disputes between States and Nationals of other States, opened for signature 18 March 1965, 575 UNTS 159, (entered into force 14 October 1966) (ICSID Convention).

[2] United Nations Commission on International Trade Law Arbitration Rules (1976). Throughout this chapter reference is made to the 1976 version of the UNCITRAL Rules. UNCITRAL adopted a revised version of the UNCITRAL Rules (Revised UNCITRAL Rules) on 29 June 2010, which took effect from 15 August 2010; available at www.uncitral. org/pdf/english/texts/arbitration/arb-rules-revised/arb-rules-revised.pdf (last accessed 19 January 2011).

[3] The awards in most of the cases conducted under the original ICSID Rules were published in the ICSID Review, the ICSID website or ILM. Since April 2006, Art. 48(4) of the ICSID Rules provides that ICSID 'shall promptly include in its publications excerpts of the legal reasoning of the Tribunal' regardless of whether the parties have consented to the publication of the award.

[4] See http://icsid.worldbank.org/ICSID/FrontServlet?requestType=CasesRH&actionVal=List Cases (last accessed 19 January 2011).

decided thereunder.[5] Practice guides to ICSID arbitration have been produced by specialists.[6] ICSID recently released a report of statistics about all cases it has ever administered.[7] The ICSID website contains a bibliography of 648 publications about ICSID (and two items about investor–State arbitration under the UNCITRAL Rules).

By contrast, information about investor–State arbitration under the UNCITRAL Rules is less readily accessible, due to different publicity requirements and the fact that no single institution is responsible for administering all cases under the UNCITRAL Rules.[8] Although it is a challenge to find out about investor–State cases under the UNCITRAL Rules, one cannot assume that such cases are any less worthy of attention. They are significant in terms of their volume, the guidance they may offer on procedural and substantive questions, and the impact that they have on the parties, stakeholders and public in each case.

It is possible to glean from various public sources significant numbers – over 120 – of investor–State cases brought under the UNCITRAL Rules. One might assume that even more investor–State disputes have been taking place away from the public eye. One source suggests that in recent years there were more investor–State arbitrations commenced under the UNCITRAL Rules than the ICSID Convention.[9] As discussed below, it appears safe to estimate that at least 25 per cent of new investor–State arbitrations are initiated pursuant to the UNCITRAL Rules. As one indication of the increase in investor–State disputes under

---

[5] See e.g. C. Schreuer *et al.* (eds.), *The ICSID Convention: A commentary,* 2nd edn (Cambridge University Press, 2009); R. Happ, *Digest of ICSID Awards and Decisions: 2003–2007* (Oxford University Press, 2009); E. Gaillard, *La Jurisprudence du CIRDI (ICSID Case Law)* (Paris: Pedone, 2010), II.

[6] See e.g. L. Reed, J. Paulsson and N. Blackaby, *Guide to ICSID Arbitration* 2nd edn (The Hague: Kluwer, 2010).

[7] ICSID Secretariat, *The ICSID Caseload: Statistics,* 2 (2010), http://icsid.worldbank.org/ICSID/Index.jsp (last accessed 21 January 2011).

[8] For general commentary on the UNCITRAL Arbitration Rules (not specific to investor–State disputes), see J. J. van Hof, *Commentary on the UNCITRAL Arbitration Rules: The application by the Iran–US Claims Tribunal* (The Hague: Kluwer, 1991); D. Caron, L. Caplan and M. Pellonää, *The UNCITRAL Arbitration Rules: A commentary* (Oxford University Press, 2006); J. Paulsson and G. Petrochilos, *Revision of the UNCITRAL Arbitration Rules* (Report Commissioned by UNCITRAL, 2006), www.uncitral.org/pdf/english/news/arbrules_report.pdf (last accessed 19 January 2011); J. Castello, 'UNCITRAL Rules' in F.-B. Weigand (ed.), *Practitioner's Handbook on International Commercial Arbitration,* 2nd edn (Oxford University Press, 2009).

[9] L. Peterson, *Investment treaty news: 2006 – A year in review* (2006), www.iisd.org/pdf/2007/itn_year_review_2006.pdf (last accessed 19 January 2011).

the UNCITRAL Rules, the Permanent Court of Arbitration in The Hague (the PCA) has administered over fifty such cases in the last ten years compared to none in the previous decade.[10]

The purpose of this chapter is to shed some light on the number and nature of investor–State disputes submitted to arbitration under the UNCITRAL Rules, a lesser-explored 'parallel universe' to the well-understood ICSID system. The aim is to assist those advising investors and States should they face an UNCITRAL arbitration either by choice (at the stage of drafting an investment agreement or when a dispute has already arisen) or otherwise. Section II covers preliminary issues, including a brief description of the UNCITRAL Rules, an examination of the circumstances in which parties to an investor–State dispute may find themselves submitting to UNCITRAL arbitration, and information about the numbers of investor–State disputes actually submitted to UNCITRAL arbitration. Section III highlights some of the practical and legal features of UNCITRAL arbitration that may distinguish it from ICSID arbitration. Section IV contains some conclusions and considers recently proposed and enacted revisions to the UNCITRAL Rules that account for their application to investor–State disputes.

II Preliminary matters

A What are the UNCITRAL Rules?

The United Nations Commission for International Trade Law (UNCITRAL) was established in 1966 as a subsidiary body of the General Assembly of the United Nations.[11] While international arbitration is one facet of UNCITRAL's work, UNCITRAL itself is not an arbitral institution and has no role in the day-to-day running of any arbitrations.

The UNCITRAL Rules provide a comprehensive set of procedural rules upon which parties may agree for the conduct of arbitral proceedings. The UNCITRAL Rules were designed for use in any type of

---

[10] Data about PCA cases which the parties have agreed to make public are available at the PCA website, www.pca-cpa.org (last accessed 19 January 2011). The PCA is currently providing registry services in 32 investor–State disputes under the UNCITRAL Rules.

[11] The general mandate of UNCITRAL is 'to further the progressive harmonization and unification of the law of international trade': see UNCITRAL, *Origin, Mandate and Composition of UNCITRAL* (2007), www.uncitral.org/uncitral/en/about/origin.html (last accessed 19 January 2011).

commercial dispute anywhere in the world. A majority of cases under the rules are ad hoc international commercial arbitrations where the parties have agreed in their contract to submit disputes to arbitration under the UNCITRAL Rules. The UNCITRAL Rules have also been indirectly used in cases administered by regional and international arbitral institutions with rules modeled on the UNCITRAL Rules.[12] Several bodies resolving public international law disputes have also adopted and adapted the UNCITRAL Rules.[13]

Although the UNCITRAL Rules were not specifically tailored for claims brought by foreign investors against a host State government, they have actually been used in that context since 1981, when the Iran–US Claims Tribunal adopted a modified version of the UNCITRAL Rules for resolving claims in the wake of the 1979 hostage crisis and the subsequent freeze of Iranian assets by the USA.[14] More recently, the UNCITRAL Rules have increasingly been applied to investor–State disputes under bilateral and multilateral investment treaties, in which a State expresses a standing offer to arbitrate investment disputes that an investor can accept at the time a dispute arises. This trend led to the recommendation of some investor–State inspired changes to the rules, discussed in more detail in section IV.[15]

---

[12] e.g. the Australian Centre for International Commercial Arbitration; Kuala Lumpur Regional Centre for Arbitration; Cairo Regional Centre for International Arbitration; and Swiss Chambers Court of Arbitration and Mediation.

[13] e.g. the PCA's various sets of Optional Rules are adapted from the UNCITRAL Rules, www.pca-cpa.org/showpage.asp?pag_id=1188 (last accessed 19 January 2011); the United Nations Compensation Commission was established in 1991 to process claims for compensation stemming from the Gulf War: see SC Res 692, UN SCOR, 2987th meeting, UN Doc. No. S/RES/692 (20 May 1991), which used the rules as a procedural fall back mechanism.

[14] Declaration of the Government of the Democratic and Popular Republic of Algeria Concerning the Settlement of Claims by the Government of the United States of America and the Government of the Islamic Republic of Iran (Claims Settlement Declaration), 1981, www.iusct.org/claims-settlement.pdf (last accessed 19 January 2011). See also G. Sacerdoti, 'Investment arbitration under ICSID and UNCITRAL Rules: Prerequisites, applicable law, review of awards', *ICSID Review – Foreign Investment Law Journal*, 19(1) (2004), 1, 8 (citing UNCTAD's explanation for the inclusion of UNCITRAL Rules as an alternative to ICSID in BITs partly because 'the successful use of UNCITRAL rules by the Iran–United States Claims Tribunals seemed to suggest that these rules were specially adaptable to investor-to-State dispute-settlement').

[15] For a discussion of the UNCITRAL Rules revision process, see J. Levine, 'Current trends in international arbitral practice as reflected in the revision of the UNCITRAL Arbitration Rules', *University of New South Wales Law Journal*, 31(1), (2008), 266; Castello, 'UNCITRAL Rules'.

B   When is there an option to submit an investor–State dispute to arbitration under the UNCITRAL Rules?

Before considering what factors may play a role in choosing UNCITRAL arbitration over other possible forms of resolving investor–State disputes, it is helpful to establish whether such a choice exists in the first place. Most investment treaties provide the investor with a choice of dispute-resolution options. Article 10(5) of the Netherlands–Argentina bilateral investment treaty (BIT) is typical,[16] in that it provides that 'the investor concerned may submit the dispute either to': (a) ICSID, or (b) an ad hoc arbitration tribunal established under the UNCITRAL Rules. The choice between ICSID and UNCITRAL (among other options) is also offered under most multilateral investment agreements.[17]

Many publicly known investor–State arbitrations under the UNCITRAL Rules involve respondent States or investors from States that have signed but not ratified the ICSID Convention (e.g. Canada, Kyrgyz Republic, Thailand), have never signed the ICSID Convention (e.g. India, Mexico, Poland, Russia), or have ratified but later denounced the ICSID Convention (e.g. Bolivia and Ecuador).[18] Thus, while some investment treaties, such as

---

[16] Agreement on Encouragement and Reciprocal Protection of Investments Between the Kingdom of the Netherlands and the Argentine Republic, signed 20 October 1992 (entered into force 1 October 1994).

[17] See e.g. Agreement Establishing the ASEAN-Australia-New Zealand Free Trade Area, signed 27 February 2009, [2010] ATS 1 (entered into force 1 January 2010), Art. 21(1) (AANZFTA); United States–Dominican Republic–Central America Free Trade Agreement, signed 28 May 2004 (entered into force for the United States on 28 February 2006; El Salvador 1 March 2006; Honduras and Nicaragua 1 April 2006; Guatemala 1 July 2006; Dominican Republic 1 March 2007; Costa Rica 1 January 2009), Art. 10.16(3) (offering ICSID, ICSID Additional Facility, UNCITRAL Arbitration Rules); Energy Charter Treaty, signed 17 December 1994, 2080 UNTS 95 (entered into force 16 April 1998), Art. 26(4).

[18] On 6 July 2009, the World Bank received a written notice of denunciation of the ICSID Convention from the Republic of Ecuador. In accordance with Art. 71 of the ICSID Convention, the denunciation took effect six months after the receipt of Ecuador's notice, i.e. on 7 January 2010. On 2 May 2007, the World Bank received a written notice of denunciation from the Republic of Bolivia, which, in accordance with Art. 71, took effect on 3 November 2007. For States that have entered BITs with Bolivia and Ecuador, the ICSID option in those BITs may be thrown into question in light of the denouncement of the ICSID Convention by Bolivia and Ecuador. Thus, Art. XIII(4) of the Agreement between the Government of Canada and the Government of the Republic of Ecuador for the Promotion and Reciprocal Protection of Investments, signed 29 April 1996 (entered into force 6 June 1997), appears to provide the investor with three choices – ICSID, ICSID Additional Facility or UNCITRAL Rules.

the North American Free Trade Agreement (NAFTA),[19] *appear* to offer the investor a choice of arbitral options, in reality, there may be no effective choice if one of the contracting parties falls into one of these categories.

Some BITs, such as the UK–Argentina BIT,[20] make the choice between ICSID and UNCITRAL subject to agreement by *both* the investor party and the State Party, and provide for UNCITRAL Rules as a default failing agreement by the parties. Different again, the Canada–Venezuela BIT provides for UNCITRAL Rules arbitration *only* if ICSID and the ICSID Additional Facility are *unavailable.*[21] Certain BITs provide for UNCITRAL Rules as the *only* arbitration option (subject to the parties agreeing otherwise), for example Article 10 of the Hong Kong–Australia BIT.[22] On the other hand, some treaties, such as the United Kingdom–Malaysia BIT,[23] provide for ICSID as the only arbitration option. Under the Egypt–Thailand BIT,[24] the only arbitration option is ICSID, but as Thailand has never ratified the ICSID Convention, the sole avenue of recourse for an investor would be the local courts.

Quite apart from treaties, investor–State disputes may be submitted to arbitration under the UNCITRAL Rules by virtue of the parties' direct choice to do so in their investment contracts, and/or if the national

[19] North American Free Trade Agreement, signed 17 December 1992, 32 ILM 289 (entered into force 1 January 1994), Art. 1120.

[20] Agreement between the Government of the United Kingdom of Great Britain and Northern Ireland and the Government of the Republic of Argentina for the Promotion and Protection of Investments, signed 11 December 1990 (entered into force 19 February 1993), Art. 8(3).

[21] Agreement between the Government of Canada and the Government of the Republic of Venezuela for the Promotion and Protection of Investments, signed 1 July 1996 (entered into force 28 January 1998), Art. 3. For interpretation of this provision, see *Nova Scotia Power Incorporated (NSPI)* v. *Bolivarian Republic of Venezuela* (Decision on Jurisdiction of 22 April 2010).

[22] Agreement between the Government of Hong Kong and the Government of Australia for the Promotion and Protection of Investments, signed 15 September 1993 (entered into force 15 October 1993), Art. 10. Similarly, Art. 8(5) of the Agreement on Encouragement and Reciprocal Protection of Investments Between the Kingdom of the Netherlands and the Czech and Slovak Federal Republic, signed 29 April 1991 (entered into force 1 October 1992), which is the basis of five of the cases listed in the Appendix, provides only for arbitration by tribunals using the UNCITRAL Rules.

[23] Agreement between the Government of the United Kingdom of Great Britain and Northern Ireland and the Government of Malaysia for the Promotion and Protection of Investments, signed 21 May 1981 (entered into force 21 October 1988).

[24] Agreement between the Government of the Kingdom of Thailand and the Government of the Arab Republic of Egypt for the Promotion and Protection of Investments, signed 18 February 2000 (entered into force).

investment legislation of the host State provides for arbitration of investment disputes pursuant to the UNCITRAL Rules.[25]

The above survey demonstrates that investors and States can find themselves in arbitration under the UNCITRAL Rules by choice of one party, by agreement of both, or by default. Whichever way it happens, it is happening increasingly often, as the following section shows.

C   The number of investor–State disputes under the UNCITRAL Rules

Unlike ICSID, there is no single repository of data about investor–State disputes under the UNCITRAL Rules. UNCITRAL itself does not possess or process such information. A 2010 United Nations Conference on Trade and Development (UNCTAD) study reported the following figures:

> Of the total 357 known disputes, 225 were filed with [ICSID] or under the ICSID Additional Facility, 91 under the [UNCITRAL Rules], 19 with the Stockholm Chamber of Commerce, eight were administered with the Permanent Court of Arbitration in the Hague, five with the International Chamber of Commerce (ICC) and four are ad hoc cases. One further case was filed with the Cairo Regional Centre for International Commercial Arbitration. In four cases the applicable rules are unknown so far.[26]

Those figures suggest that UNCITRAL cases constitute over 25 per cent of all investor–State disputes. The proportion may vary from year to year. According to one report – prepared using published data and off-the-record interviews with counsel, arbitrators and institutions – UNCITRAL cases represented 52 per cent of investor–State disputes commenced in 2006 (see Figure 17.1).[27]

---

[25] The case of *Centerra Gold Inc. (Canada) and Kumtor Gold Company (Kyrgyz Republic)* v. *The Kyrgyz Republic*, administered by the PCA, is a recent example, brought on the basis of an investment agreement and the 2003 Kyrgyz Law No. 66 on investments.

[26] UNCTAD, *Latest Developments in Investor–State Dispute Settlement*, IIA Issues Note No. 1 (2010), UNCTAD Doc. No. UNCTAD/WEB/DIAE/IA/2010/3, www.unctad.org/en/docs/webdiaeia20103_en.pdf (last accessed 19 January 2011).

[27] L. Peterson, *Investment Treaty News: 2006 – A year in review* (2006), www.iisd.org/pdf/2007/itn_year_review_2006.pdf (last accessed 19 January 2011). Peterson found that:

> the ICSID facility – the most visible and well-known forum for investment disputes – handled less than half of the treaty-based investment arbitrations launched in 2006 . . . [F]urther number of cases could have been launched without being detected . . . Certainly, it is possible that the proportion of cases taking place *outside* of ICSID is even more pronounced . . .

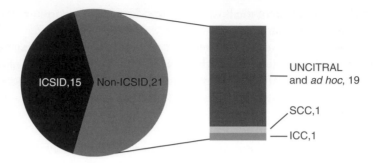

Figure 17.1: 2006 known treaty cases by rules of arbitration

In 2009, there were twenty-five cases commenced at ICSID and fifteen publicly known cases commenced under the UNCITRAL Rules. One leading commentator notes that it is possible that a 'non-trivial percentage' of investor–State arbitrations are proceeding under the UNCITRAL Rules which public sources have not managed to identify.[28] There are several other public sources from which one can estimate that at least 25 per cent of investor–State disputes are commenced under the UNCITRAL Rules.[29] Such sources cumulatively show over 120 publicly known investor–State disputes commenced since 1994, more than half of which were commenced in the last five years.

III   In what ways is investor–State arbitration under the UNCITRAL Rules really that different from ICSID arbitration?

This section draws attention to some of the differences that practitioners can expect between an ICSID arbitration and an investor–State arbitration under the UNCITRAL Rules. Two general observations are made at the outset.

---

[28] G. Born and E. Shenkman, 'Confidentiality and transparency in commercial and investor–State international arbitration' in C. Rogers and R. Alford (eds.), *The Future of Investment Arbitration* (Oxford University Press, 2009), pp. 4, 28.

[29] These sources include UNCTAD (http://www.unctad.org/iia-dbcases/cases.aspx), Investment Claims (www.investmentclaims.com), Investment Treaty Arbitration (http://ita.law.uvic.ca/), Investment Arbitration Reporter (www.iareporter.com), *Investment Treaty News* (www.investmenttreatynews.org), *Global Arbitration Review* (www. globalarbitrationreview.com), Energy Charter Secretariat (www.encharter.org) and the Permanent Court of Arbitration (www.pca-cpa.org).

First, typically investor–State arbitrations will in reality be similar in most respects under both sets of rules. One should expect that the substantive outcome of the dispute would be the same irrespective of the chosen forum to the extent the same BIT governs the dispute.[30] Procedurally also, there will be similarities, including a preliminary phase involving constitution of the tribunal, procedural conferences, establishment of a timetable, document exchanges and possibly requests to the tribunal for provisional measures. Under both systems, tribunals determine their own competence and often bifurcate proceedings into separate jurisdictional and merits phases.[31] There will usually be written and oral pleadings, and the award will be signed, reasoned and final, subject only to limited recourse for review.[32]

Secondly, factors distinct from the rules and forum can influence how an arbitration plays out in practice. These might include the amount at stake, the parties' budgets, the legal and cultural background of counsel and arbitrators, and the attitudes of the arbitrators to cross-examination and document production. Such factors can impact an arbitration's cost, speed, length and style as much as the choice of any rules.[33]

---

[30] See discussion of *Romak SA* v. *The Republic of Uzbekistan*, below in section III.G.

[31] UNCITRAL Rules, Art. 21; ICSID Rules, Art. 42; see also Revised UNCITRAL Rules, Art. 23.

[32] The fact that the two procedures can be similar in practice is illustrated by the related cases of *Suez, Sociedad General de Aguas de Barcelona SA and Vivendi Universal SA* v. *Argentine Republic* (ICSID Case No. ARB/03/19) (*Suez*); *Suez, Sociedad General de Aguas de Barcelona SA, and InterAguas Servicios Integrales del Agua SA* v. *Argentine Republic* (ICSID Case No. ARB/03/17) (*InterAguas*); and *AWG Group Ltd* v. *Argentine Republic* (*AWG*) (under the UNCITRAL Rules). Those cases arose from similar circumstances concerning all three claimants' investments in a water concession in Buenos Aires and the alleged failure by Argentina to apply a previously agreed tariff system. Claimants Suez and Vivendi relied on the Agreement between the Government of the French Republic and the Government of the Republic of Argentina on the Encouragement at Reciprocal Protection of Investments, signed 3 July 1991 (entered into force 3 March 1993) (which allowed them to choose ICSID arbitration), but the claimant AWG relied on the Agreement between the Government of the United Kingdom of Great Britain and Northern Ireland and the Government of the Republic of Argentina for the Promotion and Protection of Investments, signed 11 December 1990 (entered into force 19 February 1993) which, as noted above, requires both parties to agree on the forum, failing which arbitration under the UNCITRAL Rules is the default. The members of the tribunal are identical in all three cases and the cases are joined for all purposes. One set of pleadings was filed in all three cases, one hearing was held for all three cases at both the jurisdiction and merits phases, and one decision on jurisdiction was issued by the tribunal covering all three cases. See procedural history discussion in *InterAguas* (Decision on Jurisdiction of 16 May 2006) and *InterAguas* (Decision on Liability of 30 July 2010).

[33] See R. Dolzer and C. Schreuer, *Principles of International Investment Law* (Oxford University Press, 2008), p. 226: 'Given the freedom of arbitrators to determine the

A   *Confidentiality and publicity*

Because it affects whether we are aware of the very existence of a dispute, a natural starting place to consider the differences between ICSID and UNCITRAL is the extent to which case details are made public. Given the public-interest implications of many foreign investment disputes, the lack of transparency requirements for cases under the UNCITRAL Rules has been the source of criticism and was a hotly contested issue in discussions of the Working Group tasked with revising the UNCITRAL Rules.[34] Differences between the ICSID and UNCITRAL regimes relate to: (i) publicity about the commencement of the arbitration; (ii) submissions by non-disputing parties; (iii) public access to hearings; and (iv) publication of awards.

Under ICSID Administrative and Financial Regulation 22, the Secretary-General of ICSID is required to make public information on the registration of all requests for conciliation or arbitration and to indicate in due course the date and method of the termination of each proceeding. A list of pending and concluded cases appears on the ICSID website.

Since amendments introduced in 2006, ICSID Rule 37 provides that: 'After consulting both parties, the Tribunal may allow a person or entity that is not a party to the dispute to file a written submission with the Tribunal regarding a matter within the scope of the dispute.' Rule 37 sets out the factors a tribunal should consider in determining whether to allow such a filing. The tribunal can allow such submissions even if a party objects. Both parties have an opportunity to present their observations on non-disputing party submissions. This rule has been applied recently to allow submissions by human rights organisations in a case brought by European mining investors challenging so-called Black Economic Empowerment measures as contrary to South Africa's BITs,[35] and

---

procedure, a major difference often lies less with the written rules than with the personal background and experience of the arbitrator, especially in regard to their familiarity with the principles of common law and civil law'. Given the typically large size of claims under investment treaty claims (at least 50 cases being for claims over $100 million), it is usual that highly experienced, confident and sophisticated arbitrators are selected to oversee the procedure.

[34] See Levine, 'Current trends', pp. 279–80; Castello, 'UNCITRAL Rules', para. 16.25; Born and Shenkman, 'Confidentiality and transparency', p. 33; S. Jagusch and J. Sullivan, 'A comparison of ICSID and UNCITRAL arbitration' in M. Waibel *et al.* (eds.), *The Backlash against Investment Arbitration: Perceptions and reality* (The Hague: Kluwer, 2010), p. 95.

[35] *Piero Foresti, Laura de Carli and ors* v. *Republic of South Africa* (ICSID Case No. ARB (AF)/07/01). In that case, the NGOs were granted limited access to documents. The claimants in that case have since discontinued the proceedings.

by environmental non-governmental organisations (NGOs) seeking to participate in a case between a UK investor and Tanzania over water supply facilities.[36]

Non-parties might also attend ICSID hearings under certain conditions. Rule 32 of the ICSID Arbitration Rules provides that:

> Unless either party objects, the Tribunal, after consultation with the Secretary-General, may allow other persons, besides the parties, their agents, counsel and advocates, witnesses and experts during their testimony, and officers of the Tribunal, to attend or observe all or part of the hearings, subject to appropriate logistical arrangements.

Finally, under ICSID Institution Rule 22, the ICSID Secretary-General is required to publish, with the consent of both disputing parties, reports of awards rendered by arbitral tribunals in ICSID proceedings. Since the 2006 amendments, ICSID Arbitration Rule 48(5) provides that excerpts of the Tribunal's legal reasoning shall be published by ICSID even absent consent.

The UNCITRAL Rules, by contrast, contain no obligation on the parties or any tribunal to publicise the existence of their dispute. They are silent on the participation of non-disputing parties. With respect to hearings, Article 25(4) of the UNCITRAL Rules states that: 'Hearings shall be held *in camera* unless the parties agree otherwise.'[37] Under Article 32(5), the award 'may be made public only with the consent of both parties'.[38]

The fact that the UNCITRAL Rules do not *oblige* public disclosure of all or part of the proceedings does not mean that arbitration under the UNCITRAL Rules is always and necessarily opaque. Rather, it leaves the decisions about how public the proceedings will be in the hands of the parties and the tribunal in any given case. Here, Article 15(1) of the UNCITRAL Rules is also important as a guiding provision on the conduct of proceedings under the UNCITRAL Rules.[39]

---

[36] *Biwater Gauff (Tanzania) Ltd* v. *United Republic of Tanzania* (ICSID Case No. ARB 05/22, Procedural Order No. 5 on *amicus curiae* of 2 February 2007).

[37] See also Revised UNCITRAL Rules, Art. 28(3).

[38] See also Revised UNCITRAL Rules, Art. 34(5).

[39] Art. 15(1) provides that: 'Subject to these Rules, the arbitral tribunal may conduct the arbitration in such manner as it considers appropriate, provided that the parties are treated with equality and that at any stage of the proceedings each party is given a full opportunity of presenting his case.' See also Revised UNCITRAL Rules, Art. 17(1), which adds that: 'The arbitral tribunal, in exercising its discretion, shall conduct the proceedings so as to avoid unnecessary delay and expense and to provide a fair and efficient process for resolving the parties' dispute.'

That rule has been relied on by several tribunals to allow the participation of *amici curiae*, the first of which was *Methanex Corporation* v. *United States*,[40] involving a claim of over almost US$1 billion arising from a ban on a gasoline additive that had environmental implications. The *Methanex* tribunal held that 'by Article 15(1) of the UNCITRAL Arbitration Rules it has the power to accept *amicus* submissions' of environmental NGOs, and considered that it could be appropriate to *exercise* that power in the case, having weighed the undoubted public interest of the arbitration against other factors such as cost and the risk of imposing an extra burden on the parties.[41] This approach has been followed by other tribunals, including ICSID tribunals before the ICSID Rules were amended to provide expressly for non-disputing party submissions,[42] and was an impetus to the NAFTA Free Trade Commission issuing a statement on the participation of non-disputing parties in NAFTA arbitrations.[43]

The PCA has seen different approaches to confidentiality across its investor–State caseload. In some cases neither party wishes to make the proceedings public, and additional confidentiality provisions might in fact be included in terms of appointment or procedural orders to bolster the limited provisions present in the UNCITRAL Rules. In other cases, the party urging for the proceedings to be kept private is the respondent State. And in other cases, it is the investor who urges the proceedings be kept private, often expressing concerns about revealing business information or overly politicising a dispute.

Where both parties have agreed to publicise details of the dispute, the source of the consent and the extent of transparency varies from case to case. Two examples of PCA cases in which the parties agreed to 'full' transparency are *TCW* v. *Dominican Republic*,[44] and the *Abyei Arbitration*.[45] The former was a dispute between a US investor in the

---

[40] *Methanex Corporation* v. *United States* (Decision on *Amici Curiae* of 15 January 2001); see also *United Parcel Service of America Inc.* v. *Government of Canada* (Decision on *Amici Curiae* of 17 October 2001); *Glamis Gold Ltd* v. *United States of America* (Decision on Application and Submission by Quechan Indian Nation of 16 September 2005).

[41] *Methanex*, paras. 47–51.

[42] In *Suez*, the tribunal followed *Methanex* in allowing *amicus* briefs, on the basis that Art. 44 of the ICSID Convention gave the tribunal similarly broad powers as Art. 15(1) of the UNCITRAL Rules: see *Suez* (Order in Response to a Petition for Participation as *Amicus Curiae* of 17 March 2006).

[43] NAFTA Free Trade Commission, *Statement of the Free Trade Commission on Non-Disputing Party Participation*, www.naftaclaims.com/Papers/Nondisputing-en.pdf (last accessed 20 January 2011).

[44] *TCW Group Inc. and Dominican Energy Holidings LP* v. *The Dominican Republic*.

[45] *The Government of Sudan* v. *The Sudan People's Liberation Movement/Army*.

electricity sector and the Dominican Republic brought pursuant to the Central America–Dominican Republic–United States Free Trade Agreement (DR–CAFTA). Article 10.20(3) of DR–CAFTA gives the tribunal 'the authority to accept and consider *amicus curiae* submissions' and Article 10.21 sets out detailed provisions on transparency, including publication of documents and public hearings. On the basis of the treaty provisions and consultations among the tribunal, the PCA and the parties, all of the documents in the case, including pleadings, transcripts and orders, are available on the PCA's website. Public hearings had been planned in New York and detailed procedural directions were issued for submissions by non-disputing CAFTA Member States and interested *amici curiae*. The case settled.

The *Abyei Arbitration* between the Government of Sudan and the Sudanese People's Liberation Movement/Army was not an investor–State dispute, but a case brought under the PCA's Optional Rules for Disputes between Two Parties only one of which is a State, which are a modified version of the UNCITRAL Rules with identical Articles 24(5) and 32(4). Given the importance of that case to peace, stability and resources in the region, the parties agreed in their *compromis* and at the first procedural hearing[46] that the proceedings would be fully transparent and all the pleadings, transcripts and orders were made available on the PCA website. The hearings were open to the public (hundreds of Sudanese people, diplomats and members of the public attended), were webcast live and video-archived on the PCA's website (attracting thousands of hits). These two cases illustrate that maximal transparency is feasible for disputes under the UNCITRAL Rules, if the parties so agree.

Alternatively, parties may agree to publicise only *some* details about their case, and to do so *after* the dispute is resolved. In some PCA-administered cases, the parties have agreed to make certain details available on the PCA's website,[47] or have maintained confidentiality throughout the proceedings but agreed to publication of the award after

---

[46] Arbitration Agreement between the Government of Sudan and the Sudan People's Liberation Movement/Army on Delimiting Abyei Area (7 July 2008), Art. 8, www.pca-cpa.org/upload/files/Abyei%20Arbitration%20Agreement.pdf (last accessed 20 January 2011) and Transcript of Proceedings, *The Government of Sudan* v. *The Sudan People's Liberation Movement/Army* (Permanent Court of Arbitration, Procedural Hearing, 24 November 2008), www.pca-cpa.org/upload/files/Transcript_Abyei_241108%20_rev2.pdf (last accessed 20 November 2011).

[47] The list of cases on the PCA website includes e.g. *HICEE BV* v. *The Slovak Republic*, *Telekom Malaysia Berhad* v. *Government of Ghana* (initiated 2003), and *Centerra Gold Inc. & Kumtor Gold Co.* v. *Kyrgyz Republic* (2009).

completion of the case or a certain phase of the case.[48] This latter approach is consistent with what the authors of a recent commentary urge should be a 'balanced approach' concluding that 'confidentiality should not automatically be abandoned in favor of transparency in the investor–State context'.[49]

One commentator has observed that one reason why 'UNCITRAL investment arbitration is still an attractive alternative to ICSID arbitration' is that decisions by tribunals acting under the UNCITRAL Rules:

> have achieved a balance between the interests of those who wanted to open the proceedings to non-disputing parties and the public, on the one hand, and the interests of the parties to have an efficient dispute settlement without undue delay, extra costs and lack of confidentiality, on the other, on the basis of a flexible interpretation of article 15 of the Rules on the power of the tribunal, and article 25(4) on confidentiality.[50]

Details about investor–State disputes under the UNCITRAL Rules have come into the public domain via means other than party agreement or tribunal direction. For example, basic facts about a case can emerge via reporting obligations under securities legislation affecting publicly held companies and requests under freedom of information legislation affecting States. Details can also come to light as a result of related court proceedings.[51] Interesting questions arise about the appropriate remedy when one of the parties makes unilateral statements to the media, in the absence of consent of the parties to go public and sometimes notwithstanding confidentiality orders in place in the arbitration.

B   Institutional support

One of the main features of the ICSID Convention was the creation of a specialised centre for investor–State disputes,[52] described by Dolzer and Schreuer as follows:

---

[48] See e.g. *Eureko* v. *The Slovak Republic* (2010), *Romak SA (Switzerland)* v. *The Republic of Uzbekistan* (2009) and *Saluka Investments BV* v. *Czech Republic* (2008).

[49] Born and Shenkman, 'Confidentiality and transparency', p. 37 (offering practical ways in which tribunals can address public-interest concerns without endangering the benefits associated with confidentiality).

[50] N. Horn, 'Current use of the UNCITRAL Arbitration Rules in the context of investment arbitration', *Arbitration International*, 24(4) (2008), 587, 600.

[51] Recently, details relating to a dispute between Chevron and Ecuador have come to light as a result of the proceedings before courts in New York and a case between a telecommunications company and the Government of Belize by virtue of a Supreme Court proceeding in Belize: see e.g. www.globalarbitrationreview.com (last accessed 20 January 2011).

[52] ICSID Convention, Chapter I.

[ICSID] offers standard clauses for the use of the parties, detailed rules of procedure, and institutional support. The institutional support extends not only to the selection of arbitrators but also the conduct of arbitration proceedings: for instance, each tribunal is assisted by a legal secretary who is a staff member of ICSID; venues for hearings are arranged by ICSID; all financial arrangements surrounding the arbitration are administered by ICSID.[53]

The UNCITRAL Rules do not expressly provide for administrative support from any institution.[54] But UNCITRAL arbitration does not need to be in an administrative vacuum in a purely ad hoc sense. One practitioner observed in 2008 that:

> the fact that the parties select arbitration under UNCITRAL Rules does not necessarily deprive them of the benefits of the administrative support of an institution. In particular, the Permanent Court of Arbitration in The Hague, the world's oldest standing arbitral institution, has considerable institutional expertise in handling claims involving sovereign states and is being chosen to administer an increasing number of investment treaty cases under UNCITRAL Rules.[55]

A 2008 study found that institutional arbitration is generally preferred to ad hoc arbitration, with corporations interviewed indicating 'that the main reason for using institutional arbitration was the reputation of the institutions and the convenience of having the case administered by a third party'.[56] Most investor–State arbitrations these days are handled by an institution to some degree, whether it be the PCA, the International Chamber of Commerce (ICC), Stockholm Chamber of Commerce (SCC), London Court of International Arbitration (LCIA) or the ICSID

---

[53] Dolzer and Schreuer, *Principles of International Investment Law*, p. 223. See also Sacerdoti, 'Investment arbitration', p. 46.

[54] The PCA is the only institution mentioned in the UNCITRAL Rules, but that is in the context of its Secretary-General being the default body to designate an appointing authority for arbitrator selections and challenges where the parties have not already agreed an appointing authority: Arts. 6–8 and 12).

[55] C. McLachlan, 'Investment treaty arbitration: The legal framework' in A. J. van den Berg (ed.), *ICCA Congress Series No. 14* (Alphen aan den Rijn: Wolters Kluwer, 2009), pp. 95, 128. See also *UNCITRAL Notes on Organizing Arbitral Proceedings* (1996), paras. 21–3, www.uncitral.org/uncitral/en/uncitral_texts/arbitration/1996Notes_proceedings.html (last accessed 20 January 2011); and P.-J. Le Connu and D. Drabkin, 'Assessing the role of the Permanent Court of Arbitration in the peaceful settlement of international disputes' (2010) 27 *L'Observateur des Nations Unies* 181.

[56] Price Waterhouse Coopers and Queen Mary University, *International Arbitration: Corporate attitudes and practices 2008* (the *PWC Study*), www.pwc.co.uk/eng/publications/international_arbitration_2008.html (last accessed 20 January 2011). Note that the study was not exclusively concerned with investor–State disputes in particular, but rather international commercial arbitration generally.

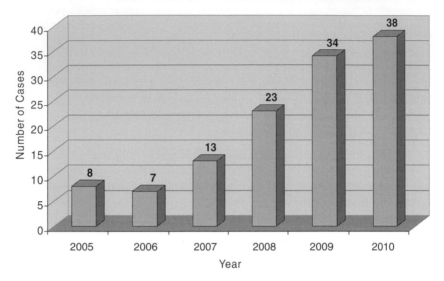

Figure 17.2:   BIT and MIT-based investor–State arbitrations administered by the PCA under the UNCITRAL Arbitration Rules

itself. As already mentioned, the PCA has seen an increase in investor–State activity, as Figure 17.2 illustrates.

Institutional administration can save on costs because it lightens the arbitrators' load with respect to administrative tasks. An institution provides support in running the case, managing deposits, maintaining archives and arrangements for hearings. The PCA benefits from highly qualified multinational and multilingual staff lawyers with experience in the public and private sector, who serve as administrative secretaries to tribunals. An institution can also serve sensitive roles as intermediary in coming to fee arrangements between the parties and arbitrators, and resolving arbitrator appointments and challenges. Having an award associated with an established organisation may also be perceived as adding a certain gravitas.[57]

For cases administered by the PCA, a respondent State may also have access to the PCA's Financial Assistance Fund to defray

---

[57] See e.g. P. D. Friedland, *Arbitration Clauses for International Contracts* (Juris, 2007), p. 40: 'an enforcing court can be assured that an award rendered under the aegis of an established arbitral institution has ensued from a proceeding under well-tested rules applied by accomplished arbitrators'; J. D. M. Lew, L. Mistelis and S. Kroll, *Comparative International Commercial Arbitration* (The Hague: Kluwer, 2003), p. 34: 'A strongly perceived advantage of institutional arbitration is the cachet behind the name of the institution.'

costs,[58] the parties may use the Peace Palace hearing facilities free of charge, and may hold hearings abroad through a network of co-operation agreements with other institutions and Host Country Agreements with PCA Member States.[59]

Parties to an investor–State dispute under the UNCITRAL Rules have a large degree of flexibility in how much administrative support they may seek from an institution, whether full service, none at all, or an 'institution-lite' model, which might, for example, entail just the management of a deposit and maintenance of an archive of correspondence.

C Appointment of arbitrators

Under both the UNCITRAL Rules and ICSID Convention, the default number of arbitrators is three,[60] but the two regimes differ when a party has failed to appoint an arbitrator or the two sides have been unable to agree on a presiding arbitrator.

Under Article 7 of the UNCITRAL Rules, if a party has failed to appoint an arbitrator within thirty days of being notified on the other party's choice, then the first party may request an 'appointing authority' to appoint the second arbitrator.[61] The appointing authority 'may exercise its discretion in appointing the arbitrator'. If there is no agreement on a presiding arbitrator in thirty days, then the presiding arbitrator shall be appointed by the appointing authority, by way of a list procedure or exercise of discretion.[62]

---

[58] A description of the Financial Assistance Fund and its Terms of Reference appear in the PCA's *Annual Reports*: see e.g. PCA, *Annual Report 2009*, http://www.pca-cpa.org/ showpage.asp?pag_id=1069 (last accessed 20 January 2011).

[59] e.g. in a recent investor–State dispute involving parties from the Americas, hearings were held in San Jose, Costa Rica, pursuant to the PCA's agreement with Costa Rica and co-operation agreement with the InterAmerican Court of Human Rights. Hearings in another investor–State dispute are to be held this year in Singapore pursuant to the PCA's agreement with Singapore and cooperation agreement with the Singapore International Arbitration Centre, and pursuant to a 2009 Host Country Agreement with the Government of Mauritius, the PCA has opened an office in Africa, operational since 2011. For practical examples of how tribunals and parties use the PCA, see *TCW* v. *Dominican Republic* (Procedural Order No. 1 of 23 June 2008), at www.server.nijmedia.nl/pca-cpa. org/upload/files/10%20PO1.pdf (last accessed 20 January 2011), or *Abyei Arbitration* (Terms of Appointment of 24 November 2008), para. 6, www.pca-cpa.org/upload/files/ Abyei_Terms_of_Appointment_signed_241108.pdf (last accessed 20 January 2011).

[60] UNCITRAL Rules, Art. 5; ICSID Rules, Art. 37(2)(b)). See also Revised UNCITRAL Rules, Art. 7(1).

[61] See also Revised UNCITRAL Rules, Art. 9.

[62] Art. 6(4) of the UNCITRAL Rules provides the following guidance to the appointing authority: 'In making the appointment, the appointing authority shall have regard to

The parties may agree upon an appointing authority in advance. Some investment treaties, including the ASEAN–Australia–New Zealand Free Trade Agreement (AANZFTA),[63] and the France–India BIT,[64] specify that the PCA Secretary-General shall serve as the appointing authority,[65] others designate the ICSID Secretary-General, President of the ICC or the ICJ, but many remain silent. If the appointing authority has not been agreed, the UNCITRAL Rules provide that a party may request the Secretary-General of the PCA to designate an appointing authority. The PCA Secretary-General has received over 400 requests to designate or act as an appointing authority under the UNCITRAL Rules since they were promulgated in 1976[66] (approximately 10 per cent in the last ten years have arisen from investor–State disputes), following a pattern of growth demonstrated in Figure 17.3.

Under ICSID Convention Article 38, if the tribunal has not been constituted within 90 days after notice of registration of the request by the Secretary-General or such other period as the parties may agree, the President of the World Bank (the Chairman) shall, 'at the request of either party and after consulting both parties as far as possible, appoint the arbitrator or arbitrators not yet appointed'.[67] Arbitrators appointed by the Chairman shall not be nationals of either party to the dispute.

such considerations as are likely to secure the appointment of an independent and impartial arbitrator and shall take into account as well the advisability of appointing an arbitrator of a nationality other than the nationalities of the parties.' See also Revised UNCITRAL Rules, Art. 6(7). The Revised Rules clarify that the parties may appoint the Secretary-General of the PCA directly as the appointing authority.

[63] Agreement Establishing the Association of Southeast Asian Nations (ASEAN)-Australia-New-Zealand Free Trade Area, signed 27 February 2009 (entered into force 1 January 2010 for Australia, New Zealand, Brunei, Burma, Malaysia, the Philippines, Singapore and Vietnam; 12 March 2010 for Thailand; 1 January 2011 for Laos; 4 January 2011 for Cambodia).

[64] Agreement between the Government of the French Republic and the Government of the Republic of India on the Encouragement and Reciprocal Protection of Investments, signed 2 September 1997 (entered into force 17 May 2000).

[65] AANZFTA defines 'appointing authority' for purposes of the Article referring to UNCITRAL Arbitration as 'the Secretary-General of the Permanent Court of Arbitration': Chapter 11, Art. 18(4)(a)(ii); France–India BIT, Art. 9(3)(b).

[66] See generally UNCITRAL, *Settlement of Commercial Disputes – UNCITRAL Arbitration Rules: Report of the Secretary-General of the Permanent Court of Arbitration on its activities under the UNCITRAL Arbitration Rules since 1976* (7 December 2006), www.uncitral.org/uncitral/en/commission/sessions/40th.html (last accessed 20 January 2011); and S. Grimmer, 'The expanding role of the appointing authority under the UNCITRAL Arbitration Rules 2010' (2011) 28 *Journal of International Arbitration* 5.

[67] See Jagusch and Sullivan, 'A comparison', pp. 81–2.

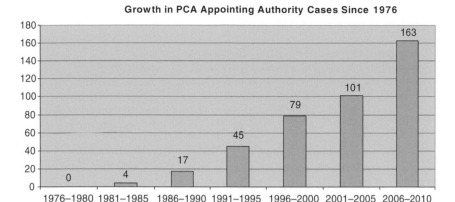

Figure 17.3:   Growth in PCA appointing authority cases since 1976

Article 40 provides that when the Chairman appoints arbitrators according to Article 38 he must do so from the ICSID Panel of Arbitrators. The ICSID Panel is comprised of up to four persons nominated by each Contracting State and ten persons designated by the Chairman. Under Article 14 of the ICSID Convention, those on the Panel shall be 'persons of high moral character and recognized competence in the fields of law, commerce, industry or finance, who may be relied upon to exercise independent judgment'. Arbitrators appointed (by the parties) from outside the Panel shall possess the same qualities.

There are thus two limitations in appointments under the ICSID Convention that are not present in the UNCITRAL Rules. First, in ICSID appointments, if the parties have not appointed arbitrators, the pool from which the Chairman can choose is limited to the ICSID Panel. Secondly, the Chairman is not permitted to appoint a national of one of the parties (even for the co-arbitrators), whereas under Article 6(4) of the UNCITRAL Rules the appointing authority is required only to take into account the advisability of appointing an arbitrator of a nationality other than the nationalities of the parties and only to do so in relation to the presiding arbitrator.

A further difference is that whereas the UNCITRAL Rules reference the need for arbitrators to be 'independent and impartial', Article 14 of the ICSID Convention refers to 'independent judgment' with no mention of impartiality, an issue discussed further below in the section on challenges.

Lastly, the timing of arbitrators' disclosures is slightly different. Under Article 9 of the UNCITRAL Rules:

> A prospective arbitrator shall disclose to those who approach him in connection with his possible appointment any circumstances likely to give rise to justifiable doubts as to his impartiality or independence. An arbitrator, once appointed or chosen, shall disclose such circumstances to the parties unless they have already been informed by him of these circumstances.[68]

Any conflict is thus likely to come to the parties' attention *before* formal appointment, which is earlier than a conflict is likely to come to the parties' attention in an ICSID arbitration, as ICSID arbitrators do not need to sign a declaration until the first session of the tribunal, *after* their formal appointment.[69]

D   Challenges to arbitrators

On the subject of arbitrator challenges, the ICSID Rules differ from the UNCITRAL Rules in terms of: (i) the timing of challenges; (ii) the standard to be applied to challenges; and (iii) the method of resolving challenges.

Article 10 of the UNCITRAL Rules provides that 'any arbitrator may be challenged if circumstances exist that give rise to justifiable doubts as to the arbitrator's impartiality or independence'.[70] Article 11 sets a fifteen-day limit from the date of appointment or of the challenging party becoming aware of the circumstances giving rise to the challenge, after which date any challenge is deemed waived.[71] The challenge must be in writing, state reasons, and be notified to the other party, the challenged arbitrator and other members of the tribunal. Under Article 12, if the other party does not agree to the challenge or the arbitrator does not withdraw, then the challenge is submitted to the appointing authority for decision.[72] The appointing authority might already have

---

[68] See also Revised UNCITRAL Rules, Art. 11.
[69] ICSID Rules, Rule 6(2). Such declaration should contain a statement of '(a) . . . past and present professional, business and other relationships (if any) with the parties and (b) any other circumstances that might cause [the arbitrator's] reliability for independent judgment to be questioned by a party'.
[70] See also Revised UNCITRAL Rules, Art. 12.
[71] See also Revised UNCITRAL Rules, Art. 13(1).
[72] See also Revised UNCITRAL Rules, Art. 13(4).

been specified in the arbitration agreement, be agreed by the parties at the time, or designated by the Secretary-General of the PCA.

Article 1 of the UNCITRAL Rules states that where the parties have agreed to refer their disputes to arbitration under the UNCITRAL Rules 'then such disputes shall be settled in accordance with these Rules *subject to such modification as the parties may agree*'.[73] Thus, the above-described procedures can be modified by the parties if they so choose. No equivalent provision exists in the ICSID Convention or Rules. While certain provisions in the ICSID Convention are predicated with the words 'except as the parties otherwise agree', those pertaining to arbitrator challenges are not.

Article 57 of the ICSID Convention provides that a party may propose the disqualification of an arbitrator 'on account of any fact indicating a manifest lack of the qualities required by paragraph (1) of Article 14'. Article 58 of the ICSID Convention provides that:

> [the] decision on any proposal to disqualify a[n] arbitrator shall be taken by the other members of the . . . Tribunal . . . provided that where those members are equally divided, or in the case of a proposal to disqualify a sole . . . arbitrator, or a majority of . . . arbitrators, the Chairman [of the World Bank] shall take that decision . . .

ICSID Rule 9 states that a 'party proposing the disqualification of an arbitrator pursuant to Article 57 of the Convention shall promptly, and in any event before the proceeding is closed, file its proposal with the Secretary-General, stating its reasons therefor'. The proposal is then submitted to the members of the tribunal and the other side. The challenged arbitrator may furnish explanations without delay. The other arbitrators shall promptly consider and vote on the proposal in the absence of the challenged arbitrator. If they are divided, then the Chairman is informed via the Secretary-General. The arbitration proceeding is suspended until a decision is taken on the challenge.

With respect to the timing of challenges, the ICSID Rules are less certain than the UNCITRAL Rules (which impose a specific time limit), because they require a party to propose disqualification 'promptly' and set the latest time at the close of proceedings. This 'anomaly' has led to the suggestion that the ICSID Rules set a period of thirty days from the date of the arbitrator's Rule 6(2) declaration or from the date when the

---

[73] Emphasis added.

challenging party knew or ought to have known of the circumstance giving rise to the challenge.[74]

It has already been noted that the ICSID Convention refers to 'independence' (in the sense of lack of connection to a party) but not 'impartiality' (in the sense of lack of predisposition). In one other respect the standard for challenges under the ICSID Convention has been described as out of line with the UNCITRAL Rules, international best practices as reflected in the International Bar Association (IBA) Guidelines on Conflict of Interest in International Arbitration,[75] national law and the rules of other arbitral institutions. Where the UNCITRAL Rules (and most other sets of rules) require the disqualification of an arbitrator if circumstances create 'justifiable doubts' as to his or her impartiality and independence, Article 57 of the ICSID Convention requires circumstances 'indicating a manifest lack of the qualities required' of arbitrators.

The difference came into play in a challenge to an arbitrator in the three Argentine water cases mentioned in note 32 – *Suez*, *InterAguas* and *AWG*. The respondent challenged an arbitrator when they learned that she was a non-executive director of a bank that held shares in two of the claimants. It was agreed by the parties that the two co-arbitrators who needed to decide the challenge for the purposes of the two ICSID cases would also decide the challenge for purposes of the UNCITRAL arbitration (the UNCITRAL Rules permitting the parties to modify any of the procedural rules set out therein).[76] The co-arbitrators described the UNCITRAL Rules test as being an objective, not a subjective, standard,

---

[74] A. Sheppard, 'Arbitrator independence in ICSID abitration' in C. Binder *et al.* (eds.), *International Investment Law for the 21st Century: Essays in honour of Christoph Schreuer* (Oxford University Press, 2009), p. 131.

[75] IBA, *IBA Guidelines on Conflicts of Interest in International Arbitration* (22 May 2004), www.ibanet.org/Document/Default.aspx?DocumentUid=E2FE5E72-EB14–4BBA-B10D-D33DAFEE8918 (last accessed 20 January 2011), Part I (General Standards Regarding Impartiality, Independence and Disclosure). Part I(1) provides that: 'Every arbitrator shall be impartial and independent of the parties at the time of accepting an appointment to serve and shall remain so during the entire arbitration proceeding . . .'; Part I(2)(b) provides that an arbitrator should be disqualified 'if facts or circumstances exist, or have arisen since the appointment, that, from a reasonable third person's point of view having knowledge of the relevant facts, give rise to justifiable doubts as to the arbitrator's impartiality or independence . . .'; Part I(2)(c) provides that: 'Doubts are justifiable if a reasonable and informed third party would reach the conclusion that there was a likelihood that the arbitrator may be influenced by factors other than the merits of the case as presented by the parties in reaching his or her decision.'

[76] See especially *Suez*, *InterAguas* and *AWG* (Decision on a Second Proposal for the Disqualification of a Member of the Arbitral Tribunal of 12 May 2008).

with the relevant question being: 'Would a reasonable, informed person viewing the facts be led to conclude that there is a justifiable doubt as to the challenged arbitrator's independence and impartiality?'[77] The bank in question was not a shareholder of the claimant in the UNCITRAL case, and so the connection was held insufficient to give rise to justifiable doubts. The approach of the co-arbitrators for the two ICSID claimants was different because the test under Article 57 of the ICSID Convention is not a 'justifiable doubts' standard but a 'manifest lack of qualities' standard. The arbitrators cited an earlier ICSID challenge decision, which described the ICSID test as setting a high threshold as follows:

> It is important to emphasise that the language of Article 57 places a heavy burden of proof on the Respondent to establish facts that make it obvious and highly probable, not just possible, that [the challenged arbitrator] is a person who may not be relied upon to exercise independent and impartial judgment.[78]

Applying the criteria of proximity, intensity, dependence and materiality, the arbitrators ultimately rejected the challenge.

Under ICSID, challenges are decided by the other two arbitrators, whereas under the UNCITRAL Rules (and most other systems), the challenge is resolved by a neutral third party (the appointing authority). This is described by one commentator as an 'unusual feature of ICSID' which makes it:

> inevitable that a challenging party will have further doubts as to whether the remaining arbitrators will have a conflict of interest themselves when determining a challenge, in that they may have been or might expect one day to be challenged themselves, and may have a (subliminal) desire to set the test at a high level.[79]

That same commentator, after providing a survey of ICSID arbitrator challenges noted that: 'It is interesting to speculate whether any of these cases would have been decided differently if (i) the test had been justifiable doubts rather than manifest lack of independent judgment and/or (ii) the challenge had been decided by a third party rather than the co-arbitrators.'[80] He recommends that the ICSID rules be changed such that (i) arbitrators must be expressly 'independent and impartial'; (ii) the 'manifest lack' of qualities test be replaced with a 'justifiable doubts' test;

---

[77] *Ibid.*, para. 22.
[78] *Compaña de Aguas del Aconquija & Vivendi Universal* v. *Argentine Republic* (ICSID Case No. ARB/97/3, Decision on the Challenge to the President of 3 October 2001).
[79] Sheppard, 'Arbitrator independence', pp. 155–6.   [80] *Ibid.*, p. 144.

(iii) challenges should be decided by an independent ad hoc challenge committee which should consider a doubt to be justifiable if a 'fair-minded and informed observer, having considered the facts, would conclude that there was a real possibility that the tribunal was not independent or not impartial'; and (iv) the time for challenging an arbitrator be a fixed period.[81]

E   Provisional measures

Provisional measures ordered by domestic courts have been described as a 'normal feature of international commercial arbitration'.[82] In the investor–State context, Schreuer, Malintoppi, Reinisch and Sinclair point out that 'provisional measures may be initiated by the host State, usually in its own courts, or by the foreign investor, usually in the courts of another State'.[83]

Under Article 26 of the UNCITRAL Rules, a party may request an arbitral tribunal to take necessary interim measures and that such interim measures may be established in the form of an interim award.[84] Article 26(3) of the Rules states that: 'A request for interim measures addressed by any party to a judicial authority shall not be deemed incompatible with the agreement to arbitrate, or as a waiver of that agreement.'

Article 47 of the ICSID Convention provides that: 'Except as the parties otherwise agree, the Tribunal may, if it considers that the circumstances so require, recommend any provisional measures which should be taken to preserve the respective rights of either party.' The interaction of Article 47 with Article 26 of the ICSID Convention has generated some controversy about whether parties to an ICSID arbitration could approach national courts for interim measures. Article 26 of the ICSID Convention states that: '[the] [c]onsent of the parties to arbitration

---

[81]   *Ibid.*, p. 156. It has become publicly known that in one ICSID case, some modifications along the lines of the above were in fact agreed by the parties in writing in 2008, the terms of which agreement were applied when a challenge arose in 2009. The parties agreed that arbitrator challenges would be resolved by the PCA Secretary-General applying the IBA Guidelines. A challenge to an arbitrator under this agreed process was upheld. The arbitrator then resigned and was replaced in accordance with Art. 15 of the ICSID Convention. Any concerns expressed by some commentators about the capacity of parties to modify challenge procedures set out in the ICSID Convention thus became theoretical.

[82]   Schreuer *et al.* (eds.), *The ICSID Convention*, p. 394.

[83]   *Ibid.*, p. 395.   [84]   Cf. Revised UNCITRAL Rules, Art. 26.

under this Convention shall, unless otherwise stated, be deemed consent to such arbitration to the exclusion of any other remedy'.

Up until an amendment to the ICSID Rules in 1984, judicial and arbitral practice and scholarly debate were sharply divided on the permissibility of provisional measures by domestic courts in the context of an ICSID arbitration.[85] The question was clarified when ICSID Arbitration Rule 39(6) was introduced, stating:

> Nothing in this Rule shall prevent the parties, provided that they have so stipulated in the agreement recording their consent, from requesting any judicial or other authority to order provisional measures, prior to or after the institution of the proceeding, for the preservation of their respective rights and interests.

Thus, provisional measures by domestic courts in ICSID arbitration are permissible *only if* the parties have expressly agreed to them in the instrument recording their consent to arbitration. One commentator has expressed some doubts about the practical significance of this difference for certain types of interim measures because of limited jurisdiction by courts over sovereign States and immunities preventing pre-award attachment of a State's assets.[86]

One new feature of the ICSID Rules with respect to interim measures is ICSID Rule 39(5):

> If a party makes a request pursuant to paragraph (1) before the constitution of the Tribunal, the Secretary-General shall, on the application of either party, fix time limits for the parties to present observations on the request, so that the request and observations may be considered by the Tribunal promptly upon its constitution.

There is no equivalent provision in the UNCITRAL Rules.

F Preliminary avenues for disposing of frivolous claims

ICSID arbitration involves two potential opportunities for a case to be dismissed at a preliminary stage. Article 36(3) of the ICSID Convention provides that the Secretary-General 'shall register the request unless he finds, on the basis of the information contained in the request, that the

---

[85] The debate is summarised in Schreuer *et al.* (eds.), *The ICSID Convention*, pp. 395–400.
[86] McLachlan, 'Investment treaty arbitration', p. 133. Jagusch and Sullivan likewise note that 'it is inherently unlikely that that the parties will reach [an agreement under ICSID Arbitration Rule 39(6)]' because one party will desire the provisional measures, while the other will oppose them: Jagusch and Sullivan, 'A comparison', p. 90.

dispute is manifestly outside the jurisdiction of the Centre'. There is no
equivalent provision in the UNCITRAL Rules, partly because there is
no equivalent to Article 25 of the ICSID Convention ('Jurisdiction of the
Centre') and partly because there is no single institution involved in
administering all cases.

However, a comparable check against the institution of manifestly
baseless claims under the UNCITRAL Rules lies in the appointing
authority process. Article 8 of the UNCITRAL Rules provides that:

> When an appointing authority is requested to appoint an arbitrator . . .
> the party which makes the request shall send to the appointing authority
> a copy of the notice of arbitration, a copy of the contract out of or in
> relation to which the dispute has arisen and a copy of the arbitral
> agreement if it is not contained in the contract. The appointing authority
> may require from either party such information as it deems necessary to
> fulfil its function.[87]

The PCA Secretary-General requires similar information in serving the
role of designating authority under the rules.[88] While the appointing
authority does not have the power to dismiss a claim, it can ensure that
the proceeding has properly been commenced by a notice of arbitration
served on the respondent, before proceeding to constitute a tribunal.

In 2006, ICSID Rule 39(5) was introduced to allow parties within
thirty days of the constitution of the tribunal and before the first session
of the tribunal to 'file an objection that a claim is manifestly without
legal merit'. The tribunal, 'after giving the parties the opportunity to
present their observations on the objection, shall, at its first session or
promptly thereafter, notify the parties of its decision on the objection'.
No equivalent exists under the UNCITRAL Rules. There have so far been
three decisions under this rule.[89] In the first two cases, the tribunals held
there to be a high threshold for any respondent wishing to make a Rule
41(5) objection. Only when a claim is clearly, certainly and obviously
without legal merits is such a preliminary objection likely to be

---

[87] See also Revised UNCITRAL Rules, Art. 6(6).
[88] See PCA, *Designation of Appointing Authority* (2009), www.pca-cpa.org/showpage.asp?
pag_id=1062 (last accessed 20 January 2011).
[89] *Trans-Global Petroleum Inc.* v. *Jordan* (ICSID Case No. ARB/07/25, Decision on the
Respondent's Objection under Rule 41(5) of the ICSID Arbitration Rules of 12 May
2008); *Brandes Investment Partners LP v. Bolivarian Republic of Venezuela* (ICSID Case
No. ARB/08/3, Decision on the Respondent's Objection under Rule 41(5) of the ICSID
Arbitration Rules of 2 February 2009); and *Global Trading Resource Corp. and Globex
International Inc.* v. *Ukraine* (ICSID Case No. ARB/09/11, Award of 1 December 2010)
(*Global Trading*).

successful. In neither case did the respondent succeed in having the case dismissed.[90] In the third case, Ukraine was successful in having the case dismissed on the basis that 'the sale and purchase contracts entered into by the Claimants are pure commercial transactions that cannot on any interpretation be considered to constitute "investments" within the meaning of Article 25 of the ICSID Convention'.[91]

G Jurisdictional limitations

Whether proceeding under ICSID or the UNCITRAL Rules, the tribunal is the judge of its own competence.[92] Both systems provide that challenges to jurisdiction be made as soon possible, and no later than in the counter-memorial or statement of defence.[93] Both systems provide that a tribunal may rule on a plea concerning its jurisdiction as a preliminary question.[94] Where the two systems diverge with respect to jurisdiction is Article 25 of the ICSID Convention.[95] There has been debate about whether the terms of Article 25 impose 'outer limits of ICSID jurisdiction', restricting a tribunal's jurisdiction beyond any limitations present in a BIT.

For example, different approaches have applied to the requirement that the dispute arise 'directly out of an investment', as well as nationality considerations set out in Article 25(2)(b) of the ICSID Convention. Writing in 2004, one commentator speculated that:

> It could happen that the subject matter of a dispute qualifies as an investment under a BIT, but does not qualify as such for the purposes of ICSID jurisdiction. This might explain the reference to arbitration under the UNCITRAL Arbitration Rules or to the rules of some private arbitral institution[s] in provisions of BITs, even when both States are

---

[90] For a discussion of this provision, see C. Lamm, H. Pham and C. Giorgetti, 'Interim measures and dismissal under the 2006 ICSID Rules' in C. A. Rogers and R. P. Alford (eds.), *The Future of Investment Arbitration* (Oxford University Press, 2009), p. 89.

[91] *Global Trading*, para. 57.

[92] See ICSID Convention, Art. 41(1); UNCITRAL Rules, Art. 21; Revised UNCITRAL Rules, Art. 23(1).

[93] See ICSID Convention, Art. 41(1), UNCITRAL Rules, Art. 21(3); Revised UNCITRAL Rules, Art. 23(2).

[94] See ICSID Convention, Art. 41(4); UNCITRAL Rules, Art. 21(4)); Revised UNCITRAL Rules, Art. 23(3).

[95] Art. 25 of the ICSID Convention provides that: 'The jurisdiction of the Centre shall extend to any legal dispute arising directly out of an investment, between a Contracting State . . . and a national of another Contracting State, which the parties to the dispute consent in writing to submit to the Centre . . .'

parties to the ICSID Convention. Under those rules, the qualification of
the dispute as arising out of an investment would be immaterial for
competence purposes.[96]

The question of whether Article 25 of the ICSID Convention imposes
criteria additional to the often broad definition of 'investment' found in
BITs was at the heart of *MHS* v. *Malaysia*,[97] where a sole arbitrator found
that the resources spent by a company that contracted with the Malaysian government to salvage a shipwreck did not constitute an investment
within the meaning of Article 25(1) of the ICSID Convention. The
claimant argued that it had made an investment as broadly defined in
the BIT.[98] However, the sole arbitrator first turned to the meaning of
'investment' in Article 25(1) of the ICSID Convention and reviewed
seven cases of importance 'to discern a broad trend which emerges from
ICSID jurisprudence on the "investment" requirement'. He identified
typical hallmarks of an 'investment', from cases such as *Salini* v.
Morocco,[99] and *Joy Mining* v. *Egypt*.[100] These hallmarks were 'Regularity
of Profits and Returns', 'Contributions', 'Duration of the Contract', 'Risks
Assumed Under the Contract', and 'Contribution to the Economic
Development of the Host State'. The arbitrator held that the question
of contribution to the host State's economic development assumed
significant importance because the other typical hallmarks of 'investment' were either not decisive or appeared only to be superficially
satisfied. In this respect, the claimant's contract was more like a normal
services contract than one that provided lasting benefit to the positive
economic development of the State. The arbitrator concluded that the
claimant's contract was not an 'investment' within the meaning of
Article 25(1) of the ICSID Convention, and, having done so, found it

---

[96] Sacerdoti, 'Investment arbitration', p. 8.
[97] *Malaysian Historical Salvors, SDN, BHD* v. *Malaysia* (ICSID Case No. ARB/05/10,
Decision on Jurisdiction of 17 May 2007).
[98] The BIT stated:

> For the purposes of the Agreement, (1)(a) 'investment' means every kind of
> asset and in particular, though not exclusively, includes: . . . (iii) claims to
> money or to any performance under contract, having a financial value; . . .
> (v) business concessions conferred by law or under contract, including
> concessions to search for, cultivate, extract or exploit natural resources.

[99] *Salini Costruttori SpA and Italstrade SpA* v. *Morocco* (ICSID Case No. ARB/00/4.
Decision on Jurisdiction of 23 July 2001), paras. 37–40.
[100] *Joy Mining Machinery Limited* v. *Egypt* (ICSID Case No. ARB/03/11, Award on Jurisdiction of 6 August 2004), paras. 31–63.

unnecessary to discuss whether the contract was an 'investment' under the BIT definition.[101]

On review by an ICSID ad hoc annulment committee, the majority sharply disagreed with the sole arbitrator and annulled his award because:

(a) it altogether failed to take account of and apply the [BIT] defining 'investment' in broad and encompassing terms but rather limited itself to its analysis of criteria which it found to bear upon the interpretation of Article 25(1) of the ICSID Convention;

(b) its analysis of these criteria elevated them to jurisdictional conditions, and exigently interpreted the alleged condition of a contribution to the economic development of the host State so as to exclude small contributions, and contributions of a cultural and historical nature;

(c) it failed to take account of the preparatory work of the ICSID Convention and, in particular, reached conclusions not consonant with the travaux in key respects, notably the decisions of the drafters of the ICSID Convention to reject a monetary floor in the amount of an investment, to reject specification of its duration, to leave 'investment' undefined, and to accord great weight to the definition of investment agreed by the Parties in the instrument providing for recourse to ICSID.[102]

A dissenting member of the ad hoc annulment committee argued that a significant contribution to the host State's economy must be made for an investment to exist.[103]

The requirement of nationality has also drawn support from some ICSID tribunals for the notion that Article 25 of the ICSID Convention sets 'outer limits beyond which party consent would be ineffective'.[104] For example, the majority in *TSA* v. *Argentina*[105] held that:

---

[101] See also *Toto Construzioni Generali SpA* v. *Republic of Lebanon* (ICSID Case No. ARB/07/12, Decision on Jurisdiction of 11 September 2009).

[102] *Malaysian Historical Salvors, SDN, BHD* v. *Malaysia* (ICSID Case No. ARB/05/10, Decision on the Application for Annulment of 16 April 2009).

[103] *Malaysian Historical Salvors, SDN, BHD* v. *Malaysia* (ICSID Case No. ARB/05/10, Dissenting Opinion of Judge Mohamed Shahabuddeen of 19 February 2009).

[104] *The Rompetrol Group NV* v. *Romania* (ICSID Case No. ARB/06/3, Decision on Respondent's Preliminary Objections to Jurisdiction and Admissibility of 18 April 2008), para. 80. See e.g. *TSA Spectrum de Argentina SA* v. *Argentina Republic* (ICSID Case No. ARB/05/5, Award of 19 December 2008) (*TSA*), para. 134, where the majority held that the criterion of 'foreign control' in Art. 25(2)(b) of the ICSID Convention imposes an objective limit beyond which the tribunal's jurisdiction cannot extend, even where a specific agreement between the States exists.

[105] *Ibid.*

> Article 25 of the ICSID Convention defines the ambit of ICSID's juris-
> diction. In other words, it defines the extent, hence also the objective
> limits, of this jurisdiction (including the jurisdiction of tribunals estab-
> lished therein) which cannot be extended or derogated from even by
> agreement of the Parties.[106]

For the majority in that case, this meant that they must pierce the veil of
a corporate entity to determine whether it was genuinely foreign controlled. Piercing through the Dutch ownership of the Argentine claimant, the majority denied jurisdiction because the latter was ultimately
controlled by an Argentine citizen.[107] The dissenting arbitrator argued
that the treaty definition of nationality must control and that the 'limit
sovereignty imposes on how international law is made, enjoins [arbitra-
tors] to vindicate, rather than ignore, the agreements reached by two
states'.[108]

The above discussion shows that under ICSID arbitration, parties
should bear in mind not only the terms of the BIT, but also possibly
the 'outer limits' of Article 25 of the ICSID Convention. One might
expect this to be a clear difference between arbitrations under ICSID and
those under the UNCITRAL Rules, but a recent case shows that even
under the UNCITRAL Rules, a tribunal might consider importing some
objective criteria into the term 'investment' as part of a Vienna Convention analysis to interpret the term as used in a BIT, even absent Article 25
of the ICSID Convention. In *Romak* v. *Uzbekistan*,[109] the tribunal held
that a one-off delivery contract for wheat did not amount to an 'investment' for purposes of the Swiss–Uzbekistan BIT.[110] The *Romak* tribunal
rejected an argument by the claimant that the definition of the term
'investment' may vary depending on the investor's choice between
UNCITRAL or ICSID arbitration, and the claimant's suggestion that
the definition of 'investment' in UNCITRAL proceedings (i.e. under the
BIT alone) is wider than in ICSID Arbitration. The tribunal considered
that such views would 'imply that the substantive protection offered by
the BIT would be narrowed or widened, as the case may be, merely by
virtue of a choice between the various dispute resolution mechanisms

---

[106] *Ibid.*, para. 134.   [107] *Ibid.*, para. 162.
[108] TSA *Spectrum de Argentina SA* v. *Argentina Republic* (ICSID Case No. ARB/05/5,
Dissenting Opinion of Grant D. Aldonas [undated]), para. 34.
[109] *Romak SA* v. *The Republic of Uzbekistan* (Award of 26 November 2009).
[110] Agreement between the Swiss Confederation and the Republic of Uzbekistan Concerning the Promotion and Reciprocal Protection of Investments, signed 16 April 1993
(entered into force 5 November 1993).

sponsored by the Treaty. This would be both absurd and unreasonable.'[111] The tribunal found that the term 'investment' in a BIT has an 'inherent meaning (irrespective of whether the investor resorts to ICSID or UNCITRAL arbitral proceedings) entailing a contribution that extends over a certain period of time and that involves some risk'.[112] The investment made by Romak did not meet those criteria.

This area remains controversial. While a party might consider that opting for arbitration under the UNCITRAL Rules could avoid any potential jurisdictional hurdles encountered by the 'outer limits' of jurisdiction set by Article 25 of the ICSID Convention, even under the UNCITRAL Rules, there is a chance that a tribunal could impose jurisdictional limitations based on the 'inherent' meaning of terms in a BIT.

H   Costs

The UNCITRAL Rules and ICSID Convention contain slightly different language with respect to costs. Article 61(2) of the ICSID Convention leaves the question of costs to the broad discretion of the tribunal.[113] The UNCITRAL Rules differ from the ICSID Rules insofar as Article 40(1) of the UNCITRAL Rules creates a presumption that the losing party will 'in principle' cover both sides' administrative costs (including the arbitrators' fees and expenses, expenses of witnesses, institutional support and any appointing authority).[114] On the other hand, the successful party's legal fees are not included in the presumption in Article 40(1), and under Article 40(2), the tribunal has a wide discretion to allocate such expenses.[115] If the tribunal does choose to allocate legal fees, the terms of

---

[111] *Romak*, para. 194.   [112] *Ibid.*, para. 207.

[113] Art. 61(2) provides that:

> In the case of arbitration proceedings the Tribunal shall, except as the parties otherwise agree, assess the expenses incurred by the parties in connection with the proceedings, and shall decide how and by whom those expenses, the fees and expenses of the members of the Tribunal and the charges for the use of the facilities of the Centre shall be paid. Such decision shall form part of the award.

[114] Art. 40(1) provides that: 'Except as provided in paragraph 2, the costs of arbitration shall in principle be borne by the unsuccessful party. However, the arbitral tribunal may apportion each of such costs between the parties if it determines that apportionment is reasonable, taking into account the circumstances of the case.' See also Revised UNCITRAL Rules, Art. 42(1).

[115] Art. 40(2) provides that: 'With respect to the costs of legal representation and assistance referred to in article 38, paragraph (e), the arbitral tribunal, taking into account the circumstances of the case, shall be free to determine which party shall bear such costs or

Article 38(1)(e) provides that legal fees will only be allocated 'if such costs were claimed during the arbitral proceedings, and only to the extent that the arbitral tribunal determines that the amount of such costs is reasonable'.

Although there are differences on the face of the two rules, there does not seem to be great difference in practice because costs decisions under either ICSID or UNCITRAL have been very specific to the circumstances of particular cases. One 2003 study comparing costs decisions under the two regimes confirmed that tribunals under either system have examined cost issues on a case-by-case basis and more often than not divided arbitration costs equally while ordering each party to bear its own legal fees.[116] A recent example of this approach being taken, despite the respondent clearly prevailing, was in *Romak* v. *Uzbekistan* (a case in which the author of the 2003 study sat as arbitrator). The *Romak* tribunal summarised the current state of play with respect to costs in investor–State arbitration under different sets of rules. The tribunal noted that the respondent had 'prevailed entirely as a matter of jurisdiction' and pondered whether 'as a consequence, the Claimant should bear more than half of the arbitration costs and/or pay the Respondent's legal fees and expenses'.[117] The tribunal observed a general trend that costs should be equally apportioned between the investor and State Parties, irrespective of the outcome, while acknowledging some exceptions for obstructive behaviour.[118] The tribunal noted that one of the reasons for this trend is that:

> investment treaty tribunals are called upon to apply a novel mechanism and substantive law to the resolution of these disputes. Thus the initiation of a claim that is ultimately unsuccessful is more understandable than would be the case in commercial arbitration where municipal law applies.[119]

Accordingly, although differences appear on the face of the ICSID and UNCITRAL Rules with respect to costs, the outcome may be similar. One may question whether, in the future as the number of investor–State disputes rises, the novelty of the legal issues will wear off so as to remove the justification for splitting costs equally.

---

may apportion such costs between the parties if it determines that apportionment is reasonable.'

[116] N. Rubins, 'The allocation of costs and attorney's fees in investor–State arbitration', *ICSID Review – Foreign Investment Law Journal*, 18(1) (2003), 109, 126.

[117] *Romak*, para. 249. [118] *Ibid.*, paras. 250–1. [119] *Ibid.*, para. 250.

Finally, as a practical matter, due to the language of Article 38(e),[120] parties to UNCITRAL arbitrations would be advised to include a claim for legal costs from the outset, and to substantiate these before the proceedings are closed.[121]

I   Annulment of awards

One of the most obvious areas of difference between investor–State disputes under the ICSID Convention and those under the UNCITRAL Rules is the review of awards. Proceedings under the ICSID Convention are self-contained and domestic courts have no power to set aside or otherwise review ICSID awards.[122] In place of domestic review, the ICSID Convention establishes a mechanism for review by an Annulment Committee on five specific grounds enumerated in Article 52(1) of the ICSID Convention:

- (a) that the Tribunal was not properly constituted;
- (b) that the Tribunal has manifestly exceeded its powers;
- (c) that there was corruption on the part of a member of the Tribunal;
- (d) that there has been a serious departure from a fundamental rule of procedure; or
- (e) that the award has failed to state the reasons on which it is based.

By contrast, investor–State awards under the UNCITRAL Rules are subject to review by the national courts at the seat of the arbitration and according to the standards of review provided for arbitral awards generally under national law.[123] Annulment could in theory be sought in hundreds of jurisdictions applying disparate approaches. But, as one commentator has observed:

---

[120] See also Revised UNCITRAL Rules, Art. 40(1).

[121] The failure by a party to do so in a recent PCA-administered investment arbitration caused some procedural issues in claiming costs after a termination order had already been issued recording the parties' settlement.

[122] Dolzer and Schreuer, *Principles of International Investment Law*, p. 223.

[123] McLachlan, Shore and Weiniger, *International Investment Arbitration*, p. 65: 'domestic courts have consistently held that non–ICSID BIT arbitrations are reviewable as "commercial" for the purposes of Article 1(3) of the New York Convention and the UNCITRAL Model Law' (citing as examples the decisions of the Supreme Court of British Columbia in *CME* v. *Czech Republic, United Mexican States* v. *Metalclad Corp.* [2001] BCSC 664; the Svea Court of Appeal in *Czech Republic* v. *CME Czech Republic BV* (Case No. T8735–01) and the England and Wales High Court in *Occidental* v. *Ecuador* [2005] 2 Lloyd's Rep. 707).

in practice, a degree of consistency has been achieved through homogen-
izing legislation (e.g., adoption of the UNCITRAL Model Law [which
provides limited grounds for review]) and through the choice of a limited
number of places of arbitration where judiciaries are perceived to be
consistent in their application of annulment standards.[124]

A study of fifty-one non-ICSID treaty awards published in the period
from 1996 to early 2008 found that all but one of them was rendered in
jurisdictions 'that most of us would consider safe havens for arbitration,
with Sweden, Canada, Switzerland, the United States and the United
Kingdom being the usual suspects'.[125] The author of that study pointed
out that choosing ICSID:

> does not necessarily mean choosing an established set of well-defined
> standards. While courts in the above jurisdictions can draw on a wealth of
> commercial arbitration cases applying the relevant standards, there are
> only fifteen ICSID annulment decisions to date that may shed light on
> how the ICSID standards will be applied.

He concluded that:

> while excesses do occasionally occur both within and outside the ICSID
> system, at least in the recent past both ad hoc committees and domestic
> courts have exercised proper restraint when reviewing treaty awards.[126]

The same author also noted a difference in mindset between ad hoc
committees (a subculture within the subculture of treaty arbitration
within the subculture of international arbitration, invariably composed
of distinguished arbitrators heavily specialised in the field) and those
who make up the 'typically sophisticated and experienced judiciary for
whom the review of treaty awards represents only a tiny little portion of
the immensely more varied mix of matters that they adjudicate on any
given day'. He suggests that the latter may be more likely to show
deference to the tribunal and less likely than an ad hoc committee to

---

[124] B. W. Daly and F. C. Smith, 'Comment on the differing legal frameworks of investment
treaty arbitration and commercial arbitration as seen through precedent, annulment,
and procedural rules' in A. J. van den Berg (ed.), *ICCA Congress Series No. 14* (Alphen
aan den Rijn: Wolters Kluwer, 2009), pp. 151, 156. See also Horn, 'Current use of the
UNCITRAL Arbitration Rules', p. 591.

[125] G. Verhoosel, 'Annulment and enforcement review of treaty awards: To ICSID or not to
ICSID' in A. J. van den Berg (ed.), *ICCA Congress Series No. 14* (Alphen aan den Rijn:
Wolters Kluwer, 2009), pp. 285, 292.

[126] *Ibid.* See also McLachlan, 'Investment treaty arbitration', p. 136 (noting that despite the
'self-contained' nature of ICSID as contrasted with investor–State disputes under
UNCITRAL being subject to national court review, 'analysis suggests a degree of
convergence').

engage in a 'detailed autopsy' of awards.[127] Two very recent decisions by ICSID annulment committees overturning the decisions of arbitral tribunals have reignited discussions about the ICSID annulment system as compared with annulment proceedings before national courts.[128]

J Enforcement

Possibly the feature of ICSID arbitration considered most attractive compared to non-ICSID arbitration of investor–State disputes is the enforcement mechanism under Article 54 of the ICSID Convention, which offers what Dolzer and Schreuer describe as 'an effective system of enforcement'.[129] Article 54 does not necessarily apply to non-pecuniary obligations imposed by an award, for which the national courts may be the only recourse.[130]

One prominent arbitrator recently recalled that 'whenever I had a case as counsel for an investor where arbitration was available under ICSID I would advise the client to use it'.[131] The reasons he gave included that:

---

[127] Verhoosel, 'Annulment and enforcement', p. 306.

[128] *Sempra Energy International* v. *The Argentine Republic* (ICSID Case No. ARB/02/16, Decision on the Argentine Republic's Application for Annulment of the Award of 29 June 2010) and *Enron Corporation and Ponderosa Assets LP* v. *Argentine Republic* (ICSID Case No. ARB/01/3, Decision on the Application for Annulment of the Argentine Republic of 30 July 2010).

[129] Dolzer and Schreuer, *Principles of International Investment Law*, p. 224. ICSID Convention, Art. 54 provides:

(1) Each Contracting State shall recognize an award rendered pursuant to this Convention as binding and enforce the pecuniary obligations imposed by that award within its territories as if it were a final judgment of a court in that State. A Contracting State with a federal constitution may enforce such an award in or through its federal courts and may provide that such courts shall treat the award as if it were a final judgment of the courts of a constituent state.

(2) A party seeking recognition or enforcement in the territories of a Contracting State shall furnish to a competent court or other authority which such State shall have designated for this purpose a copy of the award certified by the Secretary-General. Each Contracting State shall notify the Secretary-General of the designation of the competent court or other authority for this purpose and of any subsequent change in such designation.

(3) Execution of the award shall be governed by the laws concerning the execution of judgments in force in the State in whose territories such execution is sought.

[130] Verhoosel, 'Annulment and enforcement', p. 310.

[131] A. W. Driver, 'A world-class international arbitrator speaks! An interview with Judge Charles Brower', *Metropolitan Corporate Counsel*, 8 (2009), 24.

> ICSID has its own internal system for any review of awards and review is very limited, it's difficult to get a case annulled within that system and there's no other recourse because of the exclusivity of the ICSID Convention [and] . . . [Every] state party is required to enforce in its courts any ICSID award with the same force and effect as if it were a final judgment in that country, not subject to further appeal to the highest courts of that state. The defense of sovereign immunity is preserved, but still it's very helpful to claimants.[132]

However, as noted by that arbitrator, Article 55 of the ICSID Convention expressly preserves the laws relating to sovereign immunity from execution.

Outside of the ICSID system, a party must rely on the New York Convention[133] for recognition and enforcement of awards.[134] The New York Convention allows national courts to refuse recognition and enforcement on one of five grounds: (a) invalidity of the arbitration agreement; (b) lack of due process; (c) excess of mandate by the arbitrators; (d) improper constitution of the tribunal; and (e) the award is not binding or has been set aside or suspended in the country where it was rendered.[135] Additionally, the court may refuse recognition on the grounds of non-arbitrability and public policy of an enforcing State.[136]

There are no reported court decisions refusing to recognise or enforce a non-ICSID investment treaty award. Recently, a US Appeals Court confirmed an award in an investor–State arbitration under the UNCITRAL Rules.[137] According to the 2008 PwC study, parties reported high levels of compliance by States or State enterprises with arbitral awards generally. Compliance often resulted in either the renegotiation of contracts between corporations and the State, or payment of damages to the investor by State enterprises rather than by the State itself. The study actually found that corporations experienced fewer significant problems in enforcing arbitral awards against States or State enterprises than in enforcing awards against private-sector entities. Of the minority of

---

[132] *Ibid.*, p. 24.
[133] Convention on the Recognition and Enforcement of Foreign Arbitral Awards, signed 10 June 1958, 330 UNTS 38 (entered into force 7 June 1959) (New York Convention).
[134] In court proceedings instituted by Ecuador to set aside the arbitral award in *Occidental Exploration and Production Company* v. *The Republic of Ecuador* (Final Award of 1 July 2004), the England and Wales High Court held that it can review UNCITRAL awards outside the context of the New York Convention: see *Ecuador* v. *Occidental Exploration & Petroleum Company* [2005] EWHC 774 (Comm). See also Jagusch and Sullivan, 'A comparison', p. 103.
[135] *New York Convention*, Art. V(1).   [136] *Ibid.*, Art. V(2).
[137] *Argentine Republic* v. *National Grid plc*, No. 10–7093 (DC Circ., 2011).

participants that had experience of enforcing awards against States or State enterprises, over half experienced no significant problems. A small proportion had experienced significant difficulties and the interviews indicated that there was a correlation between countries where corporations experienced broader business issues and the countries where there were difficulties in enforcing arbitral awards.

It would be interesting to see this notion – that the political will of a State may be more relevant in enforcement than any particular legal rules – play out in the *Suez*, *InterAguas* and *AWG* cases against Argentina. Argentina has been held liable in all three cases, and the quantification of damages remains to be done. When the cases proceed to three damages awards against Argentina, then the differences between enforcement under Article 54 of the ICSID Convention and enforcement via the New York Convention might be measured in a meaningful and practical way.

IV   Conclusions

Investor–State arbitration under the UNCITRAL Rules continues to make up a significant proportion of the total number of investor–State arbitrations. Parties may find themselves arbitrating an investor–State dispute under the UNCITRAL Rules by choice, or because it was the only available option open to them in the circumstances. Unlike ICSID, the UNCITRAL Rules were not specifically designed for investor–State arbitration and do not operate in a self-contained system dedicated to that type of dispute. Nevertheless, as the above survey indicates, UNCITRAL arbitration presents a viable option and has become the most used alternative for investor–State disputes.

The frequent application of the UNCITRAL Rules in the investor–State context led to several suggestions for improvements and amendments to the existing rules, which had not been amended since they were promulgated in 1976. From 2006 until 2010, the rules underwent a wholesale review by a Working Group of UNCITRAL.[138] On 12 July 2010, the Working Group released a revised set of rules.

Some of the investor–State-inspired changes were of a technical (though important) nature. For example, the Working Group

---

[138] For a discussion of the Working Group's mandate and some of the key proposed changes to the Rules, see Levine, 'Current trends'; Castello, 'UNCITRAL Rules'; and Daly and Smith, 'Comment on the differing legal frameworks'.

recommended that references to a 'contract' in the first article of the rules be broadened and replaced with references to disputes arising out of a 'defined legal relationship, whether contractual or not'.[139] This will clearly encompass investor–State disputes arising out of a treaty.[140]

The special way in which consent to arbitration is formed in an investment treaty arbitration was also taken into account by the Working Group. Under an investment treaty, the State makes an open-ended offer to arbitrate investment disputes. The consent is perfected when the investor accepts that offer. Several years, even decades, might pass between the offer and acceptance. This issue came to light when the Working Group was considering which version of the rules should apply to a dispute once the revisions come into effect. This was accounted for by the following text in Article 1(2) of the Revised Rules:

> The parties to an arbitration agreement concluded after 15 August 2010 shall be presumed to have referred to the rules in effect on the date of commencement of the arbitration, unless the parties have agreed to apply a particular version of the rules. That presumption does not apply where the arbitration agreement has been concluded by accepting after 15 August 2010 an offer made before that date.

Article 33 of the UNCITRAL Rules states that the tribunal 'shall apply the law designated by the parties as applicable to the substance of the dispute. Failing such designation by the parties, the arbitral tribunal shall apply the law determined by the conflict of laws rules which it considers applicable.'[141] The revised UNCITRAL Rules remove the reference to 'determined by the conflict of laws rules' to give the tribunal greater flexibility in determining which law, or laws, would be applicable in a given dispute. This would encompass cases where, for example, the host State law as well as public international law would be applicable.[142]

The most heated debate concerning adapting the UNCITRAL Rules to investor–State disputes was whether specific changes were needed to address concerns over transparency. Two observer NGOs proposed that the rules be amended insofar as they apply to investor–State treaty

---

[139] See Revised UNCITRAL Rules, Art. 1(1).
[140] See UNCITRAL Working Group II, 'Revision of the UNCITRAL Arbitration Rules' (Report of Working Group II (Arbitration and Conciliation) on the Work of its 52nd Session, No. A/CN.9/WG.II/WP.157, 10 December 2009), www.uncitral.org/uncitral/en/commission/working_groups/2Arbitration.html (last accessed 21 January 2011).
[141] See Art. 35(1), Revised UNCITRAL Rules.
[142] *Ibid.*, Add. 2. See also the in-depth discussion of the different approaches to applicable law under ICSID and UNCITRAL in Sacerdoti, 'Investment arbitration'.

arbitrations by: (1) making the notice of arbitration publicly available; (2) making all copies of pleadings publicly available (subject to redaction of confidential information); (3) allowing for *amicus*-type written submissions to be made on behalf of non-disputing parties; (4) requiring hearings to be made open to the public; and (5) requiring publication of any decision.[143] The February 2008 Working Group meeting saw broad support for the principle of greater transparency in investor–State arbitrations that affect the public interest, but it was not agreed that such changes be introduced to the current revision of the rules, and which apply to many types of commercial arbitration, only a small percentage of which arise under investment treaties.

The issue of transparency, widely agreed to be complex and worthy of further attention, will be considered further by UNCITRAL and is now the subject of special consideration by the Working Group. Some delegations suggested it could lead to an optional or mandatory annex to the rules, a set of model provisions for inclusion in future treaties (as in the Model US BIT 2004) or some other form of instrument or guidelines. The UNCITRAL Commission itself in July 2008 supported this approach, stating that 'it would not be desirable to include specific provisions on treaty-based arbitration the UNCITRAL Arbitration Rules themselves' and agreeing that work on investor–State disputes 'should not delay the completion of the revision of the UNCITRAL Arbitration Rules in their generic form'.[144] The Commission agreed that the topic was 'worthy of future consideration and should be dealt with as a matter of priority immediately after completion of the current revision of the Rules'. As noted in section II.A above, parties to investor–State disputes under the existing UNCITRAL Rules have managed to incorporate greater transparency in their proceedings by choice, whether through detailed provisions in their consent to arbitration (as in DR–CAFTA) or at the time of the dispute.

---

[143] Center for International Environmental Law and International Institute for Sustainable Development, Submission to UNCITRAL Working Group II (Arbitration and Conciliation), *Revision of the UNCITRAL Arbitration Rules*, 12 September 2007, www.ciel.org/Publications/UNCITRAL_Arbitration_12Sep07.pdf (last accessed 21 January 2011).

[144] UNCITRAL, 'Report of the United Nations Commission on International Trade Law: Forty-first session (16 June–3 July 2008)', UN Doc. No. A/63/17, [undated]), para. 314, www.uncitral.org/uncitral/en/commission/sessions/41st.html (last accessed 21 January 2011). For the latest report of the UNCITRAL Working Group on this project, see www.uncitral.org/en/commission/workinggroups/2Arbitration.html. See also Castello, 'UNCITRAL Rules', para. 16.25.

One of the perceived advantages of UNCITRAL arbitration is the flexibility it offers to the parties throughout the process. Thus different approaches can be seen in different UNCITRAL cases with respect to confidentiality and transparency, the extent of institutional support and the chosen seat of arbitration (entailing the supervisory national jurisdiction that might play a role in granting interim relief or review of the award). The UNCITRAL Rules may also be seen as offering a standard and method of resolving arbitrator challenges more in line with generally accepted international best practices. Differences exist between UNCITRAL and ICSID with respect to the pool of available arbitrators, availability of provisional relief from courts, procedures for dismissal of frivolous claims and means of enforcement. On certain issues where the two systems appear on their face to diverge – such as cost allocation, jurisdictional limitations, and annulment – there is more convergence between the two systems than meets the eye.

18

The scope of 'amount of compensation' dispute-resolution clauses in investment treaties

J. ROMESH WEERAMANTRY AND CLAIRE WILSON[*]

I Introduction

An investment tribunal's determination of the jurisdiction granted to it by an investment treaty has often given rise to considerable controversy. The meaning of words such as 'investments' or 'investors' for purposes of establishing jurisdiction or the ability of most-favoured nation provisions to import external dispute-resolution procedures have generated much debate. These issues are now well traversed (but still not fully resolved) in numerous awards and in scholarly literature.[1] This chapter concerns a jurisdictional issue of a more recent vintage and about which comparatively little has yet been written. The issue in question relates to whether investment treaty dispute-resolution clauses that provide arbitral jurisdiction over disputes as to the 'amount of compensation' or 'compensation due' (i) permit a tribunal to determine an investor's entitlement to compensation (i.e. determining whether the host State breached the treaty's substantive provisions, thus triggering compensation obligations) *and* also to quantify such compensation (i.e. calculating the amount of compensation to be paid to the investor as a result of a treaty breach); *or* (ii) limit a tribunal solely to quantifying the amount of compensation.[2]

 For the purposes of this present chapter, 'amount of compensation' clauses can be said, for example, to take the form (with variations) of

---

[*] This chapter is based on the presentation by J. Romesh Weeramantry at the University of Sydney conference on 'International investment treaty law and arbitration: Evolution and revolution in substance and procedure', 19–20 February 2010.
[1] See e.g. ch. 2 by David A. R. Williams QC and Simon Foote in this volume.
[2] The use of the words 'entitlement' and 'quantification' have been adopted from the judgment of Justice Simon in *Czech Republic* v. *European Media Ventures SA* (2007) EWHC 2851 (Comm), para. 44.

Article 13(3) of the 1988 China–New Zealand bilateral investment treaty (BIT):

> If a dispute involving the amount of compensation resulting from expropriation referred to in Article 6 cannot be settled within six months after resort to negotiation . . . it may be submitted to an international tribunal established by both parties.[3]

This type of clause was adopted in many BITs concluded by communist States, particularly China[4] and the former USSR.[5] This treaty practice

---

[3] Agreement between the Government of New Zealand and the Government of the People's Republic of China on the Promotion and Protection of Investments, signed 22 November 1988, 1787 UNTS 186 (entered into force 25 March 1989) (China–New Zealand BIT). But compare this investment treaty with the far wider reference to 'any legal dispute' in the more recent dispute-resolution provisions contained in the Free Trade Agreement between the Government of New Zealand and the Government of the People's Republic of China ('New Zealand–China Free Trade Agreement'), Chapter 11, Art. 153, signed 7 April 2008 (entered into force 1 October 2008), www.chinafta.govt.nz (last accessed 14 February 2011). See also n. 9 below, and corresponding text.

[4] In their extensive study of Chinese BITs, Gallagher and Wenhua Shan have observed that: 'The scope of the dispute-resolution provisions in the majority of China's BITs are restrictive. The provisions limit the jurisdiction of a tribunal to questions of quantum only': N. Gallagher and Wenhua Shan, *Chinese Investment Treaties: Policies and practice* (Oxford University Press, 2009), p. 313, para. 8.29. In addition to the China–New Zealand BIT of 1988, other restrictive dispute-settlement provisions include Art. 9(3) of the Agreement between the Government of the People's Republic of China and the Government of the State of Qatar Concerning the Encouragement and Reciprocal Protection of Investments, signed April 1999; Art. 8(3) of the Agreement between the Government of the Lebanese Republic and the Government of the People's Republic of China Concerning the Encouragement and Reciprocal Protection of Investments, signed 13 June 1996 (entered into force 10 July 1997) (China–Lebanon BIT) ('If a dispute involving the amount of compensation cannot be settled within six months after resort to negotiations as specified in paragraph 1 of this Article, it may be submitted at the request of either party to international arbitration.'); Art. 9(3) of the Agreement between the Government of the Republic of Indonesia and the Government of the People's Republic of China on the Promotion and Protection of Investments, signed 18 November 1994 (entered into force 1 April 1995); Art. 4(5) of the Agreement between the Republic of Austria and the Government of the People's Republic of China Concerning the Promotion and Protection of Investments, signed 12 September 1985 (entered into force 11 October 1986) ('The investor has the right to request that the level of compensation given will be reviewed, either by the competent authorities of the State, whose authorities have taken the decision, or by an international arbitration tribunal.'); and Article 7 of the Agreement between the Government of the Confederation of Switzerland and the Government of the People's Republic of China Concerning the Reciprocal Promotion and Protection of Investments, signed 12 November 1986 (entered into force 18 March 1987) (allowing investors to bring a claim in respect of a dispute 'on the matter of compensation mentioned in Article 7').

[5] See e.g. Art. 10(1) of the Agreement between the Kingdom of Spain and the Union of the Soviet Socialist Republics for the Reciprocal Protection of Investments, signed 26 October

seems to have been generated by suspicion as to foreign investment, private enterprise and international arbitration, as well as by general concerns related to the erosion of State sovereignty.[6] Russia, for example, contended in *Berschader* v. *Russian Federation* that it was a strict point of principle for the Soviet Union that the occurrence of an act of expropriation must be determined by the courts in whose territory the expropriation was alleged to have taken place.[7] As we shall see, this contention has not been fully accepted by investment tribunals.

'Amount of compensation' clauses may be contrasted to those clauses that succinctly express a right to refer 'any dispute' to investment arbitration without elaborating on or qualifying the scope of that term. The majority of the more recent investment treaties contain such broad dispute-resolution provisions.[8] An illustration of this change in treaty formulation is apparent when the latest investment dispute-resolution provisions between New Zealand and China contained in their 2008 Free Trade Agreement (quoted below) are compared to those of the 1988 BIT between those two nations (quoted above). The 2008 provisions on their face appear to be far wider; they permit recourse to international

---

1990 (entered into force 28 November 1991) (Spain–USSR BIT) ('Any dispute . . . relating to the amount or method of payment of the compensation due under Article 6 [concerning nationalisation and expropriation] of this Agreement . . .'); and Art. 9(2) of the Agreement on Encouragement and Reciprocal Protection of Investments between the Kingdom of the Netherlands and the Union of the Soviet Socialist Republics, signed 5 October 1989 (entered into force 20 July 1991) ('Disputes concerning the amount or procedure of payment of compensation under Article 6 of this Agreement [concerning expropriation] or concerning the free transfer as defined in Article 4 of this Agreement, which cannot be settled amicably within a period of six months from the date either party to the dispute requested amicable settlement, may be referred by the investor to international arbitration or conciliation.'). As regards BITs containing 'amount of compensation' clauses signed after the breakup of the Soviet Union, see Art. 9(1) of the Agreement between the Government of the Russian Federation and the Cabinet of Ministers of the Ukraine on the Encouragement and Mutual Protection of Investments, signed 27 November 1998 ('disputes, which concern the amount, terms of and procedure for payments'). For a more detailed discussion regarding the application of BITs concluded by Soviet States see N. Rubins and A. Nazarov, 'Investment treaties and the Russian Federation: Baiting the Bear?', *Business Law International*, 9(2) (2008), 100.

[6] See e.g. *Czech Republic* v. *European Media Ventures*, paras. 11(i), 25(i) and 31. See also Rubins and Nazarov, 'Investment treaties', pp. 102–3; P. Peters, 'Dispute settlement arrangements in investment treaties', *Netherlands Yearbook of International Law*, 22 (1991), 91, 118.

[7] *Vladimir and Moise Berschader* v. *The Russian Federation* (SCC Case No. 080/2004, Award of 21 April 2006), para. 154. See also *Czech Republic* v. *European Media Ventures*, paras. 25, 31.

[8] R. Dolzer and C. Schreuer, *Principles of International Investment Law* (Oxford University Press, 2008), p. 242.

arbitration (subject to a six-month settlement period) in respect of 'any legal dispute arising under this Chapter between an investor of one Party and the other Party, directly concerning an investment by that investor in the territory of that other Party'.[9] From the treaty-making perspective of China, this general and unqualified wording is typical of the 'new generation' of Chinese BITs. In these treaties, China – in line with its new status as a capital exporter[10] – has adopted a more relaxed policy towards disputes that can be referred to international arbitration.[11]

The ensuing discussion will first deal with awards in which 'amount of compensation' clauses have been interpreted as limiting arbitration to determine only the quantum of compensation due. The effect of this interpretation is that it requires a positive determination (or admission) made by the host State or another body that an expropriation had occurred *before* recourse to international arbitration is permitted. Thereafter, the chapter will move to review awards by tribunals that have interpreted these types of clauses as permitting arbitration in relation to both the calculation of compensation as well as the determination as to whether an expropriation took place. The chapter will conclude with an analysis of both lines of divergent decisions.

II   Awards limiting jurisdiction to quantum only

A   Plama *v.* Bulgaria

One of the first awards in which the significance of an 'amount of compensation' clause was raised was *Plama* v. *Bulgaria*.[12] The tribunal in that case did not interpret that clause but made observations that merit reference in this section. The claimant attempted to establish

---

[9] New Zealand–China Free Trade Agreement, Chapter 11, Art. 152.

[10] See Gallagher and Shan, *Chinese Investment Treaties*, pp. 10–14, paras. 1.19–1.26.

[11] Examples of these 'new-generation' BITs include the Agreement between the Government of the People's Republic of China and the Government of the Republic of Benin Concerning the Encouragement and Reciprocal Protection of Investments, signed 18 February 2004; the Agreement between the People's Republic of China and the Federal Republic of Germany on the Encouragement and Reciprocal Protection of Investments, signed 1 December 2003 (entered into force 11 December 2005); the Agreement between the Government of the Republic of Trinidad and Tobago and the Government of the People's Republic of China on the Reciprocal Promotion and Protection of Investments (2002); and the Agreement between the Government of the People's Republic of China and the Government of the Union of Myanmar on the Promotion and Protection of Investments, signed 12 December 2001.

[12] *Plama Consortium Limited* v. *Republic of Bulgaria* (ICSID Case No. ARB/03/24, Decision on Jurisdiction of 8 February 2005), para. 186.

jurisdiction on the basis of a 'most-favoured-nation' (MFN) clause. The tribunal determined that it could not extend the jurisdictional rights of the claimant by applying the MFN clause because its reference to 'privileges' was related solely to substantive provisions.[13] Of interest to the present chapter is the tribunal's explicit acknowledgement that the claimant had raised the MFN claim because the BIT had restricted access to international arbitration on the merits by virtue of an 'amount of compensation' clause:

> The Claimant's position appears to be prompted by the limited dispute settlement provisions in the Bulgaria-Cyprus BIT. Said provisions are only concerned with disputes relating to expropriation, the legality of which, 'Shall be checked at the request of the concerned investor through the regular administrative and legal procedures of the Contracting Party that had taken the appropriate steps.' (Article 4.1) A dispute 'with regard to the amount of compensation . . . shall be checked either in a legal regular procedure of the Contracting Party which has taken the measure on expropriation or by an international 'Ad Hoc' Arbitration Court' (id.), which is detailed in Articles 4.2–4.5 . . . The Claimant does not invoke these dispute settlement provisions in the present case.[14]

The tribunal offers no further discussion on the relevant 'amount of compensation' clause, and did not pursue the question whether or not a tribunal had jurisdiction to hear issues concerning the occurrence of an expropriation in addition to issues of quantum.

B   Berschader v. Russian Federation

The tribunal in *Berschader* v. *Russian Federation*[15] was called upon to determine a dispute under the Belgo-Luxembourg–USSR BIT.[16] The claimant asserted that the investment had been expropriated after the government cancelled a construction contract and then ordered the police department to force the claimant's staff to evacuate the site. Article 10(1) of the Belgo-Luxembourg–USSR BIT presented an issue as to the jurisdiction of the tribunal. That provision offered investors the right to arbitrate

---

[13] *Ibid.*, para 191. For a full discussion of the application of MFN clauses and their interpretation see paras. 190–227.

[14] *Ibid.*, para. 186.

[15] *Vladimir and Moise Berschader* v. *The Russian Federation* (SCC Case No. 080/2004, Award of 21 April 2006).

[16] Agreement between the Governments of the Kingdom of Belgium and the Grand Duchy of Luxembourg and the Soviet Union on the Encouragement and Reciprocal Protection of Investments, signed 9 February 1989 (entered into force 13 October 1991).

disputes 'concerning the amount or mode of compensation paid under Article 5'. Expropriation was the subject matter of Article 5. The tribunal concluded that it lacked jurisdiction to hear this dispute affirming that a claimant would first need to prove that expropriation had occurred prior to instituting an arbitral claim pursuant to Article 10. This decision applied Article 31(1) of the Vienna Convention on the Law of Treaties ('VCLT')[17] to find that the ordinary meaning of Article 10 was clear and that it could be assumed that its restrictive wording was indeed intentional, the purpose of which was to restrict the scope of arbitration under the treaty.[18]

C   RosInvest Co. UK Ltd *v.* Russian Federation

In *RosInvest Co. UK Ltd* v. *Russian Federation,*[19] a British investor alleged that the Russian government had deliberately taken measures that affected the claimant's investment, which amounted to an expropriation by virtue of the UK–USSR BIT.[20] Similar to the *Berschader* case, the tribunal was required to ascertain whether the BIT extended jurisdiction to decide whether expropriation had occurred, rather than make a decision only upon quantum. The tribunal was required to interpret and apply Article 8(1) of the UK–USSR BIT, which provided that 'any legal disputes . . . concerning the amount or payment of compensation under articles 4 or 5' could be referred to arbitration. The tribunal interpreted this provision by applying Article 31(1) of the VCLT and found that the Article 8(1) words 'concerning the amount or payment of compensation under', according to their ordinary meaning, 'can only be understood as a limitation of the jurisdiction conferred by that clause'.[21] The tribunal further noted:

> Though no documents from the negotiation of the BIT have been produced, the Parties including the Claimant agree that the rather complicated wording in Article 8 presented a compromise between the UK's intention to have a wide arbitration clause and the Soviet intention to

---

[17] Vienna Convention on the Law of Treaties, opened for signature 23 May 1969, 1155 UNTS 331, entered into force 27 January 1980 (VCLT).

[18] *Berschader* v. *Russian Federation*, paras. 152–3, 155.

[19] *RosInvest Co. UK Ltd* v. *The Russian Federation* (SCC Case No. Arb. V079/2005, Award on Jurisdiction of October 2007).

[20] Agreement between the Government of the United Kingdom of Great Britain and Northern Ireland and the Government of the Union of the Soviet Socialist Republics for the Promotion and Reciprocal Protection of Investments, signed 6 April 1989 (entered into force 3 July 1991).

[21] *RosInvest Co.*, para. 110.

have a limited one. If that is so, it is hard to arrive at an interpretation all the same that the clause is so wide as to include all aspects of an expropriation.[22]

In support of its finding that it did not have jurisdiction over all aspects of an expropriation, the tribunal drew attention to the exception to expropriation provided in Article 5, which stipulated that expropriation could be permissible if it were (i) in the public interest; (ii) not discriminatory; and (iii) against payment of prompt, adequate and effective compensation. The tribunal was not persuaded that the reference to a dispute as to the amount or payment of compensation in Article 8 could also be a reference to the other two exception criteria in Article 5 (i.e. public interest and non-discrimination).[23] Other treaties entered into by the United Kingdom, the USSR, Russia and other States were cited to illustrate that had the parties wanted to include every aspect of expropriation within the jurisdiction of the arbitral tribunal, this could easily have been achieved in clear and unambiguous terms.[24] Despite the *RosInvest* tribunal's interpretation of Article 8, however, it found jurisdiction on the basis of the UK–USSR BIT MFN clause.[25]

D Austrian Airlines v. Slovak Republic

An 'amount of compensation' clause in the Austria–Czech/Slovak BIT[26] was at issue in *Austrian Airlines v. Slovak Republic*.[27] Once again, an important task of the tribunal was to ascertain whether the scope of the clause could allow a finding that there had been an expropriation, or whether it was restricted to an assessment of quantum. Article 8(1) of the BIT related to:

> Any disputes arising out of an investment, between a Contracting Party and an investor of the other Contracting Party, concerning the amount or the conditions of payment of a [*sic*] compensation . . .[28]

---

[22] *Ibid.*, para. 110.   [23] *Ibid.*, paras. 111–12.   [24] *Ibid.*, para. 113.

[25] *Ibid.*, paras. 132–3. The tribunal stated that: 'If this effect [application of MFN Clause] is generally accepted in the context of substantive protection, the Tribunal sees no reason not to accept it in the context of procedural clauses.'

[26] Agreement between the Republic of Austria and the Czech and Slovak Federal Republic Concerning the Promotion and Protection of Investments, signed 15 October 1990 (entered into force 1 October 1991) (Austria–Czech/Slovak BIT).

[27] *Austrian Airlines v. The Slovak Republic* (Final Award of 20 October 2009).

[28] Austria–Czech/Slovak BIT, Art. 8(1).

The tribunal considered that the above provision must be read in conjunction with paragraphs 4(4) and 4(5) of the BIT:

> (4) The investor shall have the right to have the legitimacy of the expropriation reviewed by the competent authorities of the Contracting Party, which prompted the expropriation.
>
> (5) The investor shall have the right to have the amount of the compensation and the conditions of payment reviewed either by the competent authorities or the Contracting Party, which prompted the expropriation or by an arbitral tribunal according to Article 8 of this agreement.[29]

Applying Article 31 of the VCLT, the tribunal held that the ordinary meaning of Article 8(1) was clear, i.e. it did not allow the tribunal to determine expropriation. This position was confirmed by examining the context of that provision, which includes Article 4(4) and (5). In particular, the tribunal noted that these Article 4 provisions made clear that the competent authorities of the Slovak Republic (and not the arbitral tribunal) were the entities possessing the power to determine whether an illegitimate expropriation had taken place.[30] Charles Brower concurred with this finding in his Separate Opinion.

The tribunal went further by examining the drafting history of Article 8. It noted that an early draft referred to disputes 'regarding an investment' to arbitration. However, in subsequent drafts 'amount of compensation' type words were added. Consequently, it concluded that: 'One can only deduct from this sequence of texts that the Contracting States deliberately narrowed down the initially broad scope of arbitral disputes.'[31]

III   Awards permitting jurisdiction over both expropriation and quantum

A   Sedelmayer v. Russian Federation

Sedelmayer v. *Russian Federation* appears to be one of the earliest cases in which the claimant invoked a dispute-resolution clause containing an 'amount of compensation' proviso.[32] A notable feature of this case is that Russia did not make the objection that the clause limited the

---

[29] *Ibid.*, Art. 4(4)–(5).   [30] *Austrian Airlines*, paras. 95–7.   [31] *Ibid.*, para. 107.
[32] *Franz Sedelmayer* v. *The Russian Federation* (Stockholm Chamber of Commerce, Award of 7 July 1998).

tribunal's jurisdiction only to quantum. In this case, the Germany–USSR BIT dispute-resolution clause provided claimants 'the right to submit disputes concerning the procedures and amount of compensation' to international arbitration.[33] The *Sedelmayer* award does not explore the question as to whether jurisdiction should be limited only to disputes over quantum or could be extended to determining whether expropriation had occurred in the first place. There was no detailed analysis of this point; the arbitrators in *Sedelmayer* simply concluded that the tribunal had jurisdiction over both entitlement to compensation and quantum. The tribunal then went on to conclude that Russia had committed an act of expropriation, after which it calculated the amount of compensation. Considering the paucity of reasoning in this case, it is uncertain how persuasive this decision may be in other similar disputes. This would be the case even where the Germany–USSR BIT itself was at issue.

B   Telenor Mobile Communications AS *v.* Hungary

A similar approach to that adopted by Russia in *Sedelmayer* was taken by Hungary in *Telenor Mobile Communications AS* v. *Republic of Hungary*.[34] In that case, the claimant invoked the Norway–Hungary BIT, Article XI(1) of which opened the door for international arbitration as to:

> any legal disputes between the Investor of one Contracting Party and the other Contracting Party in relation to an investment of the former either concerning the amount or payment of compensation under Article V [concerning compensation relating to war, revolution, etc] and VI [concerning expropriation] of the present Agreement, or concerning any other matter consequential upon an act of expropriation in accordance with Article VI of the present Agreement . . .'[35]

Hungary contended that the BIT conferred arbitral jurisdiction only with respect to expropriation claims, and excluded Telenor's claims for alleged unfair or inequitable treatment or failure to protect its investment. No

---

[33] Agreement between the Federal Republic of Germany and the Union of Soviet Socialist Republics concerning the Promotion and Reciprocal Protection of Investments, signed 13 June 1989 (entered into force 5 August 1991), Art. 4(3).

[34] *Telenor Mobile Communications AS* v. *Republic of Hungary* (ICSID Case No. ARB/04/15, Award of 13 September 2006).

[35] Agreement between the Government of the Kingdom of Norway and the Government of the Republic of Hungary on the Promotion and Reciprocal Protection of Investments, signed 8 April 1991 (entered into force 4 December 1992), Art. XI(1).

objection to any possible limits arising from the 'amount of compensation' clause was made by Hungary.

C   Saipem SpA v. Bangladesh

The relevant BIT dispute-resolution clause in *Saipem SpA* v. *The People's Republic of Bangladesh*[36] was contained in Article 9(1) of the Bangladesh–Italy BIT,[37] which provides:

> Any disputes arising between a Contracting Party and the investors of the
> other, relating to compensation for expropriation, nationalization, requi-
> sition or similar measures including disputes relating to the amount of
> the relevant payments shall be settled amicably, as far as possible.

Paragraph 2 of Article 9 permitted recourse to international arbitration in the event that such a dispute could not be settled amicably within six months. Bangladesh in this case did not submit any argument as to any potential limitations on jurisdiction that may be contained in the words 'relating to compensation for expropriation' or 'the amount of the relevant payments'. Much like the *Sedelmayer* and *Telenor* cases, because of the position taken by the respondent State, the tribunal in *Saipem* was not required to address whether or not limitations arose from the reference in the BIT dispute-resolution provision to 'compensation for expropriation' or 'amount of payments'.

D   Czech Republic v. European Media Ventures *(Eng. High Crt)*

The jurisdictional award issued by the tribunal in *European Media Ventures* v. *Czech Republic* on 15 May 2007 is not public.[38] However, the outcome of the award is known because it was subject to a setting aside action before Mr Justice Simon in the English High Court. In the arbitration, the tribunal was required to determine whether Article 8(1) of the Belgo-Luxembourg–Czech Republic BIT[39] granted it power to

---

[36] *Saipem SpA* v. *The People's Republic of Bangladesh* (ICSID Case No. ARB/05/07, Decision on Jurisdiction and Recommendation on Provisional Measures of 21 March 2007).

[37] Agreement between the Government of the Republic of Italy and the Government of the People's Republic of Bangladesh on the Promotion and Protection of Investments, signed 20 March 1990 (entered into force 20 September 1994).

[38] *European Media Ventures* v. *Czech Republic* (Award of 15 May 2007), cited in *Czech Republic* v. *European Media Ventures SA* [2007] EWHC 2851 (Comm) (5 December 2007).

[39] Agreement between the Belgo-Luxembourg Economic Union and the Czechoslovak Socialist Republic Concerning the Reciprocal Promotion and Protection of Investments, signed 24 April 1989 (entered into force 13 February 1992).

determine entitlement to compensation as well as quantum. That provision permitted the tribunal to consider disputes 'between one of the Contracting Parties and an investor of the other Contracting Party concerning compensation due by virtue of Article 3 Paragraphs (1) and (3)', which dealt with expropriation. The tribunal took the view that it possessed the power to determine entitlement as well as quantum. This jurisdictional finding of the tribunal was contested in the English High Court by the Czech Republic.

Mr Justice Simon considered that Article 31 of the VCLT required 'focus on the words and meaning and not the intention of one or other contracting party [to the treaty], unless that intention can be derived from the object and purpose of the treaty . . . its context . . . a subsequent agreement as to interpretation . . . or practice which establishes an agreement as to its interpretation'.[40] Consequently, the judge took into account a varied mix of contextual matters, including the intention of the BIT in question to confer a valuable right to arbitrate, Belgian and Czech Republic parliamentary materials and the contention that communist States for ideological reasons were reluctant to agree to international arbitration, which contrasted to their varied State practice (some of their treaties permitted international arbitration to decide substantive issues and others did not[41]).[42] The conclusion of Mr Justice Simon was that the contextual material did not throw clear light on the proper interpretation of Article 8 of the Belgo-Luxembourg–Czech Republic BIT and that 'the width of the arbitration clause was left unclear: possibly to the satisfaction of both sides'.[43]

After making this finding, the judge turned his attention to the ordinary meaning of the terms of the treaty provision. He indicated that the clause should not be read as meaning 'relating to the *amount* of

---

[40] *Czech Republic* v. *European Media Ventures*, para. 17.

[41] Examples provided by the tribunal of instances where the USSR agreed to submit issues of entitlement for determination by international arbitration included the Agreement between the Republic of France and the Government of the Union of the Soviet Socialist Republics Concerning the Promotion and Reciprocal Protection of Investments, signed 4 July 1989 (entered into force 18 July 1991); the Agreement between the Government of Canada and the Government of the Union of the Soviet Socialist Republics for the Promotion and Reciprocal Protection of Investments, signed 20 April 1989 (entered into force 27 June 1991); and the Agreement between the Government of the Republic of Korea and the Government of the Union of the Soviet Socialist Republics for the Promotion and Reciprocal Protection of Investments, signed 14 December 1990 (entered into force 10 July 1991). See *Czech Republic* v. *European Media Ventures*, para. 31.

[42] *Ibid.*, paras. 23, 25, 31.   [43] *Ibid.*, para. 32.

compensation'.[44] This point is significant as it highlights the importance
of the absence of the word 'amount' in Article 8(1) and suggests that the
judge's decision may have been different had there not been a 'compensation due' clause before him but an 'amount of compensation' clause.
In this respect, the view taken during the case by Toby Landau, counsel
for European Media Ventures (and later arbitrator in *Renta 4* v. *Russia*,
which will be discussed below), is noteworthy. The judgment describes
his view as follows:

> [Toby Landau] pointed out that before the fall of Communism in Eastern
> Europe, the majority of BITs specifically restricted the arbitral jurisdic-
> tion to 'the amount' and 'method' of compensation due with respect to
> an expropriation. He pointed out that no such delimiting words
> appeared in the present Treaty.[45]

Again, this passage draws attention to the significant role played by the
word 'amount'. Another important part of the judge's interpretation of
the words 'concerning compensation due' as found in Article 8 is set out
in the following passage:

> '*Concerning*' is similar to other common expressions in arbitration
> clauses, for example '*relating to*' and '*arising out of*'. Its ordinary meaning
> is to include every aspect of its subject: in this case '*compensation due by
> virtue of Paragraphs (1) and (3) of Article 3*'. As a matter of ordinary
> meaning this covers issues of entitlement as well as quantification. . . .
> [I]n determining any claim '*concerning compensation*', the tribunal must
> necessarily consider whether the events in Articles 3(1) and (3) have
> occurred, and their precise nature.[46]

Deploying these and other reasons, Mr Justice Simon concluded that the
arbitral tribunal could not only determine the quantification of compensation, but also whether an entitlement to compensation existed.[47]

E   Renta 4 v. Russian Federation

In *Renta 4* v. *Russian Federation*,[48] the BIT dispute-resolution provision
at issue was Article 10(1) of the Spain–USSR BIT, which permits arbitration of disputes 'relating to the amount or method of payment of
the compensation due under Article 6 [concerning expropriation] of this

[44] *Ibid.*, p. 43 (original emphasis).   [45] *Ibid.*, p. 26.
[46] *Ibid.*, pp. 44–5.   [47] *Ibid.*, para. 53.
[48] *Renta 4 SVSA and ors* v. *Russian Federation* (SCC Case No. V024/2007, Award on
Preliminary Objections of 20 March 2009).

Agreement'.[49] On this point, Russia contended that the tribunal possessed jurisdiction to hear claims as to quantification of compensation only after a national court had established that an expropriation had indeed occurred. The tribunal rejected this argument and found that Article 10 granted it jurisdiction to determine the occurrence of an expropriation as well as the amount of compensation to be paid.

The tribunal did not accept the approach taken in the *Berschader* award as it was based on 'seven short paragraphs' and 'does not appear to be supported by analysis'.[50] The *RosInvest Co.* award was not given weight on the basis that 'that award does not consider whether the word "payment" in the [UK–USSR BIT] may lead to consideration of the reality of its predicate: expropriation. Nor does the formulation in that treaty include the word "due".[51] The *Renta 4* tribunal also mentioned that the *RosInvest Co.* tribunal at any rate assumed jurisdiction on the basis of the MFN provision. Furthermore, one of the *Renta 4* arbitrators stated in a separate declaration that the finding in *RosInvest Co.* was not an expression of opinion on how the 'amount of compensation' clause at issue, or similar treaty clauses, relate to other claims that might be brought on an allegation of expropriation.[52]

Numerous policy-based reasons for its decision were provided by the *Renta 4* tribunal in its award, including that: (i) investment would not be promoted by a regime that gave investors access to international arbitration to determine quantum, but not whether an expropriation had occurred; (ii) if Russia's arguments were upheld, 'obtaining *any* amount of compensation according to *any* method would be hostage to the host State's self-determination as to whether it is due at all';[53] (iii) even if there had, in fact, been a decree of expropriation, a subsequent government denial that this event constituted an expropriation would prevent a claim under Article 10; (iv) the failure of Russia in *Sedelmayer* to raise the point that expropriation was not arbitrable under the 'amount of compensation' clause at issue in that case shows Russia's interpretation of Article 10 in the present case was less than fundamental; and (v) disagreement as to the quantification of compensation might refer not only to the sum of compensation, but whether compensation was due at all.

The tribunal also considered the effect of the use of the term 'due' in Article 10(1) and undertook a textual analysis of the provision.

---

[49] Spain–USSR BIT, Art. 10(1).   [50] *Renta 4* v. *Russian Federation*, paras. 25–7.
[51] *Ibid.*, para. 48.   [52] *Ibid.*   [53] *Ibid.*, para. 58 (original emphasis).

Accordingly, it was found that: 'Article 6 defines the precondition of compensation being "due" for the purposes of Article 10. It is an aspect of Article 6 which cannot be beyond the arbitrator's reach.' Taking this line of argument further, the tribunal reasoned that it had the capacity to ascertain whether the claimants' allegation of expropriation did, in fact, 'deprive' them of adequate compensation. It was concluded that this provision infers 'the power to determine whether there has been a compensable event in the first place'.[54] Also, the tribunal took the view that if Russia's contentions were correct, Article 6 might have explained how entitlement would be determined, and Article 10 might have stipulated that only an authority identified in Article 6 could establish whether compensation was due. However, the tribunal pointed out that there is nothing of the kind in the Spain–USSR BIT.[55]

F   Tza Yap Shum v. Peru

The case of *Tza Yap Shum* v. *Peru*[56] concerned a dispute submitted to arbitration under the Peru–China BIT.[57] Article 8(3) of that treaty provides: 'If a dispute involving the amount of compensation for expropriation cannot be settled within six months . . . it may be submitted at the request of either party to [ICSID].'[58]

Peru argued that the only dispute that could be settled by arbitration under this clause 'is that involving the amount of compensation owed to an investor, once the occurrence of an illegal expropriation has been confirmed'.[59] To support this assertion, two witness statements were submitted on behalf of Peru. One was from a Chinese negotiator and one by a Peruvian negotiator, both of whom had worked on negotiations associated with the Peru–China BIT. According to Peru, these statements affirmed that the parties to the treaty intended that only disputes as to quantum could be determined by ICSID arbitration.[60] It was also argued that despite the liberalisation in Peru's attitude to dispute-settlement provisions after Peru signed the ICSID Convention in 1993, China continued to maintain its position

---

[54] *Ibid.*, para. 39.   [55] *Ibid.*, para. 59.

[56] *Tza Yap Shum* v. *Republic of Peru* (ICSID Case No. ARB/07/6, Decision on Jurisdiction and Competence of 19 June 2009). The analysis contained in this chapter is based on an unofficial English translation of the award.

[57] Agreement between the Government of the Republic of Peru and the People's Republic of China Concerning the Encouragement and Reciprocal Protection of Investments, signed 9 June 1994 (entered into force 1 February 1995) (Peru–China BIT).

[58] *Ibid.*, Art. 8(3).   [59] *Tza Yap Shum* v. *Peru*, para. 134.   [60] *Ibid.*, para. 135.

that the question of entitlement to compensation could not be decided by an international arbitral tribunal.[61]

The tribunal agreed that the phrase 'involving the amount of compensation for expropriation' contained some limitation. To ascertain the exact scope of this limit, Article 8 was interpreted in accordance with Article 31 of the VCLT. Unsurprisingly, the tribunal pointed out that the phrase 'involving the amount of compensation for expropriation' could have many different meanings. However, the tribunal applied Article 31 of the VCLT to conclude that the word 'involve' means 'include'. Accordingly, it held that the BIT required that the dispute may 'include' the quantification of compensation, not that it was restricted solely to a determination of the amount to be awarded. The tribunal pointed out that other terminology (such as 'limited to' or 'exclusively') was available to the treaty negotiators that would more convincingly have restricted the application of this provision to quantification, if that were, indeed, the intention.[62] In addition, the tribunal supported its interpretation by reference to the purpose of the BIT: 'It may be assumed, in accordance with the wording of the Preamble of the BIT, that the purpose of including the entitlement to submit certain disputes to ICSID arbitration is that of conferring certain benefits to promote investments.'[63]

After examining the preparatory work of the BIT (as described in the witness statements of Chinese and Peruvian negotiators), the tribunal took the view that China was unwilling to accept the Peruvian proposal for ICSID arbitration to determine all the issues that could have arisen between an investor and China. Nonetheless, the tribunal was not persuaded that this evidence offered conclusive proof as to the scope of Article 8(3): 'it does not establish clearly if China's consent was limited only to disputes involving the amount of compensation for expropriation or if as suggested by the actual wording of the BIT it would also include disputes involving other issues addressed in Article 4 of the BIT'.[64]

Chinese legal scholars' examination of Chinese BIT practice was also considered by the tribunal as not providing definitive or convincing guidelines on the interpretation of the BIT.[65] It further considered that there was no clearly established national policy of communist governments in the 1980s and 1990s that eschewed the resolution by

---

[61] *Ibid.*, para. 136. See particularly n. 71, which confirms that the draft notice and witness statement of Mr Jianghong Fan are consistent.
[62] *Ibid.*, para. 151.   [63] *Ibid.*, para. 153.
[64] *Ibid.*, para. 171.   [65] *Ibid.*, para. 172.

international arbitration of all disputes arising out of investment treaties.[66] And citing *RosInvest Co.*, it observed that the focus of the
interpretative exercise should not be the policies of the contracting
parties but what they had agreed to in the documentation.[67] In relation
to the respondent/host State arguments made in the *Sedelmayer,*
Saipem and *Telenor* awards the tribunal said this:

> It seems that none of the governments (two of which, Hungary and
> Russia, were communist States) had even tried to argue that the expres-
> sions 'involving compensation' or 'involving the amount of compen-
> sation' established public policies and the parties' intention to exclude
> all legal issues related to expropriation from the consent to international
> arbitration. Had the restrictive interpretation been the result of a policy
> deeply enrooted (and presumably hard to negotiate), it would have been
> unlikely that the involved governments had decided not to discuss it. But
> to the moment, as can be seen in the analysis of the three Awards (which
> include the usual abstracts of the positions of the parties) that is precisely
> what happened.[68]

The tribunal criticised the *Berschader* award because it had not analysed
how 'in the real world' an expropriation dispute may arise only in relation
to valuation.[69] It also appears to give less weight to both *Berschader*
and *RosInvest Co.* for attempting to determine the intentions of the BIT
parties without the parties having produced negotiation documents or
evidence.[70] *European Media Ventures* was considered by the tribunal to be
the 'most thorough and detailed' of the decisions on point.[71]

In arriving at its final decision, the tribunal emphasised that the
overall object and purpose of the BIT was important. The preamble of
the BIT was cited in order to show that the prime purpose of the BIT was
to 'increase the flow of private investment between both Contracting
Parties'.[72] The tribunal ultimately concluded that:

> to give meaning to all the elements of the article, it must be interpreted
> that the words 'involving the amount of compensation for expropriation'
> includes not only the mere determination of the amount but also any
> other issues normally inherent to an expropriation, including whether
> the property was actually expropriated in accordance with the BIT
> provisions and requirements, as well as the determination of the amount
> of compensation due, if any.[73]

---

[66] *Ibid.*, para. 174.   [67] *Ibid.*, para. 175.
[68] *Ibid.*, para. 176 (unofficial English translation).   [69] *Ibid.*, para. 178.
[70] *Ibid.*, paras. 182–4.   [71] *Ibid.*, para. 186.
[72] *Ibid.*, para. 187.   [73] *Ibid.*, para. 188.

The decision of the tribunal was unanimous and establishes that this clause in the Peru–China BIT provides tribunals with jurisdiction to ascertain not only the quantum of compensation, but also the matter of whether expropriation had occurred in the first place. This decision is of great significance for both companies investing in China and Chinese investors establishing investments in other States since many Chinese BITs which are still operable contain this or similar dispute-resolution clauses.

IV   Conclusion

The cases discussed in Sections II and III above reveal two divergent lines of awards as to 'amount of compensation' dispute-resolution clauses. This trend may have parallels with other conflicting lines of investment awards, such as those concerning the interpretation of umbrella clauses, MFN clauses and so forth. Nonetheless, comparatively little debate has been generated among members of the investment arbitration community with regard to the disparity in interpretation and application of 'amount of compensation' clauses. It is interesting to compare this present attitude with the high level of concern that was expressed early in the new millennium, when conflicting tribunal decisions caused a number of scholars to talk in terms of investment arbitration's legitimacy crisis.[74] Perhaps the relative paucity of concern in the current discourse on interpretation of dispute-resolution clauses indicates that inconsistent decision trends have, unfortunately, become a regular, almost expected, feature of investment arbitration.

In terms of commonality, an element in many of the cases referred to in this chapter is the use of Article 31 of the VCLT in the interpretation process. But, as has been seen, due to the different ways of deploying this rule, varied outcomes have emerged. *Berschader, RosInvest Co.* and *Austrian Airlines*, for example, tended to place importance on the ordinary meaning of the treaty text. This approach contrasts with the dominant role given to the object and purpose of the BIT in the interpretative process in *Tza Yap Shum* and *Renta 4*.

Before most of the awards discussed in this chapter became known to the public, many thought that 'amount of compensation' clauses constituted a bar to international arbitration in respect of substantive

---

[74] See e.g. S. D. Franck, 'The legitimacy crisis in investment treaty arbitration: Privatizing public international law through inconsistent decisions', *Fordham Law Review*, 73 (2004), 1521.

(as opposed to quantitative) issues. It followed from this understanding that international arbitration was available only if an investor was fortunate enough to have first obtained a finding by a host State organ that its property had been expropriated.[75] This general understanding makes the approach taken by the respondents in *Sedelmayer, Telenor* and *Sapiem* all the more perplexing – why did they not make objections to the effect that the dispute-resolution clauses at issue were limited to quantifying compensation?

It is apparent from section III that the narrow view as to the scope of 'amount of compensation' clauses no longer holds true for all cases. Indeed, arbitrators in recent decisions have shown a considerable willingness to interpret these clauses expansively. The implications of this new approach are, of course, profound. Where previously in such circumstances it was considered that there existed no realistic way to bring substantive issues before an international arbitral tribunal, now – without treaty amendment or the conclusion of a new instrument – it may be possible. It will also be of considerable interest to know China's view on the *Tza Yap Shum* tribunal's dispute-resolution clause interpretation, particularly given the remarkable growth of China as a capital exporter in recent years and the consequential need to protect its investors abroad.

From the perspective of China, the most common Chinese BIT restrictive dispute-resolution clause employs the words 'involving the amount of compensation for expropriation'.[76] This is precisely the same language as that found in the 'amount of compensation' clause of the

---

[75] See e.g. L. Nottage and J. R. Weeramantry, 'Investment arbitration in Asia: Five perspectives on law and practice' in L. Nottage and V. Bath (eds.), *Foreign Investment and Dispute Resolution Law and Practice in Asia* (Routledge, forthcoming 2011); G. Smith, 'Chinese bilateral investment treaties: Restrictions on international arbitration', *Arbitration*, 76 (2010), 58, 59; Gallagher and Shan, *Chinese Investment Treaties*, p. 316, para. 8.41; K. Rooney, 'ICSID and BIT arbitrations and China', *Journal of International Arbitration*, 24(6) (2007), 689, 703–4; and P. Peters, 'Dispute settlement arrangements in investment treaties', *Netherlands Yearbook of International Law*, 22 (1991), 91, 118–19, 123–4 and 129–33.

[76] Gallagher and Shan, *Chinese Investment Treaties*, p. 313, para. 8.32. Gallagher and Shan observe that the following BITs with China include this specific provision: Agreement between the Government of the People's Republic of China and the Government of the Republic of Albania Concerning the Encouragement and Reciprocal Protection of Investments, signed 13 February 1993, Art. 8(3); Agreement between the Government of the People's Republic of China and the Government of the Republic of Bolivia Concerning the Encouragement and Reciprocal Protection of Investments, signed 8 May 1992, Art. 8(3); Agreement between the Government of the Kingdom of Cambodia and the Government of the People's Republic of China for the Promotion and Protection of

Peru–China BIT, which was interpreted expansively by the *Tza Yap Shum* tribunal. If *Tza Yap Shum* is followed, upwards of eighteen BITs with the same clause[77] may also now have the potential to be invoked to determine substantive expropriation claims – and, although not identical, there are dozens of other treaties that also have similar wording to that of the China–Peru BIT.

Investments, signed 19 July 1996), Art. 9(3); Agreement between the Government of the Republic of Chile and the Government of the People's Republic of China Concerning the Encouragement and the Reciprocal Protection of Investments, signed 23 March 1994 (entered into force 14 October 1995), Art. 9(3); Agreement between the Government of the People's Republic of China and the Government of the Republic of Croatia Concerning the Encouragement and Reciprocal Protection of Investments, signed 7 June 1993 (entered into force 1 July 1994), Art. 8(3); Agreement between the Government of the People's Republic of China and the Government of the Republic of Cuba Concerning the Encouragement and Reciprocal Protection of Investments, signed 24 April 1995, Art. 9(3); Agreement between the Government of the Arab Republic of Egypt and the Government of the People's Republic of China Concerning the Encouragement and Reciprocal Protection of Investments, signed 21 April 1994, Art. 9(3); Agreement between the Government of the Federal Democratic Republic of Ethiopia and the Government of the People's Republic of China Concerning the Encouragement and Reciprocal Protection of Investments, signed 1998, Art. 9(3); Agreement between the Government of the People's Republic of China and the Government of the Republic of Georgia Concerning the Encouragement and Reciprocal Protection of Investments, signed 3 June 1993 (entered into force 1 March 1995), Art. 9(3); Agreement between the Government of the People's Republic of China and the Government of the Republic of Iceland Concerning the Promotion and Reciprocal Protection of Investments, signed 31 March 1994, Art. 8(3); Agreement between the Government of the People's Republic of China and the Government of Jamaica Concerning the Encouragement and Reciprocal Protection of Investments, signed 26 October 1994 (entered into force 1 April 1996), Art. 8(3); Agreement between the Government of the People's Republic of China and the Government of the Lao People's Democratic Republic Concerning the Encouragement and Reciprocal Protection of Investments, signed 31 January 1993 (entered into force 1 June 1993), Art. 8(3); China–Lebanon BIT, Art. 8(3); Agreement between the Government of the People's Republic of China and the Government of the Mongolian People's Republic Concerning the Encouragement and Reciprocal Protection of Investments, signed 26 August 1991 (entered into force 1 November 1993), Art. 8(3); Peru-China BIT, Art. 8(3); Agreement between the People's Republic of China and the Republic of Turkey Concerning the Reciprocal Promotion and Protection of Investments, signed 13 November 1990 (entered into force 19 August 1994), Art. VII(b); Agreement between the Government of the People's Republic of China and the Government of the Oriental Republic of Uruguay Concerning the Encouragement and Reciprocal Protection of Investments, signed 2 December 1993 (entered into force 1 December 1997), Art. 9(3); Agreement between the Government of the People's Republic of China and the Government of the Socialist Republic of Vietnam Concerning the Encouragement and Reciprocal Protection of Investments, signed 2 December 1992 (entered into force 1 September 1993), Art. 8(3). Gallagher and Shan, *Chinese Investment Treaties*, p. 314.

[77] *Ibid.*

Nonetheless, it is certainly not the case yet that investors can become complacent and should expect consistently favourable outcomes under BITs containing these clauses. Ultimately, *Shum, Renta 4* and *European Media Ventures* are not binding on any other investment tribunal, each case turns on the specific wording of the BIT at issue, and each treaty must be interpreted separately on its own merits. It is likely, however, that the interpretation of these very specific types of clauses will continue to be the subject of still further developments in the future. What can be said at this stage is that the introduction of such a significant shift in approach illustrates the evolving nature of foreign investment law, indicates a more general state of flux within interpretative processes adopted by tribunals, and reflects the extraordinary pace with which change is currently occurring in the field.

19

Interference by a local court and a failure to enforce: Actionable under a bilateral investment treaty?

ANDREW STEPHENSON, LEE CARROLL AND
JONATHON DEBOOS

I Introduction

The New York Convention was designed to promote the enforcement of international arbitral awards, with minimal interference by the courts of the country in which enforcement is sought.[1] Accordingly, Article V of the New York Convention provides few grounds for resisting the recognition and enforcement of awards. Those grounds are limited to awards made without jurisdiction, a party being subject to some legally relevant incapacity, a failure to comply with the rules of natural justice, the composition of the tribunal being contrary to the arbitration agreement or the law of the seat, the award having been set aside at the seat, the subject matter of the dispute not being capable of resolution by arbitration in the country where enforcement is sought or enforcement of the award being otherwise contrary to the public policy of that country.[2] Importantly, the New York Convention does not allow a court asked to enforce an international award to engage in a 'merits review' of the award; that is, it is irrelevant to the question of enforcement whether the award is correct in accordance with the *lex causae*. In theory, it is only the courts of the seat of the arbitration which have jurisdiction to review the merits of an award. Whether any review is possible in those courts is not a function of the New York Convention but is determined by the

---

[1] United Nations Convention on the Recognition and Enforcement of Foreign Arbitral Awards, signed 10 June 1958 (entered into force 7 June 1959) (New York Convention); see e.g. G. B. Born, *International Commercial Arbitration: Commentary and materials*, 2nd edn (The Hague: Kluwer, 2001); L. A. Mistelis and J. D. M. Lew (eds.), *Pervasive Problems in International Arbitration* (The Hague: Kluwer, 2006).
[2] New York Convention, Art. V(1)–(2).

lex arbitri. This means that it is possible for the parties to choose a seat which does not allow a merits review of the award. If this is done, then the award will not, in theory at least, be the subject of a merits review in either the place where the award was made or the place where it is enforced. Many (but by no means all) parties will deliberately seek this outcome.

However, there are numerous examples where awards have been the subject of a merits review in the country where enforcement is sought, notwithstanding that country's ratification of the New York Convention.[3] Often that country is the home of the party required to make payment pursuant to the award and the jurisdiction where all of that party's assets are located. Therefore, if enforcement is frustrated in this jurisdiction, the award may be of no value.

Often a merits review occurs because the enforcing court has, in a domestic setting, interpreted Article V widely. For example, in *ONGC* the Supreme Court of India refused to enforce an international arbitration award on the ground that it was contrary to forum public policy. The governing law which applied to determine the substantive issues in the dispute was the law of India. The Supreme Court reviewed the award and concluded that the arbitrators had misapplied Indian law. The Supreme Court ruled that it would be contrary to Indian public policy for an Indian court to enforce an award which had misapplied Indian law. In this way, notwithstanding the narrow grounds for review stipulated by the New York Convention, the Indian court engaged in a merits review and refused to enforce the award.

Such an outcome was not intended by the New York Convention, and where such outcomes occur they frustrate the primary purpose of the New York Convention. However, once it is ratified, the New York Convention should, in theory, be incorporated into the domestic law of each State Party, and become part of each State Party's *lex arbitri.* This means that it was always possible that the domestic courts of different

[3] See e.g. *Oil & Natural Gas Corporation Ltd* v. *Saw Pipes Ltd* (2003) 5 SCC 705 (India) (*ONGC*); *Luzon Hydro Corp.* v. *Hon Rommel O Baybay and Transfield Philippines Inc.* (Decision of the Philippines Court of Appeals, Manila, of 29 November 2006, Special Former Fourth Division), CA-G.R. SP No. 94318, (*Luzon*) (Philippines), reproduced in A. J. van den Berg (ed.), *Yearbook Commercial Arbitration,* XXXII (2007), 456; *Resort Condominiums International Inc* v. *Bolwell* [1995] 1 Qd R 406 (*Resort Condominiums*) (see especially Lee J.) (Australia); and *Monégasque de Réassurances SAM (Monde Re)* v. *NAK Naftogaz of Ukraine and State of Ukraine,* 311 F 3d 488 (2d Cir, 2002) (*Monde Re*) (United States).

countries would interpret the provisions of the New York Convention differently.[4] There is nothing surprising or inappropriate about this.[5]

Of greater concern, however, are situations which can arise where a court refuses enforcement not by reference to any legitimate interpretation of the relevant law but to protect the domestic party and frustrate the award. Obviously, such decisions are not made bona fide and the court is likely to disguise the real motive for the decision. Where it does occur, a question can sometimes arise as to whether a bilateral investment treaty (BIT) can provide relief to the beneficiary of an award.

The recent case of *Saipem SpA* v. *The People's Republic of Bangladesh* provides an opportunity to explore the circumstances in which a State could breach a BIT where its local courts interfere in the proceedings of an international commercial arbitration.[6] In this case, the interference in an arbitration by a Bangladeshi court, revoking the authority of the arbitral tribunal, was held to amount to an expropriation without compensation[7] by the Bangladeshi State in contravention of Article 5 of the Italy–Bangladesh BIT.[8] The case also raises the interesting and related question of whether a State may breach a BIT by failing to provide a sufficient enforcement mechanism under the New York Convention.

II Saipem

A The facts

Saipem SpA (Saipem), an Italian company, and the Bangladesh Oil Gas and Mineral Corporation (Petrobangla), entered into a contract for the construction of a gas pipeline in Bangladesh. The contract contained an arbitration agreement referring all disputes to ICC arbitration before a

---

[4] See e.g. W. W. Park, 'Treaty obligations and national law', *Hastings Law Review*, 58 (2006), 251; K.-H. Böckstiegel, 'Public policy as a limit to arbitration and its enforcement', *International Bar Association Journal of Dispute Resolution* (2008), 123.

[5] Hopefully education programmes will help reach an international consensus about the proper interpretation of the New York Convention to avoid anomalies such as those identified in the third footnote.

[6] *Saipem SpA* v. *The People's Republic of Bangladesh* (ICSID Case No. ARB/05/7, Award of 30 June 2009) (*Saipem*).

[7] It was common ground that no compensation was paid. Therefore, the question for the tribunal was limited to whether the disputed actions constituted an expropriation within the meaning of Art. 5 of the BIT.

[8] Agreement between the Government of the Republic of Italy and the Government of the People's Republic of Bangladesh on the Promotion and Protection of Investments, signed 20 March 1990 (entered into force 20 September 1994).

three-member tribunal in Dhaka.[9] Disputes arose, and Saipem commenced arbitration in accordance with the parties' agreement. Petrobangla raised a number of jurisdictional challenges which the ICC tribunal dismissed in an award on jurisdiction.[10]

During the ICC arbitration, the tribunal denied a number of procedural requests made by Petrobangla.[11] These were: (a) a request to strike from the record the witness statement of a key Saipem witness who had not been present at the hearing (according to Saipem, due to actions taken by Bangladesh to prevent him from attending the hearing); (b) a request that all witnesses be allowed to be present in the hearing room during the entire hearing; (c) a request that a letter from Petrobangla which was not on the record be filed during the cross-examination of a witness; (d) a request to strike from the record a 'draft *aide-mémoire*' of the World Bank (which was sponsoring the project),[12] and certain cost calculations prepared by Saipem; and (e) a request that written transcripts be made of the tape recordings of the hearing.

Petrobangla reiterated these requests on two occasions before the tribunal. Petrobangla also requested the ICC tribunal to order Saipem to provide information about its insurance policy and claims made under it, which Saipem had refused to provide. The ICC tribunal issued an order that Saipem's refusal to provide the requested information would be assessed when appropriate at a later stage in the proceedings.[13]

Following the ICC tribunal's decision on these matters, Petrobangla issued proceedings in the First Court of the Subordinate Judge of Dhaka seeking to revoke the ICC tribunal's authority. The basis of Petrobangla's claim was that the arbitrators had misconducted themselves and had breached the parties' procedural rights when rejecting Petrobangla's procedural requests during the hearing.[14] Petrobangla also applied to the High Court Division of the Supreme Court of Bangladesh to stay all further proceedings of the arbitration pending before the ICC tribunal and/or restrain Saipem and/or the tribunal from proceeding further with the arbitration. The Supreme Court issued an injunction restraining Saipem from continuing with the arbitration, and subsequent decisions confirmed and maintained the stay of arbitration.

---

[9] *Saipem*, para. 10.   [10] *Ibid.*, paras. 25–7.

[11] *Ibid.*, para. 31. See also *Saipem SpA v. The People's Republic of Bangladesh* (ICSID Case No. ARB/05/7, Decision on Jurisdiction and Recommendation on Provisional Measures of 21 March 2007) (*Saipem* (Decision on Jurisdiction)), para. 22.

[12] *Saipem*, para. 6.   [13] *Ibid.*, paras. 32–3.   [14] *Ibid.*, para. 35.

The First Subordinate Judge of Dhaka revoked the authority of the ICC tribunal on the grounds that it had:

> conducted the arbitration proceedings improperly by refusing to deter-
> mine the question of the admissibility of evidence and the exclusion of
> certain documents from the record as well as its failure to direct that
> information regarding insurance be provided. Moreover, the Tribunal has
> manifestly been in disregard of the law and as such the Tribunal commit-
> ted misconduct.[15]

Further court proceedings ensued, culminating in an injunction being issued by the High Court Division of the Supreme Court of Bangladesh, restraining Saipem from proceeding with the ICC arbitration.[16] None-theless, the ICC tribunal continued and rendered an award in Saipem's favour.[17]

Petrobangla applied to the High Court Division of the Supreme Court of Bangladesh to have the award set aside. However, the Court denied the application because it considered there to be 'no Award in the eye of the law' for it to set aside. This was because the ICC tribunal's authority had been revoked and it had proceeded with the arbitration 'most illegally and without jurisdiction'. Moreover, the ICC tribunal had been 'injuncted upon by the High Court Division not to proceed with the said arbitration case any further'. Saipem did not appeal this decision.[18] Petrobangla had no assets outside Bangladesh.[19] Therefore, Saipem could not enforce the award in Bangladesh, and was unable to enforce the award outside Bangladesh.

B   The ICSID proceeding

On 5 October 2004, Saipem filed a request for arbitration with the International Centre for Settlement of Investment Disputes (ICSID).[20] At the hearing on the merits, Saipem contended that the courts of Bangladesh had acted illegally and/or without jurisdiction when revok-ing the ICC tribunal's authority.[21] Saipem argued that this denied it the right to arbitration, which was a contractual right with an economic value. It argued that the actions of the Bangladeshi courts were

---

[15] *Ibid.*, para. 40.   [16] *Ibid.*, para. 47.   [17] *Ibid.*, para. 50.   [18] *Ibid.*, paras. 49–51.
[19] *Ibid.*, para. 130.   [20] *Saipem* (Decision on Jurisdiction), para. 42.
[21] Bangladesh raised jurisdictional objections but the ICSID tribunal held that it had jurisdiction to hear the claim: *ibid.*, para. 161.

attributable to the Republic of Bangladesh and, accordingly, that the State of Bangladesh had expropriated Saipem's right to arbitration in breach of Article 5 of the Italy–Bangladesh BIT.[22] For its part, Bangladesh contended that the courts of Bangladesh had the necessary supervisory jurisdiction to revoke the authority of the ICC tribunal under Article 5 of the Bangladeshi Arbitration Act 1940.[23]

The ICSID tribunal held that the acts of the Bangladeshi courts amounted to an expropriation by Bangladesh of Saipem's investment in Bangladesh, in breach of the Italy–Bangladesh BIT. Its reasoning can be summarised as follows.

The ICSID tribunal held that the property being expropriated was 'Saipem's residual contractual rights under the investment as crystallised in the ICC Award'.[24] It held that the actions of the Bangladeshi courts amounted to an indirect expropriation as they were 'measures having similar effects' within the meaning of Article 5(2) of the Italy–Bangladesh BIT and that the actions 'resulted in substantially depriving Saipem of the benefit of the ICC Award'.[25]

The next question was whether the actions of the Bangladeshi courts (which were attributable to the State of Bangladesh) were 'illegal', thus giving rise to a claim of expropriation. Saipem argued that the actions of the courts were illegal for two reasons: first, the courts lacked jurisdiction to revoke the authority of the ICC tribunal, and secondly, revocation of the ICC tribunal's jurisdiction had been decided on spurious grounds.

The ICSID tribunal rejected Saipem's first submission. It held that the assertion of jurisdiction by the Bangladeshi courts was not illegal and that Saipem had failed to establish that the ICC Court's authority as regards revocation was exclusive under the applicable Bangladeshi law.[26] In respect of the merits of the Court's decision to revoke the authority of the ICC tribunal, the ICSID tribunal rejected, for want of evidence, Saipem's allegation that Petrobangla had acted in collusion or conspired with the Bangladeshi courts.[27] However, the ICSID tribunal found that the revocation of the ICC tribunal's authority was contrary to both the principle of abuse of rights and the New York Convention.

---

[22] *Saipem*, para. 84. Saipem did not bring a claim on the ground of denial of justice because Art. 9.1 of the Italy–Bangladesh BIT does not confer jurisdiction to the ICSID tribunal in respect of such claims.
[23] *Ibid.*, para. 86.   [24] *Ibid.*, para. 128.   [25] *Ibid.*, para. 129.   [26] *Ibid.*, para. 144.
[27] *Ibid.*, paras. 146–8.

1 Abuse of rights

In making its finding on abuse of rights, the ICSID tribunal reviewed the procedural orders of the ICC tribunal which constituted the impugned conduct and 'did not find the slightest trace of error or wrongdoing'. The ICSID tribunal held that the Dhaka court's finding that the arbitrators 'committed misconduct' lacked any justification. The Dhaka court did not refer to any Bangladeshi law which had been manifestly disregarded. It found that the Dhaka court's decision was a 'grossly unfair ruling'.[28] The ICSID tribunal said:

> Bangladesh does not even try to show that the ICC Arbitrators' conduct was somehow inappropriate, illegitimate or unfair. To the contrary, Bangladesh tries to justify the decision to revoke the authority of the ICC Tribunal exclusively on the ground that the test set forth in Article 5 of the [Bangladeshi Arbitration Act of 1940] is not stringent and leaves the authority free to extrapolate that the arbitrators may be likely to commit a miscarriage of justice. In none of its submissions in the present arbitration did Bangladesh even attempt to show that the ICC Tribunal committed misconduct and that such alleged misconduct could reasonably justify the revocation of the arbitrators.[29]

The tribunal concluded that:

> the Bangladeshi courts abused their supervisory jurisdiction over the arbitration process. It is true that the revocation of an arbitrator's authority can legitimately be ordered in case of misconduct. It is further true that in making such order national courts do have substantial discretion. However, they cannot use their jurisdiction to revoke arbitrators for reasons wholly unrelated with such misconduct and the risks it carries for the fair resolution of the dispute. Taken together, the standard for revocation used by the Bangladesh courts and the manner in which the judge applied that standard to the facts indeed constituted an abuse of right ... In conclusion, the Tribunal is of the opinion that the Bangladeshi courts exercised their supervisory jurisdiction for an end which was different from that for which it was instituted and thus violated the internationally accepted principle of prohibition of abuse of rights.[30]

2 Violation of the New York Convention

In addition to its finding that the Dhaka court had violated the principle of abuse of rights, the ICSID tribunal also held that the court's decision to revoke the arbitrators' authority amounted to a violation of Article II of the New York Convention because it de facto prevented or

---

[28] *Ibid.*, para. 155.   [29] *Ibid.*, para. 156.   [30] *Ibid.*, paras. 159 and 161.

immobilised the arbitration that sought to implement the arbitration agreement, 'thus completely frustrating if not the wording at least the spirit of the Convention'.[31] We consider below whether a State's failure to provide a sufficient enforcement mechanism under the New York Convention may amount to a breach of a BIT.

III   Discussion of the ICSID tribunal's decision in *Saipem*

A   *Generally*

This is a very interesting award because it examines the extent to which a State can be held liable in international law where a local court interferes with an arbitration. Arbitral proceedings are governed by the law of the seat of arbitration (the *lex arbitri*) and the courts of the seat have jurisdiction to supervise the arbitration including, in some jurisdictions, the power to conduct a merits review of the award, as has already been noted. In this case, the choice of Dhaka as the seat of arbitration meant that Bangladeshi arbitration law governed the proceedings as the *lex arbitri* and the Bangladeshi courts had supervisory jurisdiction over those proceedings.

The *lex arbitri*, as it is domestic law, will typically reflect the public policy of the relevant country. Public policy varies significantly from country to country so that what is regarded as misconduct in one country may not be misconduct in another. Further, public policy relevant to arbitration can change rapidly. At the time of entering into an arbitration agreement, parties should engage in due diligence to ensure the *lex arbitri* suits them and their transaction.

It is submitted that the failure of a court to apply its domestic law properly, which serves to confer an advantage on a local investor and a disadvantage on a foreign investor, may amount to an abuse of the power of the court and a failure by the State to accord fair and equitable treatment (inter alia, in the sense that it may amount to a denial of justice)[32] and a failure to provide legal protection for the

---

[31] *Ibid.*, para. 167.

[32] See e.g. C. McLachlan, L. Shore and M. Weiniger, *International Investment Arbitration: Substantive principles* (Oxford University Press, 2007), pp. 227–33; R. Dolzer and C. Schreuer, *Principles of International Investment Law* (Oxford University Press, 2008), pp. 142–4; K. Yannaca-Small, 'Fair and equitable treatment standard: Recent developments' in A. Reinisch (ed.), *Standards of Investment Protection* (Oxford University Press, 2008), pp. 111, 119–20; and J. Paulsson, *Denial of Justice in International Law* (Cambridge University Press, 2005), pp. 1, 147–57.

investment.[33] In addition, such conduct may breach an expropriation protection under a BIT, as was found by the ICSID tribunal in *Saipem*.

However, were an ICSID tribunal permitted to find that it disagreed with the policy settings reflected in the *lex arbitri* and that, without more, the application of those policy settings constituted a breach of a BIT, many decisions of 'first world' courts would be capable of challenge because of different views about policy held by an ICSID tribunal.

Let us consider the approach taken by the ICSID tribunal in the *Saipem* case. The bases on which the Bangladeshi court revoked the ICC tribunal's jurisdiction are listed at paragraph 152 of the ICSID award. In summary, the court considered the ICC tribunal's conduct to be inappropriate because it: (a) allowed the admission of a witness statement without the witness being called when (perhaps) available to give evidence; (b) admitted into evidence a document without formal proof of the document (and therefore presumably the truth of its contents); (c) either did not rule on a discovery application in relation to insurance documents or otherwise did not allow discovery; and (d) rejected an application for a written transcript.

The first two grounds appear to be based on the failure to apply common law rules of evidence that would preclude the admission of a document into evidence without oral evidence as to its authenticity and, if admitted into evidence for the purpose of proving factual matters, the accuracy of the statements made in the document. In Australia, domestic arbitrations are governed by the Commercial Arbitration Act in force in the relevant Australian state or territory. Prior to the introduction of this legislation in Australia, and also for a time in England,[34] absent anything to the contrary in the arbitration agreement, an arbitrator had to comply with the applicable rules of evidence. A failure to do so in a serious way could have grounded an application for misconduct.[35] If it was recently considered appropriate that the applicable rules of evidence apply in Australian and English arbitrations (and that a failure to apply them may constitute misconduct), how can it now be said to be inappropriate in Bangladesh? As to the third ground, in a number of common law countries an inability to obtain discovery of relevant documents would be regarded as a serious irregularity. The fourth ground is curious, as it seems that the ICC tribunal refused to allow written transcripts to be

---

[33] See e.g. Dolzer and Schreuer, *Principles of International Investment Law*, pp. 151–2.

[34] See e.g. *In re Enoch and Zaretsky Bock & Co.* [1910] 1 KB 327 and *WM Adolph & Co.* v. *The Keene Company* [1921] 7 Lloyd's Rep 142.

[35] See e.g. *Gas and Fuel Corporation of Victoria* v. *Wood Hall Ltd* [1978] VR 385.

made of the tape recordings of the hearings. Why the ICC tribunal would refuse such an application is not explained and is in any event very unusual.

When one looks at the ICSID award, the reasoning (or absence thereof) is unsatisfactory and does not provide the usual analysis which would give comfort that the decision was correct (it may be correct – it is just not apparent from the award). First, there is no explanation of the *lex arbitri* and no analysis as to why the decision of the Bangladeshi court offends the *lex arbitri*. It may be a function of the way in which the case was argued, but the award contains no detailed analysis of the reasons justifying the conclusion that the Bangladeshi court did not apply the *lex arbitri* correctly, let alone that the court was acting in bad faith. Indeed, the decision merely summarises the arguments and then reaches a conclusion.

Secondly, the ICSID tribunal appears to have proceeded on the basis that it is for Bangladesh to prove that the Bangladeshi court was correct in finding that the ICC arbitrators had misconducted themselves. As extracted above, the ICSID tribunal bemoaned Bangladesh's failure to show that the conduct of the ICC tribunal was inappropriate, illegitimate or unfair. This is curious. Saipem was the claimant and presumably the onus fell on it to prove that the Bangladeshi court's decision was not only in error (which occurs in any court system – that is why there is an appeal process), but that the error was in bad faith and constituted an abuse of right.

Thirdly, it is unclear what the ICSID tribunal considered to be the scope of a court's discretion to revoke a tribunal's authority. The ICSID tribunal said:

> It is true that the revocation of an arbitrator's authority can legitimately be ordered in case of misconduct. It is further true that in making such an order national courts do have substantial discretion. However, they cannot use their jurisdiction to revoke arbitrators for reasons wholly unrelated with such misconduct and the risks it carries for the fair resolution of the dispute.[36]

The tribunal may have been of the view that all that need be established was that the court had incorrectly concluded that there had been misconduct. If that is what is meant, then this test is far too wide. Any error can usually be rectified by an appeal. However, in a common law

---

[36] *Saipem*, para. 159.

country, if the decision is confirmed by the final court of appeal, then the ratio of that decision is the law, and, by definition, cannot be in error.

It is submitted that for Saipem to be successful in its claim for expropriation, it would have to establish the relevant Bangladeshi law and then analyse why, having regard to the facts, there was no breach of the relevant minimum procedural requirements of the *lex arbitri* which could justify a finding of misconduct. To make out the serious allegation against Bangladesh, Saipem should have been required to establish: (a) what (if any) rules of evidence or discovery of Bangladesh were required by the *lex arbitri* to be applied in the arbitration; (b) whether any relevant rules were broken by the ICC tribunal; (c) if this was the case, whether the breach was of such a magnitude to constitute misconduct in accordance with the *lex arbitri*; (d) if there was misconduct, whether such misconduct was of such a magnitude, by the standards specified by the *lex arbitri*, to justify the removal of the arbitrators; and (e) if there was no misconduct, whether the error was a consequence of a genuine mistake or some lack of bona fides.

Even if the answer to (e) is that the court did not discharge its function with bona fides, the claimant would still need to establish that there was no way in which the error could be rectified. It is submitted that it is only when mala fides have been established and the error so created cannot be rectified, it can be contended that the State has failed to provide a suitable justice system and thereby 'expropriated' the cause of action. Similar questions could be posed in relation to the refusal to allow a written transcript. In each case it is necessary to establish what the *lex arbitri* is, and whether the ICC tribunal complied with those rules.

B   Purported breach of the New York Convention

In addition to its findings on the issue of expropriation, the ICSID tribunal also contemplated that a decision to revoke an arbitral tribunal's authority may amount to a breach of the New York Convention. The tribunal said:

> Technically, the courts of Bangladesh did not target the arbitration agreement in itself, but revoked the authority of the arbitrators. However, it is the Tribunal's opinion that a decision to revoke the arbitrators' authority can amount to a violation of Article II of the New York Convention whenever it *de facto* 'prevents or immobilizes the arbitration that seeks to implement that [arbitration] agreement' thus completely frustrating if not the wording at least the spirit of the Convention.[37]

---

[37] *Ibid.*, para. 167.

Article II of the New York Convention provides:

1. Each Contracting State shall recognize an agreement in writing under which the parties undertake to submit to arbitration all or any differences which have arisen or which may arise between them in respect of a defined legal relationship, whether contractual or not, concerning a subject matter capable of settlement by arbitration.
2. The term "agreement in writing" shall include an arbitral clause in a contract or an arbitration agreement, signed by the parties or contained in an exchange of letters or telegrams.
3. The court of a Contracting State, when seized of an action in a matter in respect of which the parties have made an agreement within the meaning of this article, shall at the request of one of the parties, refer the parties to arbitration, unless it finds that the said agreement is null and void, inoperative or incapable of being performed.[38]

What the ICSID tribunal appears to be saying is that the decision by the Bangladeshi courts to revoke the authority of the ICC tribunal is conduct which fails to recognise the agreement to arbitrate. The Bangladeshi courts had jurisdiction to supervise the ICC arbitration. Such jurisdiction includes a power to revoke the authority of the tribunal if there had been misconduct on the part of the arbitrators. Accordingly, while a decision to revoke the authority of the tribunal may frustrate the arbitration, a proper decision of that type could never constitute a breach of the New York Convention. This is so because the New York Convention does not regulate the supervisory jurisdiction of the courts at the seat. If there is merit in the argument, much more needs to be established.

In order for a decision to be properly based on such a ground, the issues noted above would need to be established concerning the court's failure to follow the relevant *lex arbitri* relating to the supervision of international arbitration (i.e. what the applicable rules of evidence and discovery are under the *lex arbitri*; whether the arbitrators failed to apply any relevant rules; if so, whether such breach was of sufficient magnitude to constitute misconduct under the *lex arbitri*; and whether such misconduct was of sufficient magnitude to justify removal of the arbitrators). If the *lex arbitri* had not been properly applied it would be necessary to establish that this was not just a mere error, but was a bad-faith decision. There are no findings in relation to these matters in the *Saipem* case, nor did the ICSID tribunal seem to consider them as relevant. It is unknown whether these issues were canvassed at the

---

[38] New York Convention, Art. II.

hearing. The award, on its face, seems to suggest, by omission, that these issues were not important to the tribunal's consideration.

C   What if the reasoning in Saipem were applied to other non-enforcement decisions?

It is worth considering what the outcome would be if the reasoning of the ICSID tribunal in *Saipem* v. *Bangladesh* were applied in a number of other cases where local courts have refused enforcement. For instance:

- *Monde Re* is a United States decision in which Monde Re sought enforcement of an award rendered in Moscow in New York against Naftogaz and the State of Ukraine. The United States District Court for the Southern District of New York had dismissed the request for enforcement on the basis of *forum non conveniens*,[39] which allows courts to 'decline jurisdiction over complex and inconvenient lawsuits brought in the United States which implicate foreign parties only; require the application of foreign law; and entail no contacts with the interests of the United States'.[40] The decision was affirmed by the Court of Appeals for the Second Circuit. Could such a decision justify recourse to a BIT if one had existed?
- *Resort Condominiums* is a Queensland Supreme Court decision which concerned an arbitration arising due to a dispute over a licence agreement. The court noted that while the New York Convention states that recognition of an award may *only* be refused upon proof of one of the events listed in Article V(1), the International Arbitration Act 1974 (Cth) (which implements the New York Convention in Australia) does not contain the word 'only'. On this basis Lee J. concluded that the court had a residual discretion about whether to enforce arbitral awards.[41] This decision has been criticised,[42] and the relevant provision of the International Arbitration Act 1974 has now been amended so that such an argument is no longer available in Australia. However, the question remains if a relevant BIT existed with an appropriate provision, would the decision of Lee J. have constituted a breach of that treaty at the time it was made?

---

[39] *Monégasque de Réassurances SAM. (Monde Re)* v. *Nak Naftogaz of Ukraine*, 158 F Supp 2d 377 (US Dist. S.D.N.Y., 2001).

[40] *Ibid.*, p. 381.   [41] *Resort Condominiums*, p. 427.

[42] See e.g. M. Pryles, 'Interlocutory orders and convention awards: The case of *Resort Condominiums v. Bolwel*', *Arbitration International*, 10(4) (1994), 385.

- *Australian Granites* v. *Eisenwerk* is a Queensland Court of Appeal decision in which it was held that by agreeing to arbitration in accordance with the ICC Rules of Arbitration the parties intended to opt-out of the Model Law (which was formerly permitted under the International Arbitration Act 1974).[43] This decision was followed by the Singaporean High Court in *John Holland Pty Ltd (fka John Holland Construction & Engineering Pty Ltd)* v. *Toyo Engineering Corp. (Japan)*.[44] Both cases were the subject of heavy criticism. Subsequently, in both Australia and Singapore, the law has been changed so that the ratio of the case is not the law of either jurisdiction. Again, could such a decision be a breach of an appropriately worded BIT?

- Could the decision of the Supreme Court of India in *ONGC*, discussed earlier, constitute a breach of a BIT?

- *Luzon* is a Philippine Court of Appeals decision in which it was held that an arbitral award in respect of a contract governed by Philippine law was null and void for manifestly disregarding Philippine law and for being contrary to forum public policy.[45] The court found that the award manifestly disregarded Philippine law because the contract was governed by Philippine law and the tribunal failed to apply it correctly. Further, the award was contrary to Philippine public policy because it awarded costs to the successful party without first finding that the unsuccessful party had litigated in bad faith (which was a precondition to an adverse costs order under Philippine law).

- *Iran Aircraft Industries and Iran Helicopter Support and Renewal Company* v. *Avco Corporation* is a United States Court of Appeals decision in which the Second Circuit refused to enforce an award of the Iran–United States Claims Tribunal in favour of Iranian agencies and instrumentalities against Avco.[46] The court held that the award was unenforceable under Article V(1)(b) because Avco had not been afforded an opportunity to present its case. This was because at a pre-hearing conference (which neither counsel for the Iranian party nor the Iranian arbitrator had attended) the chairman of the tribunal had permitted Avco to substantiate its claims by submitting its audited accounts, rather than actual invoices. Subsequently the chairman of the tribunal resigned and was replaced. In its award, the

---

[43]   *Eisenwerk Hensel Bayreuth Dipl-Ing Burkhardt GmbH* v. *Australian Granites Ltd* [2001] 1 Qd R 461 (*Eisenwerk*).

[44]   [2001] 2 SLR 262. However, this decision has since been overturned by legislation in Singapore.

[45]   *Luzon*, pp. 456–73.   [46]   980 F 2d 141 (2d Cir, 1992).

tribunal rejected Avco's claims for failure to produce the actual invoices, notwithstanding its earlier ruling that audited accounts would be sufficient to prove quantum. The court refused to enforce the award because the tribunal had, 'however unwittingly', misled Avco and in so doing had 'denied Avco the opportunity to present its claim in a meaningful manner'.[47] This case appears to be justified in principle.

However, the *Avco* decision was the subject of a further claim before the Iran–United States Claims Tribunal, this time between Iran and the United States.[48] In this case, Iran argued that the United States had breached its obligations under the Algiers Accords (the agreements between Iran and the United States which, among other things, established the Iran–United States Claims Tribunal),[49] by failing to enforce the *Avco* award. The Iran–United States Claims Tribunal held that the United States had breached the Algiers Accords because the Court of Appeal's decision in *Avco* was erroneous. This was because the tribunal's award in *Avco* 'was based not on the absence of the invoices underlying Avco's claims, but on a lack of proof that those invoices were payable'.[50]

These cases demonstrate that there can be legitimate differences of opinion as to the meaning of certain provisions of the New York Convention. Of course, there can also be illegitimate bad-faith decisions by courts to protect the interests of nationals and States. However, it is submitted that international arbitral tribunals called upon to consider the conduct of a national court will need to establish bad faith in the judicial process before being able to establish a breach of a treaty by a State. Further, any tribunal called upon to rule on such case should require detailed proof of the alleged illegitimate decision. The award should set out in detail why the conduct of the court falls outside a legitimate exercise of its jurisdiction.

IV Conclusion

The New York Convention provides an effective system for the enforcement of international arbitration awards. Unfortunately, there will be legitimate differences of opinion about the interpretation of its provisions. Over time, it is hoped that an international consensus will emerge

---

[47] *Ibid.*, p. 146.
[48] *The Islamic Republic of Iran* v. *United States of America* (Award No. 586-A27-FT of 5 June 1998) 34 Iran–US Claims Tribunal Reports 39 (*Iran* v. *USA*).
[49] Algiers Accords (1981) 20 ILM 223.   [50] *Iran* v. *USA*, para. 66.

so that merits reviews of awards by courts asked to enforce awards will disappear. In the meantime the resolution of the problem caused by different interpretations of the New York Convention is most likely to be resolved by debate and criticism of existing decisions.

More problematic is where the courts of a particular country refuse to enforce an award, or where the courts of the seat interfere with the arbitral process or otherwise interfere with an award, for ulterior illegitimate reasons. Drawing a distinction between such cases and cases arising from a legitimate difference of opinion about legal principle is always likely to be difficult. However, States should be wary because the actions of its courts may give rise to a claim under a BIT.

The nature of such an allegation is obviously serious. To be made out, the claimant must discharge a significant onus. Likewise, any tribunal which concludes that such onus has been discharged should, having regard to the seriousness of the allegations, set out its full reasoning. If this does not occur it is likely that countries, particularly those who were not involved, will not understand why the defendant country was held liable, and will be concerned that a similar fate awaits it.

The ICSID tribunal in the *Saipem* case failed to set out the basis of its decision in sufficient detail to justify the conclusion reached.[51] Accordingly, it will raise concerns not only in Bangladesh but elsewhere as to the appropriateness of international arbitration as a dispute-resolution process. Where an ICSID tribunal makes a finding that the value of a cause of action has been lost due to a court process, the claimant must satisfy a heavy burden of proof, and the quality of the tribunal's reasoning must be of the highest standard.

---

[51] Arguably, it was open to Bangladesh to file an application for annulment of the award under Art. 52(1)(e) of the ICSID Convention on the ground that the 'award has failed to state the reasons on which it is based'. Bangladesh did not do so.

20

Bias challenges in investor–State arbitration: Lessons from international commercial arbitration

SAM LUTTRELL*

I Introduction

Bias challenges are part of everyday life in international commercial arbitration (ICA). ICA lawyers are now very sophisticated in their use of challenge as a means of delaying proceedings and denying the other side the arbitrator of its choice. There are various causes and effects of this phenomenon, but on balance it seems that the rate of bias challenge in ICA has increased for mostly economic reasons: from the perspective of the aspiring arbitrator, bias challenges are a valuable weapon against the cartel of 'grand old men' (and women) who get most of the appointments as arbitrators; and bias challenges have a retail aspect in that, from the client's perspective, they are a procedural device that can be deployed with great effect.[1] There are therefore aspects of 'generation conflict' and 'supply and demand' to bias challenges in ICA.

Experience has shown that investor–State arbitration (ISA) is not immune to these forces. There has been a gradual increase in the rate of bias challenge in ISA proceedings in recent years. Examples of bias challenges in ISA can be found in challenge decisions under the Convention on the Settlement of Investment Disputes between States and Nationals of other States,[2] such as *Amco Asia*

---

* Parts of this chapter are taken from ch. 7 of my book *Bias Challenges in International Commercial Arbitration: The need for a 'real danger' test* (The Hague: Kluwer, 2009). I am grateful to Associate Professor Chester Brown of Sydney University for his valuable input on the issues discussed in this chapter. Naturally, the views expressed are mine alone and any errors are for my account.

[1] S. R. Luttrell, *Bias Challenges in International Commercial Arbitration: The need for a 'real danger' test* (The Hague: Kluwer, 2009), pp. 249–56.

[2] Opened for signature 18 March 1965, 575 UNTS 159 (entered into force 14 October 1966) (ICSID Convention).

v. *Indonesia*,[3] *Vivendi Universal* v. *Argentina*,[4] *Suez* v. *Argentina*,[5] *Generation Ukraine* v. *Ukraine*,[6] and *Zhinvali Development* v. *Georgia*.[7] The challenges in these cases were all predicated upon either relationships between the arbitrator and a party or its counsel, or the arbitrator's apparent preference for one party over the other. These two broad sets of facts make up what can be called the 'common garden variety' of bias challenges in ICA. In the sense that most of the reported cases have been of the common garden variety, the pattern of bias challenges in ISA reflects the experiences of lawyers and arbitrators in ICA.

But as is well known, although their methods are similar in many respects, ISA and ICA are very different in the substantive legal sense. Whereas ICA can be used to resolve almost any contractual dispute (and therefore almost any number of related questions of law and fact), ISA is used to resolve only a limited set of substantive legal issues. The majority of these issues arise out of investment treaties (bilateral and multilateral), instruments which can be labelled 'trade constitutions' to signify the relative breadth and simplicity of their substantive provisions as compared to the complexity of private commercial agreements. This chapter will show that, in recent years, this fundamental substantive difference has caused ISA challenge jurisprudence to develop independently of ICA in certain areas, especially merits prejudgment (or what can be called 'outcome preference'). One of the tasks of this chapter is to analyse the development of the jurisprudence of merits prejudgment in ISA.

The programme will be as follows: first, this chapter introduces the general themes of bias challenges in ICA, and sets out some key terms. It then discusses the test that is most commonly applied to bias challenges in ICA, and compares this standard to the standard prescribed by the ICSID Convention. The attention of this chapter will then turn to ISA, and after conducting a brief survey of the key challenge decisions, it

---

[3] *Amco Asia Corp.* v. *Republic of Indonesia* (ICSID Case No. ARB/81/1, Decision on Proposal to Disqualify an Arbitrator of 24 June 1982), unpublished.

[4] *Compañia de Aguas de Aconquija SA & Vivendi Universal* v. *Argentine Republic* (ICSID Case No. ARB/97/3, Decision on Challenge to the President of 3 October 2001).

[5] *Suez, Sociedad General de Aguas de Barcelona SA and InterAguas Servicios Integrales del Agua SA* v. *The Argentine Republic* (ICSID Case No. ARB/03/17, Decision on the Proposal for the Disqualification of a Member of an Arbitral Tribunal of 22 October 2007).

[6] *Generation Ukraine Inc.* v. *Ukraine* (ICSID Case No. ARB/00/9, Final Award of 16 September 2003).

[7] *Zhinvali Development Ltd* v. *Republic of Georgia* (ICSID Case No. ARB/00/1, Decision on Respondent's Proposal to Disqualify Arbitrator of 19 January 2001), unpublished.

identifies primary and secondary characteristics of ICSID bias jurisprudence. It then looks at two new types of challenge that have emerged:
challenges to counsel (which can be termed '*Hrvatska* challenges') and
role/issue conflict (which can be termed '*Eureko/Vivendi* challenges').
This chapter concludes by pointing to certain lessons that ISA practitioners can learn from the shared experiences of ICA actors in the area
of bias.

II   Themes of bias challenges in ICA

It is possible to identify certain themes or patterns in both the law and
practice of bias challenges in ICA. These themes manifest at two levels:
the municipal level of the State (and its arbitration law), and the level of
practice (which includes both the jurisprudence of bias challenges and
trends in the way they are made and decided).

At the level of the State and its *lex arbitri*, the first theme to observe is
that 'appearances, not fact, are the touchstone' in lawmaking, both by
parliaments and by courts.[8] It is now well settled that, in order to
successfully challenge an arbitrator, the challenger does not bear the
burden of proving actual bias. The vast majority of national arbitration
laws – including those of all fifty-odd States Parties to the UNCITRAL
Model Law on International Commercial Arbitration – recognise an
apparent lack of impartiality or independence as a basis for challenging
an arbitrator.[9] Article 12 of the Model Law reads: 'An arbitrator may be
challenged only if circumstances exist that give rise to justifiable doubts
as to his impartiality or independence.'

The language of Model Law Article 12 has its origins in Article 10(1) of
the UNCITRAL Arbitration Rules, which date from 1976. Many non-
Model Law States have adopted similar language to the Model Law
challenge rule in their arbitration statutes. The direct effect the Model
Law has had in this area is, therefore, profound. Indirectly, the consistency
of Model Law Article 12 with General Standard 2 of the International Bar
Association's Guidelines on Conflicts of Interest in International Arbitration (IBA Guidelines) has also contributed to the export of the Model

---

[8] D. Jones, 'Conflicts of interest: Intellectual corruption – the IBA Guidelines and *Telekom
Malaysia*' (Presentation at the Inter-Pacific Bar Association 15th Annual Meeting and
Conference, Bali, 3–7 May 2005).

[9] UNCITRAL Model Law on International Commercial Arbitration, UN Doc. No. A/40/17,
Annex I (adopted 21 June 1985) (Model Law).

Law standard into non-Model Law settings, including (as we shall see) ISA generally, and ICSID arbitration specifically.[10]

At the level of the dispute, the second theme to observe is that the jurisprudence of bias challenges in ICA has now split into two main streams: rules regarding apparent *party* preferences, and rules regarding apparent *outcome* preferences. Party preferences are, in the close-knit world of ICA, predicated mostly on familiarity between party and arbitrator. Using typically common law (case-based) taxonomy, the main types of party familiarity can be characterised as follows:

1. Professional familiarity: the party and the arbitrator have or have had professional dealings, such as where the decision-maker has judged the party before, or has acted as counsel or advocate for the party in the past (*Rustal Trading* familiarity).[11]
2. Commercial familiarity: the party and the arbitrator have either continuing or past commercial dealings, or common commercial interests, such as where the arbitrator owns shares in the corporate party and therefore has an apparent 'bias by portfolio'(*Saudi Cable* familiarity).[12]
3. Social familiarity: the party (or their witnesses) and the arbitrator know or are related to one another, for example by consanguinity, marriage, membership of the same chambers or common membership of social or sporting clubs (*Laker Airways* familiarity).[13]
4. Representative familiarity: the officers, agents or servants called as witnesses by, or the advocates of, the party are professionally, socially or commercially familiar to the arbitrator, or *vice versa* (*ASM Shipping* familiarity).[14]

Each of the first three heads of familiarity can be categorised as either *pecuniary* or *non-pecuniary*. Commercial familiarity is, naturally, pecuniary in nature. The professional and social forms of familiarity are, generally, non-pecuniary (although the basis for professional familiarity may have originally been commercial familiarity). Being secondary,

---

[10] IBA, *Guidelines on Conflicts of Interest in International Arbitration* (approved 22 May 2004) (IBA Guidelines).
[11] *Rustal Trading Ltd* v. *Gill & Duffus SA* [2000] 1 Lloyd's Reports 14.
[12] *AT&T Corporation and Lucent Technologies Inc* v. *Saudi Cable Company* [2000] All ER (Comm) 625.
[13] *Laker Airways* v. *FLS Aerospace* [1999] 2 Lloyd's Reports 45.
[14] *ASM Shipping Ltd of India* v. *TTMI Ltd of England* [2005] APP.L.R.10/19.

representative familiarity may fall into either category depending upon the basis of the familiarity of the natural person and the decision-maker.

As to the rules of apparent outcome preferences, outcome preferences based on legal opinion are actionable where a decision-maker gives the appearance that they have judged the facts or merits prior to the scheduled hearing. This substantive bias may be the result of an arbitrator's prior determination of a matter that is factually or legally similar to the case now before them, their previous public expression of opinion on a legal issue that is live in the current proceedings or involvement in the facts of the dispute. The latter will include situations where the decision-maker has acted as counsel in the matter at an earlier stage. In ICA, allegations of outcome preference have arisen mostly in the context of tiered, multiparty disputes, most of which have arisen out of construction projects.

The challenge in *Qatar* v. *Creighton Ltd* provides an illustration of outcome preference in ICA:[15] the challenged arbitrator sat as arbitrator in proceedings between the prime contractor (Creighton) and its subcontractors, and then he served again in the arbitration between the prime contractor and the principal (the State of Qatar). The French Court of Cassation held that there was no basis for challenge because the arbitrator's determination in the first arbitration did not prejudice the State of Qatar in the second. More recently, the notion of outcome preference has expanded to take in opinions and preferences formed or expressed in unrelated arbitrations and non-contentious settings such as conferences and publications. This development has caused the jurisprudence of outcome preferences based on opinions as to matters of law to diverge further into two main streams:

1. Procedural outcome preference: the arbitrator appears to have pre-judged the merits of a procedural matter or a jurisdictional objection (*CalEnergy* bias).[16]
2. Substantive outcome preference: the arbitrator appears to have pre-judged one or more material substantive matters of law that are live in the dispute (*Telekom Malaysia* bias).[17]

---

[15] *Qatar* v. *Creighton Ltd* [1999] Revue de l'Arbitrage 308.
[16] *Himpurna California Energy Ltd (Bermuda)* v. *The Republic of Indonesia, Yearbook Commercial Arbitration*, XXV (2000), 109.
[17] *Telekom Malaysia Berhad* v. *Republic of Ghana* (Case Nos. HA/RK 2004.667 and HA/RK 2004.788, Decisions of 18 October 2004 and 5 November 2004, District Court of The Hague).

The *CalEnergy* challenge warrants some attention in this chapter because it arose in an investor–State dispute, which has been said to provide 'a virtual encyclopaedia of allegations of delay'.[18] In the *CalEnergy* matter, which came out of an ad hoc arbitration brought by foreign investors in the Indonesian energy sector, counsel for Indonesia challenged the chairman of the tribunal – one of the world's leading arbitrators – on the basis that his well-known commitment to international arbitration gave rise to the appearance that he had prejudged the issue of jurisdiction. Counsel claimed the chairman was:

> well known throughout the arbitration community to be on a constant crusade to elevate international arbitration, and thus the power of inter-national arbitrators such as himself, to a level above and beyond the jurisdiction of any court in the world. He has now found himself in a situation in which he believes he can prove his theory and ignore the rightful jurisdiction of the Indonesian courts, at the same time prevent-ing such courts from engaging in their proper and legal authority to review his previous decision.[19]

Although the *CalEnergy* challenge failed, it provides a useful illustration of abstraction of bias challenges in international arbitration. As the discussion of 'role/issue conflict' below demonstrates, this process of abstraction, which is being driven by the twin forces of 'generation conflict' and 'supply and demand', is gaining momentum. The protagon-ists of bias challenges are akin to 'practitioners in the Black Arts', as there is much room for the view that bias challenges are mostly tactical. Commenting on the increasing rate of challenge, the drafters of the IBA Guidelines noted:

> The growth of international business and the manner in which it is conducted, including interlocking corporate relationships and larger international law firms, have caused more disclosures [of conflicts of interest] and have created more difficult conflict of interest issues to determine. Reluctant parties have more opportunities to use challenges to arbitrators to delay arbitrations or deny the opposing party the arbitrator of its choice.[20]

As a 'non-State entity' whose members include the most prominent practitioners of ICA, the IBA is uniquely placed to provide guidance on conflicts of interest for arbitrators, and to this end, it published the

---

[18] M. W. Buhler and T. H. Webster, *Handbook of ICC Arbitration* (Sweet & Maxwell, 2005), p. 304.
[19] *CalEnergy*, p. 151.   [20] IBA, *Guidelines on Conflicts of Interest*, para. 1.

IBA Guidelines in May 2004. The working party that drafted the IBA Guidelines was made up of nineteen members, representing fourteen jurisdictions. When the IBA Guidelines were drafted, it was hoped they would be treated as persuasive authority by State courts and arbitral tribunals faced with conflict of interest issues.

The IBA Guidelines identify circumstances that may expose arbitrators to challenges for bias. They include three colour-coded lists – Red, Orange and Green. The Red List deals with situations where a conflict of interest exists. In recognition of the doctrine of party autonomy (and its limits) the Red List is split in two. The 'Non-Waivable Red List' identifies conflicts of interest where the arbitrator must not act (or must resign, if they have already entered onto the reference). The situations in the 'Waivable Red List' must be disclosed, and the arbitrator may only act where the parties are fully aware and give their express consent. The Orange List enumerates situations where a conflict *may* exist in the eyes of the parties depending upon the facts of the case. The Green List sets out matters where no conflict of interest will exist and disclosure is not necessary.[21]

In a similar vein to the IBA Working Party, which drafted the IBA Guidelines, Ahmed El-Kosheri and Karim Youssef wrote in 2007: 'In the world of globalised business and legal services in which international commercial arbitration operates, many, if not most, players are in some way acquainted with each other.'[22]

At the transnational level, the third theme to observe is the development of *lex mercatoria* rules for arbitrator bias. The *tronc commun* of the principles and doctrines of arbitrator bias as developed in State courts and parliaments is undeniable. The ongoing proliferation of the UNCITRAL Model Law notion of 'justifiable doubts', coupled with the codification of the appearance-based test in the IBA Guidelines, is consolidating the position of the rule of apparent bias. This rule is now so widely accepted that it arguably qualifies as a principle of *lex mercatoria*, or transnational customary commercial law.[23] If this is so then the universally accepted prohibition against actual bias must also qualify as custom. The existence of a *lex mercatoria* principle of apparent bias is especially important in ISA, where much of the applicable law is derived from custom.

---

[21] Luttrell, *Bias Challenges*, p. 201.
[22] M. El-Kosheri and K. Youssef, 'The independence of international arbitrators: An arbitrator's perspective', *ICC Bulletin 2007 (Special Supplement)*, 690 (2008), 48.
[23] Luttrell, *Bias Challenges*, pp. 187–209.

The fourth and final theme to observe is the increasing use of the IBA Guidelines in ICA. Indeed, this theme is inextricably linked to the third theme identified above, as it is the observance of a non-binding rule that makes it a custom, which is arguably what is happening to the IBA Guidelines.

It is true that, for the most part, the IBA Guidelines have been well received by users of arbitration, those 'users' being comprised of two groups: the first group is the parties, and the second group is made up of arbitrators, arbitration institutions and State courts. That is not to say, however, that they have enjoyed unanimous approval: one of the recurring objections to the IBA Guidelines is that their focus on 'appearances' has caused the practice of giving elaborate, American-style 'life story' disclosure to increase in ICA; another criticism is that the IBA Guidelines favour the same subjective test for apparent bias the whole way through the arbitration, and do not distinguish between the different stages of the proceedings.[24] These criticisms aside, it is now clear that the IBA Guidelines have found their place in ICA and, as will become apparent, ISA too.

It seems that the first time the IBA Guidelines were cited by a national court was in the decision of the District Court of The Hague in *Telekom Malaysia* (an investor–State dispute).[25] It is worth noting that this first case involved the curious situation of one member of the IBA Working Party (Arthur Marriott QC) challenging another member (Professor Emmanuel Gaillard, sitting as arbitrator), and the challenge being decided by reference to the rules the challenger and arbitrator both helped create. For students of customary law, *Telekom Malaysia* therefore provides a fascinating practical illustration of the 'role reversibility thesis'; it is highly likely that there will be more examples of this curious 'rule maker/rule user' dynamic in future.

Since *Telekom Malaysia*, the courts in civil law and common law States have displayed an increasing willingness at least to refer, if not rely, on the IBA Guidelines. Regarding civil law States, in *Anders Jilkén v. Ericsson*

---

[24] V. V. Veeder, 'L'Indépendence et l'impartialite de l'arbitre dans l'arbitrage international' in T. Clay and E. Jeuland (eds.), *Mediation et Arbitrage* (Litec, 2005), p. 219, English translation cited by Lord Steyn in 'England: The Independence and/or impartiality of arbitrators in international commercial arbitration', *ICC Bulletin 2007 (Special Supplement)*, 690 (2008), 96–7.

[25] Decision of the District Court of The Hague, 18 October 2004 (Challenge No. 13/2004; Petition No. HA/RK/2004.667).

AB; Re Judge Lind,[26] the Swedish Supreme Court used the IBA Guidelines in conjunction with the Swedish Arbitration Act to rule *for* disqualification. The Brussels Court of Appeal used the IBA Guidelines in *Eureko* v. *Poland* (to dismiss the challenge),[27] as did the Higher Regional Court of Central Frankfurt in *X* v. *Y* (challenge dismissed).[28]

Common law courts have also made use of the IBA Guidelines in challenge hearings. Bound by *Porter* v. *Magill*,[29] Justice Morison of the English Commercial Court considered the IBA Guidelines in *ASM Shipping*.[30] In the United States, the US Court of Appeals for the Fifth Circuit relied in part on the IBA Guidelines in *Positive Software*,[31] finding that the relevant circumstances were on the Green List. In *AIMCOR*,[32] the US Court of Appeals for the Second Circuit measured the arbitrator's non-disclosure in accordance with the IBA Guidelines (*vacatur* granted). The IBA Guidelines also appear in the judgment of the District Court of Florida in *HSN Capital LLC (USA) and ors* v. *Productora y Commercializador de Television SA de CV (Mexico)*,[33] and were treated as persuasive by the US Court of Appeals for the Ninth Circuit in *New Regency Productions Inc.* v. *Nippon Herald Films Inc.*[34]

The growing acceptance and significance of the IBA Guidelines in ICA is demonstrated by the fact that they are now being incorporated into the municipal arbitration laws of Model Law Plus States. The only current example is the United Arab Emirates (UAE), where Article 12(1)(c)–(d) of the 2008 draft Federal Arbitration Law of the United Arab Emirates (2008) are near-perfect adoptions of items (c) and (d) of the

---

[26] *Jilkén* v. *Ericsson AB*, Swedish Supreme Court, Case No. T2448–06 [2007] 3 SIAR 167, para. 174.

[27] *Eureko* v. *Poland*, R.G. 2006/1542/A.

[28] *X* v. *Y* (Decision of the Higher Regional Court of Frankfurt am Main of 4 October 2007, English translation of judgment by Richard Kreindler, Kluwer Arbitration, www.kluwerarbitration.com (last accessed 16 December 2010).

[29] [2002] 2 AC 367.

[30] *ASM Shipping Ltd of India* v. *TTMI Ltd of England* [2005] APP.L.R.10/19 (challenge upheld).

[31] *Positive Software Solutions Inc.* v. *New Century Mortgage Corp.*, 337 F Supp 2d 862, p. 865 (N D Tex, 2004) (challenge dismissed).

[32] *Applied Industrial Material Corp.* v. *Ovalar Makine Ticaret ve Sanayi, AS*, 492 F 3d 132 (2d Cir, 2007).

[33] *HSN Capital LLC (USA) and ors* v. *Productora y Commercializador de Television SA de CV (Mexico)* (Judgment of 5 July 2006, US District Court, M.D., Florida), *Yearbook Commercial Arbitration*, XXXII (2007), 774–9.

[34] *New Regency Productions Inc.* v. *Nippon Herald Films Inc.* (No. 05–55224 DC No. CV-04–09951-AHM Opinion of September 2007).

Explanation to IBA General Standard 2.[35] It is likely that more States will follow the UAE example and incorporate the IBA Guidelines into their national arbitration laws.

With these themes (or trends) in mind, we can now turn our attention to comparing the test for bias that prevails in ICA to the test for bias that prevails in ISA proceedings generally, and ICSID arbitration specifically.

III   ICA test for bias

Because there are so many different possible combinations of governing law and rules, there is no universal standard for impartiality and independence in ICA. However, certain formulations of the test for bias have enjoyed broad acceptance, chief amongst which is the wording of Article 12 of the Model Law. This makes the Model Law the most appropriate point of reference for determining the test for bias that prevails in ICA. This is so first because it is common to over fifty countries, and secondly because it has its origins in Article 10(1) of the UNCITRAL Rules, which remain the most widely used arbitration rules in the world.

To repeat, Article 12 of the Model Law reads: 'An arbitrator may be challenged only if circumstances exist that give rise to justifiable doubts as to his impartiality or independence.' The Article 12 standard for bias challenges was neatly elucidated by the appointing authority in a challenge that arose out of UNCITRAL Rules proceedings between two States in 1995. The appointing authority elaborated on the standard created by Model Law Article 12(2):

> The test to be applied is that the doubts existing on the part of the Claimant here must be justifiable on some objective basis. Are they reasonable doubts as tested by the standard of a fair minded, rational, objective observer? Could that observer say, on the basis of the facts as we know them, that the Claimant has a reasonable apprehension of partiality on the part of the Respondent's arbitrator?[36]

---

[35] S. R. Luttrell, 'The changing *lex arbitri* of the United Arab Emirates', *Arab Law Quarterly*, 23 (2009), 4. Art. 12(b) of the UAE Federal Arbitration Law 2008 reads: 'Doubts are justifiable if a reasonable and informed third party would reach the conclusion that there was a likelihood that the arbitrator may be influenced by factors other than the merits of the case as presented by the parties in reaching his or her decision.' Art. 12(1)(c) reads: 'Justifiable doubts necessarily exist as to the arbitrator's impartiality or independence if there is an identity between a party and the arbitrator, if the arbitrator is a legal representative of a legal entity that is a party in the arbitration, or if the arbitrator has a significant financial or personal interest in the matter at stake.'

[36] Challenge Decision of 11 January 1995, *Yearbook Commercial Arbitration*, XXII (1997), 227, para. 305.

In common law countries, the wording of Article 12 of the Model Law has served as a doorway for local jurisprudence. English and Commonwealth readings anchor the term 'impartiality' to public perception, observing Lord Chief Justice Hewart's famous dictum in *Sussex Justices* that 'justice must be done and be seen to be done'.[37] The courts of many other States, including those of the civil law tradition and seats supervised by the European Court of Human Rights at Strasbourg, have agreed that impartiality is a matter of 'appearances'.[38]

The broad observation of Lord Chief Justice Hewart's dictum has introduced an objective vantage – personified by the 'reasonable third person' – to Model Law jurisprudence. The process of adding the 'man on the Clapham omnibus' to the world of international arbitration has been aided by the fact that the right to an independent and impartial 'judge' is a matter of domestic (and international) procedural public policy, and a matter of human rights. I have argued that the use of the 'reasonable third person' vantage point, which is a legal fiction with origins in public law adjudication, is in many ways inconsistent with the nature and objectives of ICA. One of the main practical arguments I have made is that the tendency of common law courts to superimpose domestic standards of bias onto (or to 'domesticate') the language of Model Law Article 12 has caused the fragmentation of an otherwise uniform provision. This process of naturalisation has caused three competing tests for apparent bias to emerge:

1. The 'reasonable apprehension' test (the *Sussex Justices* test) requires that 'a fair minded and informed observer would have a "reasonable apprehension" that the arbitrator was biased'. It is derived from the judgment of Lord Hewart CJ in *Sussex Justices*. The majority of common law States follow the *Sussex Justices* test, and the test for bias under European Human Rights Law is, for all intents and purposes, the same.

2. The 'real danger' test (the *Gough* test) requires that the court must find there to be a 'real danger' of bias before apparent bias will be made out. It comes from the decision of the House of Lords in *R* v. *Gough*.[39] The *Gough* test has the highest threshold in its second limb,

---

[37] *R* v. *Sussex Justices; ex p. McCarthy* [1924] 1 KB 356, 259.

[38] For an Australian example, see *Ebner* v. *The Official Trustee in Bankruptcy; Clanae Pty Ltd and ors* v. *Australia and New Zealand Banking Group Ltd* (2000) 205 CLR 337, 376 (Kirby J.).

[39] [1993] AC 646. For a discussion of recent developments concerning the '*Gough* test', see S. R. Luttrell, 'Australia adopts "real danger" test for arbitrator bias', *Arbitration International*, 26 (2010), 4.

and a different first limb from *Sussex Justices* (*Gough* doesn't use a 'reasonable third person' vantage point).

3. The 'real possibility' test (the *Porter* v. *Magill* test) requires that a fair-minded and informed observer would say that there was a 'real possibility' that the arbitrator was biased. It comes from the 2002 decision of the House of Lords in *Porter* v. *Magill*.[40] Nearly all of the common law States that followed *Gough* now follow *Porter* v. *Magill*. The *Porter* v. *Magill* test is effectively the middle ground or 'compromise' test: its first limb (court vantage) comes from *Sussex Justices* and its second limb ('real possibility') comes from *Gough*.

The IBA Guidelines reflect the ratio in *Porter* v. *Magill*, or are at least consistent with it in the circumstances they declare 'Green' and 'Orange'.[41] This is confirmed by the recent decision of *Rompetrol Group NV* v. *Romania*.[42] In this case, which concerned a *Hrvatska* challenge to counsel rather than the arbitrator, the ICSID tribunal tacitly confirmed the compatibility of the IBA Guidelines and the 'real possibility' test in that it cited IBA General Standard 2(c) and the *Porter* v. *Magill* test in the same footnote.[43]

Let us turn now to the second phase of this comparative exercise, and consider the test for bias that is applicable in ICSID arbitration.

IV   ICSID test for bias

The *lex arbitri* of ICSID is derived from non-national sources. In order of priority, these sources are: (a) the ICSID Convention; (b) the ICSID Arbitration Rules; and (c) ICSID jurisprudence.

As in ICA, in ICSID proceedings bias challenges can be made before, during or after the award is made. There is, however, one crucial difference to ICA – in ICSID arbitration the parties *do not* have the right to plead bias at the enforcement stage. The ICSID Convention has its own enforcement mechanism and does not rely upon the New York Convention for the enforcement of ICSID awards. The ICSID Convention contains no equivalent to Article V ('refusal to enforce') of the New York Convention. The Article 54 ICSID enforcement mechanism is unidirectional: 'Each Contracting State shall recognize an award

---

[40] [2002] 2 AC 357.   [41] Luttrell, *Bias Challenges*, pp. 200–9.
[42] (ICSID Case No. ARB/06/3, Decision on the Participation of a Counsel of 14 January 2010) (*Rompetrol* v. *Romania*).
[43] *Ibid.*, para. 15.

rendered pursuant to this Convention as binding and enforce the pecuniary obligations imposed by that award within its territories as if it were a final judgment of a court in that State.'

It follows that domestic enforcement courts have no power to review ICSID awards;[44] when a Member State court is asked to enforce an ICSID award, all it is entitled to do is verify that the award is authentic. For the purposes of this study, the primary outcome of this limitation is that there is no public policy ground upon which to plead a denial of natural justice by *ex post facto* discovery of arbitrator bias. In an ICSID proceeding, the only post-award opportunity to plead bias is by application for annulment under Article 52(1)(d). The *sui generis* enforcement regime of the ICSID Convention has the secondary outcome that ICSID tribunals are not *de jure* influenced by the enforcement practices of New York Convention Member States, nor the doctrine of their courts.

A   The ICSID Convention

A party to an ICSID proceeding may directly challenge an arbitrator at the appointment stage or during the arbitral proceedings. An indirect challenge may be made by application for annulment of the award under Article 52. The provisions of the Convention which regulate direct challenges are:

1. Article 14 – Chapter 1 of the Convention sets out the process by which Contracting States may nominate arbitrators to the ICSID Panel. Under Article 13, each Contracting State may nominate four persons to the ICSID list. Article 14(1) states the qualities which a person must possess in order to be nominated as a panel member or be appointed as an arbitrator in an ICSID proceeding. The requisite qualities are (1) high moral character, (2) technical expertise, and (3) the capacity to exercise independent judgment. Regardless of whether they are party-appointed or placed by the chairman,[45] where an arbitrator does not possess all three of these essential traits, that arbitrator can be directly challenged in accordance with Article 57. It is notable that the qualities of the arbitrator do not include impartiality.[46]

---

[44] J. D. M. Lew, L. A. Mistelis and S. M. Kroll, *Comparative International Commercial Arbitration* (The Hague: Kluwer, 2003), p. 801.

[45] ICSID Convention, Art. 40(2).

[46] Notwithstanding the silence of Art. 14, ICSID tribunals seem to interpret 'independent judgement' as including a requirement of impartiality: see e.g. *Suez* v. *Argentina*, para. 42.

2. Article 57 – this article governs the process of challenging arbitrators. It allows for the challenge of any tribunal member on account of any fact indicating manifest lack of the qualities required of an arbitrator under Article 14(1) (i.e. high moral character, expertise and independent judgment).[47] This sets an 'extremely high bar for challenging an arbitrator'.[48] Significantly, vantage is not clarified: the black letters of Article 57 make no reference to any objective or 'reasonable third person' test. As will be observed, the first arm of *Sussex Justices* is, rather, a jurisprudential addition to Article 57.[49]

3. Article 58 – decisions on challenges are taken by the unchallenged members of the tribunal itself. Where the challenge is made to a member of an annulment committee, the same rule applies. Where the challenge is made to a sole arbitrator, or the tribunal or committee is split on the challenge, the chairman of ICSID shall decide finally. The decision in *Generation Ukraine* suggests that, in the rare event that the chairman himself is conflicted out, the matter will be referred to the Secretary-General of the PCA for final determination.[50]

The ICSID test for bias is therefore unique: the inter-operation of Articles 14(1) and 57 produces a rule that an ICSID arbitrator may only be challenged for bias where he or she manifestly lacks the capacity to exercise independent judgment. As far as I am aware, no other arbitral institution or law uses this test.

The key word in Article 57 is *manifest*. The *travaux préparatoires* to the ICSID Convention do not define or elucidate the expression. 'Manifest' has been interpreted to mean 'obvious or evident',[51] and to 'exclude reliance on speculative assumptions or arguments',[52] but not to bar challenges brought solely on the basis of appearances (i.e. 'manifest' does not mean *actual*).[53] And it certainly does not prevent the challenger from pleading matters unknown to, or undisclosed by, the arbitrator – the appearance does not need to be manifest at the time the arbitrator

---

[47] Art. 57 also provides that a party may propose the disqualification of an arbitrator on the basis of offence to the Common Nationality Prohibition in Chapter IV. Under Art. 40(2), arbitrators who are appointed from outside the ICSID Panel (which is the list of arbitrators) must also possess the mandatory qualities of an arbitrator under Art. 14(1), with the effect that non-list arbitrators can also be challenged under Art. 57.

[48] L. Reed, J. Paulsson and N. Blackaby, *Guide to ICSID Arbitration* (The Hague: Kluwer, 2004), p. 81.

[49] See e.g. *Suez* v. *Argentina*, paras. 39–40.   [50] *Generation Ukraine* v. *Ukraine*, para. 418.

[51] *Suez* v. *Argentina*, para. 34.   [52] *Vivendi Universal* v. *Argentina*, para. 25.   [53] *Ibid.*

sits, so long as the material facts of the challenge are proven later.[54] Professor Schreuer has said that the expression 'manifest' operates as an evidentiary condition which 'imposes a relatively heavy burden of proof on the party making the proposal [to disqualify]'.[55] As a general rule, something will be 'manifest' when the court does not need the assistance of counsel to see it. The term is not uncommon in arbitration laws: some domestic arbitration statutes, for example, allow for judicial review of awards on the basis of 'manifest error of law'.[56] Internationally, the notion of 'manifest breach of procedural fairness' is well developed in Anglo-American foreign-judgment enforcement contexts, where enforcement may be refused if the procedural public policy of the enforcing State is patently offended by the manner in which the foreign court reached its conclusion.[57]

The test created by the ICSID Convention is, on its face, closest to the *Gough* 'real danger' test. This view is based on the fact that:

1. Neither Article 14 nor Article 57 of the ICSID Convention uses the word 'reasonable' or otherwise posits a third person 'objective observer' vantage point.
2. In much of the common law world (which is where I come from), the term 'manifest' is a device of administrative law which implies court vantage and limited judicial review.
3. The use of the word 'manifest' to preface the word 'lack' in Article 57 elevates the ICSID standard above that of a simple lack of capacity for independent judgment and, therefore, into the realm of evidentiary probability.

At the level of posited law, therefore, the first comparative observation that can be made as to the test for bias in ICA and ISA is that, at least in ICSID arbitration, the bar is set significantly higher for the challenger.

B   ICSID Arbitration Rules

In ICSID arbitration the parties are afforded considerable autonomy in the selection of procedural rules – the ICSID Convention allows the

---

[54] *Ibid.*

[55] C. H. Schreuer *et al.*, *The ICSID Convention: A commentary*, 2nd edn (Cambridge University Press, 2009), p. 1202, cited in *Vivendi Universal* v. *Argentina*, para. 24.

[56] See e.g. section 43 of the Uniform Commercial Arbitration Acts of the Australian states.

[57] G. Petrochilos, *Procedural Law in International Arbitration* (Oxford University Press, 2004), p. 99.

parties to use rules other than the ICSID Rules (the most common alternative being the UNCITRAL Rules).[58] Whilst this option is rarely taken, it is still important to note that the ICSID Rules do not necessarily apply to proceedings conducted at ICSID. The UNCITRAL Rules, for example, are often selected in ISA provisions within BITs, with the result that the Article 10(1) 'justifiable doubts' standard for challenge might apply where a claim under a BIT that provides for UNCITRAL arbitration is brought together (or is consolidated) with a claim under the ICSID Convention.[59] *AWG* v. *Argentina* is, it would seem, the sole example of this combination.[60] If this is the case, then UNCITRAL Rules (and Model Law) jurisprudence may well inform the decision on challenge.

When the Model Law standard is applicable, an ICSID tribunal may consider the doctrine and case law of Model Law States.[61] ISA proceedings subject to the UNCITRAL Rules are sometimes consolidated with ICSID proceedings subject to the ICSID Rules. When a challenge is made in mixed consolidated proceedings, it will be subject to separate tests applicable under each set of rules.[62]

ICSID Rule 6 requires that arbitrators 'judge fairly'. Much like the Article 7(2) of the ICC Rules, ICSID Rule 6(2) requires that arbitrators sign a declaration of independence and provide a written statement of 'past and present professional, business and other relationships (if any) with the parties'.[63] The ICSID Rules were last amended in 2006.[64] The

---

[58] Art. 44 of the ICSID Convention provides that, unless otherwise agreed by the parties, any ICSID proceedings between the parties will be conducted in accordance with the ICSID Rules.

[59] Because Art. 10(1) of the UNCITRAL Rules employs substantially the same wording as Model Law Art. 12(2), I will not discuss the UNCITRAL Rules standard in detail here.

[60] The challenge in *AWG* v. *Argentina* arose out of ad hoc ISA proceedings that were brought by a UK claimant that was a shareholder in an Argentine company. French and Spanish shareholders commenced ICSID arbitrations – *Suez, Sociedad General de Aguas de Barcelona SA, and Vivendi Universal SA* v. *Argentine Republic* (ICSID Case No. ARB/03/19), and *Suez, Sociedad General de Aguas de Barcelona SA, and InterAguas Servicios Integrales del Agua SA* v. *Argentine Republic* (ICSID Case No. ARB/03/17). The three different proceedings were consolidated for convenience, and the challenge was heard in this mixed context.

[61] Even where the ICSID Rules apply and no municipal jurisprudence is incorporated, ICSID tribunals sometimes still resort to the case law of leading seats for guidance on challenges. See e.g. *Vivendi Universal* v. *Argentina*, para. 24, where the committee refers to the decision of the Paris Court of First Instance in *Philipp Brothers* v. *Drexel Burnham Lambert Ltd* (1990) Revue de l'Arbitrage 497.

[62] See e.g. the second challenge to Professor Kaufmann-Kohler in *Suez* v. *Argentina*.

[63] ICSID Arbitration Rules, Rule 6.

[64] The preceding amendments to the ICSID Rules took place in 1984 and 2003.

changes included an addition to Rule 6(2) requiring that the arbitrator disclose 'any other circumstances that might cause [his or her] reliability for independent judgment to be questioned by a party' and, importantly, 'assume a continuing obligation to promptly notify the Secretary-General of the Centre of any such circumstance'.[65]

The first effect of the 2006 amendments to ICSID Rule 6 is that the obligation to disclose extends beyond relationships (and, for example, into the realm of *Pinochet*-type sympathies and outcome preferences). The second effect is that, where before it was limited to past or present relationships, the Rule 6(2) obligation to disclose is now ongoing. And in *Vivendi Universal* v. *Argentina* the tribunal held that the Rule 6(2) disclosure obligation applies to members of ad hoc annulment committees as it does members of merits panels.[66] Another important jurisprudential extension of Rule 6(2) is that arbitrators have an ongoing (but limited) duty to investigate possible conflicts of interest.[67]

C   ICSID Jurisprudence

Much like the jurisprudence of a court in a civil law State, ICSID jurisprudence consists of the decisions of ICSID tribunals and the doctrine of leading scholars of foreign investment law and dispute resolution. On questions of substantive law, ICSID tribunals increasingly refer to the decisions of ICSID and other ISA panels (a juridical practice which I have identified as a causative factor in the rise in the number of role/issue conflict challenges). On procedural matters, ICSID tribunals refer to the rules of arbitration established by other international bodies, and the general principles of international arbitration.[68]

---

[65] The amendments to the ICSID Arbitration Rules came into force on 1 April 2006. Amendments were also made to the ICSID Financial Regulations.

[66] *Vivendi Universal* v. *Argentina*, para. 18.

[67] *Suez, Sociedad General de Aguas de Barcelona SA and Vivendi Universal SA* v. *Argentina* (ICSID Case No. ARB/03/19, Decision on a Second Proposal for the Disqualification of a Member of the Arbitral Tribunal of 12 May 2008), para. 47. This second challenge arose out of the ad hoc ISA proceedings brought by AWG against Argentina, which were consolidated with the ICSID cases *Suez, Sociedad General de Aguas de Barcelona SA, and Vivendi Universal SA* v. *Argentine Republic* (ICSID Case No. ARB/03/19) and *Suez, Sociedad General de Aguas de Barcelona SA, and InterAguas Servicios Integrales del Agua SA* v. *Argentine Republic* (ICSID Case No. ARB/03/17).

[68] See e.g. the decision in *Amco Asia* v. *Indonesia*, cited in M. Tupman, 'Challenge and disqualification of arbitrators in international commercial arbitration', *International and Comparative Law Quarterly*, 38(1) (1989), 44–5.

Although the ICSID Convention does not posit a doctrine of precedent, the practice of following earlier decisions is increasingly common in ICSID arbitration. The subject matter of ICSID arbitration is, in my view, the principal reason for this practice: because the same issues arise over and over between investors and host States (such as the foreign investor's entitlement to fair and equitable treatment), each award's persuasive value as an expression of customary law is increased by a recurring congruency of facts. Leading ISA practitioners have confirmed the trend towards precedent: according to Philippe Fouchard, Emmanuel Gaillard and Berthold Goldman, ICSID awards 'naturally serve as precedents';[69] Albert Jan van den Berg has observed that 'there is a tendency to create a true arbitral case law' in the field of investment disputes;[70] and in 2005 Pierre Duprey noted the similarity between ISA awards and judicial case law.[71]

There are, naturally, strong arguments against these opinions. The claim that ISA awards enjoy some kind of de facto status as precedents is weakened by the fact that the law of foreign direct investment is (in the wider context of international law) in its infancy: it may be that we are bound to see some consistency in ISA awards at this stage of the game because the rules are still primary; the appearance of consistency may well vanish once secondary rules (or '*the rules of the rules*') develop and the jurisprudence of ISA fragments. Whilst it is still too early to tell, there certainly seems to be such a thing as 'ICSID jurisprudence', and even de facto *stare decisis* in certain areas.

Against this background, it is fair to say that a *jurisprudence constante* is emerging in the area of bias challenges in ICSID arbitration. Challenge decisions often cite judgments of previous ICSID panels and the decisions of the courts of leading arbitral seats as persuasive authorities for the conclusions reached. ICSID bias jurisprudence can be said to have the characteristics which are set out in the following sections.

1   Primary characteristics

(a)   *Nemo judex in sua causa*   As is to be expected, ICSID tribunals do recognise the rule that 'no man may be a judge in his own cause':

---

[69] E. Gaillard and J. Savage (eds.), *Fouchard, Gaillard and Goldman on International Commercial Arbitration* (The Hague: Kluwer, 1999), p. 384.

[70] A. van den Berg, introductory note to P. Duprey, 'Do arbitral awards constitute precedents? Should commercial arbitration be distinguished in this regard from arbitration based on investment treaties?' in A. Schlaepfer, P. Pinsolle and L. Degos (eds.), *Towards a Uniform International Arbitration Law?* (Juris, 2005), p. 249.

[71] *Ibid.*, p. 258.

nemo judex informs the Article 14 requirement of independent judgment, and the ICSID Rule 6(2) disclosure obligation presupposes the operation of *nemo judex*. The force of this rule is also evident from the regularity with which critics of ICSID cite the Centre's institutional proximity to the World Bank: the 'cause' of the Centre is identified as the cause of its parent, and the ICSID process is said to be illegitimate as a result.[72]

(b) *De minimis non curat lex*   ICSID tribunals have consistently confirmed that the challenge and disqualification articles of the ICSID Convention are subject to *de minimis*. In pre-award challenges governed by Article 57, the circumstances which are said to deprive the arbitrator of his or her capacity to exercise independent judgment must be 'manifest' and, it follows, significantly more than trifling. Similarly, in an annulment application brought under Article 52(1)(d) the procedural breach must be 'serious'. The record confirms that Article 57 challenges are subject to *de minimis*: the tribunal in *Amco Asia* applied *de minimis* to dismiss a challenge to an arbitrator whose firm had a profit-sharing arrangement with the lawyers for the claimant, and the annulment committee in *Vivendi Universal* v. *Argentina* confirmed the availability of the exception in *obiter*.[73] In the context of Article 52, the use of the expression 'more than minimal' (to explain the meaning of the word 'serious') is a strong indication that *de minimis* functions in post-award settings as well.

2   Secondary characteristics

As to the secondary characteristics of ICSID challenge jurisprudence, we must take a closer look at the pattern of decisions. Rather than address their material facts in detail, it is appropriate to deal with the key decisions chronologically and in point form.

(a) *Amco Asia Corp.* v. *Indonesia* (1982)   Indonesia challenged the claimant's appointee on the basis that seven years earlier he had given tax advice to the individual who controlled the three corporate claimants. The arbitrator's firm also had an office and profit-sharing arrangement with the lawyers for the claimant, but neither Amco nor its controlling

---

[72] See e.g. the comments of the Bolivian Special Ambassador for Trade and Integration, cited in M. Weisbrot, 'A new assertiveness for Latin American governments', (2007), www.commondreams.org/archive/2007/06/13/1855/ (last accessed 10 December 2010).
[73] *Vivendi Universal* v. *Argentina*, para. 27.

shareholder were clients of either firm.[74] Although formally the arrangement ended before the arbitration started, for the first six months of
proceedings the two firms still shared offices.[75] Counsel for Indonesia
argued that these facts deprived the arbitrator of independence. The
challenge was dismissed: there was found to be no manifest risk of
partiality because the services rendered by the arbitrator to the claimant's principal shareholder were not in the nature of regular legal advice,
their commercial significance was minimal (the fee for the advice being
C$450), and the links between the two law firms did not 'create any
psychological risk of partiality'.[76] In stressing the significance of the
Article 57 expression 'manifest', the tribunal held that under the ICSID
Convention the challenger must prove not only the facts which indicate
a lack of independence, but also that the lack is 'highly probable', not just
'possible' or 'quasi-certain'.[77]

(b) *Zhinvali Development* v. *Georgia* (2001)   A proposal to disqualify
was made by Georgia on the basis of occasional, purely social contacts
between the arbitrator and an executive officer of Zhinvali.[78] Georgia's
challenge was decided by arbitrators Davis Robinson and Seymour
Rubins (the arbitrator challenged in *Amco Asia*).[79] They dismissed the
proposal, stressing the absence of any professional or commercial relationship between the arbitrator and the executive officer. In their unre-
ported decision of 19 January 2001, the deciding members held that
Georgia's contention that 'a merely occasional personal contact could
manifestly affect the judgment of an arbitrator, in the absence of any
further facts, was purely speculative'.[80] The *Zhinvali* challenge decision
was cited with approval by the ICSID tribunal in the challenge to
President Fortier in *Vivendi Universal* v. *Argentina*.

(c) *Vivendi Universal* v. *Argentina* (2001)   This was a challenge to the
president of an ad hoc committee convened to decide an application for
annulment of a final award. In accordance with Article 52(3) the president
of the ICSID Administrative Council appointed three list-arbitrators to
the ad hoc annulment committee. The appointees included Canadian

---

[74] The decision on the challenge to Arbitrator Rubins was not published. This summary of
the material facts draws on the discussion of the *Amco Asia* challenge in Tupman,
'Challenge and disqualification'.
[75] *Ibid.*, p. 44.   [76] See discussion of *Amco* v. *Indonesia, ibid.*, p. 45.   [77] *Ibid.*, p. 44.
[78] *Zhinvali Development Ltd* v. *Georgia*, cited in *Vivendi Universal* v. *Argentina*, para. 23.
[79] *Ibid.*   [80] *Ibid.*

Yves Fortier QC. When his fellow arbitrators made their Rule 6 declarations of independence, Mr Fortier qualified his position. After reserving its rights at first, Argentina challenged Mr Fortier. The material facts of the challenge were that one of the partners at Mr Fortier's firm Ogilvy Renault had given advice on Quebec tax law to Vivendi Universal's corporate predecessor, Compagnie Générale des Eaux. Mr Fortier was not personally involved and the tax matter was unrelated to the claim against Argentina.

The challenge was dismissed. Although they criticised the *Amco Asia* decision,[81] the committee members agreed with the earlier tribunal that the effect of Article 57 was to preclude reliance on 'mere speculation or inference'.[82] The ad hoc committee held that an arbitrator's professional relationship with a party is not an automatic basis for disqualification, and that 'all the circumstances need to be considered in order to determine whether the relationship is significant enough to justify entertaining reasonable doubts as to the capacity of the arbitrator or member to render a decision freely and independently'.[83] The test the deciding members applied was 'whether a *real risk* of lack of impartiality based upon those facts (and not on any mere speculation or inference) could *reasonably be apprehended* by either party'.[84]

(d) *SGS v. Pakistan* (2002)   SGS challenged Pakistan's party arbitrator on the basis of his connections with counsel for Pakistan. The particulars of the claimant's challenge were that three years earlier Pakistan's arbitrator had been counsel for the successful respondent in an ICSID arbitration (*Azinian* v. *Mexico*),[85] in which counsel was an arbitrator, and that the decision in *Azinian* created a reasonable appearance that the arbitrator would 'return the favour' in the instant matter. The deciding arbitrators dismissed the challenge, ruling that the claimant's challenge was 'bereft of any basis in the fact of this proceeding', and characterised the proposal as 'simply a supposition, a speculation merely'.[86] Significantly, the word 'manifest' was taken as meaning 'clearly and objectively'; the deciding members identified its function as a test

---

[81] *Vivendi Universal* v. *Argentina*, para. 22.   [82] *Ibid.*, para. 25.   [83] *Ibid.*, para. 28.

[84] *Ibid.*, para. 25 (emphasis added).

[85] *Azinian, Davitian, & Baca* v. *Mexico* (ICSID Case No. ARB (AF)/97/2, Award of 1 November 1999).

[86] *SGS Societe Générale de Surveillance SA* v. *Islamic Republic of Pakistan* (ICSID Case ARB/ 01/03, Decision on Claimant's Proposal to Disqualify an Arbitrator of 19 December 2002), para. 404.

for whether the inference that independence is lacking should be drawn.[87] In its acceptance of inference as a basis for disqualification, the *obiter* in *SGS* conflicts with other ICSID challenge decisions. Inference was expressly rejected as a basis for challenge in *Amco Asia*, and *Vivendi Universal* v. *Argentina*.[88]

(e) *Canfor Corporation* v. *USA* (2003)   This challenge arose out of arbitral proceedings brought under NAFTA Chapter 11. In July 2002, Canfor Corporation and Tembec Inc. (both Canadian producers of softwood lumber) filed NAFTA claims concerning countervailing duty and anti-dumping measures adopted by the United States in relation to Canadian softwood lumber products.[89] One year before his appointment, in a speech to a Canadian government council, the claimant's arbitrator described US government measures on softwood lumber 'harassment'. The legitimacy and effect of US government softwood lumber policy was live in the dispute. Upon learning of these comments, the US proposed disqualification.

The challenge was referred to the Secretary-General of ICSID under the Additional Facility. In March 2003 the Secretary-General wrote to the challenged arbitrator informing him that if he did not stand down a decision upholding the US challenge would be issued.[90] The arbitrator resigned. Although no formal decision was made, the Secretary-General still expressed a clear view in favour of the challenge. This decision provides an early glimpse of ICSID jurisprudence on 'issue conflict' in NAFTA proceedings.

(f) *Generation Ukraine* v. *Ukraine* (2003)   The challenged arbitrator was appointed by the Ukraine in ICSID proceedings commenced by Generation Ukraine.[91] The claimant challenged the arbitrator on the basis that he had, during his time as Deputy General Counsel of the Multilateral Investment Guarantee Agency (MIGA, which is a member of the World Bank Group) been involved in studies and investment policy reviews of the Ukraine for the OECD. The claimant's concern

---

[87] *SGS* v. *Pakistan*, para. 402.

[88] *Vivendi Universal* v. *Argentina*, para. 25.

[89] *Canfor Corporation* v. *The United States of America; Terminal Forest Products Ltd* v. *The United States of America* (Decision on Preliminary Question [2006] 18 World Trade and Arbitration Materials 4), p. 136.

[90] B. Legum, 'Investor–State arbitrator disqualified for pre-appointment statements on challenged measures', *Arbitration International*, 21 (2005), 241, 245.

[91] *Generation Ukraine* v. *Ukraine*.

was that the arbitrator had developed personal connections with Ukrainian political officials,[92] and that these personal connections would deprive him of the capacity for independent judgment. The deciding arbitrators were divided on the claimant's disqualification proposal, and in accordance with Article 58 the challenge went to the chairman of the ICSID Administrative Council for final determination.[93] It was at this point that the matter became more complicated: because the arbitrator was being challenged on the basis of his relationship with a World Bank agency (MIGA), and the person being asked to judge his independence was the president of the World Bank, there was a potential breach of *nemo judex in sua causa*.

In an ad hoc procedure that has been described as 'original and unparalleled',[94] the president of ICSID referred the challenge to the Secretary-General of the PCA in The Hague. The Secretary-General of the PCA considered the matter and made a recommendation that the proposal to disqualify be dismissed.[95] This recommendation was accepted by the chairman of ICSID, and the challenge was rejected.

This chapter will return to *Generation Ukraine* in the discussion of the challenge to Judge Brower in *Perenco* v. *Ecuador.*

(g) *Grand River Enterprises* v. *USA* (2007)   Grand River Enterprises commenced arbitration against the United States in response to agreements reached by the US government with certain tobacco companies. Like *Canfor*, the *Grand River* claim was brought under NAFTA Chapter 11.[96] Grand River – a cigarette manufacturer owned by a Canadian First Nations group – appointed Professor James Anaya as its arbitrator. The US challenged Professor Anaya on the basis that he was advocate for certain Native American groups in proceedings against the US before the Inter-American Commission on Human Rights and the UN Commission on the Elimination of Racial Discrimination (CERD). The US claimed that justifiable doubts arose as to Professor Anaya's ability to impartially judge the NAFTA claim, because his participation in the

---

[92] J. Fouret, 'The World Bank and ICSID: Family of incestuous ties?', *International Organisation Law Review*, (2007), 121, 138.

[93] *Ibid.*

[94] J. Fouret and M. Prost, 'Chronique de règlement pacifique des différends internationaux', *La Revue Québécoise de Droit International*, 16(2) (2003), 283.

[95] *Generation Ukraine* v. *Ukraine*, para. 4.18.

[96] *Grand River Enterprises and ors* v. *The United States of America* (Decision on Objections to Jurisdiction of 20 July 2006).

human rights matters suggested he had predetermined the issue of US compliance with international obligations.

The challenge went to the Secretary-General of ICSID. The relevant standard was UNCITRAL Rule 11(1). On 23 October 2007, the Secretary-General wrote to Professor Anaya informing him that his role as advocate before CERD was incompatible with his function as arbitrator in the NAFTA matter, and asked if he would continue to act as advocate in the CERD proceedings.[97] Professor Anaya responded that he would not, but that he would continue to assist law students in relation to human rights advocacy work they were doing for the Western Shoshone people. Applying the 'justifiable doubts' standard posited by the UNCITRAL Rule 11(1) the Secretary-General found that Professor Anaya's advisory work was not inconsistent with his role as arbitrator, and was not on its own enough to cause justifiable doubts to arise. The US challenge was accordingly dismissed.

(h) *Suez and ors* v. *Argentina (No. 1)* (2007) The claimants (who included French water-services multinational Suez) appointed Swiss Professor Gabrielle Kaufmann-Kohler as their arbitrator in a string of arbitrations under the ICSID and UNCITRAL Rules. After only one of the three merits hearings had been conducted, Argentina filed an Article 57 challenge to Professor Kaufmann-Kohler. The basis of the challenge was that Professor Kaufmann-Kohler had been a member of the ICSID tribunal in the first *Vivendi Universal* claim against Argentina (from which the annulment proceedings and challenge to Yves Fortier QC arose). Argentina argued that the award of US$105 million in favour of Vivendi Universal and its partner revealed 'a *prima facie* lack of impartiality . . . made evident through the most prominent inconsistencies of the award that result in the total lack of reliability towards Ms Gabrielle Kaufmann-Kohler'.[98]

The challenge failed. In respect of the UNCITRAL Rules proceeding, in which the fifteen-day time limit imposed by Article 11(1) applied, the

---

[97] C. Mouawad, 'Issue conflicts in investment treaty arbitration', *Transnational Dispute Management*, 5 (2008), 4, 9.

[98] Respondent's proposal to disqualify, para. 8, cited in Decision on a Proposal for the Disqualification of a Member of the Arbitral Tribunal, 22 October 2007, para. 13. This was the first challenge that arose out of the ad hoc ISA proceedings brought by AWG against Argentina, which were consolidated with the ICSID cases *Suez, Sociedad General de Aguas de Barcelona SA, and Vivendi Universal SA* v. *Argentine Republic* (ICSID Case No. ARB/03/19) and *Suez, Sociedad General de Aguas de Barcelona SA, and InterAguas Servicios Integrales del Agua SA* v. *Argentine Republic* (ICSID Case No. ARB/03/17).

tribunal found that Argentina's challenge was out of time.[99] The tribunal reached the same result under the ICSID Rules, holding that the challenge to Professor Kaufmann-Kohler was not 'prompt' for the purposes of ICSID Rule 9(1).[100] Although it was not strictly necessary in order to decide on the challenge, the deciding members commented in *obiter* that the challenge was without merit: it relied on the inference that Professor Kaufmann-Kohler was biased against Argentina simply because she was a member of a tribunal that made a unanimous award against the Republic six years earlier. The tribunal concluded that the effect of Article 57 was to deprive parties of the right to challenge on inference and the 'mere belief' that independence is lacking.[101]

(i) *Suez and ors* v. *Argentina (No. 2)* (2008) Shortly after the dismissal of its first proposal, Argentina challenged Professor Kaufmann-Kohler again. The second challenge was filed after Argentina discovered that in 2006 Professor Kaufmann-Kohler had been elected to the supervisory board of Swiss bank UBS. The relationship between UBS and the claimants was that UBS held a 2.1 per cent stake in Suez, and a 2.38 per cent stake in Vivendi Universal.[102] Argentina's second challenge extended to two other ICSID proceedings against the Republic in which Professor Kaufmann-Kohler was also an arbitrator.[103] Argentina's challenge also pleaded the rule in *Dimes*: as a non-executive director of UBS Professor Kaufmann-Kohler received a proportion of her remuneration in UBS stock, making her an indirect shareholder in the claimant companies.[104] Argentina alleged that Professor Kaufmann-Kohler failed to disclose these facts in accordance with ICSID Rule 6(2) and UNCITRAL Rule 9.

The challenge subject to the UNCITRAL Rules was quickly dismissed. Argentina's argument that Professor Kaufmann-Kohler was under a duty to disclose that she was a director of UBS and that UBS had interests in the international water sector was without merit. Accordingly, Professor Kaufmann-Kohler had not breached Article 9 of the UNCITRAL Rules by failing to disclose her UBS directorship, and no 'justifiable doubts' arose under Article 10(1) of the UNCITRAL Rules. The challenge subject

---

[99] *Suez* v. *Argentina*, para. 21.   [100] *Ibid.*, para. 22.
[101] *Ibid.*, para. 40.   [102] *Ibid.*, para. 12.
[103] *Electricidad Argentina SA & EDF International SA* v. *Argentina* (ICSID Case No. ARB/ 03/22); *EDF International, SAUR International SA & Leon Participaciones Argentinas SA* v. *Argentina* (ICSID Case No. ARB/03/23, Decision on Jurisdiction of 5 August 2008).
[104] *Suez* v. *Argentina*, para. 12.

to the ICSID Convention was also dismissed. The deciding members cited *Amco Asia* as persuasive authority for the proposition that Article 57 of the ICSID Convention imposes a 'heavy burden' on the challenger to prove that the lack of capacity for independent judgment is 'highly probable', not just 'possible'.[105] *SGS* v. *Pakistan* and *Vivendi Universal* v. *Argentina* were also cited in support of this interpretation.[106]

(j)   *Perenco* v. *Ecuador* (2009)   The challenge to Judge Brower arose out of an arbitration between French company, Perenco, and the Ecuadorian State oil company Petroecuador.[107] Perenco alleged that Ecuador had breached the France–Ecuador BIT by expropriating Perenco's participating interest in an oil tenement in the Amazon region of Ecuador. Perenco appointed Judge Brower as its arbitrator. The parties agreed that any challenges to arbitrators would be resolved by the Secretary-General of the PCA according to the IBA Guidelines. During the proceedings, on 6 July 2009, Ecuador formally denounced the ICSID Convention. Ecuador's reaction to the ICSID tribunal's provisional measures (which included a temporary restraining order against the State), and its withdrawal from the ICSID Convention, attracted a good deal of media attention.

In August 2009, Judge Brower was interviewed by *The Metropolitan Corporate Counsel*. After being asked to comment on Ecuador's withdrawal from the ICSID Convention, Judge Brower was asked the following question:

> Editor: Tell us what you see as the most pressing issues in international arbitration.
> Judge Brower: There is an issue of acceptance and the willingness to continue participating in it, as exemplified by what Bolivia has done and what Ecuador is doing. Ecuador currently is expressly declining to comply with the orders of two ICSID tribunals with very stiff interim provisional measures, but they just say they have to enforce their national law and the orders don't make any difference. But when recalcitrant host countries find out that claimants are going to act like those who were expropriated in Libya, start bringing hot oil litigation and chasing cargos, doing detective work looking for people who will invoke cross-default clauses in loan agreements, etc., the politics may change. After a certain point, no one will invest without having something to rely on . . .[108]

---

[105]   *Ibid.*, para. 29.   [106]   *Ibid.*
[107]   *Perenco Ecuador Limited* v. *Republic of Ecuador & Empresa Estatal Petroleos del Ecuador* (ICSID Case No. ARB/08/6, Decision on Challenge to Arbitrator of 8 December 2009).
[108]   *Perenco* v. *Ecuador* (PCA Case No. IR-2009/1), para. 26, citing Albert Driver, 'A world-class arbitrator speaks!', *The Metropolitan Corporate Counsel* (August 2009), 24.

On 19 September 2009, Ecuador filed a request for disqualification of Judge Brower with the Secretary-General of the PCA, alleging that Judge Brower's answer to the above question gave rise to justifiable doubts as to his impartiality or independence.

The Secretary-General upheld the challenge. In arriving at his decision as to Judge Brower's bias, the Secretary-General of the PCA applied General Standard 1 and General Standard 2 (Conflict of Interest) of the IBA Guidelines. The Secretary-General concluded that:

> The combination of the words chosen by Judge Brower and the context in which he used them have the overall effect of painting an unfavourable view of Ecuador in such a way as to give a reasonable and informed third party justifiable doubts as to Judge Brower's impartiality.[109]

Ecuador also argued that Judge Brower appeared to have prejudged two issues: first, the issue of whether provisional measures are legally binding under the ICSID Convention; and secondly, the merits issue of expropriation. The Secretary-General held that Ecuador's argument on pre-judgment of the provisional measures issue failed because Judge Brower was simply repeating what the tribunal had already decided. As to the merits prejudgment question, the Secretary-General concluded that Judge Brower's comments also gave rise to a justifiable doubt that he had prejudged the issue of whether Ecuador had expropriated Perenco's investment.

(k)   *Urbaser* v. *Argentina* (2010)   The decision of the Secretary-General of the PCA in *Perenco* v. *Ecuador* was distinguished by the tribunal in the recent challenge to New Zealand arbitrator Professor Campbell McLachlan QC in *Urbaser SA and anor* v. *Argentine Republic*.[110] In this case, the claimant challenged Professor McLachlan on the basis of perceived prejudgment of two merits issues live in the arbitration: the scope and application of the most-favoured nation (MFN) clause, and the availability of the customary international law defence of 'necessity'.

On MFN, the claimant pointed to a book Professor McLachlan published in 2007, in which he described as 'heretical' the jurisdictional decision in *Maffezini* v. *Spain*,[111] where the tribunal extended the application of the MFN clause to the dispute-resolution provisions of the BIT.

---

[109] *Perenco* v. *Ecuador*, para. 48.
[110] *Urbaser* v. *Argentina* (ICSID Case No. ARB/07/26, Decision on Claimant's Proposal to Disqualify Professor Campbell MacLachlan of 12 August 2010).
[111] (ICSID No. ARB/97/7, Decision on Jurisdiction of 25 January 2000).

In relation to the defence of 'necessity', the claimant relied on the fact that Professor Campbell had, in a 2008 paper, expressed the opinion that the decision of the ICSID annulment committee in *CMS Gas Transmission* v. *Argentina* – which found errors of law in relation to the defence of necessity – should be given more weight than the decision of the first instance tribunal in that case.[112] Both of the merits positions taken by Professor McLachlan were unhelpful to the claimant's case against Argentina.

The claimant's challenge to Professor McLachlan was dismissed. In terms of its contribution to ICSID challenge jurisprudence, the decision is perhaps most valuable for its practical approach to the question of academic opinions. The deciding arbitrators expressed the opinion that:

> [If the claimant was right] the mere fact of having made known an opinion on an issue relevant in an arbitration would have the effect of allowing a challenge for lack of independence or impartiality. Such a position, however, would have effects reaching far beyond what Claimants seem to sustain, and incompatible with the proper functioning of the arbitral system under the ICSID Convention.[113]

The *Urbaser* challenge decision is interesting in the context of this chapter because of the relatively low weight the deciding arbitrators placed on the IBA Guidelines – where other tribunals have taken a formalist approach to the IBA Guidelines, the arbitrators in *Urbaser* identified the IBA Guidelines as more of a 'source of inspiration' than a source of law.[114]

With these leading authorities in mind, in my view it is possible to deduce certain secondary characteristics of ICSID bias jurisprudence:

1. Something like the *Porter* v. *Magill* 'real possibility' test (or 'real risk', as it was put in *Vivendi Universal* v. *Argentina*) is used to interpret Article 57 and determine challenges to ICSID arbitrators.
2. Although the black letters of the ICSID Convention do not frame the test for bias in objective or subjective terms, ICSID tribunals have, since *SGS* v. *Pakistan*, consistently 'tacked on' the vantage of the 'reasonable third person' to make the Article 57 standard a matter of objective assessment.

---

[112] (ICSID Case No. ARB/01/8, Decision on Annulment of 25 September 2007).

[113] (ICSID Case No. ARB/07/26, Decision on Claimant's Proposal to Disqualify Professor Campbell MacLachlan of 12 August 2010), para. 46.

[114] Referring inter alia to the IBA Guidelines, the arbitrators commented (at para. 37) that 'while these texts certainly constitute a most valuable source of inspiration, they are not part of the legal basis [on which the challenge is to be decided]'.

3. The initial resistance to inference as a basis for challenge (displayed by the tribunals in *Amco Asia* and *Vivendi Universal* v. *Argentina*) has declined in recent years, and it is reasonably well settled now that an appearance of bias can be inferred from the facts, particularly where the allegation is one of merits prejudgment (see e.g. *Perenco* v. *Ecaudor*).

4. In circumstances where the challenge 'falls through the cracks of the Convention', such as occurred in the challenge to the president of the annulment committee in *Generation Ukraine*, it seems possible as a matter of custom to refer the challenge to the Secretary-General of the PCA for 'recommendation' (or outright determination, as the parties purported to do in *Perenco* v. *Ecuador*).

5. Despite the reduced weight given to them in *Urbaser* v. *Argentina*, in general ICSID arbitrators are increasingly willing to rely on the IBA Guidelines, or at least hear submissions based on them. This is evident from a number of decisions, including *Rompetrol* v. *Romania*.

These secondary characteristics are not 'stable' in the same way the primary characteristics (*nemo judex* and *de minimis*) are – the set of secondary characteristics identified here are merely trends in the form and substance of challenge decisions that emerge from a survey of leading decisions. At the same time as these lines emerge (and either brighten or fade), new doctrines and practices augment and replace them. Recently, practice has generated two new doctrines, or more properly, two new types of challenge: *Eureko/Vivendi* 'role/issue conflict' and *Hrvastska* counsel conflict.

Before moving on to discuss these new types of challenge, it is worth making one final comment on the test for bias that is applied in ICSID challenges, or rather posing the following question: why have so many ICSID tribunals applied a 'reasonable apprehension' or 'real possibility' test for bias when the ICSID Convention places an ostensibly heavier burden on the challenger, requiring that they establish a manifest lack of capacity for independent judgment?

A two-limbed answer can be offered in response to this question: first, it is a matter of policy pressure, and secondly it is a result of cross-pollination with ICA jurisprudence via the medium of the arbitrator.

As to the first limb of this answer, ICSID proceedings take place in an increasingly complex policy setting. A number of developing countries have expressed dissatisfaction with the ISA system, and some (most recently Ecuador) have denounced the ICSID Convention and certain

BITs. Charged with natural resources and socialist sentiment, Venezuela has been especially vocal in its criticism of ICSID, and other Latin American states have formed up behind it. And in August 2009, Russia gave formal notice that it no longer considers itself bound by the Energy Charter Treaty. These events suggest that there may be a crisis of confidence on the horizon and, if there is, the neutrality and fairness of the ISA system will be at the heart of it. The most recent evidence of this is the 31 August 2010 'Public Statement on the International Investment Regime' made by a group of academics from countries including Canada, England, Australia, Singapore, China and Germany.[115]

ICSID arbitrators have clearly felt the pressures of their increasingly heated geopolitical context: on North/South arbitrations, Algerian Judge Mohammed Bedjaoui has written of 'the problems of arbitral "neutrality" of the harsh times we live in'.[116] Bias challenges – where the allegation of conspiracy is most readily made – suffer the most in the North/South context; and bias challenges can become test cases for transparency in international arbitration. As former Secretary-General of the ICC Anne Marie Whitesell observed in 2007, the desirability of encouraging States to participate in international arbitration is an important policy consideration in ISA proceedings;[117] it seems that this *realpolitik* is colouring ICSID challenge jurisprudence. It should not be forgotten that, in ISA, States are well positioned to make demands, and to some extent it seems that ICSID challenge panels are giving them the test they want when they challenge arbitrators, not the test they signed up for in the ICSID Convention.

It is evident from the unique measures taken in the *Generation Ukraine* challenge that ICSID is (on an ad hoc basis) adapting its procedures where conflicts of interest arise. The involvement of the PCA in the challenge to Judge Brower in *Perenco* v. *Ecuador* may be further evidence of this process of institutional adaptation. Whether they are doing so consciously or subconsciously, ICSID arbitrators seem to be personally reacting to the policy pressures around them by adding

[115] Available at www.osgoode.yorku.ca/public_statement/documents/Public%20Statement. pdf (last accessed 10 December 2010).

[116] M. Bedjaoui, 'The arbitrator: One man – three roles', *International Arbitration*, 5(1) (1988), 7, cited in M. El-Kosheri and K. Youssef, 'The independence of international arbitrators: An arbitrator's perspective', *ICC Bulletin 2007 (Special Supplement)*, 690 (2008), 47.

[117] A. M. Whitesell, 'Independence in ICC arbitration: ICC court practice concerning the appointment, confirmation, challenge and replacement of arbitrators', *ICC Bulletin 2007 (Special Supplement)*, 690 (2008), 10.

elements of *Sussex Justices* and lowering the Article 57 test for bias. It has been said that the arbitrator's need to adhere to a strict judicial standard of independence is part of a 'broader trend towards the moralisation of international commercial law in general';[118] in this process the laws and practices of international arbitration respond to the global public interest. In ISA, the speed of this process of modification is increased by the tendency of ICSID arbitrators to refer to and follow earlier ICSID challenge decisions.

As to the second limb of this answer, the growing acceptance and application of the 'reasonable apprehension' test into ICSID jurisprudence can also be explained by cross-pollination or, perhaps more accurately, the ICA pedigree of many ICSID arbitrators. As has been observed above, the 'justifiable doubts' language of Model Law Article 12 (and UNCITRAL Rules Article 10) is so widely represented in national arbitration laws and institutional rules that it has arguably become a rule of the *lex mercatoria*. One of the things that the members of the relatively small pool of ICSID arbitrators have in common is that they either used to (or still) serve as arbitrators in strictly private international *commercial* disputes. They therefore carry the customs of ICA, which include the 'justifiable doubts' (or 'reasonable apprehension', as it is usually read) standard, in their briefcases when they cross over into ISA. It is not surprising, therefore, that ICSID arbitrators are so willing to elucidate Article 57 in these terms.

V   *Hrvatska* 'counsel conflict'

Now, turning to the first of the two new forms of bias that are emerging in ICSID law and practice, the challenge in *Hrvatska Elektroprivreda* v. *Slovenia* involved a rare form of *ASM Shipping* familiarity – where there is an objectionable familiarity between counsel and arbitrator. However, the *Hrvastka* challenge was novel in that it was made to counsel rather than the arbitrator. Given its novelty, it is appropriate to examine the *Hrvatska* decision in some detail.

By way of background, the claimant (the Croatian national electricity company) requested arbitration against the Republic of Slovenia on

---

[118] L. Gouiffes, 'L'Arbitrage international propose-t-il un modèle original de justice?', in *Recherche sur L'arbitrage en Droit International et Comparé: Mémoires pour le Diplôme D'Études Approfondies de Droit International Privé et du Commerce Présentés et Soutenus Publiquement* (Paris: LDGJ, 1997), p. 55.

4 November 2005.[119] After preliminary hearings in July 2006, the matter was booked for a two-week hearing in Paris starting 5 May 2008.[120] On 25 April 2008 the lawyers for the respondent sent the tribunal their list of attendees. The list named David Mildon QC of Essex Court Chambers as counsel for the respondent. The president of the ICSID tribunal (David A. R. Williams QC) was a door tenant at Essex Court. At no point prior had the respondent advised the tribunal or the claimant that Mr Mildon would be presenting part of its defence at the Paris hearing. The claimant wrote to the respondent seeking disclosure of the personal and professional relationship that existed between Mr Mildon and the president, clarification of the role Mr Mildon was to play in Paris, and the chronology of his engagement as counsel.[121] The respondent's lawyers replied that no relationship, professional or otherwise, existed between the president and Mr Mildon, but refused to disclose when Mr Mildon had been retained or the nature of the role he would play at the hearing.[122]

The correspondence continued: the lawyers for the claimant contended that their client (Slovenia) was entirely foreign to the London Chambers system, and derived no comfort from the status of English barristers as separate, self-employed legal practitioners. It was put that Slovenia would not have consented to the appointment of Mr Williams as president had it known that he was a door tenant in the same chambers as counsel for the respondent. The claimant identified the failure to disclose the appointment of Mr Mildon as a breach of General Standards 3 and 7 of the IBA Guidelines, which require prompt disclosure by both arbitrators and parties of problematic circumstances. The lawyers for the respondent replied that neither IBA General Standard 3 nor General Standard 7 dealt with disclosure by *lawyers*. After the respondent again refused to give the chronology of Mr Mildon's appointment, the claimant gave notice that it would make an objection to his involvement at the outset of proceedings in Paris.[123]

Slovenia objected to Mr Mildon on the first day of the hearing. The ICSID tribunal – whose members included the president – was required to determine two questions: (1) did it have the power to make an order disqualifying counsel, and (2) should such an order be made in the

---

[119] *Hrvatska Elektroprivreda dd* v. *Slovenia; Re David Mildon QC* (ICSID Case ARB/05/24, Tribunal's Ruling Regarding the Participation of David Mildon QC in Further Stages of the Proceedings of 6 May 2008), para. 3.

[120] *Ibid.*   [121] *Ibid.*, para. 4 (Claimant's letter to the Tribunal dated 28 April 2008).

[122] *Ibid.*, para. 10 (Respondent's letter to the Tribunal dated 2 May 2008).

[123] *Ibid.*, para. 10 (Claimant's letter to the Tribunal dated 2 May 2008).

circumstances.[124] With respect to the first question, the tribunal referred to ICSID Rule 6 (judge fairly), Rule 18 (notice of counsel), Rule 19 (the tribunal shall make orders required for the conduct of the proceeding), and Rule 39 (power to make provisional measures for the preservation of a party's rights).[125] ICSID Convention Article 56(1) (the immutability of ICSID tribunals) played a pivotal role: under this principle a properly constituted tribunal cannot be changed once the proceedings have begun.[126] The IBA Guidelines and their Background Information (namely Paragraph 4.5) were also cited with approval by the tribunal.[127] Relying on Schreuer's commentary the tribunal concluded that 'as a judicial formation governed by public international law' it did have the inherent power to make orders necessary to preserve the integrity of its proceedings,[128] and that this inherent power included the power to disqualify counsel.[129]

With respect to the second question, the fact that Slovenia was foreign to the London Chambers system, coupled with the respondent's conscious decision not to inform the claimant of its choice of counsel, had 'created an atmosphere of apprehension and distrust which it is important to dispel'.[130] The members decided that Mr Mildon's continued participation in the proceedings could indeed lead a reasonable observer to form a justifiable doubt as to the impartiality or independence of the president of the tribunal.[131] On these grounds the tribunal made orders that Mr Mildon could not participate any further in the proceedings.

On reading the *Hrvatska* decision, three points stand out. First, the party challenging counsel (Slovenia) was not a common law State and

---

[124] *Ibid.*, para. 12.   [125] *Ibid.*, para. 13.   [126] *Ibid.*, paras. 27–32.

[127] Para 4.5 of the Background Information to the IBA Guidelines states that:

> While the peculiar nature of the constitution of barristers' chambers is well recognised and generally accepted in England by the legal profession and by the courts, it is acknowledged by the Working Group that, too many who are not familiar with the workings of the English Bar, particularly in light of the content of the promotional material which many chambers now disseminate, there is an understandable perception that barristers' chambers should be treated in the same way as law firms.

See O. de Witt Wijnen, N. Voser and N. Reo, 'Background Information on the IBA Guidelines on Conflicts of Interest in International Arbitration', *Business Law International*, 5(3) (2004), 433.

[128] *Hrvatska*, para. 33. On the key question of inherent powers, the tribunal also referred to C. Brown, 'The inherent powers of international courts and tribunals', *British Yearbook of International Law*, 76 (2005), 195: see *Hrvatska*, n. 33.

[129] *Hrvatska*, paras. 33–4.   [130] *Ibid.*, para. 31.   [131] *Ibid.*, para. 30.

had no familiarity with the customs of the English Bar (such as the 'cab rank rule' or the status of barristers as independent sole practitioners). Secondly, the party opposing the challenge had refused to give particulars of counsel's engagement in its replies to the claimant's letters of inquiry and demand. Finally, if the tribunal did not disqualify counsel, then there would have been an appearance of partiality that would have required the president to stand down. As the proceedings were well advanced, the replacement of the president was not an option. As a matter of law, to do so would have gone against the principle of immutability enshrined in ICSID Convention, Article 56(1). But on closer examination, the decision may have broader implications for ICSID and ICA. It is fundamental that parties have the right to counsel of their choice – this is Rule 9 of the ICSID Rules. But the accepted fundamentality of the right to counsel does not, it seems, render it an absolute procedural rule: where the choice of counsel imperils the integrity of the process, the right will be trumped.

The probability of future *Hrvatska* challenges was confirmed in the ICSID case *Rompetrol Group NV* v. *Romania*,[132] in which the state respondent challenged counsel on the basis that counsel and arbitrator worked at the same firm for four years. The challenge was dismissed.[133]

VI   *Eureko/Vivendi* role/issue conflict

As has been noted above, ICSID awards appear to be (and are treated more and more like) precedents. Whilst this has gone some way to achieving the policy objective of adjudicatory consistency, it has collided with the reversible personality of the arbitrator. The problem is that, unlike in a municipal setting – where case law is generated by individuals (judges) who serve only as rule *makers* – in arbitration the rule makers are also the rule *users*; 'counsel one day, arbitrator the next'. Significantly, it is from their role as rule users that most leading arbitrators make their money: although there are some notable exceptions, for most practitioners the function of arbitrator is not especially lucrative,[134] at least not when compared to the money that can be made arguing the case. It follows that, as a precedent, an award may assume a commercial value when an arbitrator 'changes hats' to counsel: he or she may get the benefit

---

[132] *Rompetrol* v. *Romania*.   [133] *Ibid.*

[134] Y. Dezalay and B. G. Garth, *Dealing in Virtue: International commercial arbitration and the construction of a transnational legal order* (University of Chicago Press, 1996), pp. 50–1.

of a rule he or she made. If an arbitral award has weight as a precedent, can the arbitrators who made it subsequently argue for its application when they appear before other tribunals as counsel? And would there be a risk that in deciding the earlier matter they were generating case law for their client's benefit in the latter? These pressing questions are currently being debated in the context of 'issue conflict', or *Telekom Malaysia* bias.[135]

In my view, ISA (and ICSID) issue conflicts can be distinguished from issue conflicts in ICA. As already mentioned, allegations of issue conflict in ICA tend to focus on the arbitrator's previous expressions of opinion in lectures (such as occurred in *Uni-Inter* v. *Maillard*),[136] or their consecutive service in matters of similar or identical facts (which gave rise to the challenge in *Qatar* v. *Creighton*, referred to above).[137] But in ISA, issue conflicts can arise out of wholly separate (but concurrent or consecutive) arbitral proceedings. Although *Qatar* v. *Creighton* situations do sometimes arise in ISA (see for example *BG Group Plc* v. *Argentina*),[138] because of the emerging doctrine of precedent the conflict is more between *roles* than issues – between the role of rule *maker* and the role of rule *user*. This is why 'role/issue conflict' is a better name for this new type of challenge.

The appeal in *Eureko* v. *Poland* illustrates the new problem of role/ issue conflict in ISA. In the first appeal in *Eureko* v. *Poland*, Poland claimed that arbitrator Stephen Schwebel was related to the lawyers for the claimant: they had offices in the same building. The Brussels Court of First Instance dismissed Poland's challenge. On appeal, Poland raised

---

[135] In *Telekom Malaysia*, the challenged arbitrator – Professor Emmanuel Gaillard – was serving as counsel in a similar but unrelated investor–State dispute in which he was pressing an ICSID expropriation claim on behalf of a foreign consortium against the Kingdom of Morocco (*Consortium RFCC* v. *The Kingdom of Morocco* (ICSID Case No. ARB/00/6, Decision on Annulment of 18 January 2006)). The question was whether Professor Gaillard would be generating case law against his client's position in the claim against Morocco if he decided against the aggrieved investor in the ad hoc claim against Ghana. Ghana said he would, and that justifiable doubts as to his impartiality arose as a result. Judge von Maltzahn of the District Court of The Hague agreed and made orders requiring Professor Gaillard to stand down as counsel in the ICSID case or resign as chairman of the tribunal in the ad hoc matter.

[136] Decision of the Paris Court of Appeal of 5 July 1990 in *Uni-Inter* v. *Maillard* [1991] Revue de l'Arbitrage 359.

[137] See e.g. *Qatar* v. *Creighton* [1999] Revue de l'Arbitrage 308.

[138] See e.g. the challenge in *BG Group Plc* v. *Argentina* (Review of Award by the US District Court for the District of Columbia of 7 June 2010), where Albert Jan van den Berg's service as arbitrator in a string of ICC arbitrations against Argentina was said to give rise to justifiable doubts as to his independence. Argentina's challenge was dismissed by the ICC Court in an unpublished decision.

role/issue conflict. Schwebel was co-counsel with Sidley Austin in an unrelated concurrent ICSID arbitration (*Vivendi Universal* v. *Argentina*), and Schwebel and Messrs Sidley Austin cited the *Eureko* award as authority for certain propositions they were making on behalf of their clients against Argentina before the ICSID tribunal in the *Vivendi Universal* case. The legal issue common to both proceedings was the interpretation of the obligation of fair and equitable treatment – a question of law that arises in most ISAs.

The question for the court was whether Schwebel's impartiality was cast into doubt by the fact that he participated as arbitrator in the making of an award in one arbitration (*Eureko* v. *Poland*) that would be persuasive authority for his arguments as counsel in another (*Vivendi Universal* v. *Argentina*). The Brussels Court of Appeals declined to rule on Poland's additional objection: Poland failed to notify the arbitrators in accordance with the Belgian procedural rules or make the role/issue conflict argument before the Court of First Instance.

Although the Brussels Court of Appeals did not rule on the merits of Poland's challenge, there is no reason to suspect that the conclusion would have been any different to that reached by the District Court of The Hague in *Telekom Malaysia*. If anything, the evidence in *Eureko* v. *Poland* was much stronger: Schwebel actually cited his award against Poland in the submissions he made as counsel for Vivendi Universal, proving the point that in the two matters Schwebel was playing the roles of rule *maker* and rule *user* consecutively. On the other side of the Atlantic, Argentina objected to Vivendi Universal's reliance on the *Eureko* award, making a formal request to the ICSID tribunal to have any reference to the decision struck from the record. Although the merits of Argentina's objection were not formally decided by the *Vivendi Universal* tribunal, commentators have inferred from the citation of the *Eureko* decision in the final award that the ICSID tribunal rejected Argentina's position.[139]

As mentioned above, the position taken by the Secretary-General in *Canfor Corporation* suggests that role/issue conflict may well be a valid basis for proposing disqualification; and indeed, the decision in *Grand River Enterprises* suggests that even the broadest issues (such as a State's compliance with 'international commitments') may be actionable. But neither *Canfor* nor *Grand River* was decided under the 'manifest apparent bias' test prescribed by Article 57 of the ICSID Convention, and neither challenge raised the *Eureko/Vivendi* 'problem of precedent'.

---

[139] Mouawad, 'Issue conflicts in investment treaty arbitration', p. 6.

Nevertheless, given that many ICSID tribunals have displayed a preference for the *Sussex Justices* 'reasonable apprehensions of bias' standard in their interpretation of Article 57, it seems to me that a demonstrable role/issue conflict of the *Eureko/Vivendi* type would likely amount to a 'manifest lack of capacity for independent judgment' under Article 57 as it is currently being interpreted.

VII   Lessons

In my view, ISA practitioners can learn a good deal from the experiences of ICA arbitrators and lawyers in recent years. It must be accepted, however, that the lessons rely on an imperfect analogy: for mostly substantive legal reasons, the ethical hazards of the two disciplines are not shared, especially in the area of merits prejudgment. But overall these specifics do not deprive the analogy of force – the problems that ISA lawyers and arbitrators are being confronted with are, for the most part, problems that have been addressed either in practice or principle in purely commercial arbitrations.

The first lesson is that the substantive law of ISA is perhaps too 'constitutional' to be suited to ICA-style role reversibility. The system of investment treaties, which so clearly reflects the influence of a small handful of 'Model BITs' (US, UK, German etc.), is at present too conducive to merits prejudgment – or at least the appearance of it – to be operated by individuals who act as both rule makers and rule users. This systemic and structural problem may be addressed in a number of different ways, ranging from the establishment of a standing corps of arbitrators under the auspices of some world investment court to the total abandonment of the party-appointment model. However, the group of arbitrators may self-regulate this conflict of roles and issues by acknowledging a customary proscription against wearing 'both hats' (counsel and arbitrator) once one reaches a certain number of appointments as an arbitrator. Besides the normal forces that back up a customary rule, members of the ISA group will be inclined to observe this rule because it will only apply once a certain level of success has been achieved ('Oh, he doesn't do counsel work anymore'). In this sense, the rule would be a rank that members would aspire to wear, rather than avoid observing.

The second lesson is that the way a *Laker Airways* bias challenge is approached in an ISA will be informed by the nationality of the challenger. If all parties are of the Anglo-American legal tradition, the prospects of the 'same chambers' challenge succeeding drop significantly. But where the challenger can legitimately say that it has no tradition of barristers and solicitors, and can put its hand on its heart and say that it does not see the difference between a law firm and Essex Court, the challenge will be much more likely to succeed. This is a lot of the reason why Slovenia succeeded in the *Hrvatska* challenge to David Mildon QC.

The third lesson to be learnt is that bias challenges are becoming more abstract as the 'scorched earth game' of international litigation against States becomes more 'vulgar' and profitable. Large, full-service law firms are engaged in a process of intense competition for ISA work, and the desire to compete is driving lawyers to demonstrate their skills to their clients in new and different ways, one of which is the bias challenge ('Don't like him? We'll get rid of him. He used to be the Chairman's boss, you know'). The market buys the best minds, and the best minds are currently set (amongst other things) on the task of elaborating the grounds on which an arbitrator may be challenged. This competitive subtext of a bias challenge should not be discounted. My belief in this regard is grounded partly in my conviction that the logic of the proposition is sound, but partly also in the fact that I, as counsel, have felt these market forces myself. Clients ask about arbitrators and ask how to get rid of them, and these questions will persist in the future. The way I answer them will, I am sure, betray the fact that I am myself an upstart – a barbarian at the gates of the salon.

PART V

Engagement with cross-cutting issues

21

Protecting intellectual property rights under BITs, FTAs and TRIPS: Conflicting regimes or mutual coherence?

HENNING GROSSE RUSE-KHAN

I Introduction

Policy-makers, commentators and scholars are increasingly realising the impact that (international) intellectual property (IP) protection has beyond incentivising investment in innovation and creativity. IP also touches upon areas of general societal concern such as public health, access to information, the environment, climate change and food security. At a recent World Intellectual Property Organisation (WIPO) conference on these linkages, the World Trade Organization (WTO) Director-General Pascal Lamy acknowledged that 'the international intellectual property system cannot operate in isolation from broader public policy questions such as how to meet human needs as basic health, food and a clean environment'.[1]

In the most relevant multilateral agreement on IP, the WTO Agreement on Trade Related Aspects of Intellectual Property Rights (TRIPS), several provisions have been identified as providing WTO Member States, in particular developing countries, flexibility and policy space to address such public interests. In 2001, WTO Member States emphasised several of these flexibilities in the Doha Declaration on TRIPS and Public Health.

This chapter examines the policy space that States enjoy under the TRIPS Agreement and how this is affected by obligations to protect IP flowing from free trade agreements (FTAs) and bilateral investment

---

[1] P. Lamy, 'Strengthening multilateral cooperation on ip and public health' (Speech given at the WIPO Conference on Intellectual Property and Public Policy Issues, Geneva, 14 July 2009), <www.wipo.int/meetings/en/2009/ip_gc_ge/presentations/lamy.html> (last accessed 30 August 2009).

treaties (BITs). Focusing on public health, the scope of IP protection under these regimes and its impact on TRIPS flexibilities is scrutinised. Section II sets out the framework of (public-health-related) flexibilities under TRIPS. FTAs often contain substantive obligations on additional IP protection as well as investment chapters covering IP. How do these systems relate to each other and to which extent can they undermine policy space flowing from the multilateral system to address public-interest concerns? Also under BITs, IP is generally covered as a protected investment. Here, standards like fair and equitable treatment and the prohibition of expropriation raise questions of compatibility with the multilateral IP protection regime and its exceptions. Do BITs contain any safeguards for the regulatory sovereignty of the host country to accommodate sufficiently the flexibilities WTO Member States enjoy to regulate for example access to medicines? Section III, which forms the main part of this chapter, examines these issues. This chapter however aims not only to compare the substantive scope of protection for IP under TRIPS, FTAs and BITs but also, in section IV, to examine the relationship between these different systems and standards against the general international law framework to address cases of norm conflict and to achieve coherence between the distinct regimes of IP protection within international law. The main conclusion is that while IP protection under FTAs and BITs does have significant potential to constrain the use of flexibilities under TRIPS, more recent BITs increasingly contain provisions which safeguard especially the public-health related flexibilities TRIPS foresees.

II   TRIPS flexibilities

In light of the global debate about the impact of TRIPS obligations regarding patent protection for pharmaceutical inventions on public health and access to medicines, the WTO Member States in 2001 issued the Doha Declaration on the TRIPS Agreement and Public Health.[2] Recognising 'the gravity of the public health problems afflicting many developing and least-developed countries', WTO Member States agreed 'that the TRIPS Agreement does not and should not prevent Members from taking measures to protect public health'.[3] They affirmed 'that the

---

[2] Ministerial Conference, 'Doha Declaration on the TRIPS Agreement and Public Health' (WT/MIN(01)/DEC/2), 20 November 2001.
[3] *Ibid.*, para. 4.

agreement can and should be interpreted and implemented in a manner supportive of WTO Members' right to protect public health and, in particular, to promote access to medicines for all'.[4] In order to achieve this, the Doha Declaration then reaffirmed 'the right of WTO Members to use, to the full, the provisions in the TRIPS Agreement, which provide flexibility for this purpose'.[5] Amongst these 'TRIPS flexibilities', the Doha Declaration lists a number of flexibilities which are particularly noteworthy.

First, it recognises that each WTO Member State 'has the right to grant compulsory licences and the freedom to determine the grounds upon which such licences are granted'.[6] In the relevant patent context, compulsory licenses are State-imposed limits on the free exploitation of a particular patented invention by the patent-holder whereby he must grant an authorisation to produce and sell the patented product against payment of compensation.[7] These licences (or the mere threat of issuing them) can be utilised to bring down the price of the patented product and hence increase its availability especially amongst poorer parts of the population. While seldom used in practice, compulsory licensing (and the threat thereof) remains an important tool for governments to address the public interest in having easy access to a particular patented technology. In TRIPS, Article 31 provides for a long list of detailed conditions for the use of compulsory licences, such as, for instance, the need to provide adequate compensation. As confirmed by the Doha Declaration, however, the grounds for granting such licences remain free for the individual WTO Member State to decide. Further, TRIPS does not limit the issuance of compulsory licences 'to case[s] of a national emergency or other circumstances of extreme urgency or in cases of public non-commercial use'. Instead, these grounds addressed in Article 31(b) allow WTO Member States to waive, inter alia, the Article 31 requirement for previous negotiations with the holder of the IP right. The flexibility addressed in paragraph 5(c) of the Doha Declaration concerns this point: 'Each Member has the right to determine what constitutes a national emergency or other circumstances of extreme urgency, it being understood that public health crises, including those relating to HIV/AIDS, tuberculosis, malaria and other epidemics, can represent a national emergency or other circumstances of extreme

---

[4] *Ibid.*   [5] *Ibid.*   [6] *Ibid.*, para. 5(b).
[7] On compulsory licences under TRIPS see e.g. C. Correa, *Trade Related Aspects of Intellectual Property Rights* (Oxford University Press, 2007).

urgency.'[8] Hence WTO Member States have autonomy in determining the existence of a 'national emergency' and other scenarios which allow them to depart from some of the conditions for compulsory licensing under Article 31 of TRIPS. As these determinations are particularly relevant in the context of public-health crises, this possibility further enlarges the policy space of WTO Member States to address the issue of access to medicines.

The next relevant flexibility explicitly mentioned in the Doha Declaration concerns the concept of the 'exhaustion' of IP rights and the right to allow parallel imports. Generally speaking, IP rights vesting in a particular good are exhausted once the good in question has been 'lawfully'[9] placed onto the market. 'Exhaustion' thus means that the right-holder can no longer invoke his or her IP rights to control the further distribution or resale of those specific goods which have been marketed. Countries however differ on whether their national law requires the first marketing or sale of the goods to take place within their domestic market (national exhaustion), within a regional market of a free trade area or customs union (regional exhaustion) or on any national market around the globe (international exhaustion). In relation to patents, some countries have adopted the concept of international exhaustion to allow the (parallel) importation of patented drugs from countries where the patent-holder offers these medicines at a lower price in order to increase access to these medicines. Since these practices have been challenged as being inconsistent with TRIPS, the Doha Declaration clarifies that 'the effect of the provisions in the TRIPS Agreement that are relevant to the exhaustion of intellectual property rights is to leave each Member free to establish its own regime for such exhaustion without challenge, subject to the MFN and national treatment provisions of Articles 3 and 4'.[10]

In addition to these flexibilities which are explicitly mentioned in the Doha Declaration, TRIPS permits further public-health-related flexibilities. These include the right of WTO Member States to 'provide limited exceptions to the exclusive rights conferred by a patent, provided that such exceptions do not unreasonably conflict with a normal exploitation

---

[8] Ministerial Conference, 'Doha Declaration', para. 5(c).
[9] The term 'lawfully' is used here as the lowest common denominator amongst different opinions which either require such placement on the market to occur with the consent of the right-holder – while others also consider goods produced and sold under a compulsory licence sufficient to trigger exhaustion of the right to control the further resale.
[10] Ministerial Conference, 'Doha Declaration', para. 5(d).

of the patent and do not unreasonably prejudice the legitimate interests of the patent owner, taking account of the legitimate interests of third parties'.[11] However, arguably the most important TRIPS flexibility is not explicitly addressed either in TRIPS or the Doha Declaration. It is the concept of 'negative rights': IP rights as negative rights allow a right-holder to prevent anyone else from utilising the protected subject matter (and products or services containing or relying on that subject matter) in any commercially relevant way – without guaranteeing a positive (exclusive) right to exploit. Limiting IP rights as mere 'negative rights' allows governments to impose further regulatory controls on their utilisation and exploitation. An example of such a regulatory control is that certain copyrighted computer programs containing sexually explicit or violent images may not be sold freely, but only to persons who have reached a certain age. Here, regulations protecting the interests of minors limit the free exploitation of the copyrighted work – arguably without interfering with the exclusive rights in the computer program since they do not grant a positive monopoly for exploitation. In a similar fashion, a patent for a new innovative technology incorporated in a firearm does not provide the right-holder with a guarantee to commercialise the firearm without restrictions. Instead, rules on gun control and export or import prohibitions may significantly limit the trading of the patented product while leaving the negative right to exclude others from using the patented invention untouched. In the public-health context, regulatory measures such as price controls which do not affect the ability of the right-holder to exclude others from exploiting his patented drug do not infringe patent rights.

Confirming this, the WTO Panel in the *EC–Geographical Indications*[12] dispute observed:

> The TRIPS Agreement does not generally provide for the grant of positive rights to exploit or use certain subject matter, but rather provides for the grant of negative rights to prevent certain acts. This fundamental feature of intellectual property protection inherently grants Members freedom to pursue legitimate public policy objectives since many measures to attain those public policy objectives lie outside the scope of intellectual property rights and do not require an exception under the TRIPS Agreement.[13]

---

[11] TRIPS, Art. 30.
[12] *European Communities – Geographical Indications*, Panel Report (WT/DS/174R), 15 March 2005.
[13] *Ibid.*, para. 7.210.

International obligations which protect IP rights in principle[14] therefore do not constrain the ability of the national legislators to introduce limits on the commercial exploitation of the IP protected good or service, as long as this does not entail a curtailment of the 'negative right'.

III   Additional IP protection under FTAs and BITs

Throughout its history of over 130 years, the development of international IP protection has been a one-way street of continuously increasing protection. This effect is often explained by the basic principle that international IP treaties set only *minimum standards* for protection: they create a 'floor'[15] consisting of a minimum level of protection which must be available in all national laws of contracting parties – with presumably the sky being the only limit as to the further extension of IP protection. This notion of minimum standards is a central feature in the long history of international IP protection.[16] It finds express support in Article 20 of the Berne Convention which requires further agreements to 'grant to authors *more extensive rights* than those granted by the Convention'.[17]

In the current 'post-TRIPS' environment, bilateral and regional FTAs and BITs provide ample evidence for the operation of the minimum-standards principle: FTAs and BITs generally contain 'TRIPS-plus' standards which establish obligations for IP protection beyond the standards of the TRIPS Agreement. These TRIPS-plus obligations have created controversies over undue limitations of national sovereignty in areas such as public health, food security, technological advancement,

---

[14] For the special case of TRIPS, Art. 20 regarding limits on the commercial use of trademarks on goods or services see also, Correa, *Trade Related Aspects*.

[15] A. Taubmann, 'Rethinking TRIPS: Adequate remuneration for non-voluntary patent licensing', *Journal of International Economic Law*, 11(4) (2008), 927–70, 944.

[16] There are however cases of maximum standards where international IP treaties, notably TRIPS, provide 'ceilings' for the protection of IP; compare H. Grosse Ruse-Khan and A. Kur, 'Enough is enough: The notion of binding ceilings in international intellectual property protection' in A. Kur and M. Levin (eds.), *Intellectual Property Rights in a Fair World Trade System: Proposals for reform of Trips* (Cheltenham: Edward Egar, 2011), p. 359, and also available at Max Planck Papers on Intellectual Property, Competition & Tax Law Research Paper, No. 09–01, http://ssrn.com/abstract=1326429 (last accessed 28 September 2010).

[17] Berne Convention for the Protection of Literary and Artistic Works, opened for signature 9 September 1886 (as amended on 28 September 1979), Art. 20 (emphasis added), www.wipo.int (last accessed 19 October 2010).

promotion of domestic industries and access to knowledge.[18] The sheer number of these FTAs and BITs with increasing levels of IP protection, paired with the absence of an applicable most-favoured nation (MFN) and national-treatment (NT) exception in Articles 3 and 4 of TRIPS,[19] effectively globalises these increasing standards to become the international relevant standards. This section examines the extent to which TRIPS-plus standards in FTAs and BITs curtail the flexibilities and policy space left open under the TRIPS Agreement.[20] As any comprehensive evaluation of TRIPS-plus standards in FTAs and BITs would by far exceed the space available here, I limit my analysis to some examples of IP obligations in FTAs and BITs and examine their impact on the public-health-related flexibilities mentioned in section II.

A   IP and investment chapters in FTAs

Most of the FTAs negotiated between developed countries and developing countries contain chapters on IP protection and investment. The political economy behind developing countries agreeing to TRIPS-plus IP obligations lies in the trade-off that these countries (and their export-oriented industries) expect from obtaining preferential market access to major markets in the developed world. Below, some examples from FTAs

---

[18] See S. Musungu and G. Dutfield, 'Multilateral agreements in a TRIPS-plus world', Quaker United Nations Office, Geneva (2004), www.quno.org/geneva/pdf/economic/ Issues/Multilateral-Agreements-in-TRIPS-plus-English.pdf (last accessed 28 September 2010); see also K. Maskus and J. Reichmann, 'The globalization of private knowledge goods and the privatization of global public goods', *Journal of International Economic Law*, 7(2) (2004), 279–320; and South Centre, 'Analytical note: Intellectual property in investment agreements: The TRIPS-plus implications for developing countries', SC/TADP/AN/IP/5, May 2005, www.southcentre.org/index.php?option=com_content&task=view&id=81 (last accessed 28 September 2010).

[19] Distinct from the effect of Art. XXIV of GATT and Art. V of GATS (where WTO Member States can limit the benefits of further trade liberalisation to partners in regional trade agreements), any TRIPS-plus protection secured by one trading partner via an FTA is automatically and unconditionally available to right-holders from all other WTO Member States.

[20] For examples of such policy space (as pointed out and emphasised by WTO Member States), see Ministerial Conference, 'Doha Declaration', especially paras. 4, 5. For a comparative analysis of policy space under TRIPS and other core areas of WTO regulation, namely trade in goods and services, see H. Grosse Ruse-Khan, 'A comparative analysis of policy space in WTO law' (Max Planck Papers on Intellectual Property, Competition & Tax Law Research Paper No. 08–02, November 26, 2008), http://ssrn.com/abstract=1309526 (last accessed 28 September 2010).

by the US, EC and Japan are used as indicators of a wider trend of extending IP protection beyond TRIPS.

The phenomenon of demanding ever-increasing levels of IP protection in FTAs has first and foremost been attributed to those FTAs negotiated by the US. The often very detailed provisions on IP protection do not only go beyond the standards of TRIPS, but sometimes constrain the public-health-related flexibilities discussed above. For example, Article 17.9.4 of the US–Australia FTA effectively prohibits the adoption of a system of international exhaustion which would allow parallel imports (e.g. of patented drugs) from cheaper markets abroad.[21] Article 17.9.7 then limits the grounds on which compulsory licences may be granted; these are stated as being situations where the grant of such licences is necessary in order to 'remedy a practice determined after judicial or administrative process to be anticompetitive', as well as 'cases of public non-commercial use, or of national emergency, or other circumstances of extreme urgency' – if further conditions are satisfied.[22] The US–Australia FTA hence significantly curtails two (if not three)[23] of the TRIPS flexibilities all WTO Member States recognised in the Doha Declaration. The Central American Free Trade Agreement (CAFTA–DR),[24] in turn, encroaches less on the public-health-related flexibilities in TRIPS. It does not prohibit parallel imports, and nor does it limit the ability to grant compulsory licences. It does, however, constrain the policy space of WTO Member States under Article 27(3)(b) of TRIPS to exclude biological material from patentable subject matter, and sets

---

[21] US–Australia FTA, Art.17.9.4 provides:

> Each Party shall provide that the exclusive right of the patent owner to prevent importation of a patented product, or a product that results from a patented process, without the consent of the patent owner *shall not be limited by the sale or distribution of that product outside its territory,* at least where the patentee has placed restrictions on importation by contract or other means'. [emphasis added]

[22] *Ibid.*, Art. 17.9.7(b)(i)–(iii).

[23] In the compulsory licensing context, one may question whether the discretion under para. 5(c) Doha Declaration to determine autonomously whether a public-health crisis amounts to a 'national emergency' or 'other circumstances of extreme urgency' still exists under the same wording in Art. 17.9.7.

[24] Signed in August 2004, the CAFTA–DR is the first free trade agreement between the United States and a group of smaller developing economies – five Central American countries (Costa Rica, El Salvador, Guatemala, Honduras, and Nicaragua) and the Dominican Republic.

out additional conditions for the revocation of patents.[25] Finally, the patent provisions of the North American Free Trade Agreement (NAFTA) – which were negotiated almost simultaneously with the WTO/TRIPS Agreement – are more or less equivalent to the patent standards under TRIPS.[26]

The European Union (until December 2009 acting as the European Community (EC)) has traditionally not demanded 'US-style' detailed provisions on IP rights in its FTAs. Instead, the approach taken was in principle limited to obligations to accede to various international agreements.[27] An example for the 'traditional' EC approach to IP protection in FTAs[28] with developing countries is Article 46 of the Partnership Agreement between Members of the African, Caribbean and Pacific Group of States (ACP countries) and the EC and its Member States (Cotonou Agreement).[29] Its provisions on IP are particularly interesting since the EC is currently attempting to replace Article 46 with much more comprehensive and detailed IP rules negotiated in the framework of so called economic partnership agreements (EPAs) which are to supersede the Cotonou Agreement.[30] The main obligation under the traditional approach, exemplified in Article 46 of the Cotonou Agreement, is to 'ensure an *adequate and effective* level of protection of intellectual, industrial and commercial property rights, and other rights covered by TRIPS . . . *in line with the international standards*'.[31] Compared with these rather

---

[25] CAFTA–DR, Arts. 15.9.2, 15.9.4. An almost identical approach can be found in one of the most recent US FTAs – the one negotiated with South Korea; compare KORUS FTA, Arts. 18:8.2, 18:8.4.

[26] NAFTA, Art. 1709.

[27] For a comprehensive analysis of EC FTAs see Santa Cruz, 'Intellectual property provisions in European Union trade agreements' (ICTSD, Geneva, 2007), www.iprsonline.org/resources/docs/Santa-Cruz%20Blue20.pdf (last accessed 29 September 2010).

[28] One needs to add that the EC has also negotiated significantly stronger levels of IP protection which more or less require the trading partner to adopt the community *acquis* on IP protection. These types of bilateral agreements however are mainly negotiated with candidates or potential candidates for accession to the EC as well as other neighbouring countries. For details see Santa Cruz, 'Intellectual property', pp. 10–11.

[29] Cotonou Agreement (2000) OJ L317/3, amended (2005) OJ L287/1.

[30] The Cotonou Agreement has to be seen in the historical context of the special economic relationships between the EC Member States and their former colonies in Africa, the Caribbean and in the Pacific. For a detailed analysis of the EC's trade relationship with ACP countries see L. Bartels, 'The trade and development policy of the European Union', *European Journal of International Law*, 18(4) (2007), 715–56.

[31] Cotonou Agreement, Art. 46(1) (emphasis added).

ambiguous terms, the first comprehensive EPA agreed with the group of CARIFORUM States[32] contains a full chapter with detailed rules on IP protection. While this first example for a new approach does include significant TRIPS-plus obligations, notably in the area of IP enforcement, trademarks and geographical indications,[33] it also contains an explicit recognition of the 'importance of the Doha Declaration' for the issue of patents and public health.[34] Since the final version of the EC–CARIFORUM EPA lacks any substantive TRIPS-plus obligations on patent protection,[35] it arguably does not constrain any of the public-health-related flexibilities discussed above. It remains to be seen whether this approach will be continued in the other comprehensive EPAs to be signed with other regional groups of ACP countries.

Most FTAs negotiated between developed and developing countries contain an investment chapter. Chapter 11 of the US–Australia FTA, for example, deals with investment which – according to the definition in Article 11.17:4(f) – includes 'intellectual property rights'. The same definition exists under Article 10.28(f) of the CAFTA–DR, Article 10.27(f) of the US–Chile FTA, Article 10.28(f) of the US–Peru Trade Promotion Agreement (TPA), and Article 15.1:17(f) of the US–Singapore FTA, to name but a few. IP rights are, accordingly, generally considered as protected investments under the US FTAs.[36] For US IP right-holders (and those able to rely on MFN treatment under other FTAs, BITs

---

[32] The CARIFORUM countries consist of Antigua and Barbuda, Bahamas, Barbados, Belize, Dominica, the Dominican Republic, Grenada, Guyana, Haiti, Jamaica, Saint Lucia, Saint Vincent and the Grenadines, Saint Christopher and Nevis, Surinam and Trinidad and Tobago.

[33] EC–CARIFORUM EPA (CEPA), Arts. 151–64.

[34] CEPA, Art. 147 B.

[35] An early draft of CEPA however included language which could have limited the ability to opt for international exhaustion and allow parallel imports of patented medicines; see Art. 6:2 of the CARIFORUM–EC EPA, Non-Paper on Elements for a Section on IPRs: see discussion of the Non-Paper in e.g. Center for International Environmental Law, *Intellectual Property Quarterly Update* (Fourth Quarter 2006), http://www.ciel.org/Publications/IP_Update_4Q06.pdf (last accessed 4 June 2011); for an examination of the other IP provisions in the EC non-paper see Santa Cruz, 'Intellectual property', pp. 20–33.

[36] Compare however Art. 1139(g) of NAFTA which does not explicitly list IP rights but refers to 'real estate or other property, tangible or intangible, acquired in the expectation or used for the purpose of economic benefit or other business purposes'. However, the expropriation prohibition under Art. 1110 contains an exception for compulsory licences regarding IP rights which indicates that drafters understood the chapter to apply to IP rights as well.

or multilateral IP treaties), this opens the door to the substantive standards of investment protection contained in the FTAs. Hence the question arises as to what follows from the application of standards such as 'fair and equitable treatment', 'full protection and security', the prohibition of (direct and indirect) expropriation and of certain performance requirements relating to technology transfer or 'other proprietary knowledge' to IP rights.[37] In particular, do these standards provide for protection which differs from that contained in multilateral IP treaties or in the respective IP chapters of the relevant FTA? Since the substantive investment protection standards in the US FTAs are identical to those contained in US BITs, their impact on the exercise of TRIPS flexibilities will be examined in greater detail in section III.B below.

The FTAs which have to date been negotiated by the EC with developing countries do not contain any chapters or provisions on investment. This is due primarily to the lack of competence the EC has had with regard to the protection of investment under the provisions of the EC Treaty on the EC's 'common commercial policy'.[38] After the entry into force of the Lisbon Treaty in December 2009, the new Article 207(1) of the Treaty on the Functioning of the European Union (TFEU) now extends the competence of the EU for regulating its common commercial policy to 'foreign direct investment'.[39] It hence remains to be seen whether the EU will now include investment chapters in their FTAs and what kind of substantive standards these chapters may contain.[40] The impact these standards have on the availability of TRIPS flexibilities for the host State will be assessed below.

---

[37] See e.g. the provisions of Arts. 11.5, 11.7, 11.9(1)(f) of the US–Australia FTA or Arts. 10.5, 10.7, 10.9(1)(f) of CAFTA–DR.

[38] The former Art. 133 of the EC Treaty extended the EC's competence to 'the conclusion of tariff and trade agreements' and, under Art. 133(5), 'to the negotiation and conclusion of agreements in the fields of trade in services and the commercial aspects of intellectual property'.

[39] Art. 207(2)–(4) of the TFEU then contains further provisions for the internal competences, in particular the enhanced role of the EU Parliament, and voting mechanisms inter alia relating to negotiation and conclusion of agreements concerning trade-related aspects of intellectual property and foreign direct investment.

[40] A first look provides the communication by the EU Commission on an EU investment policy – see EU Commission, 'Towards a comprehensive European international investment policy' (Brussels, 7 July 2010 (COM (2010) 343 final).

B　IP as a protected investment under BITs

Already in the first modern BIT, signed between Germany and Pakistan in 1959, the definition of investment under Article 8 included 'assets such as . . . patents and technical knowledge'.[41] Today, the model BITs of most countries address IP rights.[42] While the approach in BITs differs insofar as some contain merely a general reference to 'intellectual property rights' and others include a (usually non-exhaustive) list of types of IP rights, one can conclude that BITs generally cover IP rights as protected investments.[43]

Against this background, the main question is what substantive standards of treatment an investor can expect under a BIT for his or her IP rights.[44] Within the context of this chapter, I focus on the standards concerning expropriation, since the public-health-related TRIPS flexibilities noted above seem primarily 'threatened' by the prohibition of (indirect) expropriation.[45] While this of course does not exclude the possibility that other substantive standards may play a role, most

---

[41] See Art. 8(1)(a) of the Agreement between the Federal Republic of Germany and the Islamic Republic of Pakistan on the Encouragement and Reciprocal Protection of Investments, signed 25 November 1959, *Bundesgesetzblatt* (1961) vol. II, 793 (entered into force 28 April 1962).

[42] L. Liberti, 'Intellectual property rights in international investment agreements: An overview', *Transnational Dispute Management*, 6(2) (2009), 5–9.

[43] For a comprehensive empirical analysis on how BITs cover IP rights as protected investment see R. Lavery, 'Coverage of intellectual property rights in international investment agreements: An empirical analysis of definitions in a sample of bilateral investment treaties and free trade agreements', *Transnational Dispute Management*, 6(2) (2009), 4–7 and Annex 1. The author observes that although few BITS do not explicitly address IP rights, this does not necessarily mean that they do not cover IP since BITs generally provide that the lists of covered investments are not exhaustive.

[44] For an overview see C. Correa, 'Bilateral investment agreements: Agents for new global standards for the protection of intellectual property rights?' (GRAIN Study, August 2004), www.grain.org/briefings_files/correa-bits-august-2004.pdf (last accessed 29 September 2010).

[45] There is an increasing body of literature which mainly focuses on the expropriation and compensation standard when reviewing IP rights under BITs: see M. Seelig, 'Can patent revocation or invalidation constitute a form of expropriation?', *Transnational Dispute Management*, 6(2) (2009); T.-Y. Lin, 'Compulsory licenses for access to medicines, expropriation and investor–State arbitration under bilateral investment agreements: Are there issues beyond the TRIPS Agreement?', *International Review of Intellectual Property and Competition Law*, 40(2) (2009), 152–73; C. Gibson, 'A look at the compulsory license in investment arbitration: The case of indirect expropriation', *Transnational Dispute Management*, 6(2) (2009); R. C. Bernieri, 'Compulsory licensing and public health: TRIPS-plus standards in investment agreements', *Transnational Dispute Management*, 6(2) (2009).

provisions which expressly deal with IP rights in BITs address the applicability of the expropriation standard.[46] The impact of this standard on the operation of IP law is significant, as the following example indicates. In May 2007, the US-based pharmaceutical company Merck issued the following statement on the Government of Brazil's decision to issue a compulsory licence for STOCRIN™ (efavirenz), a patent-protected drug which was to be produced by a generic manufacturer:

> This *expropriation of intellectual property* sends a chilling signal to research-based companies about the attractiveness of undertaking risky research on diseases that affect the developing world, potentially hurting patients who may require new and innovative life saving therapies . . . This decision by the Government of Brazil will have a negative impact on Brazil's reputation as an industrialized country seeking to attract inward investment, and thus its ability to build world-class research and development.[47]

Even though the TRIPS Agreement contains detailed provisions in Article 31 on the conditions and procedures for the issuance of compulsory licences, Merck did not challenge the TRIPS consistency of this measure. Instead, it chose to present the matter as a case of 'expropriation of intellectual property' – hence primarily relying on investment standards in making its case. Although Merck apparently did not take this case further – maybe because Brazil has not signed a BIT (or FTA) with the US – Merck's statement is indicative of the added value that investment standards can offer to IP right-holders. In particular the wide and effects-based notion of indirect expropriation or 'regulatory taking' which focuses on 'depriving the owner, in whole or in part, of the use or reasonably-to-be-expected economic benefits of property',[48] allows foreign IP right-holders to challenge various host State measures constraining the commercial exploitation of his IP protected goods or services. Such a standard of protection may not only affect compulsory licensing or other exceptions and limitations to IP rights, but also the concept of 'negative rights' and the principle of (international) exhaustion – both which are internationally accepted boundaries of IP protection.[49]

---

[46] On these clauses see this section as well as sections III.B and III.C below.

[47] Merck & Co. Inc., 'Statement on Brazilian government's decision to issue compulsory license for STOCRIN™' (4 May 2007), www.merck.com/newsroom/news-release-archive/corporate/2007_0504.html (emphasis added) (last accessed 29 September 2010).

[48] *Metalclad* v. *Mexico* (ICSID Case No. ARB(AF)/97/1, Award of 30 August 2000), para. 105.

[49] See section II above for details on these TRIPS flexibilities.

The main difficulty for a more precise analysis of the impact the expropriation and compensation standard has on TRIPS flexibilities lies in the indeterminate and multifaceted meaning of the term 'indirect expropriation'. A comprehensive assessment of its meaning under customary international law, the Model BITs currently in use or the increasing jurisprudence from investor–State arbitration is well beyond the scope of this chapter.[50] The criteria set forth in the US Model BIT[51] for indirect expropriation are therefore selected as a 'benchmark' test case – not least because these criteria are used in all investment chapters of recent US FTAs, and also in all recent US BITs.[52] These criteria further find support in literature and case law.[53] Some argue that they generally express international consensus as they 'do not add anything new to international expropriation law'.[54]

Under Article 6(1) of the US Model BIT, the standards pertaining to direct and indirect expropriation are addressed:

> Neither Party may expropriate or nationalize a covered investment either directly or indirectly through measures equivalent to expropriation or nationalization ('expropriation'), except: (a) for a public purpose; (b) in a non-discriminatory manner; (c) on payment of prompt, adequate, and effective compensation; and (d) in accordance with due process of law and Article 5 [Minimum Standard of Treatment] (1), (2), and (3).

Annex B of the Model BIT then further defines direct expropriation and sets out three criteria which should guide the determination of indirect expropriation.[55] Direct expropriation concerns cases 'where an investment is nationalized or otherwise directly expropriated through formal

---

[50] For an overview on expropriation in international (investment) law see A. Newcombe, 'The boundaries of regulatory expropriation in international law', (April 2005), http://ssrn.com/abstract=703244 (last accessed 29 September 2010).

[51] The 2004 US Model BIT, www.bilaterals.org/IMG/doc/2004_update_US_model_BIT.doc (last accessed 29 September 2010).

[52] Art. 6 and Annex B of the US Model BIT concern expropriation. These provisions are identical to the respective Article and Annex in the most recent US BITs (such as the US–Uruguay BIT and the US–Rwanda BIT) and with those in the US–Australia FTA and the CAFTA–DR.

[53] For a comprehensive discussion of the indirect expropriation standard and its application to IP rights see Gibson, 'Compulsory license', pp. 21–33.

[54] Newcombe, 'Regulatory expropriation'.

[55] Annex B begins by stating that 'Article 6 [Expropriation and Compensation](1) is intended to reflect customary international law concerning the obligation of States with respect to expropriation' – hence indicating that the US considers these standards as part of customary international law obligations binding on all States.

transfer of title or outright seizure'.[56] None of the acts covered under the TRIPS flexibilities discussed above would amount to such a formal transfer of title or seizure: compulsory licences, exceptions to the exclusive patent rights, parallel imports and other regulatory interference with the commercial exploitation of a patented drug (such as price controls) do not interfere with the formal ownership position of the patent-holder.[57] But do they amount to 'indirect expropriation, where an action or series of actions by a Party has an effect equivalent to direct expropriation without formal transfer of title or outright seizure'?[58]

The US Model BIT (as well as the identical text in BITs the US recently concluded) makes this determination dependant upon:

> A case-by-case, fact-based inquiry that considers, among other factors:
>
> (i) the economic impact of the government action, although the fact that an action or series of actions by a Party has an adverse effect on the economic value of an investment, standing alone, does not establish that an indirect expropriation has occurred;
> (ii) the extent to which the government action interferes with distinct, reasonable investment-backed expectations; and
> (iii) the character of the government action.[59]

The first criterion hence concerns the size and scope of the impact which host State measures implementing TRIPS flexibilities have on the economic value of the patent. This certainly depends on the individual circumstances (such as the terms of the compulsory licence, the amount and price of parallel imported drugs and the degree to which price controls affect the price set by the patent-holder). For compulsory licences, adherence to the obligation under Article 31 of TRIPS to provide for adequate compensation, 'taking into account the economic value of the authorization', may often exclude a substantial deprivation of the economic value of the patent.[60] Nevertheless, one can hardly exclude, *a priori*, that an investment tribunal would find any of these measures as having a sufficiently severe economic impact.[61]

---

[56] Annex B, section (3) of the US Model BIT.
[57] One could however discuss whether the revocation of patent – e.g. due to successful challenge of the patentability criteria – amounts to direct expropriation; on this point see, Seelig, 'Patent revocation'.
[58] Annex B, section (4) of the US Model BIT.
[59] Annex B, section (4)(a) of the US Model BIT.
[60] Cf. Gibson, 'Compulsory license', pp. 23–4.
[61] See also Lin, 'Compulsory licenses for access', p. 157.

Secondly, one needs to assess the measure's interference with 'distinct, reasonable investment-backed expectations'.[62] Here, the main question is whether the grant of the patent by the host State and the exclusivity it entails under the domestic patent law constitute State representations which in turn create legitimate expectations on which the patent-holding investor may rely. From an IP perspective, all measures backed by the public-health-related TRIPS flexibilities discussed above are internationally accepted elements of the IP system. The issuance of a compulsory licence (e.g. in order to facilitate easy access to medicines) is a common legal option in national IP laws[63] which all WTO Member States agreed in the Doha Declaration as being consistent with TRIPS. The same applies to allowing parallel imports by opting for a system of international exhaustion and for exceptions and limitations to the exclusive patent right which are consistent with the three-step test in Article 30 of TRIPS. In all cases, the grant of the patent certainly does not and cannot create any legitimate expectation that the exclusivity it confers is absolute and will remain without interference from accepted checks and balances inherent in the IP system. Instead, the expectations of the patent-holding investor are *a priori* limited by the regulatory tools the domestic IP law of the host State foresees. Even in case a host State introduces such measures[64] after the investor has obtained his patent, the international acceptance of those measures would militate against findings of interference with any legitimate expectations allegedly held by the investor.[65] This may of course be different as soon as the host State is bound by TRIPS-plus FTA obligations which curtail or prohibit the use of TRIPS flexibilities, as is the case in the US–Australia FTA.[66] These additional IP obligations, which the host State must implement in its domestic law, may

---

[62] Annex B, section (4)(a)(ii) of the US Model BIT.

[63] For a discussion of recent cases see V. Vadi, 'Access to essential medicines & international investment law: The road ahead', *Journal of World Investment and Trade*, 8(4) (2007), 523–25.

[64] Apart from the measures mentioned so far, such measures may e.g. be a new exception allowing the use of a patented drug for medical tests necessary to obtain regulatory approval for a competing drug from the drug authorities (so called regulatory approval or 'Bolar' exception) which a WTO Panel has found to be consistent with Art. 30 TRIPS; see *Canada – Patent Protection of Pharmaceutical Products* (Panel Report, WT/DS114/R, adopted 7 April 2000).

[65] Similar, Lin, 'Compulsory licenses for access', pp. 157–8, who however relies on common State practice and further considers the underlying public-policy objectives already for this second criterion.

[66] See section III.A above.

give rise to legitimate expectations such that measures contrary to them may also be actionable under indirect expropriation standards.

For regulatory measures which from the outset do not interfere with IP protection due to the 'negative-rights' character of IP rights, the grant of a patent cannot create any expectations that such measures will not be introduced in relation to the exploitation of the patented product. As has been explained above,[67] the negative right to exclude others from exploiting the patent does not entail a guarantee against State intervention such as, for instance, the imposition of conditions on the production or limitations on the use and sale of the patented product. Hence, the introduction of, for example, price controls for a certain patented medication does not interfere with the patent for that medicine. Since such a measure is outside the protection conferred by IP rights, these rights cannot create legitimate expectations as to the (continued) absence of such measures. Wherever the protected investment consists of an IP right, the grant of this right therefore does not result in legitimate expectations which stand against the introduction of measures based on TRIPS flexibilities.[68] This conclusion does not, of course, preclude the possibility that such measures may be viewed as interfering with legitimate expectations resulting from *other forms of host State representations* – such as specific assurances given to the investor regarding the exploitation of his IP protected product or service in the host State.

The third factor relevant for the determination of indirect expropriation is the 'character of the government action'.[69] Here, the further explanation in Annex B of the US Model BIT offers additional guidance:

> Except in rare circumstances, non-discriminatory regulatory actions by a Party that are designed and applied to protect legitimate public welfare objectives, such as public health, safety, and the environment, do not constitute indirect expropriations.[70]

Domestic measures implementing any of the public-health-related flexibilities in TRIPS will thus generally benefit from this presumption against indirect expropriation. So long as their character and underlying rationale consists of good-faith public-welfare goals such as facilitating

---

[67] For a discussion of the concept of negative rights see section II above.

[68] Gibson, 'Compulsory license', pp. 25–7, however argues in favour of a reasonable expectation flowing from the patent grant that there will be generally no interference during the (20-year) period of patent protection.

[69] Annex B, section (4)(a)(iii) of the US Model BIT.

[70] *Ibid.*, at section (4)(b).

access to medicines, and so long as they are non-discriminatory in nature, investors are unlikely to succeed with claims of indirect expropriation.[71] But what about measures which (although they are disguised as being motivated by public-health considerations, such as the granting of compulsory licences) pursue an industrial policy goal – such as boosting the domestic generic drug industry? The 2003 WTO waiver on Article 31(f) of TRIPS[72] addresses the lack of domestic manufacturing capacity in the pharmaceutical sector in a significant number of developing countries as a key public-health concern. It therefore offers stark evidence that building a domestic (generic) industry has certainly positive public-health implications as well and may not per se amount to a 'bad-faith' measure. Further, the compliance with TRIPS requirements for compulsory licences under Article 31 and exceptions and limitations under Article 30 should generally ensure that the effect of any bad-faith measures is marginal in its economic impact.

In sum, applying the criteria set out in Annex B of the US Model BIT to measures implementing TRIPS flexibilities will generally not support findings of indirect expropriation. This is because compliance with the relevant TRIPS provisions usually entails that the conditions for indirect expropriation are not satisfied: in the case of compulsory licences and exceptions or limitations, the consistency with the conditions under Articles 30 and 31 of TRIPS will prevent a significant economic impact.[73] For other measures such as price controls or parallel imports which may have such an impact, the other criteria will not be met: none of the measures analysed interferes with reasonable expectations resulting from the grant of a patent to an investor, on the basis that the investor has to reckon with internationally accepted checks and balances that limit the exclusivity of patent rights. Again, consistency with the global standards embodied in TRIPS is crucial – unless of course these standards are superseded by those of TRIPS-plus FTAs prohibiting the host State from relying on the relevant TRIPS flexibilities. For measures which are – due to the concept of negative rights – a priori outside the scope of IP protection, the grant of IP rights logically cannot offer any (legitimate) expectations whatsoever. IP rights do not protect expectations on return

[71] Compare also Vadi, 'Access to essential medicines', p. 518.
[72] *WTO General Council* (Decision of 30 August 2003 (WT/L/540), 1 September 2003).
[73] Apart from the aforementioned duty to offer adequate compensation under Art. 31, Art. 30 of TRIPS only allows such type of exceptions which inter alia 'do not unreasonably conflict with a normal exploitation of the patent'.

of investments other than by preventing others from using the IP protected subject matter and hence cannot be affected by limiting the exploitation of protected goods or services. Finally, while the TRIPS flexibilities usually do not require a specific public-welfare objective,[74] those referred to in the Doha Declaration will generally be relevant for public health and access to medicines. Therefore, in the public-health context, the use of compulsory licences, exceptions to patent rights, parallel importation and price controls will normally not constitute an (indirect) expropriation. Nevertheless, the 'case-by-case, fact-based inquiry' which Annex B demands may lead an investment tribunal to reach opposite conclusions. In such a case, a BIT would typically prohibit an (indirect) expropriation, unless it is (a) for a public purpose; (b) non-discriminatory; (c) carried out under due process of law; and (d) accompanied by the payment of prompt, adequate and effective compensation.[75]

These conclusions reached by applying the US Model BIT provisions on (indirect) expropriation can be extended to investor protection under other BITs such as the Canadian Model BIT. The latter contains almost completely identical language which again relies on the three criteria examined above.[76] Other recently concluded BITs do not contain a specific list of criteria to determine indirect expropriations.[77] This equally applies to the Energy Charter.[78] But since the general prohibition of expropriation is phrased in language very similar to the US Model BIT, chances are that arbitrators would rely on standards identical or similar to the three criteria as an expression of customary international law determining what constitutes an indirect expropriation.[79]

---

[74] See Arts. 31, 30 and 6 of TRIPS.
[75] Compare Art. 13 of the *Energy Charter Treaty*, 2080 UNTS 95, signed 17 December 1994 (entered into force 16 April 1998), Art. 6(1) of the US Model BIT. For a review of these conditions in contrast to the requirements for compulsory licensing under Art. 31 of TRIPS see Lin, 'Compulsory licenses for access', pp. 161–4.
[76] See Art. 13 and Annex B.13(1) of the Canadian Model BIT, http://ita.law.uvic.ca/documents/Canadian2004-FIPA-model-en.pdf (last accessed 29 September 2010).
[77] See e.g. Art. 9(1) of the Japan–Vietnam BIT or Art. 4(1) of the Germany–Afghanistan BIT.
[78] See Art. 13 of the Energy Charter Treaty.
[79] On the customary international law character of the three criteria see, Gibson, 'Compulsory license', pp. 21–33 and Newcombe, 'Regulatory expropriation'.

C Impact on TRIPS flexibilities

What then follows from the substantive IP and investment standards in FTAs and BITs for the ability of a WTO Member State to rely on the public-health-related TRIPS flexibilities? The analysis in sections III.A and III.B on TRIPS-plus IP protection suggests that certain obligations undermine the use of these flexibilities. The obligations in the US–Australia FTA on compulsory licensing and parallel imports are prime examples.[80] In contrast to the EC–CARIFORUM EPA,[81] the IP chapters of most of the earlier US FTAs generally do not contain any specific clauses which safeguard the operation of the public-health-related flexibilities. Since these TRIPS provisions are not mandatory but optional,[82] the principle of minimum standards suggests that the subsequent obligations in US FTAs will prevail, and prevent any reliance on TRIPS flexibilities.[83]

Turning to the investment chapters of FTAs, one may recall that these generally contain the same substantive standards of treatment as found in (Model) BITs. Here, the three criteria contained in the US Model BIT (and implemented in investment chapters of recent US FTAs as well as in recent US BITs)[84] generally do not support findings of (indirect) expropriation in case of measures implementing TRIPS flexibilities. If, however, an investment tribunal arrives at a different conclusion based on the individual circumstances of the case, the US BITs and FTAs contain an important safeguard which may uphold the public-health-related policy space under TRIPS: according to Article 6(5) of the US Model BIT the standards on

---

[80] See Art. 17.9(4) and (7) of the US–Australia FTA and the respective discussion in section III.A above.

[81] See Art. 147 B of the EC–CARIFORUM EPA and its analysis in section III.A above.

[82] Since Art. 1(1) 2nd sentence of TRIPS makes the right of WTO Member States to introduce more extensive protection subject to the condition that it does not 'contravene' TRIPS provisions, one could nevertheless question whether TRIPS-plus norms which curtail (optional) TRIPS flexibilities 'contravene' these flexibilities; see section III below and generally H. Grosse Ruse-Khan, 'Time for a paradigm shift? Exploring maximum standards in international intellectual property protection', *Journal of Trade, Law and Development*, 1(1) (2009), 56–102, http://ssrn.com/abstract=1457416 (last accessed 29 September 2010).

[83] The US FTAs however often contain a general provision where the FTA parties 'affirm their existing *rights* and obligations under the TRIPS Agreement' (see Art. 15.1(7) of CAFTA–DR and Art. 17.1(3) of the US–Australia FTA) (emphasis added). Whether these general provisions may be interpreted as to uphold the (optional) TRIPS 'rights' to regulate public health will be addressed in section IV below.

[84] See section III.B above.

expropriation do 'not apply to the issuance of compulsory licenses granted in relation to intellectual property rights in accordance with the TRIPS Agreement'.[85] Under Article 6(5) of the recent US–Uruguay and US–Rwanda BITs, this type of safeguard clause extends further to cover not only compulsory licences, but also 'the revocation, limitation, or creation of intellectual property rights, to the extent that such issuance, revocation, limitation, or creation is consistent with the TRIPS Agreement'. Still more comprehensive but similar language is used in the draft Multilateral Agreement on Investment (MAI) which had unsuccessfully been negotiated in the late 1990s under the auspices of the OECD:

> The creation, limitation, revocation, annulment, statutory licensing, compulsory licensing and compulsory collective management of IPRs, the withholding of authorised deductions by an entity charged with the collective management of IPRs, and the sharing of remuneration between different holders of IPRs are not expropriation within the terms of this agreement, to the extent that they are not inconsistent with specialised IPR conventions.[86]

Similar clauses exist in the investment chapters of US FTAs – however with an important distinction: Article 10.7(5) of the CAFTA–DR contains language identical to the US Model BIT safeguarding TRIPS-consistent compulsory licences, but then requires for the 'revocation, limitation, or creation of intellectual property rights' consistent with CAFTA's own IP chapter.[87]

At first sight, these safeguards for compulsory licences (and often other forms of limitations on IP rights) seem to offer sufficient security for the host State that it may continue to rely on the public-health-related flexibilities in TRIPS. At the same time, these safeguard clauses offer investors the security and predictability that TRIPS standards will govern the question of (indirect) expropriation under investment protection. A closer look, however, reveals some problems, in particular for the host State whose measures are challenged by an investor in investor–State arbitration proceedings. The main issue is that on the basis of safeguard clauses like Article 6(5) of the US Model BIT, the question of the TRIPS-consistency of a compulsory licence (or other IP

---

[85] Identical provisions exist in recent US BITs; see Art. 6(5) of the US–Uruguay and US–Rwanda BITs.

[86] See OECD, 'The Multilateral Agreement on Investment: The MAI negotiating text' (24 April 1998), p. 51.

[87] Art. 11.7(5) of the US–Australia FTA contains an identical provision.

limitation, if applicable) is tested in arbitration proceedings *outside* the (State-to-State) WTO dispute-settlement system. This represents a unique option for private parties to challenge a national measure as inconsistent with WTO law – something which in most jurisdictions cannot be tested by domestic courts.[88] The acceptance and legitimacy of any decisions on TRIPS rendered by investment arbitration panels may certainly be questionable in light of the competing jurisdiction of the WTO Panels and the Appellate Body.[89]

A more practical matter concerns the burden of proof under the safeguard clauses. Inapplicability of the expropriation standards here is generally subject to showing TRIPS-consistency of the compulsory licence or other relevant measure. The host State will normally carry this burden of proof. This however is not necessarily so under the WTO dispute-settlement system, where this matter will depend on the individual complaints.[90] In the case of compulsory licences, for instance, the complaining WTO Member State must show an infringement of one (or more) obligations the responding State has under Article 31 of TRIPS.[91] But under the safeguard clauses, the host State seems to be responsible for showing that its compulsory licence is 'in accordance with the TRIPS Agreement'.[92]

Another issue relates to the scope of the consistency test in the safeguard clauses: does a TRIPS-consistency test only mandate an isolated analysis of the provision addressing the measure at stake – for

---

[88] See e.g. the case law of the ECJ (Case C-491/01, Judgement of 10 December 2002, para. 154) and the judgment of the High Court of the Judicature at Madras in *Novartis v. Union of India* (W.P. Nos. 24759 and 24760 of 2006, 6 August 2007), para. 8.

[89] See in particular Art. 23 DSU which demands that WTO Member States when seeking redress for violations of WTO obligations 'shall have recourse to, and abide by, the rules and procedures of this Understanding'. While this obligation does not bind private investors, any WTO Member State agreeing to a BIT which allows investor–State arbitration to determine compliance of a host State measure with TRIPS may be acting in violation of Art. 23(2)(a) DSU.

[90] See e.g. *United States – Measure Affecting Imports of Woven Wool Shirts and Blouses from India*, Appellate Body Report (WT/DS33/AB/R and Corr.1, adopted 23 May 1997), para. 14: 'the burden of proof rests upon the party, whether complaining or defending, who asserts the affirmative of a particular claim or defence'.

[91] This follows from the general principle expressed in n. 90 above: a WTO Member State asserting that a compulsory licence in the domestic law of another Member State does not conform to the requirements of Art. 31 of TRIPS must prove that one or more of these requirements is not adhered to. However, under the exception provision of Art. 30 of TRIPS the party asserting the exception bears the burden of proving compliance with the conditions of that exception; *Canada – Patents*, para. 7.60.

[92] See Art. 6(5) of the US Model BIT.

example Article 30 of TRIPS regarding exceptions to patent rights? This would prevent the operation of the main 'horizontal' flexibility all WTO Member States had agreed to under paragraph 5 of the Doha Declaration, which provides that:

> In applying the customary rules of interpretation of public international law, each provision of the TRIPS Agreement shall be read in the light of the object and purpose of the Agreement as expressed, in particular, in its objectives and principles.

In particular, the open meaning of several terms used in Article 30 of TRIPS (such as 'unreasonableness', and 'legitimacy')[93] can be significantly influenced by the balancing objective in Article 7 of TRIPS and the 'public-interest' principle under Article 8(1) of TRIPS. While an interpretation by an arbitration panel will usually also rely on the principles embodied in Articles 31–3 of the Vienna Convention on the Law of Treaties (VCLT) and hence is likely equally to consider the treaty's 'context' and 'objectives', the context and objectives may nevertheless mean something different here: since the questions of TRIPS-consistency are incorporated into the BIT or FTA containing the safeguard clause, an arbitration panel may struggle to avoid considering the context and objectives of the BIT or FTA as being relevant in guiding its interpretation of the consistency test. Thus, the interpretative result may well be different from the result achieved in a 'pure' WTO setting. These examples demonstrate the potential problems encountered when host States rely on TRIPS-consistency tests in order to safeguard domestic measures implementing TRIPS flexibilities.

Finally, the consistency clauses in the investment chapters of US FTAs do not in all instances refer to compliance with TRIPS as a safeguard against expropriation claims. While this is the case for compulsory licensing, acts amounting to 'revocation, limitation, or creation of intellectual property rights' must be consistent with the FTA's own IP chapter.[94] This excludes (indirect) expropriation claims against, for example, a TRIPS-consistent exception under Article 30 or revocation under Article 33 of TRIPS only insofar as the exception or revocation is also consistent with the TRIPS-plus standards of the FTA's IP chapter. As discussed

---

[93] e.g. TRIPS, Art. 30 provides: 'Members may provide limited exceptions to the exclusive rights conferred by a patent, provided that such exceptions do not unreasonably conflict with a normal exploitation of the patent and do not unreasonably prejudice the legitimate interests of the patent owner, taking account of the legitimate interests of third parties.'

[94] See Art. 11.7(5) of the US–Australia FTA and Art. 10.7(5) of CAFTA–DR.

above, the US–Australia FTA limits, inter alia, the flexibilities of Articles 6, 30 and 33 of TRIPS regarding parallel importation; 'Bolar exceptions';[95] and patent revocation in a significant way.[96] In scenarios like these, TRIPS-flexibility safeguards are subject to the TRIPS-plus obligations emanating from the FTA's IP chapter.

The impact of IP protection under FTAs and BITs on the ability of States to use public-health-related policy space under TRIPS is therefore determined by three issues. The first of these is the degree to which the substantive protection standards in an FTA or BIT go beyond the obligations contained in TRIPS. Here, IP chapters in some of the US FTAs curtail the flexibilities mentioned in the Doha Declaration to a significant extent. Investment protection (under BITs or FTAs) in turn does not seem to interfere with the public-health-related discretion WTO Member States enjoy under TRIPS – at least as far as expropriation standards are concerned. The second issue is the existence of specific consistency clauses which uphold TRIPS flexibilities on public health and access to medicines. While some of these clauses can be found in IP chapters of recent EU EPAs, they are far more common in (BIT or FTA-based) investment protection provisions. Here, indirect expropriation standards do not apply to TRIPS- (or FTA IP chapter-) consistent compulsory licences, exceptions and limitations or revocations of patents. The third relevant issue is that the implications of these safeguard clauses have to be examined against the background of investor–State arbitration. As investors have the unique opportunity to bring claims directly against a host State, the TRIPS-consistency clause opens doors for private arbitration over compliance with WTO/TRIPS obligations. This in turn raises several issues concerning legal standing, interpretation, and burden of proof, as well as broader questions of legitimacy and the acceptance of arbitral awards judging the TRIPS-consistency of, for example, a compulsory licence issued by the host State.

IV   Conflicting regimes or coherence?

The preceding analysis has identified varying degrees of overlap as well as difference in the substantive standards of protection pertaining to IP rights. It has further identified specific norms which aim to uphold State

---

[95] Compare the explanation in n. 64 above.   [96] See US–Australia FTA, Art. 17.9(4)–(6).

sovereignty in choosing from distinct options the multilateral IP standards leave especially in the public-health context. These norms however entail new problems, which again are primarily based on differences between the international systems of IP and investment protection. Against this background one may ask whether we are looking at conflicting regimes addressing the same subject matter, or whether there is harmony and coherence between these two bodies of law. This section gives an overview on specific and more general norms in international law which may be helpful in determining conflict, tension or coherence between traditional IP law and international investment law. It however does not purport to 'resolve' any specific cases of conflict in a struggle for unity in public international law.

Since FTAs and BITs as international treaties would be born into the existing body of international law[97] – including TRIPS – their relations with TRIPS would be governed by international law. Resolution of norm conflicts in international law is, first and foremost, achieved by the principle of harmonious interpretation and systemic integration which operates as a presumption against conflict.[98] This would require a treaty interpreter to aim for a coherent and mutually consistent interpretation of FTA, BIT and TRIPS rules as much as possible to avoid norm conflicts between the two treaties. However, the limits to this approach are set out in the customary international law principles of treaty interpretation which are primarily to be found in Articles 31–3 VCLT. If the ordinary meaning and context of the two relevant treaty terms, understood in light of their respective treaty object and purpose, do not allow a mutually consistent understanding of the two terms or provisions, a harmonious treaty interpretation is not possible.

Whether a harmonious interpretation is an option in relation to TRIPS flexibility norms and subsequent TRIPS-plus FTA and BIT obligations is of course a matter dependant on the individual circumstances. In cases of concrete and well-defined FTA provisions such as those of the US–Australia FTA on compulsory licensing, this however appears doubtful; as section III has indicated, these provisions generally contain

---

[97] See International Law Commission (ILC), 'Conclusions of the work of the Study Group on the Fragmentation of International Law: Difficulties arising from the diversification and expansion of international law' (2006), para. 7, http://untreaty.un.org/ilc/texts/instruments/english/draft%20articles/1_9_2006.pdf (last accessed June 2010); J. Pauwelyn, 'The role of public international law in the WTO: How far can we go?', *American Journal of International Law*, (95) (2001), 535–78.

[98] ILC, 'Conclusions'; C. McLachlan, 'The principle of systemic integration and Article 31(3)(c) of the Vienna Convention', *International Comparative Law*, 54 (2005), 279.

explicit prohibitions of something TRIPS (sometimes equally explicitly) allows. There is no ambiguity in these TRIPS-plus treaty terms which makes them open to a harmonious interpretation. In the case of the broad investment protection standards in BITs, however, the situation is different. The prohibition of expropriation for example should leave sufficient room for an understanding, based on the notion of systemic integration under Article 31(3)(c) of the VCLT, which 'takes into account' TRIPS flexibilities on compulsory licensing as 'other rules of international law applicable in the relations between the parties'.[99] Such an approach, however, is not necessary where more concrete definitions of the term expropriation exist (such as the case in the US Model BIT) or where TRIPS consistency clauses explicitly safeguard the reliance on TRIPS flexibilities (again such as the case in US Model BIT, recent US BITs and investment chapters of FTAs as well as the MAI draft).

Resolving norm conflicts then is first of all a matter of defining what constitutes a true 'conflict' of norms.[100] In a strict sense, only a direct incompatibility, i.e. where complying with one rule necessitates the violation of another, is considered as a conflict.[101] The WTO Appellate Body seems to follow this view.[102] But this is not the only perspective on norm conflict: a wider understanding also takes into account (optional) rights given by treaties and finds conflicts also when one treaty obligation limits or prevents the exercise of a right provided for by another treaty.[103] In the TRIPS context, choosing a narrow or wide understanding of conflict is particularly relevant. Under the narrow approach, additional IP protection flowing from FTAs or BITs whose application does not necessitate the violation of a TRIPS obligation constitutes no conflict. But under the wider notion, a TRIPS-plus rule in an FTA or BIT may be in conflict with an optional TRIPS provision as soon as it limits the ability of a WTO Member State to exercise a 'right' or flexibility

---

[99] VCLT, Art. 31(3)(c).

[100] Instructive on this topic in general is J. Pauwelyn, *Conflict of Norms in Public International Law* (Cambridge University Press, 2003).

[101] *Ibid.*, pp. 166–7, citing W. Jenks, 'Conflict of law-making treaties', *British Yearbook of International Law*, 401 (1953), 426, 451.

[102] See *Guatemala – Antidumping Investigation Regarding Portland Cement from Mexico (Guatemala – Cement)*, Appellate Body Report WT/DS60/AB/R (5 November 1998), para. 65, where the Appellate Body defined conflicts as 'a situation where adherence to the one provision will lead to the violation of the other provision'.

[103] Pauwelyn, 'The role of public international law', p. 551; for an overview on various different approaches to 'conflicts' or 'inconsistencies' see ILC, 'Conclusions', and Pauwelyn, *Conflict of Norms*, pp. 167–74.

TRIPS provides for. If in such cases TRIPS were to prevail, it would make TRIPS flexibilities inviolable and untouchable – almost as inalienable rights of WTO Member States which cannot be taken away. As the analysis below will show, the relevant conflict norms provide answers whether TRIPS flexibilities or TRIPS-plus provisions prevail in the cases at stake here.

When examining the relation between two or more bodies of (international) law pertaining to the same subject matter, 'conflict norms' from either of these sources, as well as those from general international law, may provide answers. In the case at hand, the WTO/TRIPS Agreements forms one body of law, while FTAs and BITs form another. In the following, I examine whether these bodies contain any conflict norms which may provide guidance on which system or which individual rule prevails in case they differ in substance.

As discussed above, the main concept in international IP law which governs the relation amongst different agreements addressing the same subject matter is that of 'minimum standards'.[104] In principle, subsequent treaties can establish additional protection for IP, but may not curtail the protection provided in earlier treaties. In the second sentence of Article 1(1), TRIPS addresses this issue of additional protection: however not in relation to (subsequent) international agreements, but to the domestic IP laws of WTO Member States.[105] The second sentence of Article 1(1) of TRIPS authorises members to grant more extensive protection than is required by TRIPS – with the qualification that such protection 'does not contravene the provisions of the Agreement'. In the context addressed here, the main importance of this qualification lies in its capacity to establish a condition on the ability to introduce more extensive IP protection: TRIPS-plus protection must not contravene TRIPS.[106]

This leads to the question whether the domestic implementation of an FTA or BIT rule setting IP protection standards which curtail any of the public-health-related flexibilities in TRIPS 'contravenes' the respective TRIPS flexibility provision. While findings of contravention would not directly amount to inconsistency of the FTA or BIT rule with Article 1(1)

---

[104] See section III above for further details.

[105] In the end, this may lead to the same result: While countries may conclude *inter se* agreements without directly violating Art. 1(1) of TRIPS, any domestic implementation of IP protection which 'contravenes' TRIPS provisions would be inconsistent with TRIPS.

[106] For an analysis of this qualification and its implications for the principle of minimum standards, see Ruse-Khan, 'Time for a paradigm shift?'.

of TRIPS, the FTA or BIT TRIPS-plus rule may run afoul of Article
41(1)(b)(i) of the VCLT. This general treaty law rule limits the ability to
enter into *inter se* agreements modifying existing treaties to cases where
the modifications are 'not prohibited by the treaty' and do 'not affect
the enjoyment by the other parties of their rights under the treaty'.[107] On
the other hand, such a result seems to contradict the overall notion of
optional flexibilities in TRIPS: a WTO Member State may choose to
implement them in its domestic IP laws (i.e. to exercise its right) – but
may equally choose not to do so. If a WTO Member State thus decides
to waive its right to use a certain flexibility which it has under TRIPS,
this is equally a way of exercising its right and part of the flexibility
TRIPS provides. Applying the qualification in the second sentence of
Article 1(1) to prevent a WTO Member State from doing so in effect
turns the optional rule into a mandatory one. The 'non-contravention'
qualification in the second sentence of Article 1(1) hence cannot function to safeguard TRIPS flexibilities against WTO Member States which
decide not to exercise them. Since a TRIPS-plus rule in national law thus
does not contravene an (optional) TRIPS flexibility norm, an FTA or
BIT provision requiring the introduction of such a rule equally is 'not
prohibited by the treaty' in the sense of Article 41 of the VCLT. TRIPS
thus does not contain a conflict rule that would prohibit WTO Member
States from entering into FTAs or BITs which curtail the public-health-
related TRIPS flexibilities.

The next bodies of law to look at for a relevant conflict norm then are
the FTAs and BITs which limit the ability of the contracting WTO
Member States to use the policy space in TRIPS. In the opening provisions of the IP chapters in most US FTAs, the 'parties affirm their rights
and obligations with respect to each other under the TRIPS Agreement'.[108] But again, this clause cannot be applied to uphold an optional
provision in TRIPS which other provisions of that very same FTA IP
chapter override. Arguably, committing oneself not to use a TRIPS
flexibility (in full or at all) is a way of exercising the right to use the
flexibility. The recent EU EPAs in turn do provide for specific norms

---

[107] The latter alternative however would imply that other WTO Member States have a
'right' for their nationals to be able to exercise TRIPS flexibilities under the domestic
law of the WTO Member State which has agreed to additional protection in a FTA or
BIT. On the application of Art. 41 of the VCLT in relation to TRIPS and TRIPS-plus
FTAs see A. Mitchell and T. Voon, 'Patents and public health in the WTO, FTAs and
beyond: Tension and conflict in international law', *Journal of World Trade*, 43(3) (2009),
571–601.

[108] See Art. 17.1(3) of the US–Australia FTA; Art. 15.1(7) of CAFTA–DR.

which safeguard public-health-related flexibilities in TRIPS.[109] Finally, the same applies to general conflict clauses in FTAs which establish that 'in the event of any inconsistency between this and the WTO Agreement, the WTO Agreement shall prevail to the extent of the inconsistency'.[110] For the reasons addressed in relation to the second sentence of Article 1(1) of TRIPS above, inconsistency with TRIPS (as an agreement annexed to the WTO Agreement) does not include scenarios where the contracting parties agree not to exercise a right under TRIPS.

The investment chapters of FTAs as well as BITs often contain the specific safeguards for TRIPS-consistent compulsory licenses, exceptions or other limitations discussed above. Where they exist, these consistency clauses can ensure that investment standards – especially relating to (indirect) expropriation – do not interfere with the exercise of TRIPS flexibilities. But they allow investors to bring the issue of TRIPS-consistency into investor–State arbitration. This implies a significant departure from the WTO/TRIPS system which in turn challenges the substantive coherence established by these consistency clauses in the first place.[111] Furthermore, the consistency clauses of some US FTAs do sometimes refer to their own TRIPS-plus IP standards instead of TRIPS as a benchmark.[112] This deferral is also inherent in more general norms in investment chapters which state that 'in the event of any inconsistency between this Chapter and another Chapter, the other Chapter shall prevail to the extent of the inconsistency'.[113] A TRIPS-plus IP obligation from the IP chapter thus prevails over investment protection standards in case the latter are interpreted to offer less IP protection. This could arguably even lead to overriding specific TRIPS-consistency clauses safeguarding the compulsory licensing flexibilities under Article 31 of TRIPS if the IP chapter of the FTA curtails those flexibilities.[114] In a similar manner, 'non-derogation' clauses in BITs may lead to additional IP protection deriving from other 'international legal obligations' (such

---

[109] See Art. 147(B) of the EC–CARIFORUM EPA and the respective discussion in section III.A above. For an analysis of these TRIPS safeguard clauses see H. Grosse Ruse-Khan, 'The international law relation between TRIPS and subsequent TRIPS-plus free trade agreements: Towards safeguarding TRIPS flexibilities?', *Journal of Intellectual Property Law*, 18(2) (2011).

[110] See e.g. Art. 12 of the JEPA signed with Indonesia.

[111] For a discussion of the implications, see section III.C above.

[112] See Art. 11.7(5) of the US–Australia FTA and Art. 10.7(5) of CAFTA–DR.

[113] See Art. 10.2(1) of CAFTA–DR and Art. 11.2(1) of the US–Australia FTA.

[114] Compare the interplay of Arts. 11.2(1) and 17.9(7) of the US–Australia FTA which may be interpreted to render the safeguard in favour of TRIPS- (but not IP chapter-) consistent compulsory licences under Art. 11.7(5) useless.

as in FTA IP provisions) to prevail over more limited protection standards under the BIT.[115] Again, safeguard clauses for compulsory licences or other TRIPS flexibilities may be overridden by these additional protection standards whenever those interfere with the policy space TRIPS provides.

This brief review of 'conflict norms' in TRIPS, FTAs and BITs confirms the continued relevance of the minimum-standards approach in international IP law: subsequent treaties generally extend, rather than curtail, the protection available for right holders. In particular, IP chapters of FTAs add new layers of protection which often take away policy space under TRIPS. Although TRIPS subjects the ability to introduce additional protection to the requirement not to 'contravene' TRIPS provisions, this only helps safeguarding mandatory (rather than optional) limits to IP protection in TRIPS.[116] The same result follows from WTO or TRIPS consistency clauses in FTAs. As for the substantive investment standards under FTAs and BITs, on the other hand, any potential extension of IP protection is often subject to clauses safeguarding some of the TRIPS flexibilities (especially concerning compulsory licences). But wherever (FTA-based) TRIPS-plus provisions are applicable between the parties, these – rather than TRIPS and its flexibilities – will form the consistency benchmark. Furthermore, the investor's right to challenge TRIPS consistency in investor–State arbitration adds one of the main features of BITs to the international IP system.

V   Conclusion

This chapter has analysed the flexibilities TRIPS provides for public-health-related measures adopted by WTO Member States. It has shown how TRIPS-plus rules in FTAs and BITs affect the ability to exercise these flexibilities. In essence, the interplay between TRIPS, FTAs and BITs gives a good example for the dynamics of the minimum-standard approach. Ever increasing standards of protection on the regional and bilateral level are eroding the optional policy space on the multilateral level. However, as emphasised by all WTO Member States in the Doha Declaration, these flexibilities are crucial for addressing public-health concerns.[117] They are equally relevant for balancing IP incentives to innovate with access to the protected subject matter in other areas of

---

[115] See e.g. Art. 16 of the US Model BIT.

[116] For a discussion on such mandatory limits or 'ceilings' in international IP law and especially TRIPS see, Grosse Ruse-Khan and Kur, 'Enough is enough'.

[117] See section II above.

public concern (such as climate change and food security). As new layers of IP protection are added, the ability of countries to ensure that this balance is tailored to their domestic concerns is being continuously reduced.

This impact follows in particular from the concrete and detailed IP protection obligations set out in the IP chapters of FTAs. The more general and ambiguous investment protection standards in BITs and investment chapters of FTAs, on the other hand, arguably permit an interpretation which aligns these standards with the TRIPS flexibilities. The prohibition of expropriation, for example, can be understood in a manner which does not interfere with the concept of negative rights and the ability to introduce (TRIPS-consistent) compulsory licences. Here, TRIPS flexibilities may guide their interpretation under Article 31(3)(c) of the VCLT. The expropriation criteria in the US Model BIT and various consistency clauses in BITs and in some FTAs support these findings and thereby offer further opportunities for achieving coherence in international law. However, this struggle for coherence between distinct bodies of international law cannot provide any meaningful help wherever a real impact on TRIPS flexibilities (in form of reducing policy space) exits. As this analysis has shown, it is not the open investment protection standards which curtail these flexibilities on a substantive level. This is done instead by explicit TRIPS-plus standards in IP chapters of FTAs. As 'flexibilities', those TRIPS provisions which are derogated from are optional rather than mandatory in nature. They cannot, therefore, be upheld against subsequent mandatory provisions which constrain their operation.

A main conclusion then follows that TRIPS flexibilities are primarily under threat from concrete and precise TRIPS-plus obligations in IP chapters of FTAs. Due to the different modes for achieving coherence discussed above, the application of substantive investment protection standards to IP on the other hand does not pose this threat. It nevertheless adds a novel element to the TRIPS-plus world, by allowing private investors to challenge the consistency with TRIPS in investor–State arbitration.

22

Stabilisation clauses and sustainable development: Drafting for the future

ANTONY CROCKETT*

I Introduction

'Stabilisation clauses' are a common feature of long-term investment contracts between foreign investors and host States, particularly in the developing world. Following the execution of the contract, which will typically be governed by the domestic law of the host State, changed political and economic circumstances may lead the government to change the law. The change in law may amount to bona fide law reform, but the government may also change the law in a capricious or opportunistic way. The essential purpose of stabilisation clauses is to impose some constraints on the host government's ability to amend domestic law in a way which affects the investment contract, including by providing that the investor shall be compensated if detrimental changes in law occur. In one sense, stabilisation clauses can be seen as straightforward contractual devices which allocate the risk of a change in law to the party best placed to avoid it. In another sense, and to the extent that stabilisation clauses attempt to address the special risks created by the State's capacity to exercise sovereign powers to affect its contractual relationship with the investor, they are properly seen as a creature of international investment law.

The use of stabilisation clauses to deter host States from amending domestic law has led to allegations that they represent an obstacle to sustainable development. In particular, it has been suggested that stabilisation clauses may discourage governments from introducing or enforcing laws relating to the protection of human rights,[1] and

---

* The views expressed in this chapter are the personal opinions of the author.
[1] See e.g. Amnesty International, *Human Rights on the Line: The Baku–Tbilisi to Ceyhan Pipeline Project* (2003), www.amnesty.org.uk (last accessed 16 February 2010); Amnesty International, *Contracting Out of Human Rights: the Chad–Cameroon Pipeline Project* (2005), www.amnesty.org (last accessed 12 July 2009).

environmental conservation.[2] Criticism of stabilisation clauses has mainly been targeted at projects in the energy and natural resources sectors, where the potential for negative impacts on human rights and the environment is often considerable. These are also sectors in which investors are exposed to significant political and economic risks. Their upfront capital investment – often measured in hundreds of millions or even billions of dollars – may only be recovered over the (very) long term. The stability and predictability of the legal and regulatory framework is fundamentally important for investors who are risking capital in host States that have a 'volatile legal and institutional system . . . which the foreign company (often quite legitimately) does not trust'.[3]

With this background in mind, the challenge considered in this chapter is how the foreign investor's requirement for a stable and predictable legal framework can be reconciled with the host State's right to regulate. Section II briefly surveys the history of stabilisation clauses and comments on the debates regarding the effect of stabilisation clauses under international law and their relevance in the age of investment treaties. Section III introduces and considers the criticisms that have recently been directed at stabilisation clauses. Section IV explores the use of 'carve-outs' to protect the ability of host States to legislate with respect to environmental and social matters. Concluding remarks are included in Section V.

II A brief history of the evolution of stabilisation clauses

A significant majority of contracts executed between host States (or, as is increasingly the case, State entities) and foreign investors is solely and exclusively governed by the State's domestic law. It is rarely the case that express provision is made in the contract for the application of international law. This creates two problems. The first, which led lawyers to develop stabilisation clauses, is that the host State is able to change the law, including in order to invalidate or revise contracts with foreign investors and to deny the investor any remedy. The second problem, which is particularly relevant to the discussion in this chapter, is that

---

[2] See e.g. L. Cotula, 'Reconciling regulatory stability and evolution of environmental standards in investment contracts: Towards a rethink of stabilization clauses', *Journal of World Energy Law and Business*, 1(2) (2008), 158.

[3] T. W. Waelde and G. Ndi, 'Stabilizing international investment commitments: International law versus contract interpretation', *Texas International Law Journal*, 31 (1996), 215, 223.

defining the legitimate scope of the State's powers vis-à-vis the foreign investor can be exceedingly difficult where one is prevented from paying regard to international law. In other words, 'there may be situations where the Contracting State is entitled to change the law though the result be to the detriment of the alien contractor. The point is that the definition of these situations must itself be a question of international law.'[4]

By the mid-twentieth century, the practice of including stabilisation clauses in concession contracts as a protection against expropriation and other similar forms of unilateral host-government interference was well established.[5] The classic approach to stabilisation purported to insulate the contract from any subsequent legislative or administrative actions that affected its terms. 'Freezing clauses', as the relevant provisions came to be known, provided that the contractual terms would prevail over any inconsistent laws or regulations passed subsequent to the execution of the contract. The strictest forms of freezing clause provide that the applicable law of the contract is the law in force at the date of its signing.[6] Because the duration of many investment contracts (particularly in the energy and natural-resources sectors) is measured in decades, the notion which takes expression in a freezing clause – that the law will not, or should not, change during the life of the investment – flies in the face of political and economic realities.[7] Freezing clauses also suffer from the fundamental weakness of being themselves vulnerable to changes in the host State's law.[8]

International law, of course, provides that foreign investors (and their investments) are entitled to a minimum standard of treatment, including the non-discriminatory application of the host State's law.[9] As a result, including a reference to international law in the governing

---

[4] R. Jennings, 'State contracts in international law', *British Yearbook of International Law*, 37 (1961), 156, 182.

[5] In his separate opinion in the *Kuwait* v. *Aminoil* arbitration Sir Gerald Fitzmaurice credited US companies with the development of stabilisation clauses in concession contracts in Latin America following a series of nationalisations on that continent: *Government of Kuwait* v. *American Independent Oil Company* (Award of 24 March 1982), 21 ILM 976, 1052.

[6] A. F. M. Maniruzzaman, 'The pursuit of stability in international energy investment contracts', *Journal of World Energy Law and Business*, 1(2) (2008), 121, 122–6.

[7] A. Redfern and M. Hunter, *Law and Practice of International Commercial Arbitration*, 4th edn (Sweet & Maxwell, 2004), p. 118.

[8] Maniruzzaman, 'The pursuit of stability', p. 138.

[9] See e.g. A. Newcombe and L. Paradell, *Law and Practice of Investment Treaties: Standards of treatment* (The Hague: Kluwer, 2009), pp. 234–52.

law clause is supposed to introduce an additional degree of stability.[10] The post-World War II period witnessed considerable innovation and experimentation by (predominantly American and European) international lawyers seeking to develop mechanisms and theories of host State responsibility under international law for breach of contract; the origins of the 'umbrella clause' commonly found in bilateral investment treaties (BITs) can be traced to this period.[11] Arbitrators also demonstrated some creativity in fashioning solutions to the dilemma faced by investors whose petroleum concessions had been declared invalid by host country governments. Even in the absence of express provision for the application of international law to a contractual dispute, a number of tribunals were prepared to imply an intention to subject the contract to international law in order to engage the host State's international responsibility.[12]

The so-called 'internationalisation' theory has been highly controversial.[13] On one side of this debate, where there is evidence of the parties' intention to 'internationalise' the contract (such as a stabilisation clause, or an agreement to submit disputes to international arbitration), contracts which are governed by the domestic law of the host State are said to also be subject to fundamental principles of international law – for example, the requirement that agreements must be performed in good faith and the rule that States may not rely on their internal domestic law in defence of a breach of an international obligation.[14] Other highly qualified publicists deny that any intention to apply international law should be presumed in the absence of an express choice of law,[15] and, further, that the application of international law does not lead automatically to the conclusion that the provisions of a contract

[10] Maniruzzaman, 'The pursuit of stability', pp. 124–5.

[11] A. Sinclair, 'The origins of the umbrella clause in the international law of investment protection', *Arbitration International*, 20(4) (2004), 411.

[12] See e.g. M. Hunter and A. Sinclair, '*Aminoil* revisited: Reflections on a story of changing circumstances' in T. Weiler (ed.), *International Investment Law and Arbitration: Leading cases from the ICSID, NAFTA, bilateral treaties and customary international law* (London: Cameron May, 2004), p. 347.

[13] See e.g. A. F. M. Maniruzzaman, 'State contracts in contemporary international law: Monist versus dualist controversies', *European Journal of International Law*, 12(2) (2001), 309.

[14] *Ibid.*, 316.

[15] See e.g. Rosalyn Higgins, *Problems and Process: international law and how we use it* (Oxford University Press, 1994), p. 141: 'the best way to avoid sole reliance on domestic law is, one has to say, by having a governing law clause that introduces international law. If, in the bargaining process, the private party has been unable to accomplish this, it seems doubtful that international arbitrators should remedy that which one of the negotiating parties was unable to achieve.'

will remain immutably valid where under the host State's domestic law it was (or has become) a nullity.[16]

It is beyond the scope of this chapter to attempt to settle these disagreements. Of course, the internationalisation debate (and the dilemma faced by investors unable to persuade the host State to agree to subject the contract, one way or another, to international law) has been, to a large extent, rendered academic by the adoption of the ICSID Convention,[17] and the proliferation of bilateral and multilateral investment treaties.[18] This is not to say that the vexed question of the status and effects of State contracts in customary international law has been resolved;[19] rather, the path leading to the application of international law in disputes between foreign investors and host States has been (mostly) cleared of obstacles.

Simultaneously with these developments, freezing clauses have fallen out of favour. They are rarely encountered in practice, except in older agreements.[20] It has been suggested that the trend away from freezing clauses may be due to concerns that such clauses will ultimately prove unenforceable.[21] This trend is also, at least in part, explained by the fact that BITs provide more robust protection against expropriation. Another important factor is that it has become less likely for States to be directly party to contracts with foreign investors. The increasing involvement of State-owned companies (particularly national oil companies) in the development of energy and natural resources in many countries has

[16] See e.g. M. Sornarajah, *The International Law on Foreign Investment*, 1st edn (Cambridge University Press, 1994), pp. 424–6.

[17] Convention on the Settlement of Investment Disputes between States and Nationals of other States (ICSID Convention), opened for signature 18 March 1965, 575 UNTS 159 (entered into force 14 October 1966).

[18] At the end of 2008, there were more than 2,600 BITs: see United Nations Conference on Trade and Development (UNCTAD), *Recent Developments in International Investment Agreements (2008–June 2009): IIA Monitor No. 3* (2009), UNCTAD Doc. No. UNCTAD/WEB/DIAE/IA/2009/8, www.unctad.org (last accessed 8 December 2010).

[19] See e.g. J. Crawford, 'Treaty and contract in investment arbitration', *Arbitration International*, 24(3) (2008), 351.

[20] A. Sheppard and A. Crockett, 'Are stabilisation clauses a threat to sustainable development?' in M. C. Segger, A. Newcombe and M. Gehring (eds.), *Sustainable Development in International Investment Law* (The Hague: Kluwer, 2010), pp. 335, 343. See also, J. Nwaokoro, 'Enforcing stabilization of international energy contracts', *Journal of World Energy Law and Business*, 3(1) (2010), 103, 106.

[21] See e.g. A. Shemberg, *Stabilization Clauses and Human Rights: A research project conducted for IFC and the United Nations Special Representative of the Secretary General on Business and Human Rights* (11 March 2008), www.business-humanrights.org (last accessed 10 January 2010), p. 33.

forced lawyers to reconsider how to address what can be described as 'change in law risk' in circumstances where it is not possible to obtain protection in the form of a direct undertaking from the host State.

One solution has been to include an 'economic equilibrium' clause in the contract. Unlike a freezing clause, an economic equilibrium provision does not seek to prevent the application of new laws or regulations. Instead, it typically provides that in the event of a 'change in law' affecting the investor's returns, the host State or State entity, as the case may be, is required to take steps to restore the original economic equilibrium of the contract. What constitutes a 'change in law' for the purpose of an economic equilibrium clause is usually broadly defined. For example, Pakistan's model host government agreement for private-sector power-generation projects defines 'Change in Law' to include, inter alia: 'The adoption, promulgation, repeal, modification or reinter-pretation after the date of this Agreement by any Public Sector Entity of any Law of Pakistan (including a final binding and non-appealable decision of any Public Sector Entity).'[22] In some cases, the definition may expressly encompass changes in international law affecting the contract, including the adoption of treaties. For example, the definition of 'Change in Law' included in the Host Government Agreements for the Baku–Tbilisi–Ceyhan (BTC) pipeline provides that:

> If any domestic or international agreement or treaty; any legislation, promulgation, enactment, decree, accession or allowance, or any other form of commitment, policy or pronouncement or permission has the effect of impairing, conflicting or interfering with the implementation of the Project or limiting, abridging or adversely affecting the value of the Project or any of the rights, privileges, exemptions, waivers, indemnifications or protections granted under this Agreement . . . it shall be deemed a Change in Law.[23]

Although it is often said that the primary concern of investors is that the fiscal regime will change to their disadvantage,[24] an important secondary concern addressed by stabilisation clauses is the predictability and stability of non-fiscal regulations, particularly any preconditions for the renewal of licences or other operational consents. This is one reason that

---

[22] Private Power and Infrastructure Board of Pakistan, *Standardized Implementation Agreement* (Draft dated 15 May 2006), www.ppib.gov.pk (last accessed at 28 October 2010) (emphasis added).

[23] See e.g. Art. 7.2(vi) of the Georgian Host Government Agreement cited in Maniruzzaman, 'The pursuit of stability', p. 135.

[24] See e.g. Shemberg, *Stabilization Clauses and Human Rights*, pp. 48–49.

contractual definitions of 'change in law' are usually framed in broad terms. On the State side, governments may seek to limit the operation of an economic equilibrium clause by including requirements that the provision will only be triggered by a change in law which has a material adverse effect on the investor. As further discussed in section IV, it is also increasingly common for the definition of change in law to contain exceptions or carve-outs to allow changes in environmental and social laws and regulations.

Economic equilibrium clauses occasionally provide that additional costs incurred by the investor as a result of a change in law will be borne by the State in a stipulated manner. For example, in the case of production-sharing contracts in the oil and gas industry, an economic equilibrium provision may require a reduction in the State's share of production to offset costs incurred by a foreign investor as a result of the change in law.[25] Other forms of economic equilibrium clause are silent as to the precise steps which shall be taken in order to restore the economic equilibrium. In these examples, a change in law may merely trigger an obligation of the host State to enter into negotiations with the investor in order to make the necessary changes. When negotiations fail, and in the absence of very clear contractual criteria, it is doubtful that an arbitral tribunal can revise or adapt the contract.[26]

The few available awards (and most academic commentary) regarding the enforceability of stabilisation clauses suggest that they enhance the remedies available to the investor in the event of unilateral host State conduct in breach of the clause, but they do not operate to restrain the breach (i.e. an arbitral tribunal has no power to reinstate the contract or award specific performance).[27] The apparent absence of arbitral awards dealing with the enforcement of stabilisation clauses in recent years, particularly the more modern types of economic equilibrium clause, leads to the conclusion that stabilisation clauses are primarily relied upon to force governments to the negotiating table when they might otherwise simply terminate the contract.[28] As has already been noted

---

[25] Maniruzzaman, 'The pursuit of stability', p. 127.

[26] K. P. Berger, 'Renegotiation and adaption of international investment contracts: The role of contract drafters and arbitrators', *Vanderbilt Journal of Transnational Law*, 36 (2003), 1347.

[27] See e.g. P. Cameron, *International Energy Investment Law: The pursuit of stability*, (Oxford University Press, 2010), p. 93.

[28] *Ibid.*, p. 425: 'It remains a feature of dispute settlement between host states and foreign investors that these are usually settled by negotiation based on the terms of the investment contract . . . A stabilization clause in the contract greatly improves the investor's bargaining position.'

above, the decline in popularity of freezing clauses may also be connected to the fact that investment treaties provide better protection against expropriation. Stabilisation clauses have not, however, become redundant. In particular, there is an important linkage between stabilisation clauses and the fair and equitable treatment (FET) standard contained in many investment treaties and which is arguably an evolving standard of customary international law.[29]

The stability and predictability of the legal framework in the host State has been identified as a key principle embraced by the FET standard.[30] In relation to a claim brought under the US–Ecuador BIT dealing with changes in the interpretation of tax regulations, the tribunal in *Occidental* v. *Ecuador* said, regarding the FET standard, that:

> The relevant question for international law in this discussion is ... whether the legal and business framework meets the requirements of stability and predictability under international law. It was earlier concluded that there is not a VAT refund obligation under international law . . . but *there is certainly an obligation not to alter the legal and business environment in which the investment has been made.*[31]

In the more recent case of *Parkerings-Compagniet AS* v. *Lithuania,* the tribunal observed:

> It is each State's undeniable right and privilege to exercise its sovereign legislative power. A State has the right to enact, modify, or cancel a law at its own discretion. Save for the existence of an agreement, in the form of a stabilisation clause or otherwise, there is nothing objectionable about the amendment brought to the regulatory framework existing at the time an investor made its investment. As a matter of fact, any businessman or investor knows that laws will evolve over time. What is prohibited however is for a State to act unfairly, unreasonably or inequitably in the exercise of its legislative power.[32]

The key to reconciling the *Occidental* v. *Ecuador* decision (which says that the FET standard requires that the legal environment must not be altered) with the observation made in *Parkerings* (which regards

[29] Sheppard and Crockett, 'Are stabilisation clauses a threat?', pp. 345–50. See also, Maniruzzaman, 'The pursuit of stability', pp. 147–50; S. Schill, *The Multilateralization of International Investment Law* (Cambridge University Press, 2009), pp. 78–81.

[30] R. Dolzer and C. Schreuer, *Principles of International Investment Law* (Oxford University Press, 2008), pp. 133–47.

[31] *Occidental* v. *Ecuador* (LCIA Case No. UN 3467, Final Award of 1 July 2004), pp. 64–5 (emphasis added).

[32] *Parkerings-Compagniet AS* v. *Lithuania,* (ICSID Case No. ARB/05/8, Award of 11 September 2007), para. 332 (*Parkerings*).

ANTONY CROCKETT

evolution of the host State's law as inevitable) is the concept of legitimate expectations. While on its face the *Parkerings* award suggests that a stabilisation clause, without more, creates a legitimate expectation that the law will not change,[33] it is submitted that a more nuanced approach is required, as follows:

> it is entirely legitimate for investors to seek guarantees that the host government will not introduce new laws that fundamentally alter the legal framework affecting the investment, particularly fiscal laws. However, it is highly unlikely that an investor can legitimately claim to have expected (when it made its investment) that environmental or social policies in the host country would remain entirely static and the government would not wish to introduce legislation that reflected evolving international standards, especially when required to do so by any treaty it has entered into or by general international law. The investor should be protected from arbitrary or discriminatory laws, but not bona fide law reform that complies with the international law standard of fair and equitable treatment.[34]

The FET standard is, arguably, qualified by the concept of 'equitable treatment', so that a tribunal is entitled to give 'due weight to the proper public purposes which the host State may wish to protect in determining whether the standard is breached'.[35] In the author's view, the legitimate scope of a stabilisation clause does not include domestic laws subsequently required to implement international law relating to human rights or the environment. Investors should not seek (and governments should not offer) to prevent the introduction or implementation of bona fide human rights or environmental legislation,[36] and it is inimical to the

---

[33] *Ibid.*, para. 331: 'The expectation is legitimate if the investor received an explicit promise or guaranty from the host State.'

[34] Sheppard and Crockett, 'Are stabilisation clauses a threat?', pp. 349–50. See also, the award in *Saluka Investments BV (The Netherlands)* v. *The Czech Republic* (Partial Award of 17 March 2006), para. 305 (*Saluka*):

> No investor may reasonably expect that the circumstances prevailing at the time the investment is made remain totally unchanged. In order to determine whether frustration of the foreign investor's expectations was justified and reasonable, the host State's legitimate right subsequently to regulate domestic matters in the public interest must be taken into consideration as well.

[35] C. McLachlan, L. Shore and M. Weineger, *International Investment Arbitration: Substantive principles* (Oxford University Press, 2007), p. 262.

[36] A. Crockett and T. Edjua, 'Human rights are not negotiable', *International Financial Law Review*, 28(7) (2009), 50.

objectives of sustainable development to do so. In the next section of this chapter, it will be seen that the failure to specify social and environmental exceptions to broadly drafted stabilisation commitments has exposed otherwise well-meaning investors to the criticism that the contracts they had negotiated posed a threat to human rights in the host country.

III   Stabilisation clauses in the spotlight: Is it all about scope?

Two reports by Amnesty International (Amnesty) criticising the host government agreements executed in connection with the Baku–Tbilisi–Ceyhan (BTC) and Chad–Cameroon pipeline projects (provocatively entitled *Human Rights on the Line* and *Contracting Out of Human Rights*) are credited with drawing widespread attention to the argument that stabilisation clauses have hampered the ability of governments to introduce human rights reforms.[37] Amnesty criticised the economic equilibrium clause contained in the host government agreement signed between the BTC investor consortium (BTC Co) and the Turkish government as follows:

> While Turkey remains bound by its international human rights obligations, it has undertaken in the Host Government Agreement (HGA) to pay the consortium substantial compensation for any changes in law or other actions that will disturb the economic equilibrium of the project. It is thus caught between two sets of requirements – to live up to its undertakings to its citizens, and to live up to its undertakings to the consortium. Each step in the former direction will carry the price tag of damages – which can easily amount to many millions of pounds. In this way, the HGA creates disincentives for Turkey to become more integrated into international human rights norms. At the very least, it may have to enter reservations exempting the project from any new international standards it subscribes to. The effect of being faced with punitive costs for protecting the human rights of those affected by the pipeline is likely to have a chilling effect on Turkey's ability to improve its general human rights record.[38]

In 2005, Amnesty attacked the host government agreements executed in connection with the Chad–Cameroon pipeline project in similar terms:

> The stabilising conditions of the project agreements are sufficiently vague that they could be used in an attempt to undermine the requirement of progressive realisation of human rights. The agreements could discourage

---

[37] Shemberg, *Stabilization Clauses and Human Rights*, p. 1.
[38] Amnesty International, *Human Rights on the Line* (2003), p. 5.

Chad and Cameroon from taking positive steps that would impose costs
on the consortium without its consent, even if such steps are intended to
advance human rights. Human rights law requires governments to take
steps to improve peoples' health, environment and working conditions.
At the same time, Chad and Cameroon are threatened under the investment agreements with penalties for breaching the 'stabilisation of law'
provisions. The obligation to comply with human rights commitments
ought to take precedence over duties according to an investment agreement. *Amnesty International believes that this has to be made explicit.*[39]

Amnesty specifically rejected arguments that the Chad–Cameroon consortium's undertaking to comply with international best practice and
company codes of conduct with respect to environmental and social
standards was sufficient to allay fears that the host government agreements would lead to negative human rights impacts.[40] Amnesty argued
that international human rights law should take precedence over industry
standards,[41] that host government agreements should incorporate an
explicit commitment by the parties to uphold human rights and that
they must not undermine the ability of the host State to meet its
international obligations.[42]

A number of environmental non-governmental organisations (NGOs)
criticised the stabilisation clause contained in a Production Sharing
Contract between the investors and the Russian Federation relating
to the development of oil and gas fields off Sakhalin Island.[43] The
clause provided that the project should be exempt from any changes in
Russian law adopted after 31 December 1993 which would infringe the
investors' rights under the agreement. The clause did not include a
carve-out for environmental or social matters, although the contract
did require the project company to comply with standards generally
accepted in the international oil and gas industry.[44] Peter Cameron
suggests that the company (and international lenders to the company)
did not try hard enough to identify the right balance between its
legitimate requirements for *economic* stability and environmental protection, concluding that 'there is a real question as to the adequacy of
relying on the incorporation of industry standards and guidelines as a
source of content for environmental actions',[45] especially where the
relevant provisions are vague and open to broad interpretation.[46]

---

[39] Amnesty International, *Contracting Out of Human Rights* (2005), p. 30 (emphasis added).
[40] *Ibid.*, p. 31.   [41] *Ibid.*, p. 8.   [42] *Ibid.*, p. 41.
[43] Cameron, *International Energy Investment Law*, p. 385.   [44] *Ibid.*
[45] *Ibid.*, p. 386–7.   [46] See also, Cotula, 'Reconciling regulatory stability', p. 177.

From a legal standpoint, the argument that stabilisation clauses may have a 'chilling effect' on environmental regulation or human rights standards in host States is well made. To date, however, it has not been proven that stabilisation clauses have had this effect in practice. Nevertheless, strident civil-society criticism of stabilisation clauses, particularly their potential negative impact on human rights,[47] attracted the attention of Professor John Ruggie in the context of his mandate as the Special Representative of the Secretary-General on the Issue of Human Rights and Transnational Corporations and Other Business Enterprises.[48] The International Finance Corporation (IFC) agreed to sponsor a study to investigate these concerns (the UN–IFC Study). The principal research question of the UN–IFC Study was framed as follows: 'Can stabilisation clauses create obstacles to applying new social and environmental legislation to investment projects in the host state; and if so, to what extent?'[49] In order to answer this research question, seventy-six contracts and twelve model contracts containing stabilisation clauses were examined. In addition, various stakeholders including negotiators, lawyers, lenders and civil society were interviewed.[50]

It was found that more than half of the contracts surveyed which related to countries outside the OECD provided investors with exemptions (or a right to claim compensation) from any new laws having an adverse impact on the investment in question, *including* environmental and social laws.[51] In other words, the stabilisation clauses contained in these contracts did not include carve-outs for environmental and social matters. Although the UN–IFC Study did not identify any specific instance where an investor had relied on a stabilisation clause to claim an exemption (or compensation) in the face of new environmental or social laws, the following conclusion was reported:

> Evidence supports the hypothesis that some stabilization clauses can be used to limit a state's action to implement new social and environmental legislation to long-term investments. The data show that the text of many clauses applies to social and environmental legislation, so that investors are able to pursue exemptions or compensation informally and formally.[52]

---

[47] Shemberg, *Stabilization Clauses and Human Rights*, p. vii–viii.
[48] Office of the High Commissioner for Human Rights, Human Rights Resolution 2005/69, E/CN.4/2005/L.10/Add.17, www.business-humanrights.org (last accessed 10 January 2010).
[49] Shemberg, *Stabilization Clauses and Human Rights*, p. viii.   [50] *Ibid.*, p. ix.
[51] *Ibid.*, p. ix.   [52] *Ibid.*, p. x.

It is difficult to identify evidence that stabilisation clauses in fact have a negative impact on environmental or social law reform in host countries.[53] This observation serves to put a proposal recently made by the International Bar Association (IBA) – effectively calling for a ban on stabilisation clauses – into perspective.

In early 2010, an IBA working group submitted a response to the OECD Consultation on an update of the OECD Guidelines for Multinational Enterprises (MNEs). Three paragraphs of the IBA response warrant quotation *in extenso*:

> V. Amendment to Chapter II - General Policies
>
> 92. The OECD should consider rewriting paragraph 5 in chapter II entitled 'General Policies', which now reads:
>
>> [MNEs should] [r]efrain from seeking or accepting exemptions not contemplated in the statutory or regulatory framework related to environmental, health, safety, labour, taxation, financial incentives, or other issues.
>
> It would be revised to read as follows:
>
>> [MNEs should] [r]efrain from seeking or accepting exemptions ~~not contemplated~~ in the statutory or regulatory framework, *including by way of government contracts*, related to environmental, health, safety, labour, taxation, financial incentives, or other issues. *MNEs should refrain from asserting or advancing any claim against a host government or another party with respect to laws, regulations or measures relating to human rights, health, safety or the environment.*
>
> 93. The words 'not contemplated' should be deleted to ensure that MNEs do not seek to have exemptions that are already contemplated in host government laws and regulations applied to them with respect to these issues. Notably, a number of developing countries have already granted MNEs exemptions in their statutory and regulatory frameworks in relation to these issues. The words 'including by way of government contracts' should be added following 'in the statutory or regulatory framework'. This is because the SRSG [i.e. Professor Ruggie] and others are concerned that many governments, particularly, in developing countries, have included stabilization clauses in their contracts with foreign investors that prohibit them from applying regulation to investors or require them to compensate investors for the economic impact such regulation may have.

---

[53] Sheppard and Crockett, 'Are stabilisation clauses a threat?', pp. 341–2. See also, Cameron, *International Energy Investment Law*, p. 391.

94. The last added sentence is desirable in light of the fact that SRSG and others are concerned that many bilateral investment treaties ('BITs') and host government agreements may permit foreign investors to seek compensation from governments for such regulation before international arbitral tribunals. In fact, a number of governments have recently launched reviews of their own BITs. The United States has, for example, embarked on a review of its Model BIT, which it adheres to closely in its BIT negotiations with other countries. The BIT review follows campaign pledges by US President Barak Obama, in which he committed to 'ensure that foreign investor rights are strictly limited and will fully exempt any law or regulation written to protect public safety or promote the public interest'. South Africa has also launched an official policy review of its BITs, explaining that 'the Executive had not been fully apprised of all the possible consequences of BITs,' including for human rights, when the young post-apartheid government began entering into BITs in 1994. Norway, countries that acceded to the European Union in 2004 and 2007, and a number of countries in Latin America, including Ecuador, are also reviewing their BITs.[54]

In the author's view, the IBA proposal is ill-considered.[55] If accepted, it would lead to the entirely unsatisfactory result that OECD investors would be in breach of the OECD Guidelines if they sought to negotiate almost any form of stabilisation clause. Advocating a wholesale prohibition on stabilisation clauses is an unnecessary and unwarranted overreaction.[56]

[54] IBA, *IBA Working Group on the OECD Guidelines for Multinational Enterprises: Response to the OECD Consultation on an Update of the OECD Guidelines for Multinational Enterprises* (31 January 2010), www.ibanet.org (last accessed 8 December 2010), pp. 33–4.

[55] When the IBA Working Group responded to the earlier consultation on the terms of reference for the update of the OECD Guidelines the proposed changes to para. 5 of chapter II of the Guidelines had the support of 'several', but not all, members of the group: see IBA, *IBA Working Group on the OECD Guidelines for Multinational Enterprises: Response to the UK Consultation on the Terms of Reference for an Update of the OECD Guidelines for Multinational Enterprises* (30 November 2009), www.ibanet.org (last accessed 3 November 2010), pp. 33–4.

[56] An equally unbalanced proposal recently subscribed to by a number of distinguished legal scholars calls on States to 'review their investment treaties with a view to withdrawing from or renegotiating them . . . [and to] take steps to replace or curtail the use of investment treaty arbitration': see Osgoode Hall Law School, *Public Statement on the International Investment Regime* (31 August 2010), www.osgoode.yorku.ca/public_statement/ (last accessed 3 November 2010). Interestingly, it is also stated that: 'Although not without flaws, investment contracts are preferable to investment treaties as a legal mechanism to supplement domestic law in the regulation of investor–State relations because they allow for greater care to be taken and greater certainty to be achieved in the framing of the parties' legal rights and obligations.'

Insisting that host States should have an unfettered right to change the terms of a contract arguably undermines States' ability to attract investment required for development.[57] Furthermore, the proposed requirement that OECD investors should refrain from bringing claims against governments with respect to measures relating to environmental or social matters fails to recognise the risk that a government may well use human rights or environmental laws in the manner of a 'Trojan Horse' – that is, in order to disguise measures that are harmful to an investment project but which lack genuine links to human rights or environmental concerns.[58]

While pointing to best practice in the form of carve-outs for environmental and social matters, the UN–IFC Study acknowledges that investors are entitled to protection against arbitrary or discriminatory conduct by host States.[59] Similarly, in his most recent report to the Human Rights Council, Professor Ruggie adopts a more pragmatic approach:

> The Special Representative encourages States to ensure that new model BITs combine robust investor protections with adequate allowances for bona fide public interest measures, including human rights, applied in a non-discriminatory manner . . . [S]tabilization clauses, where they are used, should meet the twin objectives of ensuring investor protection and providing the required policy space for States to pursue bona fide human rights obligations.[60]

Safeguarding the host State's right to regulate with respect to environmental and social matters is not incompatible with the protection of foreign investment. Stability is, after all, a synonym for balance.

The next section considers the challenges of drafting for the future. Investors (and States) face increasing pressure to rethink traditional approaches to stabilisation. Their lawyers will be forced to innovate,

---

[57] On the economic and policy objectives of States when entering into investment treaties, see J. Paulsson, 'The power of States to make meaningful promises to foreigners', *Journal of International Dispute Settlement*, 1(2) (2009), 341. See also Waelde and Ndi, 'Stabilizing international investment commitments', pp. 259–60.

[58] See Cotula, 'Reconciling regulatory stability', p. 174.

[59] Shemberg, *Stabilization Clauses and Human Rights*, p. 37.

[60] 'Report of the Special Representative of the Secretary-General on the issue of human rights and transnational corporations and other business enterprises, John Ruggie: Business and human rights: further steps toward the operationalization of the "protect, respect and remedy" framework' (9 April 2010), UN Doc. No. A/HRC/14/27, www.business-humanrights.org (last accessed 3 November 2010), p. 6.

which also means resisting the 'natural desire' to search for comfort in old precedents.[61]

IV   The balancing act: Eliminating the threat to sustainable development whilst preserving a stable and predictable legal framework for investors

It is highly unlikely that an investor who includes a broadly drafted stabilisation clause in a contract intends to use the clause to prevent or deter legitimate law reform with respect to environmental or social matters. Instead, the tendency to draft in broad terms is probably linked to the fact that it is difficult to identify in advance every potential adverse change in law. However, in seeking the widest possible scope of protection, investors have exposed themselves to the accusation that their contractual arrangements endanger the human rights of host country populations. The stigma attached to being the subject of a report by Amnesty International or Global Witness is something most investors will be concerned to avoid.[62] In the wake of the negative publicity generated by *Human Rights on the Line*,[63] the BTC consortium executed the BTC Human Rights Undertaking in which it agreed not to rely on the economic equilibrium clauses contained in its contracts with Azerbaijan, Georgia and Turkey in order to challenge the introduction of new environmental or social laws.[64] But, as is illustrated below, the undertaking was not without limitations. Investors wary of the risk that environmental and social exceptions may be abused are likely to include additional devices to guard against arbitrary or discriminatory host State conduct.

The BTC Human Rights Undertaking prevents the consortium from relying on the stabilisation clauses contained in the HGAs with Azerbaijan, Georgia and Turkey to oppose or advance any claim in respect of:

> regulation by the relevant Host Government of the human rights or health, safety and environmental ('HSE') aspects of the Project in its territory in a manner (1) *reasonably required* by international labor and

---

[61] P. Butt and R. Castle, *Modern Legal Drafting: A guide to using clearer language*, 2nd edn (Cambridge University Press, 2006), p. 15.

[62] See e.g. Global Witness, *Heavy Mittal* (2006), www.globalwitness.org (last accessed 3 November 2010).

[63] Amnesty International, *Human Rights on the Line*.

[64] The Baku–Tbilisi–Ceyhan Pipeline Company, *BTC Human Rights Undertaking* (22 September 2003), www.bp.com (last accessed 3 November 2010).

ANTONY CROCKETT

human rights treaties to which the relevant Host Government is a party from time to time, and (2) otherwise as required in the public interest in accordance with domestic law in the relevant Project State from time to time, provided that such domestic law is *no more stringent than* the highest of European Union standards as referred to in the Project Agreements, including relevant EU directives ('EU Standards'), those World Bank Group standards referred to in the Project Agreements, and standards under applicable international labor and human rights treaties.[65]

There is scope for argument as to precisely what this clause means. In particular, it is not clear whether the requirement that domestic law be 'no more stringent' than the highest international standard is additional to the requirement that the relevant host State regulation is 'reasonably required' by international labour or human rights treaties.[66]

The 'no more stringent' requirement seeks to use international standards (including treaties) as an objective benchmark for the assessment of future domestic regulation. The BTC consortium had promised to comply with a raft of international technical, environmental and social standards. At the same time, an appendix to each HGA detailing these standards (and added after the NGOs had criticised the original agreements) contained an additional stabilisation provision relating to environmental matters and stating that 'in no event shall the project be subject to any [new domestic standards] to the extent that they are different from or more stringent than the standards and practices generally operating in the international petroleum pipeline industry for comparable projects'.[67] The 'no more stringent' requirement contained in the Human Rights Undertaking is linked backed to the 'standards referred to in the Project Agreements'. To the extent that this includes industry

---

[65] *Ibid.* Clause 2(a) (emphasis added).

[66] The use of 'and' (rather than 'or') to link the two limbs suggests that any new HSE regulation must be 'reasonably required' pursuant to the terms of an international labour or human rights treaty *and* 'no more stringent than' the highest of the various international standards referred to. One difficulty created by this interpretation is that it would appear to prevent the host States from introducing new regulations required to implement international environmental treaties. An earlier agreement signed by the host governments and the consortium in response to the NGO criticisms but prior to the execution of the Human Rights Undertaking suggests that this was not the intention. The so-called 'Joint Statement' clarifies that the inter-governmental agreement (IGA) signed in connection with the pipeline 'commits each State to the application of environmental standards no less stringent than [EU standards]' as such standards evolve over time. The Joint Statement did not say that the IGA committed the host States to apply human rights or labour standards equivalent to EU standards. See further, Cameron, *International Energy Investment Law*, pp. 402–7.

[67] P. Cameron, *International Energy Investment Law*, p. 405.

standards and practice, it is doubtful whether the reference provides an objective or appropriately well-defined benchmark for assessing the stringency of new environmental laws.[68]

Quite apart from the issue of whether it is legitimate for the petroleum industry to assign to itself the right to define the stringency of the environmental requirements it shall be subject to, other objections can be made, such as the following:

> The weakness of these provisions is their vagueness . . . the wording is elusive and no international standards applicable in the petroleum industry have been clearly defined . . . Yet the elusive wording may also be a strength, as reference to standards external to the contractual relationship introduces an element of flexibility [enabling] evolution in applicable environmental standards despite broad stabilization clauses.[69]

Most investors will, of course, be unconcerned if the law evolves in a reasonable and predictable way (provided no great harm is caused to their investment). The challenge is to protect against the risk of arbitrary or discriminatory measures whilst preserving the host State's right to regulate, including in accordance with evolving international norms. Although it has been repeatedly cited as an example of best (or at least better) practice, it is not clear that the BTC Human Rights Undertaking achieves this.

The BTC Human Rights Undertaking is in some ways analogous to the non-precluded measures (NPM) clauses contained in some BITs which 'seek to protect State freedom of action in certain domains of public policy from the restrictions or limitations that would otherwise be imposed by a BIT'.[70] An NPM clause defines the range of 'permissible objectives' (e.g. the protection of national security, health, safety or the environment) and then imposes a 'nexus requirement'[71] such that the measure taken by the State must be linked to the range of permissible objectives (e.g. the measure must be *necessary* to achieve a permissible objective).[72] In the case of BTC, the nexus requirement is that a measure must be 'reasonably required by international labor and human rights

---

[68] Cotula, 'Reconciling regulatory stability', p. 177.   [69] *Ibid.*

[70] W. W. Burke-White and A. von Staden, 'Investment protection in extraordinary times: The interpretation and application of non-precluded measures provisions in bilateral investment treaties', *Virginia Journal of International Law*, 48 (2007), 307.

[71] *Ibid.*

[72] See e.g. Art. XI of the United States –Argentina BIT: 'This Treaty shall not preclude the application by either Party of measures necessary for the maintenance of public order, the fulfilment [*sic*] of its obligations with respect to the maintenance or restoration of international peace or security, or the Protection of its own essential security interests.'

treaties'. It is unclear how this requirement should be interpreted, in particular whether it requires a tribunal to determine the nature and extent of the host State's obligations under international law.

In BIT jurisprudence, where the nexus requirement under an NPM clause is that the measure be 'necessary', there is debate as to whether this means that the State can only take the measure if it has no other alternative or whether the State has a broader discretion.[73] In customary international law, the 'necessity' defence can only be invoked if the measure taken is the only means available to safeguard an essential interest.[74] The 'least restrictive alternative test' developed in the World Trade Organization (WTO) dispute-settlement system allows States a substantial margin of discretion in determining the level of protection they wish to achieve based on the State's assessment of the risk in question (e.g. risks to public health or the environment). In accordance with this test, States are not necessarily precluded from taking measures which achieve a level of protection higher than international standards. States are required, however, to ensure that the measure taken is the least restrictive alternative in terms of its impact on the State's obligations under the relevant international trade agreement. In most cases this will mean that a party wishing to complain about a measure has to demonstrate that there was a reasonably available alternative which would have had a lesser impact on international trade.[75]

This brief segue into a discussion of public law standards of review is not intended to suggest that stabilisation clauses should henceforth be drafted so as to provide the investor with a contractual right to a process of quasi-administrative review equivalent to that undertaken by WTO dispute-settlement panels (or, as some commentators argue, by investment treaty tribunals).[76] Quite the opposite; any such proposal would be highly controversial,[77] and devising the appropriate contractual terms

---

[73] Burke-White and von Staden, 'Investment protection in extraordinary times'. See also, *Continental Casualty Corporation* v. *Argentina* (ICSID Case No. ARB/03/9, Award of 5 September 2008), paras. 22–34.

[74] International Law Commission, 'Draft Articles on responsibility of states for internationally wrongful acts, with commentaries' (2001), UN Doc. No. A/56/10, Art. 25(1)(a).

[75] See F. Ortino and E. Petersmann (eds.), *The WTO Dispute Settlement System, 1995–2003* (The Hague: Kluwer, 2003).

[76] G. van Harten and M. Loughlin, 'Investment treaty arbitration as a species of global administrative law', *European Journal of International Law*, 17(1) (2006), 121. See also, S. Schill (ed.), *International Investment Law and Comparative Public Law* (Oxford University Press, 2010); Daniel Kalderimis's chapter in this volume.

[77] The role of WTO dispute-settlement panels and investment treaty tribunals in reviewing State measures relating to environmental or other matters in the public interest has been

would present a formidable challenge. To the extent that this is what some draftsmen are trying to achieve when they qualify exceptions for environmental and social laws with nexus requirements such as 'necessary' or 'reasonably required', they are being overly ambitious. A more practical approach – which also reflects the reality that 'stabilisation clauses play a role in the *negotiation* rather than the arbitration of change' – is to include provisions designed to ensure that the investor's interests and views,[78] as well as relevant international standards, are taken into consideration if the government decides that a change in law is required.

In this perspective, referencing international standards in the contract is not intended to provide a benchmark to be used by a tribunal to assess whether a new environmental or social law falls outside the scope of a stabilisation clause.[79] Even where benchmarks are provided, many commercial arbitrators will be eminently unsuited, in terms of both qualifications and outlook, to determine whether a particular new environmental or social measure is necessary to fulfil the host State's international obligations. References to international standards can, however, inform the negotiations which an investor, facing a change in law which it has determined will materially impact its investment, will seek to have with national regulators. To facilitate negotiations there must be a requirement that the host State notify the investor in advance of any change to existing environmental or social standards.[80] Ideally, there should also be an express obligation to negotiate or consult with the investor. The Model Host Government Agreement published by the Energy Charter Treaty Secretariat provides an example:

Article 16 Environmental Protection and Safety

1. The environmental and safety standards applicable to the Project shall be as set forth in Appendix III, Part II. The Host Government agrees to the standards set forth in Appendix III, Part II and consents to any action taken by or on behalf of the Project Participants in conformity therewith, provided however that the Host Government shall be

highly controversial. Conferring powers of administrative review on arbitral tribunals established pursuant to contract would be even more so.

[78] Cameron, *International Energy Investment Law*, p. 425.

[79] It is often the investor that first proposes the inclusion of references to international standards in an investment contract. In many cases, the investor has an interest in defining the environmental and social standards that will apply to its operations because domestic law standards do not exist or are significantly lower than international standards. Investors may also be subject to pressure from other stakeholders, notably international lenders and shareholders, to comply with international standards.

[80] Cameron, *International Energy Investment Law*, p. 384.

entitled to vary the standards set forth in Appendix III, Part II, following due consultation with the Project Investors, and in line with the relevant environmental protection and safety standards applicable to similar projects.

2. The Project Investors shall observe the standards referred to in paragraph 1 of this Article.[81]

Because the FET standard permits the investor to expect that the host State will comply with its contractual obligations and imposes a general duty on the State to ensure that the investor has an opportunity to be heard before a decision is taken which affects the investor's interests,[82] negotiating in good faith with the investor may help the State to avoid an investment treaty claim. Discussion and negotiation may also lead to the identification of alternative measures which achieve the desired environmental or social objective but have a lesser impact on the foreign investor. Imposing an obligation on States to negotiate with investors should not be seen as a threat to the progressive realisation of human rights (or higher environmental standards) and it does not give undue precedence to investors' rights or commercial expedience.[83] It is consistent with theories of 'responsive regulation' which posit that better policy solutions are likely to be found if private firms (and other stakeholders) are given an opportunity to influence regulatory design.[84]

Investors and governments should be discussing and negotiating environmental and social matters long before they enter into a contract. A stabilisation clause which contains no carve-outs for environmental and social regulation is an indicator that they have failed to do so. A general undertaking by the investor to comply with 'prevailing industry standards' or 'good oilfield practice' is no longer enough. In his most recent report, Professor Ruggie has said that there is 'an urgent need for all parties, including State and company negotiators and their legal and financial advisors, to consider the human rights implications of

---

[81] Model Host Government Agreement between/Among the Government of State [. . .] and the Project Investors concerning the [*insert Project name*] Pipeline System, in Energy Charter Secretariat, *Model Intergovernmental and Host Government Agreements for Cross-Border Pipelines*, 2nd edn (2007), p. 37, www.encharter.org/index.php?id=329 (last accessed 8 December 2010).

[82] Sheppard and Crockett, 'Are stabilisation clauses a threat?', pp. 345–8.

[83] Amnesty International, *Contracting Out of Human Rights* (2005).

[84] See I. Ayres and J. Braithwaite, *Responsive Regulation: Transcending the deregulation debate* (Oxford University Press, 1992). See also J. Braithwaite, 'Responsive regulation and developing economies', *World Development*, 34(5) (2006), 884 (arguing that developing States with limited regulatory capacity might benefit from a responsive approach to regulation).

long-term investment projects at the contracting stage, thereby reducing subsequent problems'.[85] States and investors both stand to gain from a proactive approach and by benchmarking standards which are capable of evolution.[86] In this sense, stabilisation clauses could come to be known as flexibility clauses. The more flexible the contract, the more durable it is likely to be in the face of changing environmental and social standards.

V   Conclusions

By including a stabilisation clause in their contracts, investors and States signal their intention that the agreement shall have a long life. Failing to make provision for the evolution of environmental and social standards is inconsistent with this intention. However, despite the recent criticism of stabilisation clauses by human rights and environmental groups there does not appear to be any evidence that they are actually used to deter legitimate law reform. Nevertheless, investors will come under increasing pressure to include carve-outs for environmental and social matters in order that the host State is free to introduce new legislation and regulations as international standards (and the host State's international obligations) evolve. In order to protect against the risk that governments will abuse these carve-outs, contracts may identify internationally accepted standards as a benchmark for assessing future domestic legislation.

There is scope for debate, however, as to whether such benchmarks would allow a tribunal to reach a determination that a new host country regulation lacked a bona fide linkage to the host State's international obligations. To the extent that the adjudication of disputes involving carve-outs would require an administrative review exercise (applying international law) similar to that undartaken by investment treaty tribunals, there are strong arguments that the FET standard provides a more effective (and acceptable) standard for the identification of arbitrary or unreasonable measures.[87] Certainly, the legitimate expectations of the investor are very important and this chapter has identified a number of parallels between stabilisation clauses and the FET standard. In particular, the protection of foreign investors against arbitrary or

---

[85] *Report of the Special Representative of the Secretary-General on the Issue of Human Rights,* p. 6.
[86] See also Cameron, *International Energy Investment Law,* pp. 408–9.
[87] L. Cotula, 'Pushing the boundaries vs Striking a balance: Some reflections on stabilization issues in light of *Duke Energy International Investments v. Republic of Peru', Transnational Dispute Management,* 1 (2010).

discriminatory changes in law and the preservation of a stable and predictable legal environment is a common goal.

It has also been argued that the functional value of a stabilisation clause in the face of a proposal by the host government to introduce new environmental and social measures is that it facilitates negotiations between the investor and the host State. If the issue has to be referred to arbitration, the stabilisation clause has failed to achieve its primary purpose. The FET standard requires that due weight be given to the proper public purposes a State may have in mind when it introduces measures affecting a foreign investor. Similarly, when drafting a stabilisation clause, due recognition should be given to the prerogative of States to regulate matters in the public interest, including environmental and social matters. But the analogy with investment treaties should only be taken so far. When drafting stabilisation clauses, lawyers should focus on ensuring that the contract is able to adapt to and survive the evolution of environmental and social standards in the host country. Except in the absence of an applicable investment treaty, we should not attempt to recreate in contractual form the type of rights investors may enjoy under investment treaties.

23

A new investment deal in Asia and Africa: Land leases to foreign investors

ANASTASIA TELESETSKY

I Introduction

In the last decade, Ethiopia has made a concerted effort to attract foreign direct investment. The website for the Ethiopian Investment Commission, a federal government agency tasked with promoting Ethiopia as an investment destination, boasts of Ethiopia's 'abundant natural resources: such as land, water, minerals, and population of over 70 million potential consumers'.[1] While Ethiopia touts the availability of surplus lands for investors and offers investment incentives such as exemption from export custom duties, the United Nations World Food Programme provided food to 10 million individuals in 2009 and expected to provide food to 9.5 million individuals in 2010.[2]

'Free investment', like 'free trade', has been embraced as a panacea for States lagging behind in the world economy. Yet as the idea of 'free investment' follows 'free trade', citizens in many of the poorest States are increasingly emerging on the losing end of the globalisation spectrum. It seems that in spite of global rhetoric of 'raising the floor' for all citizens, 'free investment' policies and the laws that support these policies may in fact hurt the very communities the investment is putatively intended to help.

Events currently unfolding in several Asian and African States are particularly illustrative of these trends. Take, for example, the recent situation in Madagascar, a State that is 'natural resource rich' but 'international currency poor'. In 2009, President Rajoelina rose to power as the transitional leader of the country after former President Ravalomanana

---

[1] Ethiopian Investment Commission, *Country Overview*, www.ethiomarket.com/eic/ (last accessed 16 December 2010).

[2] United Nations World Food Programme, *Ethiopia Operations*, www.wfp.org/countries/Ethiopia/Operations (last accessed 16 December 2010).

entered into a 99-year land-lease agreement to permit the South Korean firm Daewoo to produce corn and palm oil for export back to South Korea on 3.2 million acres of land, half of Madagascar's arable land.[3] Daewoo intended its investment to bolster South Korea's food security so that South Korea would no longer be the world's third-largest corn importer. Smallholder farmers responded with outrage as the deal would damage their livelihoods. In cancelling the approximately $12 an acre investment deal, President Rajoelina indicated that the agreement ran counter to the public interest because the sale or rent of land to foreign investors was explicitly prohibited by the constitution.

The Madagascar deal is not an isolated contract. With allegedly 90 per cent of the arable land outside of forests and fragile ecosystems already in production, there is a scramble by well-heeled arid countries and their investors to find the last green pastures.[4] Generally, the overseas land-lease deal-makers comprise a combination of investment managers, World Bank consultants and State and intergovernmental officials. Responding to investment managers' appraisals that the agricultural sector has been 'overlooked',[5] and that Africa is 'the one continent that remains relatively unexploited',[6] influential institutional investors, including representatives of the largest pension funds and university endowments, have expressed interest in making sizable financial investments in overseas agribusiness.[7] It is also clear that overseas investors have high expectations of profits on agribusiness ventures, including 25 per cent annualised returns.[8]

Pundits and politicians have sharply criticised large-scale foreign land leases. The editorial page of the *Financial Times* characterised the private industries engaged in the leases as 'rapacious' and 'positively

[3] BBC News, 'Madagascar leader axes land deal' (19 March 2009), www.news.bbc.co.uk/2/hi/africa/7952628.stm (last accessed 16 December 2010).

[4] A. Rice, 'Is there such a thing as agro-imperialism?', *New York Times* (16 November 2009).

[5] M. Scott, 'Agriculture: A growing investment', *Financial Times* (14 March 2010), www.ft.com/cms/s/0/e656b546–2e08–11df-b85c-00144feabdc0.html (last accessed 16 December 2010).

[6] Rice, 'Is there such a thing' (quoting Susan Payne, Chief Executive Officer (CEO) of Emergent Asset Management).

[7] H. Knaup and J. von Mittelstaedt, 'Foreign investors snap up African farmland', *Der Spiegel* (30 July 2009), www.spiegel.de/international/world/0,1518,639224,00.html (last accessed 16 December 2010).

[8] 'Down on the farm: Investing in agriculture', *Camden FB News Release* (5 March 2010), citing Peter Halloran, CEO of Pharos Financial Advisors, www.pharosfund.com/pdfs/FB%20-%20Mar%2010.pdf (last accessed 16 December 2010).

neocolonial'.[9] Libyan leader Muammar al-Gaddafi, speaking at the Food and Agricultural Organisation of the United Nations (FAO) in 2009, described the overseas leases as a kind of 'new feudalism'.[10] In spite of the cautionary tale of Madagascar, however, the agricultural deals continue to unfold without obvious benefits to either ecological integrity or to local communities dependent on a healthy environment for their sustenance.

In the case of Madagascar, there have been no repercussions under international investment law as a result of the government reneging on the lease agreement.[11] However, Madagascar did not have a bilateral investment treaty (BIT) with South Korea that would have conferred on South Korean investors the ability to pursue legal grievances before international arbitration panels. But what if the investor had not been a Korean firm but rather a Chinese, Swiss, South African, French, Belgian, German or Swedish private company? Madagascar has BITs with each of these States that protect the investment expectations of foreign direct investors. Would an arbitral tribunal have found a compensable expropriation or would Madagascar as a World Food Programme recipient be entitled to protect the public interest in its arable land at the expense of private investors?

This chapter examines the current phenomenon of foreign direct investment (FDI) fuelling large-scale overseas agribusiness and asks whether current international investment law undermines the public interest in a safe environment, healthy ecosystems, and meaningful employment. The term 'public interest' as used in this chapter refers to the protection of environmental integrity values from the perspective of the ecosystem, and labour rights from the perspective of individuals and local communities. This chapter starts with an examination of the recent trend in granting large-scale land leases. In the second and third sections, the chapter explores respectively aspects of current international investment law that threaten the public interest and then proposes how investment treaties could be structured to better protect the public interest.

---

[9] 'Food security deal should not stand', *Financial Times* (19 November 2008) (copy on file with author).

[10] S. Brown and S. Kovalyova, 'Gaddafi asks Food Summit to stop Africa "landgrab"', *Reuters* (16 November 2009), www.reuters.com/article/idUSTRE5AF29V20091116 (last accessed 16 December 2010).

[11] See Madagascar Law No. 2007–036. Before the negotiations with Daewoo had begun, Madagascar has promulgated investor-friendly laws to permit foreign legal entities the ability to lease land.

II   Dynamics of large-scale land leases

With the increasing trend towards global urbanisation in countries that have until recently been largely agricultural economies,[12] few individuals know the source of their food before it arrives at the market and few will care as long as the food is cheap, plentiful and sanitary. The same is true for biofuels: as long as there is ample affordable fuel to put into the tank, many consumers will not seek to know the provenance of such energy.

Yet as the production sites for commodity food products and biofuels proliferate, there are very real food security concerns for large numbers of people in Africa and Asia. Focusing national investment strategies on generating food and fuel for export raises ethical dilemmas about what the external market simplistically depicts as necessary for economic growth. If sub-Saharan Africa's population grows from 770 million in 2005 to 1.5–2 billion in 2050, as predicted, [13] Africa will need its arable but currently uncultivated lands to feed its growing population, not to feed or fuel markets overseas. In October 2009 at the 2050 High-Level Experts Forum, the FAO indicated that an additional $83 billion per year would be needed to feed the world's growing population. Given the rising food demands in India, China and the Middle East/North Africa, FAO advises that almost one-third of that investment ($29 billion), should be spent in India and China and $10 billion in the Middle East and North Africa to improve their domestic agricultural sectors.[14] Yet India, China and numerous Middle Eastern and North African States are looking outside of their own boundaries for less expensive approaches to meet their national commodity demands.

To private agribusiness interests seeking under-utilised land and water, Africa is perceived as a buyer's market. For example, out of 807 million hectares of cultivable land, only 197 million hectares are under cultivation.[15] A jointly sponsored World Bank and FAO study

---

[12] J. Watts, 'China's soil deterioration may become growing food crisis', *The Guardian* (23 February 2010) (predicting an urban population growth in China from a share of 47% to 75% of the total population).

[13] FAO, '2050 – Africa's food challenge: Prospects good, resources abundant, policy must improve' (28 September 2009), www.fao.org/news/story/en/item/35770/icode/ (last accessed 16 December 2010).

[14] FAO, *2050: How to Feed the World – Issue Brief on Investment* (High-Level Expert Forum: Rome, 12–13 October 2009), p. 3.

[15] L. Cotula *et al.*, *Land Grab or Development Opportunity: Agricultural investment and international land deals in Africa* (London/Rome: FAO, International Institute for Environment and Development and International Fund for Agricultural Development, 2009), p. 59.

proposes intensifying agriculture in a 400 million hectare area that it refers to as the 'Guinea Savannah', which includes portions of twenty-five countries: Senegal, Sierra Leone, Guinea, Mali, Cote D'Ivoire, Burkina Faso, Ghana, Togo, Benin, Nigeria, Cameroon, Chad, Central African Republic, Sudan, Ethiopia, Uganda, Kenya, Tanzania, Angola, Democratic Republic of Congo, Angola, Zambia, Malawi, Mozambique and Madagascar.[16] The study observes that these areas will require mechanisation and proposes large-scale mechanised farming for the production of staple goods.[17] The study acknowledges that there may be environmental impacts from such intensification, including excess use of chemicals, damage to natural habitats from irrigation, release of sequestered carbon, and salinisation of soil, but suggests that these impacts may be less costly for the environment than continued expansion of agriculture into other fragile areas.[18]

Financing this proposed agricultural intensification of approximately 400 million hectares of land in Africa is FDI.[19] The beneficiaries of developing large-scale mechanised agribusiness in the Guinea Savannah lands will be private agribusiness firms, international agricultural investment funds, and possibly government officials from investment ministries either in terms of kickbacks or career promotion. There are no obvious direct benefits for the environment or communities in terms of habitat protection or community job generation. Despite these concerns, however, the process for large-scale, foreign-owned agricultural investment is already underway. Investors from China, Korea, Saudi Arabia, Qatar, India and other States have used FDI, including sovereign wealth funds, to lease approximately 50 million acres of land within Africa for large-scale export-oriented agribusiness of either biofuels or commercial staples.[20] Even though some local communities have protested against

---

[16] G. Larson, 'Awakening Africa's sleeping giant: Prospects for commercial agriculture in the Guinea Savannah and beyond', *World Bank and FAO Agricultural and Rural Development Note*, 48 (2009), 1 (FAO and World Bank 2009 Report/The Report). All but six of these countries are classified by the United Nations as 'Least Developed Countries'.

[17] *Ibid.*, p. 9.   [18] *Ibid.*, p. 11.

[19] 400 million hectares is roughly about half the size of Canada.

[20] FAO, *Foreign Direct Investment: Win-win or land grab?* (World Summit on Food Security: Rome, 16–18 November 2009), p. 1, www.svt.se/content/1/c8/01/86/34/32/k6358e.pdf (last accessed 16 December 2010) (50 million acres covers approximately the lands of Great Britain, Scotland, and Ireland).

the cultivation of non-food crops such as feed for livestock or jatropha grass as a precursor for biofuel, FDI investors continue to gain access to arable lands.[21]

A   Lessors

Governments within the Guinea Savannah area have launched successful campaigns to attract agribusiness-related FDI. For example, in Ethiopia, the government has attracted $800 million of annual agricultural investments by countries such as Saudi Arabia. As a result of its overseas agricultural investments, arid Saudi Arabia unexpectedly became the world's sixth-largest wheat exporter in the 1990s.[22] All the while, Ethiopia and other land-leasing States remain the recipients of World Food Programme Aid. In spite of sizable portions of the Ethiopian population depending on external food aid, Ethiopia has declined to make new land leases conditional on the requirement that investors preferentially supply local markets in the event of a national food crisis.

Sudan has also been successful in attracting Middle Eastern investors. It is one of the seven countries hosting half of the remaining cultivable land acres in the world,[23] and it receives irrigated water from the White and Blue Nile. Even though Sudan is currently importing food to meet its citizens' needs, Qatar has invested in export agriculture projects in Sudan,[24] and the United Arab Emirates-based Abu Dhabi Fund for Development has leased Sudanese farmland to grow animal feed, maize, beans, and potatoes for export.[25] Sudan is the site of the UN World Food Programme's largest assistance effort: 11 million people in Sudan are classified as 'food insecure', with 32 per cent of all children identified as malnourished.[26]

---

[21] British Broadcasting Corporation, Channel BBC2, *Future of Food: Episode 2* (24 August 2009) (quoting a community member in India on jatropha cultivation: 'The problem we have with jatropha is that we can't eat it. We can't burn it; we can't use it for anything. The poor have to make their living from the land. Jatropha is only useful for fuel. As we don't have a vehicle it is of no value to us. Also, a big problem is that if our animals eat jatropha they die.')

[22] Knaup and von Mittelstaedt, 'Foreign investors'.

[23] Cotula, Vermeulen, Leonard and Keeley, *Land Grab*, p. 60. The other States are Angola, Democratic Republic of Congo, Argentina, Bolivia and Colombia.

[24] *Ibid.*, p 36.   [25] *Ibid.*, p. 39.

[26] United Nations World Food Programme, 'Sudan: Ten hunger facts' (19 April 2010), www.wfp.org/stories/sudan-10-hunger-facts-nation-goes-vote (last accessed 16 December 2010).

With rapidly growing populations, Asia and Africa are the two most populous regions in the world respectively, and neither continent has truly surplus agricultural lands. Much of the land currently offered for lease by States to foreign investment firms is occupied or used in some fashion by small-scale farmers whose customary rights to the lands remain unrecognised by their governments' land-tenure systems. States continue to offer choice arable lands even though, as of 2002, in both Africa and Asia 1.4 billion people (one-sixth of the world's population at the time) were living on fragile lands not suited to agricultural intensification.[27]

B   Lessees

A number of States, including China, India and the United Arab Emirates are engaged in promoting the acquisition of large-scale land leases. It is of particular note that, in preparation for its investment in Africa, China has entered numerous BITs over the past decade with African States.

China is currently feeding 22 per cent of the world's population with 10 per cent of the world's arable land.[28] With serious concerns about soil deterioration due to nutrient exhaustion and industrial pollution, China has begun turning its attention abroad for locations to grow certain commodity crops.[29] At the 2006 Beijing Summit of the Forum on China–Africa Cooperation, President Hu Jintao pledged that China would create a China–Africa Development Fund. Since this fund was launched, it has focused substantial resources on making new investments and acquiring existing enterprises in the agribusiness sector.[30] Organised as a private equity fund, the fund has received $1 billion of funding from the China Development Bank and has agreed to pledge up to $5 billion to Chinese corporations to invest in African business.[31] China is also interested in entering the fuel market and recently signed a memorandum of understanding with the Democratic Republic of Congo

---

[27] World Bank, *Atlas of Global Development* (2007), p. 99.
[28] Watts, 'China's soil deterioration'.   [29] *Ibid.*
[30] China–Africa Development Fund (the Fund), *Investment Targets*, www.cadfund.com/en/Column.asp?ColumnId=74 (last accessed 16 December 2010).
[31] G. Jian, *Chairman's Message for the China–Africa Development Fund*, www.cadfund.com/en/Column.asp?ColumnId=13 (last accessed 16 December 2010).

for one of the largest single land leases on record: approximately 3 million hectares to grow palm oil for biofuels.[32]

Countries such as the United States are supplying both direct and indirect financing for these large-scale land leases. Directly, United States private investors such as Dominion Farms Limited (Dominion), an Oklahoma-based agribusiness, are leasing acreage in Africa with the intention of bringing 'America-style agribusiness to Africa', replete with chemical inputs.[33] Indirectly, Morgan Stanley and other financial firms are creating agricultural funds designed to capitalise specifically on overseas agribusiness profits.[34] Some of the rationales proffered for overseas agribusiness investment raise ethical issues about both the rule of law and the legitimacy of investors' expectations. For example, Jarch Capital (Jarch), a US investment company, has been seeking large-scale agricultural land leases in southern Sudan because, as Philippe Heilberg, founder of Jarch, unapologetically stated, 'when food becomes scarce, the investor needs a weak state that does not force him to abide by any rules'.[35]

Overseas land-leasing in food insecure countries is not limited to Africa. Middle Eastern countries are also seeking to lease large-scale land-holdings in South Asia and many States are offering such leases on very favourable terms. For example, the government of Pakistan offers 99-year leases of agricultural lands with unrestricted repatriation of all profits and produce.[36] With shrinking water tables in their own countries and current food importation rates of between 60 and 80 per cent, a number of Arab Gulf States have expressed interest in Pakistan's open-ended offer.[37] In the case of future threats to national

---

[32] Centre for Chinese Studies, *Evaluating China's FOCAC Commitments to Africa and Mapping the Way Ahead* (January 2010), p. 47, www.ccs.org.za/wp-content/uploads/2010/03/ENGLISH-Evaluating-Chinas-FOCAC-commitments-to-Africa-2010.pdf (last accessed 16 December).

[33] J. Silver-Greenberg, 'Land rush in Africa', *Businessweek* (25 November 2009), www.businessweek.com/magazine/content/09_49/b4158038757158.htm (last accessed 16 December 2010) (referring to the lease of 17,000 acres in Kenya by Dominion, which has been criticised on a number of levels, including for causing flooding as a result of installation of a dam and contaminating drinking water with fertiliser).

[34] *Ibid.*

[35] Knaup and von Mittelstaedt, 'Foreign investors'.

[36] N. Sadeque, 'Giving away the family silver', *Newsline* (26 October 2009), www.newslinemagazine.com/2009/10/giving-away-the-family-silver/ (last accessed 16 December 2010).

[37] *Ibid.* Bahrain has initiated a long-term lease for rice production; the United Arab Emirates is leasing 370,657 acres of agricultural land near a dam; and Qatar Livestock has invested more than $1 billion for the rights to large tracts of land in Pakistan's Sindh and Punjab regions.

food security, the Pakistani government has publicly indicated that they will not interfere with these foreign-owned investments in agri-business, the result of which is that investors will still be offered freedom of choice even where the host State is experiencing food shortages. Commenting on a Saudi Arabian investment, the Pakistan Investment Minister stated to the press that the Saudi investors would be able to remove 'one hundred per cent crop yield to their countries, even in the case of food deficit'.[38]

C   Social and environmental impacts of FDI-fuelled large-scale agriculture

There is little analysis of the effect of the current agricultural land-leasing boom on fragile and already stressed ecosystems. However, potential concerns are identifiable. In this regard, the owners of the agribusiness ventures in question are primarily private companies focused on acquiring foreign leases to satisfy production demands in their home countries or other lucrative markets. Some of these ventures are bankrolled by hedge funds, pension funds and sovereign wealth funds that expect short-term return on their capital. Assigned generally thirty- to fifty-year leases, these foreign-owned ventures do not have strong economic incentives to steward the land assigned to them in order to ensure long-term environmental protection for biodiversity, water quality or soil productivity. In fact, companies such as Hebei, a Chinese agribusiness company growing rice, wheat and corn in Uganda, have made it clear that they intend to increase their land leases and farm the leases in a 'cost effective manner'.[39] No mention is made of farming in an environmentally protective manner.

In the FAO and World Bank 2009 Report, which describes the Guinea Savannah as the next locus for major agricultural investment,[40] only about 12 of the 195 pages of the report analyse the environmental impacts of the proposed release of 400 million acres of African land to intense agricultural production. Using African case studies of Mozambique, Nigeria and Zambia, the author observes that existing agricultural

---

[38] Cotula et al., Land Grab, p. 87 (citing S. Shah, 'Corporate farming raises concerns among local growers', The News (Pakistan) (28 January 2009)).
[39] S. Edward, 'Chinese investors descend on Masindi', Uganda Observer (11 October 2009), www.observer.ug/index.php?option=com_content&view=article&id=5472:chinese-invest-ors-descend-on-masindi&catid=38:business&Itemid=68 (last accessed 16 December 2010).
[40] Larson, 'Awakening Africa's sleeping giant'.

intensification for the purposes of commercial farming and subsistence-farming practices has already led to biodiversity and soil impacts. The potential toll of large-scale commercial agriculture is foreshadowed in details provided by the report. For example, in Zambia the decline in soil productivity has been attributed to continued applications of inorganic fertilisers without adequate crop rotation,[41] two practices common to large-scale commercial agriculture. In addition to soil-quality issues, there are also concerns surrounding water resources. Presently, water quality is not a problem in locations such as Mozambique because smallholder farmers apply only small quantities of fertiliser, pesticides and herbicides to their crops.[42] However, this would almost certainly change if conventional agricultural practices are permitted on the scale favoured by agribusiness.

The report suggests that large-scale farming operations may be reasonable for cultivating the 'under-utilised' Guinea Savannah lands in order to meet global food and energy needs.[43] The choice of the word 'under-utilised' to describe African land resources reinforces the current impulses of investment-hungry government ministries to conclude land deals rapidly with willing investors without any meaningful environmental or social review. Such review seems unnecessary in light of the conclusion of the report's authors, that: 'Environmental change is an inevitable outcome of economic growth and development. Economic activity, including commercial agriculture, qualitatively transforms the physical environment within which it takes place – that is inevitable.'[44] No mention of mitigation is made in the report.

In spite of the report's fatalism, there need be nothing inevitable about habitat destruction, soil mining and water pollution, if proposed and existing land-lease investments are properly conditioned at the outset and subsequently monitored by independent environmental experts. Pre-investment environmental impact analysis and third-party auditing of farming practices are essential to ensuring that the latest manifestation of the 'green revolution' does not environmentally bankrupt already fragile lands in Africa and Asia. Precautionary safeguards are needed if the Report's authors are correct that 'a significant share' of the Guinea Savannah will have to be converted to intensive agricultural use in order 'to feed the world, meet the growing demand for agricultural raw materials, and generate the feedstuffs needed for production of

---

[41] *Ibid.*, p. 170.   [42] *Ibid.*   [43] *Ibid.*, p. 175.   [44] *Ibid.*, pp. 171–2.

biofuels'.[45] Yet developing rules or frameworks for environmental safeguards alone will not be enough to promote environmental protection where credible legal enforcement mechanisms are lacking.[46]

In the existing leases between foreign investors or host States, no regard has been paid to generating new legal rules to avoid long-term impacts of soil erosion, soil mining, habitat and biodiversity loss, environmental pollution or intensive water usage associated with industrial agribusiness. With regard to soil quality, the current leases between investors and States do not incorporate future costs of rehabilitating the soil into the lease prices. For example, in Ethiopia an Indian agribusiness company, Karuturi Global, is paying – depending on the location of the land – between $1 and $8 per hectare every year for the life of the 50- to 99-year leases.[47] Yet estimates (in 1990s terms) for the cost of rehabilitating degraded lands range between $400 per hectare to restore rainfed cropland and $2,000 per hectare to improve irrigated land.[48]

In addition to environmental impacts, the current structure of agribusiness investment fails to address systematically local community concerns about income generation, job opportunities, and sustainable livelihoods. Large-scale mechanisation of agribusiness investments is unlikely to generate jobs for many small-scale farmers. Even where jobs are offered to the community by an investor, there are concerns captured by al-Gaddafi's comment at the FAO that local workers, in contrast to foreign workers, will be subject to a new serfdom where they labour for others without generating lasting benefits from their labour.[49] Government land agents indicate that one of the attractions of some of the host States offering land leases is that labour is cheap.[50] Where this is the case, workers are especially vulnerable to exploitation. This concern has been realised in Ethiopia, where workers at Karuturi Global, which has leased 300,000-plus acres of land in Southern Ethiopia, are paid less than the

---

[45] *Ibid.*, p. 171. [46] *Ibid.*, p. 191.

[47] X. Rice, 'Ethiopia – country of the silver sickle – offers land dirt cheap to farming giants', *The Guardian* (15 January 2010), www.guardian.co.uk/world/2010/jan/15/ethiopia-sells-land-farming-giants (last accessed 16 December 2010).

[48] H. E. Dregne, and N.-T. Chou, 'Global desertification dimensions and costs' in H. E. Dregne (ed.), *Degradation and Restoration of Arid Lands* (Lubbock, Texas: International Center for Arid and Semiarid Land Studies, 1992), pp. 249–81.

[49] Brown and Kovalyova, 'Gaddafi asks'.

[50] J. Vidal, 'How food and water are driving a 21st-century African land grab', *The Guardian* (7 March 2010), www.guardian.co.uk/environment/2010/mar/07/food-water-africa-land-grab (last accessed 16 December 2010) (quoting from an Ethiopian land agent who indicates that the cheap labour and the good climate are attracting Chinese, Saudi Arabian, Turkish and Egyptian investors).

World Bank's poverty threshold of $1.25 per day even though the company expects to exceed annual earnings of $100 million by 2013.[51]

In spite of the numerous environmental and social impacts of overseas land leasing, however, the current momentum in concluding such land deals raises the question of whether leasing land should be regarded as a potential 'win-win' situation, as posited by FAO briefings, or rather as a Faustian bargain. Given the current investment law structures, the answer most likely depends on whether you are a private investor, a member of a community in which land is being leased or a threatened species of flora or fauna.

III   International investment law context for overseas land-leases

In the colonial era, there was little effort on the part of the occupied power to attract investment from colonial powers. If anything, efforts were made to repel investment in hopes of colonisers abandoning their colonial enterprises. After independence, however, a number of States in Africa and Asia actively sought FDI to attract international currency to the State and provide States with entry into global markets.

For States deemed to be politically unstable, investment protection guarantees are essential to attract FDI. One of the universal guarantees in international investment law principles is an investor's right to be protected from expropriation. When this right was first codified in the earliest BITs, parties were concerned about arbitrary physical seizure of private assets by governments and the subsequent nationalisation of private assets. In the 1960s and 1970s, the seizure of assets was a real threat as recently independent States pursued Marxist-oriented ideologies and promoted new anti-capitalist international economic orders.

Over time, the universal prohibition on expropriation of investment was extended beyond physical seizures to discriminatory regulatory frameworks. This shift may have made sense where States were passing economic regulations targeted at a particular investor such as arbitrary taxes. But in a controversial case, an international arbitration panel made general observations suggesting that States' capacities to regulate for the public interest may still require compensation even where an investor's reasonable expectations would have been limited based on the location of the investment and the nature of the investment activity.

---

[51] J. McClure, 'Ethiopian farms lure investor funds as workers live in poverty', *Bloomberg* (31 December 2009), www.bloomberg.com/apps/news?pid=20601080&sid=aeuJT_p-SE68c (last accessed 17 December 2010).

In *Santa-Elena* v. *Costa Rica*,[52] the tribunal was called upon to rule on the merits of a US$1.9 million State valuation of a parcel of land versus a US$6.4 million private valuation. Instead of focusing on the narrow matter before the court, the tribunal announced dramatically that:

> taking for a public purpose does not affect the nature or the measure of compensation to be paid for the taking . . . the purpose of protecting the environment for which the property was taken does not alter the legal character of the taking for which adequate compensation must be paid. The international source of the obligation to protect the environment makes no difference . . . where property is expropriated, even for environmental purposes, whether domestic or international, the state's obligation to pay compensation remains.[53]

This seemingly innocuous commentary on the law of takings opens the door to larger and more complicated questions. In the *Santa Elena* case, the State agreed for the purposes of the case that an expropriation had taken place. But what would the outcome have been if Costa Rica had resisted characterising their State actions as expropriatory and simply passed regulations prohibiting the use of the particular land for anything other than conservation purposes, because of certain populations of internationally protected species that could not be relocated to other lands?

There is a possibility that the *Santa Elena* case will be re-enacted in future disputes over agribusiness activities on leased lands. Governments may allocate large tracts of land only to find that there are important species unique to the leased lands that can only be effectively preserved *in situ*. *Santa Elena* tells us that if a government seeks to regain control of the land via an expropriatory decree, they should expect to pay compensation as at the date of the taking. But what if a government simply regulates land usage, thereby prohibiting planting on a portion of leased land characterised as a fragile ecosystem? Would these regulatory actions be categorically classified as expropriations under international investment law?

In *Tecmed* v. *Mexico*,[54] the tribunal was called upon to decide whether an administrative decision by the Mexican environmental agency not to renew a permit for a Spanish investor to operate a landfill of hazardous waste was an expropriation of an investment. The *Tecmed* tribunal referred to the controversial language in *Santa Elena*, opining that fulfilling environmental obligations, including any international obligation, may still result in a

---

[52] *Compañia del Desarrollo de Santa Elena SA* v. *Costa Rica* (ICSID Case No. ARB/96/1, Final Award of 17 February 2000).

[53] *Ibid.*, paras. 71–2.

[54] *Tecmed* v. *Mexico* (ICSID Case No. ARB(AF)/00/2, Award of 29 May 2003).

compensable expropriation.[55] The *Tecmed* tribunal went one step further by
indicating that the BIT in question was not explicit in:

> stating that regulatory administrative actions are *per se* excluded from the
> scope of the Agreement, even if they are beneficial to society as a whole –
> such as environmental protection – particularly if the negative economic
> impact of such actions on the financial position of the investor is suffi-
> cient to neutralise in full the value, or economic or commercial use of its
> investment without receiving any compensation whatsoever.[56]

This decision was a clear rejection of the balancing of State environmental
interests with State obligations to investors. The tribunal strongly endorsed
the evaluation of investment disputes starting from the perspective of private
investor expectations and not from the perspective of the public interest.

Reflecting on the *Tecmed* findings, what might a tribunal do if an investor
claims expropriation when the State terminates a lease early because of
concerns about an investor's activities on water quality or the viability of
neighbouring smallholder farms whose soil is being contaminated by pesticide run-off? Should a tribunal entertain a claim that an investor could not
reasonably foresee potential cancellation of leases based on long-term application of noxious chemicals or overdrafting of water resources?[57]

These cases provide the context for reflecting on the proliferation of
foreign investment in agribusiness. As noted above in the case of Madagascar, Daewoo had no obvious recourse to international investment
dispute-resolution mechanisms. But what if instead of a South Korean
corporation, the corporation had been a Chinese corporation and was
able to invoke the Madagascar–China BIT which provides certain substantive protections?[58] The following subsections evaluate three investment mechanisms that might be relied upon by private investors to
defeat the public interest. These interlocking mechanisms are umbrella
clauses, lack of performance standards and stabilisation clauses.

A   Umbrella clauses

One component of many BITs, including recent treaties between China
as well as Korea and several sub-Saharan African nations, is an umbrella
clause that protects any agreements that a private investor of a State

---

[55] *Ibid.*, para. 121.   [56] *Ibid.*   [57] *Ibid.*, para. 149.
[58] Agreement on the Promotion and Reciprocal Protection of Investments between the
Government of the Republic of Madagascar and the Government of the People's Republic
of China, signed 21 November 2005 (entered into force 1 June 2007).

Party to a BIT may enter into with the government of the other State Party.[59] For example, in a number of BITs entered into between China and African States, the States are required 'to ensure at all times that the commitments it has entered into vis-à-vis investors of the other Contracting Party shall be observed'.[60]

Recent tribunal decisions support broad investor protection under BITs. In *LG&E* v. *Argentina*,[61] the tribunal characterised an umbrella clause in the US–Argentina BIT,[62] as creating 'a requirement by the host State to meet its obligations towards foreign investors, including those that derive from a contract'.[63] In other words, umbrella clauses open the door for private investors to receive international investment protection for private investment contracts that have not been subject to public review.

---

[59] Of the approximately 2,500 BITs in existence, about 40% of them contain some form of umbrella clause: see e.g. K. Yannaca-Small, 'Interpretation of the umbrella clause in investment agreements' (Organisation of Economic Cooperation and Development Working Paper on International Investment No. 2006/3, October 2006), p. 5.

[60] Agreement between the Government of the People's Republic of China and the Government of the Republic of Uganda on the Reciprocal Promotion and Protection of Investments, signed 27 May 2004 (not yet in force at 1 June 2010), Art. 11 (China–Uganda BIT); see also Agreement on the Promotion and Protection of Investments Between the Government of the People's Republic of China and Republic of Benin, signed 18 Feb 2004 (not yet in force at 1 June 2010), Art. 10(2) (China–Benin BIT); Agreement between the Government of the Republic of China and the Kingdom of Swaziland on the Promotion and Reciprocal Protection of Investments, signed 3 March 1998 (not yet in force at 1 June 2010), Art. 10(2) (China–Swaziland BIT); Agreement between the Government of the People's Republic of China and the Government of the Republic of Djibouti on the Promotion and Protection of Investments, signed 18 August 2003 (not yet in force at 1 June 2010), Art. 10(2) (China–Djibouti BIT); in the case of the Republic of Korea's BITs see e.g. Agreement between the Government of the Republic of Korea and the Government of the Islamic Republic of Mauritania for the Promotion and Protection of Investments, signed 15 December 2004 (entered into force 21 July 2006), Art. 10(3) (Republic of Korea–Mauritania BIT); Agreement between the Government of the Republic of Korea and the Government of the Democratic Republic of Congo for the Promotion and Protection of Investments, signed 17 March 2005 (not yet in force at 1 June 2010), Art. 10(3) (Republic of Korea–DRC BIT); and Agreement between the Government of the Republic of Korea and the Government of Burkina Faso for the Promotion and Protection of Investments, signed 26 October 2004 (not yet in force at 1 June 2010), Art. 10(3) (Republic of Korea–Burkina Faso BIT).

[61] *LG&E* v. *Argentina* (ICSID Case No. ARB/02/1, Decision on Liability of 3 October 2006) (*LG&E*).

[62] Treaty Between United States of America and the Argentine Republic Concerning the Reciprocal Encouragement and Protection of Investment, signed 14 November 1991 (entered into force 20 October 1994).

[63] *LG&E.*, paras. 169–75.

In a BIT with an umbrella clause, international investment tribunals would have the opportunity to interpret the nature of stabilisation clauses within investor and host State agreements that would otherwise be subject only to domestic legal proceedings. This aspect of protecting private contracts could prove particularly insidious in the context of large-scale land leases, since most of the leases are negotiated behind closed doors, are not subject to an adoption process requiring public review and are kept confidential by governments.[64] The relationship between investor-agreement stabilisation clauses and State environmental-protection regulations will be discussed in more detail in the third subsection.

B   Lack of performance standards in BITs to protect public interest

States can enter general exceptions to exclude certain subjects from the scope of BITs. These exceptions often include language to protect the parties' taxations policies, essential security interests, financial institutions and rights for cultural differentiation.[65] Some States have also negotiated general exceptions for protection of health and the environment, although such cases are rare in the field of BITs between States with investors buying land leases and States offering land leases.[66] Most of the negotiated exceptions for health and environment appear in BITs negotiated by States who have domestically prioritised environmental protection,[67] or by parties with equal negotiating power (e.g. Japan and the Republic of Korea).

---

[64] H. Avril, 'Africa: Land grabs continue as elites resist regulation', *Inter Press Service* (13 April 2010), www.ipsnews.net/news.asp?idnews=51018 (last accessed 16 December 2010).

[65] United Nations Conference on Trade and Development (UNCTAD), *Bilateral investment treaties 1995–2006: Trends in investment rulemaking* (2007), pp. 80–92.

[66] *Ibid.*, p. 87.

[67] Countries and organisations with strong domestic laws to protect the environment include Argentina, Australia, Brazil, Canada, Chile, France, Germany, Ecuador, the European Union, India, Ireland, Israel, Mexico, Mongolia, Nigeria, Peru, the Philippines, Poland, Portugal, Russian Federation, South Africa, Spain, Taiwan, Thailand and the United States: see J. Lee, 'Underlying legal theory to support a well-defined right to a healthy environment as a principle of customary international law', *Columbia Journal of Environmental Law*, 25 (2000), 283, 289; see e.g. Agreement between the Government of the Argentine Republic and the Government of New Zealand for the Promotion and Reciprocal Protection of Investments, signed 27 August 1999 (not yet in force at 1 June 2010) (Argentina–New Zealand BIT), Art. 5:

In addition to exempting certain matters from BIT protection, some States have explicitly stated that domestic environmental and labour regulations will not be relaxed to permit investment which would otherwise violate the regulations. In a BIT between the Netherlands and Costa Rica,[68] the parties agreed that the BIT would be applied 'in accordance with the laws and regulations of the [Host State], including its laws and regulations on labour and environment'.[69] Likewise in a BIT between the Belgo-Luxembourg

> The provisions of this Agreement shall in no way limit the right of either Contracting Party to take any measures (including the destruction of plants and animals, confiscation of property or the imposition of restrictions on stock movement) necessary for the protection of natural and physical resources or human health, provided such measures are not applied in a manner which would constitute a means of arbitrary or unjustified discrimination.

Agreement between the Government of Australia and the Government of the Republic of India on the Promotion and Protection of Investments, signed 26 February 1999, [2000] ATS 14 (entered into force 4 May 2000) (Australia–India BIT), Art. 15: 'Nothing in this Agreement precludes the host Contracting Party from taking, in accordance with its laws applied reasonably and on a non-discriminatory basis, measures necessary for . . . the prevention of diseases or pests'; Agreement between the Government of Canada and the Government of the Republic of Armenia for the Promotion and Protection of Investments, signed 8 May 1997 (entered into force 29 March 1999) (Canada–Armenia BIT), Art. 17:

> Provided that such measures are not applied in an arbitrary or unjustifiable manner, or do not constitute a disguised restriction on international trade or investment, nothing in this Agreement shall be construed to prevent a Contracting Party from adopting or maintaining measures, including environmental measures: . . . (b) necessary to protect human, animal or plant life or health; or (c) relating to the conservation of living or non-living exhaustible natural resources if such measures are made effective in conjunction with restrictions on domestic production or consumption.

See also Treaty between the United States of America and the Oriental Republic of Uruguay Concerning the Encouragement and Reciprocal Protection of Investment, signed 4 November 2005 (entered into force 1 November 2006) (US–Uruguay BIT), Art. 12: 'Nothing in this Treaty shall be construed to prevent a Party from adopting, maintaining, or enforcing any measure otherwise consistent with this Treaty that it considers appropriate to ensure that investment activity in its territory is undertaken in a manner sensitive to environmental concerns'.

[68] Agreement on Encouragement and Reciprocal Protection of Investments between the Republic of Costa Rica and the Kingdom of the Netherlands, signed 21 May 1999 (entered into force 1 July 2001) (Costa Rica–Netherlands BIT).

[69] *Ibid.*, Art. 10.

Economic Union and Zimbabwe,[70] the parties agreed that each party
had the right 'to establish its own levels of domestic environmental
protection and environmental development policies'.[71]

While the BIT language quoted above suggests a transition in the
relationship between FDI-rich nations and FDI-poor nations, developing States in Africa and Asia seem to be reluctant to promote domestic
environmental or labour regulations that might interfere with investment opportunities, especially from less environmentally progressive
States such as China and South Korea. In order to appear attractive to
investors, many developing States agree readily to allow investors full
access to international arbitration and ensure regulatory stability.
Developing States that raise the issue of environmental protection and
basic labour rights during their BIT negotiations generally relegate any
references to these interests in the preambles and do not provide separate
operational articles. For example, in the BITs between China and
Guyana,[72] and between China and Trinidad and Tobago,[73] there are
references that investment objectives should be achieved without 'relax-
ing health, safety, and environmental measures of general application'.[74]
However, no reference is made to the evolving nature of health and
environmental standards in these States.

In addition to preambular or 'general exception' language, some States
have indicated that investments will be required to comply with certain
performance standards that protect national environment and health
concerns. For example, in the Peru–El Salvador BIT,[75] Article 5 permits
States to enforce a law or rule that 'requires that an investment employ a
technology to comply with general application regulations with regular

---

[70] Agreement between the Belgo-Luxembourg Economic Union and the Federal Democratic Republic of Ethiopia on the Reciprocal Promotion and Protection of Investments,
signed 26 October 2006 (not in force at 1 June 2010) (Belgo-Luxembourg–Ethiopia BIT).

[71] Ibid.

[72] Agreement between the Government of the People's Republic of China and the Government of the Republic of Guyana on the Promotion and Protection of Investments, signed
27 March 2003 (entered into force 26 October 2004) (China–Guyana BIT).

[73] Agreement between the Government of the Republic of Trinidad and Tobago and the
Government of the People's Republic of China on the Reciprocal Promotion and
Protection of Investments, signed 22 July 2002 (entered into force 24 May 2004)
(Trinidad and Tobago–China BIT).

[74] China–Guyana BIT (preamble); Trinidad and Tobago–China BIT (preamble).

[75] Agreement between the Government of the Republic of Peru and the Government of the
Republic of El Salvador on the Promotion and Reciprocal Protection of Investments,
signed 13 June 1996 (entered into force 15 December 1996).

application to health, safety, and environment',[76] even where the law or rule would otherwise be considered a prohibited performance requirement. Under Article 3 of the Jordan–Kuwait BIT,[77] the parties may explicitly permit performance requirements where they are 'vital for public health, public order, or the environment'.[78]

In spite of these BITs that explicitly protect public-interest concerns, performance requirements in investment treaties are generally discouraged because of the impact they could have on distorting free trade. As a result, most BITs contain no performance requirements, while other BITs prohibit a broader range of performance requirements such as technology transfer requirements or requirements to use domestic suppliers. Notably, none of the major States involved in large-scale land leasing have specific performance requirements for environmental or labour protection within their BITs.

C   Investor–State agreements and stabilisation clauses

In addition to BITs, the legal framework for agribusiness leases also includes individual host State agreements with foreign investors. The content of these agreements, and the negotiations that lead to these agreements, are largely confidential and not subject to public review or public challenge.[79] Where contracts have been made public, there is often no explicit requirement by a State or a community that an investor will pursue environmentally sound agricultural practices.[80]

Where States already fail to address in their contracts the application of existing environmental laws to investors, they are even more unlikely to address the application to investments of evolving domestic or international standards for long-term environmental protection. Arguably,

---

[76] *Ibid.*

[77] Agreement between the Government of the Hashemite Kingdom of Jordan and the Government of the State of Kuwait for the Encouragement and Protection of Investments, signed 21 May 2001 (not yet in force at 1 June 2010).

[78] *Ibid.*, Art. 3(5).

[79] L. Goering, 'African farmland leases threaten to drive conflict, but rules could help', *AlertNet* (29 March 2010) (copy on file with author) (quoting Namanga Ngongi, President of the Bill and Melinda Gates Foundation-funded NGO, Alliance for a Green Revolution in Africa: 'The real issue in Africa is a lot of these deals are done in secret. The small-holder farmers who stand to lose their land are not consulted. No one is sure the amount of money declared is the real amount.'); see also Cotula *et al.*, *Land Grab*, p. 69.

[80] See e.g. the contract between an Indian agribusiness company, Varun Agriculture SARL, and the Madagascar Farmer's Association, cited in A. Üllenberg, *Foreign Direct Investment (FDI) in Land in Madagascar* (Eschborn: Deutsche Gesellschaft, 2009), pp. 33–5.

the failure to articulate clear standards of care for investor conduct in the State-investor agreements may lead investors to rely on certain expectations regarding their investment. For example, assume that under the current State regulatory regime endosulfans (hazardous insecticides nominated for a global ban because of their toxicity) could be legally applied to crops in a given State that is leasing land. What happens when an investor leases a large tract of land with the expectation of applying endosulfans as the insecticide of choice in order to generate larger yields of commodity crops? What would the outcome be if the State bans the application of endosulfans five years after the agricultural lease began and requires instead far more expensive and less effective pest treatments? Arguably, if an investor is now unable to achieve the needed minimum large yields to ensure a profit because of the new prohibition on a substance that was legal when the investment began, then the investor might be in the position to argue that the regulatory change has adversely affected reasonable investor expectations leading to an expropriation. The case becomes particularly interesting where endosulfan usage in a country is limited to foreign investors.

The outcome of such a case would be uncertain and would depend on what the parties had negotiated and what expectations investors could reasonably hold. On the one hand, there is the approach taken in the *Santa Elena* case where the decision to protect the natural habitat was held compensable. On the other hand, there is the outcome in the *Glamis Gold* case,[81] where the arbitrators decided that there had been no expropriation and that the regulations imposed on the investment were supported by legitimate public-policy goals of protecting the environment and cultural resources. Which logic will govern in future arbitrations will depend on the composition of a given tribunal, fact-specific considerations and the contents of the governing BIT and investor–host State contract.

Some governments have agreed to limit prospectively a State's future regulatory flexibility over an investment by signing formal stabilisation clauses in an investor–host State contract.[82] Some of these clauses

---

[81] *Glamis Gold Ltd* v. *The United States of America* (Award of 8 June 2009), www.state.gov/documents/organization/125798.pdf (last accessed 17 December 2010).

[82] W. Smith, 'Unleashing entrepreneurship' in L. Brainard (ed.), *Transforming the Development Landscape: The role of the private sector* (Washington DC: Brookings Institution Press, 2006), p. 33. According to a World Bank survey of perceptions of business risk by foreign investors, 28% of the firms listed policy uncertainty as their primary concern. For more on stabilisation clauses, see especially ch. 22 by A. Crockett in this volume.

prohibit the application to an investment of any new laws or regulations subsequently passed by the government. Other forms of stabilisation clauses recognise that while States are entitled to change laws and rules, foreign investors who are required to comply with new national laws must be fully compensated for their compliance costs (e.g. costs of installing pollution equipment or disposing of waste in an environmentally responsible manner).[83]

Investors rely on stabilisation clauses as a tool to prevent governments from changing the terms of a concession agreement by imposing new conditions. Stabilisation clauses are negotiated as 'risk-mitigation tools' to provide for long-term predictability and protect large-capital investment from regulatory expropriation.[84]

Stabilisation clauses are problematic for developing and transitional countries that promulgate new laws and do not pay compensation to investors. For example, in investment contracts between either an OECD country and a non-OECD country or two non-OECD countries, host States have agreed in some instances to waive the application of future labour and environmental laws, to lock-in a certain water usage for an investment and to waive fiscal and customs laws that create financial barriers for an investment.[85] In contrast, in investment contracts between two OECD countries, the foreign investor is often expected by the host State to absorb the risk of new health and safety laws unless the laws are somehow discriminatory towards foreign investors.[86] In a 2009 study qualitatively reviewing investment agreements for the UN's Special Representative to the Secretary-General on Business and Human Rights, forty-four out of seventy-five non-OECD contracts and models gave foreign investors exemptions from new laws or offered compensation for complying with new laws. Significantly, none of the OECD country contracts or models offered exemptions from new laws.[87]

In some instances, stabilisation clauses could operate to constrain any meaningful changes in host State policy because of fears that the

---

[83] A. Shemberg, *Stabilisation Clauses and Human Rights: A research project conducted For IFC and the United Nations Special Representative to the Secretary General on Business and Human Rights* (27 May 2009), p. 9, para. 32, www.ifc.org/ifcext/sustainability.nsf/ AttachmentsByTitle/ p_StabilizationClausesandHumanRights/$FILE/Stabilization+Paper. pdf (last accessed 17 December 2010).
[84] *Ibid.*   [85] *Ibid.*, p. 30, para. 97 and p. 31, para. 98.   [86] *Ibid.*, p. 29, para. 90.
[87] *Ibid.*, p. ix.

host States will be held financially accountable for a regulatory expropri-ation.[88] Tribunals that have been otherwise unwilling to restrict the regulatory authority of States have suggested in their awards that the existence of a stabilisation clause may result in a finding of necessary compensation even though a State is otherwise legitimately exercising its regulatory powers. Earlier arbitration cases involving stabilisation clauses focused on actions by the State which would have been protected under sovereign immunity but for the existence of a stabilisation clause. For example, in *AGIP* v. *Republic of Congo*,[89] the tribunal agreed that the government could not apply an ordinance to an investment that would change the private character of the investment. Finding the State in breach of its agreement, the tribunal stated:

> These stabilisation clauses, freely accepted by the Government, do not affect the principle of its sovereign legislative and regulatory powers, since it retains both in relation to those, whether national or foreigners, with whom it has not entered into such obligations, and that, in the present case, changes in the legislative and regulatory agreements stipu-lated in the agreement simply cannot be invoked against the other contracting party.[90]

The protection of the content of a stabilisation clause might make sense in the context of a nationalisation of an investment focused on pecuni-ary gain to a State.[91] However, upholding a stabilisation clause in the event of a non-discriminatory regulatory change to protect human or environmental health at the expense of legitimate non-investment public interests suggests a violation of a government's social contract between itself and its citizens.

While stabilisation clauses should be waived when certain non-derog-able rights are at issue (for example, rights to water), there is no indica-tion that a tribunal must find such a waiver. A report on stabilisation clauses drafted on behalf of the International Finance Corporation (IFC) found that:

---

[88] *Ibid.* Broad stabilisation clauses, with exemptions from new laws, are found in invest-ment contracts from Sub-Saharan Africa; Eastern, Southern Europe and Central Asia; and the Middle East and North Africa.
[89] *AGIP SpA* v. *People's Republic of the Congo* (ICSID Case No. ARB/77/1, Award of 30 November 1979).
[90] *Ibid.*, para. 86.
[91] Stabilisation clauses do not necessarily prohibit nationalisation: see *Government of Kuwait* v. *American Independent Oil Company* (Award of 24 March 1982), 21 ILM 976, p. 1023.

Evidence supports the hypothesis that some stabilisation clauses can be used to limit a State's action to implement new social and environmental legislation to long-term investments. The data show that the text of many clauses applies to social and environmental legislation, so that investors are able to pursue exemptions or compensation informally and formally.[92]

Recent tribunals have not provided clear signs that stabilisation clauses will be waived. For example, in the NAFTA arbitration between Methanex Corporation and the United States,[93] even though the tribunal found in favour of broad police powers for States, it indicated that stabilisation clauses might trump these powers. In other words, a State can contract away its police powers. As the *Methanex* tribunal found:

> As a matter of general international law, a non-discriminatory regulation for a public purpose which is enacted in accordance with due process and, which affects, inter alios, a foreign investor or investment is not deemed expropriatory and compensatory *unless specific commitments had been given by the regulating government to the then putative foreign investor contemplating investment that the government would refrain from such regulation.*[94]

For private citizens living in countries where transparency and accountability are chronic problems, the *Methanex* tribunal's response is unsatisfactory. While perhaps the United States and Canada can be held to their contractual investment promises made in the spotlight of public scrutiny, it does not follow that all States must be held to the same standards of protecting contracted investment obligations at the expense of protecting the public interest.

For fear of alienating investors, States remain passive in terms of proactively implementing international environmental obligations or creating new national obligations. For example, because Brazil's tanneries compete with higher-quality tanneries in Europe and cheaper tanneries in Asia, Brazil has been unwilling to pass strict regulation to control effluents from tanneries for fear of disrupting the limited market share that they have secured.[95] As a result, foreign investors financially

---

[92] Shemberg, *Stabilisation Clauses and Human Rights*, p. x, n. 70.
[93] *Methanex Corporation* v. *United States of America* (Final Award of the Tribunal on Jurisdiction and Merits of 3 August 2005), www.state.gov/documents/organization/51052.pdf (last accessed 17 December 2010).
[94] *Ibid.*, para. 7 (emphasis added).
[95] N. Mabey and R. McNally, *Foreign Direct Investment and the Environment: From pollution haven to sustainable development* (World Wildlife Fund UK, 1998), p. 33, http://www.wwf.org.uk/filelibrary/pdf/fdi.pdf (last accessed 17 December 2010).

benefit from the setting of artificially low standards to protect the local market even at the expense of the public interest in access to clean water. Overseas agricultural land leases are likely to be beset with the same unattractive trade-offs.

D Protecting the public interest

This chapter proposes amending or renegotiating BITs to include explicit language to protect the public interest. The challenge in reforming BITs is to balance the 'need for order and the need for change'.[96] This section reviews efforts by several States to incorporate environmental and labour issues as priority areas for international trade and investment negotiations. Drawing on recent developments in environmental protection language in US Free Trade Agreements, this chapter proposes a similar comprehensive approach to public-interest protection for investment treaties.

Obligations under international investment law need to be recalibrated to ensure that a State's public-interest obligations are not compromised.[97] Articles 5 and 6 of the Belgo-Luxembourg and Ethiopia

---

[96] T. Franck, *Fairness in International Law and Institution* (Oxford University Press, 1998), p. 23.

[97] Belgo-Luxembourg–Ethiopia BIT. In addition, some language to protect the environment is found in a number of recent BITs: see e.g. the Agreement between the Government of the Republic of Finland and the Government of the Kyrgyz Republic on the Promotion and Protection of Investments, signed 3 April 2003 (entered into force 8 December 2004) (Preamble) (Finland–Kyrgyzstan BIT); Agreement between the Government of the Republic of Mozambique and the Government of the Kingdom of the Netherlands Concerning the Encouragement and the Reciprocal Protection of Investments, signed 18 December 2001 (entered into force 1 September 2004) (preamble) (Mozambique–Netherlands BIT); Agreement between Japan and the Socialist Republic of Vietnam for the Liberalization, Promotion and Protection of Investment, signed 14 November 2003 (entered into force 19 December 2004) (Japan–Vietnam BIT), Art. 21, which provides that:

> The Contracting Parties recognise that it is inappropriate to encourage investment by investors of the other Contracting Party by relaxing environmental measures. To this effect each Contracting Party should not waive or otherwise derogate from such environmental measures as an encouragement for the establishment, acquisition or expansion in its Area of investments by investors of the other Contracting Party.

Agreement between the Government of the Republic of Korea and the Government of the Republic of Trinidad and Tobago for the Promotion and Protection of Investments, signed 5 November 2002 (entered into force 27 November 2003) (preamble) (Republic of Korea–Trinidad and Tobago BIT) and the US–Uruguay BIT. Language to protect health and safety standards is found in the Agreement on Encouragement and Reciprocal Protection of Investments Between the Kingdom of the Netherlands and the Republic of Namibia, signed 26 November 2002 (entered into force 1 October 2004) (preamble)

BIT represent a shift in this direction.[98] Article 5 provides that each party has 'the right . . . to establish its own levels of domestic environmental protection and environmental development policies and priorities, and to adopt or modify accordingly its environmental legislation'.[99] In addition, the parties agree that they will 'strive to ensure' not to 'waive or otherwise derogate from, or offer to waive or otherwise derogate from [domestic environmental legislation] as an encouragement for the establishment, maintenance or expansion in its territory of an investment'.[100] Article 6 provides that each of the parties has the right to establish 'its own domestic labour standards, and to adopt or modify accordingly its labour legislation', including by improving labour standards to be 'consistent with the internationally recognised labour rights' including

(Netherlands–Namibia BIT); and the Agreement between the Swiss Confederation and the United Mexican States on the Promotion and Reciprocal Protection of Investments, signed 10 July 1995 (entered into force 14 March 1996) (Switzerland–Mexico BIT), Protocol, Addendum to Art. 3, which provides that:

> it is inappropriate to encourage investment by relaxing domestic health, safety or environmental measures. Accordingly, neither Party should waive or otherwise derogate from, or offer to waive or derogate, such measures as an encouragement for the establishment, acquisition, expansion or retention in its territory of an investment of an investor. If either Party considers that the other Party has offered such an encouragement, it may request consultations.

Language to protect labour rights is found in the Agreement between the Government of the Republic of Austria and the Government of the Republic of Armenia for the Promotion and Protection of Investments, signed 17 October 2001 (entered into force 1 February 2003) (Preamble) (Austria–Armenia BIT); the Netherlands–Namibia BIT and the Agreement between the Government of the Republic of Finland and the Government of the Republic of Nicaragua on the Promotion and Protection of Investments, signed 17 September 2003 (not yet in force at 1 June 2010) (Preamble) (Finland–Nicaragua BIT).

[98] *Ibid.*

[99] *Ibid.*, Art. 1(5) defines 'environmental legislation' to encapsulate:

> any legislation of the Contracting Parties, or provision thereof, the primary purpose of which is the protection of the environment, or the prevention of a danger to human, animal, or plant life or health, through: a) the prevention, abatement or control of the release, discharge, or emission of pollutants or environmental contaminants; b) the control of environmentally hazardous or toxic chemicals, substances, materials and wastes, and the dissemination of information related thereto; c) the protection or conservation of wild flora or fauna, including endangered species, their habitat, and specially protected natural areas in the Contracting Party's territory.

[100] *Ibid.*, Art. 5(2).

the right of association; the right to organise and bargain collectively; a prohibition on the use of any form of forced or compulsory labour; a minimum age for the employment of children; and acceptable conditions of work with respect to minimum wages, hours of work and occupational safety and health.

In 2004, the US initiated an effort to reform its Model BIT to further protect environmental and labour rights.[101] In its Model BIT, the US added Article 12, 'Investment and Environment'. Using language very similar to NAFTA, the US proposes in the first portion of Article 12 that:

> The Parties recognise that it is inappropriate to encourage investment by weakening or reducing the protections afforded in domestic environmental laws. Accordingly, each Party shall strive to ensure that it does not waive or otherwise derogate from, or offer to waive or otherwise derogate from, such laws in a manner that weakens or reduces the protections afforded in those laws as an encouragement for the establishment, acquisition, expansion, or retention of an investment in its territory.[102]

The second paragraph of Article 12 of the US Model BIT states that:

> Nothing in this Treaty shall be construed to prevent a Party from adopting, maintaining, or enforcing any measure otherwise consistent with this Treaty that it considers appropriate to ensure that investment activity in its territory is undertaken in a manner sensitive to environmental concerns.[103]

Taken at face value, the language in this section seems to maintain the hierarchy of investor rights over environmental laws since any measures that may be adopted, maintained or enforced as environmental measures must be 'otherwise consistent with this Treaty'.

While no mention is made in the main text of the US Model BIT of whether implementation of future environmental or labour protection measures would require compensation, Annex B provides important qualifications on what types of measures will be considered exempted from requirement for compensations. The United States agrees that:

---

[101] Treaty between the Government of the United States of America and the Government of [Country] Concerning the Encouragement and Reciprocal Protection of Investment (US Model BIT).

[102] *Ibid.* The language used in the US Model BIT was adopted in the recently negotiated USA–Uruguay BIT and Agreement between the Government of the United States of America and the Government of the Republic of Rwanda Concerning the Encouragement and Reciprocal Protection of Investment, signed 19 February 2008, not yet in force at 1 June 2010 (US–Rwanda BIT).

[103] *Ibid.*

> Except in rare circumstances, non-discriminatory regulatory actions by a
> Party that are designed and applied to protect legitimate public welfare
> objectives, such as public health, safety, and the environment, do not
> constitute indirect expropriations.[104]

While Article 12 does little to strengthen a State's confidence in promulgating new environmental laws and regulations, Annex B does provide
some assurance that as long as the law is 'non-discriminatory' no
compensation would be payable by a State 'except in rare circumstances'.[105] This 'rare circumstances' exception may be an allusion to
contracts that contain negotiated stabilisation clauses. What is surprising
about the US Model BIT is that the language from Annex B regarding
environmental regulations has not been incorporated explicitly in Article
12 but rather remains in an annex that is referenced by Article 12.

   While the US Model BIT and the discussions surrounding it are
generating useful synergies between domestic environmental law,
domestic labour law and international investment law, a better model
for harmonising investment law with environmental and labour laws is
the approach taken by the United States in some of its recently signed
free trade agreements (FTAs).

   In a 2009 FTA between Peru and the United States, the parties devoted
two separate chapters to ensuring that trade and environmental policies,
as well as trade and labour rights, are mutually supportive.[106] Using
similar language to the Belgium–Luxembourg BIT, Article 18.1 of the
US–Peru FTA acknowledges that the parties should establish their 'own
level of domestic environmental protection and environmental development priorities, and to adopt or modify accordingly its environmental
laws and policies', and that the parties have an obligation 'to continue to
improve [their] respective levels of environmental protection'.[107]
Regarding its environmental obligations, parties are required under the
FTA to 'adopt, maintain, and implement laws, regulations, and all other
measures to fulfill its obligations' under a negotiated list of multilateral
environmental agreements which both States have ratified.[108] The list of

---

[104] *Ibid.*   [105] *Ibid.*
[106] United States–Peru Trade Promotion Agreement, signed 12 April 2006 (entered into
       force on 1 February 2009) (last accessed 17 December 2010) (US–Peru FTA).
[107] *Ibid.*
[108] *Ibid.* Art. 18.2. Annex 18.2 provides for seven agreements requiring compliance and
       domestic implementation: Convention on International Trade in Endangered Species of
       Wild Fauna and Flora; Montreal Protocol on Substances that Deplete the Ozone Layer;
       Protocol of 1978 Relating to the International Convention for the Prevention of
       Pollution form Ships; Convention on Wetlands of International Importance Especially

multilateral environmental agreements can be amended. Parties are additionally required to 'not waive or otherwise derogate from, or offer to waive or otherwise derogate from' environmental laws in order to encourage trade or investment unless there is a provision of law providing for the waiver and the waiver is not inconsistent with shared obligations under multilateral environmental agreements.[109] The agreement further provides for the creation of an Environmental Affairs Council with officials from environmental ministries to oversee the implementation of the Free Trade Act's environmental chapter and to promote public participation.[110]

While the environment chapter of the US–Peru FTA fails to require any enforcement of host-country domestic environmental laws that do not involve matters outside of the annex of multilateral environmental agreements that both parties have ratified, it does make a significant contribution to strengthening State power over investors by acknowledging that States have the requisite sovereignty to both make environmental laws and then to change those environmental laws to improve environmental protection.

One approach to achieving higher levels of environmental protection within investment activities is to require existing and future investors not only to enforce or encourage the enforcement of domestic environmental laws but also to ensure that existing and future investments comply with substantive changes and revisions to environmental laws. The US–Peru FTA contemplates this possibility in its investment chapter, where the parties agree that:

> Provided that such measures are not applied in an arbitrary or unjustifiable manner, and provided that such measures do not constitute a disguised restriction on international trade or investment, restrictions [related to preferential purchases within a host country in order to achieve a certain percentage of domestic content and to transfer technology] shall not be construed to prevent a Party from adopting or maintaining measures, including environmental measures: (i) necessary to secure compliance with laws and regulations that are not inconsistent with this Agreement, (ii) necessary to protect human, animal, or plant life or health, or (iii) related to the conservation of living or non-living exhaustible natural resources.[111]

---

as Waterfowl Habitat; Convention on the Conservation of Antarctic Marine Living Resources; International Convention for the Regulation of Whaling; and Convention for the Establishment of an Inter-American Tropical Tuna Commission.

[109] *Ibid.*, Art. 18.3(2)–(3).   [110] *Ibid.*, Art. 18.6.   [111] *Ibid.*, Art. 10.9(3)(c).

The choice of the terms 'adopting or maintaining' suggest that yet to be drafted environmental measures will be applied to existing investors as long as the laws 'are not applied in an arbitrary or unjustifiable manner' and 'do not constitute a disguised restriction on international trade or investment'. By indicating that States are free to adopt measures 'necessary to protect . . . life or health' and 'related to the conservation of living or non-living exhaustible natural resources', the US and Peru have extended their existing WTO obligations under Article XX(b) and (g) to the field of investments. The decision to attach explicitly the Article XX exceptions to investment is inherently fair and complies with obligations under the Agreement on Trade-Related Investment Measures (Agreement on TRIMs).[112] Why should foreign investors, who presumably expect some of their products or services to enter the channels of global or regional trade, have legal protection that is not available under parallel trade agreements?

The content of the US–Peru FTA provides a better model for protecting the public interest than the proposed US Model BIT and should be used to inform the general drafting approach for future BIT negotiations or renegotiations. Instead of relying on vague umbrella clauses that could encompass the problematic stabilisation clauses described above, a BIT that safeguards the public interest should have lengthy chapters detailing the obligations of the parties to protect the public interest.[113] Like the US–Peru FTA, the legal expectations of the parties as to their shared rights and responsibilities could be enumerated in a negotiated index. Unlike the US–Peru FTA, the index need not be limited to international agreements to which both States are parties, but could easily be extended to domestic laws that provide local implementation for international obligations undertaken by one party.

An obvious critique of this proposal is that host States that are currently leasing large-scale land holdings such as Ethiopia and Sudan will be unlikely to adopt language similar to the Belgium–Luxembourg BIT, the US Model BIT or the US–Peru FTA.[114] Land-leasing States do

---

[112] Art. 3 of the Agreement on TRIMs provides that all exceptions under the GATT such as Art. XX will also be applied to the TRIMs agreement.

[113] The chapter on environment under the US–Peru Free Trade Agreement is 22 pages while the chapter on labour rights is 10 pages.

[114] Countries such as Sudan which are receiving attention do not have BITs with the States where the private investors hail from (e.g. United States, Saudi Arabia, Qatar, China, South Korea).

not want to create any additional legal deterrents to investment.[115] As such, these States will be less likely to include in any future BIT an annex of specific environmental obligations – even when these environmental obligations are shared between the parties. Developing countries are often the most vocal proponents of detaching environmental and labour regulations from investment because they feel that it reduces their competitive edge to attract FDI.

Yet for host country governments that are struggling to attract investors while trying to protect socio-environmental rights, the possibility of having an amendable list of environmental and labour agreements and laws creates a different power dynamic than that which currently exists between developing States and private investors.

One of the major advantages of highlighting specific international environmental and labour obligations in BITs is that it could empower host States to make needed domestic law changes that will safeguard the public interest. Where a host State makes changes to an internal law in order to harmonise its law with its existing international obligations, a host State may be able to garner both the political support of other treaty parties as well as economic support from other treaty parties to implement new obligations. In either case, implementation of obligations under an international labour treaty or environmental treaty may insulate a host State from any potential claims of regulatory expropriation.

IV Conclusion

In a globalised world FDI is essential, but the question remains what kind of investment a State should host in light of its obligation to protect the public interest. Can land-leasing States with valuable resources – large tracts of relatively fertile land with available sources of irrigation water – negotiate agreements that protect both the interests of private investors and the public interest?

The current approach to international investment in agribusiness is fraught with problems in terms of ossifying conventional agribusiness practices with high chemical usage and low wages. States with land to

---

[115] See e.g. S. McCrummen, 'The ultimate crop rotation: Wealthy nations outsource crops to Ethiopia's farmland', *Washington Post* (23 November 2009), www.washingtonpost.com/wp-dyn/content/article/2009/11/22/AR2009112201478.html?nav=emailpage (last accessed 17 December 2010) (citing the Chief General Manager for Indian-based company Karuturi Agro Products, Hanumantha Rao, who states that the Ethiopian government has imposed few requirements on his company).

lease have the opportunities to push innovation while protecting their public interest. Entrepreneurs both global and local can rise to the challenge of ensuring that agribusiness investments do not make already poor countries poorer and unhealthier.

Instead of taking the position that imposing public conditions on an investment might 'scare off investors',[116] States should require best environmentally protective practices to be employed. States can likewise require local capacity training in these best practices so that local entrepreneurs will develop high-value skills for the regional agribusiness markets. The technologies to promote water conservation and soil conservation are ready for large-scale implementation. Water efficiency companies are emerging to assist farmers in cutting water consumption. Products such as a biochar, made from chicken manure or sugar cane leftovers, can be applied to crops rather than chemical fertilisers which are both economically costly for farmers and environmentally dangerous in terms of long-term carbon dioxide emissions.

We should expect States to demand more of their private investors. States with the ability to lease arable land have a high-demand commodity and need not be cowed by sophisticated private investors who present a 'take it or leave it' offer. With fuller awareness of the normative and legal power of the contemporary international investment framework, States should demand contract and treaty conditions that will create an investment climate which not only protects investors' expectations but also safeguards the public's interest in a safe environment and meaningful employment. Otherwise international investment law interpreting investment treaties will simply entrench poor decisions of weak States for decades to come.

[116] *Ibid.*

24

Thirst for profit: Water privatisation, investment law and a human right to water

EMMA TRUSWELL*

I Introduction

Water is both a valuable commodity and the subject of an emergent human right. These characteristics have proven to be an uncomfortable combination as the scarcity of fresh water has intensified the movement towards a human right to water in parallel to increasing private control over water utilities. At international investment law, contracts for the provision of water utilities continue to be governed by general legal frameworks. In this regard, when a foreign corporation or consortium supplies water to a city or region, that contract operates under the same legal principles that would safeguard any other investment, being those contained within a bilateral investment treaty (BIT) and enforced by international arbitral tribunals. Thus, despite the unique qualities of water, the legal obligations of a host government to protect the foreign investor are not moderated by that government's own responsibility to provide safe water to its citizens.

This chapter examines the interaction between international investment law and issues surrounding the provision of fresh water. In particular, it examines how arbitral tribunals have dealt with the failure of contracts to manage privatised water supplies in developing countries by focusing on three cases of water privatisation: Cochabamba in Bolivia, Buenos Aires in Argentina and Dar es Salaam in Tanzania. Each of these cities privatised their water supplies following World Bank pressure in the late 1990s or early 2000s. City governments undertook a tender process and awarded a contract for water services to a foreign

* Thank you to Dr Kate Miles for her valuable assistance in helping me to craft this chapter. Any errors or omissions, as well as the views expressed, are, of course, my own.

private consortium offering low water prices.[1] Following the takeover, the consortiums found water provision less profitable than their forecasts had predicted.[2] Their subsequent attempts to increase water prices triggered processes which, in each case, led to the city authorities resuming control over water supply and investors taking claims to the International Centre for Settlement of Investment Disputes (ICSID) for breaches of the governing BIT. Despite the similar facts giving rise to these claims, their outcomes were not guided by consistent principles. The case against Bolivia was settled for a nominal sum. Argentina and Tanzania were both found in breach of their obligations under BITs, but only Argentina was required to pay damages.

This chapter argues that host States need greater certainty in managing private investment contracts governing the supply of their water by foreign consortiums. Section II discusses the nature of water as a resource, especially the nascent human right to water and its interaction with water pricing. Water investments are considered in section III, which outlines inherent difficulties in private water provision that have contributed to the breakdown of investment agreements. No consistent principles have yet emerged to govern water service contracts as distinct from general investment services contracts. The current state of investment law relating to water is addressed in section IV, which focuses on *Biwater Gauff (Tanzania) Ltd* v. *Tanzania* and *Azurix Corp.* v. *Argentina*,[3] two recent water cases concerning privatisations of the water utilities of cities in Tanzania and Argentina. Finally, section V suggests legal developments which might enable States to better manage vital water services, even after privatisation to a foreign consortium.

II Water: A unique resource

Water is a biological necessity, scarce environmental resource, valuable commodity and emergent human right. These characteristics have shaped the business opportunities water produces, the difficulties in its privatisation and the actions of government in prematurely ending contracts for water provision.

---

[1] See e.g. X. Rice, 'The water margin', *The Guardian* (16 August 2007), www.guardian.co. uk/business/2007/aug/16/imf.internationalaidanddevelopment (last accessed 26 January 2011).

[2] *Biwater Gauff (Tanzania) Limited* v. *United Republic of Tanzania* (ICSID Case No. ARB/ 05/22, Award of 24 July 2008), para. 789.

[3] *Azurix Corp.* v. *Argentina* (ICSID Case No. ARB/01/12, Award of 14 July 2006).

A   Essential for human life

The movement towards the recognition of water as a human right is based upon the simple biological fact that every person needs water to survive. Unlike other resources, water can be neither substituted nor artificially produced. The argument that follows appears straightforward – if water is necessary to sustain human life, and if basic human requirements are protected by human rights, there must therefore be a human right to water. If such a right were recognised at international law, States would be under an obligation to afford water access to their citizens. Where a host State repudiated a foreign investment contract for water provision, that State might argue in an investment tribunal that they did so in order to protect the right to water of their people. Nonetheless, the nature of water as a biological necessity should, of itself, be sufficient to influence treatment of water contracts by investment tribunals, even while the human right to water remains nascent.

A human right to water is frequently declared,[4] but is not universally accepted.[5] Historically, a right to water was considered implicit in rights to food, health, human well-being and life.[6] Although a right to water is not contained within the text of a universal human rights instrument, it has been suggested that water is so obviously vital to human life that early drafters of human rights instruments did not feel that a right to water needed to be stated.[7]

More recently, a right to water has been made explicit in instruments that require States to ensure that water, alongside other necessities, is available to groups which require special protection.[8] A right

---

[4] See e.g. W. Schreiber, 'Realising the right to water in international investment law: An interdisciplinary approach to BIT obligations', *Natural Resources Journal*, 48 (2008), 432; World Health Organisation, *The Right to Water* (Health and Human Rights Publication Series, No. 3, 2003).

[5] M. A. Fitzmaurice, 'The human right to water', *Fordham Environmental Law Review*, 18 (2006–7), 537.

[6] K. Conca, 'The United States and international water policy', *Journal of Environment and Development*, 17(3) (2008), 215, 225; Fitzmaurice, 'Human right to water', p. 540; A. Cahill, 'The human right to water – a right of unique status: The legal status and normative content of the right to water', *International Journal of Human Rights*, 9(3) (2005), 389, 391.

[7] R. Brown, 'Unequal burden: Water privatisation and women's human rights in Tanzania', *Gender and Development*, 18(1) (2010), 59.

[8] Fitzmaurice, 'Human right to water', p. 544.

to water is enjoyed, for example, by prisoners of war,[9] women[10] and children.[11] The Convention on the Rights of the Child is the most widely ratified human rights instrument, and it is hard to fathom a State fulfilling its obligation to provide water to women and children but not to the general population. Recognising water as a necessity rather than a right, the 1997 United Nations Convention on Non-Navigational Uses of International Watercourses requires that special regard be given to vital human needs in resolving conflict between the uses of international watercourses.[12]

The United Nations Committee on Economic, Social and Cultural Rights adopted General Comment No. 15 in 2002,[13] which declared that a human right to water is contained within Articles 11 and 12 of the International Covenant on Economic, Social and Cultural Rights (ICESCR).[14] This General Comment provided that: 'The human right to water entitles everyone to sufficient, safe, acceptable, physically accessible and affordable water for personal and domestic uses', including to prevent death by dehydration and avoid water-related disease and for consumption, cooking, personal and domestic hygienic requirements.[15] Like other rights contained within the ICESCR, the right to water is to be realised progressively on the basis of the resources available to States. The immediate obligations for States contained within General Comment No. 15 are to ensure that any water is provided in a non-discriminatory way, and to take steps towards the full realisation of the articles from which the right to water is derived.[16]

---

[9] Under the Geneva Convention Relative to the Treatment of Prisoners of War, opened for signature 12 August 1949, 75 UNTS 135 (entered into force 21 October 1950), Art. 26 states that: 'Sufficient drinking water shall be supplied to prisoners of war.'

[10] In the Convention on the Elimination of All Forms of Discrimination against Women, opened for signature 1 March 1980, 1249 UNTS 13 (entered into force 3 September 1981), Art. 14(2h), with a focus on rural women, ensures the right to enjoy adequate living conditions, particular water supply.

[11] In the Convention on the Rights of the Child, opened for signature 20 November 1989, 1577 UNTS 3 (entered into force 2 September 1990), Art. 24 provides that children are entitled to the enjoyment of the highest attainable standard of health – including 'provision of adequate nutritious foods and clean drinking-water'.

[12] Fitzmaurice, 'Human right to water', p. 544.

[13] Economic and Social Council Committee on Economic, Social and Cultural Rights (General Comment No. 15, 2002: The Right to Water, Arts. 11 and 12 of the International Covenant on Economic, Social and Cultural Rights, UN Doc: E/C.12/2002/11, 20 January 2003) (General Comment).

[14] International Covenant on Economic, Social and Cultural Rights, opened for signature 19 December 1966, 993 UNTS 3 (entered into force 3 January 1976) (ICESCR).

[15] General Comment, para. 2.   [16] Ibid., para. 17.

The clear logical derivation of the General Comment from recognised human rights conceals challenges and ambiguities relating to its recognition by States, the content of such a right and access to resources. First, critical States do not recognise that water is a human right. The United States, for example, has argued that civil and political rights should be the focus of human rights law, as these create the necessary conditions for the provision of human needs such as water.[17] On 28 July 2010, the UN General Assembly adopted a resolution, which declared 'the right to safe and clean drinking water and sanitation as a human right that is essential for the full enjoyment of life and all human rights'.[18] While no country voted against the resolution, forty-one countries abstained including Australia, Canada, Japan, the United Kingdom and the United States. The reluctance of powerful countries (and major aid donors) to define access to fresh water as a human right will delay the rights-based treatment of water access under international law.

Secondly, those most in need of water often live in those States least capable of its provision. States with limited resources cannot afford the infrastructure required to provide safe water in sufficient quantities to all their citizens, especially those in rural areas, small towns and on urban outskirts.[19] While recognition of a human right to water under the ICSCR creates a State obligation to take concrete steps towards its fulfilment,[20] it does not require that the international community gives assistance necessary for poorer States to provide potable water to those most in need.

Thirdly, a right to water would be more difficult than some other rights to determine, to measure and to monitor. General Comment No. 15 made reference to World Health Organisation (WHO) standards to determine the precise obligations of government for water provision.[21] In 2003, the WHO published *The Right to Water*, a document predicated on the assumption following General Comment No. 15 that such a right exists. The WHO explains that the right to water creates an obligation for governments to provide non-discriminatory access to sufficient, acceptable, physically accessible and affordable water.[22] Each of these

[17] Conca, 'The United States', p. 226.
[18] General Assembly Resolution 64/292, 'The human right to water and sanitation', UN Doc: A/Res/64/292.
[19] J. Budds and G. McGranahan, 'Are the debates on water privatization missing the point? Experiences from Africa, Asia and Latin America', *Environment and Urbanization*, 15 (2003), 87, 88.
[20] General Comment, para. 17.   [21] *Ibid.*, para. 12.
[22] WHO, *The Right to Water*, p. 12.

obligations is further defined by the WHO: a basic level of water service, for example, requires the provision of 20 litres of water per person per day, close enough that a round trip takes no more than thirty minutes.[23] Domestically and internationally, even making an accurate assessment about which citizens have access to a basic level of water services presents considerable practical challenges, especially as water needs and availability can change rapidly.

Nonetheless, as access to sufficient safe water is essential for the fulfilment of other explicit rights contained within general instruments, a human right to water is likely to become accepted at international law over time. In the interim, dialogue about whether access to water is a human right should not distract from the central fact of the necessity of water. Indeed, this fact alone should be sufficient to influence the treatment of water contracts by investment tribunals.

B   Scarce environmental resource

While water is arguably the content of a human right, it is also a tradable commodity. Under economic orthodoxy, the price determined by a perfectly functioning water market would reflect both the scarcity and value of water. The reality of water pricing is, however, far more complex. Value in a traditional market is determined by consumers' ability and willingness to pay, but the life-giving properties of water are theoretically of equal value to all people, regardless of their purchasing power. A high water price may discourage overuse by industry and households, but such a price signal should have no effect on that part of demand for water that is derived from biological needs. Further, where it is provided, water is generally supplied by a monopoly, as competition in the water market is minimal. Thus, the price of water is not a function of a competitive market but an administrative decision.[24]

A water price nonetheless serves two important functions. Even though the water market does not result in efficient rationing, a water price performs some rationing function by helping to reduce excessive water use. To ensure that essential water is available to a growing global population, effective use must be made of existing resources. The value people place on a resource increases when they are required to pay for it,

---

[23] *Ibid.*

[24] V. Petrova, 'At the frontiers of the rush for blue gold: Water privatisation and the human right to water', *Brooklyn Journal of International Law*, (31) (2005–6), 577, 592.

rather than receiving it for free. Charging a price for water encourages users to monitor their water use more carefully and may therefore reduce consumption. Secondly, collecting a fee from water users helps to cover the high costs of providing water. The body that supplies water must pay to build and maintain water collection facilities and infrastructure, test and treat water, transport water effectively, fix leaks quickly, and connect water to growing populations. In developing countries especially, payments by water consumers are an important source of revenue to cover the cost of water supply.

The price of water has serious consequences for social equity and for public health. Access to affordable potable water helps to prevent disease by ensuring hydration and improving hygiene. On the other hand, a household that is not connected to public water or that simply cannot afford to pay for it will turn to alternatives that may be harmful. The World Bank has estimated that households will not purchase water when it costs more than 5 per cent of their income.[25] Above this level, people will find water in other ways – often from polluted puddles or streams. Connection costs are another way in which water pricing can entrench inequality. The poorest members of society often live in those areas furthest from central water supplies. Communities in urban outskirts, for example, grow quickly and erratically, which makes water connection and transportation difficult. To cover these costs, public and private water suppliers often charge a connection fee.[26] Poor households that might have otherwise afforded the relatively low price per litre of public water may be unable to pay the lump sum fee for connection, and so are forced to depend on the more expensive, less frequently tested water sold by private street vendors.[27]

The price of water is therefore critical. It should be high enough to discourage excessive consumption and cover at least some of the costs of water provision, but not so high as to make water unaffordable. Maintaining a price for water that vulnerable members of society can afford may prevent recovery of the full cost of water provision, which helps to explain why water pricing has proved one of the greatest challenges for private water investors.

[25] CBC News, 'Whose hand on the tap?: Water privatisation in South Africa' (February 2003), www.cbc.ca/news/features/water/southafrica.html (last accessed 30 January 2011).
[26] See e.g. A. S. Holland, *The Water Business* (Macmillan, 2005), p. 24.
[27] Petrova, 'At the frontiers', p. 587.

III   The water business

Private-sector control over water supply remains limited compared with other utilities, but has grown fairly steadily for the past two decades. Approximately 5 per cent of the world's population receives their water from the private sector.[28] The provision of water is an attractive business opportunity, as water utilities are usually monopolies selling an essential resource. Nonetheless, generating a profitable water supply is made difficult by costly infrastructure, few opportunities to add value and the limits of a population's ability to pay for the water they need.

Decisions by governments to privatise their water supplies have often been influenced by external pressures. During the 1990s especially, the World Bank encouraged developing countries to privatise utilities including water, sometimes as a condition for receiving critical loans.[29] This movement towards services provision by the private sector was part of an ideology that stressed the efficiency of private management, but was also a pragmatic response to the need for large-scale investment in water infrastructure that developing country governments could not afford.[30] The privatisation of the water supply in Dar es Salaam, Tanzania provides an example of the process. The Tanzanian government managed its privatisation of Dar es Salaam water under World Bank supervision from 1997. The government requested bids from private actors, and awarded the lease contract to supply water to City Water, a predominantly international consortium that promised low water tariffs and considerable infrastructure investment.[31] In the proceedings that ultimately took place at ICSID, both Tanzania and an *amicus* brief suggested that the low prices of City Water's bid were miscalculated, perhaps to increase their chance of winning the contract; City Water claimed that the information they received from Tanzania was inaccurate. The tribunal concluded that the winning bid was 'poorly prepared'.[32] In effect, an inaccurate bid price was rewarded by the receipt of a water supply contract. Without the ability to fully recoup costs, the investment quickly floundered.

Even without an incentive to underestimate likely water prices, the costs of water provision are difficult to predict: the quantity of water available for supply is dependent on weather patterns; water

---

[28] Budds and McGranahan, 'Are the debates on water privatization missing the point?', p. 88.

[29] Petrova, 'At the frontiers', p. 585.

[30] Schreiber, 'Realising the right to water in international investment law', p. 446; Petrova, 'At the frontiers', p. 585.

[31] *Biwater Gauff*, paras. 102–3.   [32] *Ibid.*, para. 789.

infrastructure is expensive to build, monitor and maintain; water must be connected to growing populations, depending on the contract; and payment for water can be more difficult for a non-State actor to collect. When conditions change and the cost of water provision increases, there are few options to recoup costs except to raise water tariffs. As a consequence, large numbers of people who could previously afford water become unable to do so, particularly in developing countries.

The most dramatic example of the consequences of unaffordable water was the water war that erupted in Cochabamba, the third-largest city in Bolivia, in the early months of 2000. Privatisation of the city's water utilities following pressure by international organisations led to management by Bechtel and price rises of up to 300 per cent. Mass protests were organised in which 100,000 took to the street, one person was killed and more than one hundred were injured.[33] As a result, the contract was cancelled, and public water provision was resumed. Bechtel commenced proceedings at ICSID, but an international civil society campaign initiated by the journalist Jim Shultz was so successful that Bechtel settled its claim in January 2006 for a token sum, and a statement by the Bolivian government explained that the contract was ended due to civil unrest and not the actions of international shareholders.[34]

The foreign investment element of water investment is important. When the sale of public water utilities results in management by a domestic private actor, as occurs most often in developed countries, the contract is simply managed by the domestic legal system and governments will generally retain the ability to renegotiate the agreement in the public interest. The governments of such countries also have considerable bargaining power in their dealings with companies based within (or even outside) their jurisdiction. For example, the municipal water utilities in Atlanta, Georgia were privatised in 1999 and managed by United Water, the US subsidiary of the French environmental giant Suez. Four years later, following poor maintenance and a deterioration in water quality, the City of Atlanta resumed control over the water supply. There were no international investment proceedings; the two parties declared a 'joint decision to dissolve the relationship' and negotiated a settlement in which United Water paid net compensation to the City of Atlanta.[35]

---

[33] Holland, *The Water Business*, pp. 24–6.
[34] P. Harris, 'Bechtel, Bolivia resolve dispute', *Bilaterals.org* (19 February 2006), www.bilaterals.org/article.php3?id_article=3612 (last accessed 30 January 2011).
[35] City of Atlanta, 'City of Atlanta and United Water announce amicable dissolution of twenty-year water contract', Press Release of 24 January 2003, www.atlantaga.gov/media/

When a developing economy privatises its water provision, however, the successful bidder that takes over a lease contract for water utilities is generally a foreign company or consortium – and the legal consequences when the arrangement is unsuccessful are very different. Foreign investors are protected by the BIT, which was negotiated between the host State and the investor's national government. BITs exist primarily to attract foreign investment and, as such, are crowded with protections for investors more than for host States. Of particular relevance to water contracts, investors receive protection under the requirement that expropriation of an investment by State action be compensated, and the obligation that a State afford fair and equitable treatment to foreign investments.[36] Many actions by States that reduce the ability for foreign investors to make a profit can be legally challenged by proceedings before an international tribunal, most often an ICSID tribunal, which has the capacity to award substantial damages to an aggrieved investor.

IV State of the law

Foreign private water consortiums have had limited success to date receiving compensation from international investment tribunals for breaches of BITs following the repudiation by host States of water investment contracts. While this suggests that essential freshwater receives special treatment from investment tribunals, no clear principle has emerged to govern such cases. The two case studies below concern developing States, Tanzania and Argentina, which privatised parts of their water supply, then cancelled long-term contracts with foreign investors due to delivery problems. In both cases, the foreign investor brought claims to ICSID under the governing BIT. The Republic of Tanzania avoided paying compensation because the investing company had no value at the time of the expropriation. Argentina was required to pay damages for breach of its BIT with the United States, and while it successfully delayed the payment for several years, its application to have the award annulled was rejected. These two cases between them contain the most extensive discussion to date by ICSID tribunals concerning issues raised by private water contracts.

unitedwater_012403.aspx (last accessed 30 January 2011); CBC News 'No silver bullet: Water privatisation in Atlanta – a cautionary tale' (5 February 2003), www.cbc.ca/news/features/water/atlanta.html (last accessed 30 January 2011).
[36] Schreiber, 'Realising the right to water in international investment law', 447–64.

A   Biwater *v.* Tanzania

Dar es Salaam in Tanzania is a city of 3.5 million people, of whom only 100,000 have access to running water.[37] As part of a general push towards utility privatisation, the World Bank and International Monetary Fund, alongside the United Kingdom government, allocated funds to improve water infrastructure in Dar es Salaam on the condition that the water system be operated by a private actor. The Republic of Tanzania requested bids; City Water – a consortium including the British company Biwater, the German engineering firm Gauff, and the Tanzanian investor Superdoll Trailer Manufacturing Company – offered a very low water price,[38] and was chosen as the winning bidder in late 2002. City Water was awarded a ten-year contract to provide water and sewerage services on behalf of the Tanzanian public corporation responsible for such services.[39] The consortium also committed to bill consumers and to collect revenue, maintain and invest in infrastructure and to make new connections.

City Water's management of Dar es Salaam's water and sanitation services commenced in 2003. Problems began immediately and, within two years, the operation had become financially unviable. City Water's promised extension of water services and infrastructure investments had not taken place, and the consortium collected less revenue than the public corporation had done before it. City Water could not afford to pay for utility maintenance as the water pricing contained within its bid had drastically underestimated the costs of service provision. City Water sought a renegotiation of the terms of its contract, but was not permitted a sufficiently high price rise by the Tanzanian water authority to rescue its finances. In May 2005, the Tanzanian Minister of Water and Livestock Development purported to terminate the agreement and withdraw financial privileges that had previously been afforded to City Water. Most controversially, following a press release declaring the contract at an end, on 1 June 2008, the Tanzanian government deported the senior management of City Water, seized the company's assets and took over its management.[40]

Biwater Gauff commenced arbitration proceedings under the ICSID Convention in August 2005. Arbitrators Gary Born, Toby Landau QC and Bernard Hanotiau delivered the final award on 24 July 2008, which held that, although several of the actions of the Tanzanian government breached the governing BIT, Tanzania was not liable for damages.

---

[37] Rice, 'The water margin'.   [38] *Ibid.*
[39] *Biwater Gauff*, para. 9.   [40] *Ibid.*, para. 15.

The repudiation of the Biwater Gauff contract was not of itself a violation of the BIT, as Tanzania acted in its capacity as a contractual partner rather than exercising its governmental authority through actions *iure imperi*.[41] In assessing the claim by Biwater that Tanzania had carried out an expropriation, the tribunal considered the cumulative effects of behaviour by the government. It held that the combination of the minister's press comments, the political rally, the withdrawal of VAT exemption on purchases, the occupation of City Water's facilities, the usurpation of management control and the deportation of City Water staff constituted an expropriation of the investment of Biwater under the BIT. These same actions were also held by the tribunal to constitute a breach of the obligation under the BIT to provide Biwater fair and equitable treatment in governmental dealings with its investment.[42]

In separately determining remedies, the tribunal focused on whether Tanzania's actions in violation of the BIT had caused the loss suffered by Biwater.[43] It found that a combination of errors and mismanagement on the part of Biwater – poor bid preparation, failure to make early changes, difficulties in management and implementation leading to lack of income and the failure of the contract renegotiation process – meant that City Water had already ceased to be viable by the time of Tanzania's illegal actions.[44] As such, the tribunal concluded that 'none of the Republic's violations of the BIT caused the loss and damage for which BGT now claims compensation', and that Biwater's damages claims must therefore be dismissed.[45]

The reasoning of the tribunal makes few references to the importance of State control over critical water supply and does not appear to give this consideration significant weight. The tribunal considered, when deciding to accept an *amicus* brief, that the arbitration 'raises a number of issues of concern to the wider community in Tanzania', quoting from the award in *Methanex* v. *United States* in explaining that: 'The public interest in this arbitration arises from its subject-matter.'[46] The tribunal laid out the main arguments of the *amicus* brief in its decision, including their statement that water had been recognised as a human right by the United Nations Committee on Economic, Social and Cultural Rights.[47] The *amicus* expressed the opinion that the obligations of foreign investors

---

[41] *Ibid.*, paras. 458, 492.   [42] *Ibid.*, para. 605.   [43] *Ibid.*, para. 779.
[44] *Ibid.*, para. 789.   [45] *Ibid.*, para. 807.
[46] *Ibid.*, para. 358, referring to *Methanex Corp.* v. *United States* (Final Award of the Tribunal on Jurisdiction and Merits of 3 August 2005).
[47] *Biwater Gauff*, para. 379.

are at their highest where an investment concerns issues of human rights and sustainable development.[48] While the tribunal stated that it 'has found the *amicus*'s observations useful' and that the *amicus*'s argument had informed the tribunal's analysis, the award makes no further reference to the existence of a human right to water, nor gives any discussion of the consequences of such a right for investment law.

The second major consideration given by the tribunal to the nature of the subject matter of the dispute was rather more practical. Deciding that the tight timetable set by Tanzania for contract renegotiation prior to expropriation did not constitute a breach of the obligation to afford fair and equitable treatment, the tribunal reasoned that: 'At least in theory, and viewed at that time, this crisis could have threatened a vital public service and the situation therefore had to be resolved one way or the other in the near future.'[49] While the necessity of public water supply received little attention in the award, nonetheless the outcome reached by the tribunal effectively supported the decision by a State to take drastic measures to regain control of its water supply from a private supplier whose performance had been poor.[50]

B   Azurix *v.* Argentina

The province of Buenos Aires began the process of water privatisation in 1996, awarding a thirty-year contract to operate its water services to Azurix, owned by Enron.[51] The relationship broke down from 2001. The ICSID tribunal later constituted to consider this breakdown held that the Provincial government inaccurately blamed Azurix for a number of problems that arose with the water supply, including price rises and an algae outbreak.[52] The water contract, the tribunal found, was 'based on certain factual assumptions that did not turn out to be correct'.[53] The tribunal was critical of the Provincial government's 'unhelpful attitude',[54] for failing to deliver on promised infrastructure,[55] and for interference in the water contract for political gain.[56] In particular, the tribunal isolated public statements by the Provincial governor and other officials advising citizens not to pay their water bills to be verging on bad faith.[57] In October 2001, after a denial by the Province of any contractual breaches, Azurix terminated the water

---

[48] *Ibid.*, para. 380.   [49] *Ibid.*, para. 654.   [50] *Ibid.*, para. 486.
[51] *Azurix Corp.* (Award), paras. 38, 41, 55.   [52] *Ibid.*, para. 144.   [53] *Ibid.*, para. 143.
[54] *Ibid.*, para. 320.   [55] *Ibid.*, para. 155.   [56] *Ibid.*, para. 144.   [57] *Ibid.*, para. 376.

contract. This termination was rejected by an Executive Order of the Province in November 2001.[58] In February 2002, Azurix filed for bankruptcy and the Province then terminated the agreement in March 2002, alleging the fault of Azurix.[59]

The tribunal held in a decision of July 14 2006 that the actions of the Province did not amount to an expropriation due to the retention of control by Azurix over the water contract. They did, however, constitute a breach of the standard of fair and equitable treatment[60] and of the duty to afford full protection and security,[61] and were arbitrary.[62] Azurix was awarded damages of US$165.2 million, less than one-third the amount they had requested.[63] While Argentina successfully applied for a stay in its obligation to pay damages based on its costs following the Argentine financial crisis of the early 2000s, its attempt to annul the award was declared unsuccessful on 1 September 2009.[64]

Consideration of the significance of the subject matter of the contract was more extensive but less favourable in the *Azurix* award than it was in the *Biwater* decision. While acknowledging, for example, that Argentina raised the issue of compatibility of the applicable BIT with human rights treaties, the tribunal wrote that it 'fails to understand the incompatibility in the specifics of the instant case', given that services to consumers continued throughout the relevant period. Perhaps, had water services been threatened, human rights considerations might have been given greater weight (and analysis) by the investment tribunal. In its discussion of expropriation, the tribunal considered the application of an exception to State liability for expropriation where economic harm has been caused by a State's actions with legitimate public purpose.[65] It was sceptical of such a principle, given that a wide variety of expropriatory measures by a State could be considered to be for a public purpose and that such an exception would undermine the purpose of expropriation provisions. It explained, 'the issue is not so much whether the measure concerned is legitimate and serves a public purpose, but whether it is a measure that, being legitimate and serving a public purpose, should give rise to a compensation claim'.[66]

---

[58] *Ibid.*, para. 244.   [59] *Ibid.*, para. 245.   [60] *Ibid.*, para. 377.   [61] *Ibid.*, para. 408.
[62] *Ibid.*, para. 393.   [63] *Ibid.*, para. 442.
[64] *Azurix Corp.* v. *Argentine Republic* (ICSID Case No. ARB/01/12, Decision on Annulment of 1 September 2009).
[65] *Azurix Corp.* (Award), para. 310.   [66] *Ibid.*

V   Water and investment law

The importance of affordable, safe public water supply will generally require that foreign private water providers be subject to some State regulation. Such flexibility could be incorporated into investments in three main ways. In descending order of legal centralisation, a consistent treatment of water contracts could emerge from the awards of international investment tribunals; water (perhaps alongside other vital resources or rights) could be subject to special provisions within BITs; and the contracts governing water services could contain provisions that permit States to intervene when water supply was under threat.

The most practical solutions of these options are special legal treatment by investment tribunals and within individual water contracts. While a public purpose exception has not yet evolved to the point of receiving consistent treatment by tribunals, it offers the opportunity for States to use as a defence the vital nature of actions or regulations, even if they impair the profitability of a foreign investment. There are few areas in which the consequences of a malfunctioning international investment can be as harmful for communities as poor water services. Nonetheless, such a change would take place only gradually (aided, perhaps, by clearer recognition at international law of a human right to water), and remains controversial.[67] This gives States little guidance in attempting to resolve quickly a developing problem with a private water provider.

Careful design of water services contracts to permit a State to intervene in the interests of serious risk to public health may be a more effective option for newly negotiated private water contracts. A definition of public-health risk drafted by both the private investor and the State actor would assist government later in knowing when and how to take action in the case of service deterioration. It would also make plain the nature of the obligation by the private company to the communities it services and the consequences of mismanagement.

VI   Conclusion

Foreign investment in privatised water services can be a vital source of capital, paying for costly infrastructure to provide safe water to those who might otherwise live without it. To date, water investments have

[67] *Ibid.*

soured for a combination of reasons: the incentive for companies to underestimate water price, the inherent difficulties in making profit from water provision and the lack of options available to governments when a private water operation is not run well.

Even before access to safe water is universally recognised as a human right, the biological necessity of fresh water is sufficient reason for private water contracts to receive special treatment under investment law. Foreign investment in a city's water supply should be one of several reasonable options available to a government seeking to improve water infrastructure for its citizens. However, it can only be an acceptable policy choice if governments have the ability to protect the continuity and affordability of water for their citizens. A water business is more likely to be viable if a consortium can plan the investment on its own terms subject to requirements set by a government with the power to end an investment that causes harm to its citizens.

Given the nature of the interests involved, it is likely that the inter-action between international investment law and the provision of water services will continue to generate controversy, especially as a human right to water becomes more broadly recognised. This chapter has argued for the development of a more balanced approach to the accom-modation of all those relevant interests. In so doing, it has proposed several possible mechanisms through which such a goal could be achieved, but also recognises that the exploration of the issues surround-ing investment law and water are very much in their infancy and will continue to evolve over time.

25

Economic development at the core of the international investment regime

OMAR E. GARCÍA-BOLÍVAR

I Introduction

It is well known that a dispute will only fall within the jurisdiction of the International Centre for Settlement of Investment Disputes (ICSID) if the dispute directly arises out of an 'investment', as is provided by Article 25(1) of the Convention for the Settlement of Investment Disputes between States and Nationals of other States (ICSID Convention).[1] However, not only does the ICSID Convention fail to provide any definition of what constitutes an 'investment', the drafters of the ICSID Convention, in fact, made an express decision not to include such a definition. This absence has given rise to interesting issues of interpretation as ICSID tribunals have sought to arrive at an understanding of how the term 'investment' should be properly understood for the purposes of the ICSID Convention. Various elements have been proposed in defining what is and what is not 'an ICSID investment', including the existence of contribution, certain duration, risk, participation, and contribution to the development of the host State.[2] In considering these characteristics of an 'investment', this chapter argues that the most important element is the aim of furthering the economic development of the host State. Indeed, it is argued that this constitutes the most critical element in any definition of investment as it is understood under the ICSID Convention.

At a fundamental level, the arguments put forward in this chapter are grounded in the nature of the State itself. Inarguably, the welfare and

---

[1] Convention for the Settlement of Investment Disputes between States and Nationals of other States, opened for signature 18 March 1965, 575 UNTS 159 (entered into force 14 October 1966) (ICSID Convention).

[2] See e.g. *Salini Costruttori SpA and Italstrade SpA* v. *Morocco* (ICSID Case No. ARB/00/4, Decision on Jurisdiction of 23 July 2001), para. 52.

development of their nationals and residents is of primary concern to States. It is also clear that in promoting that development, significant amounts of capital can be required. Accordingly, a range of strategies is often adopted by States to attract that capital, a key one of which is enhancing the domestic investment climate through entering into international legal instruments that provide protection to foreign investment. In concluding international investment agreements (IIAs), States agree to grant international protection to foreign investments – and, in return, they expect to attract the capital needed to promote their economic development. For host States, this assumption is a central, if often unarticulated, rationale behind the conclusion of the agreement. For this reason, it is important to consider the intention of States when entering into IIAs and to gain a proper understanding of why the treaties were concluded. This understanding could, in turn, influence the interpretation of the IIAs' provisions under international law. The argument presented in this chapter is that this type of analysis should play an important role in the interpretation and application of IIAs, and in adjudicating fair solutions to the disputes that might arise between investors and States.

II Intentions of States in international investment law

The regime for the international protection of foreign investment is sustained by two streams. On the one hand, foreign investors and their investments are granted international protection through IIAs. On the other hand, the regime is informed by principles of customary international law and general principles of law that have evolved over time. Differing somewhat from the formation-process of customary international law and general principles of law, IIAs embody the express manifestation of States' intentions. There are, however, even then, unspoken assumptions contained within these agreements. For example, it is clear that States enter into IIAs which grant protection to foreign investments in the expectation that this will enhance the chances of attracting capital, and that this will, in turn, promote their economic development. This rationale, however, does not innately extend to a willingness to attract any kind of foreign capital, at all costs. Rather, the intention of States in devising a set of policies aimed at protecting the interests of foreigners should be considered, interpreted rationally, and examined in good faith, taking into account all the relevant circumstances – and this should include the anticipated development benefits of those policies.

Development – generally understood as the general welfare of a people[3] – is a key goal of States, and capital is but a means of financing it. Traditionally, the development trajectories of many States have been self-financed through revenues obtained from either direct exploitation of each country's resources or by collecting duties from those that have conducted business within their boundaries. Over time, the sources of capital have expanded to include the obtaining of credit and the provision of international aid. And more recently, countries have rightly appreciated that foreign investment could also be a significant means of financing and promoting the welfare of their peoples.

As a way of enhancing their attractiveness to foreign investors, a substantial number of countries have granted to foreign capital internationally-enforceable treatment guarantees through IIAs. On the assumption that such guarantees will diminish the non-commercial risk of doing business in certain States, many capital-exporting States have entered into these agreements. From the perspective of the host State, the rationale for doing so, of course, has been to attract the much-needed capital that would finance the development projects and policies of the country, not simply foreign capital per se. In this sense, foreign investments are in the same category as public revenues, credit and aid – they are all means to finance the development of the recipient State.

Bearing this in mind, it becomes clear that it is important to consider in the interpretation of IIAs the intention of States when entering into those agreements. In some cases, that interpretation is relatively straight-forward as the IIA itself identifies the intentions of the States Parties, and sets out the object and purpose of the agreement. But in other instances, the States' intentions are not expressly stated. Where this is the case, it is suggested that the approach adopted by the arbitrators should be one of looking at all the surrounding circumstances, not only at the preamble and preparatory work, but also at the *raison d'être* of the States them-selves as well as the reasons for entering into the agreement – in other words, the promotion of the welfare and development of communities within the host State.

---

[3] See e.g. Amartya Sen, *Development as Freedom* (1999), p. xii: 'Development consists of the removal of various types of unfreedoms that leave people with little choice and little opportunity of exercising their reasoned agency. The removal of substantial unfreedoms, it is argued here, is constitutive of development.'

III Economic development as expressed in relevant international instruments

A The relevance of the parties' intentions in treaty interpretation

According to Article 31(1) of the Vienna Convention on the Law of the Treaties (VCLT), treaties shall be interpreted 'in good faith in accordance with the ordinary meaning to be given to the terms of the treaty in their context and in the light of its object and purpose'.[4] Article 31(2) of the VCLT goes on to provide that the 'context', for the purposes of treaty interpretation, shall include the text of the treaty, including its preambles and annexes, as well as any subsequent agreement regarding the interpretation of the treaty, and any subsequent practice in the application of the treaty.[5] Article 32 provides further that 'Recourse may be had to supplementary means of interpretation', including the *travaux préparatoires* of the treaty, and the circumstances of its conclusion, 'in order to confirm the meaning resulting from the application of article 31, or to determine the meaning when the interpretation according to article 31: (a) leaves the meaning ambiguous or obscure; or (b) leads to a result which is manifestly absurd or unreasonable'.[6] These provisions of the VCLT have been accepted by the International Court of Justice and by the international community as expressions of customary international law.[7] Thus, when called upon to interpret IIAs, arbitrators should make an effort to understand the intention of the State Parties when entering into these agreements. The difficulty that arises, of course, is when the purpose is not given a detailed articulation in the wording of the treaty, as is the case with a significant number of IIAs. This absence of a fully expressed purpose can prove problematic for host States when protection is sought by investors pursuant to an IIA with a stated purpose of promoting foreign investment that does not make reference to the development of the State Parties. Discounting the full purpose of the IIA from the host State's perspective may confer the treaty's protection to foreign investments that could be detrimental to the development

---

[4] Vienna Convention on the Law of Treaties, opened for signature 23 May 1969, 1155 UNTS 311, Art. 31(1) (entered into force 27 January 1980) (VCLT).

[5] *Ibid.*, Art. 31(2).   [6] *Ibid.*, Art. 32.

[7] e.g. *Kasikili/Sedudu Island (Botswana/Namibia)* [1999] ICJ Rep, p. 1059, para. 18; see also *Phoenix Action Ltd* v. *Czech Republic* (Decision on Jurisdiction of 15 April 2009), para. 76; see also *Malaysian Historical Salvors Sdn Bhd* v. *Malaysia* (ICSID Case No. ARB/05/10, Decision on Annulment of 16 April 2009), para. 56.

policies of the host State rather than supportive.[8] This would lead to a result quite contrary to the original intention of the State Parties in concluding the agreement and, accordingly, such an approach should be avoided by arbitrators in interpreting IIAs in disputes between host States and investors.

B   Economic development as a goal of relevant international instruments

1   The International Centre for Settlement of Investment Disputes

Support for the position advocated in this chapter can be drawn from a number of international instruments. In particular, the ICSID Convention has addressed the question of the purpose of IIAs by means of textual reference to economic development in its preamble where it states: 'Considering the need for international cooperation for economic development, and the role of private international investment therein.'[9]

While the report from the Executive Directors states that the primary purpose of the Convention is to stimulate international investment flows, it underlines the body's desire to address the interests of both investors and States:

> 12. . . . Adherence to the Convention by a country would provide additional inducement and stimulate a larger flow of private international investment into its territories, which is the primary purpose of the Convention.
>
> 13. . . . The provisions of the Convention maintain a careful balance between the interests of investors and those of host States.[10]

Giving further weight to the importance of economic development to the relationship between foreign investors, capital flows and host States, there is also a clear link between ICSID and the World Bank, which has strong developmental goals in its lending practices. From the preamble

---

[8] Examples of detrimental foreign investments protected under IIAs are provided in Howard Mann, *Private Rights, Public Problems: A guide to the NAFTA's controversial chapter on investor rights* (Winnipeg: IISD, 2001), http://www.iisd.org/publications/publication.asp?pno=270 (last accessed 5 November 2010).

[9] The full text of the ICSID Convention, Regulations and Rules are available on the World Bank website: www.worldbank.org/icsid (last accessed 5 November 2010).

[10] Report of the Executive Directors of the International Bank for Reconstruction and Development on the Convention on the Settlement of Investment Disputes between States and Nationals of other States, www.worldbank.org/icsid (last accessed 5 November 2010).

of the ICSID Convention it can be seen that the fifth preambular paragraph states: 'Desiring to establish such facilities under the auspices of the International Bank for Reconstruction and Development.' The purpose of the International Bank for Reconstruction and Development (IBRD), one of the entities that comprise the World Bank, is, among others, to facilitate and encourage international investment for: (a) productive purposes; (b) for the development of the productive resources of countries to increase productivity, standards of living and conditions of labour.[11] Thus, investments not devoted to productive purposes, such as those undertaken solely for private gain and speculative purposes, and those that do not develop the productive resources of the host State and do not impact positively the productivity or increase the standards of living or labour conditions, are contrary to the objectives of the World Bank and should, therefore, also be considered to fall outside the ambit of ICSID.

Furthermore, ICSID is, of course, part of the World Bank Group, together with the IBRD and other multilateral institutions. As portrayed by the World Bank Group on its website, ICSID complements the overall mission of the group on helping 'People help themselves and their environment by providing resources, sharing knowledge, building capacity and forging partnerships in the public and private sectors'.[12]

The level of co-operation between ICSID and the World Bank Group exceeds that of merely sharing premises, as Article 2 of the ICSID Convention states. There is a financial linkage, as any excess in expenditure which the Centre cannot meet shall be borne by the Bank.[13] There is also an operational linkage as the president of the Bank is also the chairman of the Administrative Council of ICSID,[14] and has the authority, among other things, to appoint arbitrators in given circumstances.[15] More importantly, perhaps, there is also a shared cultural approach. Embedding ICSID within the World Bank framework inherently places it within a context of framing capital flows as a means to an end, rather than as the goal themselves. In particular, this contextual setting necessarily requires an emphasis on the developmental benefits of investment

---

[11] IBRD Articles of Agreement, Art. I, http://web.worldbank.org/WBSITE/EXTERNAL/ EXTABOUTUS/0,contentMDK:20049563~pagePK:43912~menuPK:58863~piPK:36602,00. html#I1 (last accessed on December 6, 2010).

[12] See the website of the World Bank at: http://web.worldbank.org/WBSITE/EXTERNAL/ EXTABOUTUS/0,pagePK:50004410~piPK:36602~theSitePK:29708,00.html (last accessed 5 November 2010).

[13] ICSID Convention, Art. 17.   [14] *Ibid.*, Art. 5.   [15] *Ibid.*, Art. 38.

inflows for recipient States. Thus, ICSID is not just another arbitration centre. It is a unique arbitration facility with a purpose that goes beyond the resolution of disputes between investors and States. It has an institutional role designed by the parties to the ICSID Convention, but it also has a mission that needs to be consistent with the multilateral entities with which it is associated – and that purpose cannot be detached from the promotion of the economic development of host States.

2   International investment agreements

The preamble to the Energy Charter Treaty,[16] a multilateral treaty which includes provisions on the promotion and protection of investments, expressly states that the Charter's measures to liberalise the energy sector are meant to spur economic development likened to economic growth: 'Wishing to implement the basic concept of the European Energy Charter initiative which is to catalyse economic growth by means of measures to liberalize investment and trade in energy.'[17]

In contrast to the ECT, the majority of IIAs contain either no reference to economic development or use ambiguous language in defining their object and purpose and limit their purpose to the promotion and protection of foreign investment, requiring those seeking to interpret them to engage in a deeper teleological interpretation. The issue of interpretation is often further complicated in the case of investment provisions within free trade agreements. For example, Chapter 11 of the North America Free Trade Agreement deals with investments but does not mention economic development.[18] For this reason, it is suggested that the purpose, objective and preambular statements of NAFTA as a whole should be applicable to the investment chapter. In particular, several statements in the preamble indicate that the treaty's obligations are to be considered in a broader context. This is evidenced by the State Parties resolving to:

---

[16] Energy Charter Treaty, opened for signature 17 December 1994, (1995) 34 ILM 360 (entered into force 16 April 1998) (ECT).

[17] *Ibid.*, preamble. Art. 2 of the ECT reinforces the economic development objective by referring to the Charter's general objectives, stating, 'This Treaty establishes a legal framework in order to promote long-term cooperation in the energy field, based on complementarities and mutual benefits, in accordance with the objectives and principles of the Charter.'

[18] North American Free Trade Agreement, signed 17 December 1992, United States–Canada–Mexico, 32 ILM 289 (entered into force 1 January 1994) (NAFTA), www.international.gc.ca/trade-agreements-accords-commerciaux/agr-acc/nafta-alena/texte/index.aspx (last accessed 5 November 2010).

CONTRIBUTE to the harmonious development and expansion of world
trade and provide a catalyst to broader international cooperation; . . .

ENSURE a predictable commercial framework for business planning and
investment; . . .

UNDERTAKE each of the preceding in a manner consistent with environmental protection and conservation;

PRESERVE their flexibility to safeguard the public welfare;

PROMOTE sustainable development;

STRENGTHEN the development and enforcement of environmental laws
and regulations; and

PROTECT, enhance and enforce basic workers' rights.[19]

Taken together, these statements point to an overarching approach,
intended to inform the implementation of NAFTA, that has a broader
focus than solely that of trade and investment promotion. The factors
for consideration are, indeed, even more expansive than the concept of
economic development, although clearly encompassing it, and also
include wider social, human rights and environmental aspects.

Similarly, the 2004 US Model BIT also emphasises the implicit bargain
between capital-exporting and host States, recognising that 'agreement
on the treatment to be accorded such investment will stimulate the flow
of private capital and the economic development of the parties' and
states that signatories agree that 'a stable framework for investment will
maximize effective utilization of economic resources and improve living
standards'.[20] Thus, there is an indication that the intention of State
Parties entering into agreements based on this Model BIT is also to
encourage economic development within the host State through foreign
investment inflows as well as to provide international protection for
those investments. The interdependence between the provision of protective treatment for investment and the stimulation of economic development has, perhaps, not been spelled out in the clearest of ways, and
this lack of express linkage within the operative text of the treaty could
give rise to different interpretations. However, the fact that the preamble
of the Model BIT refers specifically to economic development should be
taken to indicate that the purpose of agreements following this model
is to protect foreign investments so as to attract capital and foster
the economic development of the State Parties involved. On this basis,

---

[19] *Ibid.*, preamble.

[20] Treaty between the Government of the United States Of America and the Government
of [Country] Concerning the Encouragement and Reciprocal Protection of Investment
(US BIT Model (2004)), http://ita.law.uvic.ca/investmenttreaties.htm (last accessed
5 November 2010).

it may be possible to develop this line of reasoning further and argue that treaty protection should be denied to investments that are not beneficial for the economic development of the recipient country.

Other BITs also include references to the promotion of economic growth in the economies of the States Parties. The BIT between Cuba and the United Kingdom, for instance, illustrates the manner in which the assumption that foreign investment promotes economic growth is often found in IIAs. It highlights the desire of the parties to create favourable conditions for foreign investment while recognising that the agreement will 'contribute to the stimulation of business initiative and will increase prosperity in both States'.[21]

The BIT between Germany and Israel also mentions the effect that investor protection will have on mutual prosperity, but the language is ambiguous and fails to make a strong case on behalf of economic development as the purpose for protecting foreign investments.[22] Provisions expressed in such a form could certainly provide grounds for a narrow interpretation of the intention of the parties to the agreement. In so doing, this could circumscribe the discretion implicitly bestowed on host States to limit the scope of the treaty's protection to solely those investments that enhance their development trajectories.

Another objective common to many IIAs is the enhancement of economic co-operation. For instance, the stated purpose of the Sweden–Venezuela BIT is the intensification of economic co-operation for the mutual benefit of both countries and for the creation of conditions conducive to investment.[23] The Spain–China BIT also highlights the desire of the parties to develop their economic co-operation.[24] In the

[21] Agreement between the Government of the United Kingdom of Great Britain and Northern Ireland and the Government of the Republic of Cuba for the Promotion and Protection of Investments, signed on 30 January 1995 (entered into force 11 May 1995), www.unctad.org/sections/dite/iia/docs/bits/cuba_uk.pdf (last accessed 5 November 2010).

[22] Treaty between the Federal Republic of Germany and the State of Israel concerning the Encouragement and Reciprocal Protection of Investments, signed on 24 June 1976, www.unctad.org/sections/dite/iia/docs/bits/germany_israel.pdf (last accessed 5 November 2010).

[23] Agreement between the Government of the Kingdom of Sweden and the Government of the Republic of Venezuela on the Promotion and the Reciprocal Protection of Investments, signed on 25 November 1996 (entered into force on January 5, 1998), www.unctad.org/sections/dite/iia/docs/bits/sweden_venezuela_sp_eng.pdf (last accessed 5 November 2010).

[24] Acuerdo para la Proteccion y Fomento Recipricos de Inversiones entre el Reino de Espana y la Republica Popular de China, signed on 6 Feburary 1992, www.unctad.org/sections/dite/iia/docs/bits/spain_china_sp.pdf (last accessed 8 December 2010).

BIT between Germany and the People's Republic of China, the parties express a desire to develop bilateral 'economic cooperation' and 'to create favorable conditions for investment' between signatories.[25] The China–Argentina BIT also includes economic co-operation and the creation of favourable investment conditions amongst its objectives, recognising that 'the promotion and protection of such investments through an agreement stimulates business initiatives in this field'.[26]

Non-governmental organisations have also expressly articulated the implicit intentions of host States in entering into IIAs. Of particular note is the 2005 International Institute for Sustainable Development (IISD) draft Model Agreement on International Investment, which defines its purpose as the promotion of long-term investment that supports sustainable development.[27] The Model also refers to a necessary balance between the rights and obligations between and among investors and host countries.

In summary, the manner in which IIAs tend to define their purpose leaves significant room for interpretation contrary to the interests and unstated objectives of party States when protecting foreign investments. This is clearly unsatisfactory, but with arbitral interpretations of IIAs that accurately reflect the implicit intentions of host States, the potential negative impact on their economic development could be lessened.

IV   Economic development as considered in the jurisprudence of arbitral tribunals

Most cases on the relevance of economic development in international investment law have dealt with it in the context of an ICSID protected investment. As the ICSID Convention does not define the term 'investment', tribunals have considered whether there are criteria that can be read into its provisions to determine when an investment has been made

---

[25] Agreement between the People's Republic of China and the Federal Republic of Germany on the Encouragement and Reciprocal Protection of Investments, signed on 1 December 2003, www.unctad.org/sections/dite/iia/docs/bits/china_germany.pdf (last accessed 8 December 2010).

[26] Agreement between the Government of the People's Republic of China and the Government of the Argentine Republic on the Promotion and Reciprocal Protection of Investments, signed on 5 November 1992, www.unctad.org/sections/dite/iia/docs/bits/argentina_china.pdf (last accessed 8 December 2010).

[27] The IISD Model International Agreement on Investment for Sustainable Development is available at the IISD website: http://www.iisd.org/publications/pub.aspx?id=685 (last accessed 5 November 2010).

for the purposes of the ICSID Convention; this being an issue that, in principle, is very important for jurisdictional reasons.

To date, the most emblematic case has been that of *Salini*, which gave rise to what is now known as the '*Salini* test'. In *Salini Costruttori SpA and Italstrade SpA* v. *Morocco*,[28] the tribunal considered the criteria generally identified by the Convention's commentators, indicating that those were: 'contributions, a certain duration of performance of the contract, and a participation in the risks of the transaction'.[29] The tribunal also noted that 'one may add the contribution to the economic development of the host State of the investment as an added condition'.[30] On the facts, the tribunal found that a highway construction contract fulfilled the criteria. Even with respect to the component of 'risk', the tribunal indicated that a construction project which lasts for several years, for which total costs cannot be established with certainty in advance, created an undeniable risk for the contractor. Thus, a construction operation could be qualified as an investment, and the disputes that arose directly out of it were susceptible to being heard by a tribunal established under the ICSID Convention. In connection with the economic development requirement, the tribunal commented that in most countries construction of infrastructure falls under the tasks to be carried out by the State or by other public authorities. It then mentioned that the highway in question served the public interest and that the claimant companies were also able to provide the host State with know-how in relation to the work.[31]

The tribunal also expressed the view that the elements to be considered when determining whether there is an investment for the purposes of the ICSID Convention may be 'interdependent', in the sense that 'the risks of the transaction may depend on the contributions and the duration of the performance of the contract'.[32] In this regard, the tribunal held that the conditions were to be assessed 'globally'.[33]

Notably, for the tribunal to reach the conclusion that economic development was one of the elements to take into account in order to determine the existence of an investment under the ICSID Convention, it looked at the purpose of that treaty as mentioned in its preamble.[34]

---

[28] *Salini Costruttori SpA and Italstrade SpA* v. *Morocco* (ICSID Case No. ARB/00/4, Decision on Jurisdiction of 23 July 2001).
[29] *Ibid.*, para. 52.
[30] *Ibid.* See also Christoph Schreuer *et al.*, *The ICSID Convention: A commentary*, 2nd edn (Cambridge University Press, 2009), Art. 25, paras. 153–74.
[31] *Salini* v. *Morocco*, para. 57.   [32] *Ibid.*, para. 52.   [33] *Ibid.*   [34] *Ibid.*, para. 52.

The tribunal went on to identify at least two of the criteria needed for an investment to contribute to the economic development of the host State: (a) the investment should be beneficial to the public interest; and (b) there should be some transfer of know-how.[35]

The *Salini* test has been followed by tribunals in many subsequent disputes, some in whole, some in part and some with subtle changes.[36] Others have taken a different approach in connection with the fourth criterion. One such case of significance is *Malaysian Historical Salvors Sdn Bhd* v. *Malaysia* (*MHS*).[37] In this award, subsequently annulled by an ad hoc Annulment Committee, the sole arbitrator found that a positive and significant contribution to the economic development of the host country was a requirement for the investment to come under the protection of the ICSID Convention. Significantly, the tribunal held that enhancing the gross domestic product (GDP) of the local economy was the factor that determined the criterion of economic development.[38] The tribunal then qualified this, and stated that the enhancement of GDP would have to be by more than a small amount in order for the investment to be protected by the ICSID Convention. The tribunal stated:

> The weight of the authorities cited above swings in favour of requiring a significant contribution to be made to the host State's economy. Were there not the requirement of significance, any contract which enhances the Gross Domestic Product of an economy by any amount, however small, would qualify as an 'investment'.[39]

As noted above, the award in *MHS* was subsequently annulled by an ICSID ad hoc Committee on the issue of whether or not there had been an 'investment'.[40] But one of the members of the ad hoc Committee, Judge Mohamed Shahabuddeen, issued a strong dissenting opinion in

---

[35] The tribunal said: 'It cannot be seriously contested that the highway shall serve the public interest. Finally, the Italian companies were also able to provide the host State of the investment with know-how . . .': *ibid.*, para. 57.

[36] e.g., *Joy Mining Machinery Limited* v. *Egypt* (ICSID Case No. ARB/03/11, Decision on Jurisdiction of 23 July 2001), para. 53; *Jan de Nul NV* v. *Egypt* (ICSID Case No. ARB/04/13, Decision on Jurisdiction of 16 June 2006), para. 91; *Helnan International Hotels A/S* v. *Egypt* (ICSID Case No. ARB/05/19, Decision on Jurisdiction of 17 October 2006), para. 77; *Malaysian Historical Salvors Sdn Bhd* v. *Malaysia* (ICSID Case No. ARB/05/10, Award on Jurisdiction of 17 May 2007), paras. 73–4.

[37] *Malaysian Historical Salvors Sdn Bhd* v. *Malaysia* (ICSID Case No. ARB/05/10, Award on Jurisdiction of 17 May 2007).

[38] *Ibid.*, para. 123.   [39] *Ibid.*

[40] *Malaysian Historical Salvors Sdn Bhd* v. *Malaysia* (ICSID Case No. ARB/05/10, Decision on Annulment of 16 April 2009).

which he stressed the importance of economic development in the definition of investment under ICSID. In his dissenting opinion, he observed that:

> An ICSID investment might indeed be made in favour of private entities but not for their own enrichment exclusively: only on the basis that, though made in favour of private entities, such an investment would – not might – promote the economic development of the host State.[41]

He also noted that:

> the preamble [of the ICSID Convention] reflects an inference that the very purpose of an ICSID investment is to contribute to the economic development of the host State. . . . it is not merely that 'international investment plays a role in economic development' of the host State: international investment must play a role in the economic development of the host State if the investment is to rank as an ICSID investment and be entitled to the protection of the ICSID settlement procedures; that requirement is a condition of an ICSID investment.[42]

In an earlier case, *Ceskoslovenska obchodni banka, a.s.* v. *Slovak Republic* (*CSOB*),[43] it was concluded that the investment had to have a positive impact on the host State's development. The tribunal considered that the phrase found in the preamble to the ICSID Convention 'permits an inference that an international transaction which contributes to cooperation designed to promote the economic development of a Contracting State may be deemed to be an investment as that term is understood in the Convention'.[44] In an indirect fashion, this viewpoint had previously been alluded to by the ICSID tribunal in *Amco* v. *Indonesia* when it concluded that:

> The Convention is aimed to protect, to the same extent and with the same vigour the investor and the host State, not forgetting that to protect investments is to protect the general interest of development and of developing countries.[45]

Thus, if one combines the criteria for determining a contribution to economic development as applied by the ICSID tribunals in *Salini*, *MHS*

---

[41] *Ibid.* (Dissenting Opinion of Judge Mohamed Shahabuddeen), para. 17.

[42] *Ibid.*, paras. 28–9.

[43] *Ceskoslovenska obchodni banka, a.s.* v. *Slovak Republic* (ICSID Case No. ARB/97/4, Decision on Jurisdiction of 24 May 1999).

[44] *Ibid.*, para. 64.

[45] *Amco Asia Corporation* v. *Indonesia* (ICSID Case No. ARB/81/1, Decision on Jurisdiction of 25 September 1983); See also *ibid.* (Award of 20 November 1984).

and *CSOB*, it can be concluded that the investment must: (a) be made for the public interest; (b) transfer know-how; (c) enhance the GDP of the host State; and (d) have a positive impact on the host State's development.

In direct contrast, other tribunals considering the term 'investment' within the meaning of the ICSID Convention have taken a markedly different approach to the element of a contribution to economic development. Most significantly, the majority of these cases have one element in common – they have rejected or downplayed the criterion of economic development due to the perceived difficulty or impossibility of ascertaining its scope.

At one end of the spectrum, the ad hoc Annulment Committee in *Patrick Mitchell* v. *Democratic Republic of Congo* watered down the importance of the criterion, stating that:

> The existence of a contribution to the economic development of the host State as an essential – although not sufficient – characteristic or unquestionable criterion of the investment, does not mean that this chapter must always be sizable or successful; and, of course, ICSID tribunals do not have to evaluate the real contribution of the operation in question. It suffices for the operation to contribute in one way or another to the economic development of the host State, and this concept of economic development is, in any event, extremely broad and also variable depending on the case.[46]

A more explicit dismissal of the criterion can be found in *L.E.S.I. SpA et ASTALDI SpA* v. *Algeria*. In this award, the tribunal took the view that it did not seem necessary that the investment contribute to the economic development of the country; this was a condition that the tribunal considered to be difficult to establish, and one that was implicitly covered by the other three elements of an 'investment'.[47]

In *Phoenix Action Ltd* v. *Czech Republic*, the tribunal did not exactly deny that contribution to economic development was a criterion in defining an ICSID protected investment, although, in practical terms, it comes close to doing so. Rather, the tribunal rejected its applicability based on the logistical difficulties in measuring a contribution to development. It stated: 'It is the Tribunal's view that the contribution of an international investment to the *development* of the host State is

---

[46] *Patrick Mitchell* v. *Democratic Republic of Congo* (ICSID Case No. ARB/99/7, Decision on Annulment of 1 November 2006), para. 33.

[47] *L.E.S.I. SpA et ASTALDI SpA* v. *Algeria* (ICSID Case No. ARB/05/3, Decision of 12 July 2006), para. 73(iv).

impossible to ascertain – the more so as there are highly diverging views on what constitutes "development".[48] Subsequently, however, the tribunal stated: 'The Tribunal wishes to recall that the object of the Washington Convention is to encourage and protect *international investment made for the purpose of contributing to the economy of the host State* . . . This has to be read in light of the first words of the Preamble of the ICSID Convention, referring to "the need for *international cooperation for economic development,* and the role of private international investment therein."'[49]

Thus, the tribunal did, in fact, point out that the purpose of the ICSID Convention was to encourage foreign investment for economic development. That being the case, it should have followed that for investments to be protected under the ICSID system they would have needed to have contributed to the economic development of the host country. The tribunal, however, declined to engage with such an approach and, instead, adopted a frustratingly contradictory position, the effect of which is arguably to deny the full realisation of the purpose of the Convention.

More recently, in *Saba Fakes* v. *Turkey* the tribunal held that while Article 25(1) of the ICSID Convention provides for an objective definition of an investment, this definition is comprised of three criteria, namely (i) a contribution, (ii) a certain duration, and (iii) an element of risk. The tribunal added that: 'Neither the text, nor the object and purpose of the Convention commands that any other criteria be read into this definition.'[50] However, the *Saba Fakes* tribunal accepted that the economic development of a host State is one of the proclaimed objectives of the ICSID Convention.[51] But it said that this objective was not 'in and of itself an independent criterion for the definition of an investment'.[52] It followed, for the tribunal, that the promotion and protection of investments in host States was expected to contribute to their economic development: it would be 'an expected consequence, not a separate requirement'.[53] Accordingly, the tribunal refused to interpret Article 25(1) in its context and in light of the object and purpose of the ICSID Convention, even though it had admitted that the economic development of the host State was an objective of the ICSID Convention. The tribunal considered that States did not pursue foreign investment as

---

[48] *Phoenix Action Ltd* v. *Czech Republic* (ICSID Case No. ARB/06/5, Decision on Jurisdiction of 15 April 2009), para. 85 (emphasis in original).
[49] *Ibid.,* para 87 (footnotes omitted) (emphasis in original).
[50] *Saba Fakes* v. *Turkey* (ICSID Case No. ARB/07/20, Award of 14 July 2010), para. 121.
[51] *Ibid.,* para. 111.   [52] *Ibid.*   [53] *Ibid.*

a means of financing that development but as an end per se. Thus, a contribution to the economic development of the host State was not a defining requirement for an investment to be protected by the ICSID Convention.

Other tribunals have looked at the purpose of IIAs, not so much to constrain explorations into the definition of economic development, but to consider the goal of protecting the interests of the investors. For example, in *Siemens AG* v. *Argentina*,[54] the tribunal analysed the purpose of the Germany–Argentina BIT to find that the agreement was meant to promote investment and create conditions favourable to investors. The tribunal ruled that the BIT should be interpreted in this way, stating that: 'The Tribunal shall be guided by the purpose of the Treaty as expressed in its title and preamble. It is a treaty "to protect" and "to promote" investments . . . The intention of the parties is clear. It is to create favorable conditions for investments and to stimulate private initiative.'[55] In this case, the analysis of the treaty's purpose of promoting investment allowed the tribunal to extend the treaty's protection beyond its text. In a further example of this type of analysis, the tribunal in *MTD Equity Sdn. Bhd. and MTD Chile SA* v. *Chile* referred to the BIT's purpose, stating that: 'in terms of the BIT, fair and equitable treatment should be understood to be treatment in an even-handed and just manner, conducive to fostering the promotion of foreign investment'.[56]

In a recent case which was not brought under the ICSID Convention, *Romak* v. *Uzbekistan*, the tribunal constituted under the UNCITRAL Rules analysed the term 'investments' under the BIT between the Swiss Confederation and the Republic of Uzbekistan. Stating *a priori* that the tribunal was not bound to follow previous arbitral decisions, it categorised the approaches of previous arbitral tribunals into the 'conceptualist' approach, under which there is a definition of 'investment' that entails certain elements which must be present in order to assert jurisdiction *ratione materiae*; and the 'pragmatic' approach under which the presence of certain non-concurrent elements typical of investments is required for the same purpose.[57] Based on Articles 31–2 of the VCLT the tribunal

---

[54] *Siemens AG* v. *Argentina* (ICSID Case No. ARB/02/8, Decision on Jurisdiction of 3 August 2004).

[55] *Ibid.*, para. 81.

[56] *MTD Equity Sdn. Bhd. and MTD Chile SA* v. *Chile* (ICSID Case No. ARB/01/7, Decision of 25 May 2004), para. 113.

[57] *Romak SA (Switzerland)* v. *Republic of Uzbekistan* (Award of 26 November 2009), para. 197.

concluded that it needed to construe the term 'investments' in good faith in accordance with its ordinary meaning in its context and in light of the object and purpose of the treaty, for which it had to analyse the BIT's preamble.[58] It then stated that 'investments' under the Switzerland–Uzbekistan BIT had an inherent meaning 'entailing *contribution* that extends over a *certain period of time* and that involves some *risk*',[59] thus discarding the requirement of a contribution to the host State's economic development.

The discourse surrounding economic development as a criterion for an 'investment' has largely centered on the ICSID Convention. However, since many other IIAs also contain references to economic development as the *leitmotiv* of States to enter into them, it is foreseeable that tribunals could be exposed to circumstances where interpretation of the intention of the State Parties would have to be considered. In those cases, the analysis would inevitably turn to the issue of economic development as a criterion of the investment. Of course, in the absence of any reference to economic development in the relevant IIAs, the task of the tribunals will be more complicated.

Where investor–State disputes are determined in fora other than ICSID, the so-called economic-development defence to object to the jurisdiction of a tribunal is probably not possible. Only if the relevant IIA has made references to economic development as the reason for the parties to grant international protection to foreign investments could that argument be submitted. But in such a hypothetical situation, the tribunals would most likely consider the defence on the merits. For now, it seems that cases under ICSID will dominate the discussion on the analysis of economic development as an outer limit of a protected investment.

V   Economic development: A measurable concept

The search for prosperity has been the main drive behind the development of rules of international law on foreign investment. From the perspective of host States, however, that promise of prosperity is linked to the implicit bargain contained within IIAs – international protection for foreign investments in exchange for the expectation of increased capital supportive of domestic development programmes. That intention is articulated clearly in some IIAs, but not so much in others. And

---

[58] *Ibid.*, para. 206.   [59] *Ibid.*, para. 207 (emphasis in original).

from the inconsistencies in approach evident in recent jurisprudence, it seems that there is little consensus on the extent to which contribution to economic development is determinative of an investment's entitlement to protection under IIAs. The divergence of opinion seems to stem from the difficulties associated with how to define and measure economic development and in ascertaining what constitutes relevant contributions towards it. However, rather than failing to give effect to this important criterion by placing it in the 'too-hard basket', as several tribunals appear to have done, this chapter argues that further intellectual engagement with the concept is, in fact, what is required. Indeed, in-depth analysis and exploration into its nature, not less, would most likely lead to a more sophisticated understanding of its operation within IIAs. It is suggested that future tribunals should seek to provide a comprehensive analysis of questions such as: (i) how economic development should be defined within the context of IIAs; (ii) what amounts to a contribution to economic development; (iii) how a positive contribution to economic development can be measured; and (iv) whether any 'negative' factors related to the investment or conduct of the investor (such as breaches of human rights, corruption or harm to the environment) are relevant in determining whether the investment has made a positive contribution to the economic development of the host State.

Economic development is certainly a concept that can be very broad and can, potentially, encompass many disparate elements. However, through a review of the relevant documents and cases, several factors have emerged that point to certain non–exclusive criteria for determining when an investment has made a contribution to the economic development of the host country. The jurisprudence indicates that an assessment will be made of the following: (a) the extent to which the investment benefits the public interest; (b) whether any transfer of technological knowledge or 'know-how' from investor to the host State has taken place; (c) the degree to which the investment has enhanced the GDP of the host country; and (d) whether the investment has had a positive impact on the host State's development. A hermeneutic analysis of the ICSID Convention and the World Bank's constitutive instruments also reinforces this approach, emphasising that investments are to be made for: (a) productive purposes as opposed to speculative purposes; and (b) for the development of the resources of countries so as to increase productivity, standards of living and conditions of labour.

Similarly, as ICSID is part of the World Bank Group, the wording of World Bank documents should also be of assistance in delineating what is meant by 'economic development' in the context of IIAs. Of particular note in this regard are the 1992 Guidelines for Treatment of Foreign Investors. Although, not a binding document, it does provide a set of recommendations intended to be incorporated into States' domestic regulations on the treatment of foreign investment. In its preamble, it states that it is recognised that: 'A greater flow of foreign direct investment brings substantial benefits to . . . the economies of developing countries . . . through greater competition, transfer of capital, technology and managerial skills and enhancement of market access and in terms of the expansion of international trade.'[60] This statement provides a useful indication of factors to take into account when assessing the extent to which an investment has contributed to or encouraged the creation of such conditions within the host State. In such an analysis, for example, a tribunal may well need to consider whether the investment exhibits attributes that could contribute to the realisation of any of the listed beneficial conditions or whether it could be taken to reflect at a more general level the advancement of these goals. Accordingly, it can be seen that there are ways to ascertain the contribution to economic development of a foreign investment. Indeed, there are, of course, already very specific tools that can be utilised to assess contributions to the local economy. For example, the impact of the investment on the host State's GDP is one indicator that can be easily measured by comparing the value of the goods or services produced by the transaction with reliable data on the overall value of goods and services produced in the given country in a given period of time (as may be provided by e.g. the World Bank). It must be borne in mind, however, that economic growth is distinct from economic development. Focusing solely on the positive impact of an investment on the GDP cannot in itself be conclusive in determining whether an investment has contributed to the economic development of a country. It is, of course, a *prima facie* indicator of positive contribution. However, an investment might enhance the GDP and yet be detrimental to the economic development of a country as when, for example, human rights standards are violated. It is to take account of such circumstances that a more sophisticated approach needs to be developed to the relationship between contribution to economic development and availability of protection under the treaty – one in which

---

[60] Guidelines on Treatment of Foreign Investments, World Bank (1992), www-wds. worldbank.org/external/default/WDSContentServer/WDSP/IB/1999/11/10/000094946_ 99090805303082/Rendered/PDF/multi_page.pdf (last visited 5 November 2010).

the contribution is assessed per se and then, if it suffices on this *prima facie* basis, is examined for any negative factors that may cancel out its apparent positive impact on the economic development of the host State. If, upon analysing the facts, it is concluded that the investment has not contributed to the economic development of the host State, it should also follow that the investment falls outside the limits of the protection granted by ICSID.

VI Conclusion

Although this is still very much a contentious area of international investment law, it is clear that several factors need to be satisfied under the test of whether an 'investment' has contributed to the economic development of the host State. If an investment is contrary to the public interest, has not generated any knowledge transfer to the host State, has not enhanced the economy or its productivity, has not increased the standards of living of the host country or the labour conditions, it almost certainly has not made a contribution to the economic development of that country. Given specific references in the relevant IIAs, that investment should be denied protection either at a preliminary jurisdictional stage or at a final merits stage.

This chapter has considered the conditions necessary for an 'investment' to come within the ambit of protection of the ICSID Convention, and has analysed the various criteria which have been proposed by tribunals. It has argued that the most important of the criteria is whether the investment has made a contribution to the economic development of the host State of the investment. This is because the main motive for developing countries to enter into IIAs is to attract foreign capital to assist the development of their economy. This factor is an important consideration in the interpretation of IIAs, and this should not be overlooked by future tribunals so that they may arrive at a sustainable outcome in adjudicating disputes.

26

Regulatory chill and the threat of arbitration: A view from political science

KYLA TIENHAARA[*]

I Introduction

The academic literature on international investment treaties, foreign investment contracts and investor–State dispute settlement is dominated by legal analysis. This is understandable in light of the complexity and, until recently, relative obscurity of the field. However, it is imperative that scholars from other disciplines now become more actively engaged in the critical debates surrounding investment law and investment arbitration in particular. One example of an issue that has been inadequately addressed and often prematurely dismissed by legal scholars is 'regulatory chill'. Fundamentally, the notion of regulatory chill suggests that investment arbitration – as an institution – may *influence* the course of policy development.[1] For reasons that will be laid out in this chapter, investigating regulatory chill requires methods and approaches more familiar to political scientists than to lawyers.

II The regulatory chill hypothesis

Soloway suggests that the 'meaning of the term "regulatory chill" is not clear'.[2] This is a fair critique; the vast majority of scholars and non-governmental organisations (NGOs) that have referred to regulatory chill in the context of discussions about investor–State dispute

[*] The author would like to thank David Schneiderman, Kate Miles and Jonathan Bonnitcha for their thoughtful comments on an earlier draft of this chapter.
[1] In the international relations literature, institutions are defined as relatively stable sets of related norms and rules that pertain to State and non-State actors and their activities: see J. Duffield, 'What are international institutions?', *International Studies Review*, 9 (2007), 1.
[2] J. Soloway, 'NAFTA's Chapter 11: Investment protection, integration and the public interest', *Choices*, 9 (2003), 1, 18.

settlement have not precisely articulated what their understanding of the term is. That being said, it should be self-evident that these commentators were not implying that regulators would 'cease to adopt any new regulations and that the entire environmental regulatory framework [would grind] to a halt'.[3] Similarly, it is highly unlikely that anyone who has expressed a concern about regulatory chill would argue that regulators should be permitted to discriminate, 'unduly',[4] against foreign investors.[5]

However, the ambiguity in the literature has led to some understandable confusion. Some authors appear to consider regulatory chill to be a *broad* phenomenon whereby regulatory progress is dampened across all areas that impact on foreign investors because government officials are aware of, and seriously concerned about, the risk of an investor–State dispute arising. In other words, policy-makers take into account potential disputes with foreign investors before they even begin to draft a policy and prioritise avoiding such disputes over the development of efficient regulation in the public interest. This type of chilling effect would be quite difficult to measure, although one could use detailed surveys or in-depth interviews with regulators to at least gauge their awareness of and concern about investment arbitration. A second conceptualisation of regulatory chill commonly employed by authors and commentators focuses on the chilling of *specific* regulatory measures that have been proposed or adopted by governments. This form of regulatory chill would emerge only when a government has been *made aware* of the risk of an investor–State dispute by an investor or group of investors that oppose the adoption or enforcement of a regulatory measure. This form of regulatory chill is the focus of the remainder of the chapter.

In order to define more precisely this form of regulatory chill, we can formulate it as a hypothesis. This requires identifying several key variables. The following description of the dependent variable is proposed: *the enactment and/or enforcement of bona fide regulatory measures*. It is acknowledged at the outset that the terminology 'bona fide regulatory measures' is potentially problematic; opinions on what qualifies as

---

[3] *Ibid.*

[4] With the important caveat that it is sometimes *necessary* to 'discriminate' against certain industrial sectors for environmental or health reasons: see K. Miles, 'International investment law and climate change: Issues in the transition to a low carbon world', Inaugural Conference of the Society of International Economic Law, Geneva, 15–17 July 2008, Online Proceedings Working Paper No. 27/08, p. 33, www.ssrn.com (last accessed 16 December 2010).

[5] Soloway, 'NAFTA's Chapter 11', p. 18.

'bona fide' will no doubt be varied amongst States, investors, arbitrators and other observers. Nevertheless, the use of this terminology signals recognition that some regulatory measures may be designed solely with discrimination or protectionism in mind and that the 'chilling' of such measures can more appropriately be described as a State's compliance with its international obligations.[6] It is also conceded that this dependent variable, as it stands, would be nearly impossible to measure. Even if one were to focus on a specific area of regulation within a specific level of government within a specific country, it is hard to imagine how one could develop a baseline of 'normal' regulatory activity (in terms of both content and rate of development) against which to measure variation. As such, for the sake of testability, the focus of investigation needs to be further narrowed to a specific bona fide regulatory measure (or set of bona fide regulatory measures) that is (are) the subject of an investor–State conflict.[7] The baseline thereby becomes the original (proposed) measure(s); if a government abandons, significantly alters, or fails to enforce the measure(s), this represents a decline in the dependent variable.

Next we can turn to the independent variable. It is worth noting that there are many options that an investor has when faced with a conflict with a government over regulation. He or she can lobby or negotiate directly with the government; delegate resolution of the conflict to a third party (e.g. an arbitral tribunal); utilise reputation and shame sanctions;[8] enlist the assistance of his home State; and/or *threaten* to exit the State's jurisdiction or to utilise one of the measures listed above. In the present context, we are primarily concerned with an investor's use of the threat of arbitration. As explained further in the next section, it is not the *actual* threat that is critical but rather *the government's perception of the threat of arbitration.*

As with the dependent variable, measurement of this independent variable is challenging: how does the researcher know how high the perceived threat of arbitration is? A considerable amount of decision-making is not made out in the open, even in democratic countries,

[6] The underlying assumption being that States intended for blatant discrimination or acts of direct expropriation to be the subject of investor–State disputes, but did not intend or anticipate that bona fide regulatory measures would be called into question.
[7] The term 'conflict' is used here as distinct from 'dispute', which in the literature commonly signifies that the matter has reached the stage of arbitral proceedings.
[8] T. Ginsburg, 'International substitutes for domestic institutions: Bilateral investment treaties and governance', *International Review of Law and Economics*, 25 (2005), 107.

and governments may be wary of admitting that they have capitulated to investor demands because they were concerned about being sued (not least because this might raise questions about why the government agreed to submit itself to arbitration in the first place). Conversely, governments could theoretically use the existence of a threat of arbitration as an *excuse* to retract a policy proposal that was, for other reasons, losing support. In such a situation, researchers might end up mislabelling cases of 'political cover' as examples of regulatory chill.[9] Ultimately, it is not possible to open up the minds of regulators and peer in to see what they are *really* thinking, but careful research based on interviews, media reports and observance of government behaviour can produce a reasonable approximation.

Unfortunately, it is rare that a political phenomenon can be adequately explained by one independent variable. In this regard, it is worth noting that scholars have suggested that regulatory chill could occur as a result of government fear of the threat of industrial flight (or non-entry of investment).[10] Although it is not the focus of the present chapter, it is important to keep the issue of industrial flight in mind when discussing the 'arbitral' regulatory chill hypothesis. These two 'fear factors' are, in fact, very difficult to untangle; arbitration can be seen as a prelude to investor exit and furthermore, as discussed below, one of the costs of arbitration for States is a detrimental impact on its 'investor friendly' reputation.[11]

While an increase in either the threat of arbitration or the threat of industrial flight would be expected to cause a decline in the dependent variable, other extraneous variables (e.g. public demand for regulation or the existence of an international commitment to regulate) could counteract this effect. There are simply not enough known cases of investor–State conflict involving a threat of arbitration to allow researchers to control extraneous variables; as should be evident at this point, research on regulatory chill does not lend itself to statistical analysis. However, researchers conducting intensive case studies can make

[9] K. Tienhaara, *The Expropriation of Environmental Governance: Protecting foreign investors at the expense of public policy* (Cambridge University Press, 2009), p. 263. For a discussion of political cover in the context of trade agreements, see T. Allee and P. Huth, 'Legitimizing dispute settlement: International legal rulings as domestic political cover', *American Political Science Review*, 100 (2006), 219.

[10] J. Clapp, 'What the pollution havens debate overlooks', *Global Environmental Politics*, 2 (2002), 11, 17.

[11] See text accompanying nn. 27 and 28 below.

reasonable inferences about the relative importance of various factors in the outcome of an investor–State conflict.

Taking into account the above, the following working formulation of the regulatory chill hypothesis is proposed: *In some circumstances, governments will respond to a high (perceived) threat of investment arbitration by failing to enact or enforce bona fide regulatory measures (or by modifying measures to such an extent that their original intent is undermined or their effectiveness is severely diminished).*

The caveat 'in some circumstances' may appear, at first glance, to diminish the value of the hypothesis. However, as long as researchers are careful to account for the role of extraneous variables (which make up the 'circumstances'), the hypothesis remains useful. The caveat merely indicates that the hypothesis and any research that springs from it should be thought of as having explanatory rather than predictive value.

III   Critiques of the regulatory chill hypothesis

There has been an attempt in the previous section to respond to one of the major critiques of the regulatory chill hypothesis – that it is not precisely defined. This section provides rebuttals to three further critiques that have emerged in the investment law literature.

A   Regulators are not aware of the threat of arbitration

Coe and Rubins argue that one of the problems with the regulatory chill hypothesis is that 'it assumes that regulators are aware of international law'.[12] Although the authors acknowledge that with an increasing number of investor–State disputes 'regulators may be more conscious of the prospect of liability than ever before', they maintain that the actions of many States are 'clearly uninformed by the dictates of international law'.[13]

As of 2009, eighty-one countries had direct experience with investment treaty arbitration.[14] In those countries awareness is likely to be higher, but

---

[12] J. Coe Jr and N. Rubins, 'Regulatory expropriation and the *Tecmed* case: Context and contributions' in T. Weiler (ed.), *International Investment Law and Arbitration: Leading cases from the ICSID, NAFTA, bilateral treaties and customary international law* (London: Cameron May, 2005), pp. 597, 599.

[13] *Ibid.*

[14] United Nations Conference on Trade and Development (UNCTAD), *Latest Developments in Investor–State Dispute Settlement: IIA Issues Note No. 1* (2010), UN Doc. No. UNCTAD/WEB/DIAE/IA/2010/3.

there may certainly be regulators in areas that have not been the subject of a dispute that have never even heard of a bilateral investment treaty (BIT). That being said, their lack of awareness is irrelevant; as noted above, regulators can be *made aware* of the key aspects of international investment law by investors and their lawyers when a conflict arises. In fact, a lack of knowledge about the specificities of investment law makes the threat of arbitration all the more potent, because regulators will be less likely to recognise when an investor is bluffing.

In summary, this critique may be fitting to claims about a broad arbitration-induced chilling effect on regulation, which would seem to require a reasonable level of regulator awareness of investment law. However, most commentators are equally, if not more, concerned about governments capitulating to specific investor threats to arbitrate and, in such cases, this critique is immaterial.

B   Governments can expect to win cases when regulation is bona fide

In the same article, Coe and Rubins go on to make a more substantial critique:

> the regulatory chill thesis assumes that the prospect of having to pay compensation will cause States to forbear from taking action, despite compelling regulatory objectives. While the apprehension of international liability may prompt reflection and careful tailoring of means to ends, it seems less likely to cause abandonment of legislation at the heart of a government's mandate. Indeed, to the extent a government *has the machinery* to defend such claims, it *might well expect victory*, since expropriation claims often fail.[15]

The first aspect of this statement that deserves scrutiny concerns the capacity of a government to engage effectively in arbitration: do most governments have the 'machinery' to defend claims?

As Salgado notes, 'a tribunal's ability to reach fair and just results largely depends on its ability to consider all interests affected by the proceeding' which, in turn, depends on the parties being well represented.[16] In any form of litigation, the level of expertise of a party's lawyers will likely be a decisive factor in the outcome of the dispute, but in the specialised area of investment arbitration the importance of

---

[15] Coe and Rubins, 'Regulatory expropriation', p. 599 (emphasis added).
[16] V. Salgado, 'The case against adopting BIT law in the FTAA framework', *Wisconsin Law Review* (2006), 1025, 1036.

having access to legal expertise is magnified.[17] While developed countries
will likely have sufficient in-house expertise, developing countries will
generally not. Hiring representation from an international law firm that
has specialists in the field of investment arbitration can overcome this
problem and also has a number of other advantages. For example, as a
result of the fact that not all awards are published, firms that are regularly
involved in investment arbitrations are likely to have access to a broad
range of tribunal decisions on which to base their case, while government
counsel are forced to rely on 'scattered and incomplete sources'.[18] However, while hiring outside counsel can be advantageous, it may not always
be a feasible option for developing countries. Large law firms often have
long-term relationships with multinational corporations and such relationships may prevent a firm from representing a developing country in
an investor–State dispute.[19] If a law firm is available, the next question
becomes whether a developing country can afford its services. Gottwald
notes that the hourly rates for lawyers in elite firms can range from US
$400 to US$600.[20] When a team of lawyers is retained for arbitral proceedings that are drawn out over a period of several years, the result can be
a colossal legal bill.

As a result of these obstacles, developing countries often rely on
government attorneys regardless of their experience or access to necessary
resources. As Gottwald found, 'this can lead to shocking disparities in the
quality of legal representation between investor claimants and developing
nation defendants'.[21]

The second aspect of the above-quoted statement by Coe and Rubins
that deserves further attention is the notion that governments 'might
well expect victory' in investment arbitration (if their regulation is
bona fide). This argument has also been put forward by other authors
that have provided an analysis of existing arbitral awards (typically

[17] E. J. Gottwald, 'Leveling the playing field: Is it time for a legal assistance center for
developing nations in investment treaty arbitration?', *American University International
Law Review*, 22 (2007), 237, 252.
[18] A. Cosbey *et al.*, *Investment and Sustainable Development: A guide to the use and potential
of international investment agreements*, (Winnipeg: International Institute for Sustainable
Development, 2004), p. 7. Similarly, Gottwald suggests, in 'Leveling the playing field',
p. 256, that: 'Developing country counsel seeking to find relevant precedent are forced to
engage in a kind of legal scavenger hunt through scattered and incomplete sources for
past arbitral awards.'
[19] Personal communication with Mahnaz Malik of Mahnaz Malik International Law
Counsel, 14 December 2008 (copy on file with author).
[20] Gottwald, 'Leveling the playing field', p. 254.   [21] *Ibid.*

Metalclad,[22] *S. D. Myers*[23] and *Methanex*),[24] in an attempt to discredit the regulatory chill hypothesis.[25]

There are three major problems with this line of reasoning. First, it is peremptory: proponents of the 'might well expect victory' argument ignore the substantial debate in the literature about the tribunal decisions in cases such as *Metalclad* and *S. D. Myers* and are dismissive of any suggestion that *there were legitimate public-interest issues at stake* in these cases.[26]

Secondly, the argument neglects to account for the fact that States can incur high costs through investment arbitration even if they 'win' a case. In addition to the legal costs and fees associated with investment arbitration (which may be awarded to one party or divided between the parties), there is also the reputational effect that investor–State disputes have.[27] Allee and Peinhardt have found that the existence of arbitral proceedings against a government, regardless of the eventual outcome of the dispute, has a negative impact on the State's reputation in the eyes of foreign investors.[28] Their data suggests that States are likely to receive less foreign direct investment following an investor's lodging of a BIT claim. Other possible negative impacts that could worry a host government faced with a dispute include strained relations with the government of the investor's home State (which may be an important trading partner or provider of financial aid) and/or with the World Bank.[29]

---

[22] *Metalclad Corporation* v. *The United Mexican States* (ICSID Case No. ARB(AF)/97/1, Award of 30 August 2000).

[23] *S. D. Myers Inc.* v. *Canada* (First Partial Award of 13 November 2000, Second Partial Award of 21 October 2002 and Final Award of 30 December 2002).

[24] *Methanex* v. *United States* (Final Award of 3 August 2005).

[25] S. W. Schill, 'Do investment treaties chill unilateral State regulation to mitigate climate change?', *Journal of International Arbitration*, 24 (2007), 469; see also, Soloway, 'NAFTA's Chapter 11'.

[26] See e.g. L. Dhooge, 'The North American Free Trade Agreement and the environment: Lessons of *Metalclad Corporation* v. *United Mexican States*', *Minnesota Journal of Global Trade*, 10 (2001), 209; B. T. Hodges, 'Where the grass is always greener: Foreign investor actions against environmental regulations under NAFTA's Chapter 11 – *S. D. Myers Inc.* v. *Canada*', *Georgetown International Environmental Law Review*, 14 (2001–2), 367.

[27] A. van Aaken, 'Perils of success? The case of international investment protection', *European Business Organization Law Review*, 9 (2008), 1, 14.

[28] T. L. Allee and C. Peinhardt, 'Contingent credibility: The reputational effects of investment treaty disputes on foreign direct investment' (2008), unpublished, www.psweb.sbs.ohio-state.edu/intranet/gies/papers/Allee%20Peinhardt%20Sept2009.pdf (last accessed 15 December 2010).

[29] On the links and possible conflicts of interest between the International Centre for Settlement of Investment Disputes (ICSID) and the World Bank, see J. Fouret, 'The

Thirdly, and perhaps most importantly, the 'might well expect victory' argument is based on an assumption that regulators are *perfectly rational*; in reality, all humans experience 'bounds' on their rationality as a result of time constraints and, critically, limits on the availability of information and their cognitive ability to absorb and understand it.[30] Ironically, as noted above, some critics of the regulatory chill hypothesis have argued that regulators have little *awareness* of (let alone *comprehension* of) the intricacies of investment law, which actually supports the contention that regulators are operating under bounded rationality.

It is worth pointing out that decision-makers have particular difficulty dealing with uncertainty,[31] which is rife in the rapidly evolving area of international investment law. Awards rendered in investment arbitration are only binding on the parties involved in the dispute; the rulings of tribunals are said to have no *stare decisis*. Hence, tribunals do not have to base their decisions on those of previous tribunals. Furthermore, unlike in the realm of trade disputes, there is no appellate body to ensure consistent interpretation of investment treaties. As a result, there have been cases where several awards have been issued addressing the same facts where panels have reached diverging conclusions. This has led to what some have termed a 'legitimacy crisis' in international investment arbitration.[32]

Given the above, the critical question becomes: what do regulators *believe* about investment arbitration? Clearly, the beliefs of regulators will vary between States and even between government departments within a State and will depend on their prior experience with arbitration as well as the level of information and advice that they have access to. However, some statements by government officials clearly indicate that they believe that investment arbitration is a threat to *bona fide* regulation. For example, Dr Perera, a legal advisor in the Sri Lankan Ministry of Foreign Affairs, has stated:

World Bank and ICSID: Family or incestuous ties?', *International Organizations Law Review*, 4 (2007), 121.

[30] H. A. Simon, *Models of Man: Social and rational* (London: John Wiley and Sons Inc., 1957); see also, H.A. Simon, 'Rationality in political behaviour', *Political Psychology*, 16 (1995), 45.

[31] B. Jones, 'Bounded rationality and public policy: Herbert A. Simon and the decisional foundation of collective choice', *Policy Sciences*, 35 (2002), 269, 273.

[32] S. Franck, 'The legitimacy crisis in investment treaty arbitration: Privatising public international law through inconsistent decisions', *Fordham Law Review*, 73 (2005), 1521.

Sri Lanka believes that an expansive interpretation of regulatory measures could circumvent the national policy space hindering the government's right to regulate, creating a risk of 'regulatory chill', with governments hesitant to undertake legitimate regulatory measures in the public interest for fear of claims for compensation being preferred by investors.[33]

There is also evidence to suggest that government officials in some countries, particularly in Latin America, believe that investment arbitration has a structural bias that favours investor claimants.[34] Of course actions also often speak louder than words, and one can extrapolate from the recent initiatives taken by governments – to change model BITs, to renegotiate or terminate treaties, and even to withdraw from the ICSID Convention – that they have serious concerns about investment arbitration.[35]

In summary, regulators faced with the prospect of an investor–State dispute are forced to make an *ex ante* assessment about possible outcomes, with time and resource constraints, in an environment of uncertainty. The notion that regulators operating under such conditions will simply move forward with confidence about their pending 'victory' in a dispute is highly implausible. Regulators in developing countries are likely to be especially cautious given the limited capacity of their governments to engage in arbitration.

---

[33] A. R. Perera, 'Technical assistance and capacity building: Lessons learned from experiences and the way forward' (Symposium Co-organised by ICSID, Organisation for Economic Co-operation and Development (OECD) and the United Nations Conference on Trade and Development (UNCTAD) – Making the Most of International Investment Agreements: A Common Agenda, Paris, 12 December 2005).

[34] See e.g. E. Mekay, 'Bias seen in int'l dispute arbiters', *IPS News Service* (19 June 2007).

[35] See e.g. G. Gagné and J. Morin, 'The evolving American policy on investment protection: Evidence from recent FTAs and the 2004 Model BIT', *Journal of International Economic Law*, 9 (2006), 357 (on changes to the US model BIT and the absence of an investor–State dispute-settlement clause in the 2005 Australia–US Free Trade Agreement); C. M. Ryan, 'Meeting expectations: Assessing the long-term legitimacy and stability of international investment law', *University of Pennsylvania Journal of International Law*, 29 (2008), 725 (on the Bolivian withdrawal from ICSID, other developments in Latin America and the absence of an investor–State dispute-settlement clause in the Japan–Philippines Economic Partnership Agreement); A. van Aaken, 'Perils of success? The case of international investment protection', *European Business Organization Law Review*, 9(1) (2008), 1 (on the omission of the controversial fair and equitable treatment standard from the Economic Cooperation Agreement between India and Singapore); and UNCTAD, *Recent Developments in International Investment Agreements (2008–June 2009): IIA Monitor No. 3* (2009), UNCTAD Doc. No. UNCTAD/WEB/DIAE/IA/2009/8 (on the denunciation of BITs).

C   There is no evidence to support the regulatory chill hypothesis

Soloway has argued that the 'literature supporting the contention that regulatory chill does exist is largely anecdotal and has not been adequately substantiated'.[36] At the time that she was writing, this was probably an unfair critique; after all, investor–State dispute settlement was only just beginning to gain notoriety and research in the area was in its infancy. Furthermore, most commentators were not asserting the existence of regulatory chill, but rather suggesting that it might occur; raising the alarm, but also recognising the need for further research. In recent years, much research has been conducted which, at the very least, lends credibility to the hypothesis, even if it does not definitively prove it. Before turning to the evidence, it is worth briefly exploring the issue of burden of proof.

Been and Beauvais argue that:

> Those concerned about the role NAFTA may play in chilling desirable regulations, however, have the benefit of the status quo on their side: Because international compensation requirements were construed fairly narrowly prior to NAFTA, caution requires that those arguing for a more expansive compensation requirement bear the burden of proof both that the requirement will deter inefficient regulation effectively and that it will not over deter efficient regulation.[37]

Regardless of whether or not one agrees with this statement, it does seem fair to point out that those commentators who assert that regulatory chill *does not exist* are themselves often guilty of failing to substantiate adequately their arguments. For example, Schill contends that 'investment treaties neither obstruct nor chill state regulation that aims at reducing greenhouse gas emissions'.[38] However, he arrives at this bold conclusion through a legal analysis of existing investor–State awards. Regardless of how well-reasoned Schill's analysis might be, it is entirely insufficient to support a claim that regulatory chill does not exist for the reasons discussed above (bounded rationality, capacity, etc.). Soloway's argument that the increasing volume of new environmental legislation in Canada can dispel concerns about NAFTA Chapter 11 causing regulatory chill is equally unhelpful.[39] As Toellefson notes, 'drawing conclusions

---

[36] Soloway, 'NAFTA's Chapter 11', p. 19.

[37] V. Been and J. C. Beauvais, 'The Global Fifth Amendment? NAFTA's investment protections and the misguided quest for an international "regulatory takings" doctrine', *New York University Law Review*, 78 (2003), 30, 134.

[38] Schill, 'Do investment treaties chill', p. 470.   [39] Soloway, 'NAFTA's Chapter 11', 19.

about the Chapter's impact on, or irrelevance to, the appetite of governments to engage in policy innovation based on the volume, as opposed
to the content, of regulatory measures is hazardous'.[40]

Setting aside the issue of burden of proof, let us turn to the evidence
that might support the regulatory chill hypothesis. Despite the serious
methodological challenges that researchers in this area face, there is a
growing body of work based on detailed case-study analysis. The following
is a brief overview of some of the key cases available in the literature:

- The Government of Canada settled a dispute with Ethyl Corp., paying
  the company compensation and retracting its ban on the gasoline
  additive MMT. There are differing views on whether the government
  capitulated because it was concerned that it would lose the NAFTA
  Chapter 11 suit or if other factors (such as an internal legal case on the
  issue brought by several provinces that the government lost) were of
  primary significance.[41]
- Members of the insurance industry threatened action under NAFTA
  Chapter 11 when provincial governments within Canada put forward
  plans for providing public auto insurance. This has been cited as a key
  factor in those plans being shelved.[42]
- Tobacco companies threatened NAFTA Chapter 11 suits against
  Canada on two occasions (first in 1994 and then again in 2001) when
  the federal government proposed changes to cigarette packaging and
  labelling. The arbitration threats have been cited as a possible factor in
  the government's decision not to move ahead with the measures in
  1994, although a Charter of Rights claim by R. J. Reynolds Tobacco
  may have also been relevant.[43]

---

[40] C. Tollefson, 'NAFTA's Chapter 11: The case for reform', *Choices*, 9 (2003), 48, 49.

[41] In support of the former argument, see H. Mann, 'Private rights, public problems:
A guide to NAFTA's controversial chapter on investor rights' (Winnipeg: International
Institute for Sustainable Development and World Wildlife Fund, 2001). In support of the
latter argument, see S. E. Gaines, 'The masked ball of NAFTA Chapter 11: Foreign
investors, local environmentalists, government officials, and disguised motives' in J.
Kirton and V. W. MacLaren (eds.), *Linking Trade, Environment, and Social Cohesion:
NAFTA experiences, global challenges* (Aldershot, Hampshire: Ashgate, 2002), pp. 103–29.
For a view suggesting that both the arbitration and the internal legal case were relevant,
see D. Schneiderman, *Constitutionalizing Economic Globalization: Investment rules and
democracy's promise* (Cambridge University Press, 2008), pp. 129–34.

[42] S. Shrybman and S. Sinclair, 'Public auto insurance and trade treaties', *Briefing Paper:
Trade and Investment Series (Canadian Centre for Policy Alternatives*, 5(1) (2004)).

[43] Schneiderman, *Constitutionalizing Economic Globalization*, pp. 120–9. Interestingly, one
of the companies that threatened the Canadian government – Philip Morris – recently
initiated arbitration against the Uruguayan government over its cigarette packaging

- Indonesia exempted a number of foreign investors from a ban on open-pit mining in protected forests after receiving threats of arbitration claims in the range of US$20–30 billion. The timing of the government's actions, statements to the media and other factors suggest that the government was strongly motivated to remove the threat of arbitration.[44]

The next section will provide a summary of two further cases.

IV Examining investor threats to arbitrate: Two case studies from Costa Rica

It is axiomatic that not every threat to arbitrate will result in a government capitulating to investor demands. In some instances the government will call the investor's bluff and the matter will be dropped. In others, the threat will be acted upon but the government will choose to defend its regulatory measures and proceed to arbitration. The political machinations that occur when an investor makes a threat to arbitrate are worth exploring regardless of the final outcome. Detailed analysis can further our understanding of the circumstances in which regulatory chill is most (or least) likely to occur. In this section, two cases of investor–State conflict in Costa Rica are presented. In both cases, an investor threatened to take the government to arbitration, but the outcome of each case is markedly different.

A Harken Energy

In 1994, the Government of Costa Rica passed a Hydrocarbons Law as part of a series of measures designed to implement a structural adjustment programme. This law opened Costa Rica to foreign interests in oil and gas exploration. In 1997, the Ministry of Environment and Energy (MINAE) opened a round of bidding for oil and gas exploration

policies. Reports have suggested that the government might have been willing to settle with the company (see Luke Eric Peterson, 'Uruguay hints at compromise in arbitration with Philip Morris', *Kluwer Arbitration Blog* (28 July 2010)). However, at the time of writing it appeared that the government would defend its regulatory measures in arbitration.

[44] S. G. Gross, 'Inordinate chill: BITs, non-NAFTA MITs, and host-State regulatory freedom: An Indonesian case study', *Michigan Journal of International Law*, 24 (2003), 893; see also, K. Tienhaara, 'What you don't know can hurt you: Investor–State disputes and the environment', *Global Environmental Politics*, 6 (2006), 73; Tienhaara, *The Expropriation of Environmental Governance*, pp. 217–27.

concession blocks on land and offshore. In 1998 MKJ Xploration, a Lousiana-based company, acquired four concession blocks – two onshore and two offshore.[45] Texas-based Harken Energy later purchased an 80 per cent stake in the project under the subsidiary Harken Costa Rica Holdings (together, Harken).

In 1999, protests began over the seismic tests that were being carried out in one of Harken's offshore concessions. Environmentalists expressed alarm over the potential impacts on marine life, and noted that wildlife reserves existed close by, including two sites registered under the Ramsar Convention on Wetlands (Ramsar).[46] Fishermen and members of the tourism industry also voiced concerns about the impacts that oil exploration could have on their livelihoods.[47]

Meanwhile, communities in the vicinity of the land concessions filed a petition with the Constitutional Chamber of the Supreme Court (Sala IV), claiming that the bidding process had been flawed as there had been no prior consultation with them.[48] In 2000 the court ruled in favour of the petitioners, citing irregularities in the bidding process and a lack of public consultation.[49] The decision annulled Harken's concessions.[50] Opposition groups celebrated the decision, but Harken maintained that the project was still viable as the court had not made a decision on the validity of oil exploration, but only on the way that the contract had been awarded.[51] The company filed a motion for relief, claiming that it had been denied the opportunity to make its case heard before the court. Subsequently the court amended its decision so that only the two land concession blocks held by Harken were annulled, leaving the marine concession blocks unaffected.[52] The company welcomed this decision, as it had conducted the bulk of exploration work in the offshore blocks, and it later decided to give up its contractual

---

[45] M. V. Cajiao, 'The case of oil exploration in the Caribbean off Costa Rica: Legal background', *Environmental Law Alliance Worldwide* (24 March 2009), www.elaw.org/offices/ELAW+Costa+Rica/caribbean+oil+exploration (last accessed 15 December 2010).

[46] 'Oil exploration protested', *Tico Times* (10 December 1999); see also, J. M. de Oca Lugo, 'Costa Rica rejects oil exploration near Ramsar sites', *Ramsar News Release* (7 March 2002), www.ramsar.org/cda/en/ramsar-news-archives-2002-costa-rica-rejects-oil/main/ramsar/1-26-45-87%5E20194_4000_0__ (last accessed 15 December 2010).

[47] 'Oil drilling plans denounced', *Tico Times* (1 September 2001).

[48] Cajiao, 'The case of oil exploration'.   [49] 'Oil drilling plans denounced'.

[50] 'Court orders halt to oil drilling', *Tico Times* (14 September 2000).

[51] 'Oil firm: Project not dead yet', *Tico Times* (29 September 2000).

[52] 'Oil firm faces deadline to clarify report', *Tico Times* (2 February 2001).

rights in the land blocks rather than proceed with consultations with the indigenous communities.[53]

While Harken's offshore concessions had not been annulled, the company still had to obtain approval for its environmental impact assessment (EIA). In 2001, Costa Rica's environmental agency (SETENA) outlined numerous legal and technical elements that were missing from Harken's EIA. These included the failure to address the potential effects of an oil spill and to provide measures for containment in the event of a spill.[54] Environmental groups also sought an external review of the EIA with the assistance of the International Union for the Conservation of Nature. Two independent experts were hired to review the EIA as well as an Addendum to the EIA that the company produced in response to SETENA's concerns; they found that both the EIA and the Addendum failed to adequately address the potential scope and cumulative effects of oil exploration in the area.[55]

In late February 2002, SETENA made its final decision, providing fifty-five reasons for rejecting Harken's EIA. The reasons provided by SETENA relied heavily on the precautionary principle; international agreements such as Ramsar; decisions of the Sala IV; the lack of resources in the country to deal with oil spills; and deficiencies in the company's application. Harken maintained that the decision to reject the EIA was based on a lack of understanding about the technology that would be employed in the operation and filed an appeal.[56]

2002 was an election year in Costa Rica and oil and mining were hot campaign issues. All three of the leading candidates for the office of president voiced their opposition to oil exploration in the country.[57] Abel Pacheco was elected in a closely fought race, and in his inaugural address in May he declared 'peace with nature'. On Earth Day, he placed a moratorium on future oil and gas exploration as well as on large-scale open-pit mining projects.

In October 2003 Harken submitted a request for arbitration to ICSID under the terms of its concession contract (CAFTA–DR was not yet in force and the US and Costa Rica do not have a BIT). Harken claimed it

[53] 'Oil firm out of Indian land', *Tico Times* (23 March 2001).
[54] 'Oil firm faces deadline'.   [55] *Ibid*.
[56] Harken Energy Corporation, *SEC Form S-3: Registration Statement for Securities Offered pursuant to a Transaction* (filed 3 June 2002), www.secinfo.com/dRE54.31Wm.htm (last accessed 15 December 2010).
[57] 'Texas oil a slippery issue in Costa Rica', *CNN* (1 February 2002), www.articles.cnn.com/2002–02–01/tech/costa.rica.oil_1_oil-drilling-texas-oil-green-turtles?_s=PM:TECH (last accessed 15 December 2010).

had lost US$9–12 million in exploration activity and costs related to administrative and legal procedures, but the company reportedly sought US$57 billion in damages and lost future profits. President Pacheco flatly refused to consent to arbitration and pointed out that Harken's contract required the company to exhaust local remedies.[58] Furthermore, he argued that the company had not met its environmental requirements, which was grounds for termination of the contract. On the other hand, Harken's CEO suggested that SETENA's decision had been politically motivated, that a fair hearing in Costa Rica would be impossible and that the company 'would prefer to reserve the decision to the panel of unbiased and fair international arbitrators'.[59] A representative of the NGO Oil Watch Costa Rica suggested that the threat of arbitration was 'a bluff intended to give the company a stronger negotiating position', and a lobbyist of the company admitted that the company would be willing to back down for a US$10 million settlement.[60]

Only seventeen days after the initial request to ICSID, Harken dropped the case as a 'good faith' act and sought negotiations.[61] President Pacheco called the withdrawal a 'triumph for reason and justice'.[62] Negotiations ensued and at one point Costa Rica was apparently willing to pay Harken between US$3–11 million, as this was 'cheaper than being sued' and 'preferable to facing retaliatory sanctions from the US government'.[63] In a resolution signed by the president in 2005, the Costa Rica government formally cancelled Harken's concession contract.[64] The details of any settlement that might have been agreed by the parties have not been publicised.

B   Vannessa Ventures

In the late 1990s, Placer Dome Inc. of Canada explored for minerals on two properties in the far north-west corner of Costa Rica, near the

---

[58] Natural Resources Defense Council and Friends of the Earth, *The Threat to the Environment from the Central America Free Trade Agreement (CAFTA): The case of Harken Costa Rica Holdings and Offshore Oil* (undated), www.citizen.org/documents/HarkenCRfactsheet.pdf (last accessed 15 December 2010).

[59] 'Pacheco stands firm against oil drilling', *Tico Times* (3 October 2003); see also, 'U.S. oil company withdraws request', *Tico Times* (10 October 2003).

[60] 'Pacheco stands firm'.   [61] 'Harken stopped arbitration', *La Nación* (4 October 2003).

[62] 'U.S. oil company withdraws request'.

[63] 'Government, Harken to negotiate settlement', *Business News Americas* (13 January 2004).

[64] 'Government cancels Harken exploration concession', *Business News Americas* (3 March 2005).

Nicaraguan border.[65] Subsequently, these properties were acquired by Lyon Lake Mines Ltd, another Canadian company. In June 2000, Lyon Lake sold the rights to Vannessa Ventures (Vannessa), also incorporated in Canada.[66] The Crucitas project developed by Vannessa consisted of ten gold-mining concessions covering an area of 176 square km.[67] Vannessa set up a subsidiary in the country, Industrias Infinito SA, submitted a feasibility report to the government in 2001 and received an exploitation permit in 2002, only days before a presidential election.[68]

As noted above, following his election to office President Pacheco put a moratorium on open-pit mining. However, Vannessa assumed that its existing permits would not be affected and continued with the development of its project. The company contracted a Costa Rican consulting company to produce an EIA and submitted it to SETENA in March 2002.[69] In August of that year, the Sala IV ruled on an appeal of the open-pit mining moratorium brought by a representative of the Costa Rican Chamber of Mines. While the court upheld the moratorium, it affirmed the legality of concessions which were issued before the moratorium was put in place. The Environment Minister said that he would respect the decision, but also indicated that the government was ill-equipped to properly regulate and monitor large-scale gold mines.[70]

With the court decision Vannessa Ventures could be confident that its mining licence remained valid but it still faced a second hurdle: the approval of its EIA. In March 2003, a year after it had submitted the EIA, Vannessa filed an injunction to obtain a resolution on its approval or rejection. SETENA responded that the EIA was below standard and would not be approved. Vannessa subsequently filed an appeal with SETENA and requested that the Supreme Court review the decision. The company declared that 'the political environment that manifests itself in the declarations and actions of the President and Minister may

---

[65] D. B. Doan, *The Mineral Industry of Costa Rica* (Reston, VA: US Geological Survey, 1998), p. 1.

[66] P. Velasco, *The Mineral Industries of Central America: Belize, Costa Rica, El Salvador, Guatemala, Honduras, Nicaragua, and Panama* (Reston, Virginia: US Geological Survey, 2000), p. 2.

[67] 'Multi-million ounce Crucitas gold project acquired', *Vannessa Ventures News Release* (17 May 2000) (copy on file with author).

[68] 'Vannessa advances multi-million ounce Crucitas gold project', *Vannessa Ventures News Release* (22 January 2002) (copy on file with author).

[69] 'Vannessa submits Crucitas environmental impact study', *Vannessa Ventures News Release* (19 March 2002) (copy on file with author).

[70] 'High Court gives go-ahead to open-pit mine in north', *Tico Times* (25 October 2002).

have involuntarily influenced the legal and administrative process and resulted in unfair treatment of Infinito and its shareholders'.[71] As a result, the company felt that the principles of fairness, transparency and non-discrimination found in the Canada–Costa Rica BIT had been violated.[72] Erich Rauguth, a senior mining consultant for Vannessa, further stated, 'In reality we've been expropriated'.[73] The company noted in a news release that, if it proceeded with international arbitration under the BIT, 'Effective compensation would be based on the loss of return on investment that can reasonably be expected to materialise', which Vannessa estimated at the time to be approximately US$200 million.[74]

Despite its bold statements, the company continued to pursue a response from SETENA on its appeal and took the issue to the local courts. The Supreme Court found in its favour, requiring SETENA to respond to Vannessa's appeal within five days.[75] The approval process thereafter recommenced and in March 2004 the company appointed a technical commission to deal with additional issues raised by SETENA.[76]

In late 2004 environmentalists brought a case to the Sala IV, arguing that Vannessa's exploitation permit was awarded prior to the company receiving the required environmental approvals and that, as such, it should be annulled.[77] In December 2004 the court upheld the injunction, finding that the process of awarding the mining concession had violated the Central American Biodiversity Agreement and Article 50 (on the right to a healthy environment) of Costa Rica's Constitution.[78] In April 2005 the company asked the Sala IV to reconsider, clarify and add to its ruling. Vannessa also filed a request to advance the international arbitration process with ICSID in July 2005. In a news release the company stated that it sought restitution of its contractual rights and

---

[71] *Ibid.* Vannessa changed its name in May 2008 to 'Infinito Gold Ltd' (Infinito).

[72] Agreement between the Government of Canada and the Government of the Republic of Costa Rica for the Promotion and Protection of Investments, signed at San José 18 March 1998 (entered into force 1 November 2002). The definition of investment under the BIT covers 'rights, conferred by law or under contract, to undertake any economic and commercial activity, including any rights to search for, cultivate, extract or exploit natural resources': Art. 1(g)(vi).

[73] 'High Court sides with gold mining company', *Tico Times* (13 June 2003).

[74] *Ibid.*   [75] *Ibid.*

[76] 'Vannessa ventures updates shareholders on its activities', *Vannessa Ventures News Release* (26 April 2004) (copy on file with author).

[77] 'Clarification of Supreme Court decision on Crucitas concession', *Vannessa Ventures News Release* (5 December 2006) (copy on file with author).

[78] 'Court annuls gold mining concession', *Associated Press* (12 December 2004).

US$5 million in legal and administrative costs. In lieu of restitution it
sought lost profits of US$240 million, plus US$36 million in expenses
and compound interest.[79] The company made it clear that it was advancing the arbitration process in order to protect its claim under the time
requirements of the BIT, and that it would halt the process if SETENA
provided approval of the EIA in the interim.[80]

It was later clarified that the Sala IV ruling only partially annulled the
company's exploitation permit, allowing Vannessa to make corrective
action by submitting an EIA and holding a public meeting about the
project.[81] In September 2005 SETENA approved the company's EIA.[82]
Industrias Infinito's Chief Executive Officer, Jesus Carvajal, noted that
the arbitration request to ICSID had been crucial, stating, 'This kind of
pressure helped SETENA resolve the issue.'[83] The company reported that
the approval of the EIA was 'sufficient reason for the investor Vannessa
Ventures, to consider the withdrawal of the arbitration presented before
[ICSID]'.[84]

Although Vannessa's decision to drop the arbitration request signals
the close of this case for the purposes of this chapter, it is worth noting
that the company's saga is ongoing. President Pacheco's successor,
Oscar Arias, lifted the moratorium on open-pit mining in 2008, which
was then reinstated by President Laura Chinchilla in 2010 (her first act
as president). The ban does not affect Vannessa's (the company is now
known as Infinito Gold) project, but there has been continued pressure
on the government to annul the company's concession. In late July 2010,
a government-commissioned study indicated that to do so would be very
costly: it estimated that $1.7 billion in compensation would be required
to cover the company's expenses as well as lost 'future earnings'.[85] It is
not clear how this sum was calculated, or why it is so much higher than
the claim quoted in Vannessa's 2005 request for arbitration, although

---

[79] 'Vannessa updates Crucitas developments', *Vannessa Ventures News Release* (22 July 2005)
(copy on file with author).
[80] *Ibid.*
[81] 'Update – Supreme Court decision on Crucitas concession', *Vannessa Ventures News
Release* (22 December 2006) (copy on file with author).
[82] 'Crucitas environmental submission approved', *Vannessa Ventures News Release* (1 September
2005) (copy on file with author).
[83] 'Vannessa secures Crucitas enviro permit', *Business News Americas* (1 September 2005).
[84] 'Mining company considers withdrawal of international arbitration', *Infinito News Release*
(2 September 2005), www.infinito.co.cr/comunicados/2005/pr_september2_2005.pdf
(last accessed 16 December 2010).
[85] 'Costa Rica says it would have to pay $1.7 billion to annul mining concession', *Tico Times*
(28 July 2010).

presumably the unprecedented rise in the price of gold in the interim would have significantly affected the value of the company's lost future profits. In any case, the government decided that it could not afford such a high sum and would not take any further action. However, environmental groups in the country have pressed on with legal actions and they were rewarded for their efforts in November 2010 when a Costa Rican court ruled that Vannessa's concession was illegal.[86] At the close of 2010, the company was considering its options for appeal and had not ruled out the possibility of once again bringing the case to ICSID.

C   Analysis

These two cases have many similarities: they occurred in the same country at the same period of time (under the same government); they both concerned controversial resource extraction projects; and they both directly pertained to EIAs that were widely viewed as inadequate. What separates the two cases is their ultimate outcome. In the Vannessa case the government allowed the project to go ahead despite concerns about the EIA. In the Harken case, the government rejected the project outright. What explains the difference in outcomes?

Although the moratorium on oil and open-pit mining projects is relevant to understanding the context in which these investor–State conflicts occurred, it is the EIA policy that is the dependent variable in each case. The companies involved in these conflicts would argue that the (initial) decisions made by SETENA that rejected their EIAs should not be considered bona fide and were rather a result of political pressure from an administration opposed to mining and petroleum exploitation. However, in the Harken case, at least, there was an independent external review of the EIA conducted, which supported SETENA's position. In the Vannessa case, where the project involves the clearing of large areas of forest that are home to two endangered species of birds, it is also hard to imagine that there were no legitimate environmental concerns at stake.

SETENA's approval of Vannessa's EIA despite concerns about deficiencies in it can, therefore, be viewed as non-enforcement of the EIA policy (i.e. a decline in the dependent variable). In the Harken case, the policy was enforced and therefore there was no change in the dependent variable. In terms of the independent variable, in both cases there was

[86] 'Costa Rican court strikes down Las Crucitas gold mine project', *Tico Times* (24 November 2010).

a threat of arbitration, but the key question is how the government *perceived* the threat in each case. On the one hand, the government appeared to view Harken's arbitration threat as hollow; the company's contract stipulated a requirement to exhaust local remedies and no BIT or regional investment agreement with Harken's home State (the USA) was yet in place (if CAFTA–DR had been in force, it is possible that the outcome of the conflict might have been different). On the other hand, in the Vannessa case the threat of arbitration was more palpable, given that the Canada–Costa Rica BIT was in force and clearly covered the company's investment.

In neither case was it evident that the threat of industrial flight was a concern; in fact the aim of the moratorium was to ensure no further investment in extractive projects, which is unsurprising given the focus of the Costa Rican government at the time on promoting ecotourism. However, the role of other variables cannot be entirely ruled out. For example, diplomatic pressure on governments, applied by the home State of the investors, could have also contributed to the outcome in each case. Vannessa enlisted the support of the Canadian Embassy 'to encourage transparency and due process from the Costa Rican government',[87] and there were reports that the US Embassy had become involved in the Harken case. Although the US Ambassador to Costa Rica maintained that he was only assisting the company insofar as to ensure that it was treated fairly by the government, activists remained suspicious.[88] Their cynicism was fuelled by the fact that US President George W. Bush was a former Harken board member. However, others believed that the US pressure was actually on Harken to withdraw its arbitration request, as it could have complicated the negotiations for CAFTA–DR.[89] Thus, the discrepancy in the treatment of Harken and Vannessa might be explained by the fact that Canada urged the Costa Rican government to resolve the conflict, while the US instead might have pressured the investor to drop its arbitration request.

V   Conclusion

As has been noted throughout this volume, the field of investment law has been evolving rapidly in recent years. It has been difficult for many

---

[87] 'Crucitas update', *Vannessa Ventures News Release* (14 April 2003) (copy on file with author).

[88] 'Costa Rica just says no to oil development', *Environmental News Network* (20 September 2002).

[89] 'Pacheco wins one with reversal by Harken energy', *A.M. Costa Rica* (6 October 2003).

practitioners, let alone government regulators, to keep up with developments in the myriad cases being resolved under various contracts, treaties and sets of arbitral rules. Given the current state of flux, it is unsurprising that researchers are largely preoccupied with analysing arbitral awards. However, it is important that scholars recognise that many conflicts between investors and States will never reach the stage of formal arbitration proceedings. Arbitration is a high-risk, high-cost option for both governments and investors. In contrast, the threat of arbitration is cheap and potentially very effective, even in cases where experts might predict that a State would be successful if it took its chances with a tribunal.

The overall aim of this chapter has not been to argue that regulatory chill will always, or even frequently, result from an investor's threat to arbitrate; in fact the Costa Rican cases show that investor–State conflicts are often quite complex and outcomes will depend on a number of factors. Rather, the key objectives have been to dispel some misconceptions about how regulators behave that are evident in the legal literature, and to provide a solid foundation on which future empirical work on regulatory chill could be based. It is hoped that the reader may have also been persuaded that the repeated dismissals of the regulatory chill hypothesis by some practitioners and legal scholars are both premature and lacking in analytical rigour.

Legal scholars with a genuine interest in exploring the interconnections between investment law and other areas of law and policy must begin to look beyond arbitrator-authored texts. It is also important that political scientists and scholars from other fields of social science become, as have some economists recently, much more involved in debates about the current and future framework for international investment protection. Some cross-fertilisation and collaboration between disciplines is already occurring, but it could be significantly advanced if established investment law scholars clearly indicated that they were open to considering new perspectives and ideas, even those that might challenge some prevailing views within the field.

PART VI

Conclusions

27

Evolution or revolution in international investment arbitration? The descent into normlessness

M. SORNARAJAH

I Introduction

There is evident disquiet about foreign investment arbitration.[1] Some of the titles of the papers in this collection demonstrate that disquiet. There is need to explore the schisms that have opened up in the last few years in a field that was a dormant area of international law not so long ago. A book written just three years ago was euphoric in proclaiming that there was such common ground in the law that was being evolved by arbitration tribunals that it was possible to speak of almost a common law on foreign investment.[2] A more recent book even contemplates the possibility of multilateral rules on foreign investment having evolved as a result of investment treaties and intepretations placed on them by arbitral tribunals.[3] Another work seeks to virtually codify the rules created through investment arbitration with Diceyan pomp.[4] Some have contemplated the creation of a regime on foreign investment resulting from the treaties and the arbitrations based on them. There is an argument that the developments relating to treaties and investment arbitration has brought about a regime which supposes the existence of community expectations about norms and their enforcement.[5]

---

[1] This is evidenced in the literature with a whole book appearing with a title that indicates concern. See Michael Waibel *et al.* (eds.), *The Backlash against Investment Arbitration: Perceptions and reality* (The Hague: Kluwer, 2010).

[2] Campbell McLachlan, Laurence Shore, and Matthew Weiniger, *International Investment Arbitration: Substantive principles* (Oxford University Press, 2007) paras. 1.48–1.56.

[3] Stephan Schill, *The Multilateralisation of International Investment Law* (Cambridge University Press, 2009).

[4] Zachary Douglas, *The International Law of Investment Claims* (Cambridge University Press, 2009).

[5] See e.g. Jeswald Salacuse, 'The emerging global regime for investment', *Harvard International Law Journal*, 51 (2010), 427; see also Jeswald Salacuse, *The Law of Investment Treaties* (Oxford University Press, 2010).

Another collection, while conceding the problems that have arisen, contains attempts at apologetic justification.[6] There are even efforts to constitution-alise the principles on foreign investment that have been created.

All this comes at a time when the law is hurtling into 'normlessness'[7] as a result of State reactions to expansive interpretations placed on treaty prescriptions.[8] There has been resistance to the manner in which treaties have been interpreted in arbitral awards to create obligations binding on States far beyond what was originally intended in the treaties. The assumption of this near legislative power by arbitrators chosen without a mandate to fulfil such a function has resulted in responses by States which undermine considerably the existing system of investment treaty arbitration. The creation of wide preclusions to State liability that could arise under the treaties prevents further expansionism. Some States have withdrawn from the system and others have threatened to do so. Some States have embarked on reviews of the utility of the system.[9] In response, some arbitrators, at least, are imposing stringent restrictions on the jurisdictional threshold which will considerably restrict the number of arbitrations that would be brought. They also show a tendency to rein in the expansionism that was initiated by another group of arbitrators. These disparate trends show neither evolution nor revolution but an ongoing conflict that either will bring a new system – resulting in a revolution – or will keep the old, simply because one or the other of the camps wins the tussle.

Much of the turbulence in the field has been caused by the immense activity in investment treaty-making and the profusion of arbitral awards resulting from disputes based on jurisdiction assumed under these treaties. It has become a lucrative area of practice as many inter-national firms and arbitrators have jumped into the area to fish in its troubled waters. The malaise that afflicts the law must be identified. It lies not in any style in interpretation of treaties or the differences in the wording of the treaties but in the fact that a large number of arbitrators

[6] Waibel *et al.* (eds.), *The Backlash against Investment Arbitration.*

[7] A coined word denoting intense norm conflict, similar to the concept of 'anomie' as used by the sociologist, Robert Merton: see e.g. Robert Merton, 'Norm structure and anomie', *American Sociological Review*, 3 (1938), 672.

[8] M. Sornarajah, 'Towards normlessness: The ravage and retreat of neo-liberalism in international investment law', *Yearbook of International Investment Law and Policy*, 2 (2010), 595.

[9] South Africa announced a review and has released a report. The United States also has a pending review of investment treaties. States like Argentina and the Czech Republic have expressed displeasure.

sought to give new ideological interpretations to the treaties. This is a fact that must be squarely faced. The ideology of neoliberalism dominated the last decade of the twentieth century until the 'free fall'[10] of the world economy in 2008. Many arbitrators sought to give effect to what was the dominant economic thought of the period in their awards. In so doing, they took the law on expansionary paths it was not intended to take. The awards were dictated by an ideological fervour of the times which did not permit any contrary ideas to stand in the way of articulation of principles that were based on free-market fundamentalism. Arbitrators readily assumed this role because of their own natural inclination towards such a view but also because it profited the profession they belonged to. They were however met with objections by arbitrators with a fidelity to the neutrality that is the basis of arbitration and to the tenets of arbitration not to go beyond the mandate that was entrusted to them by the parties. It is this tussle that marked the descent into 'normlessness'[11] that has ensued.

This chapter describes the nature of the normlessness and contemplates the possible outcomes. It puts forward the view that the law has been taken back to the situation of the period of a similar chaos when the clash between the capital-exporting and capital-importing nations regarding the New International Economic Order (NIEO) resulted in two sets of norms. The investment treaty system was to settle rules of investment protection as between the parties. The evolution of the system has been subjected to severe strains as a result of arbitral adventurism motivated by ideological considerations. This chapter begins by identifying the old conflict that existed and its attempted solution through bilateral investment treaties. It characterises that settlement itself as flawed because it contained asymmetric rules that were exploited by a self-serving legal profession and arbitrators to the detriment of

[10] Joseph Stiglitz, *Free Fall: America, free markets and the sinking of the world economy* (New York: W. W. Norton, 2010). In an earlier book, Stiglitz had described the last decade of the twentieth century as the 'roaring nineties': Joseph Stiglitz, *The Roaring Nineties* (London: Penguin Books, 2003). It was during this decade that investment treaties proliferated.

[11] 'Normlessness' is a concept that has an affinity to the theory of anomie put forward by the sociologist, Robert Merton. Merton explained crime on the basis of the existence of groups which did not accept the rules stated by the community but accepted their own values and norms. When large-scale dissent of this sort takes place, a situation of '*anomie*' results giving rise to crimes as behaviour which is in accordance with one set of norms but which is criminal according to the other set of norms. The notion is varied here to indicate the existence of two sets of norms both of which have credible claims to legality, resulting in a chaotic schism.

developing countries when they increased the asymmetries by building more-onerous rules of investment protection on the basis of nebulous provisions in the investment treaties.

II   The old conflict

I had identified the area of international law on foreign investment as an area of intense norm conflict since its beginning.[12] The law was never settled simply because of the interests at conflict. In the beginning, the law was very much regional, confined to the investment relations between the US and Latin America. In the rest of the world, investment took place in the colonial context. The regional law was based on the conflict between the international minimum standard and the Calvo doctrine. The conflict was never settled, though power equations clearly favoured the international minimum standard. The conflict was universalised in the period of decolonisation with the former colonial powers subscribing to the international minimum standard and the newly independent States supporting sovereignty-based control norms in documents associated with the New International Economic Order. Investment treaties which began life in 1959 and had reached the figure of around 400 by the 1990s[13] were a symbol of these conflicts of norms. In the last decade of the twentieth century, the 'roaring nineties', the number of treaties catapulted to reach almost 3,000. States sought to bring about settled rules by signing treaties bilaterally so as to escape the conflict of norms that existed on the international scene. They were very much *lex specialis* in origin. The fact that the developing States were signing bilateral investment treaties while maintaining a stance that favoured the NIEO approach has been variously explained.[14] The truth is that neither the developing States nor the developed States were prepared to make a multilateral treaty. The failure of the effort of

---

[12] M. Sornarajah, *The International Law on Foreign Investment*, 3rd edn (Cambridge University Press, 2010).

[13] According to Kenneth Vandevelde, there were 386 treaties by 1989: Kenneth Vandevelde, 'A brief history of international investment agreements' in Karl Sauvant and Linda Sachs (eds.), *The Effect of Treaties on Foreign Direct Investment: Bilateral investment treaties, double taxation treaties, and investment flows* (Oxford University Press, 2009), p. 16.

[14] See Andrew Guzman, 'Why LDCs sign treaties that hurt them', *Virginia Journal of International Law*, 38 (1998), 639. The explanation is contested by Jose Alvarez, 'The once and future foreign investment regime' in Mahnoush Arsanjani *et al.* (eds.), *Looking to the Future: Essays on international law in honour of Michael Reisman* (Leiden: Martinus Nijhoff, forthcoming 2011), pp. 607, 614.

the OECD to make a multilateral agreement on investment confined to developed States attests to this fact. It is evident that like the developing countries, developed countries too were adopting a duplicitous attitude for though they made bilateral treaties, they would not participate in a multilateral treaty even among themselves. The developing States made bilateral treaties yet did not change their domestic laws on investment or their contractual practices significantly in response to these treaties. In fact, as has been held, the protected investments under the treaties depended on the manner of the admission of the investment into the host State as well as its subsequent conduct.[15]

In hindsight, it is possible to conclude that a larger number of the treaties that were made in the 1990s were made in the belief that investment treaties will promote flows of investment into developing States, and international financial institutions assiduously promoted this belief. But considerable doubt has been cast on this view.[16] Judging by the views stated by mid-level developing countries like South Africa, it is clear that the developing countries lacked any idea as to the implications of the treaties they were making. They were misled into the belief that economic development was not possible unless foreign investment flows occurred and that such flows would occur only if investment treaties were made.

It would be a gross error to say that these treaties contributed to customary international law or confirmed pre-existing customary international law. The treaties were not sufficiently uniform to create such law. Each treaty was separately negotiated and constituted a particular balance of rules struck through negotiations. Though their outer form was similar, they did not subscribe to the same rule. The argument that the Hull standard of compensation has become customary international law, which is the usual illustration put up by those who argue that customary international law has been created by the treaties, does not hold water. It is true that a large number of the treaties contains the Hull standard. But to determine the extent of the protection they give to investment through the operation of the Hull standard, one has to take into consideration the nature of the definition of the protected

---

[15] *Fraport AG Frankfurt Airport Services Worldwide* v. *Philippines* (ICSID Case No. ARB/03/25, Award of 16 August 2007).

[16] There is a spate of economics literature which has examined whether investment treaties do in fact promote investment flows into developing countries. The conclusions to be derived from these studies are not conclusive but they do throw some doubt on the main belief with which these treaties are concluded: see especially the various contributions in Sauvant and Sachs (eds.), *The Effect of Treaties on Foreign Direct Investment*.

investment which varies with treaties, the scope of the host State's entry laws which regulate such protected investment (as the investment has to be made in accordance with such laws) and a host of other limiting factors which are unlikely to be the same in each treaty. There is nothing to indicate that BITs have been followed by changes in internal laws. Rather, the constitutions of most developing countries reflect the doctrine of permanent sovereignty over natural resources and the contract forms preferred, like the production-sharing agreement, emphasise host State control rather than external control through treaty principles. Despite the existence of these treaties, international law on foreign investment retains the original flaw of discordant interests that characterised its creation in the practice of the United States and the Latin American States. Though American writers may pretend that what the US espoused was customary international law, that was never in fact the case.[17] The Latin Americans clearly did not accept these norms and the newly independent States of Asia and Africa did not accept them either. It is a facet of American exceptionalism to pass off the prescriptions of the United States as international law. The prescriptions were made through weak sources of international law which included official statements, awards of bilateral arbitral commissions imposed on States and writings of American publicists, highly qualified no doubt. These prescriptions were always contested by Latin American States. Later, they were contested by Asian and African States through the NIEO resolutions. The fact that these resolutions are said to be weak sources[18] is of little consequence as what is claimed by American writers to be customary international law also depend on weak sources of law. And further, the fact that investment treaties were made in a particular decade does not alter the picture simply because the treaties did not contain rules of uniform application.

The investor–State dispute-settlement provision was not a feature of the early treaties.[19] It became routine in later times. The treaties made in the 1990s uniformly contained such provisions. Nevertheless, it must be remembered that early treaties did not have such provisions and this is

---

[17] e.g. Alvarez, 'The once and future foreign investment regime', p. 619.

[18] e.g. ibid., p. 618.

[19] Aron Broches, 'Bilateral investment treaties and the arbitration of investment disputes' in Jan Schultsz and Albert Jan van den Berg (eds.), *The Art of Arbitration: Essays on international arbitration: Liber amicorum Pieter Sanders* (The Hague: Kluwer, 1982) distinguished between the types of dispute-settlement clauses found at the time of his writing in the different investment treaties. It was exceptional to find treaties with unilateral rights of arbitration in the foreign investor, a feature that was to become common in treaties concluded in the last decade of the twentieth century.

THE DESCENT INTO NORMLESSNESS

matched by new treaties which are dispensing with the investor–State dispute-settlement provision.[20] Investment treaty arbitration took off only with the discovery of the technique of founding jurisdiction on the basis of dispute-settlement provisions of investment treaties in *AAPL* v. *Sri Lanka*, though treaties containing similar language had existed for some time. This phenomenon of startling significance for international law – enabling individuals or corporations, not bearers of personality in positivist international law to sue States – had gone unnoticed by the most percipient commentators of the period who commented on the treaties prior to 1990, the year of *AAPL* v. *Sri Lanka*, where the technique was first recognised. Since the recognition of establishing jurisdiction through investment treaties came to be recognised, the number of arbitrations sky-rocketed, leading no doubt to the economic development of arbitrators and law firms and to the detriment of the developing States to which the system was supposed to bring economic development. These trends were promoted through the repeated appointment of arbitrators prone to promote expansionist views of the law based on investment treaties. There is considerable doubt in modern literature as to whether investment treaties promote flows of foreign investment and thereby lead to the economic development of host developing States.[21] It would appear that the sovereignty costs of the investment treaties and the consequent risk of investment arbitration far outweigh the elusive benefits that investment treaties bring to developing States. This would be particularly so because of the expansive interpretations that arbitrators have placed on provisions in the investment treaties, thereby subjecting States to greater risk of investment claims. The mathematical calculations made on the basis of damages awarded[22] do not

---

[20] See e.g. the Australia–United States Free Trade Agreement, www.dfat.gov.au/fta/usfta/index.html (last accessed 7 December 2010); and the Philippines–Japan Economic Partnership Agreement, www.mofa.go.jp/policy/economy/fta/philippines.html (last accessed 7 December 2010), both of which lack investor–State arbitration provisions. Since the *SGS* case (*SGS Société Générale de Surveillance SA* v. *Republic of the Philippines* (ICSID Case No. ARB/02/6, Decision on Jurisdiction of 29 January 2004)), the Philippines has demonstrated a reluctance to make treaties with such provisions. The Australia–United States Free Trade Agreement is explained on the ground that the two countries have the same common law system. This is not much of a rationalisation as there are other States with which the US has made treaties which also have common law systems (such as e.g. Singapore).

[21] See e.g. the ch. 6 by Jonathan Bonnitcha in this volume and the references cited therein.

[22] The argument is sometimes made that the awards eventually given are small in comparison with the huge claims that are made. This is beside the point. There are reputational costs to the State arising from allegations of unfair treatment. Besides, the need to mount defences to spurious claims involves costs that a developing country can hardly bear. It

outweigh the risk of spurious claims brought by law firms that fish for such litigation and mount them on the basis of fanciful theories of jurisdiction and substantive claims, resulting in litigation and reputational costs to the respondent States. Besides, since the system has been shown to be so expansive, the threat of arbitration has become a powerful way of bringing pressure on States to desist from environmental and other measures to promote the public welfare.[23] In the light of these developments, States are taking measures which may result in the demise of investment arbitration, though the euphoric phase is still showing signs of life. This may be due to the fact that the profession which created the goose that laid golden eggs may be afraid to admit that goose is nearing its end. There is also considerable academic effort in keeping the system alive as academics also generate wealth and fame for themselves through their association with the legal profession in the lucrative endeavour that investment arbitration presents.

Signs of the decay of the system are evident. The mildest reaction is that newer treaties show that there are broad and uncertain defences that are being created. The national security exception is stated almost always in subjective terms in the newer treaties.[24] Exception is made for interferences that can be justified on grounds of health, morals or public welfare. There are exceptions relating to interferences justified on the need for environmental safeguards and human rights considerations. The treaties state that 'except in rare instances', an expropriation would be treated as regulatory. The formula of anything 'tantamount to an expropriation' which enables fanciful expansion of the concept of expropriation goes missing in the new treaties. The possible expansion of the 'fair and equitable treatment' on the basis of arbitral imagination is restrained by tying it to customary international law in most of the newer treaties. In some, the phrase is simply not used. One would think that these are reactions of the developing world. On the contrary, these are changes that can be found in the American and Canadian treaties as well as in the more recent treaties made by developing countries. The new ASEAN Comprehensive Investment Agreement, which came into

---

also is apparent that a State which hires foreign firms stands a better chance of success, thereby creating more work for foreign law firms and greater costs for respondent States.

[23] The *Ethyl* case is the obvious example (*Ethyl Corporation* v. *Canada* (NAFTA, Decision on Jurisdiction of 24 June 1998)). The extent of the pressure brought cannot be quantified. See especially Kyla Tienhaara, *The Expropriation of Environmental Governance: Protecting foreign investors at the expense of public policy* (Cambridge University Press, 2009), ch. 8.

[24] The new Model BITs of the United States and Canada are indications. The many cases against Argentina may not have been possible if there had been a subjective statement of national security in the US–Argentina BIT.

force in 2010, contains the traditional statements on investment protection but also includes wide statements of defences to responsibility along
similar lines that are identified above. It is still to be determined what the
extent and scope of these express defences are.

What was described was the mildest reaction by the States to the
present crisis. This reaction preserves the system. It introduces what
commentators have optimistically described as balances into the treaties.
The so-called balance itself destroys the purpose of investment protection which was the solitary concern of the older treaty system as well as
of customary international law. The change must be noticed. It obviously results from the fact that the shoe is on the other foot.[25] The
erstwhile capital-exporting States are becoming massive recipients of
capital. They are becoming respondents in arbitrations. They may soon
become targets of even larger numbers of claims. They are quick to break
down the law that they had so assiduously created knowing well that it
could become the stick to beat them with. Since the retreat is most
visible in the US Model BIT, one could argue, taking a leaf from
American exceptionalism, that the old law that the US created has been
severely undermined. In fact, the displeasure with the new Model BIT is
expressed by the veterans of American international law who can see
their preferred system crumbling before them.[26]

There have been more severe reactions than the creation of defences.
Some treaties leave out investor–State arbitration altogether.[27] This

---

[25] In the context of NAFTA, the United States and Canada have faced many arbitrations
under provisions which they designed for use exclusively against Mexico. The unin-
tended consequence was that they became respondents. Though the United States is yet
to lose a case, it is obvious that it has taken measures to change the law. The NAFTA
Commission, in its Interpretive Statement of 31 July 2001, removed the possible uses of
the fair and equitable treatment standard which was fast becoming the obvious avenue
for further arbitration by coupling it with customary international law, thereby removing
an important breach through which further cases could have been mounted.

[26] See e.g. the view of Judge Schwebel on the US Model BIT (2004): Stephen Schwebel, 'The
United States 2004 Model Bilateral Investment Treaty: An exercise in the regressive
development of international law', *Transnational Dispute Management* (2006), 2, www.
transnational-dispute-management.com.

[27] See e.g. the Australia–United States Free Trade Agreement, www.dfat.gov.au/fta/usfta/
index.html (last accessed 7 December 2010); and the Philippines–Japan Economic
Partnership Agreement, www.mofa.go.jp/policy/economy/fta/philippines.html (last
accessed 7 December 2010). This could well become the pattern for future Philippines
treaties as the country has had to face many arbitrations recently, principally *Fraport
AG Frankfurt Airport Services Worldwide* v. *Philippines* (ICSID Case No. ARB/ 03/25,
Award of 16 August 2007) and *SGS Société Générale de Surveillance SA* v. *Republic of the
Philippines* (ICSID Case No. ARB/02/6, Decision on Jurisdiction of 29 January 2004). It

again keeps the treaty system but forestalls its extensive use as State-to-State arbitrations have been a rarity in the field. If it gathers steam, it will undermine considerably investor–State arbitration, which is the life-blood of the present legal industry. It will send ICSID into the old days of lugubrious slumber. The case-load of ICSID seems to be on the increase but one has to wait and see whether the newer treaties will have an impact on the number of arbitrations once they take hold. The prospects of winning an arbitration diminish considerably in the light of the new defences that have been recognised as well as the responses of States which have explored further defences in existing international law like the necessity defence.

The more disconcerting phenomenon is the withdrawal of some States from the system. It would appear that many States which have been at the wrong end of the stick have withdrawn or are contemplating withdrawal. It is well known that Ecuador and Bolivia have withdrawn from the system and that Venezuela has withdrawn petroleum disputes from the system. There have been many threats from Argentina which, as is well known, is faced with over fifty arbitrations arising from its economic crisis. The Argentinian cases, as they hang around, will be illustrative to other States of the predicament they can get into as a result of investment treaties. The Argentinian cases demonstrate a tenacity in the respondent State to try out novel defences. It appears to be succeeding. It has exploited to the fullest the existing system and, in the process, successfully demonstrated its flaws. The presence of this constant demonstration does little good for the system. Argentina has also consistently threatened withdrawal. With the presence of Brazil, the most successful Latin American State which developed without investment treaties, it could well be that the Calvo doctrine will be back in Latin America.[28] Indeed, some writers are thinking out loud as to whether the United States is following the Calvo doctrine in its approach to the subject of investment arbitration. There are reviews of the investment treaty system in the United States and South Africa. South Africa has declared that it had made its existing investment treaties without fully understanding its

---

is reported that Thailand will show reluctance to include arbitration clauses in its State contracts after losing in *Walter Bau AG* v. *Thailand* (Award of 1 July 2009). Reactions in Pakistan to a series of investment arbitration awards were similar. The Pakistani Attorney-General remarked that the claims made exceeded the foreign exchange reserves of Pakistan.

[28] Ignacio Vincentelli, 'The uncertain future of ICSID in Latin America', *Law and Business Review of the Americas*, 16 (2010), 409.

implications. Norway experimented with a model BIT which, had it been approved, would have been a turn around on investment protection. It was replete with articulations of the concern with environmental and other interests in the area.

Clearly, despite the vestiges of the old euphoria with investment arbitration, all is not well with investment arbitration. It is necessary to ask what led to this present position where there is neither 'evolution' nor 'revolution' as the title to the Sydney conference suggests, but a descent into the morass of 'normlessness'. If 'revolution' there be, then it is that dissent is growing and changes will have to occur. There may well be signs of this but the revolution is yet to turn the corner. It is more likely that the investment treaty system will go into disuse because of the uncertainties opened up by the extent of the defences that have been created both in the new treaties as well as in some arbitral awards. It may no longer be wise for foreign investors to bring claims as they cannot, as in the past, be assured of victory. Since tribunals are moving away from the practice of bifurcating costs and asking the losing party to pay more by way of costs, there would be an increasing deterrence to bring claims against States. There will be changes taking place. This chapter now examines what has brought the law in the area to the present situation which has been described and contemplates the possible future outcomes.

III   On killing the goose that laid the golden eggs

The fairy tale of the goose that laid golden eggs is a tale of greed.[29] The tale of investment arbitration is also a tale of greed.[30] Greed subverted a worthwhile system that could have matured to serve its genuine purpose

---

[29] In the fairy tale, the couple who owned the goose thought that its innards would be made of gold and dissected the goose to find the gold. It was a normal goose with normal innards. The fanciful thinking of the couple killed the goose and denied them of a steady income. So, too, ordinary treaties have been given extraordinary meanings to support spurts in arbitration. The system has been strained and may have to shut down, killing off a lucrative business because of the haste of some arbitrators to structure a system which the States did not want and that too at a time when the structure of investment flows were changing with the erstwhile capital exporters becoming the largest recipients of foreign capital. The elite few within the multinational law firms practicing in this area also jumped onto the bandwagon and fashioned fanciful theories of litigation on the basis of nebulous language in the treaties. The interaction between two small bands, arbitrators and a group of lawyers dominating, both intent on building up a lucrative business for themselves in the field, has led to the present morass.

[30] I have written a longer paper on this subject suggesting that there was a build up of an international law of greed in the neoliberal age: M. Sornarajah, 'A law for need or a law

had it not been subverted through greed and by an ideology that supported greed. Fanciful litigation theories based on the interpretations of terms of treaties which the parties never intended became the cause of a spurt in litigation. A small group of lawyers cornering the field of investment arbitration for themselves and an equally small group of arbitrators finding repeated appointment in the field have between them succeeded in tearing the system apart.[31] The academic profession has joined in to grab the crumbs from the table. The young are subverted by the extent of the lucre that is supposed to lie at the end of the rainbow. The field has begun in recent times to see challenges to arbitrators alleging bias and challenges to lawyers wearing different hats during their careers. It is an unhappy tale of unscrupulous greed thriving on a system that was purportedly built to ease poverty in the developing world. What follows is a short and incomplete list of the excesses that have been committed through arbitral adventurism. The list serves to identify the malaise that afflicts investment arbitration.

A   Exorbitant theories of jurisdiction

The idea that there could be arbitration of investment disputes at the unilateral instance of a foreign investor is an innovation that is startling in the context of any legal system – more so in that of international law, which did not, at least in the view of positivist international lawyers, recognise the personality of multinational corporations. In 1990, the year of the award in *AAPL* v. *Sri Lanka*, the case that initiated treaty-based investment arbitration, the common law did not recognise contracts that confer rights on third parties. The civil law systems were wary

for greed? Restoring the lost law in the international law of foreign investment', *International Environmental Agreements: Law Politics and Economics*, 6 (2006), 329. Others have remarked on a change within law towards a loss of values and an assumption that wealth creation should be the only touchstone for the validity of laws: see Anthony Kronman, *The Lost Lawyer: Failing ideals of the legal profession* (Cambridge, MA: Harvard University Press, 1993). See also Anthony Kronman, *Education's End: Why our colleges and universities have given up on the meaning of life* (New Haven, CT: Yale University Press, 2007).

[31] On repeat appointments of arbitrators, see Daphna Kapeliuk, 'The repeat appointment factor: Exploring decision patterns of elite investment arbitrators', *Cornell Law Review*, 96 (2010), 47. It is interesting to see to what extent these 'elite' arbitrators have contributed to the making of expansive interpretation of treaties and inquire whether they are appointed to perform this very task. There does not seem to be any extraordinary expertise in them in the field of investment law. Many did not even have a demonstrated grounding in international law or even public law.

of stipulations in favour of third parties (*stipulatio alteri*), though they had come to accept them in a limited number of situations.[32] The common law due to the existence of the doctrine of consideration for the making of contracts did not admit stipulations in favour of third parties, until it was changed by legislation. As a general principle of law, the validity of a *stipulatio alteri* would have been exceptional in most legal systems in 1990. The idea that international law had progressed towards the recognition of stipulations in favour of yet-unknown individuals and corporations would indeed be a novelty of immense proportions for a law still considered to be in a primitive state. Not only was the stipulation made in favour of entities lacking capacity in terms of international law but the entities may not have even been in existence at the time the stipulation was made.[33] Yet, investment arbitration has come to be based on that idea, which has been extended beyond the limits of credibility by arbitrators. There is no doubt that the ordinary meaning of the dispute-settlement provision in the treaties admits of the view taken in *AAPL* v. *Sri Lanka* and the cases since then in permitting jurisdiction on the basis of an appropriately worded dispute-settlement provision in investment treaties. It is to be admitted that the large number of treaties made in the 1990s do ordinarily provide for investor–State arbitration. Yet, there are theoretical difficulties that attend this conclusion.

Added to the theoretical difficulties inherent in the situation, the extensions made to the notion of jurisdiction on the basis of BITs have been subjected to severe strain. Thus, tribunals have held that jurisdiction could be invoked by citizens of a State against their own State merely by incorporating a company in the other treaty partner.[34] This defeats the whole purpose of the BIT as it is the State's own funds that are being re-routed into the State through the medium of the company incorporated abroad. It also defeats the purpose of the ICSID Convention which is to provide arbitration to aliens and not to citizens of the respondent State. There is a clear subversion of the reasons why investment treaties are made and the reason for the creation of ICSID. Though

---

[32] In terms of Roman law, the *donatio mortis causa* and the *fideicommissum* are given as examples.

[33] Both in the English concept of a trust and the Roman law concept of a *fideicommissum*, the ultimate beneficiaries were not known but the immediate transferee was known and a commitment was imposed on him.

[34] *Tokio Tokeles* v. *Ukraine* (ICSID Case No. ARB/02/18, Decision on Jurisdiction of 29 April 2004); the strong dissent of the chairman, Prosper Weil, contains the reasons why the decision is based on an exorbitant extension of jurisdiction.

the textual interpretation of the treaty may be satisfied, its purpose is defeated by holding that incorporation in another State with a treaty with their home State is sufficient to enable proceedings to be brought. Further, it has been held that companies could migrate into States with better investment protection and claim the protection of the investment treaty.[35] Smaller States like Holland and Mauritius favour such views even though it is obvious that no capital has really flowed from the State of migration into the host State which is being sued. There is a definite subterfuge involved in these arguments which are tainted with an obvious fraud on the part of the claimants. Yet, arbitrators have been willingly complicit in such fraud because it is convenient for them to create jurisdiction in such cases rather than lose out on business. It is difficult to find any kinder explanation for this obvious expansion of the circumstances in which jurisdiction can be established. The fact that the words may support the conclusion does not justify an international judge permitting an obvious fraud on the system. These are cases which have caused considerable disquiet but the theories of jurisdiction based on such ideas seem to be on the increase and are known to be actively encouraged by law firms which advise clients to incorporate in third States which have treaty protection in anticipation of disputes.[36] Such cases defeat the premises on which investment arbitration is based. In more recent investment treaties, States have sought to avoid such results through the inclusion of 'denial of benefits' provisions which entitle a State to deny protection for corporations which do not have any meaningful link with the other State Party to the treaty.

Equally interesting is the current debate on the definition of an 'investment'.[37] It must be noted that there are cases in which no investment could possibly have taken place. Thus, in the recent case, *Romak SA v. The Republic of Uzbekistan*, the claim concerned contracts for the sale of cereals. Even a neophyte would recognise that a sales contract could not be regarded as an investment in respect of which a treaty claim can be made. Yet, the tribunal went through the motions of deciding the dispute. At the end, after denying jurisdiction, it held that costs should be borne equally when it was pretty obvious that this was a vexatious

---

[35] *Aguas del Tunari* v. *Bolivia* (ICSID Case No. ARB/02/3, Decision on Jurisdiction of 21 October 2005).

[36] In *Conoco-Philips* v. *Venezuela* (ICSID Case No. ARB/07/30), a pending case, jurisdiction is based on such corporate migration in anticipation of the dispute.

[37] See e.g. ch. 3 by David A. R. Williams QC and Simon Foote and ch. 25 by Omar Garcia Bolivar in this volume.

case that a developing State had needlessly to defend, it being apparent that there was no investment that was capable of protection under the treaty.

More disconcerting is the manner in which the debate on the criteria for identification of a foreign investment has been undertaken. The so called *Salini* criteria included economic development as a criterion especially where ICSID arbitration is involved. This criterion was emphasised in the decision on annulment in *Patrick Mitchell* v. *Democratic Republic of the Congo*.[38] It has generally been accepted that the concept of investment has an objective criteria. In any event, many BITs specify in their preambles that the object of the treaties is to promote economic development. Developing States make investment treaties which involve considerable erosion of their sovereignty in the belief that the treaties will promote the flow of foreign investment and thereby foster economic development. Whatever its correctness, it is this belief that justifies the sacrifice of sovereignty. It is also a reason why they accept ICSID arbitration which also has been sold to them on the basis that acceptance of such an argument and the consequent exclusion of their own judicial sovereignty over investment disputes, as required by the Calvo doctrine and Article 2(2)(c) of the Charter of Economic Rights and Duties of States, will promote economic development.

It now appears that in a system that has been built up on the promise of economic development as the *quid pro quo* for surrendering sovereignty, some arbitrators would hold that an investment would be entitled to protection even when it is clearly shown to be of no value in promoting economic development. In the decision on annulment in *Malaysian Historical Salvors Sdn Bhd* v. *Malaysia*, the majority took the view that the criterion of economic development was not necessary for the identification of a foreign investment that is protected by an investment treaty or is capable of generating a dispute that could be settled before ICSID.[39] Both conclusions go against the basic suppositions of investment treaties as well as of the ICSID Convention. The World Bank has no mandate to provide general arbitration services. The only justification for the creation of ICSID, an arm of the World Bank, is that it is based on the rationale, false or true, that its existence will create investor confidence and result in flows of investment into its

---

[38] *Patrick Mitchell* v. *Democratic Republic of the Congo* (ICSID Case No. ARB/99/7, Decision on Annulment of 1 November 2006), paras. 27–33.

[39] *Malaysian Historical Salvors Sdn Bhd* v. *Malaysia* (ICSID Case No. ARB05/10, Decision on Annulment of 16 April 2009), paras. 58–80.

developing-country members. Economic development lies at the very root of ICSID arbitration. A transaction which does not satisfy the criterion of economic development cannot qualify for jurisdiction under the ICSID Convention.[40] The decision on annulment would convert any commercial dispute into a foreign investment dispute as long as there is a transborder flow of assets. This is of course not the purpose of investment arbitration or of investment treaties. Again, the expansion suggested in *Malaysian Historical Salvors* goes beyond the intention of the parties and will undoubtedly provoke a reaction of concerned States.

Another potential source of discord has been opened in the award in *Phoenix Action Ltd* v. *Czech Republic*.[41] There is a passage in the award which states the view that a contract that involves genocide or torture cannot found jurisdiction. The present writer has argued for such a principle on the basis of *ius cogens* principles and suggested that there was a doctrine of arbitrability in investment law that denied jurisdiction in disputes violating such principles.[42] The proposition was cast in wider terms to include principles such as self-determination, bribery and contracts made by non-representative governments. One would think that in all these instances too, where principles of *ius cogens* are violated, it is unlikely that the element of economic development can be satisfied. Eventually, there would be a coalescence of investment arbitration situations with the situations under the Alien Torts Act so that all issues

---

[40] The criteria including economic development as indicia for a protected investment, as stated in *Salini Costruttori SpA and Italstrade SpA* v. *Morocco* (ICSID Case No. ARB/00/4, Decision on Jurisdiction of 23 July 2001), para. 52, was to a large extent based on the statement in the first edition of Schreuer's commentary: Christoph Schreuer, *The ICSID Convention: A commentary* (Cambridge University Press, 2001), p. 140. In the second edition, the requirement of economic development is stated in a muted fashion: see e.g. Christoph Schreuer *et al.*, *The ICSID Convention: A commentary*, 2nd edn (Cambridge University Press, 2009), p. 134. ICSID, unlike other arbitral institutions, was set up to provide for the arbitration of investment disputes on the assumption that such arbitration gives stability to foreign investment, thereby promotes flows of foreign investment and hence leads to economic development. Any investment that does not coincide with these aims cannot qualify as investment under the ICSID Convention. The sole arbitrator in *Malaysian Historical Salvors Sdn Bhd* v. *Malaysia* (ICSID Case No. ARB05/10, Award on Jurisdiction of 17 May 2007) made the mistake of going off on a tangent in stating his own theories on the definition of investment rather than making a straightforward finding of fact that the services contract involved in the dispute was not a foreign investment transaction protected by the BIT or by the ICSID Convention.

[41] *Phoenix Action Ltd* v. *Czech Republic* (ICSID Case No. ARB/06/5, Award of 15 April 2009).

[42] M. Sornarajah, *The Settlement of Foreign Investment Disputes* (The Hague: Kluwer, 2001), pp. 186–8.

relating to violations of the environment or human rights will impact investment arbitration. When this happens, the system of investment arbitration will be threatened with collapse as its primary purpose of investment protection will become untenable. Avenues have been created for States to plead such issues, particularly when the claimant seeks to advance arguments relating to the fair and equitable treatment standard. The respondent State could then argue that the tribunal should take account of the impact of the foreign investment on the environment or the human rights situation within the State. Economic development is associated with both concerns.

States have also hit back at the expansion of investment by requiring strict proof of compliance with the local laws in making the investment,[43] and seeking to challenge the original contract on the basis of which entry was made on grounds such as fraud or bribery.[44] These developments also introduce uncertainty into the law so that investment protection is not going to be easily achieved. It is, for instance, often the case that foreign investment is tainted by bribery.

The instability introduced into the law through expansionist interpretations has led States to explore all possible avenues of resisting jurisdiction. At least, so far, this has been done within the system, through withdrawal. Ecuador and Bolivia demonstrate the more extreme responses to such arbitral activism. The nature of State resistance on the basis of increasing challenges to jurisdiction will significantly erode the importance to foreign investors of investment treaty arbitration. Some argue that this withdrawal may set a trend for the return of older stances hostile to arbitration in Latin America.[45] Indeed, at a much earlier stage, there are increasing challenges mounted to the appointment of arbitrators.[46] Some of the successful challenges demonstrate the incestuous nature of investment arbitration where a small clique of persons act as

---

[43] *Fraport AG Frankfurt Airport Services Worldwide* v. *Philippines* (ICSID Case No. ARB/ 03/ 25, Award of 16 August 2007); *Inceysa Vallisoletana S.L.* v. *El Salvador* (ICSID Case No. ARB/03/26, Award of 2 August 2006).

[44] For fraud, see *Feldman* v. *Mexico* (ICSID Case No. ARB(AF)/99/1, Award on Merits of 16 December 2002); for bribery, see *African Duty Free Ltd* v. *Kenya* (ICSID Case No. ARB/00/7, Award of 4 October 2006).

[45] Vincentelli, 'The uncertain future of ICSID in Latin America'. It appears from this article that the Venezuelan Supreme Court has held that despite the existence of unilateral consent by the State in a BIT for arbitration, there must in addition be a written unequivocal consent to arbitrate in the specific case. Decision 1541 of the Venezuelan Supreme Tribunal; 17 October 2008.

[46] See e.g. ch. 20 by Sam Luttrell in this volume.

counsel on the sides of both claimants as well as respondent States and also sit as arbitrators. They also become the 'highly qualified publicists' in the area, writing up their opinions as articles to be published in glossy journals run by their clique. The fact that these arbitrators are increasingly challenged on account of bias also exhibits the rot that is setting in at the very core of arbitration.

B   Neoliberalism and substantive law on investment protection

Neoliberalism has distinct tenets that have been worked out by its proponents. Its central themes of protection of property and contracts have been present in the international law on foreign investment from the time of the theory of internationalisation. Its new themes have been to address it through a redefined rule of law that conveys the messages of market fundamentalism and liberalisation of the flow of assets. The rule of law as a Diceyan concept which stood as a bulwark to protect the citizen against public power has now been given other garbs to protect private power and promote market fundamentalism. Courts and judicial tribunals have been pressed into service. The messages assume authority as they are included in the package that has come to be known as the 'Washington Consensus'.[47] The law assumes an instrumental role in purveying the tenets of neoliberalism. The message is addressed through the law so that there would be no gainsaying. The increasing judicialisation of the messages in terms of domestic law has been commented upon.[48] The same phenomenon is to be found in international law, particularly in the law relating to international trade and international investment. The role of the dispute-resolution machinery, strongest in terms of international law mechanisms, is well known. The arbitral tribunals in investment imitate this role, though they may not have the same status.

---

[47] See e.g. Rudolf Dolzer and Christoph Schreuer, *Principles of International Investment Law* (Oxford University Press, 2008), p. 11:

> The common core of the policies embodied in investment treaties, in the Washington Consensus, and in the principle of good governance lies in the recognition that institutional effectiveness, the rule of law and an appropriate degree of stability and predictability of policies form the governmental framework for domestic economic growth and also for the willingness of foreign investors to enter the domestic market.

[48] See e.g. Ran Hirschl, *Towards Juristocracy* (Cambridge, MA: Harvard University Press, 2004).

Once the tenets are stated, ridicule and condemnation await those who seek to contest the messages. Those who state the messages are given status within the establishment. Chairs are given at universities to practitioners in the field either because academics want a share of the golden eggs or because legitimacy has to be given to the messenger. Either reason indicates decrepitude in academic life. Individuals come to play leading roles in the process of the use of the law in conveying the messages of neoliberalism. One has to conform to the rules to belong to the arbitral fraternity. The rules require promotion of neoliberal tenets of the institutions which control arbitration.

Fortunately, there is another type of arbitrator. These arbitrators owe fidelity to the rules of arbitration which demanded neutrality. Schisms that developed relating to substantive rules relating to investment arbitration reflect that they were the results of deep-seated ideological conflicts rather than the result of differences in terminology in the different treaties or the dominance of the field by commercial arbitrators who did not understand the implications of the public law features of the contracts they were dealing with.[49] Lawyers work on the premise that they are trained to find and apply the law. They do not work on the distinction between private and public law. Neither of these explanations fit. The commercial arbitrators who sit in investment arbitration have the undoubted capacity to master the area. They are simply predisposed to neoliberalism as the practice of the profession at the particular period of time requires such an inclination. The schisms have occurred in awards involving disputes containing the same facts,[50] or in disputes that involved the same clause in treaties of the same State.[51]

The schisms are recognised as a problem. The attempt to solve them by creating an appellate body has been given up. This is sensible. It would be unsound to build a superstructure on rotting foundations. They will have the same types of arbitrators. The problem will be compounded.

---

[49] See especially Gus van Harten, *Investment Treaty Arbitration and Public Law* (Oxford University Press, 2007).

[50] See e.g. *CME Czech Republic BV* v. *Czech Republic* (UNCITRAL Arbitration, Partial Award of 13 September 2001); *CME Czech Republic BV* v. *Czech Republic* (UNCITRAL Arbitration, Final Award of 14 March 2003); *Ronald Lauder* v. *Czech Republic* (UNCITRAL Arbitration, Final Award of 3 September 2001).

[51] Compare e.g. *SGS Société Générale de Surveillance SA* v. *Islamic Republic of Pakistan* (ICSID Case No. ARB/01/13, Decision on Jurisdiction of 6 August 2003); *SGS Société Générale de Surveillance SA* v. *Republic of the Philippines* (ICSID Case No. ARB/02/6, Decision on Jurisdiction of 29 January 2004).

With these remarks, I now turn to demonstrate the view taken by looking at just two areas in which there has been expansion and reactions to such expansion. The first is the situation relating to the interpretation of the fair and equitable treatment standard in investment treaties and the second relates to the course of developments in the law on expropriation. I have in a more detailed study subjected other areas of the law to similar analysis,[52] but it is sufficient for the purposes of these comments to illustrate the propositions I wish to make with these two areas as briefly as possible.

1   The fair and equitable treatment standard

This was a standard that has been referred to in treaties for many years but it remained dormant until 2000. Professor Schreuer has suggested that in five years, from 2000 to 2005, this amorphous standard has been given new meaning which has given rise to liability of States under this standard. So, whereas the meaning of the international minimum standard which has been used for so many years still remains contentious, we are told that the fair and equitable treatment standard has a meaning which has developed in just five short years. The reason for the sudden attention being given the fair and equitable treatment standard is that there is no wind behind expropriation claims once it became clear that the attempted extension of expropriation through the phrase 'tantamount to an expropriation' did not succeed. Reisman and Sloane believed this phrase, which was to provide the new bridgehead for neoliberal expansion, was brought to a brutal end the very year the article appeared by the formulation in the 2004 US Model BIT.[53] The 'international minimum standard' was a non-starter because of the high standards required by the rule in the *Neer* claim.[54] The effort to deviate from the *Neer* claim did not succeed. The only remaining option for the neoliberal thrust was to focus on the moribund provision of the fair and equitable treatment standard and to breathe life into it.

One can almost trace the origin of the idea. In his paper at the ASIL Conference in 2005, Professor Orrego-Vicuña suggested on the basis of his interpretation of English administrative law that legitimate expectations of a foreign investor resulting from promises held out to him at the time of his entry by the authorities of the host State should be

---

[52] See e.g. Sornarajah, 'Towards normlessness'.

[53] Michael Reisman and Robert Sloane, 'Indirect expropriation and its valuation in the BIT generation', *British Yearbook of International Law*, 74 (2004), 115.

[54] *Neer*, 4 UNRIAA 60 (US–Mexican General Claims Commission, 1926).

protected and that this could be achieved through the fair and equitable treatment standard.[55] As a proposition of English administrative law, the conclusion drawn is clearly incorrect. Legitimate expectations are protected in English law through a right to a hearing before there is an administrative interference. There is only one case in which it has given rise to a substantive right.[56] The position is similar in European administrative law as well as in the administrative law of Commonwealth States. The plain fact is that administration through changes in tax and other regulatory laws would be well-nigh impossible if substantive rights were to be given to all whose expectations have been dashed.

There was given sufficient opportunity to translate this error into investment law through a series of ICSID awards. *Dicta* was built up which recognised a substantive rule that violation of commitments made at the time of the entry would amount to a violation of the fair and equitable treatment standard as it would interfere with the legitimate expectations of the foreign investor. The fair and equitable treatment standard has now been reinterpreted to include a substantive rule relating to legitimate expectations. The result is as if a stabilisation clause, though not negotiated by the parties, is driven into every foreign investment transaction as the expectations created at the commencement of the contract are frozen for all time.

The concept of legitimate expectations was in fact discussed in *Aminoil* which also concerned stabilisation clauses. In *Aminoil*, it was held that a negotiated stabilisation clause, while valid to maintain some stability for the initial period of the investment when the project had not yet established itself, cannot be considered as freezing the law of the

---

[55] Francisco Orrego Vicuña, 'Foreign investment law: How customary is custom?', *Proceedings of the American Society of International Law*, 99 (2005), 97, 99–100.

[56] *R* v. *North and East Devon Health Authority; ex p. Coughlan* [2001] QB 213. The House of Lords has recognised that there is a concept of substantive legitimate expectations. *R* v. *Ministry of Defence; ex p. Walker* [2000] UKHL 22, [2000] 1 WLR 806. Professor Paul Craig, on whose academic writings this exceptional category was constructed by the English courts, has observed that this rule is confined mostly to cases where representations were made to one person or a few people. He pointed out that there are two lawful exercises of power: the initial promise, and the later policy change. He suggested that the notion of abuse of powers be used to reconcile the two conflicting exercises of power. A substantive legitimate expectation could be frustrated where there is an overwhelming public interest but whether such a public interest existed or not is a matter for the courts. See Paul Craig, 'Grounds for judicial review: Substantive control over discretion' in David Feldman (ed.), *English Public Law*, 2nd edn (Oxford University Press, 2009), pp. 737–8. See further Sornarajah, *The International Law on Foreign Investment*, pp. 354–5, n. 97.

host State for the whole duration of the contract.[57] The major significance of *Aminoil* was that it accepted that, the stabilisation clause
notwithstanding, changed circumstances that upset the contractual equilibrium should lead to the restoration of that equilibrium through
renegotiations. There is good basis for such a course in different national
systems. It is also a sound policy to follow in relational contracts for
friction would be reduced and the contract kept alive if the inflexible rule
of contractual sanctity gives way to a rule that promotes constant efforts
to make changes in the light of external circumstances that bring about
changes that make the contract less profitable to one of the parties or its
performance more onerous.

The legitimate expectations rule, formulated as a substantive rule,
leads to inflexibility in the light of dramatic changes in circumstances.
The rule was applied in the context of the Argentine economic crisis
which tribunals are slowly coming to recognise as involving a situation
of necessity.[58] Clearly, that was a situation for not stating an inflexible
rule on contract or investment protection. The more the tribunals stress
investment protection at all costs and evolve inflexible rules, the greater
the chances that States are going to ditch the system that acts as a
hindrance to taking measures to cope with difficult situations that arise
such as economic crises. The over-zealous creation of new doctrines may
lead to good business for arbitrators in the short term but in the long
run, it would be counterproductive as States would rebel against a
system that ties their hands precisely in situations where definite action
on their part is necessary. In any event, the legitimacy of the process of
such law creation in the field has been rightly subjected to doubt.

State reaction could be swift. In the context of NAFTA, the interpretive statement of the NAFTA Commission put an end to arbitral activism
that was contemplated in *Pope and Talbot*.[59] The linking of the fair and
equitable treatment standard to customary international law standards
has now passed into treaty language. It is found in the Canadian and US
Model BITs as well as in other newer treaties. In some of the newer
treaties the standard is not even mentioned. There is some effort to
isolate the experience in NAFTA as confined to NAFTA and maintain the

[57] *Government of Kuwait* v. *American Independent Oil Company* (Award of 24 March 1982),
21 ILM 976.
[58] See e.g. *Continental Casualty Company* v. *Argentina* (ICSID Case No. ARB/03/9, Award of
5 September 2008).
[59] *Pope & Talbot Inc.* v. *Canada* (UNCITRAL Arbitration, Award on the Merits of Phase
2 of 10 April 2001), paras. 105–18.

new development that the fair and equitable treatment standard is an autonomous standard in other treaties. Again, this is an attempt to treat other States as not equal to the developed States that were affected by the interpretations of NAFTA. The history of the fair and equitable treatment standard shows its strong nexus with the customary law international minimum standard.[60]

It is an effort reminiscent of the old idea of economic development agreements which involved doctrines applied to developing countries but not to precisely the same type of contracts made in developed countries. This inequality in treatment is no longer tenable. Many of the States of the so-called developing world can hardly be so described. Many – China, India, Brazil, Singapore, Malaysia, etc. – send large investments into the US and Europe which are now the largest receivers of capital. In a few years, it would be the US, Europe and Japan, the triad that makes instrumental international law, which may come to squeal about what is stated as the fair and equitable treatment standard.

The idea that standards of governance must be imposed again brings back notions of the old habits about civilised nations giving the law to the barbarians. The fair and equitable treatment standard is represented as containing standards of governance which are all taken selectively from the legal systems of the Western world which is fast diminishing in significance as a provider of norms to the rest of the world. It is a part of the neoliberal misadventure that sought to spread the norms of market fundamentalism to the rest of the world. When that project floundered in the West with the economic fall of 2008, it could hardly be expected that the norms it generated were suitable for application universally. The use of the fair and equitable treatment standard to drive the tenets of contractual sanctity and property protection is an instrumental use of the law done without a mandate from the affected States. It is also a task performed by arbitrators whose authority to so extend the law must be contested. As in the past, where, sordidly, some of the great names in international law collaborated in the creation of a one-sided law supporting the theory of internationalisation of foreign contracts, favouring the interests of multinational corporations to the detriment of developing countries, so too law is being created by a handful of men and a few women that is to be regarded as international law. The democratic legitimacy of this fraternity to so create law that is binding on States is extremely suspect. I raise the question whether the law that has been

---

[60] See e.g. ch. 4 by Martins Paparinskis in this volume.

created serves the need of humanity or serves the greed of a few whose interests have been furthered.[61]

International law, constructed through power, has hidden the role of private power to create its norms through recourse to doctrinal positions. Despite the fact that the British and Dutch East India Companies conquered nations and exerted power in large parts of the world, they had no personality in international law and the myth was maintained that they could not be subjected to international law though the whole project was to create and conserve advantages for these corporations through principles of freedom to trade and the freedom of the high seas. Private power continues to be used to create doctrines for the modern multinational corporations through the use of low-order sources of international law like the decisions of tribunals and the writings of 'highly qualified publicists' who are no more than hired guns writing their legal opinions as academic articles and having them cited by their fraternity as highly persuasive authority. They speak of a *'jurisprudence constante'* when the concept is leaking so profusely. The fact is that since they have appeared on both sides, their legal opinions vary so much depending on the highest bidder. Such mercenary lawmaking that conserves the interest of the handful will result in the system being treated with contempt. The quick rush to find a *'jurisprudence constante'* and the efforts to create a multilateral system through the interlinking of these awards and treaties when all efforts at multilateral codes have failed and the effort to constitutionalise the economic norms based on these awards are symbols of this malaise. It is also disconcerting for me, as an older academic, to see how academic writing of many younger colleagues coalesces in support of these developments though it is very obvious that the trends are one-sided and this creates problems of justice. Little criticism is made of these trends. Sadly, one has to concur with Dean Kronman's view of the Lost Lawyer – that in the changed world the values of humanity and statesmanship that dictated the legal profession have been lost and have been replaced by purely mercenary values of career advancement.[62] This is not to deny the need for a law on investment protection. There is need for investment protection but it must not be created capriciously to favour one side without recognising the problems that States are faced with or looking at the issues involving economic development, poverty, welfare needs, the environment and

---

[61] I have addressed this more fully in Sornarajah, 'A law for need or a law for greed?'.
[62] Kronman, *The Lost Lawyer*.

other factors on which there is much international law that is relevant to the issue of investment protection.

2 Expropriation

The second theme that I shall deal with is expropriation. Not that there are no other examples. The field is replete with them indicating the descent into normlessness. I choose expropriation to illustrate the descent. The law on expropriation was expanded well beyond its moorings in the physical taking of property and its subsequent assimilation of indirect takings bringing about results similar to physical dispossession. But, the phrase 'tantamount to an expropriation' began to appear in investment treaties signalling a possible third category of expropriation. Reisman and Sloane, writing in 2003, regarded the future course of expropriation law as depending on identifying this category of expropriations.[63] It seemed to be a category limited only by the imagination of North American lawyers who had strayed into the subject as a result of NAFTA. Fancy theories of litigation were the basis of new claims. In *Ethyl Corporation* v. *Canada*,[64] an announcement of a ban on a petrol additive manufactured by the US claimant suspected to be a carcinogen was alleged to be an expropriation as it caused the value of the shares in the American company to fall. Canada settled the case, paying compensation. Canada also is reported to have given up legislation requiring warnings regarding health hazards of smoking on cigarette cartons as claims relating to expropriation were threatened. Clearly, at this stage, there was a belief in governments that regulation or even threats of regulation against foreign investment would be 'tantamount to expropriation'. Awards like *Santa Elena* v. *Costa Rica* and *Ethyl* v. *Canada* helped to accentuate that fear with views that environmental legislation would still be considered expropriation whatever the public merits of the legislation are.[65] The fear had to be removed. *Methanex* v. *US* removed that fear by creating an exception for regulatory expropriation which socked a huge hole in perceptions regarding the scope of expropriation and the confident prediction that the future course of the law lay with

---

[63] Michael Reisman and Robert Sloane, 'Indirect expropriation and its valuation in the BIT generation', *British Yearbook of International Law*, 74 (2004), 115.

[64] *Ethyl Corporation* v. *Canada* (NAFTA, Decision on Jurisdiction of 24 June 1998).

[65] *Compania de Desarrollo de Santa Elena SA* v. *Costa Rica* (ICSID Case No. ARB/96/1, Award of 17 February 2000); *Ethyl Corporation* v. *Canada* (NAFTA, Decision on Jurisdiction of 24 June 1998). The cases are fully dealt with in Tienhaara, *The Expropriation of Environmental Governance*.

the category of expropriation regarded as 'tantamount to expropriation'. So, another neoliberal project was brought to an end. The newer treaties contain such a broad exception of regulatory takings that the scope of expropriation law has to undergo a fundamental change. It would of course be argued that the development should be limited to NAFTA, a favoured neoliberal response. It is not likely that this view would be adopted. The newer treaties are already incorporating similar restrictions in other regions.

IV   The future of investment arbitration

At present, it would seem that the future of investment arbitration based on treaties is bleak. The reaction of States to the ready manner in which such arbitrations are brought indicates disenchantment with the system.

V   Conclusion

Conventional works seek to analyse this area as if there is nothing wrong that is taking place. These are views of those who have a vested interest in the law remaining as it is and the neoliberal trends stabilised and advanced. That may be a possible course the law will take. But it is unlikely to be so. We have already seen the response of withdrawal in Latin America and it could well be that that part of the world will revert to the Calvo clause. The other pronounced response has been to emasculate the treaties by consciously providing defences. States that have been respondents have already started exploring defences while treaties remained wedded solely to the idea of protection. States have explored and established defences such as the need for economic development in bringing the case within the notion of investment and the requirement that the entry should have conformed to the laws of the host State and have explored limitations inherent in time factors. The limits of defences such as necessity in terms of public international law and its application in the investment context remain to be worked out. States are becoming smart, too, and will explore defences more fully. That is again a response which will greatly weaken the law by introducing imprecision. The third and the most damaging of the developments is that defences have come to be expressly introduced into the treaties making the treaty instrument unstable and inherently worthless to the investor.

Clearly, the law in this area is marked with norm conflicts similar to the one that existed prior to the certainties of the neoliberal times. With the economic crisis and the retreat of neoliberalism, dissent against the neoliberal norms will gather vigour. The foreign investors themselves will see little value in such an uncertain system. It is clear that a change has to come about which will significantly undermine the existing system.

28

Evolution or revolution?

SIR FRANKLIN BERMAN KCMG QC

I   Introduction

The purpose of the closing chapters is to undertake a broader evaluation of the evolution of investment treaty law and arbitration – to assess in other words whether it amounts to a veritable revolution. To do that, it is necessary to examine both substance and procedure and the present is a particularly apposite moment to look at them both. The task is at the same time not an especially easy one, given the momentum which continues to build up in the pattern of use of investment treaty arbitration, leading to internal pressures from within the arbitration system (or systems) itself (themselves), and simultaneously pressures from outside as the product of external expectations. The drive of that momentum is well reflected in the chapters of this book.

That investment arbitration is developing is not in doubt. The process of development has been taking place for some years and certainly will continue. Its striking present feature is the steep pace of this development, brought about largely (if not entirely) by the surprising, and therefore also unforeseen, acceleration in the pace of use. That has in turn accelerated, even if it has not directly caused, the rate at which the characteristic features of the system – procedure as well as substance – have been exposed to challenge in the demanding laboratory of case-experience. Testing to destruction can be as valid an element in social engineering as in civil engineering.

Does that justify talking in terms of 'revolution'? I would think not, partly because one could not define revolution – at least not in this context. So any treatment would be unscientific, and therefore of no great objective value. More valid might be to pose the question whether the whole area of investment treaty arbitration is a kind of revolution in itself, despite its long roots in international law of a more traditional kind. That theme has certainly been heard, though it seems to be of speculative interest only, without much in the way of practical application.

It therefore seems more profitable – bearing in mind once again the need to look at procedure as well as substance – to organise the evaluation in this chapter around a related theme which is also reflected in other chapters, namely that of 'legitimacy'; to examine, in other words, the 'long roots' mentioned above of the elements of the current rapid change and how they justify themselves within the system of international law. Coupled with that legitimacy will be the themes of 'proficiency' and 'professionalism', because of the close links and interplay between them, so that a comment on one often turns out to have wider ramifications which turn it into a comment on all three.

II 'Legitimacy': Is investment treaty arbitration private or public?

Connected with the idea of 'legitimacy' and what it entails, it is a question constantly heard whether investment treaty arbitration is essentially a public process or a private process. When it is said that the international investment treaty system has a public aspect, it seems frequently to be intended that the system *necessarily* had a public aspect, that the public aspect is inherent in it. The question has been nicely put as follows: do we see this as a case of private law serving public interests, or is it a case of public law serving private interests? Similarly, it is asked whether the arbitrator is a justice administrator or a service provider. These seem all to be different ways of introducing the public theme into the analysis and understanding of the phenomenon of investment treaty law and arbitration.

That a public element of some kind exists is clear on all hands, but merely to state that as a proposition doesn't give the proposition content or answer the question: how much of a public element is there in institutions that have at least part of their origin in private law? Nor, self-evidently, does it answer the more important question: if there is a public element, what does it entail, what does it have as its consequences? While therefore one could accept the existence of a public element as a given without drawing automatic conclusions from that, if a point was reached at which the asserted public interest began to override the private element, then it would pose some very hard questions about whether one was in the presence of an attempt at distortion of the system as it already exists – or at least the creation of a new imbalance within it. On the other hand, the introduction of a public element in such a way as to enhance or support the vindication of private interests, but to see that that is done in a properly balanced way, is a much more intriguing concept and one which opens vistas for the future that are undoubtedly worth exploring.

To look at all those questions, irrespective of whether they are questions about law or procedure or questions as to the public element, requires one to ask where this body of law comes from; what is its origin, legally speaking? The rubric of this book itself (investment treaty law and arbitration) offers of course a clue to the answer: the law comes, at least in an immediate sense, from treaties; and treaties are legal instruments, legal instruments concluded between States consisting of terms agreed between them. Contemporary law and international practice now enlarges the field somewhat, because it is recognised that treaties can be entered into by international institutions other than States. And the primary new element in this context, which has been the subject of much recent comment, is the lumbering intrusion onto the scene of the European Union, a heavyweight, but one whose footsteps are uncertain and might turn out to be quite shaking for the foundations of investment treaty arbitration.[1] But that is by way of aside, as the full implications can't yet be foreseen.

Nevertheless, the foundation remains treaties, and treaties are instruments concluded in principle between States. However the investment treaties now under examination are treaties concluded between States for the benefit of individuals (or private interests); that surely is their defining feature. If so, then we have what might be called a classic third-party situation, of the kind foreseen many years ago in the Vienna Convention on the Law of Treaties in its Section 4 (Articles 34–6) entitled 'Treaties and Third States'.[2] Except that it isn't the classic third-party instance at all, because in this particular case the benefits are being conferred upon third parties who are not themselves States, whereas the circumstance envisaged in the Vienna Convention on the Law of Treaties of 1969 was the State-to-State one.[3] Nonetheless, although this represents a deviation from the classic third-party situation, it is far from unique in contemporary international law. Exactly

---

[1] See e.g. ch. 10 by P. J. Cardwell and D. French in this volume.

[2] Vienna Convention on the Law of Treaties, opened for signature 23 May 1969, 1155 UNTS 311 (entered into force 27 January 1980), Arts. 34–6.

[3] See also the Vienna Convention on the Law of Treaties between States and International Organizations or between International Organizations, opened for signature 21 March 1986, UN Doc. A/Conf.129/15 (not yet in force at 21 January 2011), Arts. 34–6, which adds international organisations to the category of treaty-making entities.

the same kind of description could be given to human rights treaties: they are treaties concluded between States for the purpose of conferring benefits on or protecting the interests of non-States, specifically natural persons and also corporate economic entities. The point is not only that the third-party factor in the special form just described is an essential element that must be recognised, but also that it must have an effect on the way the operation of the treaty system develops. A treaty system created in order to confer benefits on entities within the private sphere will not develop in the same way as if the treaty system had been conceived of as operating entirely between States or at the governmental level. This has shown itself to be true in the human rights field, and there is no reason to suppose that a somewhat similar dynamic will not apply in the investment treaty field.[4] At all events, one conclusion that can immediately be drawn is that treaties concluded by States for the protection of individual and private interests can't create law just 'for' the investor, simply by virtue of the fact that such treaties have been brought into being by States. At the same time, this kind of treaty can't create law simply 'for' the States because that is not the purpose for which they were conceived; the essential purpose is something rather different. At least that serves as a reminder that a balance has to be struck in all cases. And, as we shall see, the balance is one of rather an unusual character.

But to pose the question of balance immediately brings us back to the public–private divide mentioned at the beginning of this chapter. Does the fact that investment treaties cannot create law just 'for' the investor, and the fact that they are the product of agreement between one State and another, bring with it a 'public' element? And if it does, is that simply a matter of *process*, which should influence the way in which investment tribunals handle the questions increasingly posed about openness of procedures and openness to outside interventions? And if so, why and in what sense should that be a question for individual *tribunals* to settle (so inevitably piecemeal and ad hoc), rather than a public-interest question that ought to have been settled by the States whose actions created the treaty and therefore the processes under it? Or does it go beyond process to become an influence on the *law* to be applied by the tribunal to the dispute, so that the tribunal, in place of the traditional function of determining the rights and interests of the parties

---

[4] But 'somewhat similar' only; for a discussion of some of the differences see *RosInvestCo UK Ltd* v. *The Russian Federation* (SCC Case No. Arb. V079/2005, Award on Jurisdiction of October 2007), paras. 37 *et seq.*

before it, should be expected to render an award that takes into account other – presumptively public – interests even though they are not advanced before it by the public party to the case, namely the respondent State? Or should the tribunal give additional weight to the public interests advanced by the respondent party on the basis that they are also being urged on it by others – in which case how does it square that with the strict and absolute equality between the parties which lies at the heart of all judicial processes?[5] The answers are by no means easy, and defy the simplistic and often emotional responses that are sometimes to be heard.

III   The applicable law

At this point it is time to return to the question where the law comes from; what is its origin, in legal terms? We know where the law comes from in the literal and obvious sense that you find it in the terms of the legal instrument or instruments that is (or are) being applied. There is however a less trivial sense to the question where the law springs from, and who are its creators, a sense that raises important questions about its ascertainment and interpretation. Of one thing we can at least be certain: the law is not the creation of arbitrators or of arbitral tribunals.[6] The task, and whole function, of a tribunal set up under an investment treaty is to apply to the case in front of it designated and pre-identified rules of law. This is reflected, for example, in Article 42(1) of the ICSID Convention, which provides that:

> The Tribunal shall decide a dispute in accordance with such rules of law as may be agreed by the parties. In the absence of such agreement, the Tribunal shall apply the law of the Contracting State party to the dispute (including its rules on the conflict of laws) and such rules of international law as may be applicable.[7]

If a tribunal were to apply the wrong set of rules, its award would be open to annulment under Article 52(1)(c) on the grounds that it had

---

[5] And which forms part of the 'fundamental rules of procedure' absorbed expressly into the ICSID system under Art. 52(1)(d) of the ICSID Convention: Convention for the Settlement of Investment Disputes between States and Nationals of other States, opened for signature 18 March 1965, 575 UNTS 159 (entered into force 14 October 1966) (ICSID Convention).

[6] Though sometimes, when you hear the arbitrators themselves talk about their work and that of other tribunals, you might gain a different impression.

[7] Note in particular the objective, not subjective, way in which the last phrase is framed.

'manifestly exceeded its powers'. In other words, it is wise to treat with an element of healthy scepticism such suggestions as one may hear from time to time that it is the arbitration community which has brought into existence a vibrant new body of international law, or that what tribunals ought to be doing is to extend that law into new areas. It is not possible to say that investment treaty law is the creation of tribunals and arbitrators when it is plainly the creature of the instruments that lay down or identify the law and the rules which tribunals and arbitrators then have to put into effect. Naturally, though, applying the law, or 'putting it into effect', inevitably entails a degree of development, but that is a different matter entirely. Development of the law is a natural part of the judicial process, especially of course at the stage when the law in question is still relatively *un*developed, and it happens in various ways: both by articulating and describing the underlying concepts and by putting them into practice in particular circumstances and against particular sets of facts.

To go back to the ICSID example mentioned above, the delicate and sensitive area lies of course within the second of the two sources of law listed in Article 42(1): 'and such rules of international law as may be applicable'. It raises immediately the question, what 'rules of international law' are these? Obviously, first and foremost amongst them – at least in an investment treaty case – will be the terms of the treaty itself. It would be inconceivable for the terms of the treaty not to be found to be 'applicable' and indeed to be directly applied by the tribunal in its award. But are there in addition rules of general 'international law' that might also be 'applicable', and if so how? Are they displaced by the terms of the treaty, or would they themselves overlay the terms of the treaty, or operate in some sense along with the terms of the treaty? So simple and obvious a question ought to be capable of a direct and authoritative answer. But it's not, because the relation between treaty and custom, central though it is to the architecture of international law, remains something of a priestly mystery, to be approached only by the initiated.[8] The particular delicacy lies therefore in that part of the function of an investment tribunal that might lie in ascertaining what are the

---

[8] Art. 38 of the Statute of the International Court of Justice, widely regarded as the leading text on the sources of international law, seems on its face to give primacy to the treaty, but, as the Court's jurisprudence shows, so simplistic a proposition is no more than a starting point: Statute of the International Court of Justice, opened for signature 26 June 1945, 3 Bevans 1153 (entered into force 24 October 1945). For a contribution on the relationship between treaty law and customary international law in the realm of international investment law, see ch. 4 by M. Paparinskis in this volume.

'applicable rules of international law' for the purpose of proceeding to 'apply' them to a case before it. And one may take it, in broad terms, that this generalised reference to 'international law' means, in reality, customary international law, so that the function divides into two parts: *first* the ascertainment of the mixture between treaty law and customary law that will be applied to the case in hand; and *secondly* the determination of the actual content of those rules of customary law. Both of those are, it should be recognised, 'creative' functions: the calling in, on the one hand, of general international law to illuminate, to supplement, or even on occasion to change the 'colour' of the specific terms the Contracting Parties adopted in their treaty, but even more so, on the other hand, the conjuring up (from whatever are the available sources) of what is deemed to be the accepted rules of customary international law the Contracting Parties had in mind as the background and framework to their treaty bargain.

Now the thought that a competent tribunal, in ascertaining and applying customary international law, might also *develop* it, is extremely familiar to all of us as students of international law. There is nothing unique or even special about it in this particular area of international practice except for the fact that there are lots of cases, thus many occasions for the process to take place, and a steadily increasing body of reference points for each successive tribunal to steer itself by. Apart from the fact, then, that there are so many cases, the process is perfectly familiar and not one would have thought in any essential sense exceptional. The unusual feature – which does distinguish investment treaty arbitrations from, shall we say, the Iran–United States Claims Tribunal or the standing international courts up to the International Court of Justice itself – is the dispersed nature of the process: no standing body building up its own stock of jurisprudence, no doctrine of precedent, and a pressing need therefore for any given tribunal to sort through the prior arbitral awards cited to it in order to decide which decisions and which *dicta* are sound and worth following and which are not.

And finally, to revert for the very last time to the public–private divide, if it is to customary international law that we have to look to provide the source for the proposition that there are external public interests to which a tribunal ought to pay regard, there will be a heavy burden to be borne in finding the appropriate techniques to ascertain both the constituent elements of the customary rules and how they interrelate, in a legal sense, with the treaty rules and national laws that particular tribunals are directly charged with applying.

Let us, however, bring the matter down from this general level of international judicial process to the level of investment treaty arbitration, and in particular to the body of law that comes into play in this field. If one looks at the kind of things that have been said and written, there seem to have been three propositions out in the ether at different times. One proposition is that we are really talking about customary law, about what people refer to as the 'minimum standard' under customary international law (a question-begging term in itself) – though the 'minimum standard' as developed by treaties and by tribunals. Another proposition is that this is a self-contained regime, conceived as being the law of particular treaties and groups of treaties, where the population of treaties is essentially bilateral though now there is the interesting and important intrusion onto the scene of multilateral treaties, beginning with a restricted multilateral case like the North American Free Trade Agreement (NAFTA),[9] but moving on to the much broader multilateral case of the Energy Charter Treaty.[10] The third proposition is that the body of applicable law is indeed an amalgam of treaty law and customary law, but that its development has reached the point where it is at the given moment and can't go back. To use a metaphor, there is something like a ratchet; or, to use another, the tide can't be turned. Proposition 1 amounts to saying that there is no qualitative difference in this field between treaty law and customary law; that what masquerades as the law of particular treaties is in reality general international law applicable as such even in the absence of treaty; but that the measure of that general customary law is the content of the treaties – together with the way they have been interpreted and applied. Proposition 2 would hold that this is a self-contained body of international law, a special regime similar to human rights or the law of armed conflict, which advances in its own way and at its own pace, and is not therefore tied to the sluggish processes for the development of customary law. Proposition 3 was epitomised by the reaction in some quarters to the binding interpretation given by the NAFTA Free Trade Commission, on behalf of the NAFTA Treaty Parties, to Article 1105.[11] If those are, then, the three common propositions, it becomes clear when you reflect on them that

---

[9] North American Free Trade Agreement, opened for signature 17 December 1992, 32 ILM 289 (entered into force 1 January 1994) (NAFTA).

[10] Energy Charter Treaty, opened for signature 17 December 1994, 34 ILM 360 (entered into force 16 April 1998).

[11] See NAFTA Free Trade Commission, *Notes of Interpretation of Certain Chapter 11 Provisions* (31 July 2001), www.naftalaw.org (last accessed 21 January 2011).

you can't espouse all three of those propositions at the same time; in my view it is not even possible to espouse two out of those three propositions at the same time. The propositions are different and mutually exclusive. To hop from one of them in one particular corner of the woods when it suits the argument to another one of those propositions in a different corner of the woods when it suits another part of the argument is not a legitimate way for lawyers to analyse problems or to decide cases. At some point, therefore, the legal community has to clear its collective mind as to the real nature and source of this area of law. It may be that this is a particularly stimulating time to start that clearing of the minds, for example because Proposition 3 (that you can't go backwards) is currently being falsified by a substantial amount of activity which is taking place at this moment by governments in the exercise of their normal treaty-making capacity. Why would one be so interested, for example, in the new Model BITs produced by some of the governments especially active in the field if it were not for the fact that the new models foreshadow new treaty-making designed to set the level of protection for investments at a chosen point that may well not correspond with past decisions by investment tribunals?[12] New treaty mechanisms are apparently being developed, in a most interesting way, to enable the operations of these treaties to be kept in track with broader developments in the international field.

IV Treaty interpretation

It is time at this point in the argument to move on to the question of treaty interpretation. This is a matter of essential importance because, whichever of the three crude propositions mentioned above one is most attracted by, the core task conferred upon an investment tribunal is, obviously, to make sense of the treaty under which it is created and operates. In the case of an ICSID tribunal, it is, self-evidently, operating under two treaties: the relevant treaty and the ICSID Convention,[13] both of which the tribunal is bound to apply. And the first step towards application is interpretation. That is the function of a dispute-settlement process; it interprets the relevant texts and applies them to the particular circumstances of the dispute. To begin therefore with interpretation, we

---

[12] For a discussion of the new generation Model BITs, see especially ch. 13 by S. Spears in this volume.

[13] Except for the rather rare case (rare, that is, in the ICSID system) where consent to arbitration is given under contract or ad hoc.

should not underestimate the huge benefit we enjoy in having under the Vienna Convention on the Law of Treaties a universally recognised 'golden rule' of interpretation surrounded by other rules expressed in terms that have a good correspondence with the experience of international life. How then should we react to the anguished cries that the Vienna Convention is not solving our problems for us, culminating in the truly horrible idea that we should have a new Vienna Convention the purpose of which would be to interpret the rules laid down in the Vienna Convention in order to give answers to the problem of interpretation that come before tribunals and parties! That is not the function of rules of interpretation. The rules of interpretation are not there to provide the answer to a particular question of interpretation; they give you the techniques by which you find the answer to your question. One of the main reasons that the Vienna Convention provisions on interpretation have stood up so extraordinarily well is what they choose not to say. One big achievement of the Vienna Convention was to sweep away the cobwebs, the old maxims about interpretation *contra preferentem, in dubio mitius*, in favour of sovereignty, or whatever. All those have gone and in their place what we have is good, sound, general principles indicating what one can recognise as more than just the international lawyer's approach to interpretation, but a good guide to interpretation for any interpreter interpreting any serious legal text. So the Vienna Convention gives us interpretative techniques, techniques which incidentally it says have to be applied 'in good faith' in finding the meaning of treaties – for the purpose of applying them, something which the Convention reminds us has also to be done in good faith.[14] It then becomes incumbent upon those concerned with investment treaty arbitration to be serious in a professional way about applying those techniques and applying them properly. The Vienna Convention offers a good overview of the materials which an interpreter can legitimately bring to bear on a question of interpretation, and some idea of how they relate to one another, what their ranking is in relation to one another. All of that is perfectly well applicable to the interpretation of investment protection treaties.[15]

Amongst those techniques and materials, one of the things that the Vienna Convention reminds us about is *language*. But should we need reminding? Given that no more than a tiny minority of investment

---

[14] Vienna Convention, Art. 26.
[15] Subject to one particular small problem discussed below.

protection treaties is concluded in one language only, it is a source of astonishment to see parties or their counsel producing arguments based entirely on one of the language texts of the treaty, and not even thinking it necessary to tell the tribunal that the other language versions have been consulted or (until probed perhaps by the tribunal itself) confirming that all the language texts have the same meaning. Occasionally, of course, they do not have the same apparent meaning, and then the Vienna Convention techniques have to be used to reconcile what might be on the surface differences between the language texts.

Another element, which takes pride of place, is *context*: if there is one basic thing the Vienna Convention says, it is that a single article of a treaty may not be extracted and interpreted on its own as if it was a self-standing tablet of stone; that is not a legitimate method of interpretation.[16] But even extremely reputable international lawyers are not always immune to the temptation.[17]

In addition to languages and context, and the principle of good faith, there is also the part to be played by the treaty's *object and purpose*. It would surely be wrong to take too narrow a view of 'object and purpose', for example by claiming that the object and purpose of investment treaties is to protect the investor. If we go back once again to the public/private divide discussed earlier, an arbitrator typically finds himself looking, at a certain point in its lifetime, at a treaty which was intended to operate over a substantial period of years, and therefore to develop in its operation. Doesn't that necessarily imply that the elements of the public interest mentioned earlier might be ones that could legitimately be brought into the process of interpretation as part of the presumed object and purpose of the treaty in circumstances in which the treaty parties haven't defined expressly in golden letters what the object and purpose was in their minds? That would seem to be a perfectly possible approach – so long as it is borne in mind that deducing the object and purpose is specific to the particular treaty under discussion, and doesn't admit of general postulates.

[16] Though, sad to say, that is what one sees people doing all the time, as e.g. in much of the discussion about the fair and equitable treatment standard.
[17] One ICSID annulment proceeding shows a tribunal taking the interpretation of a particular clause and particular words in a particular clause without once troubling to look whether those words or similar words were used in the same sense or in other senses in other parts of the treaty or at least what the other articles in the treaty provided and what light they might cast on the important question before it: *Empresas Lucchetti SA and Lucchetti Peru SA v. Peru* (ICSID Case No. ARB/03/04, Decision on Annulment of 5 September 2007, Dissenting Opinion of Sir Franklin Berman of 13 August 2007).

There is, in other words, a lot which is good in the Vienna Convention rules, and nothing more is needed other than to use them seriously and imaginatively. However there is, as indicated above, one small problem, namely that the Vienna Convention rules are designed for the case in which one party to the treaty is disputing with another treaty party the meaning of their treaty, and that is not the investment arbitration case. What an investment treaty tribunal has before it is always a respondent State which is party to the treaty and a claimant which is not party to the treaty, because the claimant is one of those private interests for whose benefit the treaty was negotiated. This unequal opposition may create problems for the process of interpretation of which one ought to be conscious. That doesn't mean that the standard tenets of interpretation become inapplicable, but they have to be applied in a sensible way. An area in which they have a particular impact is the question of preparatory work (*travaux préparatoires*); what access does the claimant investor have to the preparatory work of the treaty, what insight can counsel representing an investor give the tribunal into what went on in the negotiation of the treaty? Very little, unless it is one of those rare cases in which either the records of the negotiation were published or there is a good public record on both negotiating sides of the treaty – for example when the treaty was submitted for approval to the national parliaments. The point at issue here offers one a vivid illustration of the cardinal tenet that the purpose of interpretation is to ascertain the meaning of the text agreed upon, not the intentions of the parties at the time they negotiated it. It is notoriously difficult to discern the intention of the parties after the event, particularly when the details of the negotiations are, as usual, shrouded in some obscurity, and it is almost impossible to do so when you have before a tribunal two parties, one of which is privy to details of the negotiation and one the other one of which is not. One might simply observe *en passant* that this particular difficulty is multiplied to the nth degree when the issue arises through the invocation of a most-favoured-nation clause. That brings one back once more to the essential principle which a professional tribunal must always bring to bear to the conduct of a case: the preservation of the equality of the rights of the parties as litigants before it.

V   Issues of quality

That equality brings one naturally to the question of quality: quality of process and quality of result, two elements that are linked to one another and very intimately linked as well to the question of legitimacy. Quality implies many things: quality of treaties, tribunals, arguments and awards. To begin with quality of treaties, it is no good States complaining afterwards about the results that come out of the application of their treaties if they negotiated bad treaties in the first place. The responsibility for what goes into the text of a treaty is that of the negotiating parties and if, for example, a State decides to accept a particular clause proposed to it in a treaty without discussion, that is something which has its consequences – namely, that the clause will be interpreted and applied in accordance with its terms. A central purpose of international law is to protect the sanctity of treaties and treaties must be taken to mean what they say.

Coming beyond that to the operation of tribunals, the thesis of this chapter is that parties get the awards they deserve – which refers, of course, not to the merits of the award (who wins or loses), but the quality of the award as a legal judgment. What we ought to focus on here is the quality of the argument which counsel for the litigating parties produce to tribunals. An arbitral tribunal is no god-like body in the clouds whose task it is to produce the final statement of the law and practice on an abstract problem. The function of a tribunal is to judge a case fairly on the basis of the argument presented to it by both parties on a footing of equality. If an arbitral tribunal either departs completely from the terms of the argument put to it by the parties, or fails to take account of the argument put to it by the parties, it runs the risk of not only the disapprobation of its peers but also of legal annulment or judicial non-recognition. The process of the production of an arbitral award is directly influenced – and should be so influenced – by the way in which the parties decide to argue their cases before the tribunal. The tribunal is not free to shake off all that argument as if it was simply a tiresome distraction which should have no effect on the production of its award. If the critics see awards with which they are not satisfied, it might be worth their paying a little attention to the way the parties chose to deploy their cases before the tribunal.

Another component of quality is of course the quality of the tribunal itself: how do you compose a tribunal, how do you choose the members? There undoubtedly are problems in this area, but are they in any sense unique to the investment treaty field? In truth, problems of the composition of tribunals of an international character exist across the entire international field. Anybody who has ever paid any attention to elections to the International Court of Justice or the International Criminal

Court, or to the composition of even well-established tribunals like the European Court of Human Rights and the European Court of Justice will know that the process of finding, selecting and composing the tribunal is not a straightforward one. The more international the tribunal becomes, the more complicated the choice of the judges becomes. The same can indeed be said of ICSID when it comes to performing its statutory function of putting together or proposing names for a tribunal or its president or for an ad hoc annulment committee. What can ICSID do except operate on the basis of the Panels established pursuant to Section 4 of the ICSID Convention, namely the material given to it.[18] And who gives the material to ICSID? It is not some abstract process of judgment; rather, it is the States Parties to the Washington Convention.[19]

The nub of the argument is that there are indeed problems about the composition of arbitral tribunals, but there are problems about the composition of courts and tribunals everywhere. It is very striking indeed that, if one asks fellow lawyers about the process of nominating and choosing judges for the superior courts in their own countries, the almost invariable response is a litany of difficulties and problems, and sometimes great political controversy or unsettled issues, over the composition of national courts. The issue is terribly important and it is terribly difficult, but it is in no sense unique to the arbitration system.

As to the awards themselves, what characterises the quality of an award isn't the absolute rightness and wrongness of the final decision, but the quality of the reasoning and the explanation that goes into it. It is sometimes said that what the parties to a commercial contract really want is a result; they want it quick, definitive, precise; they don't care that much about the reasoning; what they want is an answer. If that is the case in commercial arbitration (and *quaere* whether it is), it certainly is not the case in investment treaty arbitration where you have governments or government agencies involved, and where you may have the presence of the broader public interests referred to above. Here the reasoning does matter, and, although the reasoning may be a product initially of the way the parties have put their cases to the tribunal, its quality is the ultimate responsibility of the tribunal itself.[20] That is what

---

[18] ICSID Convention, Arts. 12–16.

[19] Subject only to the limited number of panel members designated under Art. 13(2) of the ICSID Convention.

[20] See especially T. Landau, 'Reasons for reasons: The tribunal's duty in investor–State arbitration' in A. J. van den Berg (ed.), *ICCA Congress Series No. 14* (Alphen aan den Rijn: Wolters Kluwer, 2009), p. 187.

distinguishes a good decision from a bad one. There is a public market-place out there in which the good decisions are the ones which survive (or the decisions which survive are the good ones); whereas the ones that are not good become sidelined, are not frequently cited or approved by the commentators, and they don't enter into the bloodstream. It is the good ones that enter into the bloodstream, and the good decisions are characterised by the quality of their reasoning. In other words, although there is a marketplace, and although it is absolutely true that arbitration is a service industry, it is emphatically not a service like any other. The plumber is not expected to give you a full written report on his analysis of your pipes and exactly the reasons why he has chosen the particular remedy for dealing with them and what he anticipates the consequences to be. A judge is. That is exactly what distinguishes the legal process from the others: that parties have to enunciate their cases clearly and persua-sively and the tribunal has to justify the results it reaches.

VI   Conclusion

The conclusion seems to be that a little bit of modesty is not a bad thing; it would certainly become the arbitration community in the area of investment treaties. Nor is there any need for panic; things aren't as bad as they seem, or if they are as bad as they seem they are equally bad in other areas of the law. The keyword is *professionalism*; this is a professional activity, not a form of political activism. As a powerful professional activity, it is one in which its participants have professional duties and ethics, again because it is the law and not because it is other things. The process by which results are arrived at matters, and all of those with an interest in investment arbitration are participants in that process and in making it work.

INDEX

abuse of rights, by domestic courts 435
access
  to counsel, for developing States
    611–13
  to investment arbitration
    as public interest issue 307–8
    and rule of law 142–3
    for SWFs 177–9
    waiver/'no-U-turn' model of 345–8
  to markets
    BIT provisions on 179–81
    EPA provisions on 218
  to patented technology, through
    compulsory licensing
    487–8
ACP (African, Caribbean and Pacific)
    States, and EU
    209–15, 493
ad hoc investment arbitrations
  bias challenges in 30–1
  versus institutional arbitration 383–4
administrative law, global 148, 159
  investment arbitration as 7, 145–7,
    155–7, 159
admissibility
  of claims, and investor misconduct
    196–7, 198, 199–200
  of interpretative materials 73, 76–7
  and jurisdiction 192–3, 198
  powers of arbitration tribunals to
    rule on 193–6
Africa
  food security concerns in 542
  foreign land leases in 542–4
agency rights, in investor–State
    arbitration 81–2, 84
Ago, Roberto 249, 250, 252, 270

Ahdieh, Robert 299
Albania, bilateral investment treaty with
    Greece, arbitration on 231–3
Alexandrov, Stanimir A. 33–4
Allee, T. L. 613
Alvarez, José 93–4
amici curiae participation in
    arbitration 158–9, 299,
    360–2, 581–2
  by EU Commission 8, 310–14,
    319–20, 330–3, 335–6
  by EU Member States 314
  ICSID rules on 303, 304–5
  NAFTA rules on 305–6, 321–2,
    357–8, 360–2
  by NGOs 319, 327–30, 378–9,
    380
  by sub-national government units
    303–5, 307, 314–15
    practice 310–14
    Quechan Indian tribe as 306–7,
    310, 361–2
  rules and impediments 308–10
  in UNCITRAL arbitrations 380
  see also non-disputing parties'
    participation
Amnesty International, on negative
    impact of stabilisation
    clauses on human rights
    525–6
'amount of compensation' clauses
    409–11, 412
  arbitration on 425, 428
    limited to jurisdiction over
    quantum 412–16, 425–6
    not limited to jurisdiction over
    quantum 416–25, 426–7